CHILD AND ADOLESCENT
DEVELOPMENT
IN CULTURAL CONTEXT

CHILD AND ADOLESCENT
DEVELOPMENT
IN CULTURAL CONTEXT

Jennifer E. Lansford, Doran C. French, and Mary Gauvain

 AMERICAN PSYCHOLOGICAL ASSOCIATION

Published by
American Psychological Association
750 First Street, NE
Washington, DC 20002
https://www.apa.org

Order Department
https://www.apa.org/pubs/books
order@apa.org

In the U.K., Europe, Africa, and the Middle East, copies may be ordered from Eurospan
https://www.eurospanbookstore.com/apa
info@eurospangroup.com

Typeset in Meridien and Ortodoxa by TIPS Technical Publishing, Inc., Carrboro, NC
Printer: Gasch Printing, Odenton, MD
Cover Designer: Nicci Falcone, Potomac, MD

Library of Congress Cataloging-in-Publication Data
Names: Lansford, Jennifer E., author. | French, Doran C., author. | Gauvain, Mary, author.
Title: Child and adolescent development in cultural context / by Jennifer E. Lansford, Doran C. French, and Mary Gauvain.
Description: Washington, DC : American Psychological Association, [2021] | Includes bibliographical references and index.
Identifiers: LCCN 2020042983 (print) | LCCN 2020042984 (ebook) | ISBN 9781433833038 (paperback) | ISBN 9781433833281 (ebook)
Subjects: LCSH: Child psychology—Cross-cultural studies. | Adolescent psychology—Cross-cultural studies. | Child development—Cross-cultural studies. | Adolescence—Cross-cultural studies. | Ethnopsychology.
Classification: LCC BF721 .L365 2021 (print) | LCC BF721 (ebook) | DDC 155.4—dc23
LC record available at https://lccn.loc.gov/2020042983
LC ebook record available at https://lccn.loc.gov/2020042984

https://doi.org/10.1037/0000228-000

Printed in the United States of America

10 9 8 7 6 5 4 3 2 1

BRIEF CONTENTS

CONTENTS

PREFACE

A Note to Instructors

Despite the importance placed on culture in many theoretical models of human development, the majority of empirical research on child and youth development, parenting and peer relationships, and children's adjustment historically has been conducted in the United States, Canada, and Western Europe. Arnett's (2008) analysis of the research participants in the most influential journals in six subdisciplines of psychology from 2003–2007 revealed that 96% of the participants were from Western industrialized countries, with 68% from the United States; thus, 96% of the research participants in these studies came from countries with only 12% of the world's population. At the time, Arnett's findings were viewed as a clarion call for broadening the representation of children and youth in developmental research. Unfortunately, an analysis conducted later found similar patterns. Nielsen et al. (2017) reported that in 2015 less than 8% of the world's children were included in developmental research appearing in high-impact journals, and over 95% of papers were authored by scientists working in Western settings. Clearly, more needs to be done so that developmental science, and the scientists doing the work, better represent the world in which we live.

The primary research focus on youth in Western countries is especially concerning because findings from Western, educated, industrialized, rich, and democratic societies may not generalize to the majority of the world's population (Henrich et al., 2010). In the recent past, empirical studies of children and adolescents from historically underrepresented countries have multiplied as scholars have realized that fully understanding development requires studying children and youth as they live and grow in the many different cultural contexts that human beings inhabit. To meet this goal, college and university courses on child development will need to "catch up" to the direction in which the field is moving. Namely, rather than treating culture as a sidebar, it is necessary to acknowledge that development can and does differ across cultures and that it does so for a very simple reason. The human species has been able to adapt over time to create and thrive in many different social and environmental conditions. The broad range of cultures in which human beings live, and in which young people grow to become productive and contributing community members, is a key facet of human adaptation. Knowing more about culture and how it shapes development will advance understanding of our species and, in turn, enrich developmental science. Therefore, it is important for students today to understand how children and adolescents develop in cultural context. This book does just that.

To date, there is no other textbook that is ideal for a course on culture and child development. Most child development texts provide a chronological progression starting with prenatal development and advancing through infancy, the toddler years, and through the life span, with culture integrated only peripherally, if at all. Instructors who want to attend to culture in a more sophisticated way must then find additional readings to supplement the text. Students are left with a perspective on development that is biased toward how European American children from middle-class backgrounds develop, which does them a disservice because development is highly culturally contingent. It also makes students ill-equipped to live in an increasingly global world that is regularly infused with knowledge of and contact with people from across the planet.

To address this critical gap, this book describes how the many aspects of child growth and development—physical, emotional, cognitive, and social—are embedded in and affected by culture. Each chapter focuses on culture in relation to a specific domain of child development. The book begins with a general introduction chapter that provides an overview of culture and major theories that have been used to understand child development and culture, followed by a methods chapter that describes how researchers study child and youth development in cultural contexts. Each subsequent chapter focuses on a topical domain (e.g., cognition, emotions, peer relationships, family relationships, transition to adulthood) to help readers understand that the development of human behavior, values, social relationships, ways of seeing the world, language, and thought processes cannot be considered separate from culture. We highlight recent research on child and youth development in different cultural contexts. We also review classic theories and research and describe how they have been extended and still apply to the study of human development in cultural context.

Culture is a very broad construct. It includes not only country and ethnicity but also a range of formative experiences in people's lives. For example, individuals sometimes define their cultural groups in terms of religion, gender identity, or ability (e.g., deaf culture). All of these definitions and cultural identities have merit. In this book, we primarily focus on cultural groups defined by geography and ethnicity. We also provide examples of how experiences within a country or ethnic group can differ on the basis of intersecting identities related to gender, socioeconomic status, religion, and other factors.

We view this book as being appropriate for a variety of audiences, including advanced undergraduate students, graduate students, and professionals. Our intended undergraduate audience includes students majoring in psychology, human development and family studies, sociology, or cultural anthropology. We anticipate that courses using this book would be considered upper-level courses. Many students would probably have had a previous course on developmental psychology, but that would not necessarily be a required prerequisite.

This book is also appropriate for graduate seminars focusing on culture and child development, and for use in research universities, liberal arts colleges, and community colleges. It can serve as a core text that could be supplemented with additional readings as needed.

Each chapter is written to stand alone in case instructors want to cover certain topics but not others, in which case they can assign only specific chapters. Furthermore, the chapter order is not rigid, so if instructors want to present topics in a different order, they can assign chapters in whichever order works best with their lesson plans. The discussion questions at the end of each chapter and the list of additional resources in the Appendix can be used to supplement coursework as desired.

In addition to instructional purposes, the book is also suitable for use as a personal reference for professionals, including clinical psychologists; social workers; family therapists; and other practitioners who work with diverse children, adolescents, and families in applied settings. Practitioners can use the book as a resource to enhance their understanding of the role of culture in child and adolescent development. The book is unique in bringing together research from multiple theoretical perspectives and applying research in multiple topic areas. As such, it can be a useful introduction and overview of issues pertinent to understanding development within a cultural context.

A cultural approach to developmental science strives to advance knowledge about the development of children and youth around the world and provide basic scientific information to inform policies and programs that impact children and families both locally and globally. This contribution depends on using the best practices of the scientific discipline, and that effort begins by including a broad representation of people from around the world, both as research participants and as investigators. It was with this goal in mind that we wrote this book. We aim to encourage future generations of developmental scientists and practitioners to understand and appreciate the cultural nature of childhood and human psychological growth. To this end, we hope the information provided throughout the book demonstrates the great value of integrating culture in all aspects of research and practice in developmental science as we move forward.

CHILD AND ADOLESCENT
DEVELOPMENT
IN CULTURAL CONTEXT

1

Development and Culture

Theoretical Perspectives

Young novice Buddhist monks walk for morning alms in Myanmar.

American poet Mark van Doran (1894–1972) wrote, "There are two statements about human beings that are true: that all human beings are alike, and that all are different. On those two facts all human wisdom is founded." Consideration of this paradox is central to our understanding of culture and the subject matter of this book.

Imagine looking at a crowd of people from a distance through a telescope that has a very wide range of magnification. With no magnification, objects are identifiable as people, but it is impossible to differentiate between them. At the highest level of magnification, no two people are the same. At intermediate levels of magnification, different commonalties, such as age or sex become apparent. At a slightly lower level of magnification, we can begin to see other

https://doi.org/10.1037/0000228-001
Child and Adolescent Development in Cultural Context, by J. E. Lansford, D. C. French, and M. Gauvain

commonalities in terms of behavior, beliefs, and customs that we group under the construct of culture.

Psychologists and other social scientists, depending on the focus of their work, have taken different stances regarding the importance of culture. Some researchers are interested primarily in aspects of human behavior (e.g., cognition, perception, neuroscience) that apply to all people, and thus, they may not appreciate the importance of studying culture. In contrast, others argue that it is important to understand specific individuals and societies with all their complexity, and thus, it is problematic and sometimes impossible to make broad generalizations about culture.

Our stance is that children and adolescents grow up in a culture, and their behavior, values, social relationships, ways of seeing the world, language, and thought processes cannot be understood separate from culture. In this chapter, we first discuss definitions of cultures; present an overview of various theoretical models that help us to understand how culture is an essential aspect of the lives of children and adolescents; review approaches that researchers have used to categorize cultures; and finally, address questions pertaining to the origin, maintenance, and transformation of culture.

WHAT IS CULTURE?

Anthropologists, psychologists, and other social scientists have proposed multiple definitions of culture. Anthropologists often use Kroeber and Kluckhohn's (1952) definition of culture. Notice that this definition includes a large set of attributes that range from tangible objects (e.g., artifacts) to symbolic forms (e.g., traditional ideas and values):

> Culture consists of patterns, explicit and implicit, of and for behavior acquired and transmitted by symbols, constituting the distinctive achievements of human groups, including their embodiments in artifacts; the essential core of culture consists of traditional (i.e., historically derived and selected) ideas and especially their attached values; cultural systems may on the one hand be considered as products of action, on the other as conditioning of further action. (Kroeber & Kluckhohn, 1952, p. 181)

It is useful to separate this dense and complex sentence into its multiple components. First culture consists of patterns of behaviors. We discuss throughout this book the importance of looking at daily, repeated, and sometimes mundane activities. Second, symbols are the major achievement of human groups; patterns of behavior are often learned through symbols, and culture is passed onto others through symbols. Third, ideas and values are at the core of culture. Finally, culture arises from activity. In other words, the regularities of behavior create culture, and culture defines and regulates further action.

A particularly important component of Kroeber and Kluckhohn's (1952) definition of culture is the focus on symbols. This aspect of culture was also highlighted by anthropologist Clifford Geertz (1973), who emphasized the roles of communication and knowledge, both of which are symbolic. He wrote, "the culture concept . . . denotes a historically transmitted pattern of meanings embodied in symbols, a system of inherited conceptions expressed in symbolic form by means of which men communicate, perpetuate, and develop their knowledge about and attitudes toward life" (p. 89).

In subsequent chapters, we highlight the symbolic aspects of culture by discussing the importance of meaning systems by which people interpret some behavior as appropriate or inappropriate, or normal or pathological. Moreover, highlighting meaning systems also connects culture and religion. For C. Geertz (1973), religion is an aspect of culture that can provide people with ways of interpreting the world and with an organized and comprehensive system of meaning and values.

Both of these definitions consider culture to be a uniquely human phenomenon, as do most other definitions of culture. There is some evidence, however, that nonhuman animals may have some elements of culture. This issue is discussed in Research Highlight 1.1.

We conclude this section with the simple but elegant definition proposed by cultural psychologist Richard Shweder (2003). He suggests that culture is the "goals, values, and pictures of the world or ideas about what is true, good, beautiful, and efficient" (p. 11).

RESEARCH HIGHLIGHT 1.1

Do Nonhuman Animals Have Culture?

With evidence that some species exhibit behavior patterns that we typically ascribe to culture, there has been speculation that the construct of culture can be generalized beyond humans. There are multiple examples in which a small group of primates learns novel behaviors that are then passed on to subsequent generations of this group. For example, more than 50 years ago a group of primatologists documented the invention of sweet potato washing in a group of Japanese macaques. Whitten et al. (1999) identified 39 patterns of behavior that were present in some chimpanzee groups but not in others that were not explainable by ecological variables.

Van de Waal et al. (2013) used an experimental paradigm to explore social learning of food preference in wild vervet monkeys. They introduced dyed maize, half blue and half pink, to the troops. Chemicals were added to one color of maize to make it distasteful (blue for two groups and pink for another group), and this color was consequently avoided. After 4 months, the distasteful substance was removed, but despite the tastefulness of both colors, the groups continued to refrain from eating the previously distasteful color. Newly born infants copied the preferences of their mothers. Most interestingly, 15 males immigrated to new groups from other groups, 10 of which had previously been taught a food preference that differed from that of their new group. Most of these males quickly adopted the preference of their new group. Thus, there is clear evidence that social learning was occurring.

Obviously, there is a big step from this simple social learning to human culture, and most researchers do not believe that nonhumans have culture. The monkeys appeared to learn food preference by imitation, and there did not appear to be active teaching. Further, a key element of culture is the use of symbols and the development of meaning systems; these elements are absent in nonhuman species. Finally, it is unknown how long these preferences are maintained. Nevertheless, it appears that some aspects of culture are present in nonhumans.

ETIC AND EMIC PERSPECTIVES ON CULTURE

We return to the telescope metaphor introduced earlier in this chapter to discuss an issue central to the study of culture—emics and etics. The distinction between these constructs is central to how we study culture and has been the subject of considerable debate. This concept is elaborated in Chapter 2.

Emic approaches focus on the uniqueness of individual cultures. At one level of magnification, we see aspects of behavior, meaning, and relationships that are unique within each culture and are generally studied from the perspective of cultural insiders. Some researchers have emphasized that it is important to study individual cultures in depth to see how elements are systematically interconnected. For example, French and his colleagues (2012) studied how Islam is interconnected with parenting, peer relationships, and conceptions of social competence in Indonesian children and adolescents.

In contrast, *etic* approaches focus on how elements of culture are common across multiple cultures. To return to our telescope metaphor, at a lower level of magnification, some of the details of group uniqueness become blurred and we can begin to see commonalities across cultures. For example, despite the obvious differences between South Korea and China, both are heavily influenced by Confucianism, and there are some commonalities across the two countries with respect to the importance of education, peer relationships, conflict management, and the hierarchal structuring of relationships. Later in this chapter, we discuss several etic theories (e.g., individualism/collectivism) that group multiple cultures based on shared characteristics.

Throughout the book, we discuss both etic and emic studies with the perspective that considering both types of approaches in combination provides us with valuable lessons about culture. We recognize that people within different cultures differ from each other in multiple ways and that each culture has its unique history and ecological conditions and has developed various ways of finding meaning, managing relationships, raising children, and organizing other aspects of culture. At the same time, there are commonalities across cultures, and we can gain perspective by looking at elements that are shared across cultures despite the presence of unique aspects within each culture. One of the central issues is whether aspects of culture are unique or generalizable. For example, we can ask whether moral values that are present in one culture are also present in others and can consider whether aspects of culture in these countries explain similarities and differences.

CONCEPTUAL FRAMEWORKS FOR UNDERSTANDING CULTURE AND CHILD DEVELOPMENT: MICRO AND MACRO MODELS

We present seven frameworks for understanding culture and human development. We first discus four models that focus on how culture influences individual behavior or interactions; we refer to these as microsocial models. Next, we review three models that examine cultures according to a taxonomy or system of classification; we refer to these as macrosocial models. We use the term "model" to refer to these various frameworks because they highlight fundamental principles of culture in a way that is useful but not necessarily in full detail. These conceptual frameworks can overlap with the emic and etic perspectives discussed previously. The microsocial models primarily focus on the emic aspects of culture, and the macrosocial models focus on etic aspects of culture.

Microsocial Models

In this section, we describe four models that are useful for understanding how individual action, social behavior, and relationships exist within a cultural context.

Biosocial-Systems Model

Urie Bronfenbrenner (1979) introduced an extremely influential ecological model that describes the interrelations between biological and social aspects of human development. This model describes how individuals and relationships exist within a nested set of environmental and cultural contexts. A depiction of this model is presented in Figure 1.1 (we simplified this diagram by omitting some of the arrows that connect elements within and across the various

FIGURE 1.1. Selected Elements of Bronfenbrenner's Ecological System

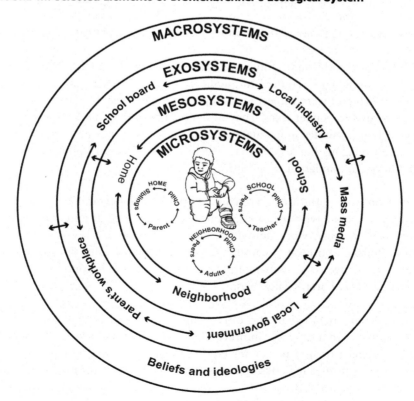

regions). At the center of the diagram is the individual child, who brings a variety of attributes (e.g., genetic endowment, history, cognitive ability, personality) to his or her connection to the world.

Microsystem. Depicted in the next circle, the microsystem, are contexts that are typically inhabited by the child (these include family, peer groups, neighborhood, classrooms, or instructional groups). The individual within these contexts interacts with others (e.g., peers, parents, teachers) while engaging in tasks (e.g., playing ball, watching television) in a setting (e.g., school, home, neighborhood). Later in this chapter, we expand on these elements in our discussion of activity settings.

Mesosystem. The next ring, the mesosystem, includes the interrelations between microsystems. The mesosystem comprises the various microsystems in which the child engages and the relations among them. As such, they exist whenever individuals move across microsystems. For example, children move from their family, their grandparents' home, school, neighborhood, and sports teams. These microsystems are interconnected through children and others who also are present in multiple microsystems. Children learn to navigate between and among these different microsystems.

The challenge of balancing the demands of multiple microsystems and moving between them is amplified for children who are immigrants. Eldering (1995) detailed the complexities of the mesosystem for Moroccan families who migrated to the Netherlands to work in skilled-labor occupations. Many of these families maintained their connections to Morocco through dual citizenship, interactions with family members in both countries, and involvement with the Moroccan community living in the Netherlands. The Moroccan immigrant children were required to attend local schools where they learned to speak Dutch and were subject to rules pertaining to social behavior, including those related to gender roles. They became embedded in a secular education system that promotes individuality and contrasts with the more interdependent and religious framework that structured their lives at home and within the Moroccan immigrant community.

Exosystem. In the third ring are contexts that are not typically inhabited by children but can have a major effect on them. These include parental employment (e.g., income, work hours), decisions of school boards and local businesses, media, and local government. We will see in a later discussion how economic changes (e.g., moving from a barter to a market economy) can lead to changes in children's daily lives.

Macrosystem. Included in the outer ring—the macrosystem—are societal characteristics that can have indirect effects on children. For example, beliefs and ideologies related to gender equality can contribute to equal educational opportunities for boys and girls. The inclusion of culture in the macrosystem is important in illustrating how culture impacts not only individuals, but also multiple ecological elements that have direct and indirect effects on children.

Chronosystem. It has become clear that an additional element—historical time—needs to be added to the Bronfenbrenner model. The chronosystem encompasses the entire ecological system as changes over time occur in both children and the environment. All of the nested levels are affected by the time period in which children live and also by the changes that occur in these various levels of the ecosystem as the child grows. For instance, 40 years ago, when the model was first introduced, technology was not included. Today, technology in various forms, such as cell phones and personal computers, needs to be included because of how it affects the way children interact with others and with the world around them.

Conclusions. An important aspect of the biosocial-systems model is that the various ecological components between and across levels of human experience are interconnected. For example, parental employment exerts a major impact on the daily interactions between parent and child, and can indirectly—through financial resources—impact the school the child attends, the neighborhood in which the child lives, and the peers with whom the child interacts. Some cultural psychologists argue that individuals, social interaction, and institutions are more strongly interconnected with culture than is evident in this model. For instance, Rogoff (2003) suggested that rather than depicting people and social interactions as distinct from culture, individuals and social interactions are actually inseparable from culture. To some extent, Bronfenbrenner acknowledged the interconnections with culture by suggesting that elements in any given ring are linked with processes occurring in other rings. In the following sections, we explore other models that explicitly connect cultural processes with children's interactions.

The Sociocultural Perspective

Lev Vygotsky, a Russian psychologist (1896–1934), developed a cultural–historical framework that describes the connection between culture and human development that has been extremely influential. Michael Cole (1966), an American psychologist, explained this view as follows: "The central thesis of the Russian cultural–historic school is that structure and development of human psychological processes emerge through culturally mediated, historically developing, practical activity" (p. 109). The three major components of this statement are outlined next.

First is the premise that cultural tools (also known as artifacts) mediate individual actions. These tools include not only tangible objects, such as computers, but also language, knowledge, and practices. Thus, when children perform a task, they do so by using tools, and those tools mediate the association between children and activities.

Second, children in each generation must relearn cultural tools. This is true not only with respect to language but of other artifacts as well. In later chapters, we discuss a variety of tools (that we group under the category of "scripts") that children use to manage conflict, effectively use aggression, and make moral judgments.

Third is the principle that children's everyday activities and social interactions are an essential aspect of learning and development. Everyday activities and social interactions, both the people with whom children engage and the types of ideas these people pass on to children, are inherently cultural. In activities and interactions, children learn cultural tools and how to use them through a process of engaging in activities with the assistance of more skilled individuals (e.g., older peers, parents, or teachers). Central to understanding how individuals learn new competencies is the "zone of proximal development" (ZPD). The ZPD refers to processes that are being developed but are not yet fully mature. Individuals attain maturity in two ways. First, through individual activity that can involve play and imagination, children may repeatedly practice tasks (e.g., shopping, having a party), and by so doing increase their level of mastery. Second, the most important way that children gradually gain mastery of skills is through the guidance provided by others. This form of guided learning, sometimes called apprenticeship, has been an important topic of study in cultural psychology. Researchers have explored how children gain cultural knowledge through formal instruction and by interacting with adults and older peers in situations in which learning occurs. In addition to formal instruction, cultural learning occurs as parents and others guide the child as they participate in repeated daily activities (Rogoff, 2003).

The cultural–historical model was informed by research conducted by Luria (1976), a student of Vygotsky, in remote villages in the former Soviet Union. This research investigated how changes in the people of this region resulted from the transition into the Soviet socialist economy that included literacy programs and group work. These economic changes led to cognitive changes as people shifted from using concrete to more abstract thinking. This study foreshadowed two ways that the sociocultural perspective continues to have a major impact on the study of culture. First is that cultural tools (e.g., computers, education, farming methods) lead to long-lasting changes in people and culture. Second, this perspective has been influential for understanding the interrelations among culture, education (formal and informal), and cognitive development. Throughout this book, we will continue to explore these themes.

Activity Settings

Children's interactions occur within contexts of space, time, and activities that are intertwined with cultural practices and meanings (Farver, 1999). These contexts are labeled *activity settings*, a concept that is a central focus of the behavioral-setting model developed by John Whiting and Beatrice Whiting (see B. B. Whiting & Edwards, 1988) in the Six Cultures Study. This approach also has roots in the biosocial-systems model (Bronfenbrenner, 1979) and the sociocultural perspective. A related perspective, described in the next section, is the developmental niche, proposed by Super and Harkness (1986).

The essential feature of the activity-setting model is that children learn culture by participating in interactions in settings and engaging in specific tasks with particular individuals. Cultural rules and practices play a central role in this process by defining who is in the setting; the tasks performed in these settings; and the meaning of the settings, participants, and activities. Children's participation in everyday activity settings is particularly significant for development. The repeated and reinforced nature makes activity settings a powerful context for learning because they provide multiple opportunities (trials) to practice new behaviors, see other people (models) doing these behaviors, and obtain feedback regarding performance (instruction, guidance, reinforcement).

As B. B. Whiting and Edwards (1988) explained,

> Our theory holds that patterns of social behavior are learned and practiced in interaction with various types of individuals in a variety of settings. In part, the effects of culture on these patterns in childhood are a direct consequence of the settings to which children are assigned and the people who frequent them. Socializing agents orchestrate children's participation in learning environments by assigning children to some and prohibiting others. (p. 35)

The concept of activity settings is illustrated by Dyson's (2010) anthropological study of girls in an Indian Himalayan village. Friendships between girls typically developed among children who worked together (e.g., gathering leaves to feed animals). There were rules the children followed during these activities, such as young girls should be the ones doing the tasks, children must assist each other to accomplish the tasks, and children who differ in caste should not become friends.

According to B. B. Whiting and Edwards (1988), children's social behavior is primarily a function of the settings that they frequently occupy. These settings are determined by ecological parameters (e.g., economy, physical environment) and cultural beliefs regarding what children of a given age and sex can and should do. Caregivers have the greatest impact on child development by assigning children to activity settings. For example, having children attend school puts them in settings that provide them with opportunities to interact with nonkin peers of their same age and sex. Super and Harkness (1986) made the following observation about Kokwet children living in rural Kenya:

> Children from late infancy through middle childhood spend most of their time in mixed-age, mixed-sex groups of children from the same or neighboring households. The tendency for boys and girls to associate more with same-sex peers did not emerge until after the age of six, when they were considered old enough to leave their homesteads and seek companions. Thus, it appears that the question of developmental trends in children's choice of companions cannot be addressed independently of the settings of their daily lives. (p. 553)

As noted in the previous example, children have limited freedom to select their peers because of their restricted independence. Consequently, they typically interact only with others in their kin network, neighborhood, school, activity groups, or others that they meet through their caregivers' social networks. To the extent that these groups are homogenous, children tend to interact with others with whom they share economic levels, education, and religion. Consequently, children living in the same culture may experience very different environments and companionship opportunities.

A major factor of children's interactions is the extent to which they associate with people of the other sex. Some gender segregation occurs because boys and girls have different interests and different styles of interaction (Maccoby, 1990). Also, as was the case for the Kokwet children, sufficient numbers of same-sex age-mates are needed to enable children to form same-sex playgroups. In some cultures (e.g., some Arab countries), interactions between nonkin members of the opposite sex are regulated (Booth, 2002). Other variations may be a function of differences in the settings that boys and girls occupy. For example, the activities of boys (herding) and girls (assisting mothers with cooking and caregiving) in a Giriama rural Kenyan community led to segregation and, consequently, boys and girls engaged in very different activities, which afforded children different learning opportunities (B. B. Whiting & Edwards, 1988).

Children's activities are infused with cultural meanings. Consider Farver's (1999) comparison of preschool classrooms attended by European American and Korean American children. In the Korean American classrooms, children were encouraged to work at their tables independently on study materials provided by the teacher. In contrast, European American students were encouraged to move around to different activity stations in the classroom and engage with their peers. These patterns reflect cultural differences in the meaning of learning. Korean American teachers in this study tended to focus on individual achievement and did not view play with peers to be important. On the other hand, the European American teachers viewed play and social interaction between the children to be important aspects of the preschool experience.

Participation in settings that vary by activities and companions affords children different learning opportunities that may have implications for both gender roles and personality. In their landmark Six Cultures Study, B. B. Whiting and Whiting (1975) enlisted teams of researchers who observed children between the ages of 3 and 11 in six countries: Kenya, the Philippines, Japan, India, Mexico, and the United States. They observed children's daily interactions with others, paying particular attention to the activity settings of children of different ages, gender, and cultures. The researchers concluded that participation in various activity settings was associated with learned behavior. In particular, they suggested that gender differences across cultures were associated with engagement in tasks and settings that elicited either aggression or nurturing behavior.

As part of the Six Cultures Study, Ember (1973) investigated what happened when boys from the Luo population of Kenya engaged in activities that are typically handled by girls in this culture (e.g., taking care of younger children, fetching water and firewood, making meals). In one community, because of the insufficient population of girls, boys did work that was usually done by girls.

Boys who took care of younger children inside the home were more prosocial and less aggressive than boys who did not engage in such activity. Ember interpreted these findings as evidence that gender differences are partly a function of the activities in which boys and girls engage.

The Developmental Niche

Super and Harkness (1986) expanded the activity-setting model to include both cultural customs and parental beliefs in the *developmental niche* model. These researchers adapted a concept from biological ecology, the ecological niche, and used it to describe the relation between humans and the cultural environment.

The developmental niche includes three subsystems that connect human development directly to culture: physical and social settings, child care customs, and the psychology of caregivers. Physical and social settings include the various environments that children and others inhabit. Childcare customs include typical child-rearing practices regarding sleep, eating, education, play, and work.

The third element of the developmental niche is the parental beliefs and values that are associated with activity settings and cultural customs that guide behavior. An illustration of the intertwining of customs and parental beliefs with activity settings is reflected in the way that Kokwet (Kenya) parents addressed children's language learning. Mothers expressed the belief that children learned to talk more from other children than from parents, and consequently, Kokwet mothers talked less to their 2- and 3-year-old children than did American mothers.

We return in subsequent chapters to the importance of the microsocial models described here. In particular, in Chapter 3, we describe the sociocultural perspective in relation to cognitive development. In Chapter 10, we discuss how children and adolescents in different cultures spend their time in various activity settings and the implications of recurring activities for individual development and cultural differences.

Macro Models: Classifications of Cultures

A number of attempts have been made to construct classification systems that group cultures into categories (i.e., etic models). In this section, we review three models that have been particularly influential: Fiske's (1992) taxonomy of elementary forms of sociability, Triandis's (1995) conceptualization of individualism and collectivism, and Markus and Kitayama's (1991) theory of culture and the self. Each of these models is potentially important for understanding the connections between culture and human development.

Elementary Forms of Sociability

Alan Fiske (1992) argued that across cultures, individuals use four elementary forms of human relations or sociability to organize their social interactions. These four forms—communal sharing, authority ranking, equality matching, and market pricing—are used in combination and for different purposes. Fiske developed this model based on his ethnographic fieldwork of the Moose community in Western Africa. Although the Moose people use all four forms of interaction, they use them in different contexts and with different frequency than they are used in the United States. In examining these forms of social relations, it is useful to think about how to distribute a valuable resource among members of a group. We will see that these forms of social relations lead to differences in how people conceptualize and accomplish the distribution of resources.

Communal sharing. Communal sharing (CS) forms of sociability involve the distribution of a resource without regard to individual contributions. For example, all members of a community may take food from a hunt regardless of whether or not they had participated. CS typically occurs within a defined group of others, such as a family, village, or collective of some type. Note that people may engage in CS for a specific purpose (e.g., distributing food) but not use CS to share other resources (e.g., money). People are not required to contribute equally to the resources but are obligated to share with others.

Fiske (1992) suggested that land is an important shared commodity in many cultures. He noted that the Moose people do not own land, and unoccupied space can be used by anyone who requests it. It was also common to establish shared grazing lands in the early history of the United States. In the 1600s, Boston Common, which is currently a large park, was shared grazing land that could be used by all inhabitants.

Communal sharing invariably entails divisions into ingroups (those with whom resources are shared) and outgroups (those not entitled to the resources). Although individuals are expected to exhibit kindness and altruism toward members of the ingroup, they may behave aggressively toward outsiders.

Authority ranking. Authority ranking (AR) describes how resources in the form of tangible objects, privileges, or power are provided to people based on their status ranking. An example of this was provided by Triandis's (1994) description of meal times in traditional Chinese families in which the grandfather eats first, followed by other males in descending age order, and then females by descending age. The privileges that high-ranking individuals experience are accompanied by obligations to be generous and protect others. This is reflected in Confucianism within which the leader is obligated to be virtuous and support others.

It is common in many cultures for social relations to be structured by AR. In traditional Indonesian Javanese culture, social relations are hierarchical, and there is a general principle that no two individuals are equal. This structure is reflected in the Javanese language, which requires the parties of a conversation to define their relative status using terms such as older brother and younger brother. Individuals who meet for the first time may go through an extensive exploration of their attributes (e.g., age, profession, education, marital status, number of children) to identify a characteristic that can be used to determine status. As we will see later in Chapter 8 on conflict management, AR systems streamline decision making and reduce conflict as subordinate individuals are expected to acquiesce to the higher ranking individual.

Equality matching. The focus in equality matching (EM) social exchanges is to ensure that each individual gets an equivalent amount. An unequal distribution in a particular instance results in an obligation to correct this deficit in the future. EM is an aspect of social relations in most cultures and is sometimes reflected in moral values and conceptions of justice. It can also be a factor in aggression such that an action by one party requires an equivalent or proportional response, thus leading to "eye for an eye" revenge.

Market pricing. The essence of market pricing (MP) is proportionality. Thus, individuals could receive a share of the resource in proportion to their input, or in proportion to some other criteria (e.g., need, merit). Social relations based on MP are viewed as contractual and, consequently, they exist to the extent that each party attains proportional value.

Asocial or null relationships. The four forms of sociability described previously apply to interactions that are governed by social rules. There are some relations between people that occur when there is no expectation of sociable relations. For example, thieves are likely not concerned with establishing and maintaining relationships.

Combining the forms of sociability. Fiske (1992) proposed that the four forms of sociability exist in all cultures, but they are uniquely combined and used for different relationships and contexts. He suggested that there is high agreement between members of a culture as to what form of sociality should exist for different types of social transactions between particular individuals in specific contexts. These forms of sociability are significant for development because children need to learn and practice relational behaviors that are socially appropriate in their cultural setting. In many countries, an initial socialization goal is for children to understand and function within hierarchies. For example, in traditional Javanese culture, children need to learn different forms of language to communicate with authority figures (e.g., their father) and with their peers. These forms of relationships also pertain to understanding how children in different cultures develop friendships (see Chapter 7), manage conflict (see Chapter 8), and share with each other (see Chapter 14).

These modes of sociability are also relevant to understand the categorical systems of cultures that we discuss next. Although each of the modes is present in all types of cultures, certain relational forms are more prominent in some cultures than they are in others. For example, in the United States, market pricing is more common than in some other cultures, and in Indonesian Javanese villages, communal sharing is common but is coordinated with authority ranking.

Individualism and Collectivism

The interest in individualism and collectivism grew out of Hofstede's (1980, 1991) highly influential study of 116,000 IBM employees worldwide. Based on the questionnaire responses, Hofstede grouped countries that were similar in each of four dimensions (i.e., power distance, individualism, uncertainty avoidance, and masculinity). Most of the subsequent attention has been focused on the individualism/collectivism dimension.

Triandis (1995) spent more than 40 years empirically researching the individualism/collectivism dimension by developing measures of the construct and exploring multiple characteristics of cultures that are associated with these dimensions. In this research, individualism and collectivism pertain to groups (i.e., societies, countries) in which most of the people view the world in a particular way.

Various definitions have been proposed for individualism/collectivism. Triandis (1995) suggested that individualism incorporates the idea of autonomous individuals as the unit of analysis, whereas collectivism incorporates the idea that groups are the unit of analysis and individuals are tightly intertwined parts of these groups. Thus, relationships among individualists are seen as contractual and are based on concerns of costs and benefits. In contrast, relationships among collectivists may be fixed, defined by firm boundaries between ingroup and outgroup membership. Kagitçibasi (1994) referred to individualism as the "culture of separateness" and collectivism as the "culture of relatedness."

In reviewing the history of individualism and collectivism in research, Triandis and Gelfand (2012) found that the distinction between individual autonomy and the group permeates many cultural aspects including law, religion, and philosophy. One especially influential example was presented by German sociologist Ferdinand Tönnies (1855–1936), who contrasted two types of social groups. *Gemeinschaft* refers to social groups and communities that are based on kinship and neighborhood relationships that reflect mutual affection and a sense of community. In contrast, *Gesellschaft* refers to social groups and communities that emphasize individualism with people connected through mutual self-interest. This distinction is used by Greenfield (2009) in her theory of cultural change and will be discussed later in this chapter.

Triandis (1995) suggested that four attributes of individualism and collectivism exist across cultures. First, collectivism is associated with the interdependence of the self, whereas individualism is associated with the independence of the self. This view of self permeates a variety of aspects of life including the distribution of resources, conformity to the group, and an emphasis on personal uniqueness and expression. Second, among collectivists, individual goals are closely aligned with group goals; this is not the case, however, for individualists. This alignment is particularly relevant when group and individual goals diverge. Third, social behavior in collectivist cultures is guided by obligations to others and social rules. In contrast, social behavior in individualistic cultures is more often directed by self-needs, contractual relationships, and personal attitudes. Fourth, there is a focus in collectivist cultures on maintaining relationships even when they are problematic. In individualistic cultures, however, the focus is on appraising the advantages and disadvantages of relationships with the goal of distancing oneself from those that are problematic.

Vertical and horizontal individualism and collectivism. Triandis (1995) suggested that it is useful to divide the individualism and collectivism dimensions into vertical and horizontal subgroups. The vertical dimension incorporates inequality and relative status and power, whereas the horizontal dimension incorporates ideas of equality and reticence to stand out. Singelis et al. (1995) developed a scale that measures these dimensions. Vertical individualistic cultures tend to emphasize competition, achievement, and relative status ("It is important that I perform my job better than others"; "Without competition, it is not possible to have a good society"). Triandis suggested that the United States fits into the vertical individualistic category, noting that there is an ethos of the importance of being "above average." Australia and Sweden are typical of horizontal individualistic countries because there is a perspective that individuals are equally free to live their lives and be treated similarly and have equal status (e.g., "I enjoy being unique and different from others in many ways"; "I am a unique individual").

The distinction between vertical and horizontal can also be applied to collectivist countries. Vertical collectivists are focused on fulfilling their duties and conforming to authorities and the group, thus willing to accept authority and inequality within the group ("I usually sacrifice my self-interest for the benefit of the group"; "I would do whatever would please my family, even if I detested the activity"). In contrast, horizontal collectivists focus on cooperation with others and tend to see group members as equal ("It is important to maintain harmony within my group"; "I feel good when I cooperate with others"). According to Triandis (1995), examples of vertical collectivist cultures include South Korea, Japan, and India. Horizontal collectivism appears to be more strongly applicable to groups within countries (e.g., the Israeli Kibbutz) and less applicable to entire countries. Indonesian traditional village social structures incorporate some elements of horizontal collectivism. Note, however, this culture also includes elements of hierarchal structures typical of vertical collectivism, illustrating the difficulty of applying the vertical/horizontal dimension to collectivism at the country level.

Correlates of individualism and collectivism. There has been extensive study and discussion of the characteristics associated with individualism and collectivism (see reviews by Triandis, 1995; Triandis & Gelfand, 2012). Among these characteristics are attributions, self-definition, goals, emotions, cognitions, norms, values, language, group processes, and leadership. Some of these will be discussed later in this book. For example, in Chapter 8, we describe how the models of individualism and collectivism are relevant to understanding how individuals in different cultures manage conflict; in Chapter 12, we discuss the pertinence of this construct to understanding shyness and social withdrawal; and in Chapter 14, we discuss the use of this construct to understand prosocial behavior and morality.

Critique of individualism and collectivism. Oyserman et al. (2002) provided a comprehensive review of the theory and empirical findings that pertain to individualism and collectivism. An important conclusion from their analysis is that individualism and collectivism are not opposite poles of a unidimensional construct; instead, elements of each exist in all societies.

Although North Americans and people in other Western countries tend to be higher in individualism and lower in collectivism than people in other countries, there are some notable exceptions. A comparison of European Americans with South Korean and Japanese adults using self-report measures of individualism and collectivism yielded inconsistent findings. This study is important because much of the research assessing country differences in individualism and collectivism has included comparisons of these countries. In several studies, there were no differences between these countries on individualism and collectivism, and in some studies Japanese scores were lower on collectivism than those of European Americans.

It is also important to reiterate that individualism and collectivism are applied to countries, but this does not mean that everyone in these countries shares these worldviews. Some of these differences are explained by natural variation in individual needs and characteristics within mostly homogenous countries and some by the presence of diverse populations in more heterogeneous countries. For example, Asian Americans score lower than European Americans in both individualism and collectivism, whereas Latino Americans score lower in collectivism but not individualism.

Some differences between countries are explained by the specific content of the scales used to measure individualism and collectivism. For example, people in the United States typically rate the importance of group harmony and obligations to others in the group lower than those in most other countries, but they also rate "sense of belonging to ingroups" highly. Thus, the extent to which U.S. participants score highly on collectivism is partly a function of the extent to which items tapping these different aspects are included in the measure. These findings illustrate that the extent to which a country is seen as collectivist or individualistic is a function of the definitions of the constructs.

Finally, there are questions as to whether or not individualism and collectivism can be assessed using self-report measures. First, it is uncertain if individuals can report their implicit values pertaining to their views on individualism and collectivism using rating scales. Second, there are concerns regarding difficulties of comparing the results from questionnaire measures across cultures, a topic that we will consider in the next chapter.

Independent and Interdependent Views of the Self

Markus and Kitayama (1991) refined the individualism and collectivism model by focusing on cultural differences that can be explained by variation in how individuals construe the self. The central thrust of their argument is that there are cultural differences in the extent to which persons tend to see the self as either independent or interdependent.

Clifford Geertz (1973) described the independent self as

> a bounded, unique, more or less integrated motivational and cognitive universe, a dynamic center of awareness, emotion, judgment, and action organized into a distinctive whole and set contrastingly both against other such wholes and against a social and natural background. (p. 48)

Thus, the independent self is autonomous and defined by internal attributes rather than by relationships with others or with the attributes of others. This view of the self appears to be typical in the United States and many other Western countries.

Contrary to the independent self, the interdependent self is construed as interconnected with others. Individuals see their actions as contingent upon the actions, thoughts, and feelings of other people in the relationship, and individuals are motivated to maintain their relationships with others. Consequently, individuals' views and actions may be more likely to depend on interpersonal context. The interdependent self is thought to be typical of populations in many countries in Asia, Africa, and Central and South America.

There are implications of these different self-views for relationships. Independence implies a focus on maintaining boundaries between the individual and others in ways that entail continuing appraisal of the advantages and disadvantages associated with the relationship. On the other hand, interdependence carries with it a focus on maintaining relationships and being attuned to the feelings of others. An extreme example of this is the ideal of South Korean friendships that is captured by the word "cheong." This ideal stresses a very high degree of empathy, which enables individuals to understand the feelings of others and anticipate their needs (S. Lee, 1994). This interdependence, however, is usually limited to members of a select group of insiders, which raises a general issue that the notion of interdependence incorporates the idea of a boundary between those inside and outside the group. In addition to consequences for relationships, independent and interdependent views of the self have implications for cognition, emotion, motivations, and goals.

Cultural differences are expected when cognitive activities are somehow connected with this self-view. For example, people with interdependent notions of the self tend to view objects in relational terms, whereas those with independent notions of the self tend to view the relations among objects in more conceptual or categorical ways. This was assessed using the cognitive style task of sorting objects (e.g., doghouse, dog, child) that can be grouped conceptually (dogs and children are living) or relationally (dogs sleep in houses). Consistent with expectations, Chinese children more often chose relational alternatives than did U.S. children (Chiu, 1972).

Emotional expression is also expected to differ as a function of views of self. In this regard, it is useful to consider whether emotions are self-focused and consequently associated with independence (e.g., anger, pride, sadness), or other-focused, such as those that involve taking the perspective of others (e.g., sympathy, shame). It is hypothesized that those with independent self-views are more likely to exhibit self-focused emotions than are those with interdependent construals of the self.

Finally, it is thought that views of the self have implications for motivation. Marcus and Kitayama (1991) suggested that individuals with an interdependent view of the self should be highly motivated to express and engage in actions that enhance their relationships with others (e.g., nurturance, help giving). Consistent with this perspective, Hau and Ho (2010) suggested that Chinese youth see educational achievement in part as a social obligation to their parents and their family. Social motivations can coexist with self-focused motivation as shown in findings that, consistent with Confucianism, Chinese youths' achievement is also viewed as self-cultivation. An additional self-focused aspect of motivation is the goal of striving for self-worth, which is often exhibited by people in the Unites States through attempts to take credit for success and to blame others or external factors for failure. Conversely, Chinese individuals display self-enhancement under certain conditions, but more typically provide credit to the group rather than to the individual and tend to be modest about their successes in their presentations to others (Kwan et al., 2010).

Critique of Markus and Kitayama's view of the self-system. Matsumoto (1999) argued that Markus and Kitayama's (1991) model has been highly influential in developing a theory that explains why cultural differences exist across many of the areas of focus in psychology. In his view, this perspective was consistent with a contemporary psychological view: "It made conceptual sense, fit with previous theories, and appeared to explain a lot of data" (p. 292). Matsumoto (1999), however, went on to suggest that one of the major problems is that there have been few empirical tests of these ideas. Whereas the model presumes that culture leads to self-construals that then lead to outcomes (cognition, motivation, emotion), research based on this model has mostly explored country differences. Moreover, investigators typically assume that people differ in self-construals and that these differences lead to the particular outcomes. The causal links, however, have not been demonstrated.

Other weaknesses of this theory are similar to those we described previously regarding the individualism and collectivism model and how countries actually differ on these dimensions. In particular, there is mixed empirical evidence indicating that the United States differs from South Korea or Japan in either individualism or collectivism, or with respect to independent and interdependent construals of the self.

This brings us back to some of the questions that were raised previously and will continue to be important questions throughout the book. First is the idea of whether countries can be grouped into categories (e.g., as typically exhibiting independent or interdependent views of the self). Second is the question of measurement and availability of appropriate instruments (typically questionnaires) to measure key constructs.

Implications of the individualism/collectivism and the independent/interdependent models for understanding development. Both of these models have been highly influential in the study of human development. For example, Chen (2011) attributed some of the differences between Chinese and Canadian children on dimensions such as shyness to respective cultural features of group orientation versus individual orientation, a dimension that maps closely to the individualism/collectivism and independent/interdependent constructs. In subsequent chapters in this book, the pertinence of the individualism/collectivism dimension to friendships (Chapter 7) and prosocial behavior (Chapter 14) are discussed. In these chapters, however, it is noted that the individualism/collectivism model does not appear to explain cultural differences in either help-giving or friendship, and consequently, the appropriateness and limitation of these models for understanding cultural variation in developmental processes needs to be carefully considered.

WHERE DOES CULTURE COME FROM?

It is useful to think of culture in the context of adaptation. Cultural systems enable people to survive by providing them with an organized system of practices that facilitate subsistence, child-rearing, and safety. An essential aspect of culture emphasized in this book is the mechanisms that exist to socialize children and provide them with the skills and practices, values, and belief systems that enable them to prosper as children and subsequently as adults.

Niche Construction, Culture, and Evolution

Evolutionary biologists have explored how humans use cultural innovations to alter their environments and develop within them. This process, labeled as either *niche construction* or *ecosystem engineering*, has been well documented in nonhuman animals who modify their environments, creating new ecologies (Odling-Smee et al., 2003). For example, beavers dam streams and, by doing so, create their own habitats. Furthermore, by changing their environment, animals change their odds of survival and reproductive success with the consequence that these cultural adaptations can lead to changes over time in the gene pool.

Humans have rapidly changed their habitats by making cultural adaptations (Flynn et al., 2013). For example, the transformation from hunter–gatherer to agricultural methods of subsistence was accompanied by very large increases in the size of groups, which required people to learn to develop cooperative and harmonious relationships with others. This also enabled specialization of roles (e.g., artists, government officials, teachers), the formalization of religion, and stratification by wealth and power.

Cultural adaptation has also enabled humans to live in extremely inhospitable environments. Boyd et al. (2011) detailed the immense cultural knowledge necessary for Central Inuit people to survive in the extremely harsh ecology of the Arctic Circle (e.g., making caribou clothing, constructing homes from snow, mastering seal hunting techniques, making archery bows from local materials). Innovations were gradually developed and passed onto successive generations through social learning. As an illustration of the complexity of knowledge needed to inhabit this land, Boyd et al. point to several examples of the "lost European explorer experiment" (e.g., Franklin Expedition of 1845–1846; Roald Amundsen expedition of 1903–1904), in which European travelers stranded in the Artic perished despite being initially well-stocked with food and equipment. These explorers did not have the cultural tools necessary to survive in this environment and did not develop them before their supplies ran out.

Ecological changes that persist over a sufficient period of time can lead to changes in the genetic pool. The most common example is the domestication of cattle and consumption of milk from dairy cattle being associated with changes in the presence of the gene that makes it possible to tolerate lactose (Gerbault et al., 2011).

Subsistence Demands and Culture

Most of the focus in the study of culture has been on how variations in subsistence demands are associated with cultural variation under the assumption that different qualities are necessary in different environments. This view—*subsistence theory*—was presented by Nisbett and Cohen (1996), who distinguished cultures based on herding from those based on farming. Herding cultures emphasize the individual toughness that is needed to protect herds and instill fear in potential thieves. These qualities are less important in agricultural communities in which the ability to develop harmonious relationships with others and develop complex social structures may be more important.

The association between subsistence patterns and culture is illustrated by wet rice agriculture, a major crop in Asia (e.g., southern China, Indonesia, Thailand, Philippines, and Vietnam) that supports high population densities because of the large yields and high calorie content of rice. Farmers plant rice in small plots (paddies) that are surrounded by built-up earth barriers to hold water, which are filled and drained periodically (see photo). It is necessary to construct a large irrigation infrastructure, maintain harmonious relationships with those in neighboring plots, and recruit a large labor force at various times during the season. These agricultural demands are thought to have led to cultures across the rice-growing regions that emphasize cooperation with others, formation of systems of mutual dependence and obligation, and the development of conflict-management systems that promote harmonious relationships within the community. Societies that are similar in subsistence demands,

The demands of wet rice agriculture have led to a cultural emphasis on cooperation, mutual dependence, and harmonious relationships.

however, do not necessarily meet their needs in the same way. In Javanese wet rice culture, a social structure based on shared community labor, group decision-making, and group intervention to resolve conflicts evolved. In contrast, Chinese agricultural communities developed a hierarchical system that relied on leaders to organize groups of farmers and manage conflict with others (Peregrine & Ember, 2001).

Talhelm et al. (2014) expanded the arguments of subsistence theory based on differences in the cultural demands associated with herding and farming to argue that different forms of agriculture (i.e., wet rice agriculture and wheat farming) partially explain cultural differences between northern and southern China. While wet rice agriculture entails interdependent social structures because of the need to maintain large-scale irrigation systems and bring together large labor pools, wheat farming does not require irrigation and thus requires about half the labor demands of rice farming. Consequently, Talhelm et al. suggested that cultures in wet rice-producing regions tend to be more interdependent than cultures existing in wheat-producing areas. Research Highlight 1.2 describes a study that supports this idea.

FACTORS THAT ACCOUNT FOR CULTURAL VARIATION

Cultures are complex and cannot be explained simply by ecological demands. Cohen (2001) outlined a number of factors that explain the diversity of cultures.

First, there are often multiple ways to deal with the same ecological demands, and consequently, populations may address these demands in different ways. The previous example of wet rice agriculture illustrates this point. Although

---

RESEARCH HIGHLIGHT 1.2

Cultures of Rice Versus Wheat Farming in China

To test their hypothesis that cultures in wet rice-producing regions are more strongly interdependent than cultures in wheat-producing areas, Talhelm et al. (2014) looked at Han ethnic group members from different regions in China that share a common language and history but differ in the predominant agricultural crop. The Yangtze River divides the northern wheat-growing region of China from the southern rice-growing region.

In the study, college students from wheat- and rice-production areas were compared on several tasks that had been previously used to assess independence and interdependence with findings consistent with the hypotheses. Students from the two areas were shown pictures of objects such as a train, bus, and tracks and asked to pair two of the objects. People from independent cultures tend to pair items symbolically (e.g., the train and bus go together because they are vehicles), whereas those from more interdependent cultures tend to pair items by function (e.g., trains and tracks go together because trains run on tracks). As expected, students from rice-producing areas used more functional comparisons than those from wheat areas. In addition, participants completed a loyalty/nepotism task in which they imagined going into business with an honest and a dishonest friend and rated how much money they would invest with each. Consistent with expectations that students from rice-growing regions would show more ingroup loyalty, they were less likely to punish the dishonest friend than were students from wheat-growing areas. The authors suggested that agricultural differences (as well as those between farming and herding) might account for some regional and cultural differences.

---

they share similar needs to construct complex irrigation systems and meet the intensive labor requirements of rice farming, societies differ in how these needs are addressed. A social structure evolved in Bali, Indonesia, based on shared community labor, group decision-making, and community intervention to resolve conflicts. In contrast, Japanese farmers tended to solicit the assistance of nonfarming kin to help during times that require intensive labor (Talhelm & Oishi, 2018).

Second, cultural characteristics that were developed in response to ecological needs at one point in time may persist long after these needs changed. For example, Nisbett and Cohen (1996) suggested that the higher violence rates in the southern United States stem from the initial settlement of this region by Scotch–Irish immigrants who came from herding cultures. It was important for herders to defend their livestock and respond aggressively to thieves and others who threatened their livelihood. Nisbett and Cohen argued that despite economies being vastly different from what existed in the home countries of immigrants, aspects of the herder culture continued in the new world and are reflected in violence rates and retribution exhibited by some people residing in the southern United States.

Third, many of the characteristics of the original culture tend to persist despite the influx of new members. This is illustrated by de Tocqueville's (2000) observations that perspectives on independence and self-reliance in the United States in 1835 stemmed from the beliefs of the original New England settlers. These ideas continue to flourish in the contemporary United States (Bellah et al., 1985). Nevertheless, the influx of new members can often bring about modifications as elements of the immigrants' cultures are transformed and incorporated into the established local culture.

Fourth, cultures can be profoundly influenced by wars and conquests. Political historian Francis Fukuyama (2011) suggested that the different societal structures of China and India are traceable to histories of intertribal warfare that united China into a single semihomogenous state, and the absence of such unifying wars in India. Another example is Mexico. Catholicism came to Mexico during the 15th century as a product of the Spanish conquest. The Catholicism of Spain, however, was not adopted in its entirety in Mexico, but rather transformed as it incorporated multiple aspects of Indigenous religions.

Fifth, it is common for elements of one culture to be adopted and blended into another culture. This is selective, as some elements are adopted, and others are not. In addition, cultural elements are often transformed rather than being adopted in their original form. For example, Arab traders in the 13th century gradually introduced Islam into Indonesia, which eventuated in Indonesia being the home of the world's largest Muslim population. The forms of Islam, however, vary in different parts of Indonesia as this was blended, depending on the region, with Buddhist, Hindu, and local religious elements (e.g., spiritualism and belief in the supernatural).

Sixth is the importance of ideas and innovation. Dramatic examples are in the development of religion. Islam, the youngest of the world's major religions, originated in Mecca during the 7th century at the time of prophet Muhammad. Today, it is the world's second largest religion. A variation of the idea that innovations and events can dramatically change culture is apparent by how the presence of an individual (e.g., Hitler, Gandhi) can have a profound effect on culture. A further illustration of the effect of innovations on culture is in the history of the use of chopsticks in Asian countries. Chopsticks originated in China sometime before 1200 BC, and this innovation was spread by traders to other countries along with other elements of Chinese culture. The current use of chopsticks generally corresponds with the extent of historical Chinese influence. These utensils became widely used in Japan, Korea, and Vietnam but not in Thailand or Indonesia, as they were more strongly influenced by India than by China.

The influences described previously have helped shape and continue to shape cultures and contribute to their diversity. Because there are so many forces that can shape cultures, some of which may be unique to a specific group, it is unlikely that explaining variations across cultures will be possible using simple classification systems such as individualism and collectivism. Instead, cultures are constructed from multiple elements that are combined in unique ways.

CULTURAL CHANGE

The forces described in the previous section can also contribute to cultural change. Cultures are constantly changing; sometimes this happens gradually and other times this is rapid. Societal changes caused by forces such as modernization, technological advances, wars, or political changes are associated with long-term changes in children's development.

There are numerous examples of how societal changes have led to long-term changes in cognitive functioning. As noted previously, Luria and Vygotsky (Luria, 1976) conducted one of the first studies demonstrating this point by showing how political changes and literacy instruction in remote villages in the former Soviet Union led to the development of abstract thinking. In another widely cited series of studies, Saxe (2012) documented how introducing a market economy into remote villages in Papua New Guinea led to the transition from using a simple, limited numeric system based on counting body parts to a more abstract number system.

Greenfield (2009) developed a general theory of cultural change based on the results from multiple studies. Her central thesis is that the transition from Gemeinschaft communities to Gesellschaft societies is associated with multiple changes in behavior, childrearing, and cognition. As noted earlier in this chapter, according to the framework advanced by Tönnies (1957), Gemeinschaft communities are typically insular, rural, low in technology, have limited role specialization, and have limited formal education. In contrast, Gesellschaft societies are urban, complex, connected with the outside word, and rely on schools to provide education. Transitions from Gemeinschaft to Gesellschaft are often associated with a shift from collectivism to individualism, lowered expectations that children will care for their elderly parents, transition to more abstract styles of thinking, diminished sharing, and an increased emphasis on ownership and individual rights. Although it is more common to shift from Gemeinschaft to Gesellschaft structures, a move in the opposite direction is possible.

There are many variations of cultural communities that incorporate elements of Gemeinschaft and Gesellschaft structures. Along these lines, Chen (2015) suggested that although there is abundant evidence that is consistent with the Greenfield model, there are a number of nuances that should be considered. First, he noted that most cultures have become diverse and complex, and as such, they incorporate both individualistic and collectivist value systems that are applied in different contexts and for different purposes. Second, as societies transition from Gemeinschaft to Gesellschaft, elements of the earlier social organization are preserved and new elements are transformed rather than adopted in their complete form. Therefore, Chen suggested that movement toward independence does not necessarily reduce the need to attain social integration and connectedness, and as such, people may create structures that accommodate both. Finally, he noted that much of the current research pertaining to cultural change has focused on cognitive change. He suggested that further attention should be devoted to understanding how cultural change affects relationships and social functioning.

Finally, it is important to understand how broad changes in society, economic systems, and the community at large translate into the everyday experiences of children. Gauvain and Munroe (2019) discussed several examples in which introducing a market economy with accompanying parent employment led to changes in the daily life of children who moved from home apprentice-ships of traditional crafts and small industries to formal schooling. This also affected how children spent their time, the settings they occupied, and the tasks in which they engaged. In other words, major changes in the village ecology translated into the regular activity settings of childhood, which are the contexts in which development unfolds.

CONCLUSION

In this chapter, we discussed definitions of culture and both micro- and macro-theories. Both the range and number of possible influences explains why cultures are so different, despite sharing some commonalities. In subsequent chapters, we will use these theories and explanations to explore cultural variation in multiple aspects of development.

Although much of the research on culture and human development has focused on group differences, it is essential to consider the diversity that exists within groups. One source of this variation is social class, which can include a variety of indicators of relative social position such as income, occupation, and education. The potential confound between social class and culture has received less attention than it should. Consider, for example, that two middle-class women in China and the United States may have much in common and may watch the same movies, read the same magazines, and may have even attended similar colleges. Thus, despite being from different cultures, these two women may have more in common with each other than either of them do with women from lower socioeconomic backgrounds within their own cultures. The potential confound of social class and culture has received the most attention in the literature on ethnic comparisons in the United States. Such studies frequently sample differences between populations on a specific dimension (e.g., parenting, social adjustment, and academic success) by focusing on majority and minority populations, and then attribute any differences to ethnicity rather than social class (Marks & Garcia Coll, 2018; McLoyd, 1990).

In the chapters that follow, it is important to remain cognizant that underlying differences between cultures and countries, there is likely large variation between individuals in that culture. In the next chapter focused on methodology, we consider approaches to exploring this variation.

For additional resources, see the Appendix.

DISCUSSION QUESTIONS

1. How might we explain differences between cultures that are in geographic proximity and that have common patterns of subsistence? In thinking about this, it is helpful to think about a few cultures (e.g., Italy vs. the Netherlands; China vs. Japan; Brazil vs. Colombia).

2. How do cultures change over time?

3. What are the advantages and disadvantages of different models of culture?

4. Do nonhumans have culture? Why or why not?

5. What activity settings do you inhabit, and what are the cultural meanings associated with these settings?

2

Methods for Studying Development and Culture

Researchers often spend time doing fieldwork to understand child development in different cultural contexts.

Researchers who study human development in cultural context use the scientific method to formulate and carry out their investigations. They create hypotheses on the basis of theory and use systematic techniques, both quantitative and qualitative, to collect and analyze data to test the theory. As with all research in developmental science, care is needed in selecting a sample, designing a study that taps development in some way, and ensuring that all ethical protections are in place (J. G. Miller et al., 2015). It is also vital for the researcher to have extensive knowledge of the culture(s) being studied and to use methods that are not biased in favor of any particular views about culture or ways of life.

https://doi.org/10.1037/0000228-002
Child and Adolescent Development in Cultural Context, by J. E. Lansford, D. C. French, and M. Gauvain

Examining culture and human development does not require that new methods be devised. Much of the contemporary research on culture uses established research methods. Yet, in many cases, the limitations of these methods for doing cultural research are evident. Of particular concern is the representativeness of the sample, which in any research can impede the interpretation and generalization of results. This issue is compounded by cultural inquiries because much of the developmental research is overrepresented by one group—middle-class children of European American ancestry (Nielsen et al., 2017). Even when this group is not included in a study, researchers may rely on findings from research that used this group to generate research questions about culture and development, formulate assessment methods, or to use as a basis of comparison for children living in other cultural settings. This approach not only threatens external validity, it introduces a standard of development—one that is based on untested assumptions of universality—to gauge child development in cultural circumstances that differ substantially from the original tested group.

In this chapter, we describe research methods that strive to avoid these limitations. We review several topics ordinarily covered in a research methods course, such as the identification and validity of independent and dependent variables, sampling methods, and qualitative versus quantitative approaches. Our purpose is not to review these topics comprehensively, but rather, to make it clear how accounting for culture requires a reappraisal of the decisions researchers make when they launch an investigation and decide who to study, what to study, and how to do the study.

When researchers study cultural contributions to human development, several goals guide their work. They hope to obtain knowledge that provides insight about human development as it occurs *in situ*—the place where the child's development originated—and has taken shape and is expressed. Researchers also strive to increase appreciation of development in its various forms. There are many viable and valuable ways to live life, and cultural approaches to human development should make this reality clear. Finally, researchers want to reflect the lived experiences of children and youth around the world as accurately as possible (Rogoff et al., 2018). With these goals in mind, whatever method is used will rely on the natural variation that exists across cultural settings to investigate the systematic relations between social and environmental conditions and human development. This is not a new approach. It was used in the early 20th century by renowned anthropologist Margaret Mead, who helped pioneer research on culture and human development.

Determining the appropriate method of study is only one aspect of conducting valid and useful research on culture and development. Other important aspects include deciding which culture(s) and topic(s) to study. Both need to be chosen carefully to have the potential to broaden knowledge of human variation and, in many cases, provide information that cannot be obtained by studying young people in a single culture. And, as we discuss later in the chapter, an important consequence of this research is wider appreciation of the need to examine carefully, and sometimes alter, established methods of psychological research.

One way that researchers have tried to address these concerns is to collect data in various cultural settings with a wide range of participants and incorporate diverse cultural perspectives and methods (Blicharska et al., 2017). This strategy enhances the validity of the findings. As Bornstein (2002) pointed out, "The larger the number of methods, ages, or cultures studied, the more compelling is the conclusion that observed findings can be validly attributed to the theoretical dimension of interest" (p. 262). Nonetheless, researchers also need to acknowledge that no single study can measure all or even many elements of a culture. Studying culture is like studying any complex process, such as human biology, where investigators accept that there are many ways of approaching a topic. For example, in studying stress and health, some researchers focus on biochemical processes, such as cortisol levels, and others look at structure, such as the cardiovascular system. This complexity has not stopped researchers from examining the many relations between the biological system and health. To do their work, researchers clearly and purposefully focus on certain aspects of biology that may be affected by stress. Similar tactics are needed in studying culture and human development.

Finally, care must be taken at every stage in designing and carrying out cultural research because implicit biases can diminish the value of the work in many ways—through the research questions asked, the methods used, the interpretation of results, and the characterization and evaluation of participants and their social groups in light of the results (Medin et al., 2010; van de Vijver et al., 2010). When such biases occur in research with cultural and ethnic groups, they can reflect systemic biases that help to maintain prejudicial views toward these groups. This situation is especially destructive when it is carried out in the name of science. Science is presumed to be an objective way of understanding the world and those who inhabit it. People often trust results claimed to be scientifically based. However, when studies that use biased methods are called scientific, their results are not scientifically based and they do not advance understanding. Rather, they perpetuate unfounded and unjust views of social groups.

Implicit biases are especially worrisome in intervention research that aims to put children or youth on the "typical or normative developmental course"—a course that is often based on prior research conducted in a different cultural setting, with a narrow cultural sample, or is based on a nonscientific view regarding the optimal course of development (Verma & Cooper, 2017). To reiterate, there are many viable and valuable ways to live life and any purported scientific findings that deny this reality need to be examined very, very closely. In the end, it is important to understand that a scientific study is only as objective as the methods it uses.

SELECTING A CULTURE AND TOPIC OF STUDY

The selection of cultural settings for research has both ideal and practical dimensions (van de Vijver et al., 2010). Although a random sample of cultures would be useful, such research is difficult, if not impossible, to conduct. In most research, practical matters dictate which cultures are studied. Like psychological research more generally, cultural research often relies on convenience sampling. Researchers draw from cultural groups to which they have or can gain access. Convenience sampling can be particularly problematic in cross-cultural research (van de Vijver & Leung, 2000). For example, if a study involves adolescents from secondary schools in countries that differ dramatically in rates of secondary school enrollment, the sample will be more representative of adolescents in countries with higher rates of enrollment than in countries with lower enrollment rates. Using stratified random sampling or other sophisticated sampling strategies can enhance confidence in the representativeness of the samples and make more apparent the differences between economically advantaged versus disadvantaged youth or between urban and rural samples.

The sampling constraints in cultural research make it especially important for the research to be guided by theory and accompanied by a clear rationale for studying a topic in a particular culture or cultures. For example, an aspect of development may be predicted by theory (or prior observation) to vary in systematic ways in the cultures that are the focus of the research. Chavajay and Rogoff (1999) used this approach to study attention, a basic cognitive process, in young children in two cultural settings, a traditional Maya community and an urban region in the United States. Based on prior observations, the researchers hypothesized that children in these two groups would differ in how they apply their attention when they work on an activity. Indeed, children in these two communities were observed to allocate their attention differently when they worked on problem-solving activities. Specifically, the Maya children were more likely to focus on two or more aspects of an activity simultaneously, while the U.S. children tended to focus on the steps of the activity sequentially or on one aspect at a time. The careful selection of cultural groups enabled the researchers to advance theory by showing how attention—a universal characteristic of cognitive development—is organized by culture, an insight that could not have been obtained by within-culture analysis or by studying cultures in which such differences do not occur.

Cultural Variation in the Meaning and Goals of Behavior

In conducting cross-cultural research, selecting the topic of study and choosing the methods to use are complex and difficult decisions. This is because behaviors that appear similar across cultures may not have the same meaning or value. Consider for example the questions that children pose to adults that ask for an explanation ("Daddy, why are you doing that?"). In some cultures, such questions may be welcomed and highly valued as they are seen as signs that the child possesses certain positive characteristics (e.g., curiosity, intelligence). In other cultures, however, like those with strict authority relations across generations, such questions may be interpreted differently, perhaps even negatively (e.g., as disrespectful or insolent; Gauvain et al., 2013). Even when behaviors are similar across cultures, they may have different consequences for development. For example, comparisons in China, Japan, and the United States have found that the developmental pattern of learning to count may unfold similarly across cultures, but it has different relations to future mathematics learning (Stevenson & Stigler, 1992).

It is also important to understand that the same developmental outcome may exist in two cultures, but the means by which the cultures reach this outcome can differ. In other words, behaviors may differ in form but they serve the same function in the cultures. This type of commonality is referred to as *functional equivalence* (Goldschmidt, 1966). For example, socialization in all cultures is directed toward mature competence, yet the definition of mature competence and how it is obtained varies across cultures. In some cultures, maturity occurs after a youth successfully undergoes a ritual during puberty that marks the transition into adulthood, whereas in other cultures it is based on marriage or financial independence from parents.

The idea of functional equivalence is theoretically and methodologically important. On a theoretical level, it underscores the fact that there are many pathways of human development (Greenfield, 2009). Indeed, the wide range of cultures on the planet today testifies to this facet of human adaptation. Methodologically, functional equivalence presents difficulties in designing research and interpreting results. As illustrated earlier regarding children's use of explanatory questioning, two behaviors may be similar in form in two cultures, yet they may play very different roles or be seen differently across cultures. The functional role of behavior may also change over time within a culture. Consider how financial independence from parents has a different meaning when a society is economically strong and stable than when it is undergoing high rates of inflation or severe economic inequality as we see in the world today.

Culture as a Research Variable

In most research about culture, the individuals under study, or participants, are identified by the culture to which they belong. That is, culture is treated as a category and not as the complex and dynamic social–psychological process that it is. Many faulty assumptions underlie this practice. In some studies, culture is used as if it is an independent variable. Recall that in experimental research, some variables are independent variables and some are dependent variables, and different levels or states of the independent variable are used to determine or test how the dependent variable, the main object of study, relates to these differences. In experimental studies, the independent variable is manipulated, and participants are randomly assigned to different levels or states of the variable. This practice is impossible for culture because people cannot be randomly assigned to a culture. Thus, although culture might be used to identify and differentiate groups of participants in a study, culture cannot be manipulated as if it is a true independent variable.

While it may be clear that culture cannot be used as an independent variable in experimental research, problems arise when culture is used as if it is an independent variable in quasi-experimental and naturalistic research. Developmental psychologist Beatrice Whiting (1975) referred to this practice as the problem of the "packaged variable." According to Whiting, social scientists often study important dimensions of human experience, such as age, gender, social class, and culture as if they are independent variables. Yet none of these dimensions is a true independent variable. Rather, they are social categories that represent a set (or package) of information about a person's lived experiences. In other words, these dimensions are not psychological variables at all; they are social categories that indicate information about a person's psychological experience. For instance, many psychological researchers are interested in contributions of gender to cognition and in order to investigate it, they compare the behaviors of males and females on some cognitive activity or measure. When gender differences are found, what do they mean? They may suggest biological differences between males and females, although most research indicates that such differences are rarely, if ever, biologically based (Hyde, 2014). It is more likely that the observed gender differences result from living one's life as a male or female in a particular cultural setting and perhaps at a particular point in history (e.g., before or after women's suffrage, the availability of safe and accessible contraception, or the #MeToo movement).

In like manner, culture is a packaged variable. It contains experiences that may, indeed, relate to developmental outcomes. Finding a relation between culture and a psychological measure does not, however, tell us what aspect of culture is important in explaining this relation. As a result, the finding does not represent the end of the scientific inquiry—it is, in fact, the beginning. Much work remains to determine how an individual's participation in a culture pertains to the behavior in question. To do this investigative work, B. B. Whiting (1975) recommended that researchers collect detailed descriptions of the living and learning environments of a culture, an approach that has been developed in activity setting analysis discussed in Chapter 1 (Farver, 1999). Whiting also recommended that researchers remember that cultural processes and practices are connected to each other. That is, culture contains many different behaviors and ways of understanding the world that are connected in a larger, overarching system. As such, a single attribute of a culture may not explain the psychological finding, but instead a constellation of cultural factors is responsible.

Juang and Nguyen (2009) attempted to unpack culture to understand the factors that contribute to the development of problem behavior (e.g., misconduct, delinquency, substance use, risky sexual behavior) in Chinese American adolescents. Although it has been shown that Asian American youth as a group, including those of Chinese ancestry, exhibit lower levels of problem behavior than those in other ethnic groups, it is unknown what psychological aspects explain why these adolescents engage in or desist from such behavior. After looking at multiple possible contributors, the researchers found that neither generational status nor involvement in Chinese culture (i.e., behavior, attitudes, or values) predicted problem behavior. Instead, adolescents' sense of family obligation and expectations of autonomy predicted problem behavior.

Age as a Variable in Cultural Research

Developmental psychologists often include age as a "packaged variable" in their research. In fact, age is used so widely in developmental research that we rarely question what it means when it is used as a psychological variable. The implicit assumption is that age is a fixed biological description of a person that determines, in some way, how development unfolds. Yet a person's age by itself is not psychologically informative. Rather, what is informative is what age stands for in a culture, including the biological (or maturational) changes it signals, the experiences that individuals have over a certain period of growth, and expectations regarding children and youth at a particular point in time. Even the use of age as a marker for development is more prominent in some cultures than others (Rogoff, 2003).

We are not suggesting that the relation between age and maturation is irrelevant. Cultural practices and expectations often build on maturational events, but the ages when certain experiences or behaviors occur may differ greatly. For example, motor development in the first year of life has a wide maturational timetable, and the way it unfolds is defined by culture. Caregiving practices determine the opportunities infants have to develop motor skills, including the age at which children begin to sit on their own (Karasik et al., 2015). These practices reflect many factors including cultural routines (e.g., how infants are carried), expectations about when infants should have certain motor skills, and what is safe and appropriate for infants to do at certain ages. Research by Karasik and colleagues shows that the range of possible motor behaviors in infancy is much broader than was previously assumed, and that the variation results from cultural experiences that support and encourage motor development early in a child's life.

Stated more generally, findings from cross-cultural research reveal that development is not solely determined by biological maturation. Instead, culture plays a large role in the nature and timing of change from one phase of development to another. And cultures differ markedly in the experiences that children have by a given age that contribute to psychological development. Consider the fact that 8-year-olds in one culture may not be permitted to cross the street alone, while 8-year-olds in another culture travel long distances on their own to collect water or carry out other household tasks (Putnick & Bornstein, 2016). Cultures also vary in what is expected of children at certain ages. In many small-scale traditional societies, children as young as 6 years of age are expected to care for younger siblings, whereas this expectation occurs much later, perhaps not until the teenage years, in most industrialized societies (Lancy, 2008). In cultures with compulsory schooling, a child's age in years is confounded and correlated with how long the child has attended school. This occurrence makes it very difficult to disentangle which aspects of development result from increase in age, more years of schooling, or a combination of the two (van de Vijver et al., 2010).

SELECTING PARTICIPANTS FOR A STUDY: CULTURE AND INDIVIDUAL DIFFERENCES

So far, we have discussed how a culture is selected for study. Now we turn to selection of participants within a culture. As in most research, it is important to select participants as randomly as possible. Yet, this can be difficult to accomplish even in a familiar culture such as the United States where participants are often drawn from university and college communities that differ on many dimensions from communities without such institutions. Given the difficulty of obtaining a random sample, it is important to describe research participants thoroughly and consider the limitations to generalization that may result from sampling.

The selection of research participants raises questions about individual differences within a culture. Individual differences such as a child's age, interests, capabilities, and other aspects of psychological functioning, like emotionality, are pertinent to studying psychological development in any culture. All of these factors contribute to a child's socialization experiences, and this variation, explained by D'Andrade (1984), provides a complexity that is vital to the maintenance of culture itself. This is because cultures need an ongoing source of individual variation to ensure there is sufficient diversity within the group for approaching and solving problems that emerge (Gauvain, 2009). For example, individual variation in responding to the environment, such as emotional reactivity and how goals are approached, can lead to different ways of dealing with unforeseen circumstances. These variations may be especially important in sustaining a culture during periods of uncertainty or instability (e.g., rapid and widespread changes resulting from environmental or social crises), which are times when unforeseen and unfamiliar problems can arise and need to be solved in order for the culture to survive.

Does the converse experience hold—does culture contribute to individual differences? It may, for instance, by setting the boundaries or consequences associated with the expression of certain characteristics or traits. This does not mean that individuals who have certain characteristics are not a part of a culture, but rather that cultures may respond to these characteristics in different ways, which then affects their further development. This point is well illustrated by looking at cultural differences regarding the acceptance of shyness, a topic that we will consider in greater depth in Chapter 12. Chen and his colleagues (see Chen, 2012) found that shyness of children in Chinese and Canadian cultures is viewed differently among community members, including peers. In China, shyness is considered a sign of maturity and is associated with peer acceptance, whereas in Canada shyness is viewed more negatively and is associated with peer rejection. Thus, over time, culture can contribute to how individual characteristics, such as shyness, develop and contribute to social experience and development.

It is important to remember that although much of the research covered in this book describes practices and behaviors that are widely shared or displayed in a culture, there is individual variation within cultures, and this variation is important theoretically and empirically. Theoretically, it underscores the active contributions of individuals, including children and youth, in creating culture. As such, it challenges deterministic views of psychological functioning and of culture itself. In empirical terms, individual variation is the norm not the exception. Even in research examining cultural routines and practices, individuals differ in the degree to which they adhere to these practices, which can have direct implications for psychological development (H. Betancourt & López, 1993). For instance, children who live in very religious families will engage in certain cultural practices more than children whose families are less religious. These differences, in turn, affect whom children interact with on a regular basis and what they learn from these experiences.

SELECTING A RESEARCH METHODOLOGY: QUALITATIVE AND QUANTITATIVE METHODS

Collecting data about development in culture begins with making several decisions about which method(s) to use. For example, imagine a researcher wants to study the typical activities of young children in a certain cultural community. How might she go about collecting the data? Clearly, she cannot study all of the children in the community, so she needs to select a sample, a meaningful and manageable size group comprised of individuals who are representative of the children living there. That is, the children being studied should possess the same characteristics of the larger population. Identification of the sample also depends on the method of data collection the researcher plans to use.

Cross-cultural research relies on both qualitative and quantitative methods of study. In this chapter we describe both of these methods, but first we provide information about how the discipline of anthropology has influenced the ways in which psychologists study culture and human development. Anthropological studies of childhood not only predate psychological research on this topic, they helped to promote research on child development in cultural context and also influenced the content areas that are studied. The primary contributions from anthropology include the ethnographic method, the idea that cultures can be identified on some dimension that can then be used to understand a culture or compare across cultures, as well as techniques for observing children in naturalistic settings and for interviewing people who have different cultural histories than the investigator.

Anthropological Approaches

In the early 20th century, anthropologists began to study young people living in non-Western settings to determine whether or not their development followed the same course researchers had identified among children living in Western industrialized societies (LeVine, 2007). As the research progressed, one conclusion became clear: Understanding children and their acquisition of culture, referred to as *socialization*, was an immense undertaking. This insight emerged gradually and surprised many cross-cultural researchers who, for a long time, assumed that the acquisition of culture was straightforward and that children ultimately became adults of the same general makeup as their forebearers. That is, these early researchers were making assumptions about the nature of children and childhood that have since been challenged.

Ethnography

Ethnography is a qualitative method of inquiry that includes in-depth and detailed observation and description of a culture and its people in their environment as they go about their lives. By the 1930s, cross-cultural studies of children started to appear in ethnographies with some regularity (Munroe & Gauvain, 2010). Developmentally oriented ethnographies were mixed in coverage. Some were full-fledged ethnographies of childhood, some were part of a more general ethnographic study, and others focused on specific aspects of child experience like task responsibilities; play activities; and events associated with age, such as initiation ceremonies.

This early work influenced later research because it helped establish socialization, education, and developmental transitions (childhood to adolescence, adolescence to adulthood) as standard topics of study. It is worth noting that most of this early research occurred prior to the introduction of formal schooling and other forces of modernization—including the prolonged absence of many adult males because of extensive migratory wage labor—causing substantial changes across societies almost everywhere. Consequently, the contributions of these early researchers remain among the most valuable sets of empirical information about child life before the onset of these massive societal changes that continue today.

Cross-Cultural Comparison

Another contribution from anthropology is the method of cross-cultural comparison in which each culture is treated as a coherent unit, a technique called *holocultural research* (Ember & Ember, 2001b). This approach was introduced in the early 1950s by anthropologist John Whiting and psychologist Irvin Child (J. W. M. Whiting & Child, 1953), who wanted to study the long-term effects of early experiences on personality. Whiting and Child were influenced by Freudian theory and aimed to test these ideas across cultural settings. To do so, they used the Cross-Cultural Survey, an archived ethnographic resource now called the Human Relations Area Files (HRAF; Ember & Ember, 2001a; Murdock et al., 2000). This large, now computerized database archive (https://hraf.yale.edu)

includes an extensive set of ethnographic materials on past and present cultures from around the world. Whiting and Child compiled and analyzed the childrearing information available in the HRAF from a world sample of 75 societies.

The holocultural approach has been used for surveying socialization practices and certain childhood experiences, such as mothering, that are viewed as central to human development in the study of Western children. For instance, one such study by Weisner et al. (1977) included more than 150 small-scale societies. These researchers found that infant caregiving solely by the mother occurred in just 3% of the cases, and that care of young children exclusively by the mother did not occur at all. These findings led to the conclusion that many functional systems of caregiving for young children, in addition to maternal care, exist around the world.

Despite the utility of this method, researchers were limited to information available in the archives that was often collected for other purposes or to answer a different set of questions. To address this problem, John and Beatrice Whiting launched the Six Cultures Study of Socialization (SCSS) in the mid-1950s (B. B. Whiting & Edwards, 1988). Separate research teams who used a common method of study were sent to six countries spread over four continents. The clearinghouse for the data was at Harvard University, led by Beatrice Whiting. The project produced several influential writings in cross-cultural methods, including a set of monographs on each culture with detailed descriptions of socialization practices (B. B. Whiting, 1963), a volume on the relations between sociocultural contexts and children's behavior in daily settings (Whiting & Whiting, 1975), and a methodological guide for cultural-developmental inquiry (J. W. M. Whiting et al., 1966).

The SCSS led the way in illuminating the broader contexts (techno-economic, social-organizational, ecosystem) within which human development occurs and the effects of those contexts on children's social behavior including helping behavior, seeking attention, dominance, and aggression. The monographs from the field sites provided a level of detail on childhood—from birth to adolescence—that had not been available previously in the anthropological literature. This approach furthered the growing tendency to include information on socialization and child life in standard ethnographies. The emphasis on how the environment impacts cultural learning was especially formative for later approaches including the developmental niche (Super & Harkness, 1986), ecocultural theory (Weisner, 1997), and bio-ecocultural models (Worthman, 2010). With that said, the SCSS culture-sampling was limited. All but one of the six cultures practiced sedentary agriculture, there was no urban sample (but one suburban U.S. community), and there were no hunter–gatherers or nomadic pastoralists. We refer to information from the SCSS in various chapters in this book.

Naturalistic Observation

One innovation in the SCSS project pertained to naturalistic observation, which continues to be important for studying children in cultural context. In the SCSS project, researchers used repeated 5-minute observational protocols over a fixed period of time with 3- to 11-year-old children in the different cultural samples (Whiting & Whiting, 1975). Anthropologists created these running narratives as they followed children in their daily activities. This work generated a set of 12 "summary act categories" (e.g., offering help, reprimanding) that occurred commonly across the six cultures, but with different frequencies across the communities. As a result, this method offered quantitative comparability both within and among cultures. Ultimately, many others adopted this method, or a similar technique (e.g., see Ember, 1973; Harkness & Super, 1985; Hewlett, 1991; LeVine et al., 1994; Nerlove et al., 1974; Rogoff, 1981; Weisner, 1979).

One drawback of this approach is the lack of interobserver reliability. This limitation was overcome with the "spot observations" method (Munroe & Munroe, 1971), which focuses on recording an individual's activity at the initial moment of observer–participant contact. In other words, two observers record the behavior at the same time, and the recordings are compared for consistency or interrater reliability. With that said, a main limitation of this technique is that it does not allow for the measurement of ongoing behavior sequences. Although the use of spot observations and more continuous records of an ongoing behavior would be optimal, the research time and effort required have seldom been available.

Anthropologists have used naturalistic observations to uncover aspects of human behavior and development that would otherwise be difficult to obtain. For example, in the 1960s, researchers examined the subsistence lifestyle of foraging hunter–gatherers because it was believed to characterize human society until the emergence of agriculture about 10,000 years ago. A project with the Botswana !Kung people led to generalizations that were assumed to apply to all foragers, including the idea that males in these societies play a minor role in rearing small children (Konner, 1977). Later research among the Aka people, central African foragers, disputed this view. Hewlett (1991) found that Aka fathers were within reaching distance of their infants 50% of the time, and they held their babies "at least five times more than fathers in [all] other human populations" (Hewlett 1992, p. 153). These observations made it clear that evidence from a single hunter–gatherer society was not enough to generalize to the entire group. The observations also suggested that patterns of child experience among foragers were not attributable to evolutionary factors, but rather to specific adaptive pressures in the environment (Lancy, 1980). More generally, these findings highlight the problem that occurs when societies with similar lifestyles are assumed to have similar customs and childrearing practices.

Systematic Field Observations

In the 1960s, another type of cross-cultural research emerged, often involving anthropologists and psychologists working in teams, that built upon laboratory techniques used to study children's cognitive performance (e.g., see M. Cole et al., 1971; M. Cole & Scribner, 1974; Dasen, 1977; Dasen et al., 1978; Greenfield,

1974; Irwin & McLaughlin, 1970; Price-Williams, 1962; Serpell, 1979a; Wagner, 1978). Until that time, most cultural developmental research focused on children's social behaviors (play, skills, social interaction, work contribution) and socioemotional development.

Soon after this research began, it was found that children in traditional societies did not perform as well on cognitive tasks as those in urban-industrial environments. The differences appeared on a wide variety of tests, including Piagetian "stage" attainment; logical reasoning; moral reasoning; memory; and even on nonverbal, hypothetically culture-free tests (for further discussion, see Dasen, 1974; Goodnow, 1976; Greenfield, 1997; Wagner, 1981). There were many reasons suggested for the poorer performance, including a lack of familiarity with the tests. Attempts to compensate or control for the discrepancies often involved a complex series of adjustments (types of tests and methods of testing) that, in the end, did not eliminate many differences in performance (e.g., Gay & Cole, 1967; Lancy, 1983).

Yet, in more naturalistic observations conducted around the same time, children in non-Western settings demonstrated impressive expertise of their everyday experiences, such as relational and spatial knowledge, classification systems, number and measurement concepts, and pattern representation—and their expertise sometimes surpassed similar behaviors observed among children in Western communities (e.g., see Greenfield & Childs, 1977; Saxe, 1981; Serpell, 1979b). Thus, although children in traditional societies displayed high levels of functioning, such competence was not easily transferrable to Western-style testing situations or activities. Because these types of activities are often the focus of Western and non-Western comparisons in children's cognitive performance, researchers suggested that schooling could account for many of the differences that were formerly explained as cultural (Rogoff, 1981). We pick up this topic again in Chapter 11.

Despite extensive research on the cultural basis of cognitive development in the latter part of the 20th century, differential performance across cultural contexts is still not well understood. Even when viable methods are used, it is clear that not all cultural variation in cognitive performance can be explained by differences in societal institutions (such as schooling). Moreover, the underlying processes of cognition and development that connect learning in cultural context to cognitive growth await specification. Yet this research, for all its limitations, was the first to use structured observations and in some cases quasi-experimental methods to try to specify some of the processes of learning that define and support cultural socialization.

Qualitative Approaches

There are three main qualitative methods of gathering data on children and youth in cultural context. Researchers either observe young people in a naturalistic setting or in one arranged for the study; they ask young people about themselves; or they interview people who are close to them. Each method has great potential for providing insight into culture and development, yet each has limitations. The choice of method ultimately depends on the culture(s) and research questions being asked. And many investigators use several methods in the same study; for example, they may observe children and interview their parents. If the findings of a variety of methods converge, researchers can reasonably conclude they are valid (Bornstein, 2002).

Observation

Many psychological researchers value observational data for studying culture and development, and they typically observe children or youth in their natural or everyday settings. Participants may be observed in and around their home; outdoors as they carry out daily activities; or in social settings with siblings, peers, or adults in the community.

When researchers observe children or youth in cultural context, they must decide what behaviors to record, how detailed the observations will be, and how frequently behaviors will be recorded. A researcher interested in a specific behavior may arrange a situation and use a structured observation. Suppose a researcher is interested in sibling play and whether older siblings help their younger siblings if they need assistance, and how they do so. The researcher may invite sets of siblings to a quiet area where certain activities or objects (such as toys) are available and ask the children to play together as she observes them. The researcher can then watch how the siblings interact and whether older children offer help or instruction, if younger children elicit assistance, and how younger children behave when assistance is provided. Maynard (2002) used this technique to learn about sibling interaction in a rural Maya community in Mexico. She found that children assume responsibility by age 4 for teaching younger siblings, and by age 8, children are quite skilled at using various instructional techniques.

Structured observations can be used to study a range of topics. For example, LeVine and colleagues (1994) investigated whether the instructional interactions that mothers provide for their young children differ in cultures with formal schooling. The researchers recorded mothers in the Gusii community of Kenya where there was little formal schooling at the time, and in U.S. middle-class families where formal schooling is widely available. Mothers taught their 6- to 25-month-old children age-appropriate tasks based on the Bayley Scales of Infant Development. Gusii mothers tended to instruct their children verbally, demonstrating the entire task in advance and telling the children to complete the task as demonstrated, and when the children completed the task successfully, their mothers did not praise them. In contrast, American mothers used verbal instruction throughout the task; often demonstrated part of the task while the children worked on it; encouraged task exploration; and when the children finished, their mothers praised them. The Gusii children were more cooperative with their mothers, but they completed the task less often than did the American children. In explaining these differences, the researchers pointed out that the Gusii mothers and children were in an unfamiliar situation; usually the children learn skills by observing older children and siblings. Also, compliance is important because Gusii children are often responsible for domestic activities, and praise is avoided at all ages because adults think it leads to conceit and undermines group solidarity. This research indicates that certain modes of instruction are more common in some cultures, and the methods mothers use to instruct children are informed by experience with formal schooling. More generally, the findings show that maternal instruction reflects cultural values and goals for children's learning and development.

In some field observations, investigators may apply a highly structured situation, such as a set of tasks used in prior research, to compare children's performance with earlier findings. To explain this approach, we draw from the concepts of etic and emic discussed in Chapter 1. If the tasks used for the study in the new culture are identical to those used in prior research, this is an etic approach because the method has not been changed in any way. If the researchers investigate this same idea, but adapt the task to the new culture—for example, by using local materials or ways of interacting with children—it is a derived etic approach because the method is based on, or derived from, the new culture. If, instead, the researchers observe children's everyday behaviors in the new culture to see if they exhibit a particular behavior of interest, they are using an emic approach because it focuses on the actual activities of children in their own cultural context.

To illustrate, consider a field study in which the investigator wants to explore children's understanding of liquid conservation, a concept introduced by Piaget, to determine whether the same age-related patterns found in Western settings hold up in another cultural context (Dasen, 1977; Price-Williams, 1962). In the late 20th century, many cross-cultural researchers studied children's understanding of conservation because Piaget claimed his age-related stages of cognitive development were universal—they would occur in all children around the world in the same sequence and at roughly the same ages. Note that only cross-cultural comparison can test this claim. If the researcher uses the same type of pitcher and beakers to hold the liquid along with the manner of questioning that Piaget used, it would be an etic approach. However, if the researcher changes the materials and questioning to reflect those used in the culture being studied, it would be a derived etic approach. Finally, if the researchers observed children to see if they exhibit understanding of liquid conservation in their everyday lives, then the research would use an emic approach.

Observational data are valid only when the observer or other features of the situation do not distort the participants' behaviors and responses, which are called *demand characteristics*. We know from research that demand characteristics can threaten the validity of the data being collected because usual or customary behaviors change in the presence of an outside observer. When parents are being observed, for instance, they tend to display less negative behavior toward their children. When data are collected in a cultural setting that is different from the researchers' culture, demand characteristics may be magnified

because the participants may feel uncomfortable and behave differently knowing that someone from outside the community is observing them.

Increasing the familiarity between the researcher and community members
helps minimize such distortions. For example, the researcher(s) may live in the
community for a period of time, perhaps months, before conducting the observations. Sometimes observers are recruited from the community and trained to
conduct the observational protocol (Munroe & Munroe, 1971). When local
observers are trained, but not informed about the study hypothesis, *observer
bias*—the tendency of observers who are knowledgeable about the purpose of
the study to be influenced by that knowledge—is reduced. For example, to
reduce bias of observers recording children's play at set intervals, the observers
would be informed about what types of play were being assessed, but they
would not know what the researchers hypothesized (e.g., that social play is
more complex than solitary play).

Interviews

Another method for gathering information about young people in a culture is
through interviews. Interviews conducted with the young person are called
self-reports, and individuals may be asked about their beliefs, behaviors, or values. Research Highlight 2.1 describes how interviews with adolescents in
tumultuous political situations can be informative about their own experiences
and concerns.

In some studies, individuals are asked about other people. For example, children could be asked about their parents or peers, or parents could be asked
about their child. Compared with adults, children (especially young children)
are less attentive, slower to respond, and have more trouble understanding the
questions being asked. Yet, despite these limitations, certain kinds of information—such as how a child feels about another person or an experience—are
difficult to obtain in any other way.

Researchers may also interview people who are close to a young person
being observed, such as family members, teachers, health care workers, and
sometimes peers. Interviews with parents and other family members can be
especially valuable because they are based on many observations across a variety of situations. And even if parents and siblings are not totally accurate in
what they report, their perceptions, expectations, beliefs, and interpretations of
events and behavior may be just as important in describing the young person's
reality (Grusec & Hastings, 2015). For example, whether or not parents have
high academic expectations for their child, the child's behavior may be greatly
influenced if she believes that her parents want her to perform well in school.

Quantitative Approaches

Quantitative methods are frequently used by psychologists to study culture.
This approach, which may involve assessment instruments—such as surveys;
questionnaires; and parent, teacher, and peer raters—can be used to compare
multiple cultures or to learn more about individual cultures.

RESEARCH HIGHLIGHT 2.1

Interviewing Adolescents About Their Life Experiences

Interviews are typically more effective with adolescents than with young children. Oftentimes, the questions developmental psychologists use when they interview adolescents are based on the researchers' own interests and research goals. However, some research involves asking adolescents about their views on the circumstances of their lives, including cultural and political matters. One goal in this research is to discover different perspectives among young people living in a community or country. This approach is based on the idea that when adolescents are asked for their viewpoint, researchers can move away from their own assumptions about what participants think and do. Developmental psychologist Colette Daiute suggests that one way to do this is to invite participants to tell a variety of stories, from a variety of perspectives, to help the researcher understand the experiences through the eyes of those who lived them.

An example of this strategy comes from Daiute's (2014) interviews with young people growing up during and after the wars that shattered the former Yugoslavia, creating mass displacements and major political and economic changes. Adolescent participants living during these postwar contexts described their own and other people's experiences, wrote letters to public officials about what could help youth to thrive in these circumstances, and narrated stories about their own personal experiences. These dynamic forms of narrating the experiences of people's lives, including their own, revealed how these youth were making sense of the situation, how they understood their lives in relation to it, and what they hoped to achieve.

This approach provides insight into developmental concerns and challenges during times of great strife, and it is especially valuable for researchers from outside the community who do not know about these experiences firsthand. It has the potential to reveal how adolescents living in complex social circumstances think and feel about them. This method has been helpful for investigating how sociohistorical events, rural versus urban residence, religious and ethnic minority status, and immigration contribute to within- and across-country variations in psychological development (Motti-Stefanidi & Asendorpf, 2017).

The quantitative approach to studying culture has been criticized partly because of a history (that unfortunately sometimes continues in the present) of researchers uncritically administering instruments developed in one country to people in another country, and then interpreting the findings as a reflection of important differences between the cultures. Such an approach is not only culturally insensitive, but is also poor science that is likely to result in misleading conclusions. In this section, we discuss ways that researchers can optimally use quantitative approaches to explore culture. We begin by discussing the need for researchers to value the knowledge of the people living in the culture.

The Importance of Insider Knowledge

In order for researchers to conduct meaningful research in a culture that differs from their own, it is essential for them to obtain insider knowledge of the culture they plan to study. Many of the methods described previously (i.e., observations, interviews, participant observation) can be used to obtain that knowledge. We strongly recommend that researchers spend time in the country they are studying. But even with extensive language study and time spent in the country, it is unlikely that they will be sufficiently knowledgeable of the nuances of cultural meaning systems without including local experts on the research team, including bilingual scholars, among others.

For example, in his studies of Islam and social competence of Indonesian adolescents, Doran French collaborated with Urip Purwono, an Indonesian psychologist who earned his degrees in the United States, along with graduate students fluent in English, parents and teachers familiar with adolescents, and a religious expert. In their study of adolescent romance and popularity, the researchers consulted with adolescents to obtain insider knowledge of these topics. These local experts helped the investigators understand the phenomena, offered advice on appropriate measures, and interpreted the meaning of the findings.

Another way that researchers can gain insider knowledge about their study is to work on a research team that includes researchers from, or familiar with, the local area where the research will be conducted (Lansford et al., 2019). Local collaborators can provide necessary insight into Indigenous beliefs and practices that can impact development, and they can help guide appropriate sample selection. A local collaborator can also provide access to resources for obtaining potential participants. For instance, if researchers are interested in cultural variation in how children learn mathematics in school, a local collaborator who is associated with schools in the area is invaluable. Local collaborators may also have knowledge of rules and regulations for conducting research in that location. Some rules may be governmental regulations regarding protection for human research participants. Other rules may be social practices or conventions about polite or acceptable behaviors (e.g., whether or not it is appropriate for youth to make eye contact with elders).

Various issues can arise when conducting collaborative international research on development. It is especially important to avoid adopting a deficit perspective. Behaviors that appear to be self-evident in one culture may not be in another, a realization that may challenge current theory and research findings (Cheah et al., 2015). For instance, meta-analyses have shown that maternal warmth and nurturance are related to more positive child development (Kawabata et al., 2011; Yap et al., 2014). Chinese (and other Asian) mothers are often characterized as being harsh in their parenting and low in warmth (Juang et al., 2013), which has led to a deficit view of Asian parenting being less adequate for child development. Some researchers (Chao, 2001; Cheah & Li, 2010) have challenged this viewpoint and proposed that warmth expressed by Asian and Asian immigrant mothers is based on their engagement in cultural practices, such as taking care of children's daily routine needs and providing guidance and educational opportunities, which often are overlooked in Western-based measures (Cheah et al., 2015).

Collaborations that include people from the culture can reduce the risk of applying a deficit perspective because they can point out biases in the research questions and measures a priori. A deficit perspective is especially likely to occur when research is conducted in situations that present risks to healthy development such as poverty, war, or other forms of adversity. International collaborations can help researchers understand how extreme circumstances may result in developmental strengths as well as vulnerabilities (Sharma & Verma, 2013). In addition, what constitutes a risk factor in one place might not in another; for example, poverty in a low-income country might entail a different set of experiences than poverty in a high-income country.

Constructing Questionnaires and Rating Scales

A persistent question that researchers have is whether or not measures have equivalent meaning across diverse cultural contexts (Knight & Zerr, 2010). To ensure the validity of research, it is important to ascertain that any measures or assessments used in a study actually measure what they are intended to measure. To establish validity of cultural research in any cultural setting, it is important for the cultural group to develop their own instruments or for cultural outsiders to work with local researchers to adapt measures developed elsewhere for use in a new cultural setting. The selection of measures can also be guided by prior research that has established a measure's cross-national validity (Duku et al., 2015).

Translation. One aspect of establishing validity involves translation. Any measure, instructions, or other written task materials need to be translated into the language used by the participants. Translating instruments from one language to another is difficult and should be approached carefully. First, it is important to realize that many of the psychological terms that are used do not have an equivalent meaning in another culture. Examples of this are "amae" in Japanese and "choeng" in Korean. Both of these convey very close relationships between people, but they are not equivalent in their meaning and cannot be translated into English.

It is optimal to have bilingual investigators and, if possible, a team of bilingual researchers to do the translation. If there is more than one bilingual researcher, they can discuss the items and arrive at an optimal solution. In addition, nonbilingual experts can participate in a focus group with the bilingual researchers interpreting the results.

At a minimum, it is necessary to conduct forward and backward translation of items. This involves translating the instrument into a new language (e.g., English to Spanish) and then having someone else who does not have knowledge of the original instrument translate it back into the original language (e.g., Spanish to English). The original and the back-translated instrument are then compared. In most cases, there will be some discrepancies between the two versions, requiring discussion and exploration to resolve. When a satisfactory translation cannot be achieved, the item will need to be eliminated. It is important to note, however, that going through the translation process as described does not guarantee that the translated item will have the same meaning as the original item. There are often subtle differences between the original words and the translated versions. This is particularly the case because language is interconnected with cultural meaning. For example, the meaning of the translated term for "shy" is invariably affected by the cultural meanings of shyness.

One common source of discrepancy between the original version and the translation pertains to valence (extent or severity). For example, consider the difference among three synonyms used to describe shyness: reserved, reticent, and fearful. There are subtle differences in the extent to which each of these English words describes behaviors that may not be captured by translation. If there are subtle differences between the original and the translated versions, it is unlikely that they would be uncovered using back-translation methods. Now we return to a point that was made earlier in this section—that the effective use of quantitative methods to study culture is built on a foundation of deep knowledge about the culture under consideration.

Rating scales. Many quantitative instruments require participants to make judgments regarding the severity, frequency, or some other quality of a behavior or characteristic. For example, a common self-report scale of loneliness includes the following item:

> How often do you feel alone? 1 (*never*) 2 (*rarely*) 3 (*sometimes*) 4 (*often*)

Or a teacher could be asked to rate a student's sympathy toward peers using the following item:

> When this child sees someone being treated unfairly, he/she sometimes doesn't feel very much pity for the person.

1	2	3	4	5	6	7
Doesn't describe child						*Describes child very well*

There are multiple problems in comparing responses across cultures to items similar to those just presented. Two of the most important are described next.

Use of extreme scores. First, there are well established differences across cultures in tendencies of respondents to use the extreme points of a scale. For example, East Asian respondents tend to use the middle points of the scale (i.e., the child is average on this dimension) more often than do European American respondents (Chen et al., 1995). Thus, to the extent that this bias exists on the items presented previously, European American respondents, as compared with East Asian respondents, would report more loneliness and teachers would report less sympathy from the child, regardless of the actual state.

One approach to addressing this issue is to apply a mathematical correction (typically labeled "standardization") to force the means and distribution of scores to be the same for each country. Although this is commonly done, it is risky. Suppose a researcher is interested in comparing personality Trait X of children in the United States and South Korea and finds that in contrast to the American participants, few South Korean children give themselves high ratings on the items used to index this trait. This pattern could occur because of cultural differences between the two countries in use of extreme scores, but it could also be that South Korean children are low on this trait. Changing the distribution would, therefore, result in children in both countries being evaluated as the same on this trait, which would be inaccurate. Consequently, using standardization when comparing scores across cultural groups needs to be done with caution.

Reference group. The reference group problem is serious, and if left unchecked, it can lead researchers to make inaccurate conclusions. This problem occurs when people are asked to make judgments about some attribute (e.g., its frequency or severity), and they often do so by referring to a population with whom they are familiar. For example, imagine two teachers, one of whom works in an upper middle-class suburban school and the other in an alternative school for students with discipline problems. It is likely that the students rated as "aggressive" by the suburban teacher would be viewed as less aggressive in their actual behaviors than those students who are rated as "aggressive" by the alternative school teacher.

The severity of the problem of reference groups is illustrated by Weisz et al.'s (1995) research comparing American and Thai children. Classroom teachers rated 5- to 11-year-old children living in the United States and Thailand using the common Child Behavior Checklist. This measure has undergone extensive validation in Thailand. Teachers rated Thai children as exhibiting much more severe problem behaviors than U.S. children, which is surprising because Thai children are typically viewed as being very well behaved. The researchers then conducted direct observations of classroom behavior and found that the U.S. students exhibited many more problem behaviors than the Thai students. The authors explained their results by describing differences in the norms of behavior used by the teachers in the two countries when completing the instrument. Given that the teachers expected the Thai students to be very obedient, even minor infractions were considered to be serious.

The problem of reference groups is of special concern whenever people make subjective judgments about themselves or another person. Consequently, it is very difficult to make comparisons across countries regarding the intensity or frequency of behavior based on subjective assessments unless it is also possible to count occurrences or use a more objective assessment to validate the judgments.

The same reference group problem can also complicate within-country comparisons of gender or ethnic groups. Whenever ratings (self, teacher, peer, parent, or clinician) are used to appraise differences, it is possible that raters will use norms that pertain to one of the groups only. For example, a girl might be rated as highly aggressive despite engaging in behavior that is typical of moderately aggressive boys.

Statistical Comparisons of Items

Difficulties may arise when researchers attempt to use measures developed in one country to assess development, parenting processes, or educational quality in a different country. Country-specific measures can avoid many of these challenges; however, there are tradeoffs between achieving cultural relevance and obtaining internationally comparable data (Bornstein, 2012). In response to these concerns, numerous measures for early development and early caregiving environments have been developed for use in low- and middle-income countries, involving national and international experts and stakeholders in a collaborative process (Raikes, 2017; e.g., see the United Nations' Sustainable Development Goals Measuring Early Learning and Quality Outcomes Project [MELQO]; Hyson, 2017).

Researchers who use measures developed in one culture to assess participants in another culture will often use analytical tools to assess the measurement equivalence of the instruments. A detailed overview of this issue would take us into some complex statistics and is beyond the scope of this book (interested readers, see van de Vijver & Leung, 1997, for more detail). We can briefly, however, discuss the importance of internal consistency.

Quantitative researchers frequently use scales that consist of multiple items. Typically, each item assesses an aspect of the construct being assessed, and the mean of the items is used as the indicator of the construct. Consider for example the UCLA Loneliness scale (Russell, 1996) that has been used across many countries. Below are five items from the 20-item scale; each is answered using a 5-point scale that ranges from *never* to *often*.

- How often do you feel that you lack companionship?

- How often do you feel shy?

- How often do you feel isolated from others?

- How often do you feel that you are no longer close to anyone?

- How often do you feel alone?

Looking at these items, it is immediately clear that each one questions an aspect of loneliness, and we would expect that people who report that an item describes them would also respond affirmatively to most of the other items in this set. We can statistically measure the frequency of this response pattern by looking at the correlations among the similar items and determining which responses to one item are correlated with responses to others. To do this, we can assess the internal consistency of the items that is typically measured using Cronbach's alpha. This provides us with an index of the extent to which people who complete the instrument and answer items that assess similar content, do so in the same way.

We can use the method just described to review the adequacy of our translated measure by assessing the extent to which people in Culture X answer the items with the same consistency as in the original population. For example, suppose we added this item: "I feel sad when I view pictures of people on Facebook or Instagram having more fun than me." We have not tested this item, but we would not be surprised to find that the responses of American adolescents would be similar to their other responses on the Loneliness scale. We would also not be surprised to discover different results in other countries. For example, both of these websites are blocked in China, so adolescents there might find this item confusing.

What should a researcher do if the internal consistency of an instrument is lower in one population than in the country in which the measure originated? First, the researcher needs to look at each item to see which ones are not associated with the others. This may uncover problems with translation or ambiguities about the meaning of the item in the new language. In some cases, however, this will reveal that the item is not appropriate to be used in that country and must be eliminated from the scale. In other cases, it might mean that the entire concept is not relevant in the country and the researchers should not use the measure.

Advantages of Using Multiple Raters and Multiple Measures

The Weisz et al. (1995) study described earlier reveals the advantages of looking at the convergence of multiple measures and/or multiple raters when conducting assessments of children both within and across cultures. We can assume that all measures have some flaws and that convergence across measures and raters can partially compensate for this.

For example, French et al. (2008) measured each construct using multiple indicators in their study of religion and social competence of Muslim Indonesian adolescents. They assessed religious involvement through a combination of adolescent self-reports of spirituality and religiosity and parent reports of the same constructs. Prosocial behavior was measured through a combination of teacher and parent reports, and problem behavior was measured through a combination of teacher, parent, and adolescent reports. Although not perfect, this approach can address some of the problems associated with using single measures. To the extent that similar patterns emerge across raters, researchers can be more confident in their conclusions.

STUDYING DEVELOPMENTAL CHANGE IN CULTURAL CONTEXT

A main focus of developmental research is on change over time, and developmentalists prefer using the longitudinal method to collect these data. In this method, the same individuals are studied at various points in their lives. For example, a child may be observed at ages 2, 3, and 4 to determine if play behaviors change over this time period. This method is difficult to use in cultural research because it often takes years to collect the data, and researchers may not have the opportunity to do so. A short-term longitudinal study in which the same people are studied for a short period of time, usually a few months, is more feasible in culturally based research. However, this approach is limited to questions about culture and development that can be addressed adequately over such a brief time period.

Consequently, researchers who study culture and development usually employ the cross-sectional method in which individuals of different ages are studied at the same point in time on the same behavior or characteristic. For instance, a team of researchers (Munroe et al., 1984) used spot observations to study the development of gender-related behaviors in 192 children who lived in four, small-scale traditional communities by observing 12 children from each community at ages 3, 5, 7, and 9. Using this method, the researchers were able to determine how gender-related behaviors differ across age levels in each community as well as age-related patterns in these behaviors across the communities. Of course, because there were different children at the various ages, the researchers were unable to determine whether the children who exhibited gender-typed behaviors at age 3 also exhibited them at age 5.

An issue that emerges in studying change over time, regardless of where the research is conducted, is generalizing across generations, called *cohort effects*. A cohort is a collection of individuals who share a characteristic, such as being born in the same time period, who are grouped together. Generational cohort effects can occur because children in one generation may grow up with experiences that differ from children in earlier generations. If the experiences differ significantly, research findings based on one generational cohort may lose relevance for another cohort. For instance, young children's learning experiences before entering primary school differ greatly for children who were born before and after the widespread use of computers and related technology, such as tablets and other mobile devices. Currently, cohort effects have great relevance to cultural research because of the massive societal changes around the world resulting from globalization, urbanization, migration, and the various types of technology available (e.g., electricity, home-based water supplies, computers, global positioning systems). These changes affect development in many ways, including alterations to the everyday experiences of children and youth (Gauvain & Munroe, 2019).

Establishing Patterns and Causes

Selecting a sample and a method for gathering information allows a researcher to describe some aspect of human development and, if possible, identify the reasons development occurs as it does in a culture. As stated earlier, experiments are typically not possible when the research question is about culture. However, it may be possible to conduct a field experiment. For instance, if a researcher is interested in the role of culture in the effectiveness of a new instructional technique in mathematics for primary school students in Germany, Japan, and the United States, a field experiment may be used. The new technique would be introduced to one classroom in each cultural setting at the same time that another technique, also standardized across the three settings, is introduced in another classroom. The researcher could then test children's mathematics knowledge in the area of instruction in the six classrooms (two in each school in each of the three cultures) both before and after the instruction to determine if there is any change in the students' knowledge, what type of change has occurred, and the magnitude and direction of change in the three settings.

Although it is possible to conduct such a study, and research described in Chapter 11 used a similar method, it provides limited information about culture. Think about what you would conclude if the intervention just described was effective in each culture, with the highest rate of learning in one culture (Japan), the lowest rate of learning in another culture (the United States), and the results for Germany falling somewhere in between. How would you explain these differences in relation to culture? There may be different cultural contributions underlying these patterns, but without further study it would be very difficult to know exactly what they are. Any number of factors may have contributed, including prior learning, instructional experience, classroom practices, or parental support.

As this example shows, even though a study can be designed and carried out across cultural settings, it may not yield insight into how culture contributes to the results unless there is further study of the aspects of culture that may have led to these differences (H. Betancourt & López, 1993; B. B. Whiting, 1975). It simply identifies differences across the cultures on whatever was measured.

Correlational Methods

Many of the questions that researchers have about culture and human development are not amenable to causal analysis. As a result, most studies rely on correlational methods. Correlational methods can tell us whether experiences of young people in a culture are related to certain aspects in the culture in a regular or systematic way and, also, the strength of the relation. For example, how does sibling caregiving in middle childhood, a common practice in many cultures in the majority world, relate to the development of empathy? The relation may be positive in some cultures, with simultaneous increases in scores on sibling caregiving and on the measure of empathy that is used. In another culture, there may be little relation between these measures, or perhaps a negative relation (as one score increases, the other decreases). Or the relation may be positive in two cultures, but with different strengths or magnitude (e.g., in one culture the relation is strongly positive and in the other it is only moderately so).

Even when there is a similar relation across two cultures, it may occur for different reasons. For instance, in one culture, early sibling caregiving may give children practice with perspective-taking, or sharing the viewpoint of another person, which is a critical component of empathy. In another culture, early sibling caregiving may reflect cultural values of responsibility and the pride children feel when they take on more mature cultural roles and responsibilities. And in another culture, it could be a combination of these two relations. We do not describe all these possible relations to complicate the matter, but rather to underscore how careful analysis of developmental processes along with a deep understanding of the cultures are needed to design and interpret studies about the relation of culture and development.

The critical point to remember about this type of research is that a correlation does not indicate causal relations between factors. It simply tells us that two factors are related to each other and the strength of that relation. Thus, the correlations between sibling caregiving and empathy do not indicate that caring for younger siblings caused greater empathy development. Any number of factors other than sibling caregiving could have improved children's empathy scores. For example, suppose that certain older siblings in a family are selected by their parents to care for their younger siblings because they see these children as caring and responsible. In other words, the older child's ability to display empathy is what led the parents to ask the particular child to care for the younger siblings.

If correlational research does not allow the researcher to determine causation, why would it be used to study culture and development? As we already discussed, many questions about culture and development are difficult, if not impossible, to study in a controlled research design that might yield causal insight. Also, understanding causal processes is not the goal of all developmental research, including research on culture and development. Many investigators are primarily interested in describing the patterns and paths of development as they naturally occur in cultural context, which is what the correlational method attempts to describe.

Case Studies and Within-Culture Analysis

In many studies, the goal is to understand the developmental pattern of an individual or group of individuals within a culture. This approach, called a case study, is similar to that used by anthropologists in ethnographies and by psychologists who conduct in-depth studies of a single child or group of children, such as a neighborhood or classroom. In the late 1800s, in one of the first recorded case studies of a child, Charles Darwin (1872) kept a diary of his infant son's emotional expressions. He then used this record as the basis for his theory of emotional development in infants and children.

Sometimes a case study provides insights or hypotheses that later investigations pursue in a more systematic fashion. For example, careful observation of one child learning a valued cultural skill as an apprentice, such as a young weaver or seafarer, may generate ideas about how learning such skills, which are often important to the livelihood of the culture, occur. The chief limitation of the single-case approach is that without further study or a larger sample, it is difficult to know if the results of the case study generalize from the one individual or group of individuals to other people, situations, or cultures.

To reprise an earlier point, the research method that a scientist uses to study development in culture depends on the questions being asked. Researchers may combine methods over a series of studies on the same topic, a tactic that can increase insight into a phenomenon (Bornstein, 2002). A researcher, for example, may start off in an unexplored area by using a correlational approach to establish some possible relations among the factors studied. The researcher may then use a more focused field study method, such as systematic observations or interviews, to achieve a clearer view of the relations among these factors. Finally, the researcher may use a single-case study, either of an individual or a group, to provide more details about the process being studied.

SOME FINAL COMMENTS ON CHOOSING A METHOD OF STUDY

Research methods are a set of tools that researchers can draw from to study what they want to learn. With that said, theoretical perspectives tend to favor some methods over others. Researchers trained in more qualitative anthropological methods often use case studies of individuals or certain groups of people to gather details about cultural experiences or activity settings. Researchers interested in how children learn particular cultural skills tend to rely on structured observation because this method permits close inspection of how learning occurs. Researchers interested in adolescent development in cultural context often rely on interviews and surveys because adolescents are at an age when they are able to describe their own impressions (attitudes, opinions) of their experiences.

Of course, researchers with differing theoretical perspectives can and do use similar methods, so what would distinguish their investigations? A main difference is in the way the researchers interpret the data they collect. For a researcher interested in sociocultural theory, an observation of a child playing with an age-mate may provide information about social influences on children's learning. In contrast, an ethologist, who is interested in how behaviors reflect evolutionary adaptations, may interpret the very same behavioral observations in relation to peer dominance hierarchies and their role in human survival. If a researcher does not make their theoretical orientation about the study clear, it is often possible to detect it by examining how the data are interpreted.

Overall, developmental research strives to increase knowledge about children and youth, with the hope that the lives of young people will benefit from this knowledge. To understand and support human development around the globe, we believe it is necessary to study the full range of cultural contexts in which development occurs (Lansford et al., 2019). Yet, as we said earlier, the samples included in most developmental research currently fall far short of this goal, and individuals from Western industrialized settings are overrepresented (Nielsen et al., 2017).

One promising way to broaden the reach of developmental research is for researchers to engage in international collaborations to collect data in a wide range of countries and incorporate diverse cultural perspectives (Blicharska et al., 2017). It is essential to study children in their own cultural context in ways that respect local values and practices. This type of inquiry will not only advance understanding of development more generally, it can have practical use by informing international nongovernmental organizations (INGOs) that provide aid to cultural communities through new policies and programs that affect children and their families.

In recent years, many INGOs have focused on the experiences of very young children. This work is partly motivated by the UN Sustainable Development Goals (SDG; UNICEF, 2016), particularly Subgoal 4.2 that stresses the importance of early child development and care, including preprimary education. Much of this work is directed toward children living in poverty, which presents great risks to healthy development. These efforts have benefited many children as seen from assessments of physical development, cognitive and language skills, and socioemotional competencies (Engle et al., 2007). Yet, despite these positive outcomes, some scientists worry that this work is often based on assumptions that undermine the communities it aims to help (Kjørholt, 2019). Of particular concern is when INGOs offer immediate or short-term assistance for poor children and their families, yet they do little to create long-lasting structural changes in the socioeconomic conditions and governmental policies that cause the poverty (Penn, 2019). Also, for these efforts to succeed in the long term, they need to involve the community from the onset and be aligned with local values, practices, and priorities.

The research movement known as Indigenous Psychologies can play an important role here. This approach uses empirical methods to describe the historical foundations and strengths of a community and its members, including the way that children are cared for and educated (Nsamenang, 2015). The goal is to create a psychology from within, one that understands people on their own terms, while at the same time searching for universal principles of human behavior (Allwood & Berry, 2006). A key feature of this approach is the use of methods that are meaningful and appropriate in a culture and, therefore, they are able to reveal the knowledge and skills of its people (Rogoff et al., 2017). Research Highlight 2.2 describes one such study in which the researcher used culturally appropriate methods to study the perceptual skills of Zambian children.

In addition to providing insight about development in the local context, this type of information can broaden psychological theory. Nsamenang's (1992) Indigenous research in African communities, for example, produced a theory that describes the sociogenic nature of human development over the life span, including how communities prepare young people for adult life through participation in social and household activities and family caregiving. This view of human development differs greatly from theories introduced by European American scholars that tend to characterize human development as inherently individualistic.

According to Nsamenang (2015), the most effective interventions integrate the best of past and present local practices to build on a community's strengths. The potential of Indigenous psychologies to inform and guide INGOs is great, and their impact can be increased through global networking and capacity-building (Marfo, 2011). Capacity-building is especially important because it involves training young community members in qualitative and quantitative research methods so they can carry out research that is locally relevant and informs developmental science more generally.

RESEARCH HIGHLIGHT 2.2

Studying Children's Perceptual Skills With Culture in Mind

The familiarity that participants have with the materials and tasks used in a study affects how well they can perform. This issue is illustrated in a classic study conducted by developmental psychologist Robert Serpell (1979b) about children's perceptual skills. Serpell compared the ability of 8- to 12-year-old Zambian and British children at copying visual displays. The children were presented with visual displays and then asked to reproduce them in four different ways. One way was a paper-and-pencil task, and children were asked to draw the display. This task was more familiar to the British children, all of whom were in school. It was also typical of the types of tasks used at the time to study children's perceptual skills. A second task involved the children reproducing the display with strips of pliable wire, a common type of material that the rural Zambian children in the study used during play to create handmade toys. The third task involved reproducing the model with plasticine or clay, which was of equal familiarity to both cultural groups. The fourth required the children to reproduce the shapes that an adult model displayed with his hands, which was considered a universal experience and, therefore, familiar to all the children.

The Zambian children did much better than the English children in copying the model with strips of wire. The English children performed better when copying the models with pencil and paper, a common activity among English but not Zambian children, many of whom were not in school. The children performed similarly on the two tasks that were less familiar to both of them, copying the models with clay and reproducing the positions of adults' hands. Thus, regardless of cultural background, performance on the tasks (good and poor) was better explained by children's cultural experiences than by inherent individual differences in perceptual skills. Serpell concluded that it is not the children's perceptual competence that is being studied here, but rather how a specific medium of representation coincides with the child's prior experience, much of which is regulated by culture. Although this study was conducted decades ago, it remains relevant because it clearly demonstrates how methods that are based on Indigenous materials and practices can provide more accurate and useful assessments of children's understanding and skills.

ETHICS OF CULTURAL RESEARCH WITH YOUNG PEOPLE

Regardless of the research strategy used, it is critical for any research project to be conducted ethically and respect the rights and privacy of the participants and the cultural community in which they live. To ensure that researchers adequately protect participants, government review boards and professional organizations in nations around the world have developed guidelines and codes of conduct for research. For instance, the American Psychological Association (APA, 2017) has established a set of ethical principles for psychologists and a code of conduct. In addition, all legitimate research projects involving young people (and adults) are scrutinized and approved by review boards at the institutions where the researcher is based, including colleges and universities. This review ensures that researchers follow ethical guidelines.

There are a number of unique challenges in protecting human subjects in culturally based research (J. G. Miller et al., 2015; Petersen, 2017). A critical aspect is informed consent, which is agreement to participate in a study based on a clear understanding of its purposes and the procedures to be used. In a cultural setting where research is uncommon or the procedures the researcher plans to use are unfamiliar, the researcher is obliged to make clear to potential participants exactly what will be asked of them in the study. When participants are young children, parents or legal guardians must provide informed consent on their behalf. In some cultures, authority to provide consent for participants extends beyond the individual or, in the case of children, parents. For instance, in some Native American tribal communities, consent also needs to be obtained from a tribal authority (Norton & Manson, 1996). Finally, although participants may be informed in their consent materials that they can withdraw at any time without consequences, cultural norms of interpersonal obligation or authority relations may interfere with the individual's ability to do so.

Ideas and norms about privacy also differ greatly across cultures. In some cultures, especially small communities, privacy may be difficult to obtain because people know much about one another or see each other regularly during the day. The privacy afforded to young people, especially adolescents, varies across cultures and can determine who needs to be informed about their participation in a study. There are ongoing debates in countries around the world, including Kenya and the United States, about the rights of adolescents to participate in research, especially health-related studies, without parental permission (C. Liu et al., 2017; Marsh et al., 2019). Respecting the rights and expectations regarding privacy in a culture is necessary for conducting ethical research. It also conveys a researcher's genuine interest in and sensitivity to the culture and its members, which, in turn, helps ensure the integrity and quality of the research.

Participants also have the right to not be harmed. This includes protection not only from physical harm, but also from psychological and emotional harm, such as feeling uncomfortable or embarrassed. Some procedures that are considered standard in Western studies may be inappropriate or uncomfortable for people living in certain cultural settings. For example, studies that separate parents and young children may lead to great discomfort for the participants, an experience that would also interfere with the validity of the data collected. Research that involves individuals who are vulnerable in a community, such as individuals who are impoverished, homeless, or ill may also create distress for participants. Children and youth in countries experiencing war or other forms of strife may be especially fearful and need protection from any experiences that could harm them or jeopardize their safety.

A number of other ethical issues can arise in international collaborations, especially when researchers from high-income countries conduct research in low-income countries. This type of research raises issues about power differentials, language barriers, and the need for capacity-building in low-income countries. In international research, it is especially important not to engage in extractive science in which a researcher from one (typically higher income) country collects data in another (typically lower income) country and publishes the findings without coauthorship from the other country (Koller et al., 2017).

This strategy exploits local collaborators and fails to build capacity in the low-resource settings in which it occurs. Extractive research occurs not only in international studies but also within high-income countries when researchers from outside the community conduct research in ethnic minority or socioeconomically disadvantaged communities. In contrast, an ethical approach recognizes that understanding and respect for the local context is vital to collecting useful data and interpreting the findings. Local researchers are essential to this process because they can bring insight to findings from their communities through their own experience and knowledge of the setting.

Beyond practical matters, there are other ethical concerns when researchers from one culture study people from another culture. These concerns, many of which have been mentioned in this chapter, stem from implicit biases that may be inherent in the topics or questions studied by the researcher, how the researcher perceives and evaluates the behaviors of others, and the kinds of comparisons and interpretations that occur. As developmental psychologist Susan Goldberg (1977) wrote many years ago,

> As long as social science is dominated by Westerners, we will discover only what Western ideologies unveil. When we are willing to lay ourselves open to the scrutiny before which others lay themselves bare for us, we will understand ourselves differently. (pp. 595–596)

CONCLUSION

Over the last 4 decades, a great deal of progress has been made in methods for studying the role of culture in human development. The ultimate goal is to produce the best developmental research possible by attending to the full range of contexts in which children and youth develop. Studying children and youth only in select countries or cultural contexts risks yielding a biased understanding of human development because physical, emotional, social, cognitive, and behavioral growth is rooted in people's daily experiences, which differ widely across cultures. International research involving investigators from different countries, including the communities where the worked is conducted, is needed. Teams of researchers working on an even keel is the best way to ensure that theories, empirical approaches, measurement tools, and interpretations of findings are culturally meaningful, which, in turn, will improve the scientific rigor, quality, and impact of developmental research.

For additional resources, see the Appendix.

DISCUSSION QUESTIONS

1. Why is it important for researchers who are designing a culturally based study to be aware of any assumptions they have about the universality or normative development of a behavior?

2. What methods do researchers typically use when studying the everyday experiences of children in cultural context? What are the strengths and weaknesses of these methods?

3. For Beatrice Whiting, age and culture are "packaged variables." What does this mean and how can this idea be helpful for designing culturally based studies of children and youth?

4. If you were planning a study that involves interviewing adolescents from another culture, what aspects of young people's lives today would you want to learn more about and how would you determine if your method is culturally appropriate?

5. What should researchers do if the requirements for human subject protections in the culture they plan to study are different from their culture?

3

Culture and Cognitive Development

Cognitive development is shaped by social relationships and education.

People use thinking skills to understand the world around them and to solve many types of problems. *Cognition* is the term used for the mental activity through which human beings organize and use knowledge. Cognition includes many mental processes such as perception, attention, learning, memory, and reasoning. During development, children and youth acquire a vast array of knowledge and cognitive skills, which they use to guide action to reach their goals.

This chapter describes the relation between culture and cognitive development. It is clear from research that in order to understand human thinking and its development, culture must be considered (Greenfield et al., 2003). Culture determines the knowledge and skills that young people learn, when and how they learn them, and the value that is placed on certain types of knowledge and

https://doi.org/10.1037/0000228-003
Child and Adolescent Development in Cultural Context, by J. E. Lansford, D. C. French, and M. Gauvain

skills. Culture also provides formal and informal settings of learning, and children's experience in these settings affects how cognitive skills are used (Correa-Chávez et al., 2015).

An important part of this process is learning the symbols, or sign systems, and tools that the culture uses to support thinking and intelligent action (M. Cole, 2006). Symbols include language and other ways of representing thought, such as literacy and the numbering system. Tools are objects and material resources, such as computers, that support and extend thinking. Symbols and tools are valued by cultures because they help people complete activities of daily life. In fact, once a cultural tool is used to support an activity, it is hard to imagine how the activity would be possible without the tool. Think for a moment about memory and how you use literacy to help you remember class material. In class, you listen closely to the lecture and take notes on the material for later review; you do not try to memorize everything the instructor says. The cultural tool of literacy transforms how you use memory by replacing rote memorization with an external record—either on paper or a computer—of important class material. This record extends your memory capacity beyond the limits of memorization, and because you have a tangible record of the class material, you can refer to it later. However, a new memory task is introduced, remembering where you kept the record when you want to study for a test.

Cultural signs and tools are shared by community members and passed across generations in the process of cognitive socialization (Gauvain & Perez, 2015). As we discussed in Chapter 1, during socialization, parents and others ensure that the behaviors, attitudes, skills, and motives of young people conform to those endorsed by and practiced in their society. As this definition implies, much of socialization involves learning culturally appropriate ways of thinking and acting. Research on cognitive socialization examines what young people learn, including how more experienced cultural members pass on valued ways of thinking and acting to children and youth. It investigates similarities and differences across cultures in the knowledge and cognitive skills young people acquire as well as whether any particular knowledge or cognitive skills are universal, that is, appear in all cultures.

The human brain is equipped at birth to learn and learn quickly, and much of this learning occurs socially right alongside other cultural members who care for and support the child's development (M. H. Johnson, 2010). Cultural knowledge and ways of thinking are conveyed to young community members through direct social contact (e.g., social interaction, instruction) and less socially direct contact. Nonetheless, social forms of information, including rituals, customs, and shared symbols and tools, are exchanged. In this chapter, we concentrate on four social learning processes: observing, sharing, transmitting, and participating.

We begin by describing the sociocultural approach to cognitive development, a theoretical view that concentrates on how the social and cultural worlds support the development of human thinking. Then we turn to processes of social learning, describing four ways that cultural knowledge and skills become part of an individual's cognitive development. The next section illustrates connections between culture and cognitive development by looking closely at research in three areas: memory, problem solving, and spatial thinking. Throughout the chapter, we focus on both the process and content of human cognition. Process describes how thinking works (e.g., memory, problem solving). Content pertains to domain-specific skills and knowledge (e.g., spatial thinking). We provide diverse research examples to validate the significant role of culture in cognitive development.

THE SOCIOCULTURAL APPROACH TO COGNITIVE DEVELOPMENT

Contemporary research on culture and cognitive development has been greatly influenced by the ideas of Russian psychologist Lev S. Vygotsky (1896–1934) and his colleagues (Daniels, 2017). These theorists were interested in how social and cultural experiences contribute to individuals' psychological development by transforming basic cognitive abilities, such as innate perceptual and memory skills, into complex cognitive functions tailored to the needs and interests of the culture.

This transformation largely occurs through interaction with more experienced cultural members, such as parents, teachers, and older children, who pass on valued knowledge and ways of thinking. For instance, when a child and a more experienced partner solve a problem together, the child receives guidance that helps them understand and participate in problem solving that reflects the culture in some way (e.g., that a complete solution is more valued than a speedy one). The transformation is also aided by learning to use cultural symbols and tools to support and extend thinking, as illustrated in our earlier example about how literacy aids your memory and review of class material.

In the sociocultural approach, the term *mediator* refers to cultural ways of thinking and acting because mediators come between, or mediate, people's experiences with the world (M. Cole, 2005). During development, children learn to use different types of mediators (such as language, counting, and writing) that are passed across generations and used to support individual thinking and action. For example, when children learn language, words become integrated with thoughts and affect how children process information. Mediators are important for psychological development because they originate from and, therefore, represent the culture. Thus, as children and youth develop competence with cultural mediators, their thinking and intelligent actions are increasingly aligned with the people around them, which, in turn, allows young community members to interact with and learn from their elders in meaningful ways.

Developmental scientists who adopt a sociocultural approach use these ideas to study the relation between culture and cognitive development (M. Cole, 2006; Rogoff, 2003). Some of this research will be used later to illustrate connections between culture and the development of memory, problem solving, and spatial thinking. But first, we describe social processes that help children and youth develop the knowledge and cognitive skills used in their culture.

SOCIAL LEARNING PROCESSES THAT CONNECT INDIVIDUAL COGNITIVE DEVELOPMENT WITH CULTURE

During development, children and youth learn knowledge and cognitive skills that are important in their culture. In the main, these skills are learned socially. Interactions with adults—particularly caregivers—and older children are especially important because they are the most immediate representatives in children's lives who can share cultural ways of thinking and acting.

Many social processes help children and youth learn about their culture. Here we focus on four processes: observing, sharing, transmitting, and participating (see Table 3.1). Although these processes are not the only means through which culture becomes part of individual cognitive functioning, researchers have identified them as particularly important. These processes appear to be universal supports for cognitive development, but their importance varies across cultures. For instance, cultures with formal schooling emphasize transmission methods (e.g., instruction), whereas children who live in settings with limited or no access to formal schooling learn much about culture through observation (Lancy et al., 2010).

Observing

People frequently display cultural behaviors around children, and these demonstrations influence children's future behaviors. Children learn these behaviors by observing, that is, by attending closely to other people's behavior in a nonintrusive manner (Bandura, 1986). Children are active in this process in that, even very early in life, they show intrinsic motivation in selecting and attending to social behaviors (Meltzoff et al., 2009). They also need to concentrate to learn a behavior and make sense of it in the immediate context and relation to their own goals (Gaskins & Paradise, 2010). The individuals (or models) being observed may not be aware that they are being observed, and they do not do anything to encourage or support the learning. Given the nature of observational learning, it is restricted to overt or perceptible information.

Two types of observation are especially important to cultural learning—emulation and imitation (Tomasello, 2016). *Emulation* occurs when a learner observes the goal-directed actions of another and then tries to obtain the same goal without duplicating the actions of the model. For example, after seeing a child walk across the park to get a ball, another child walks to the equipment storage box to get a ball. In *imitation*, the learner reproduces the observed actions to achieve a specific goal. For example, after a child sees his father choose a book from the bookshelf and begin to read it, the child chooses a book from the bookshelf and begins to read it. For imitation to be effective, the observer needs to understand the intentions of the model doing the behavior.

Observational learning begins early in life. Late in the first year of life, infants' observational learning skills are clearly apparent as they learn many behaviors by watching others around them (Jones, 2007). In a study in which

TABLE 3.1. Four Social Learning Processes Important to Cognitive Development From a Cultural Perspective

Social learning process	Typical focus of learning	Role of learner	Role of other person(s)	Child–other person relationship
Observing	Discrete behavior of another person	Observer who selects and attends to another person's behavior and remembers the behavior to use later to meet personal goals	Model who may or may not be aware of being observed	In same physical setting, otherwise need not be related in any way
Sharing	Conveying knowledge from one person to another for the purpose of sharing it	Interactive partner who shares knowledge with another, or the person with whom knowledge is shared	Interactive partner who shares knowledge with another, or the person with whom knowledge is shared	Reciprocal
Transmitting	More experienced person teaches less experienced person a skill or under-standing of something	Engaged learner who gradually assumes responsibility for an activity under the tutelage of a more experienced person	Supportive instructor who guides the learner and gradually transfers responsibility for the activity to the learner	Learner and teacher
Participating	Cultural activity with an identifiable goal and means to reach the goal	Participant who takes part in an authentic cultural activity with the intention to learn about it	Actor who engages in a cultural activity that is the focus of the learning and provides support for appropriate learner involvement	Inexperienced participant and experienced participant

Note. From "Cognition in Childhood Across Cultures," by M. Gauvain and C. Nicolaides, in L. A. Jensen (Ed.), *The Oxford Handbook of Human Development and Culture: An Interdis-ciplinary Perspective* (pp. 198–213), 2015, Oxford University Press. Copyright 2015 by Oxford University Press. Adapted with permission.

mothers recorded their young children's imitative behaviors, the mothers reported that the children, who ranged from 12 to 18 months of age, learned an average of one or two new behaviors a day just by watching others, often their siblings (R. Barr & Hayne, 2003). By 16 months of age, infants can learn a set or sequence of modeled behaviors, though they are biased toward behaviors that are intentional rather than accidental (Carpenter et al., 1998). Young children's tendency to imitate has been found in many cultures, including San communities of the South African Kalahari Desert (Nielsen & Tomaselli, 2010). Furthermore, observational learning early in life is not limited to older or more experienced models. At 30 months of age, children can learn problem-solving strategies by watching same-age peers (Brownell et al., 2006).

Cross-cultural research, including the Six Cultures Study discussed in Chapter 2, has found that children spend the majority of their waking hours watching others (B. B. Whiting & Edwards, 1988). This suggests that they have ample opportunity to learn a variety of skills through observation. Observational learning is especially common for routine cultural behaviors because of their frequent occurrence, public display, and consistency in performance across cultural members. Opportunities for learning by observation are enhanced because young children are often in the close company of adults and older children engaging in routine cultural behaviors. For instance, children in the Warao community of South America will grip a canoe handle for the very first time, without prior instruction, in the same way as older members of the group (Wilbert, 1979), and girls in Chiapas, Mexico, learn to operate a complex foot loom solely by observing an experienced weaver (Childs & Greenfield, 1980).

Observational learning is also seen in children's play behaviors. For example, when girls in the Okavango Delta of Botswana play house, they will pound a stick on the dirt in the same way that mature community members use a mortar and pestle to crush grain (Bock & Johnson, 2004). Eight- to 10-year-old Kpelle boys in Liberia practice climbing trees with a strip of bamboo wrapped around the tree and each end of the strip in their hands, a technique used by older villagers for climbing palm oil trees (Lancy, 1996). Boys practice this skill on coconut trees, which are curved near to the ground, rather than on palm oil trees, which are tall and straight and would be far more dangerous.

As these examples suggest, what children learn through observation is often opportunistic—instigated by what children see and hear around them. Children take an active role in this learning by choosing what they attend to and then, later, by using the learned information to pursue their own goals.

Sharing

Cultural learning also occurs when knowledge is communicated from one person to another for the purpose of mutual understanding or sharing. The intent in these exchanges is to involve someone in something that another person knows or is thinking about, rather than teaching the person something. These exchanges are reciprocal; both parties are involved as equal partners, albeit with different capabilities defined by developmental status. Examples include conversations about the past or the present as events unfold and joint narratives about reminiscing or storytelling. Sharing information is not restricted to overt behavior or verbal communication, nor does it always have to be initiated by a more experienced person. Even very young children will use pointing to share information (e.g., a sight or sound) with someone else (Liszkowski et al., 2004). The emphasis and emotional register when information is shared convey cultural values about what knowledge is important to share and how others in the group feel about it (Goodnow, 1990).

Infants are interested in sharing activities with their caregivers beginning early in life. In a classic study, Bruner and Sherwood (1976) observed how 6-month-old infants actively participate in turn-taking routines with their mothers, like in the game of peek-a-boo. This type of early, ritualized play is especially rich for social learning because it involves an enjoyable activity with a constrained and repeated set of behaviors and rules associated with them. Later in their first year, infants are able to reliably look at the same place or object the adults did, a process referred to as shared or joint attention (Moore & Dunham, 2014). Joint attention is often accompanied by speech, such as object labeling, and is related to language development in young children. A positive relation between joint attention and language development has been discovered across cultures, even in settings where children are often carried on their caregivers' backs, such as the Ngas culture of Nigeria (J. B. Childers et al., 2007). This finding suggests that the connection between joint attention and language learning is not dependent on cultural practices that include high rates of face-to-face contact between caregivers and young children.

Researchers have found that there is cultural variation in the methods caregivers use to establish and engage in joint attention and object-play with young children (Adamson & McArthur, 2014). Research with middle-class urban families in the United States, France, and Japan identified differences in how mothers directed the attention of their 5-month-old infants (Bornstein et al., 1991). U.S. mothers were more likely to encourage the infants to look at objects, and U.S. and Japanese mothers often directed infant attention to themselves, whereas French mothers rarely did so. Among the !Kung San people, a hunter–gatherer society in Africa, adults neither encourage nor prohibit infants' exploration of objects. But if the infant offers an object to the caregiver, joint attention and object exploration are similar to that seen in other cultures (Bakeman et al., 1990). During joint play, dyads of mothers and their 12- to 24-month-old children in a Maya community in Guatemala attended to several objects or events simultaneously, while U.S. dyads of similar composition attended to one event or object at a time, or alternated back and forth between items (Chavajay & Rogoff, 1999).

Caregivers and children also share cultural values and other cultural information when they converse about the past and as events unfold in the present. Mullen and Yi (1995) found that European American mothers made more references to the thoughts and feelings of their children, whereas Korean mothers made more references to social norms. Similarly, when observing families telling stories involving 2½-year-old children in middle-class Taiwanese and European American families, the Taiwanese stories tended to emphasize moral and social standards, reflecting cultural values regarding proper conduct, respect for others, and self-control (P. J. Miller et al., 2012). In contrast, the European American stories mostly focused on entertainment and affirmation of the child as an individual. Also, when the child's past transgressions were discussed, the misdeeds were understated and recast to emphasize the child's strengths. These patterns are consistent with socialization goals and values in these communities and suggest that during mother–child conversations about the past, children learn what aspects of the past are considered important to talk about and remember in their culture.

Other research has confirmed these findings. The conversations of European American parents and their preschoolers tend to emphasize a person's individual attributes, whereas conversations between Taiwanese parents and their preschoolers largely focus on social relationships (Q. Wang, 2013). There is also cultural variation in conversational style. European American parents are more likely to use an elaborative and child-centered approach when reminiscing with their children, while Chinese parents are more likely to use a pragmatic, mother-centered approach (Q. Wang et al., 2010).

The nature of sharing changes as a child develops cognitive and social skills. The development of language and symbolic understanding, in particular, enables children to talk with others about events and ideas outside the immediate circumstances. As children get older, they also increasingly share knowledge and learn about culture as they play with and solve problems with other children (Göncü & Gaskins, 2006).

Transmitting

Societies make a huge investment in educating young members about the culture. Explicit efforts to transmit cultural ways of thinking and acting emerge in early childhood and take on an increasingly important role with development. These efforts occur in both informal and formal settings in which learning occurs. We refer to these processes as *transmitting* to emphasize that there is intention to pass cultural knowledge onto children.

According to Vygotsky (1978), cultural knowledge is transmitted to young community members during social interaction in a child's "zone of proximal development" (ZPD). The ZPD is the child's region of sensitivity for learning, defined as the difference between a child's "actual developmental level as determined by independent problem solving" and their "potential development as determined through problem solving under adult guidance or in collaboration with more capable peers" (Vygotsky, 1978, p. 86). Language, discussed in Chapter 4, plays a central role in interactions in the child's ZPD because it gives children access to the ideas and understandings of other people and, by extension, the social and cultural context of development.

Parents and other more experienced cultural members (e.g., older siblings, teachers) transmit cultural knowledge through formal and informal instruction, play, and by making technology and other learning tools available to children (Gauvain & Perez, 2015). Assistance from a more experienced partner that is targeted at the child's ZPD can help a child engage in more advanced levels of competence. This is because more experienced partners aid a child's learning by adjusting the amount and type of assistance to fit with the child's learning needs. In an early, classic paper on this topic, Wood and Middleton (1975) called the assistance provided by a more experienced partner a "scaffold," and they labeled the process *scaffolding*.

By carefully monitoring the child's progress, the more experienced partner arranges the task so it is manageable for the child and provides support when needed, with the goal that the child will eventually be able to do the task on their own. More experienced partners scaffold children's learning in various ways including modeling new problem-solving strategies, encouraging the child's engagement, and taking on the more difficult parts of the activity so the child can concentrate on other parts. Developmental researchers have used these ideas to investigate children's learning in many areas of cognition including attention, memory, problem solving, and planning. In general, the findings show that children's understanding and cognitive skills can indeed be improved when adults or more skilled peers provide children with appropriate support for learning (Gauvain, 2001).

Instruction in the child's ZPD may be particularly useful for transmitting cultural knowledge and skills that children are expected to eventually handle mostly on their own or entirely error free (Gauvain, 2005). This includes knowledge needed in situations when adult supervision cannot be guaranteed, such as information that may protect children or others in the environment (e.g., which plants are poisonous, how to make medicines), in circumstances where the stakes are high (e.g., economic exchanges), when traditional practices are important to maintain (e.g., ritual practices; methods of doing an important activity such as weaving), and in conveying skills that involve mainly mental activity. For example, Lancy (1996) observed scaffolding among Kpelle adults and boys in Liberia when the children learned to play Malaŋ, a traditional game that relies on the use of mental strategies. Child-directed, trial-and-error learning may be more common when cost does not matter or innovation is desired (Tanon, 1994). Research Highlight 3.1 describes a classroom in which the teacher uses the ZPD in a way that respects the child's own cultural experience.

Informal instructional interactions of the type described in the ZPD may be more common in some cultures and reflect experience with formal schooling. In Chapter 2 we described research by LeVine and colleagues (1994) in which Gusii mothers in Kenya and middle-class American mothers in the United States were observed as they taught 6- to 25-month-old children age-appropriate tasks. Recall that Gusii mothers, who had little experience with formal schooling, tended to instruct their children verbally, demonstrate the entire task in advance,

RESEARCH HIGHLIGHT 3.1

Using the Zone of Proximal Development to Integrate Cultural Learning in the Classroom

Vygotsky's notion of the "zone of proximal development" (ZPD) was used as the basis for the theory of instruction adopted by the Kamehameha Early Education Program, or KEEP, in Hawaii (Tharp & Gallimore, 1988; Tharp et al., 2007). In this program, which ran for 15 years, Native Hawaiian children received language instruction as well as instruction in other subjects, such as reading, all based on the ZPD concept. The program was learner-centered, and it was designed to incorporate the cultural knowledge, skills, values, and beliefs that children bring to the classroom.

The KEEP program used a technique called instructional conversation. It focused on how the cultural practices that Native Hawaiian children experience at home when they talk with others could be incorporated into classroom learning. For instance, the Native Hawaiian tradition of storytelling was used to develop the classroom practice of "talk-story," an approach to literacy instruction in which the teacher and the children jointly produced narratives about the focus of the day's lessons. This technique involves overlapping speech, turn-taking, and joint construction of a story. Its main emphasis is social participation, along with story creation and comprehension.

The KEEP teacher would use modeling, questioning, and feedback to scaffold children's learning. In the following exchange a teacher uses repetition, rewording, and expansion as she questions the child and seeks to clarify his statement (Tharp & Gallimore, 1988, p. 143):

CHILD: Probably, probably have snow on the . . . stuff and . . . thing, thing was heavy and thing fall.

TEACHER: Oh, you mean there might be so much snow and ice on the plane that it couldn't fly?

Notice how the teacher extends the child's utterance, using some of the child's own words, and also provides some semantic recoding of what the child said (e.g., "on the stuff" becomes "on the plane"). In this exchange, the teacher's goal is to help the child develop language skills. The teacher is guided by the overarching principle of instructional conversation, and what she offers is intended to encourage further communication with the child on the topic.

This program builds on the cultural experience children have when they begin school, rather than ignoring this rich foundation of learning. The use of this culturally supportive technique improved the standardized reading scores of Native Hawaiian children. Based on their research at KEEP, Tharp and Gallimore (1988) argued that minority individuals or other "nonstandard dialect speakers" can benefit greatly from opportunities to converse throughout goal-oriented activities with a responsive yet uncritical teacher who speaks standard English and respects the cultural information the child brings to the classroom.

and direct the children to do the task exactly as the mothers had done. This approach does not easily allow for the type of moment-to-moment modifications described in interactions in the child's ZPD. In contrast, American mothers, who had extensive schooling experience, used verbal instruction and demonstration throughout the task, which provides more opportunity for assistance calibrated to the learner's immediate needs.

A culture's emphasis on formal schooling also affects other types of experiences children have outside of school. In fact, research has found that parents will prepare children for the classroom even before they enter school by engaging them in activities or communicative exchanges similar to those in school. These efforts include small lessons about how things work, talking on a sustained topic about things that are not the current focus of activity, and asking questions for which the person posing the question already knows the answer (Greenfield, 2009; Tudge et al., 2003).

Cultural knowledge is also transmitted in more formal learning situations when children learn how their culture interprets the natural and social worlds, the values the culture places on certain ways of thinking, and the tools and technologies the culture uses to support thinking (Serpell & Hatano, 1997). Although teachers play a central role in transmitting cultural knowledge at school, peers also contribute in activities such as peer tutoring and collaborative learning, and parents and siblings often help children with their homework (Gauvain, 2016).

Participating

Much of cultural learning occurs as children participate in authentic activities alongside older children or adults engaged in the daily pursuits of life (Rogoff et al., 2003). In these experiences, children learn about the culture through joint actions with other community members as they strive toward a practical and meaningful goal. Learning through participation may be especially important in cultural settings where explicit instruction is uncommon (Lancy et al., 2010).

By "authentic activities" we mean goal-directed activities that pertain to the livelihood of the culture. These activities are aimed toward practical purposes and are not designed to teach children. Rather, they provide children with an introduction to and practice with cultural activities in the context of their actual use. Participation in authentic activities also gives children exposure to other community members as they use cognitive skills and cultural tools, both symbolic and material, to carry out the activities. These experiences help prepare children to become mature cultural members. According to Rogoff (2003), cognitive development is apparent by how children's roles and responsibilities change as they participate in authentic cultural activities.

The concept of guided participation is used to describe how adults support children's learning during participation in everyday cultural activities (Rogoff, 1990). Guided participation includes directing the child's engagement in the activity, albeit in a way suited to the child's skills and interests. In one form of guided participation, called learning through intent community participation, children actively seek ways to participate in the authentic activities of their community alongside more experienced cultural members (Rogoff et al., 2003). Children direct their attention in a sustained and resolute manner toward what they want to learn, and they also may be allowed to listen in on the conversations of more experienced individuals. For example, in Zinacanteco, a Maya community in Mexico, much of the skill of weaving is transferred through generations as apprentice weavers, usually young girls, sit or stand quietly alongside their mothers or older sisters and watch as they weave (Childs & Greenfield, 1980). The learner's attention is focused on behaviors important to learning the skill and this attention is permitted for lengthy periods of time, which in other circumstances might be considered intrusive or rude.

Children's participation in authentic cultural activities differs across cultures and is affected by many factors (Lancy, 2018). In some cases, increasing participation by young people may reflect social and cultural needs related to economic or subsistence demands (e.g., agriculture). Opportunities to learn through participation also change as children develop cognitive skills, and some may be regulated by maturation. For example, between 5 and 7 years of age, children in communities worldwide experience a shift in the assignment of roles and responsibilities to them (Sameroff & Haith, 1996). This transition may help prepare them for middle childhood, a period when children begin to participate in activities that contribute in substantive ways to the community.

Although learning by participating has roots in observational learning, these processes differ in several ways. Observational learning is opportunistic and behaviorally focused; the child incorporates what is observed into his or her own behavioral repertoire, and it may be used later to meet the child's own goals. In contrast, learning through participation is focused on the activity as a whole, and involves recognition of the purpose of the activity and some sense of its place in the culture. For example, when a child observes as a more experienced community member engages in a routine cultural practice such as preparing food or weaving cloth, the learner's focus is on how the goal—that is making food to eat or weaving cloth to use in some way, each an understandable and meaningful activity—is achieved in their culture. As a result, the learned behavior is tied to a cultural activity and goal, not solely to the child's own activity.

To summarize, these four types of social learning play significant roles in cognitive development and enable children and youth to acquire knowledge and skills that are useful in their culture. Although the four learning processes are described separately, they often occur side-by-side and sometimes build on one another. For instance, when a child and an adult share a memory or reminisce, the adult may pause and give the child a brief lesson about moral responsibility (P. J. Miller et al., 2012).

THE ROLE OF CULTURE IN DEVELOPING IMPORTANT COGNITIVE CAPABILITIES

We now turn to research findings that demonstrate the relation between culture and cognitive development. We describe cultural contributions in the development of two cognitive processes, memory and problem-solving, and relation to the cognitive domain of spatial thinking.

Memory

Human memory and culture are closely entwined over the course of development. Social and cultural context provides children and youth with information about what they should remember and how to go about remembering it. We describe this connection with research on the development of two types of memory: autobiographical and strategic.

Autobiographical Memory

Autobiographical memory is the recollection of significant personal experiences and it serves a variety of functions (Bauer & Fivush, 2010). It contains knowledge of a person's history, both the individual's own experiences and in relation to others, that helps to define social and personal identity. It is a conversational tool that helps people develop and maintain relationships. And because individual life stories reflect cultural values, beliefs, and practices, they contribute to the maintenance and intergenerational transmission of these important components of culture.

Autobiographical memory emerges early in life. By age 2, children have good understanding and memory of meaningful everyday routines and events (e.g., going to a restaurant; Bauer & Fivush, 2010). Between 20 and 24 months of age, children begin to make reference to events in the more distant past and participate in joint reminiscing, though their role changes with development. At age 2½, children need help from adults when communicating about specific events, but by age 3, children begin to handle these conversations more on their own.

Research demonstrates that the way in which mothers engage in joint reminiscing with young children is related to the quality and duration of children's autobiographical memories (Cleveland & Reese, 2005; Jack et al., 2009). When mothers use an elaborative communication style, which involves asking open-ended questions about a memory, children remember more detailed information about the past event than when mothers use a pragmatic communication style, which uses closed-ended questions mainly about facts (Howe et al., 2003). There appears to be cultural variation in these types of interactions. Q. Wang and colleagues (2010) found that European American parents are more likely to use an elaborative style when reminiscing with their children whereas Chinese mothers are more likely to use a pragmatic style.

Research has found associations between children's autobiographical memories and a culture's emphasis on individualism versus collectivism. As young as 3 to 4 years of age, the autobiographical memories of people living in individualistic societies tend to emphasize unique personal attributes and qualities, whereas autobiographical memories of people living in more collectivistic societies tend to focus on social connectedness and relationships (Q. Wang, 2013). These patterns are related to the recall of early memories. European American adults, consistent with an emphasis on personal uniqueness, tend to recall earlier and more detailed childhood memories about the self than East Asian adults do.

When examining cultural differences in relation to broad cultural values, such as individualism and collectivism, it is important to recognize that not all members of any culture behave in exactly the same way when they interact with children about autobiographical memories. This variation is demonstrated in research that examined the use of elaboration during joint reminiscing by middle-class mothers and preschool-aged children in three Western cultures: Berlin; Stockholm; and Tallinn, Estonia (Tõugu et al., 2012). All these cultures value autonomy (personal uniqueness, independence) over relatedness (interdependence, social relationships). Yet within these cultural groups, researchers found differences in mothers' use of open-ended questions, statements, and verbal confirmations—all aspects of an elaborative reminiscing style.

Research has also shown cultural variation in how children participate and how parents support them during joint reminiscing, and these variations are related to the development of autobiographical memory. Schröder and colleagues (2012) hypothesized that during joint reminiscing with their mother, children in Germany—an autonomy-oriented context—would be motivated by self-expression, whereas children in India—a relatedness-oriented context—would be motivated by parental expectations. In both cultures, they found that maternal elaborations contributed positively to children's memory recollection during joint reminiscing. However, German mothers' support for their children's self-expression at 19 months predicted children's elaborations at age 3. In India, children's memory elaborations at age 3 were predicted by children's willingness at 19 months to carry out their mothers' requests during joint reminiscing. As this research shows, cultural contributions to the development of autobiographical memory appear in the content of these memories and the manner in which children learn to communicate them.

Strategic Memory

Strategies are deliberate techniques used to enhance cognitive performance. A memory or mnemonic strategy helps a person retain and retrieve information from the memory system. Examples include rehearsal, organization, and elaboration. Children's use of mnemonics improves substantially between 5 and 10 years of age (Schneider, 2010).

Similar to autobiographical memory, the development of strategic memory is aided by social and cultural experience. Interaction with adults helps children acquire and improve memory strategies by giving them exposure to and practice with new strategies (Gauvain, 2001). During joint memory activities, adults help children understand how strategies can be used to overcome the capacity limits of memory, for example, by telling children that putting items in categories can aid memory because they can use the category labels to recall the items later.

Cross-cultural research has demonstrated that certain memory strategies, such as rehearsal and hierarchical organization, are more common among individuals from societies that emphasize formal schooling than among individuals from societies where there is no formal schooling or it is less important (Rogoff, 2003). Consider that in school, remembering often occurs for the sake of remembering itself (e.g., remembering lists of words, events, or dates in order to be tested on them later). Experience in school gives children substantial practice with remembering lists of unrelated words or facts, which also happen to be the types of activities typically used in laboratory memory tests.

This association may have societal implications within cultures as well. Recall that earlier in the chapter we described research indicating that parents prepare children for the classroom before they actually begin school by engaging them in activities similar to those at school, such as remembering dates or playing games that involve labeling groups of objects or other items (e.g., words). However, in some ethnic communities in the United States, parents and children engage in memory activities that differ from the type emphasized in school, which can make the transition from home to school difficult for these children compared with those from European American backgrounds. In a landmark study, Heath (1983) found that in African American communities, verbal explanation is highly valued and activities such as oral storytelling help children develop memory strategies aligned with these practices, such as narrative accounts. This method of remembering is extremely effective, yet it is rarely used as a memory strategy in the classroom. As a result, African American children are less prepared for the memory demands of school—not because they lack strategic memory skills, but because they are less familiar with the memory strategies typically used in school.

Other cultural practices may also play a role in strategic memory development. Research comparing Lao and American children's performance on memory-span tasks (e.g., auditory, verbal) found few cultural differences (Conant et al., 2003). But there were differences in the visual and cross-modal memory span that favored Lao children. The results are explained by associations between the tasks and literacy training in the Lao language, which alters the presentation of vowels and consonants to modify sounds and, consequently, puts more demand on visuospatial processing than English literacy training does.

Overall, research suggests that there are direct connections between culture and the development and use of strategic memory. What social-cultural learning processes might contribute to strategic memory performance? To answer this question, Mistry (1997) described three ways that memory is integrated with culture, all of which have developmental implications. The first is that memory strategies are culturally derived tools of thinking that have been developed and are maintained by cultures for the purpose of aiding memory. As such, the development and use of memory strategies follows a course similar to that of other cultural tools (e.g., literacy) in that more experienced community members aid children in acquiring, selecting, and using these strategies. For instance, whether rehearsal—a common technique for remembering information—is used as a mnemonic strategy depends on whether the culture and its institutions, such as school, encourage its development and use by young community members.

Second, people use memory strategies that are culturally valued and useful. That is, these strategies help individuals attain their goals, and they often do so by making use of other features or practices of the culture. For example, long-term memory storage and retrieval in literate cultural communities relies heavily on written accounts. Such accounts are very effective when they are used, but their effectiveness depends on availability, that is, whether the written record is present when the memory is needed. In nonliterate cultural communities, long-term memory storage and retrieval relies on the oral tradition, which has a long history in the form of epic poems, songs, and even the rhymes that young children learn and pass onto one another, often during play (D. C. Rubin, 1995). This type of memory strategy is very effective for learning lengthy sequences of information, and it does not rely on producing an external record.

Third, to understand how memory works it is necessary to study it in use. That is, the activities in which memory is used are organized by the culture and the goals that guide remembering in this context. For instance, in a now-classic study, Hutchins (1983), found that traditional Micronesian seafarers developed a navigational system that was not reliant on modern instruments. Instead, they use a complex set of principles to guide their travels, involving extensive memorization aided by the use of cultural myths as mnemonics. Learning these myths is a valued cultural activity, especially for young people desiring to become navigators one day.

To recap, both autobiographical and strategic memory processes are affected by the cultural activities and tools that support these mental processes. Children develop both of these important memory types by engaging in everyday cultural activities. This development is greatly informed by more experienced individuals who model and promote the types and uses of memory that are valued in the culture.

Problem-Solving Skills

Problem solving is a cognitive activity aimed at reaching a goal. It involves identifying the goal, defining the steps to reach the goal, executing the steps, monitoring progress toward the goal, and overcoming obstacles that arise until the goal is reached. The ability to solve problems is a central feature of human intelligence and a core achievement of psychological development.

Effective problem-solving depends on how well a person understands or encodes the problem and the strategies used to solve it. As children get older, they encode more features of a problem, focus their attention more effectively, and use more strategies, which are conscious cognitive or behavioral activities that enhance problem-solving performance. Because of the complexity of problem-solving, this skill develops over a long period of time. Rudimentary skill at solving problems is present in infancy, while competence at solving complex problems continues to develop through adolescence and into early adulthood and can vary substantially across cultures (Haun, 2015).

Throughout development, the ways in which people solve problems are informed by culture. Culture affects the types of problems people solve, the manner in which they solve them, and the tools and other resources they use (Goodnow, 1990). Children learn much about solving problems from people with whom they have regular contact, typically more experienced community members such as parents, older children, and teachers. When people solve problems together, they often convey cultural knowledge and values about problem-solving, such as the types of problems the culture views as worthwhile ("It is important for you to know this") and preferred ways of solving a problem ("This is the way to do it").

When and how people solve problems is often organized around cultural values and goals, such as cooperating with others or maximizing efficiency. Children in cultures that value slow and considered performance, such as the Native American Navajo community, solve problems more deliberatively than children in the European American community where speed of performance is important (Ellis & Gauvain, 1992). In cultures where social relationships are important, such as Native Hawaiians and the Māori people in New Zealand, children place social cooperation above individual performance when they solve problems with others (Mackie, 1980; Speidel et al., 1989). In many African cultures social responsibility is a preeminent concern, and children's everyday problem-solving reflects this value (Serpell, 2011).

Solving problems often involves cultural tools, both symbolic (e.g., literacy, numerals) and material (e.g., maps), and during development, children learn to use these tools to help them solve problems (M. Cole, 2006). Decades ago, psychologist Jerome Bruner (1964) referred to these tools as "cultural amplifiers" because they magnify or enhance the way individuals solve problems. He viewed cultural tools as fundamental to mental functioning because they inform people's representations of the world, help define the types of problems people solve, and determine the way people solve them. For instance, spatial navigation is greatly affected by the availability of maps and other navigational devices in the culture. Cognitive development entails the integration and use of material-representational forms of this sort, and cultural agents (e.g., parents, peers) convey their significance and use. We return to this topic in the next section on spatial thinking.

Research has examined how specific cultural tools, such as writing systems, common folk tales, and spatial techniques, influence the nature and development of problem-solving. A study comparing Chinese and Greek children showed that Chinese children as young as age 4 performed differently than Greek children on cognitive tasks, and these differences were related to the visual and spatial demands of the Chinese writing system (Kazi et al., 2012). Thus, it appears that the writing system used in a culture affects how children solve problems that draw from skills related to this practice.

When cultural information is available, problem-solving improves. Logical problem-solving with analogies—a form of reasoning that seeks similarities across two entities or systems—is facilitated when the analogy is based on cultural information, such as familiar stories. Chen et al. (2004) demonstrated that analogies based on *Hansel and Gretel*, a common American folktale, aided problem-solving among U.S. college students, while analogies based on the common Chinese tale *Weighing the Elephant* enhanced the problem-solving of Chinese students.

Other cross-cultural comparisons have found associations between practical everyday experiences and problem-solving, including symbolic and representational forms used for solving mathematics problems. And these relations may alter over time as the everyday experiences of people in the culture change. As a case in point, developmental psychologist Geoffrey Saxe (2014) studied the Indigenous mathematics practices in the Oksapmin community in Papua New Guinea over a 25-year period. Early in his research, Saxe learned that these people use a 27-part body-counting system to enumerate and communicate amounts. In this system, each body part has a distinct numeral value associated with it, for example, when someone points to the 14th body part (the nose), the person is indicating that there are 14 items (e.g., objects, people) in a set or grouping. When Saxe returned to the community many years later, he found that new methods were being used to communicate numerical amounts, and the new methods were based on the body-counting system. For example, if after touching a particular body part (e.g., the nose, which equals 14), and the person uttered a certain word, such as "fu," the speaker was indicating that the value associated with the body part should be doubled (in our example, it would be 28). When Saxe investigated the reasons underlying this change, he found that in the intervening years, the Oksapmin had become involved in a cash economy, which made it necessary to calculate and communicate values greater than 27.

Everyday experience affects how individuals solve many types of problems, including those that are spatial in nature (Liben & Christensen, 2010). Children who live in communities where extensive spatial exploration occurs, such as Logoli children in Kenya, exhibit high-level skill at solving spatial problems. Researchers found a positive relation between the distance these children regularly traveled from their village and their skill at solving spatial problems (Munroe & Munroe, 1971). But not all spatial experiences mattered. In a later investigation, the research team found that children's directed distance from home—that is travel while doing a goal-directed activity such as herding livestock, weeding crops, or running errands to neighboring villages—was related to spatial problem-solving skills (Munroe et al., 1985). Children's free time playing outdoors, even when it occurred at some distance from the home, did not relate to these skills.

The way that adults help children develop cognitive skills also varies based on the adult's own experience, including their schooling. We touched on this relation earlier when we discussed research by LeVine and colleagues (1994), who observed how Gusii and North American mothers instructed their infants. In later research, developmental psychologist Pablo Chavajay (2006) observed mothers in a Guatemalan Maya community, who had differing amounts of formal schooling, discuss with their children (ages 6–12) how to solve a drinking-water shortage in the village. He found that Maya mothers who had little schooling (0–2 years) allowed their children to participate in joint problem-solving in whatever way the children wanted. In contrast, Maya mothers who had several years of schooling insisted on turn-taking and they made regular assessments (evaluations) of the children's learning, behavior that is similar to school practices. Although these differences are likely related to the mother's school experience, they may also reflect other factors. For example, mothers in this community who attended school are more likely to come from middle-income households than mothers who do not attend school.

As these research examples show, the relation between everyday experiences and the development and use of problem-solving skills reflects the inherently social and cultural nature of this important cognitive ability.

Spatial Cognition

Spatial cognition is critical to survival. It allows us to navigate through environments, give and follow directions, remember where we put objects, and solve many other problems of daily living. The importance of spatial knowledge has led cultures to create a variety of practices and tools for understanding space and solving spatial problems (Gauvain, 1993). Children learn cultural ways of talking about and using space by interacting with more experienced partners, and this learning begins quite early. The amount of spatial language parents used with their children from age 14 to 46 months is related to children's production of spatial language and predicts their performance on spatial problem-solving tasks at age 54 months (Pruden et al., 2011). Mothers' use of spatial language during picture-book reading with preschool age children helps children learn about spatial-graphic representations (i.e., understanding how distance is represented in a picture; Szechter & Liben, 2004).

Cultural contributions to spatial thinking are apparent in the way that people describe space in oral and written forms. For instance, researchers have identified two way-finding strategies that people use in giving directions. One strategy concentrates on routes and uses a first-person perspective as if someone is moving through the space. Route directions include information such as left and right turns and landmarks along the way. The other strategy is called a survey, and it uses a third-person perspective. Survey descriptions describe the entire space as a whole and often use cardinal directions (e.g., north, south) and include details about locations and sometimes distances. A common type of survey description depicts a space as it would appear to someone looking down from above, referred to as an aerial or bird's-eye view. There are cultural differences in the use of these way-finding strategies, and they reflect many factors, including the tools available in the culture and cultural values about how to represent space.

There are many cultural tools that aid thinking, and children learn to use them when they are quite young, which suggests they can play an important role in cognitive development (Vygotsky, 1987). For instance, cultural ways of representing large-scale space, such as maps, help children obtain insights about a space that would not be possible otherwise (Liben, 2001). And this learning occurs early; even preschool children have a basic understanding of what maps represent (e.g., show locations) and how they can be used (e.g., to find a place; Liben, 2009).

Cartography or written maps are mainly found in literate cultures. They rely on various conventions of representation, including symbols and images, to describe a space and the locations or areas within it. Maps, which often show an aerial view of the space, are survey descriptions. Consequently, survey descriptions are more common in cultures where maps are widely available (Uttal, 2005). Research conducted in the United States has found that the skill for devising, understanding, and using maps increases from early to middle childhood (Liben & Downs, 2015). As with other cognitive skills, children learn how to understand maps with the help of more experienced cultural members.

The appearance of maps and the information represented in them differs across cultures. In the late 1800s, anthropologist Franz Boas (Müller-Wille, 1998) visited traditional Inuit communities in the Arctic region and wrote about maps he saw drawn on a variety of materials including snow, paper, antlers, and even walrus tusks. These maps were not like cartographic maps that include precise distances between locations. Rather, they emphasized local place names and the relative location and direction of important sites in the area, which sometimes spanned as much as 500 miles across. In landscapes like the Arctic, this type of map is highly functional. Changing conditions in the environment (e.g., melting ice, snow drifts) can alter the distance one has to travel between locations, which makes information about relative location more useful than precise distance. In this sense, these maps depicted spatial information that was adapted to the geography of the region.

Historically, many Indigenous cultures did not use written maps to describe spatial information. Their mappings were in the form of oral narratives, stories, songs, dances, or art, the segments or sections of which (e.g., lines, paragraphs, hand formations, areas of a painting) follow an ordered sequence of movement, locations, and sometimes temporality (D. C. Rubin, 1995). These mappings are route-based, and the information included in them can be extensive, which puts great demand on memory. The fact that mappings are set in familiar places, include actions that occur at specific locations, and are often repeated in conversation and storytelling helps people remember them.

Mappings are highly valued by cultures because they contain place names and spatial relations that show connections between people and their habitat. The ability to understand and use this information is very important, and young community members learn it during travel and in conversations with more experienced community members. For example, the songlines created by Aboriginal Australian people describe paths across the vast desert where these people live. The paths are believed to be ones that were traveled by the ancestors. When writer Bruce Chatwin (1987) searched for the meaning of the songlines, he was told, "a song was both a map and a direction-finder. Providing you knew the song, you could always find your way across country" (p. 13).

Mothers teach young children the songlines, often drawing sketches in the sand to illustrate the paths the ancestors used.

Ideas about the value and utility of cartographic maps and Indigenous mapping cannot be separated from social history, especially colonialism. Geographer Denis Wood (1993) distinguished mapping, which is common across cultures, and mapmaking, which is a specific way of representing space in literate cultures. Colonial powers often establish dominance and ownership of Indigenous lands by replacing Indigenous place names with names that are important to the colonists and by "remapping" the region with their mapmaking techniques. In essence, the methods of one culture replace the local, Indigenous way of representing the landscape. This practice is often justified by claiming that colonist's mapmaking techniques are more accurate and useful than traditional methods. Note that this justification is based on the cultural values of the colonists regarding how spatial information should be represented and what kind of spatial information is most useful (Crampton & Krygier, 2006).

The tools people use to communicate about and travel in space have changed greatly in recent years with the introduction of computerized navigational aids such as geographic information systems, global positioning systems (GPS), and geo-visualization tools. Real-time navigational information available in handheld computers, such as mobile or cellular phones, helps people plan routes that can be updated with current traffic and weather conditions. Even people living in geographically isolated regions of the Majority World use these tools to help them complete activities that are spatial in nature, such as finding clean water for livestock and household use (Mpogole et al., 2008). According to geographer Roger Downs (2014), these new spatial tools are changing how people understand and relate to the world. They allow people to travel farther, visit new places, and get lost less often. Yet Downs pointed out that people may become dependent on them and, also, that their regular and exclusive use may lead people to abandon more traditional methods of thinking about and using space. And as a result, traditional methods would no longer be transmitted across generations. They would, in effect, become extinct. Research Highlight 3.2 describes how the use of new mapping technologies is affecting the Sami Indigenous culture.

We need to learn more about the development of spatial thinking with the widespread use of these new technologies. It seems clear that these types of tools are unlikely to go away any time soon. In fact, they are already influencing geography instruction in K-12 classrooms in the United States (Collins, 2018).

Researchers have also found cultural differences in the way language is used to describe the relations of objects or places in space, and these differences reflect the frame of reference people use in understanding space. Majid and colleagues (2004) focused on three ways of describing spatial relations. One way uses relative terms, which is based on the viewers' own perspective (e.g., the spoon is to the right of the fork); another uses absolute terms and is based on an external framework (e.g., the spoon is to the north of the fork); and the

RESEARCH HIGHLIGHT 3.2

Mapping the Arctic Among the Sami People of Scandinavia

The Sami people are a reindeer-herding culture who live in Fennoscandia, the northern region of the Scandinavian peninsula. They are closely connected to the environment where they live and they have devised elaborate mappings of the terrain that include many Indigenous place names and information about how the Sami people interact with the landscape. Their mappings, for example, include journeys during reindeer migration and the paths of important mythological characters (e.g., the sacred bear). Sami place names and mental maps have been transmitted orally over many generations. Cogos et al. (2017) described how, traditionally, Sami children learned place names, spatial locations, and the topography of the region when they accompanied elders during reindeer migration. The elders described this process as learning step by step, as one remarked, like "explaining a recipe without a book" (p. 46).

But in recent years, this practice has changed. Younger Sami generations now use written maps and map technology, such as GPS and online digital maps, to learn about the environment. Indigenous place names and journeys are not on these maps. However, there have been efforts to maintain the role of elders by having them tell younger generations about traditional place names and important journeys when referring to locations on the written and digital maps. And it is possible that some map technologies, such as those that allow users to relabel place names, may help to maintain cultural mapping practices (Cocq, 2015). Even so, the Sami people are concerned that they are losing their identification of and connection to the landscape because, as Cogos and colleagues (2017) explained, "such media still emanate from a Western conception and fail to convey the Sami way of seeing the land" (p. 50).

third uses intrinsic terms and focuses on the relation of items to each other without reference to personal or external coordinates (e.g., the fork is at the nose of the spoon). The researchers found that English speakers mainly use relative and intrinsic frames of reference. The Guugu Yimithirr people, an Australian Aboriginal group, however, use an absolute frame of reference when they describe spatial information. For instance, when they describe the placement of objects on a tabletop or locations in a landscape, they use cardinal directions, such as north, south, east, and west. And their behavior corresponds to these descriptions. When asked to place objects on a tabletop in the same way that the objects were arranged on a table in another room, which was directly across the hall, these speakers used an absolute frame of reference (Levinson, 1996). That is, they placed the book to the north of the cup, whereas English speakers placed the book to the right of the cup.

Similar patterns have been found in research with children. Dutch and Namibian elementary school children (≠Akhoe Haiǁom speakers) differ in the spatial frame of reference used in speech (Haun et al., 2011). Dutch children are more likely to use relative terms, and Namibian children are more likely to use absolute terms. Moreover, when children in this study were instructed to use their nondominant frame of reference, they had difficulty doing so and performed poorly. This research suggests that spatial cognition and the language of a culture are deeply connected.

Geographical or environmental factors of a region can also inform how people use language to describe space. People from the midwestern United States, a region characterized by grid-like property boundaries, tend to use a survey or third-person perspective when giving directions. People from the Netherlands, where more natural features are used to define boundaries, tend to use route or first-person perspectives (Hund et al., 2012). Thus, the frames of reference people use in describing space are shaped by the environment and by cultural methods for describing space that have developed over time.

Cultural ways of thinking about space also contribute to how people solve problems that are not spatial. In one study, 3- to 7-year-old Australian Aboriginal children identified and manipulated spatial patterns in order to solve nonverbal addition problems more than same-age English-speaking Australian children, who relied on counting words to solve the problems (Butterworth et al., 2011). Aboriginal children's success with solving the problems by using spatial methods reflects traditional techniques of way-finding in the region where they live, along with informal instructional practices that emphasize spatial thinking (Kearins, 1986). In other research, culturally specific reading patterns in how information is spatially presented in a text can influence whether the future is perceived as occurring in a forward direction and the past in a backward direction (consistent with English left-to-right reading pattern) or whether the future is perceived as occurring in an upward manner and the past in a downward manner (consistent with vertical reading patterns, e.g., Mandarin; Bowerman & Choi, 2003; Majid et al., 2004).

Human spatial understanding is vital to everyday functioning, and culture informs our knowledge of space and how we use space for a variety of activities. Culture contributes to the development of spatial thinking by providing techniques for exploring, remembering, and talking about space, and more experienced cultural members help children acquire this knowledge.

CONCLUSION

To become mature members of the community, children and youth need to learn as much as they can about their culture. Research in diverse areas of cognition has found that gradually, over the course of development, the knowledge and cognitive skills valued in a culture become part of the thoughts and actions of young community members. To describe how this process occurs, we used sociocultural theory, which focuses on how the social world, especially interactions with adults and more experienced peers, helps young people engage in and learn about their culture. The cultural nature of learning is also present when children are alone and involved in cultural activities, and when they use the material tools and symbolic resources of the culture to carry out their own goal-directed actions. As cultural symbols and tools are integrated with individual cognition, children become intellectually connected with other cultural members and with the culture itself.

Many processes of learning contribute to this endeavor including the observation of cultural behaviors, sharing of cultural knowledge in reciprocal exchanges, explicit efforts to transmit cultural knowledge and ways of thinking, and participation in the practices and institutions of the culture. The influence of any particular learning process and how these processes are implemented varies across cultures and illustrates how cognitive development is both embedded in culture and unfolds in unique ways across cultural settings. These different social processes are robust and contribute to cognitive development in many important areas of intellectual growth, including memory, problem-solving skills, and spatial thinking.

For additional resources, see the Appendix.

DISCUSSION QUESTIONS

1. Why do we describe cognitive development as a cultural process?

2. Why are there cultural differences in the use of the four processes of social learning described in this chapter?

3. What are the benefits and problems associated with passing cultural ways of thinking and acting across generations?

4. Does autobiographical memory make individuals similar to or different from other people in their culture?

5. In examining relations between new geospatial technologies and cognitive development, Downs (2014) claimed that this cultural change will redefine the self. What do you think he means by this?

4

Sociolinguistics

Conversations between parents and young children are important for children's language acquisition.

anguage is central to children's socialization into culture, and it plays a dual role. Much of socialization occurs through language, and children are socialized to use language (Duranti et al., 2011). Learning "through" and "about" language largely occurs during everyday interactions of young people and other community members. During these interactions, children learn the sounds and words in their language along with the conventional and socially acceptable ways that people express themselves in their culture. They also learn about concepts and ways of thinking that are important in their culture, which helps to align children's ideas and the manner in which they express those ideas with the people around them (Fitnera & Matsui, 2015). Finally, they develop awareness of and sensitivity to the immediate context in which language is used, an understanding that is critical to effective communication.

https://doi.org/10.1037/0000228-004
Child and Adolescent Development in Cultural Context, by J. E. Lansford, D. C. French, and M. Gauvain

Sociolinguistics is the study of how language is used, including how language varies across societal members and social conditions. Effective social communication acknowledges (or indexes) important aspects of the sociocultural world including social norms, social status, social identity and roles, the nature of personal relationships, and one's familiarity or association with the community at large (Ochs & Schieffelin, 2016). When children use language according to their cultural practices, they display their membership in and commitment to the values and behaviors of the group (Sterponi, 2010). And in so doing, young community members help to maintain the social and cultural order.

In this chapter, we describe language socialization. We begin with an overview of what language is and describe the main theories of how language develops. Then we turn to what is known about how children learn to understand and use language in ways that are appropriate in their culture. Throughout the chapter, we refer to ideas from the sociocultural approach (described in Chapter 3), which views language as a primary tool of cognitive development in childhood (Vygotsky, 1987).

WHAT IS LANGUAGE?

Language is a system of communication in which words are combined in rule-governed manners that enable speakers to produce an infinite number of messages (Hoff, 2014; MacWhinney, 2015). Communication through language is a two-way process; we send messages to others via productive language, and we receive messages by using receptive language.

Language serves various purposes for the developing child (Parrish-Morris et al., 2013). It helps children interact with and communicate information to others. It provides a way for children to express their feelings, wishes, and ideas. Children use language to influence the behavior of other people and to explore and learn about the environment. Language can also help children use their imagination to escape from reality (Taylor, 2013). Finally, language has intrapersonal functions in that it helps children organize their perceptions and thinking, control their actions, and modify their emotions.

Research on language and its development is divided into four main areas: phonology, semantics, grammar, and pragmatics. *Phonology* is the study of sounds of a language, including intonation patterns, and the rules about how sounds are put together to form spoken words. *Semantics* pertains to word meanings, word combinations, and how words are used in phrases and sentences. *Grammar* involves the structure of language and consists of two parts: morphology and syntax. *Morphology* focuses on the smallest units of meaning in a language, such as prefixes and suffixes, and how they can be used to alter root words (e.g., to make plurals and past tense). *Syntax* focuses on how words are combined into sentences and includes rules for expressing grammatical relations such as questions, negation, and possession. *Pragmatics* deals with the preferred and expected manner of communication in sociocultural situations.

It concentrates on rules for using language in context, such as how to take turns when speaking, remain silent while others speak, and adjust speaking in different settings (e.g., more quietly indoors than outdoors).

In practice, these various aspects of language are not always easy to separate. For instance, it is important that children learn to use language in ways that respect the social roles and status of community members because it helps prepare children for their future roles and relationships in society (Ochs, 2002). This understanding is marked linguistically in many ways, including with phonology (e.g., learning appropriate pitch and tone for speaking with elders or when at home, school, or church), semantics (e.g., titles for various social roles), syntax (e.g., appropriate use of formal and informal verbs), and various pragmatic forms (e.g., politeness, honorific and respectful language). Together these different aspects of language create *communicative competence*, a notion introduced by linguist Dell Hymes (1974) to describe the ability to convey thoughts, feelings, and intentions in a meaningful and culturally patterned way. Because there are cultural contributions to all these areas of language development, we describe research findings in each to convey a sense of how deeply culture is integrated with language and its development.

THEORIES OF LANGUAGE DEVELOPMENT

There are long-standing debates about how language develops in childhood, and several theories have been proposed to describe this process. The theories can be distinguished by their emphasis on biological versus experiential contributions.

Theories that emphasize biological contributions are called *nativist* views. These theories claim that the human child is biologically predisposed to acquire human language. In other words, language ability is an inherited species-specific characteristic. The most influential advocate of this view is linguist Noam Chomsky (1968), who proposed that children are born with an innate mental structure that he called a language acquisition device, which enables them to learn language early and quickly. Evidence supporting this view includes the existence of common structural features across languages (e.g., all languages have grammar with certain formal properties such as subject-predicate relation in sentences). Also, there appears to be a sensitive period for learning language (Slobin, 1985, 1992). Before puberty, a child may achieve the fluency of a native speaker in any language without special training, but after puberty, it is more difficult to do so. To illustrate, on an English grammar test, native speakers of Chinese and Korean who had immigrated to the United States before they were 7 years old scored as well as native speakers of English (Newport, 1990). However, the older the immigrants were when they arrived in America, the more poorly they performed on the test. This type of result is not unique to the English language, which is considered to be difficult to learn. In a study including Italian families that immigrated to Canada, researchers found that children who were over the age of 6 when they arrived tended to maintain a hint of their Italian accent (Flege et al., 1999). Research Highlight 4.1 describes research with deaf children and adults regarding the idea of a sensitive period of language learning. Yet, even if there is a sensitive period for language learning, it is not clear what the underlying cause may be. Perhaps as children get older and their vocabulary increases, there is greater likelihood of word interference in learning a second language (Kroll & Tokowicz, 2005). Others contend that there may be social reasons. Compared with older children, younger nonnative speakers get more support from their family in learning a second language and they also are more readily integrated into peer social groups that provide access to conversation that is matched to the child's cognitive level (Sokolov, 1993). Overall, the nativist view has been met with much criticism. Critics point to the wide variety of grammatical and syntactic rules in the world's languages and how the communicative context, especially adult–child communication, contributes to the pacing and scope of language development.

Other theories view language as an emergent property of experience and focus on how language is learned in childhood. Behavioral psychologist B. F. Skinner (1957) suggested that children learn language first by attending to linguistic input, then by reproducing this input, and then by using basic principles of learning, such as imitation and reinforcement, which support repro-

---

RESEARCH HIGHLIGHT 4.1

Language Learning of Deaf Children

In 1977, Nicaragua opened its first school for deaf people. Prior to this, deaf students were severely limited in the social interaction and conversations they could have with others at school. In the new school, children and adults were taught to lip-read and to speak Spanish as best as they could. This approach yielded little success, but the students were able to interact using gestural communication. Gradually, a rudimentary sign language emerged among the students. As new students of various ages entered the school, they learned this language from the current students.

Senghas and Coppola (2001) studied this gestural language. They were especially interested in this language use in relation to how long a student had been at the school and the age at which the student started. If the complex grammar of language existed only among the children in the school, then it could be concluded that the ability to learn this grammar was related to innate abilities of children before they reach the cutoff (around puberty) for the sensitive period of language learning. However, if these complex components of the language were found only in adults learning the new sign language, researchers could conclude that higher cognitive levels are needed to grasp the hardest parts of language.

The investigators found that the most complex speech patterns were evident in children under age 10. The adults did not use these structures in either speech comprehension or production. Thus, children were able to create and learn gestures that conveyed complex linguistic structures, whereas adults who were past the sensitive period for language learning were unable to do so. This finding provides strong support for the idea that human beings are designed to learn language at an early age. It also highlights the important contribution of social experience in this learning.

---

duction and increase the likelihood it will be retained (or not). This experiential explanation of language development is problematic on various levels (Hoff, 2014). Although learning principles may be used to modify language usage once it is in place, these principles cannot explain how children learn the enormous number of reinforcement linkages needed to communicate effectively. Viewing learning strictly by itself also cannot account for the regular sequence of language development across cultures or the fact that children learn to speak grammatically correctly even though their parents do not systematically reinforce it. Finally, learning views portray the child as a passive figure in language development, when in actuality children play active and inventive roles as they discover, apply, and modify language for their own use. To illustrate, young children will produce creative utterances, such as using regular verb forms for irregular verbs (e.g., saying "goed" instead of "went"). This way of speaking, which is referred to as overregularization, is neither reinforced nor modeled. Although these types of words are infrequent in a young child's lexicon, they nonetheless occur and have been found in several languages. Clahsen et al. (2002) found overregularizations in the vocabulary of Spanish-speaking children who were between the ages of 2 and 5. Children also actively modify language use across social contexts to serve their own needs. Paugh (2005) observed that adults—both parents and teachers—in Dominica in the West Indies encourage children to speak English, the official language used in school, because it is associated with prestige and social mobility. Nonetheless, the children use the local creole language called "Patwa" when they play with peers.

Most contemporary language theorists hold an *interactionist* view, arguing that human infants are biologically prepared to learn to speak language and that they learn to do so in the context of spoken language (K. Nelson, 2007; Tomasello, 2003). Psychologist Jerome Bruner (1983), an early advocate of this view, proposed that the social environment provides the child with a language acquisition support system. Caregivers aid language development by using simplified language—called *child-directed speech*—when talking with children, by playing nonverbal games (e.g., peek-a-boo) with them that model turn-taking, an important language-related skill, and by using other techniques that support children's efforts to communicate. For instance, in child-directed speech, caregivers speak in short, simple sentences that refer to concrete objects and events; they repeat important words and phrases; and they talk more slowly and in higher-pitched voices, enunciate clearly, and often end sentences with a rising intonation (Fernald, 1992). Newborns and 4-week-old infants prefer to listen to child-directed speech than to adult-directed talk (R. P. Cooper & Aslin, 1990), even when the speech is in a nonnative language (Werker et al., 1994). Child-directed speech is also related to various positive outcomes in language development, including better speech perception and a larger vocabulary. Such relations have been found for a diversity of languages including English, Japanese, and Korean (S. Lee et al., 2008; Werker et al., 2007).

There is substantial variation across cultures in how the social world contributes to language development, which suggests that there is no universal pattern of social-linguistic support. Research has shown that children learn language through various methods including the aforementioned child-directed speech, as well as by direct instruction—social interactions in which adults and children are conversational partners—and overhearing the conversations of others around them (Akhtar, 2005; Ochs & Schieffelin, 2016). Variation across cultures in how adults speak to children reflects many factors, including cultural beliefs about childrearing and how children learn (Lieven & Stoll, 2010). In a now-classic study, Schieffelin and Ochs (1986) observed that caregivers in some cultures, such as the Kaluli people of Papua New Guinea and American Samoa, do not simplify their speech when talking with infants and young children. Rather, when children in this community begin to utter words, adults speak to them as if they are adults, and the children still become competent users of the language. Thus, it appears that although child-directed speech may aid language development, it is not required to learn language. What is required is the opportunity for children to participate in a language community in which people interact and talk with one another.

Not all interactivist views of language learning concentrate on supportive social behaviors. Some emphasize the role of more general cognitive capabilities, particularly learning to understand and use symbols (Callaghan, 2013). Other cognitive abilities that develop over the first years of life also contribute to language development. Social-cognitive skills, in particular, provide children with information about other people and their behaviors, including how language is used to support and carry out activities. Between 9 and 12 months of age, one important way that infants learn words, especially nouns, is by paying close attention to the gazes of their social partners as they look at and label objects in the process of joint attention (Adamson et al., 2005). Infants also need to learn about action words and how they relate to goal-directed behavior. By the end of the first year, infants' ability to comprehend behavioral intention bolsters their ability to understand communication as it relates to the actions of others (Tomasello et al., 2005).

A recent, interactionist view of early language comprehension, called *categorical speech perception*, focuses on very young infants' capacity for receptive language (Aslin & Newport, 2012). Research based on this approach has found that infants are able to discriminate among consonant sounds (e.g., *p, b, m, n, d*) as early as the first month of life, and by 2 months of age they can recognize some vowel sounds (e.g., /a/ and /i/; Aslin, 1987). In other words, human infants are active listeners who parse the vocalized sounds around them into units of meaning that resemble syllables and words. The capability to identify and group patterns in sounds may be an inherent property of the mammalian aural system (J. L. Miller & Eimas, 1994). When young children are exposed to their native language as it is spoken around them, they use this capability to distinguish and categorize phonemes in their native language.

LANGUAGE DEVELOPMENT IN CULTURAL CONTEXT

In the following section, we look more closely at the four main areas of language development: phonology, semantics, syntax, and pragmatics. In addition to describing important changes with age in each of these areas, we explain how children's experiences in culture contribute to their development.

Phonology: The Sounds of Language

Phonology involves the sounds of language, which includes the pronunciation of vowels and consonants, intonation, and regional accents and dialects. In order to become effective communicators, children need to identify and distinguish the specific phonological attributes or sounds of their language. Between 6 and 9 years of age, children are able to pronounce the sounds of their language correctly most of the time (Kent, 2005).

Because there is substantial variation in the sound systems used across languages, learning speech sounds differs for children growing up in different cultural settings. For example, although the average number of consonant sounds across languages is around 24, in some languages, such as Rotokas, which is spoken in Papua New Guinea, there are very few consonant sounds (about six). In other languages (e.g., such as dialects of the Khoisan language spoken in Botswana and Namibia), there are numerous consonant sounds (around 122), including several types of clicks (Maddieson, 2005).

Perception of the sounds of language develops very early, well before infants can speak. Infants show an interest in the sound of human language at a very young age. At 3 months of age, infants prefer the sounds made by humans when they speak versus other natural sounds (e.g., vocalizations by monkeys; Shultz & Vouloumanos, 2010). As described previously in relation to categorical speech perception, younger infants attend to patterns of sounds in language; for instance, 8-month-olds can recognize and remember groupings of sounds that resemble words (the first syllable is always followed by a specific second syllable; Saffran et al., 1996). Because this skill develops in relation to the speech sounds the infant actually hears, the ability to distinguish and categorize phonemes narrows over the first year of life and becomes specialized to the sounds of their own language (Werker et al., 2007). To illustrate, in one study of infants of English-speaking parents, the infants could distinguish between sounds that are unique to the Swedish language until they were 6 months old, but after this age they could no longer do so (Kuhl et al., 1992). In another study, 9-month-old American infants were no longer able to perceive Dutch words they had previously recognized, and Dutch infants were similarly unresponsive to English words they had previously recognized (Jusczyk et al., 1993). Interestingly, this developmental change is not restricted to vocalized language sounds, the same pattern occurs for infants learning sign language (Palmer et al., 2012).

Another important aspect of early language development is sound production. Babies produce many types of sounds from birth onward. Crying, which
begins at birth, is a way of indicating distress. By the end of the first month of
life, babies produce a string of vowel-like sounds, called cooing, during social
exchanges with caregivers. Cross-cultural studies of early vocalizations have
found that infants will make positive sounds when they gaze into their parents'
eyes (Keller, 2002). Infants' negative vocalizations usually elicit a response
from caregivers, often touching or holding. A comparison of two communities
in the Central African Republic, Aka foragers and Ngandu farmers, and one
urban community in the United States revealed no differences in how often
caregivers showed affection toward their infants, but there were differences in
the frequency and nature of caregiver responses to infant fussiness and crying
(Hewlett & Lamb, 2002).

The first strings of language-like vocalizations appear in the middle of the
first year of life when babies begin to babble. This early sound production,
which includes combinations of consonants and vowels, follows an orderly
sequence and the kinds of sounds babies make when they babble are similar
across different language groups. For instance, Chinese, American, and Ethio-
pian babies babble similar consonant-vowel combinations, even though they
are exposed to different phonemes in their native languages (Thevenin et al.,
1985). Later in the first year, cultural differences in the prespeech sounds that
babies make begin to emerge. Around 8 months of age, babies exposed to one
of two different native languages, Arabic or French—languages that differ in
voice quality and pitch, begin to show differences in their babbling (Ingram,
1989). Japanese and French words contain more nasal sounds than Swedish
and English words, and late in the first year of life, the babbling of French and
Japanese babies contains more nasal sounds than that of Swedish and English
babies (De Boysson-Bardies et al., 1992).

What sounds occur in a baby's early language? As a general rule, the sounds
that appear reflect the frequency with which the sounds are used in the language. For example, the sound of /v/ is used infrequently in English, thus it
occurs relatively late in the language development of English-speaking children. In languages in which the /v/ sound is more common, such as Swedish
and Estonian, it occurs earlier in children's speech development (Vihman,
2004). The difficulty level of a sound is also a factor. Although isiXhosa-speaking
children in South Africa have mastered most of the sounds of this complex
language by age 3, it is not until age 4 or 5 that the children are able to make
the various click sounds used in this language (Maphalala et al., 2014).

The speech sounds that young children make help them to develop skill
with communicative exchanges (Golinkoff, 1983; Kuhl, 2009). Early in life,
babies produce sounds that provide them with their first experiences as a communicative partner. These early exchanges are called "pseudo-conversations"
because infants have little control over their input behaviors, and the adults are
largely responsible for maintaining the flow of the exchange. For instance, in a
classic study that reviewed these types of interactions, Snow (1977) describes

how a baby may utter a sound such as a gurgle and then her mother replies by speaking to the infant, who responds in some way, and then the mother reacts to the response. According to Snow, what makes these interactions conversation-like is that they are reciprocal. That is, information flows in both directions, from infant to mother to infant and so on. For example, in the study, 3-month-old Ann and her mother interact in a pseudo-conversation. First, Ann smiles and her mother says, "Oh what a nice smile! Yes, isn't that nice? There. There's a nice little smile." Ann then burps and her mother says, "What a nice wind as well! Yes, that's better, isn't it? Yes." Ann then vocalizes and her mother says, "Yes! There's a nice noise" (Snow, 1977, p. 12).

This type of exchange has been observed in many cultural settings, including the Zincantec Maya of Mexico, where caregivers respond meaningfully to infants' vocalizations (de Léon, 1998). By the end of their first year, infants are quite skilled at the pattern of communicative exchanges in their culture, a topic that we review later when we discuss pragmatics.

Semantics: The Meaning of Words and Sentences

Languages are made up of *words*, the linguistic symbols that represent or refer to something. Social and cultural factors affect word learning, and this process entails more than learning to pronounce the words. Rather, children learn that words represent concepts and ways of thinking that are important in their culture. And in some languages, sounds are also used to convey meaning, linking phonology with semantics. Tonal languages such as Mandarin Chinese (Xu, 1997) and Yoruba, a language spoken in Nigeria and neighboring regions of Africa (Laniran & Clements, 2003), use pitch and other sounds to distinguish words that appear the same but are actually semantically distinct.

Children usually utter their first words between 10 and 15 months of age (Fenson et al., 1994). Then, over the second year of life, they rapidly develop their mental lexicon, which includes the words that a person knows and the knowledge that he or she possesses about these words. By age 2, the average child knows approximately 900 root words, and by age 6, children know approximately 8,000 words. The remarkable growth of vocabulary over the first 5 years of life underscores the human capacity for language and communication.

Although the task of learning words seems daunting, children are quite adept at assigning (or mapping) words onto a referent. After hearing a new word only once, young children begin to develop ideas about what it refers to, a process Carey (1978) termed *fast mapping*. There also appear to be some innate principles (or constraints) that help children learn words (Markman, 1991). The first thing a child must understand about words is that they refer to something. This understanding is described in the principle of *reference*, which is the idea that words stand for objects, actions, and events. The *whole-object constraint* is the assumption that a new word refers to the entire object, not to one of its parts or properties. It is evident that even children as young as 18 months are able to use this constraint. For example, when a 2-year-old visits the zoo and hears the word "kangaroo" for the first time, the child assumes that "kangaroo" refers to the animal, not its nose, body, or behavior. Even 12-month-olds will associate novel words with whole objects rather than parts of objects (Hollich et al., 2007). Later in development children begin to understand more complex principles such as the *mutual exclusivity bias*, which is the understanding that when hearing a label or name for the first time, infants assume it describes a new object and not a familiar one. For example, in one study, four objects were placed in front of a young child; three of the objects were familiar (a ball, a shoe, keys) and one was unfamiliar (a tea strainer; Golinkoff et al., 1992). When the experimenter asked for the "glorp," children selected the tea strainer, the unfamiliar object. The children excluded the three familiar objects because they already knew their names or labels, and decided that the new name must belong to the new object.

Social and cultural experiences contribute to word learning (K. Nelson, 1996). For example, the amount of time parents spend reading to their 2-year-olds is positively related to the children's language skills at age 4 (Crain-Thoreson & Dale, 1992). Young children are not passive recipients when they learn words from others. Children between the ages of 3 and 5 show a preference for information provided by a native speaker of their language rather than a nonnative speaker (Kinzler et al., 2011), suggesting there is a bias in early word learning that favors members of the same cultural group.

As to what words children learn first, some research suggests that nouns (object names) are learned more easily than verbs (J. B. Childers & Tomasello, 2002), while other research has found the same proportion of nouns and action words in children's early vocabulary (Schwartz & Leonard, 1984). Still other research (Huttenlocher et al., 1983) has shown that children learn some action words more easily than others, especially in certain circumstances. For example, 2-year-old children learn words for actions they can actually do themselves (e.g., walk) before words for actions they cannot yet do (e.g., skip).

Whether nouns or verbs dominate a young child's lexicon varies by language. Whereas nouns tend to dominate the first words uttered by young English-speaking children, Tardif (1996) found that 21-month-old children learning to speak Mandarin Chinese used equal numbers of verbs and nouns. This difference may reflect the fact that in some Asian languages, verbs play a prominent role in speech and often occur at the end of a sentence, which garners attention (Hoff, 2014). Japanese children also have fewer nouns in their early vocabulary than English-speaking children. The fact that Japanese mothers spend less time labeling objects than American mothers may also account for the lower rate of noun production among young Japanese children (Fernald & Morikawa, 1993).

Syntax: The Grammatical Structure of Language

Children's first words are often used to express complex ideas usually found in the sentences of older individuals. For instance, when a young child points to a toy on a high shelf and says "Down," the child is requesting that the toy be taken down from the shelf. In this sense, the child is using a one-word phrase to express a complete thought, called a *holophrase*. Between the ages of 1 and 2, children begin to put two words together in what is called *telegraphic speech*. This speech form generally includes nouns and verbs (and sometimes adjectives), but it omits other parts of speech such as articles and prepositions. In a study on young children's speech across languages, psycholinguist Dan Slobin (1985) found that children's two-word sentences are remarkably similar in terms of the relationships between the words, or the basic structure or grammar the sentences contain. For instance, a child's description of events or situations has a similar structure, such as "baby go" (English), "puppe kommt" ("doll comes"; German), "mam prua" ("mama walk"; Russian), "Seppo putoo" ("Seppo fall"; Finnish), "odhi skul" ("he-went school"; Luo, a language spoken in Kenya), and "pá u pepe" ("fall doll"; Samoan).

Why are children's early utterances similar across languages? Language is a way of expressing what one knows or understands about the world, and children around the world tend to have encounters with similar kinds of basic situations in life, such as the distinction between self and others, understanding of objects, and causal relations. Thus, wherever children live, their early spoken language is used to express similar ideas about the relationships and events in the world. All human languages are structured in ways that enable children to formulate and communicate this information.

The development of grammar or syntax accelerates in the third year of life as children begin to use pronouns, articles, and more elaborate verb forms (present and past tense, auxiliary verbs such as "to be"). Although most languages combine words in sentences in similar fashion, usually in the order of subject-verb-object, in some languages, these word types can appear in any order (Heath, 1984). Thus, even basic grammatical formations in simple sentences are adjusted to the language of the culture.

As children's simple sentences become more complex, they begin to be used in the form of a question or negation (Carruthers, 2020). Whereas younger children may ask a question by raising their voices at the end of an assertion, such as "sit chair," by the latter part of their third year, children begin to ask questions using more conventional forms, such as "wh" questions—those that start with the words "what," "when," "who," "why," and "which"—as well as questions that begin with "how" (Butler et al., 2020). Some researchers contend that children use certain question forms, in particular "why" questions, as a way of learning about the world (Chouinard, 2007). However, the universality of this behavior is not yet established, and it is likely that children have various ways of using language to understand the world that reflect the social conditions and practices of their culture (Gauvain & Munroe, 2020).

Children's earliest expression of negation is nonverbal, for example, by shaking the head to mean "no." Early in their second year, children begin to use the word "no" either alone or at the beginning of a phrase—for example, a child may say "No doggie" to mean the dog is not here. As children get older, they form different kinds of negatives such as the nonexistence of something (e.g., "All gone"), rejection of something (e.g., "No wash hair"), and the denial that something is true (e.g., "That not Daddy"; Bloom, 1970; Tager-Flusberg, 1985). Research has shown that these different forms of negation appear in the same order across cultures, suggesting that there may a biological basis to this syntaxial or grammatical aspect of language development (Bloom, 1991; Clancy, 1985).

The most striking evidence indicating that children may possess an innate program or template for grammar comes from research by linguist Derek Bickerton (1983, 1990), who studied creole languages around the globe. Creole languages occur when people who speak different languages end up together in a single place and want to talk with one another. Creole languages are found throughout the world including in Hawaii, New Orleans, the Caribbean, Guyana, Haiti, Nigeria, Indonesia, and the Philippines, all places where people from countries of Asia, Africa, Europe, and the Americas came together and formed polyglot or multilingual societies. In these new societies, many of which were comprised of people who were abducted and forced to work as slave laborers on colonial plantations, adults communicated among themselves with a pidgin language created out of two or more languages. Pidgin lacks grammatical complexity; its sentences are mainly a string of nouns, verbs, and adjectives. The children in these cultures, regardless of their parents' native languages, created a language derived from the pidgin language, called creole, which has a single grammatical structure and linguistic system. The creole languages that have developed in different places around the world are very similar in grammatical structure, regardless of the contributing languages. Also, creole languages persist into succeeding generations in similar form, which suggests that their use spreads rapidly. Bickerton concluded that the children were able to create and pass on languages with complex linguistic structures, whereas the adults who were past the sensitive period of language learning were unable to do so.

Some critics of this conclusion, such as Tomasello (1995), have argued that adult influences may play a role in the emergence of creole. Others argue that creole languages reveal the common properties and uses of language across cultures rather than simply reflecting properties of the human mind (Jourdan, 1991). The fact that creole languages developed a long time ago makes it difficult to know exactly what processes underlie them (Hoff, 2014). At this point, it seems that the interactionist view, which emphasizes both biological factors and environmental influences, provides a viable explanation for the emergence of creole languages.

Pragmatics: Socially Appropriate Language Use

The primary function of language is to communicate with other people. In this sense, learning to speak is learning to interact in socially appropriate and expected ways. The rules for language use are called pragmatics. There are a number of rules that children need to learn, such as how to get people to do things for them (requests) and how to thank people for their help (Ervin-Tripp, 1982). Children also need to learn how to use language properly depending on the situation they are in and the other people involved. Asking a respected elder for help is different from asking a peer. In addition, children need to know how to engage the listener and be good listeners themselves.

Children learn many of the pragmatic aspects of language very early, which indicates their importance to communication. Children as young as age 3 use different types of speech in different situations, or speech registers. For instance, they speak with a different level of formality depending on the person with whom they are speaking (Andersen, 1990). Young children also use language in ways that acknowledge culturally appropriate speech. For example, they are aware of who can or should be spoken to, allowed and prohibited topics, how to address and listen to others, and the types of responses that are expected (Sterponi, 2010).

Not all communication is verbal, and one important form of nonverbal communication is gesture. The use of gestures to communicate exists in all cultures (Kita, 2009). Gestures can be used independently (e.g., a wave or nod), or they can accompany language. The integration of gesture and speech enhances communication and they are used together throughout life (McNeill, 1992).

Some gestures appear in most cultures, such as head nodding. However, even when gestures look the same across cultures, they may not mean the same thing. For example, a thumbs-up gesture is a sign of approval in some cultures, but is an insult in others. Even when a gesture has similar meaning across cultures, its frequency of use may differ and result in different social experiences for the people involved. For example, head nodding during conversation is much more frequent among Japanese people than among American English speakers (Maynard, 1993, as cited in Kita, 2009). Some cultural differences reflect the pragmatic aspects of language, as illustrated by different types of polite greeting gestures.

Across cultures, the use of gestures to communicate increases between 6 and 36 months of age (Kwon et al., 2018). Gestures serve various functions for children (Goldin-Meadow, 2015). Very young children use them to convey their needs and interests before they can do so verbally. For example, infants will reach their arms out to the caregiver in order to be picked up. Infants use gestures to communicate interest by pointing at objects. At first this action is an expression of interest, but if others respond by labeling the object, the gesture becomes a way of gathering information and regulating the behaviors of others. This type of gesture is called a *declarative referential point* because it functions like a declarative sentence by referring to an object and relaying (declaring) information about it (e.g., look at it, name it) to another person. By 12 months of age, infants use pointing intentionally to inquire about objects and other sights in the world, and when others respond by labeling the object or event, they facilitate language development (Tomasello et al., 2007). Children in various cultures—including Japan, Peru, Canada, Papua New Guinea, India, and Maya in Mexico—use pointing in a declarative referential way before they are 1 year of age (Callaghan et al., 2011; Liszkowski et al., 2012). There are differences across cultures in the frequency with which young children use pointing to communicate, suggesting that this universal gesture is learned socially.

As children get older, gestures play an important role in learning because they provide information about what children do or do not know (Goldin-Meadow, 2009). For instance, when looking at a book with a caregiver, the child's response when asked to point to an animal tells the caregiver how to help the child learn. Teachers will use children's gestures to determine how well they are following a classroom lesson. Research Highlight 4.2 describes additional research comparing the frequency and composition of children's gesture use across cultures.

Research shows that even before children reach school age, they have learned socially appropriate ways of interacting with and learning from other people in their community. Consider requests, which are speech forms that ask for information or help from another person. Requests are important pragmatic forms for communication and learning, and young children's ability to make requests changes substantially over the first few years of life. When preschool-age children make requests, they do not usually present them in socially appropriate ways. For instance, they will use direct commands (e.g., "Give me the [toy] car"), issue statements or questions (e.g., "I need the car"; "Would you give me the car?"), and sometimes rely on indirect directives or hints (e.g., "I like the blue car the most"; Ervin-Tripp, 1982). Between the ages of 3 and 4, children's requests begin to reflect more social factors, such as the status of the listener or

---

RESEARCH HIGHLIGHT 4.2

Communicating With Gesture

The Italian culture is thought to use a high rate of communicative gestures. In one study, Iverson et al. (2008) compared gesture use in Italian and American children. The children were studied from 10 to 24 months of age and two types of gestures were examined: deictic gestures, which direct the attention or action of another person (e.g., pointing, reaching toward an object while opening and closing hand), and representational gestures, which depict an action or event (e.g., pretend movements associated with eating or dancing, conventional gestures such as a head nod). Italian children used more gestures than American children, and when communicating, American children used mostly deictic gestures and Italian children used both deictic and representational gestures—patterns that coincide with how adults in these cultures use gestures to communicate.

Research provides a glimpse into the possible source of such differences. Salomo and Liszkowski (2013) observed the social interactions of caregivers and infants, 8 to 15 months of age, in three cultural groups: Yucatec Maya in Mexico, urban Dutch in the Netherlands, and metropolitan Chinese in Shanghai. The researchers focused on the joint action of caregivers and infants and their use of deictic gestures (e.g., pointing to an object or event, showing an object in the hand). Both adults and children in the three cultures displayed deictic behaviors (mostly pointing), however, they did so at different rates, depending on the amount of joint action in the dyads. Also, in each culture, there were positive relations in the number of gestures used by the caregivers and infants. These patterns support the idea that social interaction contributes to the development of this universal form of prelinguistic behavior. An important part of development is mastery of the gestures used to communicate in a culture. This process begins early in childhood and is aided by interactions with caregivers.

interpersonal goals. They use less-direct requests with individuals of higher status or when they are trying to be polite or especially nice (e.g., when they want to get a treat from another person; Bates, 1976). As Kyratzis and Cook-Gumperz (2015) explained, "pragmatic choices, in something as apparently simple as request forms, reveal the real complexities of the discourse knowledge necessary for children to become competent communicators in everyday settings" (p. 684).

Cultures differ in the manner and frequency with which children request help and information from others. Japanese culture has an elaborate system of polite language and demeanor that even young children are expected to learn. Nakamura (1996) found that Japanese children's use of polite language when making requests varies by social context. In this study, 3-, 4-, and 5-year-old middle-class children living in Tokyo were observed over a period of 1 year in different home contexts, such as during role-play; object-play; and when interacting with parents, peers, and familiar and unfamiliar adults. These young children used a variety of polite expressions, which varied by social context. When the children addressed unfamiliar adults and during role-play when they pretended to be a person of high status (e.g., a doctor), they used more formal, polite expressions. However, when they made requests of their mothers, they used direct, informal expressions.

Other research has found that parents interpret children's requests for information differently depending on the content of the question. After observing the conversations of Mexican American parents and their young school-aged children, Delgado-Gaitan (1994) found that the parents welcomed and supported children's questions when they pertained to school matters. However, when the children asked about other topics, such as family routines, parents felt that the questions were defiant and challenging to parental authority.

Research indicates that the manner in which children make requests differs across ethnic communities even when parents and children are in the same social class group. In a classic study, Heath (1983) observed the early communicative behaviors, including requests, among children from two ethnic groups—African American and European American—both living in working-class communities in the southeastern United States. The African American children tended to ask brief, clarifying questions during a discussion about events, objects, and people in the immediate setting (e.g., "What is that?" or "What is she doing?"). In contrast, the European American children tended to ask their parents questions during conversations that involved mutual questions and answers. As we discussed in Chapter 3, these types of differences in pragmatic style can have significance beyond the home context. In this case, the conversations of the European American parents and children resemble, and possibly function as training for, the types of exchanges children will experience later in school. This situation can put African American children at a disadvantage when they begin school, not because they lack language or conversational skills, but because their prior experience includes cultural practices that are inconsistent with school practices. Stated more generally, caregiver–child conversational interactions may have consequences beyond the immediate situation in preparing children for other societal institutions and, furthermore, the practices of these institutions may favor certain cultural backgrounds more than others.

Children learn about the social aspects of language explicitly and through implicit means. In some cultures, there is direct instruction about proper language use from parents, teachers, and sometimes peers. Among a child's first lessons in communication is learning how to use polite words and phrases, such as "hello," "goodbye," "please," and "thank you" (Greif & Gleason, 1980). These simple social routines are common to all cultures (Ochs & Schieffelin, 2016). Japanese preschoolers have been observed practicing politeness routines with peers, and in some cases, children encourage each other to do so (Burdelski, 2010). However, much of children's learning about the social aspects of language occurs through implicit means, especially by observing people and by listening to and engaging in conversations with others (Akhtar, 2005; Dunn, 1988).

Children also need to learn when, where, and to whom it is appropriate to express their feelings, especially negative feelings and thoughts, such as anger (P. Miller & Sperry, 1987). Cultures differ in the amount of emotion that is ordinarily expressed through language. In some cultures, emotional communication is very important and children learn at a young age how to convey this type of information. Ochs (1986) described how young Samoan children use emotionally laden terms to refer to the self ("poor me") before they use more neutral terms ("I"). At the age of 2, Japanese children refer to their behavior and the behavior of others with words related to shame and embarrassment, while same-age English-speaking children do not use these terms (Clancy, 1999).

When discussing children's prior behaviors that involved a transgression, Mullen and Yi (1995) found that European American mothers made more references to the thoughts and feelings of the children, whereas Korean mothers made more references to social norms. Similarly, examination of stories about past experiences of 2½-year-old children in middle-class Taiwanese and European American families revealed that the Taiwanese stories tended to emphasize moral and social standards, reflecting cultural values regarding proper conduct, respect for others, and self-control (P. J. Miller et al., 1997). In contrast, the European American stories mostly focused on entertainment and affirmation of the child as an individual, and when the child's past transgressions were discussed, the child's misdeeds were understated and recast to emphasize the child's strengths. These patterns are consistent with socialization goals and values in these communities and suggest that during mother–child conversations about the past, children learn what aspects of the past are important to talk about and how to talk about them.

In social conversation, children need to be able to listen to and respond to another's speech. To do this effectively, children need to recognize when they lack understanding of something and how to request additional information in culturally appropriate ways. What skills must a child develop in order to become an effective speaker? First, the child must engage the attention of her listeners. By age 2, children are already adept at engaging the attention of a listener and responding to listener feedback (Wellman & Lempers, 1977). Children also need to adjust their speech according to characteristics of the listener—such as age and social background—and to the situation. Children as young as 2 to 3 years of age adjust their speech when talking with children of different ages; for example, they use more repetitions and more attention-eliciting words ("hey," "hello," "look") when talking to their younger brothers and sisters than to their mothers (Dunn, 1988; Dunn & Kendrick, 1982). Across cultural settings, when children play outdoors, they adjust their vocalizations to ecological and other factors (e.g., natural sounds, greater distances from others; see Göncü et al., 2007).

Children also need to learn how to be good listeners, which includes evaluating their own messages and messages received from others for clarity and usefulness. Expectations vary across cultures about who is responsible for clarifying a statement. Whereas it is common in American middle-class homes for caregivers to ask children, following an unclear utterance, to explain more about what they mean, such exchanges are rare in other communities. For instance, among the Inuit people of North American, Kaluli people of Papua New Guinea, and Samoan people in the South Pacific, it is inappropriate to question an unclear statement by asking the speaker what he or she is thinking (Ochs, 1990). Such inquiries are especially unlikely when they involve speakers of different social ranks. For example, a higher-ranked individual (e.g., an adult) would not ask for clarification from someone of lower rank (e.g., a child). The lower-ranked individual is expected to clarify the statement out of respect for the higher-ranked partner. These cultural differences are not merely communicative practices. Rather, they reflect deep cultural beliefs about knowledge and whether the knowledge in a person's mind is a legitimate object of discussion (Sterponi, 2010). Thus, when children learn ways of clarifying spoken information, they are also learning about social norms, social identity, and how people think and talk about knowledge in their culture.

Despite the presence of these various skills at early ages, other aspects of children's communicative competence still need to develop. Preschoolers are quite effective in one-to-one conversation, but they do not do as well when they must compete for their turn to speak (Ervin-Tripp, 1979). Young children are also more competent when speaking about familiar objects that are present in their immediate environment than they are when speaking about objects that are not present (absent in time or space) or their own feelings, thoughts, or relationships (Dunn, 1988; Shatz, 1983, 1994).

Pragmatic skills reflect cultural expectations regarding appropriate social behavior and, as a result, are a major component of children's socialization into culture. Research on the development of these skills indicates that preschoolers are remarkably sophisticated speakers, but because they have difficulty tracking multiple speakers and judging when it is their turn to speak, they are more effective in a one-on-one scenario than in a group. Children's pragmatic skills improve substantially from early to middle childhood through direct instruction, by observing and listening to others speak, and, most importantly, by engaging in conversation themselves.

BILINGUALISM

In many parts of the world, a majority of children are *bilingual*, that is, they have learned to speak two languages. When children learn more than two languages, they are *multilingual*. Some bilingual children learned the two languages simultaneously, which often occurs when one parent speaks one language and the other parent speaks a second language to the child. For other children, the two languages are learned sequentially, for instance when one language is spoken at home when the child is young, and the child learns a second language at school.

Although some experts have expressed concern that learning two languages interferes with children's language-learning ability more generally, research indicates that learning two languages simultaneously in childhood does not place children at a disadvantage in terms of language proficiency (Holowka et al., 2002). In fact, learning two languages may have some benefits, such as more flexibility of thought and more cognitive control (Bialystok & Craik, 2010). Bilingual children also show greater acceptance of peers from other cultural backgrounds. W. E. Lambert (1987) studied English-speaking children who participated in a French language immersion program in Quebec, Canada. Compared with pupils who were not in this program, the "immersion" students had less stereotyped attitudes toward their French Canadian peers.

One important determinant of how well children master two languages is how often they are exposed to each. Very few children, for example, who are learning Spanish and English at the same time are exposed to equal inputs of Spanish and English. In Miami, a city that is home to a large Cuban population, children who received less than 25% of their language input in Spanish were unlikely to become competent Spanish speakers (Pearson et al., 1997). As in the case of many other kinds of lessons, exposure is an important determinant of how well children will learn.

Although learning two languages may not be as problematic as originally thought, evidence of the benefits of bilingualism must be interpreted with caution. Children who are successful at multiple languages may be a select group (Diaz, 1983). We do not know how many children try to learn several languages and fall short of becoming bilingual.

CONCLUSION

Language development is a critical component of children's socialization to culture. Learning language does not solely involve vocabulary and grammar

(Fitneva & Matsui, 2015). It also involves learning how to communicate with others in the community, a practice that helps to establish and maintain a young person's community membership. Learning language also provides access to the ideas and thinking of other community members and the culture at large. Thus, learning language is inherently a social and cultural process.

Both human biology and sociocultural experience contribute to the development of language. Several facts—including that children are more effective at learning language when they are young, and that different languages have similar grammatical structures—support the idea that there are innate aspects to language development. Yet, most contemporary views of language development are interactivist, arguing that biological capabilities merge with experience to produce human language. This process is most evident in pragmatic development. In becoming competent language-users, children learn from others how to use language in ways that are appropriate in the cultural setting in which they live.

Close attention to language-specific patterns of development in various sociocultural contexts has revealed significant differences in the communicative practices of parents and other adults who talk with young children. Given that in all cultures, children develop communicative competence, these variations demonstrate the range of viable experiential support for language development. Probably the most salient result of these studies, considered together, is the discovery of immense cultural variety in rates of language development, including variation in children's agency in language learning, the degree to which more mature individuals "teach" language to young children, and the use (or nonuse) of child-directed speech. Because languages vary substantially in many of the attributes that are used to study language development, contemporary language researchers agree about the importance of studying children as they learn different languages in different social and cultural contexts.

For additional resources, see the Appendix.

DISCUSSION QUESTIONS

1. What role does language development play in children's socialization to culture?

2. How does culture contribute to an interactionist view of language development?

3. What are pragmatic skills and how might they contribute to a young person's integration into his or her culture from childhood through adolescence?

4. How do word-learning constraints aid language development and do you think these constraints are modified by culture in any way?

5. In what ways might bilingualism contribute to a child's socioemotional development?

5

Culture and Emotional Development

Children learn what emotions are appropriate to display and how to regulate their emotions in different cultural contexts.

Emotions—such as joy, fear, and anger—are subjective reactions to the environment. Emotions are usually experienced cognitively as either pleasant or unpleasant and accompanied by some form of physiological arousal. Emotions are very important to human functioning, and they are universal—experienced by all human beings. Children's emotional competence, which includes emotional expression, regulation, and understanding, undergoes enormous change from infancy through adolescence (Lewis, 2015). Children learn much about emotions through interactions with others, especially caregivers (Denham et al., 2015). During socialization, children's emotional experience and expression are increasingly aligned with the cultural context of development (P. M. Cole & Tan, 2015).

https://doi.org/10.1037/0000228-005
Child and Adolescent Development in Cultural Context, by J. E. Lansford, D. C. French, and M. Gauvain
Copyright © 2021 by the American Psychological Association. All rights reserved.

Emotions serve a number of functions in children's lives (Saarni et al., 2006). Even before babies can talk, they use nonverbal expressions like smiling and frowning to communicate pleasure or concern to their caregivers. Thus, from the beginning of life, effective emotional communication is critical to human experience. As children get older, their understanding and expression of emotions can affect their social success and mental and physical health. For example, children who are very sad and have difficulty finding relief may develop other problems such as poor concentration, limited social interactions, and low sense of self-worth. Physical health may also suffer, as evident in children reared in environments in which they are emotionally and socially deprived. These children often have difficulty regulating their reactions to stress, which may lead to problems of physical health (Gunnar, 2000). In adolescence, the ability to perceive and express emotions in ways that are socially appropriate and support personal growth is beneficial (Mayer et al., 2008). This ability is called emotional intelligence, and it is associated with fewer behavior problems, better social skills, and higher academic achievement (Rivers et al., 2012).

There are commonalities in human emotions across cultures. Around the world, people use similar facial expressions of emotion, which has led researchers including psychologist Paul Ekman (1994), a pioneer in this area of study, to suggest that producing these expressions is, in part, biologically determined. But despite some commonalities, emotional experiences differ substantially across cultural settings because culture affects how we appraise situations, experience emotions, and label and control our emotional reactions. Culture also determines how people communicate or display emotions to one another, which is important to everyday functioning. The way in which we understand and convey our emotions needs to be meaningful to and consistent with those around us.

In this chapter, we describe the development of emotions along with cultural contributions to this process. We begin by describing the main theoretical perspectives and lay out key issues for investigating emotional development in relation to culture. Next, we describe the development of emotional expression and regulation, both of which follow a course closely tied to culture. We conclude by describing how children understand emotions and learn to connect this understanding with other elements of their culture.

PERSPECTIVES ON EMOTIONAL DEVELOPMENT

There are several theoretical perspectives about how emotions develop with different theories emphasizing the biological aspects of emotions, the learning of emotions in sociocultural context, and the function of emotions in human life. This range of views reflects the complex nature of emotions and their development (Friedlmeier et al., 2015).

Biological Views

Researchers who emphasize biological contributions of emotion are interested in both universal aspects of emotional experience and individual differences in emotions that reflect inherited, maturational, or temperamental characteristics.

Universality of Emotional Expression

Research on universal aspects of emotions is inspired by ethological theory, which contends that there are species-specific emotions and related behaviors that play an important role in ensuring survival (LaFreniere, 2000). In influential early studies on the topic, researchers discovered that facial emotional expressions are similar across cultures (e.g., Ekman et al., 1987). In this research, people living in various cultures, such as the United States, Brazil, Chile, Japan, and Argentina, were shown photographs of people displaying one of six emotions—happiness, sadness, anger, fear, surprise, or disgust—and participants in all the cultures correctly identified the emotional expressions.

These findings support the claim of universality in the expression and recognition of facial emotions (Darwin, 1872; Ekman, 1994). These behaviors aid survival because they enable people to quickly and accurately communicate emotional states. They are especially important early in life because they give caregivers clues about infants' feelings—information that can be used to meet the infant's needs (Thompson, 2015). Although basic emotional expressions seem to be the same across all cultures, there are still cultural differences. The same facial expression may elicit different responses, such as culturally specific ways of soothing a crying baby. That is, even though the behaviors may have a common biological base, they are adapted to the culture.

Genetic-Maturational Factors

In other research on biological contributions, researchers investigate whether certain emotional characteristics are inherited and, also, whether genetic inheritance interacts with maturation. Research with twins, a common method for assessing inherited traits, has revealed biological underpinnings of the development of some aspects of emotions. Identical twins show greater similarity than fraternal twins in the timing of their first smiles and in their overall amount of smiling (Plomin et al., 2016). Also, identical twins are more similar than fraternal twins in their fear reactions to strangers and in their general degree of inhibition (Brooker et al., 2013).

Smiling in premature infants illustrates the role of maturational factors in emotional expression (Gatta et al., 2017). The normal conceptual age (age since conception) of a newborn is 40 weeks. Most full-term babies begin to smile at about 6 weeks after birth (46 weeks after conception). In an early study, researchers found that premature infants who are born at 34 weeks often do not smile until 12 weeks after birth, or 46 weeks since conception (Dittrichova, 1969). It seems that a certain amount of physical maturation, presumably accompanied by social stimulation, must occur before a baby begins to smile.

Temperament

Some research on the biological basis of emotions focuses on temperament, an individual's typical mode of responding to the environment (Rothbart & Bates, 2006). Temperament includes such things as one's activity level, adaptability to new situations, intensity of emotional reaction, and calming ability—behaviors that contribute to children's emotional development. Although scientists assume that temperament is, in part, genetically determined, research indicates that temperament is susceptible to environmental influences, particularly interactions among family members (Rutter, 2006).

Researchers studying temperament investigate how an infant's behavioral style interacts with the caregiving environment. In a ground-breaking study on this topic, Stella Chess and Alexander Thomas (1986) proposed a typology of temperament that classifies infants as *difficult, easy,* or *slow-to-warm-up,* and each type has a distinctive pattern of behavioral responses. Difficult infants (about 10% of all babies) sleep and eat irregularly, become easily upset by new situations, and experience extremes of fussiness and crying. Easy babies (about 40%) are friendly, happy, and adaptable. The slow-to-warm-up child falls somewhere between difficult and easy. These children have low activity levels and respond negatively to new stimuli at first, but then gradually show interest in the new experience.

According to Chess and Thomas (1986), development is affected by the compatibility of the child's temperament and the caregiving environment, which they called "goodness of fit." In this view, development progresses more smoothly when parents adjust their caregiving approach to suit the child's unique temperament. For example, fearful children develop greater self-control when their parents use gentle discipline (S. Kim & Kochanska, 2012).

Research by developmental psychologist Mary Rothbart and colleagues (Putnam et al., 2002; Rothbart & Bates, 2006) built on these three global temperament types to create six discrete categories: (a) positive affect, (b) irritable distress, (c) fearful distress, (d) activity level, (e) attention span/persistence, and (f) rhythmicity. Each of these aspects is assessed by certain infant behaviors, many of which are emotional in nature. For example, positive affect is measured by the display of positive emotional expressions, such as smiling and laughter.

There is evidence of cultural differences in newborn temperament. Chinese American babies, in contrast to European American and Irish infants, have been described as calmer, easier to console, more able to quiet themselves after crying, and faster to adapt to external stimulation or changes (Freedman, 1974; Gartstein et al., 2006; J. Kagan, 2010). Also, Chinese American infants have been observed to be less reactive and less likely to display vigorous motor activity than European American infants (J. Kagan & Snidman, 2004). There is no known explanation for these differences. Variation in temperament across cultural groups may reflect biological or genetic tendencies at the population level. Or it could reflect cultural patterns of nurturance and support regarding the expression of temperament. Or it may be some combination of both of these factors.

There are cultural differences in parents' perceptions of infant temperament, which have consequences for infants' experiences. Across East African societies, parents provide different learning opportunities for their children depending on their beliefs about their infant's temperament. In a classic study, deVries and Sameroff (1984) studied infants in three societies in this region and found that in the Digo group, parents view infants as active and able to learn within a few months after birth, and their caregiving behaviors reflect this view. In contrast, the Kikuyu group, who view their infants as passive, keep them swaddled for the first year and believe that real learning is not possible until the second year. This research suggests that a culture's view about child temperament affects children's social and learning experiences in early life.

Cultural variation also exists in how child temperament affects other aspects of parent–child interaction. Developmental psychologist Charles Super and anthropologist Sara Harkness (1994) conducted research on this topic in suburban Boston and among the Kipsigi people, a small farming community in Kenya. They found that an infant's temperament affected the caregiver–child experience differently in the two cultures. Whereas Boston infants who were low on the temperamental characteristic of rhythmicity (i.e., regularity of behavior) interacted more with their mothers than infants who were high in this characteristic, the opposite pattern emerged in Kipsigi households in which infants who were high in rhythmicity interacted more with their mothers than infants who were low in that area. To interpret these patterns, Super and Harkness looked to the ecological context. Kipsigi mothers worked many hours in the fields while another person, often an older sister, took care of the baby. Mothers returned home during daytime hours to visit with or feed the baby, which is easier to coordinate with infants who are more predictable. For Boston mothers, who were typically the sole caregiver, their responsiveness to infant behavior reflects the baby's expression of need. Super and Harkness emphasized that these maternal behaviors are not unique personal reactions to the infants' behaviors. Rather, they reflect different cultural beliefs about the importance of responsive maternal care for infant development as well as the experiences and activities of mothers and children in the two cultures.

Finally, even within cultures, temperamental differences may contribute to the type of caregiving that infants receive under certain ecological conditions, sometimes with serious consequences. Years ago, deVries (1984) found such a connection in her research among the Masai people of Kenya. She observed that during a famine, fussy, irritable infants were more likely to get a greater share of available food than calm, placid infants.

Social Learning Views

Research on learning emotions looks at the role of experience, with much of this work focused on the development of emotional control or regulation. Because young children have limited abilities to control their emotions, they receive help from others. To request help, infants signal their needs to their caregivers, who then interpret and respond with behaviors that are rooted in cultural beliefs, values, and practices. This type of exchange helps to initiate emotion socialization, the process by which children learn about emotions and how to express them in ways that are practiced in their culture (Denham et al., 2015).

Emotional socialization is an important aspect of development in culture. A primary goal of all cultures is to foster the development of competent human beings and community members (Keller, 2002). To reach this goal, children need to have an emotional sense of self as well as emotional connection to the community. In this regard, the development of emotional competence is a cultural process, one that reflects the values, norms, beliefs, and expectations of the community (P. M. Cole & Tan, 2015). Cultural value systems include ideas about the extent and type of emotional expressions that are appropriate, even from very young children. See Research Highlight 5.1 about early emotional development in the Marquesas Islands, which challenges the idea that cultures emphasize either independence or interdependence.

Socialization practices in the family, in particular, can lead to changes in children's understanding and expression of emotions, and these practices occur in various ways. Family members may serve as role models because their patterns of emotional expressiveness influence the child's emotional expressiveness. For example, a child who sees her mother react fearfully to a dog, may later imitate her and show fear toward a dog. Many studies, including research conducted in China, have found similarities between parents and their children in emotional expressiveness and emotion-related behaviors (Chen et al., 2011; Halberstadt et al., 2001).

Reactions of family members to children's emotions may encourage or discourage certain patterns of emotional expressiveness. When parents respond with enthusiasm to their smiling infant, the child's rate of smiling increases (Denham et al., 2015). Across cultures, caregivers differ in how much emotion and the types of emotions they encourage in their children (P. M. Cole & Tan, 2015).

Caregivers also socialize children's emotions by talking about emotions with their children and helping them explore their understanding of their own and other people's emotional responses. This behavior is referred to as *emotional coaching*. In one study, children in families that often discussed their feelings were better able to recognize others' emotions than children in families that discussed their feelings less often (Dunn, 2004). Cultural variation in parent–child conversation about emotions has been reported. For example, Chinese parents talk less about their own children's emotions than they do about other people's emotions (Q. Wang, 2001).

Siblings and peers also function as socializers of emotion (Chen et al., 2006). Siblings can shape each other's emotional reactions by their positive or negative responses or by alerting parents to their siblings' emotions (Dunn, 2004). Peers are also important agents of emotional socialization. When children display anger, their peers often respond with anger or rejection (Denham et al., 2015). Cross-cultural research suggests that peers may play especially significant roles in emotion socialization in some cultures. Early observations of Efe (foraging community in central Africa) infants and toddlers

RESEARCH HIGHLIGHT 5.1

Infant Learning About Emotional Expressiveness on the Marquesas Islands

Children begin to learn very early in life how emotions are expressed in their culture, and this process of emotion socialization provides insight into cultural values. In fact, some research on this topic challenges the view that Western cultures exclusively emphasize independence and non-Western cultures exclusively emphasize interdependence.

A developmental goal in all cultures is for children to grow up to become competent human beings and responsible community members. To meet this goal, children need to have an emotional sense of self and an emotional connection to the community. This merging of independence and interdependence in child socialization is evident in traditional Polynesian cultures, such as the Marquesas Islands, where children are raised to be both sensitive and responsive to the needs of others, and also self-reliant (Martini & Kirkpatrick, 1992). In toddlerhood, children are encouraged to join the sibling group and be cooperative and nondemanding. The reason is found in cultural patterns of family development. By the time children are 18–24 months of age, mothers are often pregnant with another child, and toddlers must learn that they cannot be as reliant on their mother as they had been previously.

Self-reliance at this young age is encouraged in various ways. Toddlers learn that expressions of anger, frustration, and sadness are not tolerated and that they are expected to comfort themselves. Martini and Kirkpatrick observed that toddlers learn to read contextual cues to determine when they need to be obedient and when they can express their own will, such as standing up to adult authority. In such instances, if a child assesses a situation correctly, the parent may be proud of the child who is expressing personal autonomy and beginning to understand that "willfulness has its place" (Martini & Kirkpatrick, 1992, p. 211). Through these socialization efforts, Marquesan toddlers learn to be emotionally competent individuals as well as emotionally connected members of the group.

This research provides insight into how childrearing and emotional development are deeply connected with culture and its values. But there is a postscript. The study was conducted decades ago and the childrearing practices described are changing as the society becomes increasingly Westernized, the village way of life is replaced by more urban lifestyles, and there is a shift from teaching children the traditional language to teaching them French, the language of the colonists (Tetahiotupa, 2000). These changes are buttressed by economic realities that have resulted from tourism, which has overtaken the islands and accounts for close to 80% of the economy. There have been some efforts to revitalize and maintain traditional practices, including language (Galla, 2016), especially in isolated and remote areas. But despite these efforts, it is difficult for the community to maintain traditional cultural practices and the language in the face of the pressures of globalization.

by developmental and clinical psychologist Ed Tronick and his colleagues (1992) revealed that children ages 1 to 3 spend less time with their mothers and more time with peers. By age 3, 70% of Efe children's social contact is with peers. Other research indicates that older children evaluate their peers according to the norms of the culture. In Canada, for example, children who are shy or emotionally reticent are viewed as socially incompetent by their peers and are often rejected (Chen, 2012). In contrast, Chinese children consider shyness as a sign of maturity, and shyness is associated with peer acceptance (see Chapter 12 for further discussion).

Cultures differ according to how much emotion children are expected to show and when and how they should control their emotions. Research suggests that culture may affect the socialization of emotion through parental, and even teachers' beliefs about emotion and its expression (Dunsmore et al., 2009; Parker et al., 2012). Beliefs about whether emotions are valuable, dangerous, or controllable, and also whether parents need to guide children's emotions, are related to caregivers' emotional expressiveness, reactions to children's emotional displays, and parent–child communication about emotion. Parental beliefs about emotions and parents' emotional expressiveness are, in turn, related to children's outcomes, including their ability to regulate emotions.

Emotion socialization is an active, not a passive process. Although caregivers encourage children to adopt culturally appropriate understanding and expression of emotion, children are also active agents in this process. By paying attention to emotional cues, children learn which behaviors trigger favorable or unfavorable reactions from others—information useful for their own future behaviors. Children's active role is also evident when we consider individual differences, such as infant temperament. Infants who are fussy or have irritable temperaments may be less responsive to emotion socialization efforts by caregivers, and these behaviors may be handled differently across cultural settings (J. Kagan, 2010; E. Tronick, 2007). For instance, in a sample that included parents from seven Western cultures, Super and colleagues (2008) found culture-specific patterns in parents' perceptions about what behaviors lead to a child being labeled "difficult."

Functional Views

The functional approach focuses on how emotions help people adapt to the environment and motivate behaviors that help them achieve their goals (Saarni et al., 2006). For example, when a child is trying to achieve a goal, such as staying out of danger, emotions are aroused that help the child reach the goal (e.g., fear leads the child to flee a dangerous situation). This perspective, which incorporates many features of the social learning view discussed previously, also emphasizes the role of emotions in establishing and maintaining social relationships.

According to the functional approach, people use information from others' emotional signals to guide one's own behavior (e.g., the way a potential friend reacts to a person emotionally will affect how the person feels about the friend). This perspective also focuses on how memories of past emotional experiences guide our reactions to current situations. For example, children who have been socially successful will be more hopeful and confident when trying to make new friends, whereas children who have routinely been rebuffed by potential friends will become wary and anxious. In this way, children use their memories of the emotional past to guide their adaptation in the present.

Reflecting on the Three Perspectives

The biological, social learning, and functional perspectives complement one another, and together, provide useful ideas for understanding and studying the complex process of emotional development. The function of emotions is often immediate, motivating people to understand their own and other people's feelings and carry out activities important to everyday life. Emotions also have a long-range purpose—they help to ensure individual and group survival. Emotional experiences and behavioral responses are shaped by the interplay of biological factors, social learning, and numerous forces in the environment, including culture. This process unfolds over the course of development, and children are attentive and responsive to their own emotional experiences and the experiences of those around them. As a result, children's emotional life becomes increasingly aligned with the emotional understanding and behaviors of their culture.

DEVELOPMENT OF EMOTIONAL EXPRESSION

Children express a wide range of emotions from a very early age. By expressing emotion, children communicate their feelings, needs, and desires, and they influence the behavior of other people. During development, children learn to recognize and interpret the emotional signs that other people display and how to use this information to create meaningful and effective social interactions. Emotional expressiveness has implications for social development. The extent to which a child is viewed as emotionally expressive and responsive is associated with perceptions of the child as a good and desired social partner (Denham et al., 2015). These perceptions vary across cultures and have implications for development, for example, as we noted earlier in research on cultural differences in the interpretation of shyness in children.

Researchers distinguish what are called *primary* and *secondary emotions*. Primary emotions, such as fear, joy, disgust, surprise, sadness, and interest, emerge early in life, have a large biological component, and do not require introspection or self-reflection. Secondary or self-conscious emotions, such as pride, shame, guilt, jealousy, and embarrassment, emerge later. These emotions depend on a sense of self and awareness of how other people react to our actions, both of which are related to social standards or cultural norms (Lewis, 2015).

Most parents pay a great deal of attention to their newborn's behaviors and identify the infant's emotional expressions very early. In one study, 99% of mothers said their 1-month-olds displayed interest; 95% observed joy; 85%, anger; 74%, surprise; 58%, fear; and 34%, sadness (W. F. Johnson et al., 1982). It is tempting to conclude that parents are able to read their infant's emotions, but we cannot be certain that infants are expressing the same feelings as adults when they show similar expressions. What appears to be anger in a baby may actually reflect feelings of distress or discomfort.

It is not until babies are about 2½ or 3 months old that they begin to display facial expressions of anger, interest, surprise, and sadness (Denham et al., 2015). These kinds of early emotions are probably influenced by biological factors, but over time other factors come into play, including cultural experience. Infants begin to display other emotional expressions, such as fear, around 7 months of age. It is not until age 2 or 3 that more complex emotions—such as pride and shame—emerge.

In addition to expressing emotion, it is important for developing children to learn how to recognize the emotions that other people express. Both the quality and quantity of caregiver–infant interactions make a difference in children's ability to recognize emotions. When mothers spend more time interacting directly with their babies, they are more successful at recognizing their mothers' emotional expressions (Montague & Walker-Andrews, 2002). There appears to be an emotional bias in these infant behaviors. In one early study, infants between the ages of 4 and 6 months looked at a face showing an expression of joy longer than at a face showing anger (LaBarbera et al., 1976). The researchers interpret this pattern as functional, suggesting that recognizing joy provides the infant with rewarding experiences and can help to strengthen the emotional bond between infants and caregivers.

Next, we describe some specific examples of the development of emotional expression. We begin with primary emotions and then turn to secondary emotions, all of which illustrate the functional significance of emotions for organizing how children interact with and learn from the social and cultural world around them.

Development of Some Primary Emotions: Smiling, Fear, Anger, and Sadness
Smiling
When newborn infants smile, these commonly called "reflex smiles" (P. H. Wolff, 1987) are usually spontaneous and likely depend on the infant's internal state. Most caregivers interpret these as signs of happiness, which encourages them to interact positively with the baby. In this sense, these smiles have adaptive value for the baby, ensuring critical caregiver attention and stimulation (Saarni et al., 2006).

Developmental psychologist Alan Sroufe (1996) conducted some of the early research on infant smiling and found that infants between 3 and 8 weeks of age begin to smile in response to not only internal events but to a wide range of external elicitors, including social stimuli such as faces, voices, and light touches. This "social smile," as it is called, is especially likely to occur in response to human faces and the human voice, in particular the higher-pitch sound typically produced by human females. When 3-month-old infants were shown a human face and puppets whose faces varied in their resemblance to a human face, the infants smiled almost exclusively at the human face (Ellsworth et al., 1993). This social smile is common in 3- to 4-month-old infants in a wide range of cultures, including the United States, Japan, Uganda, and Israel, suggesting that it is universal (Super & Harkness, 2009). However, the rate at which infants display this smile varies across cultures. For instance, 12-week-old German infants smile more at their mothers than same-age Nso infants in Cameroon (Wörmann et al., 2012). Researchers explain this difference by referring to child-care customs, such as in the Nso community in which emphasis is on body contact and stimulation, whereas in the German community there is more emphasis on mother–infant communication and smiling.

At 3 months of age, infants discriminately smile. They smile more at familiar faces, especially when accompanied by vocalizations (Camras et al., 1991). For example, a classic study found that 3-month-olds smile more when they receive smiles and vocalizations from their mothers than from women they don't know (Wahler, 1967). Positive emotional expressions are an important step in social communication and engagement. At 4 months of age, infants time their smiles to make their mothers smile (Ruvolo et al., 2015). By 10 months of age, babies generally reserve a special kind of smile, called a "Duchenne smile," for their primary caregiver (Messinger et al., 2001). In addition to an upturned mouth, this smile includes raised cheeks and wrinkles around the eyes, an expression that makes the smile seem heartfelt and sincere.

Cross-cultural differences in the frequency of babies' smiles are related to the social responsiveness of the baby's environment. For example, Israeli infants reared in a family environment smiled more often by the second half year than infants raised in either a kibbutz (a communal living arrangement) or an institution, where the level of social stimulation is lower (Gewirtz, 1967). Gender also seems to affect babies' smiling. In the newborn stage and later in childhood, girls generally show more spontaneous smiles than boys (LaFrance et al., 2003). Because smiling encourages social interaction, this pattern has led some researchers to suggest that girls may be biologically better prepared for social interaction than boys (Saarni et al., 2006). On the other hand, parents generally elicit and expect more emotions from girls than boys, which suggests that both biological and environmental factors need to be considered. There are also national gender differences in smiling (LaFrance et al., 2003). Compared with their peers in Great Britain, children and adults in the United States and Canada show larger sex differences in smiling. Perhaps Europeans have less stereotyped views of gender differences and treat boys and girls more similarly than do North Americans.

Fear

At the same time that babies are beginning to display signs of positive emotion, they are also learning to be fearful of some events and people, especially unfamiliar ones (Saarni et al., 2006). The negative emotional response to unfamiliar adults, called fear of strangers, emerges slowly over the first year of life (Thompson, 2015). At 4 months of age, babies smile less at unfamiliar adults than at their mothers, indicating that they recognize familiar people. The babies are not distressed, however, by the presence of strangers. Rather, they show interest in them. But, around 5 months of age, babies' interest is replaced, typically by staring at the stranger in a solemn manner. At 6 months, although babies are still most likely to react to strangers with a sober expression, they may also display distress. This distress reaction gradually increases in frequency over the next half year, and by 9 months, babies clearly express fear (LaFreniere, 2000).

Research conducted decades ago observed the emergence of stranger distress at about 8 months of age in several cultures, including the Hopi tribe, a Native American community (Dennis, 1940), and in six traditional villages around the capital city of Kampala in Uganda (Ainsworth, 1963). In some cultures, such as the Efe people in central Africa, that emphasize shared caregiving among relatives, and the Marquesas Islands, where babies are carried facing outward and spend lots of time outdoors in the company of many adults, babies show little fear of strangers (Martini & Kirkpatrick, 1992; E. Z. Tronick et al., 1992). Recent research involving Bedouin mothers and their 1-year-olds found that the babies exhibited high levels of stranger anxiety, which was unexpected because there are multiple childcare arrangements in this culture (Marey-Sarwan et al., 2016). Researchers believe that these patterns may be a result of the adverse sociopolitical climate in the North African region where Bedouins live and also because of the drastically changing lifestyle of this traditionally nomadic group. Thus, whether a baby is fearful of strangers depends on childrearing practices and other ecological conditions in the cultural setting.

Still, some kinds of fear appear to be present among children in all cultures. A common fear in childhood is associated with being separated from one's mother or other familiar caregivers. This fear, called "separation protest," emerges around 12 months of age and tends to peak at about 15 months. The timetable for when this reaction occurs is remarkably similar across diverse cultures in Guatemala and the Kalahari Desert region in Botswana (J. J. Kagan et al., 1978; Super & Harkness, 2009). Age-related declines of this distress, however, vary across cultural groups and seem to be related to children's experiences with caregivers outside the immediate family unit.

Anger and Sadness

Babies do not display facial expressions of anger or sadness until they are about 2½ to 3 months of age (Denham et al., 2015). For example, early research found that although few 1-month-olds show anger expressions when their arms are gently restrained, by the time infants are 4 to 7 months old, more than half (56%) show clear expressions of anger when restrained (Stenberg et al., 1983). This reaction is presumed to be universal, although the pattern of development varies across cultures. By 5 months of age, both U.S. and Japanese infants display similar negative reactions to restraint, but U.S. infants respond more quickly (Camras et al., 1992).

Similar to adults, infants display emotions in response to external events. In one study, when researchers offered 7-month-olds a teething biscuit and then withdrew it before it reached the baby's mouth, the babies showed anger (Stenberg et al., 1983). When inoculated by a physician, 2-month-olds respond with distress, a reaction to pain, whereas 6-month-olds respond to the same stimulus with an expression of anger (Izard et al., 1987). It seems that babies respond to emotional provocations in predictable ways at specific ages, and that anger is elicited by frustration and pain.

Sadness is a reaction to pain, hunger, or lack of control, but it occurs less often than anger. Babies become sad when there are breakdowns in parent–infant communication. For example, when a usually responsive caregiver ceases to respond to the baby's social overtures, the baby will exhibit distress and sadness (Barbosa et al., 2018). For older infants, separation from familiar caregivers can lead to sadness.

The sad reaction, along with other emotional reactions, is demonstrated in research with the "still-face" laboratory procedure or paradigm (E. Tronick, 2007). In this research, a mother sits face-to-face across from her baby, and for part of the study, she is asked to show no expression or reaction to the infant's behavior. For example, in an early study using this paradigm, mothers and infants between 3 and 9 months of age interacted normally for 2 minutes, then the mother held a still face for 2 minutes, and then the dyad interacted normally again for 2 minutes (Gianino, 1982, as described in E. Tronick, 2007). The babies were distressed during the still-face period and displayed various coping behaviors that were more complex depending on the baby's age. The infant's coping behaviors included staring fixedly at the mother, decreasing rates of smiling, showing frustration by wiggling or kicking, looking around the room at other objects, self-soothing behaviors (e.g., sucking on a body part or object such as the strap of the chair), rocking from side to side, and arching away from the mother. There are cultural differences in the extent and type of coping behaviors infants use in this situation; for instance Dutch infants display more overt distress than do Chinese infants (W. Li et al., 2019). Nonetheless, in both cultures infants showed a decrease in positive affect when presented with a still-face from their mothers or fathers. One reason for the difference may be that Chinese caregiving has more restrained positive emotions and less face-to-face interaction than has been observed in European and American caregiving situations (C. Y. Huang et al., 2017). But even with this difference, it is clear that infants expect and respond to human interaction and when they are deprived of it, they are distressed emotionally.

Anger and sadness are effective emotional signals for babies to use to elicit care and comfort from adults. In this way, they serve an important evolutionary function that promotes survival of the infant. Still, anger and sadness are distinct emotions and cultures differ in how caregivers respond to these two behaviors. For instance, mothers in cultures that value social-relational competence, such as India (Raval & Martini, 2009), tend to encourage sadness in their children more than they do anger.

Development of Some Secondary Emotions: Pride and Shame

The display of more complex or secondary emotions like pride, guilt, shame, or jealousy relies on the development of self-awareness (Lewis, 2014, 2015). These emotions, which emerge toward the middle of the second year, are called "self-conscious emotions" because children are capable at this point of having thoughts about their emotions and the relation of emotions to a sense of self. The effective use of self-conscious emotions requires the ability to differentiate and integrate multiple factors in a situation, including personal and social responsibility. For example, children may show jealousy by pouting when other children receive more desirable toys (Lewis & Ramsay, 2002). A child who is pleased with his accomplishments will show pride, but when he perceives that someone finds him deficient, he shows shame.

Pride and Shame

To differentiate the emotions of pride or shame, it is helpful to think about the contrast between "easy" and "difficult" and between "success" and "failure" and how experiences in relation to these situations may evoke an emotional response (Lewis, 2000). In one important early study, Lewis, Alessandri, and Sullivan (1992) found that by the time children are 3 years old, they are more likely to express pride if they succeed at difficult tasks than at easy ones. However, they express more shame if they fail an easy task, and they show little shame if they fail a difficult task.

Children's understanding of pride depends on their ability to entertain multiple emotions—such as pleasure at doing a task well and happiness that others appreciate the accomplishment (Lewis, 2000). It also depends on their sense of personal agency or effort. To evaluate this understanding, Thompson (1989) told stories to 7-, 10-, and 18-year-olds about accomplishments individuals achieved either by their own effort or by luck, and then asked them questions about the stories. Seven-year-old U.S. children used the term "proud" for all good outcomes regardless of whether or not the story characters had succeeded through their own efforts. The 10- and 18-year-old participants were more discriminating and realized that "feeling proud" can occur only when good outcomes are the result of a person's own effort, not because of luck or chance.

Cultural differences in children's expression of pride were observed in a comparison of the emotional reactions of Japanese, European American, and African American preschoolers after they successfully completed a task (Lewis et al., 2010). Japanese children expressed less pride than the U.S. children from both ethnic groups. This pattern is consistent with the idea that children living in more collectivist countries develop emotion display rules, such as personal modesty in the face of individual success, that reflect the cultural value of social harmony.

EMOTION REGULATION

All human beings experience distress from pain, fear, or anger, all primary emotions. People manage these experiences by regulating their response; for example, a person in pain might breathe deeply to calm himself down. Regulatory behaviors are essential to survival because a heightened emotional state is physically taxing and can interfere with mental efforts to address the problem at hand. When young infants experience distress, their neurological system is not yet mature enough to regulate the experience effectively (E. Tronick, 2007), so caregivers help infants by responding to their distress with calming or soothing behaviors. As infants mature, emotion regulation shifts from other- to self-regulation. Caregiver responsiveness differs across cultures, as illustrated in Research Highlight 5.2.

RESEARCH HIGHLIGHT 5.2

Caregiver Responsiveness Across Cultures

To study the relation between culture and caregivers' responsiveness to infants, anthropologist Barry Hewlett, and developmental psychologist Michael Lamb and colleagues studied the social organization of Aka, Ngandu, and urban European American infant experiences (Hewlett et al., 1998, 2000). The Aka hunter–gatherer or forager group, and the Ngandu people, a sedentary farming group, are neighboring cultural settings in central Africa. Both are small in scale, have little experience with consumerism, and are socioeconomically similar. Yet their subsistence practices—how they obtain the necessities of life—differ greatly.

Researchers observed caregiver proximity and responsiveness to infant distress. Caregivers and their 3- to 4-month-old infants were observed for 12 hours of their daily lives. Caregivers can respond by increasing contact, such as touching, holding, soothing, or stimulating the infant (e.g., rocking), and in more distal ways, such as vocalizations (e.g., soft shushing or singing). As to frequency, caregivers can respond every time the infant shows distress, or less often. The researchers used the time-sampling method (described in Chapter 2), and recorded caregiver behaviors (e.g., soothing, vocalizing) and infant behaviors (e.g., fussing, crying).

Aka infants showed the least amount of crying and fussing, Ngandu infants showed the most, and European American infants were in between. In all cultures, most of the time (50%–60%) when infants showed distress, caregivers responded with soothing. Aka infants were more likely to be close in proximity to their caregivers, and Ngandu infants were closer to caregivers than were European American infants. European American infants were held less often and left alone more than the other infants. Despite being physically closer to their infants, Ngandu caregivers were less likely to respond to infant distress than were European American caregivers. From these observations, Hewlett and Lamb (2002) concluded that sensitive caregiving in foraging cultures is adaptive because of the need to raise individuals who are trustworthy, autonomous, and willing to cooperate with others—all important to this lifestyle. In contrast, caregivers in agrarian and urban industrial cultures are not as responsive because the need for interpersonal trust and cooperation are not as high.

But why did the Ngandu and European American caregivers differ in responsiveness? Hewlett and Lamb (2002) suggested that cultural history and ecological affordances (e.g., objects, environmental features) promoted different patterns. Small-scale agrarian societies have closer proximity, which allows for regular visual checking of infant needs and safety. In contrast, urban European American caregivers have many objects (e.g., cribs, car seats) to help care for infants and these items have safety features that enable infants to be out of the caregiver's sight for short periods of time. Infant distress informs the caregiver to come near. This research shows how early emotional development reflects the integration of culture, social experience, and individual child behavior.

Learning to control or regulate emotional expression is challenging for infants and children (Thompson, 2015). Although young infants largely depend on caregivers to soothe them when they experience negative emotions, infants will sometimes soothe themselves (e.g., by sucking their thumb). In the first year of life, infants begin to use deliberate efforts to regulate their emotions, such as putting their hands over their face during a frightening event (Bridges & Grolnick, 1995). These methods change as children grow. In one study, 6-month-olds who encountered a stranger typically looked away or became fussy, whereas 18-month-olds were more likely to use self-soothing and self-distraction (Mangelsdorf et al., 1995).

As children get older, parents and others expect them to have more control over their emotional expression. Several behaviors accompany this greater self-control, in particular, emotional expressions become less frequent, less distinct, less intense and exaggerated, less variable, and more conventionalized to cultural norms (LaFreniere, 2000). For example, if mealtime is delayed, a hungry baby may cry in frustration, whereas an older child may instead pout and complain.

The development of emotion regulation is a cultural process. Caregivers seek to socialize these skills in children in ways that accord with the values, norms, and beliefs of their culture. For instance, in industrialized Western nations there is an orientation toward individuality, and socialization goals focus on the development of autonomy and independence (Kagitçibasi, 2005). In contrast, Eastern nations are often oriented toward interdependence, and socialization goals focus on connections with others and social expectations. As a result, children reared within an independent socialization orientation are encouraged to regulate their emotions on their own from an early age and to seek support verbally or through eye contact rather than through physical contact (Keller & Otto, 2009).

Alternative patterns are present in cultures that emphasize social relationships and responsibility. For instance, Otto and Keller (2015) observed how 1-year-old Nso infants reacted to strangers. The Nso people of Cameroon are an agrarian society that values cooperation, solidarity, and social responsibility. Women, even those with young infants, have many daily chores and, therefore, much of childrearing relies on support from extended family. Accordingly, the Nso people emphasize multiple caregivers and friendliness toward strangers. In this study, the majority of infants regulated their emotions when meeting a stranger; they were calm, showed no anxiety, and little emotional expression. However, infants of single mothers, who had less social support and more exclusive relationships with their infants, showed more apprehension toward strangers. These results suggest that infants learn how to regulate their emotions socially and when in potentially stressful situations, such as coming into contact with strangers. Both culture and the mother's own behaviors contribute to this development.

These findings are consistent with cultural differences in how much control children have over their own emotions and the age at which this control is thought to emerge. Nso mothers expect children to exhibit emotional control—such as calmness—by the time they are 3 years of age, which is much earlier than is expected by middle-class mothers in Germany (Keller & Otto, 2009). In another study, Russian and U.S. toddlers exhibited greater emotional control than Japanese toddlers (Slobodskaya et al., 2013). And in some cultures, including Japanese, young children are not expected to be responsible for their own emotional distress. For instance, Japanese mothers help their 2-year-old children manage their distress and do not reprimand them when they are distressed (Friedlmeier & Trommsdorff, 1999).

Emotional Display Rules

Emotional display rules are cultural expectations about the emotions a person should show and the circumstances in which they should appear (Saarni et al., 2006). To learn these rules, children need to be able to separate the visible expression of an emotion from its inner experience and understand that people can act differently from how they feel. For example, a person might mask an emotion (look happy when she is sad), intensify an emotion (laugh harder than he feels), or suppress an emotion (try not to laugh when it might hurt someone's feelings). Children as young as age 2 show an understanding of display rules for certain emotions, although they may base their behaviors on those of other people that are present (Lewis, 2015). Learning to use emotional display rules is especially important in middle childhood when children spend more time outside the home around people they don't know as well, including peers. Displaying emotions appropriately in one's culture is important for functioning successfully in the community. Research has found that being competent at implementing these rules is linked with better peer social relationships (Parke et al., 2006).

So how do cultural customs and values shape the way that children react to emotional events? This connection is illustrated in research on children's emotional behaviors in three cultural groups, Brahman and Tamang societies in rural Nepal and a rural town in the United States (P. M. Cole et al., 2002). The researchers studied the reactions of second, fourth, and fifth graders to emotionally difficult situations such as someone spilling a drink on their homework or falsely accusing them of stealing. Among the Tamang people, a Buddhist group who endorse interpersonal harmony, children were more likely to respond to difficult situations with shame than children in the other two groups. In contrast, children of the Brahman society, who teach self-control in social interactions and careful control of emotions, did not reveal anger or shame in response to the emotionally upsetting actions. The American children were more likely to endorse the display of anger, an emotion consistent with the American value of self-assertion. The American children were also more problem-focused and action-oriented than the children in the two Nepali groups, who were more accepting of difficult situations and less likely to try to alter the situation. All of these patterns were more pronounced among the older children. These patterns show how children begin to master the display rules of their culture.

Across cultures, there are restrictions on the overt display of emotions. Examples of emotional control can be seen in two Indonesian cultures. The Toraja people live in villages in South Sulawesi, Indonesia. Similar to many groups in Indonesia and throughout Asia, the Toraja culture emphasizes social harmony and practices emotional control in an effort to discourage anger and aggression. In early research, anthropologist Douglas Hollan (1988) described the multiple strategies used by people in this group to avoid "getting hot and staying cool," including the belief that the offending party will get what they deserve in the long run, either through intervention of the Gods or spirits. Therefore, controlling oneself either through self-control or the intervention of others is appropriate. Anthropologist Unni Wikan (1989) provided another example of extreme control of emotions in the reaction of a young Balinese woman to the sudden death of her fiancé. Consistent with the display rules of her culture, she did not express sadness to others and appeared indifferent to the event. It is not assumed in either of these cultures that individuals do not fully experience the emotions that they struggle to hide. For example, it was well understood that the young Balinese woman experienced inner turmoil.

Cultures also differ in the ways that children learn about display rules. Recall the earlier discussion of different methods of emotion socialization. In some cultures, such as China, mothers put more emphasis on teaching children display rules, akin to emotional coaching. In contrast, European American mothers tend to endorse methods, such as modeling and encouragement, which respect the child's autonomy (Cheah & Rubin, 2004).

Emotional Understanding

Not only do children act on their emotions, they also think about emotions. As they get older, they develop awareness of their own emotional experiences, the ability to discern emotions in others, knowledge about the causes and consequences of emotion, and understanding of the appropriateness of emotional expression in different contexts. Awareness of one's own emotional experience is the most basic of the emotional competence skills (Saarni et al., 2006). It emerges in the middle of the first year of life and relies on the infant's developing sense of self (Harter, 2006). Awareness of others' emotional experiences begins to appear later in the first year. This ability is clearly seen in social referencing, described by sociologist Saul Feinman (1982), which occurs when children attend to and make decisions about new or potentially fear-provoking events based on the emotional reactions of other people. Another change in emotional understanding occurs in the second year of life with the emergence of language as children begin to use emotion labels to refer to their own and others' emotions.

Preschool children develop an understanding of the existence of mental states in the self and others, including beliefs, desires, and expectations. During this period, children begin to appreciate the connection between thinking and feeling (C. Hughes, 2011). For example, children in Western industrialized cultures understand that if they receive something they want, they will feel a positive emotion, and if they do not receive it, they may feel a negative emotion.

In middle childhood (around age 7), children's understanding of the causes of emotion becomes more complex. They realize that the same situation can elicit different emotions in people. Later in childhood, children develop an understanding of how emotional expressions should be adapted to the situation and become aware of cultural display rules and emotion regulation strategies. They also come to realize that emotional expressions are produced by inner states. For example, young children often get angry when someone wrongs them, regardless of whether or not the wrongful act was intentional. Children ages 7 years and older tend to reserve their anger for situations in which they think a person intended to upset them (Thompson, 2015).

From a young age, children devise emotional scripts, a collection of ideas that enable them to identify the type of emotional reaction that is likely to accompany a particular kind of event (Saarni et al., 2006). In a classic American study, Borke (1971) told simple stories to 3- and 4-year-old children about such things as going to a party or getting lost in the woods or getting into a fight with a friend, and then asked the children to describe the emotions they thought the characters in the stories would be likely to feel. The children easily identified situations that would lead to happiness, and they were reasonably good at identifying situations linked with sadness or anger. Other research has found that 3- and 4-year-old children can also describe situations that evoked other emotions such as excitement, surprise, and fear (Lewis, 2015).

As children mature, their emotional scripts become increasingly complex. Five-year-olds generally understand only those situations that lead to emotions that have a recognizable facial display (e.g., anger as displayed in frowning) or that lead to a particular kind of behavior (e.g., sadness as displayed in crying). By age 7, children can describe situations that elicit more complicated emotions that have no obvious facial or behavioral expressions, such as pride, jealousy, worry, and guilt. By 9 years of age, children can describe situations that elicit relief and disappointment, called *counterfactual emotions* because they generate reactions different from what was expected (McCormack et al., 2016). A similar developmental sequence is found in a range of cultures (Markowitsch & Röttger-Rössler, 2009). However, the situations and reactions may differ. Children in the United States, for example, may react with anger when they are asked to stop playing and go to bed. In contrast, first graders in Nepal are happy when asked to go to bed because they co-sleep with adults, which they enjoy (P. M. Cole & Tamang, 1998).

Young children also come to understand that they experience emotions throughout time. Between 4 and 6 years of age children understand that current emotions can be affected by thinking about the past or by anticipating the future. In one study, developmental psychologist Kristin Lagattuta (2007) found that even 3-year-olds understood that someone might worry about what could happen in the future after previously having a negative experience with a certain stimulus (e.g., seeing a person or animal that had previously scared them).

Another aspect of emotional understanding that develops gradually is the awareness that a person can have more than one feeling at a time and that a person can experience two or more conflicting feelings at the same time (Larsen et al., 2007). Although toddlers may show signs of experiencing conflicting feelings, children's ability to understand and express multiple and conflicting feelings emerges slowly. It is not until about age 10 that children can conceive of opposite feelings existing simultaneously, such as feeling worried about a test and happy about an upcoming summer holiday.

Cultural variation in these behaviors, including timing or developmental onset, may reflect the types of conversations young children have with others, especially caregivers, about emotions. There are cultural differences in the frequency with which mothers rely on cognitive or mental state language when they talk with their children about emotions. Mothers in the United States use more mental-state language, such as "know," "think," and "understand," than Chinese mothers when talking with their young children about their own and other people's feelings (e.g., such as characters in a story; Q. Wang et al., 2000). This differential emphasis may reflect differing value systems. In the United States, values of autonomy and independence lead to a more child-centered socialization approach in which children are encouraged to focus on their own thoughts and ideas about emotional events. In contrast, Chinese mothers use a more socially oriented approach when they talk about emotional events with their children, one that concentrates on the transmission of socially appropriate emotional display rules.

CONCLUSION

Emotional development is a biological, social, and cultural process that includes emotional expression, emotion regulation, and emotional understanding. Culture contributes greatly to emotional development, and emotional socialization by caregivers, siblings, and peers plays a central role. These individuals act as models for emotional expressiveness, encourage or discourage certain types of emotional experience and expression, and provide "emotional coaching" by talking with children about their feelings. Siblings and peers also contribute when they express their own emotions and respond to the emotional displays of others.

The expression of emotion is an important part of communication, and in order to communicate emotions effectively, children need to learn display rules for how emotions are expressed in their culture. Learning to regulate emotions is also critical to the development of social competence, and children develop these skills gradually as they learn about the emotional display rules and coping strategies used in their culture. Children also learn about how people in their culture understand and think about emotions, which helps them calibrate their emotional experiences in social context and interpret the emotion-related behaviors of people around them.

Given the significant social contributions to children's emotion expression and regulation, it is not surprising that researchers have found cultural differences in these aspects of emotional development. Yet, much of our understanding of the connections between culture and emotional development is limited because most research includes children in industrialized nations. And when research has been conducted in nonindustrialized cultural settings, what is studied and how it is studied are largely based on Western theories (P. M. Cole & Tan, 2015). To date, studies conducted primarily in the United States reveal some commonalities, apparent universals, in emotional development, especially early in the child's life. Yet there is also substantial variation, especially as children grow up and learn culturally appropriate ways of expressing and regulating their emotions. More research is needed on how community values, beliefs, and practices affect emotional development in various cultures.

A major unresolved issue is determining whether or not an emotion—either a feeling state (e.g., worry) or expression (e.g., frown)—that looks the same across cultures is actually the same emotional experience. For many years, efforts to address this issue have relied largely on adult self-reports about the meaning of words for various feeling states (e.g., see Osgood et al., 1975). This method is not suitable for children, and more behavioral indices are needed to explore this issue developmentally.

An upcoming issue that warrants research attention concerns how emotional development occurs in the context of cultural change and immigration. Research comparing emotional development in immigrant children and children from the country of birth and the host nation has shed some light on how immigration may affect emotional development and socialization (e.g., see Q. Wang et al., 2006). More research on this topic is needed given the current massive scale of cross-national migration, much of which involves families with children. The findings will not only be informative about the relation between culture and children's emotional development, they will have important implications for the adjustment of immigrant children and their families to the new culture.

For additional resources, see the Appendix.

DISCUSSION QUESTIONS

1. Why is it important that children's emotional displays and expressions are consistent with those of their culture?

2. How do primary and secondary emotions differ, and what role does culture play in the development of each?

3. How do peers contribute to emotional development, and why is this contribution more important as children get older?

4. What do the observations of Aka, Ngandu, and European American caregivers' responsiveness to their infants tell us about the connection between culture, parenting practices, and early emotional development?

5. Why do you think there are positive relations between adolescent adjustment and emotional understanding and intelligence? Do you think these relations vary across cultures? Why or why not?

6

Culture, Child Development, and Family Relationships

Child development is embedded in nuclear and extended family relationships that are shaped by cultural contexts.

amilies are among children's most powerful socializing influences. Throughout the world, children grow up in families that are responsible for keeping them safe; providing for their physical, cognitive, and socioemotional needs; and socializing them to be competent members of their respective societies. The specific goals and behaviors that characterize family relationships differ across cultures, though.

Culture affects children's development in family contexts beginning in infancy and extending into adulthood. Culture influences when and how parents care for children, how restrictive or permissive parents are, how parents convey love and affection, and what aspirations parents have for their children (Selin & Stone, 2009). In some cultures, the norm is for children to be reared in

https://doi.org/10.1037/0000228-006
Child and Adolescent Development in Cultural Context, by J. E. Lansford, D. C. French, and M. Gauvain

extended-family households, receiving care from many relatives; in other cultures, mother–child dyads are the cornerstone of family life, and fathers are treated as "honored guests" rather than an integral part of family life. To illustrate, although both Japan and the United States are high-income, child-centered countries, they differ in various respects with regard to family relationships. Japanese mothers expect their children to have mastery of emotions, self-control, and socially correct behaviors at an early age, whereas American mothers expect verbal competence, assertiveness, and independence. Mothers in these respective societies behave in ways that are intended to socialize different values and behaviors in their children, such as strengthening closeness and dependency in mother–child dyads in Japan and environmental exploration in the United States (Bornstein et al., 2012).

In this chapter, we focus first on parent–child relationships by describing key responsibilities of parents as well as how parenting differs across cultural contexts and how culture may affect links between particular forms of parenting and child outcomes. We then consider major parenting theories through a cultural lens and how parenting changes as children develop. We next focus on sibling relationships, and finally, on family structure and extended family relationships as we consider children's development in the context of the family.

KEY RESPONSIBILITIES OF PARENTS

Key responsibilities of parents in all cultures include providing for their children's physical health and safety, cognitive stimulation, affection, and behavioral socialization to enable children to grow up to be well-functioning members of their cultural group. Biological parents, stepparents, adoptive parents, other family members such as siblings and grandparents, or nonfamily caregivers may fulfill these parenting responsibilities. We focus primarily on parents, but later in the chapter we discuss sibling and other family relationships.

Physical Health and Safety

Infants depend on their parents for their survival, and parents are responsible for promoting physical health and safety throughout childhood and adolescence. Physical health and safety are also highly dependent on nonfamily environmental factors that vary widely across countries. Infant mortality rates vary from a low of two in every 1,000 live births in Singapore, Iceland, Japan, and Monaco to a high of 110 in 1,000 live births in Afghanistan (Central Intelligence Agency, 2019). In large part, children's physical health and safety depend on factors such as malnutrition, infectious diseases, and availability of health care that vary widely based on the economic status of entire countries. However, parents also play an important role.

Physical health is largely dependent on feeding and nutrition. Guidelines developed by the World Health Organization (2018a) suggest that infants should be breastfed for the first 6 months of life, with breastfeeding supplemented by solid food until age 2 to optimize both nutrition and immune function because infants receive antibodies from their mothers through breast milk. Feeding and mealtimes remain important parts of parent–child interactions well beyond infancy. Children and adolescents are less likely to be overweight and more likely to have healthy eating habits if they eat at least three meals per week with their parents (Hammons & Fiese, 2011). Children's preferences for healthy foods resemble their parents' preferences, for better or worse (Guidetti et al., 2012).

Children's eating patterns resemble their parents' eating patterns not only because parents are generally responsible for procuring and preparing food for the whole family, but also because children model their parents in a range of behaviors that affect their physical health and safety. For example, children whose parents smoke are more likely to smoke (Vuolo & Staff, 2013). Children develop beliefs about acceptable and expected behaviors by observing their parents.

Cognitive Stimulation

Cognitive stimulation provided by parents, often through verbal interchanges with children, is important for children's language acquisition, school readiness, and academic performance. Starting before birth and continuing throughout childhood, parents are an important source of linguistic input. Fetuses can distinguish the sound of their own mother's voice from the voices of other women (Kisilevsky et al., 2003). Infants' vocalizations are highly contingent on their mothers' vocalizations to them (and, reciprocally, mothers' vocalizations are contingent on their infants' vocalizations to them), a finding that has been replicated in Argentina, Belgium, Brazil, Cameroon, France, Israel, Italy, Japan, Kenya, South Korea, and the United States (Bornstein, Putnick, Cote, et al., 2015). Children's vocabulary growth is predicted by the amount and quality of language to which children are exposed(Hurtado et al., 2008).

Children acquire language best through dyadic, contingent exchanges with their parents, rather than through hearing language passively as adults speak to each other or other children (Topping et al., 2013). In one lab-based study, mothers were asked to teach their 2-year-old child two new words, one at a time. A cell phone call from the experimenter interrupted the mother–child interaction during the teaching period for one of the two words. Mothers said the new word the same number of times in both conditions, but children learned the new word only during the teaching period that was not interrupted by the phone call (Reed et al., 2017). These findings suggest that parent–child interactions, beyond children simply hearing new words, are important to children's language acquisition.

Parents in 28 countries in more than 127,000 families with children younger than age 5 provided different forms of cognitive stimulation, including everyday conversations as well as more scripted exchanges, such as in reading, telling stories, and singing songs (Bornstein & Putnick, 2012). There was a wide variance in the amount and type of cognitive stimulation parents provided to young children. For example, almost no caregivers in Burkina Faso reported that they had read to their infants in the past 3 days, whereas more than half of caregivers in Trinidad and Tobago had read to their infants in the past 3 days (Bornstein, Putnick, Lansford, et al., 2015). Even forms of cognitive stimulation not dependent on material resources differ among caregivers across countries. For example, 35% of caregivers across all countries had told their child stories in the past 3 days, but caregivers in countries low on the Human Development Index (a composite that reflects average life expectancy, education, and gross national income per capita) were less likely to have told their children stories than were caregivers in countries high on the Human Development Index (Bornstein & Putnick, 2012). Bornstein, Putnick, Lansford, et al. (2015) found wide differences in the percentage of parents across countries who reported engaging in the behavior also were found for naming, counting, and drawing (7%–91%); playing (11%–97%); singing (10%–91%); and taking the infant or child outside (11%–94%). Researchers and educators are interested in these kinds of early interactions between parents and children because such interactions have been found to be important predictors of school readiness and eventual academic achievement in many countries (UNICEF, 2012).

Provision of Affection

Provision of affection—also known as warmth, love, and acceptance—is an important dimension of parenting. Children in all cultures need to feel loved and accepted by their parents; if they do not feel loved and accepted, their well-being suffers (Rohner & Lansford, 2017). In a meta-analysis of findings from 31 countries, boys' and girls' perceptions of their mothers' and fathers' acceptance and affection predicted better psychological adjustment, whereas feeling rejected by parents predicted children's maladaptation (e.g., Khaleque & Ali, 2017). Rohner's (2004) interpersonal acceptance-rejection theory posits that children's interpretation of their parents' behavior as indicating acceptance or rejection determines its effects on development. For example, corporal punishment and harsh verbal discipline have detrimental effects on child development in part through increasing children's perceptions of their parents' hostility as indicators of rejection (Lansford, Malone, Dodge, Chang, et al., 2010). Parental warmth, love, and affection are universally beneficial for children.

Behavioral Socialization

Grusec and Davidov (2010) described a five-domain model of parents' socialization of children (see Table 6.1). First, in the protection domain, parents provide comfort to children when they are upset, which teaches children that they are safe and helps them learn how to cope with their own distress. Second, in the reciprocity domain, parents respond to children's reasonable requests, which establishes an egalitarian relationship in which parents and children are

TABLE 6.1. Domains of Socialization: Parent–Child Relationships, Parental Behavior, and Mechanisms

Domain	Nature of parent–child relationship	Required parental behavior	Mechanism of socialization
Protection	Provider–recipient of protection	Alleviate child's distress	Confidence in protection
Reciprocity	Exchange/equality	Comply with child's reasonable requests and influence attempts	Innate tendency to reciprocate
Control	Hierarchical	Use discipline method best suited for achieving parental goal	Acquired self-control
Guided learning	Teacher–student	Match teaching to child's changing level of understanding	Internalization of language and approach used by the teacher
Group participation	Joint members of the same social group	Enable child to observe and participate in appropriate cultural practices	Firm sense of social identity

Note. From "Integrating Different Perspectives on Socialization Theory and Research: A Domain-Specific Approach," by J. E. Grusec and M. Davidov, 2010, *Child Development, 81*(3), p. 694 (https://doi.org/10.1111/j.1467-8624.2010.01426.x). Copyright 2010 by John Wiley and Sons. Reprinted with permission.

mutually sensitive to one another's requests. Third, in the control domain, parents try to mold children's behaviors by using rewards, punishments, and reasoning, drawing on the hierarchical nature of parent–child relationships, with the ultimate goal of shaping children to be able to control their own behavior. Fourth, in the guided-learning domain, parents scaffold interactions with children at particular developmental levels to help them internalize parents' ways of thinking. Fifth, in the group-participation domain, parents rely less on their own interactions with children and more on children's interactions with the entire social group to socialize children into acceptable behavior through observing how others in the group behave in everyday activities. Children are more readily socialized by their parents when parents are less controlling and rely more on the other domains. In other words, although parental control is needed in some situations, parental love, support, and guidance are critical to positive socialization and development.

Cultural contexts can affect the types of misbehavior in which children are likely to engage and also their opportunities to engage in prosocial behaviors. For example, different contexts in which Ngecha children in Gikuyu, Kenya, spent time elicited different types and amounts of prosocial behavior (de Guzman et al., 2005). In this subsistence economy, children contributed to the family's livelihood by taking care of livestock, doing household chores, and caring for younger siblings, all of which elicited nurturant and responsible prosocial behavior. Taking care of oneself and playing with other children were the activities that were least likely to elicit prosocial behavior. Because children in many industrialized countries have few opportunities to engage in work that benefits their families, they may have less access to work-related contexts that are likely to elicit prosocial behavior. Parents may need to be more mindful about socializing their children through inductive reasoning, which involves explaining why children should and should not behave in certain ways because of how their behaviors could make others feel, in order to promote prosocial behavior when their children are less able to see the direct benefits for others from their behavior (Hastings et al., 2007). Research Highlight 6.1 describes another study illustrating how parents' socialization goals and behaviors are related to the development of children's self-regulation.

Racial–Ethnic Socialization

Racial–ethnic socialization is defined as the transmission of values, beliefs, and information about ethnicity and race. The most widely accepted model of racial–ethnic socialization includes four main categories (D. Hughes et al., 2006):

1. cultural socialization—promoting racial and ethnic pride and teaching cultural practices, history, and knowledge;

2. preparation for bias—teaching children and adolescents how to cope with discrimination;

3. egalitarianism—emphasizing messages of racial equality and acceptance of diversity; and

4. promotion of mistrust—teaching caution and distrust of other groups.

Parents' racial–ethnic socialization is an important way to prepare minority youth for a multicultural world and is related to better self-esteem, academic achievement, and mental health of minority youth (D. L. Hughes et al., 2016). Racial–ethnic socialization attempts are better received by children and adolescents within the context of a warm and supportive parent–child relationship and when children regard their parents as having legitimate authority to convey such messages (Stein et al., 2018). Nonminority parents should not ignore issues related to race and ethnicity. In the United States, for example, white children whose parents address issues of white privilege and discuss systemic racism with them are more likely to be antiracist than white children whose parents disregard these issues (Hagerman, 2017).

WAYS IN WHICH CULTURE CAN AFFECT PARENTING AND LINKS BETWEEN PARENTING AND CHILD DEVELOPMENT

Parent–child relationships are grounded in family systems and cultural contexts that encompass beliefs and norms that set the stage for parenting. Parents and

RESEARCH HIGHLIGHT 6.1

Parents' Socialization Goals and Strategies Predict Children's Self-Regulation

To understand whether parents' socialization goals and strategies are related to the development of children's self-regulation, researchers conducted a longitudinal study of rural Cameroonian Nso families and middle-class German families (Lamm et al., 2018). In both countries, mothers and their 9-month-old infants came to a research laboratory that was equipped with a blanket on the floor and age-appropriate toys. Mothers were instructed to play with their infants as they normally would. Researchers video-recorded the mother–infant interactions for 10 minutes and later coded the videos regarding whether or not the mother or infant was structuring the interaction in each 10-second increment and how strongly the mother structured each increment that she was guiding. Mothers also completed questionnaires or oral interviews regarding their socialization goals, some of which were autonomy-oriented (e.g., teaching the child to express personal preferences and ideas) and some that were relatedness-oriented (e.g., helping the child learn to respect older persons). The families were recontacted when the children were 4 years old, and the children came to a research laboratory to complete the classic delay of gratification task in which a child is left alone in a room with a marshmallow and told that he or she can eat the one marshmallow immediately or wait 10 minutes until the researcher comes back into the room to be able to eat two marshmallows instead of just the one.

The researchers found that the Cameroonian Nso 4-year-olds were better at delaying gratification than were the German 4-year-olds, and children's ability to delay gratification at the age of 4 was related to their mothers' socialization goals and behaviors when they were infants. In particular, Cameroonian Nso mothers were more likely to hold relatedness-oriented socialization goals and to interact with their infants in a more directive way, whereas German mothers were more likely to hold autonomy-oriented socialization goals and to exert less structure in interacting with their infants. Socialization goals focused on respect for authority and social harmony, and socialization behaviors that were more structured subsequently predicted better delay of gratification for Cameroonian Nso children.

children observe others in their communities and form an understanding of how parents and children generally are expected to interact (Rogoff, 2003). Culture can affect beliefs and behaviors in ways that increase or decrease the likelihood of their occurrence, and the meaning that particular parenting behaviors convey in a given cultural context can affect how those parenting behaviors are related to child development (Bornstein, 2015).

Form Versus Function in Parenting

Specific parenting behaviors have been described as the "form" of parenting, and the underlying meaning of the specific behaviors has been described as the "function" (Bornstein, 1995). Envision a two-by-two matrix with forms of parenting on one axis and functions of parenting on the other (see Table 6.2). Forms and functions can be either the same or different across cultural contexts. A universal aspect of parenting occurs if both the form and function are the same across cultural contexts. For example, mothers' speech to infants (the "form") has the function of increasing the likelihood that infants will vocalize

TABLE 6.2. Forms Versus Functions of Parenting

Form	Same function	Different function
Same behavior	Cultural universalism	Plasticity
Different behavior	Context specificity	Cultural specificity

Note. From "Form and Function: Implications for Studies of Culture and Human Development," by M. H. Bornstein, 1995, *Culture and Psychology*, *1*(1), p. 125 (https://doi.org/10.1177/1354067X9511009). Copyright 1995 by Sage. Adapted with permission.

to mothers in consistent, albeit in infant-like, ways. This pattern has been found across at least 11 countries (Bornstein, Putnick, Cote, et al., 2015). By contrast, cultural specificity in parenting occurs if both the form and function are different across cultural contexts. For example, in the parenting form of orienting infants' attention (what mothers direct infants to do), in Japan, the focus is more on the mother and in the United States, the focus is more on objects (Rothbaum, Weisz, et al., 2000). The function of the behaviors observed in Japan is to promote closeness and interpersonal dependence between the mother and infant whereas the function of the behaviors observed in the United States is to promote individuation and environmental exploration.

Plasticity in this area of study describes circumstances in which the same form of parenting has different functions in different cultural contexts. As an example, establishing direct eye contact has the function of establishing mutual attention as a precursor to conversation in European American families but has the function of showing disrespect and even aggression in some Native American families (Niedźwiecka, 2020). Finally, context specificity describes circumstances in which different forms of parenting serve the same function in different cultural contexts. For example, the function of conveying love and affection to children can be accomplished in various forms, such as providing physical affection and saying, "I love you" in European American families and by providing guidance and educational opportunities in Chinese American immigrant families (Cheah et al., 2015). In some cultures, such as the Gusii people in Kenya, parents would not show affection by praising their child for fear that praise leads to conceit and rudeness (LeVine et al., 1994). Researchers have found that the function of parenting is more important than the form. That is, whether children perceive themselves as being loved and accepted is more important for their well-being than the specific behaviors parents use to convey that love and acceptance.

Mean-Level Differences in Parenting

Parents in different cultural contexts often have varied beliefs and behavior preferences. For example, in the domain of physical caregiving, infants have drastically different amounts of physical contact with their parents depending on their cultural group. Hunter–gatherer !Kung infants spend 90% of their first year of life having skin-to-skin contact with their mother or another caregiver, being carried in slings during the day and cosleeping at night. By contrast, infants in many Western cultures spend far less time in physical contact with their parents because they are often placed in strollers, infant seats, and the like, and they often sleep in separate beds and even in separate rooms (Diamond, 2012).

In the area of socioemotional interactions, parents in different cultures respond to infant crying in various ways. Early studies indicated that German parents ignored infant crying one third of the time and often waited 10 to 30 minutes when they did respond. By contrast, parents in the Efe community, a hunter–gatherer group in central Africa, responded to almost all instances of infant crying within 10 seconds (Diamond, 2012). In a classic ethnographic study of a poor, rural sample of the Gusii people in Kenya, when Gusii mothers were shown videotapes of mother–infant interactions in the United States, they were dismayed by how long it took American mothers to respond to infant crying, and were shocked to learn that mothers and infants rarely slept together (LeVine et al., 1994). In regards to play, parents in technologically advanced societies are more likely to endorse and engage in play as a way of promoting children's cognitive and social development, whereas parents in agrarian or hunter–gatherer societies are more likely to regard play as incidental to child development (Roopnarine, 2011).

Some of the largest mean-level differences in parenting behaviors have been found in the forms of discipline used, which is important because discipline is one of the main ways that parents shape children's behavior. More than 60 countries have outlawed all forms of corporal punishment, including spanking. This stance is a way to promote children's right to protection as stipulated in the United Nations Convention on the Rights of the Child, which has been ratified by all countries except the United States (see https://endcorporalpunishment. org). However, the use of corporal punishment remains widespread in other countries. In a study of parents' use of different forms of discipline with 2- to 4-year-old children in 24 low- and middle-income countries, 84% of parents in Jamaica reported that their child had experienced some form of corporal punishment in the past month compared with 28% of parents in Bosnia and Herzegovina, and 93% of Syrian parents believed it is necessary to use corporal punishment to rear a child properly compared with 4% of Albanian parents (Lansford & Deater-Deckard, 2012).

Mean-level differences in certain parenting behaviors are related to mean-level differences in corresponding child behaviors. For example, in naturalistic observations of dyads of mothers and 5-month-old infants in Argentina, Cameroon, Italy, Kenya, South Korea, and the United States, mothers in these countries differed widely in the opportunities they provided for their infants to sit independently, to sit with the support of adults or furniture, and to sit on different surfaces (Karasik et al., 2015). Mothers in Cameroon and Kenya provided the most opportunities for their infants to sit independently, and their infants were the most proficient sitters at young ages.

One explanation for mean-level differences in parenting behaviors across cultures is that parents' underlying beliefs, attitudes, expectations, and goals may also differ. For example, many parents in Bangladesh believe that showing children too much affection will spoil them. These parents also believe that speaking to infants is not important because infants cannot understand language. These beliefs have direct implications for the parents' behaviors toward infants and children in this community (Hamadani & Tofail, 2014). Mothers in Argentina, Belgium, Israel, Italy, and the United States differ in the importance they place on various aspects of caregiving. Mothers who place a high value on physical development or on social engagement, for example, behave in ways that promote these aspects of development and have infants, in turn, who become more physically advanced or engage in more social interactions with their mothers, respectively (Bornstein, Putnick, Park, et al., 2017).

Another explanation for mean-level differences in parenting behaviors across cultures is that different physical environments often call for specific types of parenting. For instance, to promote survival, parents in cultures with high infant mortality rates often engage in behaviors that prioritize physical health and safety. These behaviors include close physical contact with infants (e.g., infants being attached to mothers' bodies as they engage in daily activities) and quick responses to infants' distress (LeVine et al., 1994). In cultural contexts with low infant mortality rates where survival is less in question, parents are more likely to prioritize socioemotional and cognitive aspects of caregiving, such as reading to children (Bornstein, Putnick, Lansford, et al., 2016). Beyond survival, other features of physical environments also shape parents' behaviors. Distinct rainy and dry seasons in Nigeria that lead to fluctuations in the availability of food, for instance, result in particular Yoruba parenting practices regarding socializing children in relation to food (Babatunde & Setiloane, 2014). To socialize children to be thrifty, to delay gratification, and to demonstrate proper etiquette, parents teach children not to visit other families at mealtimes, to wait patiently for food, and to eat rare and valuable meat and fish at the end of meals. Thus, both underlying belief systems and environmental features can shape mean-level differences in parenting behaviors.

Culture as a Moderator of Links Between Parenting and Child Outcomes

Just as particular forms of parenting can serve various functions in different cultural contexts, the ways in which parenting affects child development may also differ. The acceptance and frequency of a particular parenting behavior in a given context (i.e., its cultural normativeness) relates to child outcomes. For example, in a study of mother–child dyads in six countries (China, India, Italy, Kenya, the Philippines, and Thailand), more frequent corporal punishment was related to more child aggression and anxiety in all six countries. However, the strength of the association varied across the countries, with the most detrimental effects of corporal punishment found in Thailand, where corporal punishment was least accepted by the group, and the least detrimental effects found in Kenya, where corporal punishment at the time was most accepted (corporal punishment has since then been outlawed in Kenya; Lansford et al., 2005).

The cultural normativeness of a particular parenting behavior may be an important factor in how that behavior relates to child outcomes because the meaning conveyed to the child by parents' behavior that is consistent with the behavior of others in the cultural group is likely different from the meaning conveyed by behavior that seems inconsistent with the behavior of other parents in the cultural group. If parents behave consistently with cultural norms, they are more likely to receive endorsement from other adults for their behavior, and children and parents are more likely to regard the normative behavior as justified and legitimate. However, if parents behave in ways not condoned by the larger cultural group, children may regard their parents as acting out of hostility or neglect (Lansford, Malone, Dodge, Chang, et al., 2010). Children's interpretations of their parents' behavior predict how that behavior affects children. Research Highlight 6.2 provides an example of a longitudinal study in nine countries that has examined how cultural normativeness of different parenting practices relates to youth adjustment.

RESEARCH HIGHLIGHT 6.2

Parenting in Different Cultures

The Parenting Across Cultures (PAC) project is a longitudinal study of parenting and child development in nine countries: China, Colombia, Italy, Jordan, Kenya, the Philippines, Sweden, Thailand, and the United States. Children and their parents were recruited through schools in each country when the children were 8 years old, on average. The family members have been interviewed annually for 12 years (with data collection still ongoing) about the parent–child relationship; cultural norms; and the child's behavioral, emotional, social, and academic adjustment. A team of researchers from universities in all nine countries collaborates on posing research questions, developing or adapting measures to use in all sites, analyzing the data, and disseminating the findings (Lansford, Bornstein, et al., 2016). On a range of parenting and child development variables, there are larger differences within countries than between countries (Deater-Deckard et al., 2018).

In one study using data from the PAC project, five domains of parenting (expectations regarding family obligations, monitoring, psychological control, behavioral control, and warmth) were examined in relation to five domains of later youth adjustment (social competence, prosocial behavior, academic achievement, externalizing behavior, and internalizing behavior; Lansford et al., 2018). The analyses tested whether or not the associations between parenting and youth adjustment depended on how normative the parents' behaviors were in their cultural context. When differences in links between parenting and youth adjustment were found to vary across cultures, the links were generally stronger in cultural contexts in which the parenting behavior was more normative. For example, adolescents were perceived as being more socially competent when their parents' expectations about family obligations were well aligned with the expectations of other parents in their community. The findings from this international comparative study are useful in demonstrating similarities in associations between parenting and youth adjustment across cultural contexts as well as ways in which cultural norms are important in understanding parent–child relationships.

MAJOR PARENTING THEORIES CONSIDERED THROUGH A CULTURAL LENS

Parenting theories have been proposed to provide a conceptual understanding of why parents behave as they do and how parenting is related to child development. An advantage of a good theory is that it can guide empirical studies and help make sense of research findings. The most prominent parenting theory is attachment theory, which we discuss first, followed by a number of other theories that consider parenting practices and styles.

Attachment Theory

Attachment theory was originally developed by John Bowlby (1969, 1973, 1980) and expanded by Mary Ainsworth (Ainsworth et al., 1978), based largely on Ainsworth's field research in Uganda. Attachment theory proposes that the interactions between infants and their caregivers are based on evolutionarily adaptive behaviors in which infants seek proximity to their caregivers, and caregivers provide comfort to infants, as these behaviors have benefits for infants' survival. A secure attachment relationship develops when caregivers are consistently sensitive and responsive to infants' needs, through which infants learn that they can rely on their caregivers to protect and nurture them. This parenting approach, in turn, provides a secure base from which infants can explore the world, returning to their caregivers if they become distressed. However, if caregivers are abusive toward, inconsistent with, or rejecting of their infant, the infant is not able to develop a sense of security in social relationships, which portends problems in future social relationships and may constrain the infant's exploration of the world.

Early attachment relationships form the basis of internal working models of social relationships, which are cognitive representations of expectations for one's own and others' behavior in the context of social relationships. For example, if an infant's caregivers are sensitive and responsive, the infant will come to regard themself as worthy of love and expect caring treatment from others in future social interactions, and will be able to offer sensitive and caring social behavior in return. In contrast, if an infant's caregivers are hostile and unpredictable, the infant will come to regard themself as worthless or incompetent and will expect individuals in future social interactions to be unavailable or rejecting.

The standard research protocol for measuring infant attachment is the Strange Situation Procedure, developed decades ago by Ainsworth and colleagues (1978). The protocol, which has seven distinct steps or experiences for the infant, begins with the infant (generally around 12 months of age) and caregiver together in a laboratory observation room (generally with a one-way mirror so that the session can be video-recorded and later coded). The caregiver is asked to sit without interacting with the infant as the infant explores the room, which is stocked with age-appropriate toys. The caregiver then leaves the room for a brief period of time while the infant remains alone in the room. The caregiver reenters the room for a brief reunion with the infant before leaving the room again. This time, a stranger enters the room instead of the caregiver and tries to comfort the infant. Finally, the caregiver reenters the room and reunites with the infant for a final time.

Trained observers code the infant's responses in the presence of the caregiver (e.g., whether the infant explores the room, demonstrating secure base behavior) and during the reunions with the caregiver (e.g., whether the infant seeks physical proximity during the reunion and can be comforted by the caregiver). *Securely attached* infants explore the room in the caregiver's presence, seek out the caregiver when distressed following the separation, and are comforted easily by the caregiver. *Anxious-avoidant* infants do not demonstrate overt distress during the separation from the caregiver and do not seek comfort from the caregiver during the reunion. *Anxious-ambivalent* or *anxious-resistant* infants are highly distressed during the separation but are resistant to comfort by their caregiver during the reunion. *Disorganized infants* do not behave consistently in seeking proximity or comfort and may become fearful or freeze during the reunion (Zajac et al., 2020).

Attachment theory has generated a large body of empirical research aimed at testing its tenets (for reviews, see Cassidy & Shaver, 2008; Roisman & Groh, 2011). One of the main take-home messages from this research is that the nature of infants' relationships with their caregivers is related to a number of indicators of later well-being, including emotion regulation, self-image, and competence in peer and romantic relationships (e.g., Groh et al., 2014). However, despite its theoretical relevance in various cultural contexts, the measurement of attachment security has generated controversy because the Strange Situation may not be ecologically valid in different cultures. For example, Japanese infants were traditionally cared for almost exclusively by their mothers. In the context of a relationship in which it is extremely rare for infants to be separated from their mothers, the Strange Situation invokes considerably more distress for Japanese infants than it does for, say, German infants who are often cared for in daycare centers by a number of caregivers from a relatively early age. German infants are usually not distressed at all by the Strange Situation (which is not so strange for them).

Beyond measurement issues involved in the Strange Situation, the main tenets of attachment theory may be biased toward Western ways of thinking (Rothbaum, Weisz, et al., 2000). For example, middle-class European American mothers demonstrate sensitivity by waiting for their infants to communicate their needs by crying or showing distress and then responding to the infants' distress, whereas Japanese mothers avoid situations that are stressful to their infants and anticipate their infants' needs before they show signs of distress. Parents in various cultural contexts appear to be universally responsive to infants' needs, but they demonstrate this responsiveness differently (Mesman et al., 2018). Children's social competence is also demonstrated differently in Japan and the United States. For example, working well in groups and interdependence with others are hallmarks of children's social competence in Japan, whereas autonomy and independent exploration of the environment are more valued in the United States. The point is that these various kinds of competencies are not typical of children, but rather are promoted by different caregiving patterns. As we described earlier, Japanese mothers orient infants' attention to themselves, and American mothers orient infants' attention to objects in the environment, which promotes interdependence versus independent exploration, respectively (Rothbaum, Pott, et al., 2000). Similarly, Gusii mothers in Kenya spend more time soothing their infants, whereas American mothers spend more time stimulating their infants. Also, because Gusii mothers do not believe that infants are capable of understanding language, they do not speak to them in face-to-face interactions that are common for American mothers and infants (LeVine et al., 1994). These different patterns of mother–infant interactions suggest that sensitive, responsive caregiving may take numerous forms across cultures, functioning in their own ways to promote attachment relationships.

Parenting Practices and Styles

Beyond attachment theory, other major theories related to parent–child relationships emphasize parenting practices (what parents do) and styles (how they do it, or the emotional climate of the parent–child relationship). The major dimensions underlying parenting practices and styles are warmth versus hostility—an emotional dimension—and control versus permissiveness—a behavioral dimension. Baumrind's (1967) classic parenting typology described three parenting styles: authoritarian, permissive, and authoritative. Authoritarian parents are highly controlling of their children's behavior and lack affection. Permissive parents are highly lenient and not controlling, and they are warm and affectionate. Authoritative parents are highly affectionate but also provide control by giving children rules to follow along with explanations for why they should comply.

Maccoby and Martin (1983) expanded on Baumrind's typology by describing a two-by-two matrix of parenting that was characterized by high versus low levels of demandingness (control, supervision) and high versus low levels of responsiveness (warmth, acceptance). Authoritarian parents are high on demandingness but low on responsiveness. Permissive/indulgent parents are low on demandingness but high on responsiveness. Neglectful parents are low on both demandingness and responsiveness. Authoritative parents are high on both demandingness and responsiveness. Children of authoritative parents in various cultural contexts have been found to exhibit the highest levels of social competence and academic achievement and fewest behavior problems, as opposed to children of authoritarian, neglectful, or permissive/indulgent parents (Pinquart & Kauser, 2018).

Despite the widespread advantages of authoritative parenting in a variety of cultural groups, parental warmth appears to be more universally beneficial than parental control, which appears to be more culturally variable. For example, in some cultures, parents who show warmth also show less control (e.g., a correlation of –.35 for European Americans in the United States), whereas in other cultures, parents who show warmth are also likely to be controlling (e.g., a correlation of .85 for Luos in Kenya; Deater-Deckard et al., 2011). Control may have different effects on child development depending on the meaning conveyed in particular cultural contexts. In China, a type of control known as *guan*—meaning "to govern"—has been described as involving firm control and training but also love and caring (Wu & Chao, 2011). This type of parenting shares features with authoritative parenting, and parents of Chinese origin without guan would be regarded as neglectful.

Another set of theories emphasizes how specific parenting practices may be related to children's adjustment in different ways depending on the parenting style or emotional context of the parent–child relationship (for a review, see Rudolph et al., 2017). Darling and Steinberg (1993) proposed a model of parenting with five components: (a) goals and values, (b) parenting style, (c) parenting practices, (d) child outcomes, and (e) children's willingness to be socialized. Parents' goals and values affect their parenting style (including the emotional climate in which parents socialize their children) and their parenting practices, which in turn influence children's outcomes. Parenting style can alter the effectiveness of specific parenting practices as well as children's openness to being socialized. If the overall parenting style is characterized by warmth and affection, children will be more open to their parents' socialization attempts. If the parent–child relationship is warm and loving, children are more likely to regard their parents as having legitimate authority to direct their behavior, are more compliant with their parents' requests, and internalize parents' messages more fully (Darling et al., 2005). Similar developmental patterns are found in diverse countries, including Chile, the Philippines, and the United States.

Davies and Cummings (1994) introduced the emotional security hypothesis, which states that the link between parenting and child outcomes depends on children's sense of emotional security. Children's emotional security and ability to regulate their emotions and behaviors are compromised when parents are unavailable or unpredictable. For example, parental intrusiveness, withdrawal, and rejection increase children's anger, dysphoria, social withdrawal, noncompliance, and externalizing problems. Parenting behaviors that are either too lax or too harsh can increase children's externalizing and internalizing problems. Children's culturally grounded interpretation of their parents' behavior is crucial to understanding the link between parenting and children's adjustment.

PARENTING CHANGES AS BOTH CHILDREN AND PARENTS DEVELOP

To meet the changing needs of children as they develop, parenting must also change to promote emerging skills and respond to issues that are salient at different points in development (e.g., Grusec & Davidov, 2007). As infants are establishing attachment relationships, parents' sensitive responding is critical to meet infants' socioemotional needs and, of course, infants are physically dependent on parents to meet all of their needs. As children gain motor, cognitive, and social competencies during early childhood, parents scaffold their children's experiences by providing guidance that enables children to progress to higher levels of competencies in each of these areas. Throughout childhood and into adolescence, parents provide different forms of behavioral control to prevent and respond to misbehavior, adjusting discipline strategies to the developmental level of their child (e.g., distraction for toddlers, reasoning with adolescents). Distal monitoring and supervision become more important aspects of parenting in adolescence as time with peers increases and time under the direct control of parents decreases. After puberty, adolescents increasingly focus on privilege and autonomy, whereas parents focus on risk and responsibility, which can lead to conflicts within the family.

Despite some consistency across cultures in the ways that parenting changes as children develop, differences also characterize certain aspects of change, in part because of cultural variation in what is considered developmentally appropriate and desirable at a given age. For example, an increase in autonomy during adolescence is more expected in some cultures than in others. Increases in early adolescents' autonomy in making decisions is more strongly related to life satisfaction, positive emotions, self-esteem, and reduced anxiety in the United States than in China. In the United States, an increase in autonomy during adolescence is expected, whereas in China beliefs about the importance of autonomy during adolescence are less pervasive (Qin et al., 2009). Even in countries as diverse as Chile, the Philippines, and the United States, when expectations regarding autonomy increased during adolescence, expectations that adolescents would obey their parents even if they disagreed with them were stronger in the Philippines than in Chile or the United States (Darling et al., 2005). And research involving youth in the latter years of adolescence and beyond has found cultural differences in the extent to which parents are expected to influence their offspring's lives even into adulthood (e.g., Alampay, 2014).

Culture affects not only how parenting changes as children develop, but also the extent to which parents believe they can affect children's development at all. Rural, poor Yucatec Maya parents in Mexico do not attempt to influence children's development because they believe that development steadily unfolds over time regardless of what parents do (Gaskins, 2000). Luo parents in Kenya, however, have a saying that "a tree is shaped while young, or when it is grown up it breaks," which embodies the Luo belief in parents' responsibility to influence child development to reach desired outcomes (Oburu, 2011, p. 155). Parents in some countries believe that they influence children even before they are born (e.g., Shwalb et al., 2010). In a direct comparison of parents' attributions for success and failures in caregiving situations in urban areas of China, Colombia, Italy, Jordan, Kenya, the Philippines, Sweden, Thailand, and the United

States, parents held various beliefs regarding the extent to which outcomes of caregiving situations were under their control, their children's control, or the result of factors outside of anyone's control, such as luck (Bornstein et al., 2011).

Influence in parent–child relationships occurs not only from parents to children; children also influence their parents' behaviors. Reciprocal influences between parents and children can occur in the moment, such as when a lack of maternal support leads to a child's aversive behavior, which leads to the mother's further withdrawal of support (Ravindran et al., 2019). Reciprocal influences can also occur over longer periods of development, such as when children express interest in or aptitude for an activity that parents then foster so their children can become more proficient. Thus, children elicit certain kinds of responses from their parents, and parents induce their children to behave in particular ways (Sameroff, 2009).

As their children develop, parents are developing, too. Immigration is an example of an experience that can lead to many changes in parenting, bringing challenges as well as giving parents opportunities related to their children's development. Immigrant parents more quickly adopt parenting practices of their new country than parenting thoughts or beliefs that are common in the new country (Cote et al., 2015). Immigrant parents who practice behaviors that are considered acceptable in their native country that are not practiced in their destination country can encounter resistance from both the new country and their own children. For example, traditional healing practices such as cupping (special cups placed on the skin to create suction) and coining (heated coin placed or rubbed on the skin) leave marks that might appear to be signs of abuse, which has led to reports of immigrant parents in the United States to Child Protective Services (Killion, 2017). These examples illustrate the importance of understanding parenting from a variety of culturally sensitive perspectives. Parenting, like child development, is not static but changes over time.

GENDER IN FAMILY RELATIONSHIPS

Gender is important in family relationships, in terms of boys' and girls' family relationships and in terms of similarities and differences between mothers' and fathers' parenting styles. The school enrollment rate of boys versus girls, men's and women's participation in the workforce, and expectations regarding gender-based rights and responsibilities are variable across countries. Iceland, Finland, Norway, Sweden, and Denmark show the most gender equality in health, education, economy, and politics, whereas Mali, Syria, Chad, Pakistan, and Yemen show the least equality (World Economic Forum, 2014). Gender equality issues at a societal level are sometimes instantiated in families through treatment of sons and daughters and in parenting roles of fathers and mothers.

Parents sometimes treat boys and girls differently with respect to the availability of gender-typed toys and encouragement or discouragement of particular activities at home and outside the home (Endendijk, Groeneveld, & Mesman,

2018). However, a comparison of parenting boys and girls based on numerous domains in various low- and middle-income countries showed only small differences at young ages (Bornstein et al., 2016). Boys and girls may be treated more similarly in infancy and early childhood than during adolescence, especially in countries in North Africa and the Middle East where boys have more mobility outside the home after puberty, but girls are more restricted (Ahmed, 2010). Transgender children who have socially transitioned from their sex assigned at birth to their current gender identity generally report identifying with their current gender by age 3 (Olson & Gülgöz, 2018), and from age five to 12 are indistinguishable from cisgender children with the same gender identity in terms of preferences for gender-stereotypical clothes, toys, and activities (Olson et al., 2015).

Historically, mothers have been characterized as children's primary caregivers, and fathers have been characterized as helpers, playmates, or disciplinarians (Lamb, 2010). This view is embodied in the Chinese adage, "Kind mother, strict father," a Confucian-based distinction that is also common in other Asian countries (Shwalb et al., 2010). These differences persist in many countries today. Based on analyses of nationally representative samples of more than 170,000 families in 39 low- and middle-income families, mothers spent more time as primary caregivers of young children than did fathers (Bornstein & Putnick, 2016). However, gender roles in many countries have become more equitable in recent years, and both fathers and mothers are important to child development (Kuhns & Cabrera, 2018). For instance, in countries such as Australia, Canada, and the United States, fathers' caregiving has increased over time (Bianchi & Milkie, 2010).

National policies also have the potential to influence the nature of mothers' and fathers' relationships with their children. For example, in countries with paid paternity leave that must be used or forfeited, fathers are more likely to take time off work to care for their infants and young children (International Labour Organization, 2014). Children have more similar relationships with their mothers and fathers if their fathers took leave to serve as primary caregivers than if their fathers did not take leave to serve as caregivers (McHale & Sirotkin, 2019). Overall, the roles of mothers and fathers and their treatment of sons and daughters within families have similarities with men and women's gender-based experiences at the societal level.

SIBLING RELATIONSHIPS

Whether or not children have siblings varies greatly across countries. For example, the one-child policy implemented in China from 1979 to 2015 limited urban families to one child, effectively eliminating sibling relationships for a large segment of the Chinese population (Feng et al., 2016). Even without legislation, birth rates vary dramatically in different countries. In many European countries, women have, on average, fewer than two children, whereas in many African countries, they have six or seven children on average (World Population Review, 2019). About 80% of children in the United States have at least one sibling (Livingston, 2011). In some countries, children spend more time with their siblings than with their parents (Feinberg, Solmeyer, & McHale, 2012).

Beyond the presence and number of siblings, the nature of sibling relationships also varies across countries. For example, in some countries, older children are key caregivers for their younger siblings, whereas in other countries, leaving infants and young children in the care of only slightly older siblings would be perceived as neglectful (Kramer & Hamilton, 2019; Lancy, 2008). Caring for younger siblings is an important way to contribute to the family's well-being, and has been shown to be related to the development of prosocial behavior in older siblings. In some cases, such as in Vietnam, children may be expected to work on the streets to support a brother's education or a girl may live in an orphanage to enable the family to try for more sons (Burr, 2014). In these cases, morality and what it means to be a "good child" are entwined with cultural values and knowing one's place in the social hierarchy of the family.

Sibling relationships have been characterized as sources of both conflict and support. Conflict in sibling relationships sometimes arises over perceptions of limited resources, such as parents' time, attention, or money. Particularly in low-income countries, it is common for families not to have the financial resources to send all their children to school. Thus, some children may be sent to school while others work to help enable their siblings to attend school. The quality of children's relationships with their siblings is related to important aspects of child development. For example, children who have chronic conflict with their siblings have more internalizing problems, such as depression and anxiety (Milevsky & Levitt, 2005), and externalizing problems, such as aggression (Ensor et al., 2010). Children who have warm and cohesive relationships with their siblings are less likely to have externalizing problems and more likely to have better psychological adjustment (Branje et al., 2004).

FAMILY STRUCTURE AND EXTENDED FAMILY RELATIONSHIPS

Parent–child and sibling relationships are embedded in larger family structures that are shaped by many aspects of culture. Demographic changes in many countries have led to an increase in the proportion of children born to unmarried parents, children who are reared by a single parent, children who are reared by two fathers or two mothers, children in stepfamilies, and children who live in a variety of other diverse family structures. For example, 40% of children in the United States are born to unmarried parents, and of the children who are born to married parents, about half will experience their parents' divorce (Martin et al., 2017). In some countries, being pregnant without being married is illegal and is punishable by lashings and prison (Santos, 2017), and divorce is not legal in the Philippines. Family structure is not static; children often experience changes in family structure as their parents enter and leave romantic relationships.

Experiencing parents' divorce and remarriage is stressful for children and leads to a period of adjustment for both parents and children (de Jong-Gierveld & Merz, 2013; Ganong et al., 2015). Children's behavioral and emotional problems sometimes increase around the time of family transitions but generally return to baseline levels after an initial adjustment period (Lansford, 2009). In long-term stepfamilies, 75% of adolescents described having "close" or "very close" relationships with their stepparents (Hetherington, 2006). Overall, although children of divorced parents are at somewhat higher risk of having behavioral and psychological problems than children whose parents do not divorce, most children of divorced parents do not have long-term adjustment problems.

A consistent finding from a variety of studies is that the quality of family relationships is more important than family structure for predicting children's well-being. For example, regardless of family structure, parent–child conflict, poor parent–child relationship quality, and financial distress are related to more emotional and behavioral problems in children (Murry & Lippold, 2018). Similarly, in a comparison of gay father, lesbian mother, and heterosexual parent families with adopted children in the United Kingdom, parenting stress was a better predictor of child behavior problems than family structure (Golombok et al., 2014). Parenting practices that promote children's well-being in two-parent, heterosexual families also promote children's well-being in other family structures.

Beyond variations in the family structure of parent–child and sibling relationships, extended-family relationships also play an important role in child development. Grandmothers, aunts, and other family members often share caregiving responsibilities with biological parents, and in many cases serve as primary caregivers (Keller & Chaudhary, 2017). In many cultural groups, families live in extended-family households with parenting functions performed by several family members (Sear, 2016). In many parts of the world, when parents migrate from rural areas to urban areas or even to other countries for work, children are left behind in the care of other relatives (Peng & Wong, 2016). Because important caregiving functions are performed by family members other than parents, children's attachment relationships within a whole family network would better characterize development than merely understanding children's attachment to parents (Keller & Chaudhary, 2017).

Both within and between cultural groups, expectations regarding family relationships and obligations vary. In the United States, Asian American and Latin American adolescents perceive themselves as being more obligated to help and respect extended family members than do European American adolescents (Witkow et al., 2015). In a number of countries, including China, Colombia, Italy, Jordan, Kenya, the Philippines, Sweden, Thailand, and the United States, parents who have higher expectations regarding their children's family obligations are more authoritarian and controlling but also warmer and less neglectful than parents who believe their children have fewer family obligations (Lansford, Godwin, et al., 2016). Children in most cultural groups are expected to work (e.g., doing household chores, caring for younger siblings, farming) to contribute to their family's well-being (Weisner, 2001).

A number of cultural groups have deeply embedded ideas about families that shape concepts of family obligations (e.g., *familism* in Mexico, Colombia, and other Latin American countries: Padilla et al., 2020; *hiya* and *utang na loob* in the Philippines: Alampay, 2014; traditional African concepts of family obligations: Baguma & Aheisibwe, 2011). Perceptions of family obligations are one way to characterize cultural values that shape how family members interact with one another and how children develop in the context of extended families (Chao & Otsuki-Clutter, 2011). In many countries, instilling the importance of social relationships is the most central aspect of family relationships. The Zulu people in South Africa nurture *umuntu umuntu ngabantu*, which means that a person is only a person with other people (Zimba, 2002). Likewise, the Yoruba people in Nigeria rear children using the concept of *omoluwabi*, which involves a holistic approach emphasizing loyalty to family obligations and traditions in interpersonal interactions (Akinsola, 2011). Gratitude, respect, and honor are often embedded in children's relationships with extended family members.

Family systems theory provides one framework for understanding entire families, beyond parent–child dyads and sibling relationships. This approach acknowledges that what happens in one part of the family system (e.g., between parents) often spills over into other parts of the family system (e.g., to parent–child relationships; Mills-Koonce et al., 2015).

CONCLUSION

In some ways, family relationships are similar regardless of cultural context. In particular, parents throughout the world have key responsibilities of providing for their children's physical health and safety, cognitive stimulation, affection, and behavioral socialization so that their children grow up to be competent members of their society. In other respects, family relationships differ according to the broader cultural contexts in which they are situated, both in terms of mean levels of parenting behavior types and in how particular forms of parenting function in relation to child development. Laws and norms influence whether children have siblings and, if so, the nature of those sibling relationships and the family structures in which children are reared. One of the most important family functions around the world is to provide love and affection to children, regardless of how it is demonstrated, as the grounding of their future social relationships. The involvement of extended family members and sense of familial obligation also vary across cultures, affecting the parent–child relationship.

For additional resources, see the Appendix.

DISCUSSION QUESTIONS

1. In what ways do parents affect child development similarly across cultures? In what ways do parents affect child development differently across cultures?

2. How does an understanding of cultural influences on family relationships advance understanding of child development?

3. In what ways can attachment theory, interpersonal acceptance–rejection theory, family systems theory, and the emotional security hypothesis be applied across cultures? Are there ways that the theories need to be framed to account for cultural differences?

4. What roles do child gender and parent gender play in family relationships?

5. What implications do national laws and policies have for understanding family relationships?

7

Culture and Peer Relationships

Peer relationships are important for child development, including as a source of fun and companionship as shown by these children in Mali.

During early childhood, most children throughout the world begin to interact extensively with their peers. Although this is likely universal, the extent of this involvement varies according to whether the population density is sufficient to provide peer associates. For much of human history, the populations of hunter–gatherer groups were too small to provide children with the opportunity to interact with same-sex age-mates; consequently, the mixed-age and mixed-sex peer group was ubiquitous (Konner, 1975). Currently, with the increased population density and school attendance, most children have the opportunity to select peer associates from larger groups.

Peer relationships are also subject to cultural perspectives pertaining to the importance of these relationships for the development of young children. Gaskin (2006) illustrated this in her ethnographic study of Maya children living in

https://doi.org/10.1037/0000228-007
Child and Adolescent Development in Cultural Context, by J. E. Lansford, D. C. French, and M. Gauvain

rural Guatemala. She reported that in contrast to what is typical for European American children, most of the social interactions of these children, even at school, typically occurred between siblings and cousins. These interaction patterns reflect a cultural belief that relationships between family members are much more important than those with others in the community.

In this chapter, we focus on multiple dimensions of peer relationships and how they are influenced by cultural parameters. To simplify our presentation, we use the label "children" to refer to both children and adolescents, but we clarify when the discussion pertains only to those in a specific age group. Interactions with peers occur between individuals who have different levels of relationships; here we will consider friendships, social networks, and romantic relationships. As we see later, each of these can be understood as existing within a cultural context.

ACTIVITY SETTINGS AND PEER RELATIONSHIPS

Peer interactions occur within activity settings (see Chapter 1), and it is important to consider the identity of participants in these settings. A major factor that affects children's companions is propinquity, which is defined as being in proximity to others. Children have limited options to select their peers because they often do not have the freedom to act independently of adults and often have limited transportation options. Consequently, they typically interact only with others in their neighborhood, school, activity groups, or others they meet through their parents' social networks. Because of these selection parameters, potential peer partners have similar qualities such as economic level, education, ethnicity, and religion. Cultural influences on the identity of peer companions is illustrated by Dyson's (2010) finding from her anthropological field work with girls in an Indian Himalayan village community that it was difficult for children who were members of different castes to become friends. This is also illustrated by Gaskin's (2006) findings from her study of children in a Guatemalan Maya village that it was difficult for children who were not part of kinship networks to become friends because parents and others encouraged children to primarily interact with siblings, cousins, and others with whom they were related.

Cultural variations in activity settings may have important implications for the quantity and quality of children's peer interactions. Consider, for example, typical Chinese and American middle schools. Although at first sight, both settings afford adolescents with abundant opportunities to interact with their peers, the activity settings in these schools provide different peer experiences. American students have abundant opportunities to interact with many different peers and pursue friendships and romances, and sometimes participate in bullying and aggressive behavior during recess, lunch, and transition periods between classes. Chinese students, in contrast, remain with their same classroom group throughout the school day and teachers move from class to class. Students eat lunch in their classroom and have few opportunities to interact with students who are not in their classroom group or to escape the watchful eyes of the teacher. This reflects cultural differences in the meaning of school. Chinese schools are structured to maximize academic learning. In contrast, American schools, in addition to providing academic instruction, promote athletic competition, peer socialization, and extracurricular activities.

The gender segregation in young children's peer interactions is likely universal, although the extent that this occurs varies across cultures. In some cases, boys and girls are intentionally segregated. Even when cross-gender interaction is possible, preschool- and elementary-age children often prefer to interact with same-sex peers, perhaps because they prefer the interaction styles and interests of their same-sex peers (Maccoby, 1990). In addition, the interactions of boys and girls often occur in different types of activity settings, which can occur either because of adult-imposed structures or child choice. For example, Wenger (1989) documents how the chores of boys (herding) and girls (assisting mothers with cooking and caregiving) in a Giriama rural Kenyan community provided boys with increased autonomy and greater access to peers than was afforded to girls. Across cultures, boys are more likely than girls to play away from the home (and adult supervision), which can influence the play styles and the learning opportunities of children.

Children's peer interactions typically occur in the context of activities that have a particular structure. For example, it is common for peer interaction to occur while children are engaged in studying, working, eating, or playing formal and informal games. There may be cultural patterns of interaction associated with these particular tasks, and cultural meanings are attached to these activities as illustrated by the activity setting of the high school prom in the United States. The interactions in this activity setting are culturally scripted and specify appropriate dress, location, and expected practices, and the activities have meanings that are passed from generation to generation and are presented in countless movies and books. Note that as each age cohort participates in this activity, they change it, and, consequently, transform culture over time.

The discussion of activity settings leads directly to an appreciation of how boys and girls in different cultures and economic strata spend their time. For example, American adolescents have much more discretionary time available to them (about 8 hours per day) than do either European (5½–7½ hours) or East Asian youth (4–5½ hours; Larson & Verma, 1999). These variations in available time are a product of differences in school and work commitments. The extent to which children in different cultures spend their time engaging in play, school activities, interaction with peers, or work—and the implications of this—are considered in Chapter 10.

FRIENDSHIPS

Friendships are voluntary dyadic relationships that are recognized by each participant. Whereas positive engagement in shared activities may be the basis for friendships among young children, intimacy and affection become increasingly important at older ages. The forms that friendships take across cultures are subject to cultural blueprints (McCall, 1988). These rules specify who can and cannot be friends, the characteristics of the interactions between friends, and the expected emotional connectedness.

As noted previously, some of the parameters that define interactions between peers, such as propinquity, also pertain to the identity of friends and partially explain the similarities of partners on dimensions such as social class, educational level, interests, and race. Sometimes there are specific rules defining the identity of friends. For example, there may be cultural norms that make it difficult for children who differ in ethnicity, gender, or social class to be friends.

Variation in the characteristics and cultural rules pertaining to friendship is illustrated by the comments of two college-age women about their same-sex friends. Hye-jin, a South Korean woman who was studying in the United States, expressed disappointment and frustration with her American best friends, who often arranged weekend activities with others without including or consulting her. Her comments reflect the view shared by many Koreans that friendships should be very exclusive and intimate. In contrast, Titi, a young Indonesian woman, was puzzled by email messages from her German friend (Greta), who had studied in Indonesia and had recently returned to her home country. Titi wondered why Greta regularly emailed her asking about her daily life and activities. Clearly, Greta sought to maintain the friendship despite the separation, whereas Titi's comments reflect the views common in her culture that close dyadic friendships are not strongly valued and that friendships typically do not persist across time and distance.

Much of the study of friendships and culture has focused on the characteristics of friendships among children in different cultures. French (2015) suggested that there are cultural differences in friends' intimacy, instrumental aid, exclusivity, and conflict management. At the outset of this discussion, however, it is important to reiterate that variability exists within cultures with respect to friendships. In any culture, some children have friends and others do not, and there are individual differences in the qualities of these relationships.

Intimacy

There are differences in the closeness of friendships and the level of sharing of confidences and personal information. Consider the contrast between South Korean and Indonesian friendships. South Korean friendships are strongly influenced by Confucianism, which identifies friendship as one of the five types of necessary relationships (K. Kim, 1996). These relationships are expected to be very intimate, long lasting, and held together by a shared understanding of obligations. The word *cheong* is a label for this extreme intimacy that describes a shared identity that develops between friends (S. Lee, 1994).

In contrast, a number of anthropologists have reported that friendships within many of the Indonesian ethnic groups tend to be low in intimacy. Mulder (1996) wrote that intimate and long-lasting friendships were not com-

mon or sought. Koentjaraningrat (1985) suggested that although urban Indonesian adolescents have friends, they primarily focus on participating and
gaining acceptance in larger groups instead of establishing intimate dyadic
friendships. Indeed, when asked, Indonesian adults preferred to have many
acquaintances rather than a few intimate friends, whereas Australians reported
the opposite preference (Noesjirwan, 1978).

There are other cultures in which acceptance within the larger peer group is
more important than having strong dyadic friendships. Sharabany (2006) summarized research pertaining to friendship intimacy of Arab and kibbutzim children and adolescents. The Arab population living in Israel (about 20% of the
population) typically lives in homogeneous Arab neighborhoods and their children attend separate schools. Sharabany (2006) reviewed several studies and
concluded that the Arab population is collectivist, and their group orientation
leads to a commitment to the community and the peer group in general, rather
than to specific intimate dyadic friendships. Similarly, Israeli children living in
a kibbutz (small, rural, communal, cooperative communities) preferred interactions with a large number of peers and de-emphasized the importance of
specific intimate friendships. Interestingly, the attitudes of kibbutzim youth
toward friends appear to be context-specific. Children who left the kibbutz and
moved to cities expressed the same level of intimacy with friends as their peers
who were not raised in the kibbutz.

European American adolescents tend to fall between the extremes of South
Korean and Indonesian youth in their level of intimacy with friends (French,
Lee, & Pidada, 2006). The term *friend* is used to describe a diverse set of relationships with peers; some of these are very close, and others are low in intimacy and based primarily on companionship and shared activities (Brain,
1976). Nevertheless, friendships are important for Americans, particularly children, adolescents, and older adults. As noted previously, however, there is variability within cultures; some children have very close friendships and others do
not (K. H. Rubin et al., 2015).

French, Bae, et al. (2006) conducted several studies using a variety of
approaches to assess the friendships of children and college students from
South Korea, Indonesia, and the United States. In one of these studies, 11- and
14-year-olds from Indonesia and the United States used a multi-item rating
scale to assess the intimacy of their friendships. Examples of items on the scale
used to measure intimacy were "How much do you share your secrets and private feelings with this person?" and "How much do you talk to this person
about things that you don't want others to know?" As expected, American
youth rated their friendships as more intimate than did Indonesian youth.
Research Highlight 7.1 describes another study by French, Bae, et al. illustrating that friendships differ across cultures in intimacy, exclusivity, and longevity.

It is also important to consider that there may be cultural differences in the
ways that intimacy is expressed. For example, Gummerum and Keller (2008)
suggested that Chinese youth are less likely than European youth to self-disclose
or exchange secrets.

RESEARCH HIGHLIGHT 7.1

Daily Diaries of Peer Interaction by College Students in South Korea, Indonesia, and the United States

In a study by French, Bae, et al. (2006), college students in Indonesia, South Korea, and the United States kept diaries to document the peers with whom they interacted and to rate the closeness of the relationships (i.e., close friend, companions/acquaintances, nonpeer). Students then completed a form for each interaction that lasted longer than 5 minutes every day for 2 weeks.

The following is an example form from one participant, DF. In the form, DF reported an interaction that occurred among four people (i.e., two men and two women) that lasted a little more than an hour. The interaction included one close friend, two acquaintances, and one nonpeer. This conversation was average in pleasantness, low in intimacy, and absent of conflict.

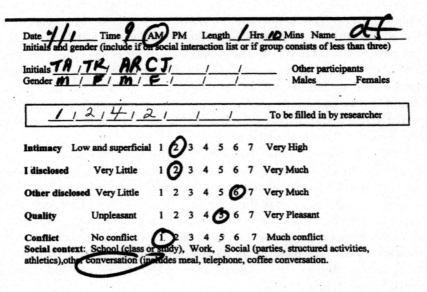

Respective numbers of reports per day for Indonesian, South Korean, and American students were 9.6, 3.6, and 4.2. When interacting with at least one friend, South Korean students reported more disclosure than Indonesian students but the same as American students. Korean students' interactions were more exclusive (interactions with close friends tended to include only close friends) than American students' interactions, and American students' interactions were more exclusive than those of Indonesian students. These patterns did not differ for men and women. Finally, Korean and American college students reported that they had known their friends longer (4.78 and 3.96 years, respectively) than did Indonesian students (2.93 years).

Instrumental Aid

One aspect of friendship that varies widely across cultures is the extent to which friends provide each other with assistance. This may include helping with chores, assisting with schoolwork, supporting friends against others, or providing money or tangible goods. Instrumental aid is likely an important aspect of friendships, but it is generally considered inappropriate to think about friendships in such utilitarian terms in Western cultures. Ideas pertaining to friendship and instrumental aid in Western cultures date from Aristotle and likely earlier. Aristotle contrasted perfect, true, and virtuous friendships between people who love each other for their own sake with imperfect forms of friendship that are based on pleasure or gain (Sherman, 1993). Nevertheless, providing help to friends is likely important in many countries, including the United States. Way (2006), for example, found that an important feature of the friendships of American low-income Black and Latino adolescents was sharing money and protecting each other from harm. She also found that help with schoolwork was a salient aspect of friendship mentioned by Asian American youth.

Numerous studies suggest that instrumental aid is an important aspect of friendship in many cultures and this is often expressed more overtly and is more socially acceptable than it is in the United States. DeRosier and Kupersmidt (1991) found that Costa Rican children reported more instrumental aid between friends than did American children, and a similar finding emerged from the comparison of Cuban and American children (GonzáLez et al., 2004). Nydegger and Nydegger (1963) found that children from the Philippines who were studied as part of the Six Cultures Study adopted adult norms of community assistance by helping their peers with their schoolwork. Finally, the importance of instrumental aid is illustrated by studies in China where children's friendships are partly based on helping each other with schoolwork (Chen, Kaspar, et al., 2004), and parents openly promote friendships between their child and academically successful peers in an effort to boost their child's school achievement (J. Li, 2012). The previous results are consistent with Tietjen's (1989) claim suggesting that instrumental aid is likely to be particularly salient in the friendships of children from collectivist cultures. It is possible, however, that instrumental aid is important in the friendships of European American youth but that they are reluctant to report this because of social desirability.

Exclusivity

An additional aspect of friendship that varies across cultures is exclusivity, which refers to the boundaries of friendships and the extent to which non-friends are allowed to permeate these boundaries. Differences between cultures in this aspect of friendship are illustrated by the diary study of South Korean, Indonesian, and American college students discussed in Research Highlight 7.1. When South Korean students were with their friends, acquaintances and non-friends were typically not present. In contrast, Indonesian students had the lowest exclusivity scores, with American students scoring between these extremes. These variations can be observed from informally watching college students in these countries as they walk in the streets around campus. It is most common for Korean students to be in same- or opposite-sex dyads or to be in mixed-sex triads that include an opposite-sex relationship partner along with a friend of one or the other partners. In contrast, Indonesian students, and to some extent American students, are more frequently in larger groups. These interaction patterns reflect the extreme intimacy of South Korean friendships that may be facilitated by being in groups comprised solely of close friends. Parents attempt to instill cultural values about exclusivity in their children at an early age. Indonesian parents reinforce the importance of children being a member of a peer group and not being an isolate. An empirical study of preschool parents' beliefs pertaining to peer relationships in four countries (Norway, Turkey, South Korea, and the United States) found that South Korean parents attached greater importance to their child developing a close relationship with a classmate than did parents in the other countries (Aukrust et al., 2003). American parents, in contrast, emphasized the importance of learning to get along well with peers in general, but were less concerned about their child developing a close and continuing relationship with another child.

Conflict

It is essential to manage conflict if friendships are to be established and maintained (Gottman & Parker, 1986). Gottman (1983) provided strong evidence of the importance of conflict management to friendship after observing previously unacquainted pairs of American preschool children in four play sessions held at the home of one of the children. The children engaged in free play, and their conversations were audio recorded and examined to determine the qualities that predicted the likelihood that the children would later become friends. Gottman found that frequency of conflict and failure to resolve conflict interfered with children's success engaging in elaborate and satisfying play, and predicted a decreased likelihood of becoming friends.

In Chapter 8, we review cultural differences in how children and adults manage conflict, suggesting that children learn cultural modes of dealing with conflict early in life and use and refine them throughout the life span. For now, it is important to note that conflict management is a crucial aspect of close relationships that varies across cultures.

SOCIAL NETWORKS

Child and adolescent peer interactions often occur within social networks, defined as groups of peers who regularly interact. Networks can include friends, playmates, acquaintances, and even enemies. These days it is common for youth to develop online social networks with peers, some of whom they will never meet in person. Networks are important because they provide a context for companionship, academic activities, delinquency, romantic relationships, and other activities to occur.

There are cultural variations in the characteristics of networks. Networks may differ in features such as size, gender composition, age homogeneity, and the extent to which members are similar to each other on such qualities as aggression, substance use, delinquency, academic achievement, and athletic skill. This was shown in the diary study of college students discussed previously (French, Bae, et al., 2006). Indonesian and American students interacted in larger groups than South Korean students. Indonesian students also interacted with more unique individuals ($n = 41.61$) than either American ($n = 21.38$) or South Korean students ($n = 21.49$). These results suggest that the networks of Indonesian students are larger and more heterogeneous than those of either South Korean or American students.

In a recent study of the characteristics of children's networks across cultures, fifth-grade children from China, Indonesia, and the United States reported their own and peers' network affiliations by listing "who hangs around with whom" (Shen et al., 2019). The data from students in each class were used to generate a mapping of social groups. Consistent with the previous results, Indonesian students were connected with more peers through network membership (12.34) than either Chinese (10.67) or American students (7.00). The American networks were less segregated by gender (14% of the children were affiliated with a member of the opposite sex) than were Chinese (10%) and Indonesian (5%) networks. Chinese students were more likely to affiliate with peers who were similar to them in academic level than were students in the other countries. Thus, there appear to be cultural parameters for networks that parallel those for friendships.

PEER INFLUENCE

Social networks are particularly important because membership in these groups may impact adjustment in multiple ways. For example, membership in an academically high-achieving network may enhance academic motivation and promote academic achievement. Conversely, membership in a group of substance-using peers is associated with increased substance use (e.g., French, Purwono, & Rodkin, 2014; M. E. Roberts et al., 2015).

Fundamental to understanding peer influence is that individuals resemble others with whom they associate in their behavior, personality, and attitudes. This similarity is commonly referred to as *homophily* and emerges from the coexistence of two processes. The first, labeled *selection*, refers to the tendency of individuals to select others who are similar to themselves. Selection processes are particularly important in explaining deviant behavior, as youth who engage in rule-breaking or substance use tend to affiliate with each other and thus contribute to the escalation of problem behavior (Dishion et al., 1996). The second process, labeled *influence*, is the tendency for individuals to become more similar over time to people with whom they interact. Dishion et al. (1996) has documented how deviant peers reinforce each other to endorse antisocial attitudes. Influence processes are complex and include modeling, reinforcement, engagement in certain activities (i.e., presence in similar activity settings), and the development of shared values (Allen & Antonishak, 2008).

There are cultural differences in the selection processes pertaining to academic success. Vitoroulis et al. (2012) compared peer and parent influences on the intrinsic academic motivation of 12-year-old adolescents in Canada, Cuba, and Spain. They found that parents had the strongest influence on the academic motivation of Cuban adolescents whereas friends had the greatest influence on Canadian adolescents. There are also differences across cultures in the selection qualities that are important. For example, the study of fifth-grade children described previously revealed that friends and network affiliates were more similar in their academic level in China than in either the United States or Indonesia. J. Li (2012) suggested that academic success is an important element in the selection of peer associates in China.

Both selection and influence processes are important, but the relative importance of each likely varies across cultures. For example, in a study of the relative importance of selection and influence pertaining to tobacco use of adolescents in six European countries (Mercken et al., 2009), selection effects emerged across all countries, but significant influence effects were found in only two countries. In the United States, it appears that selection processes explain most of the change in substance use, whereas influence may be the major factor in the tobacco and alcohol use of Chinese peers (see Research Highlight 7.2). There is a need for additional research to explore how selection and influence processes vary as a function of the target behavior, culture, and gender.

ROMANTIC RELATIONSHIPS

Adolescents in many countries begin to transition from the same-sex associations of childhood to interactions with opposite-sex peers. The timing of this transition varies across cultures, and this behavior is typically subject to strong cultural rules. In societies such as China and South Korea, teachers and parents discourage adolescents from being romantically involved during middle and high school. In contrast, in the United States and many European cultures, it is considered normal for adolescents to become romantically involved, and there are events, such as school dances, to facilitate this.

The extent to which adolescents become romantically involved varies across cultures. S. Miller et al. (2009) found that 91% of seventh-grade American adolescents reported either current or past involvement in a romance. Romantic relationships are less common in China. Among 16- to 17-year-old Chinese adolescents, only 40% of boys and 20% of girls reported having a romantic relationship, a rate considerably lower than that of Canadian adolescents (i.e., 86% of boys and 82% of girls; Z. H. Li et al., 2010).

Even in countries such as the United States, where adolescent romantic involvement is encouraged, many adolescents do not engage in this activity

RESEARCH HIGHLIGHT 7.2

Chinese Adolescents' Substance Use, Peer Selection, and Influence

DeLay et al. (2020) recently reported in a 3-year longitudinal study of middle school youth that peer selection and influence processes for tobacco and alcohol use differ for Chinese adolescents from what is typically found in other countries. This research followed adolescents over time, and complex statistical procedures (Simulation Investigation for Empirical Network Analysis [SIENA]) were used to assess the extent to which adolescents developed new friendships with youth who were similar to them in substance use (selection) or changed their behavior in ways that corresponded to the substance use of their friends (influence). Whereas selection is most prominent in the United States and Europe, influence appears to predominate in China.

On the basis of focus group discussions with Hong Kong adolescents, Yoon et al. (2015) suggested that Chinese adolescents typically congregate with friends and associates in places such as restaurants, street markets, or karaoke establishments where they can openly drink and smoke (although the legal drinking age is 18); some adolescents use substances and others do not. Peers put little pressure on one another to use substances, but adolescents may do so as a way to connect to the group. Youth smoking and drinking practices appear to correspond to Chinese adult smoking and drinking customs that have been prominent for 5,000 to 9,000 years, in which substances play an important part in celebration and are seen as a way to develop harmonious relationships. Chinese adolescents are often introduced to alcohol by their parents in family gatherings. Note that in contrast to what is typical in the United States where youth need to connect with deviant peers to obtain and use substances, Chinese adolescents can more openly purchase tobacco and alcohol and use them in public.

(Larson & Verma, 1999). Sullivan (1953) theorized that positive same-sex friendships of childhood prepare youth to develop successful romantic relationships later in life. In support of this hypothesis, French Canadian adolescents who were liked by their same-sex peers at age 12 were more romantically successful—as indexed by number of partners and time spent in a relationship—during the period from 16 to 24 years than their less-liked peers (Boisvert & Poulin, 2016). Connolly et al. (2000) further reported that the extent to which adolescents were involved in a mixed-sex social network in 10th grade predicted romantic relationships in 11th grade.

Cultural differences exist in the acceptability of adolescent romance and the timing and conditions under which this is expected to occur. Shen et al. (2020) longitudinally assessed romantic involvement of Indonesian 10th- through 12th-grade students and the relation between romance, religiosity, and problem behavior. Similar to American youth, Indonesian youth increased their progression from interest in the opposite sex to mixed-sex social activities, to dating, and then to steady dating. Although the progression was the same, Indonesian youth progressed at a slower rate than North American youth. Shen et al. suggested that Indonesian parents typically do not approve of high-school students engaging in certain types of romantic activities, and consequently, engagement in such behavior can be viewed as rule-breaking.

Consistent with this view, the progression of romantic activities was associated with problem behavior (i.e., smoking, drinking, and minor rule-breaking), suggesting that romance was associated with deviant behavior. Note that this pattern differs from what has been found for North American youth; romantic activities are associated with problem behavior for early but not late adolescence, during which time romance is viewed as normative and socially competent behavior.

In Indonesia and many other cultures, rules exist for courtship. Bennett (2005) discussed three types of courtship that were practiced by adolescents in a traditional Muslim village. Traditional courtship is widely practiced by young women ages 16 and older and involves entertaining suitors at their home in a public area (porch or sitting area) under the supervision of parents. This courtship is presumed to be a prelude to marriage. *Romance modern* activities occur in settings such as shopping malls, discos, restaurants, and bars, and it is common for these activities to occur in groups or under the chaperonage of a sibling or someone else. Finally, *romance backstreet* activities are clandestine, and may be associated with deviant activities such as substance use and minor problem behavior.

Unfortunately, most of the research on adolescent romance has been conducted in North America and Europe, so research is needed in other regions of the world. As was the case in Indonesia, it is likely that youth across the world have romantic interests but that the expression of these interests is strongly affected by cultural scripts and the activity settings that adolescents typically occupy. In many countries in Africa and Asia, research has focused on adolescent marriage (rather than romantic relationships), as 20% of girls worldwide are married before the age of 18, with prevalence rates over 50% in eight countries and as high as 76% in Niger (Girls Not Brides, 2019; see Chapter 15 for further discussion of adolescent marriage).

A major limitation of the research on culture and adolescent romance is the paucity of information pertaining to lesbian, gay, bisexual, and transgender (LGBT) youth. Because of the sensitivity surrounding this area, researchers have been reluctant to explore it, and adolescents have been reluctant to self-report their sexual identity. The reluctance of LGBT youth to report their sexual orientation and gender identity is understandable given the severe social stigma, and in some countries, criminal penalties. Consequently, much of our information about this issue has come from case studies (see Herdt, 1989), and there is a need for further research on culture and romantic partnerships of LGBT youth.

PEER STATUS

Much of the research on peer relationships has focused on status hierarchies that exist within peer groups. Dominance hierarchies and bullying are important status systems that will be discussed in Chapter 8. Two other status systems, social acceptance and popularity, are discussed next.

Social Acceptance

Social acceptance hierarchies are derived from assessments of the extent to which peers like and dislike others in their social group (Asher & Coie, 1990). A major focus of this research is the extent to which individual differences in acceptance (high positive scores and low negative scores) and rejection (low liking and high negative scores) by peers are associated with social adjustment. There is some evidence that the correlates of social acceptance differ across cultures.

Peer rejection has been consistently associated with aggression (Asher & Coie, 1990), a finding that has been replicated in diverse countries such as China (Che et al., 1995) and Finland (Salmivalli et al., 2000). It appears that rejection is more strongly associated with aggression in countries such as Indonesia and China, where interpersonal harmony is strongly valued (Chen, 2011).

Researchers have also studied cultural differences in the associations of shyness with social acceptance and rejection. In the United States, Canada, and some European countries, assertiveness is highly valued and shyness is typically associated with peer rejection. In other countries, such as China, socially reticent behavior is more accepted (Chen, 2011), and shy children have historically been more accepted by their peers. We will have more to share about this issue in Chapter 12 when we discuss culture and social withdrawal and shyness.

Popularity

Popularity is an index of visibility and social power (Cillessen et al., 2011) and is an important aspect of status in many children's groups (Adler & Adler, 2001). Although this construct overlaps with social acceptance, there are important distinctions between them. Socially accepted American youth typically exhibit low overt and relational aggression. In contrast, popular youth tend to be aggressive and display high levels of overt (i.e., physical and verbal) and relational aggression. Because popular youth also tend to be prosocial, they can be described using the bi-strategic control framework proposed by Hawley (2003), in which individuals selectively and strategically use a combination of prosocial behavior and coercion to attain status and secure resources. Hawley described this bi-strategic strategy as "Machiavellian" in reference to the Renaissance diplomat and philosopher (author of *The Prince*). In addition to aggressive and prosocial behavior, popular youth in the United States can also be physically attractive, athletically skillful, romantically involved, and engaged in minor deviant behavior.

There are questions regarding the extent to which the constellation of behavior and characteristics that are associated with popularity in the United States and Europe exist in other countries. Bellmore et al. (2011) suggested that the determinants of popularity reflect the norms and values of the culture. If this is the case, we could hypothesize that the correlates of popular status will vary across cultures. For example, perhaps the association between popularity and aggression might be lower in cultures that emphasize social harmony and avoid conflict. In addition, it is possible that the characteristics associated with popularity in the United States and Europe may reflect an emphasis on youth autonomy and beliefs regarding the encouragement of romantic involvement.

Research on popularity in China provides a test of the extent to which models of popularity are generalizable beyond North America and Europe. There is some evidence that popular Chinese adolescents are aggressive, although these effects do not appear to be as strong or consistent as the associations between popularity and aggression found in the United States (Lu et al., 2018). These results suggest that the distinction between social acceptance and popularity found in the United States also exists in China. As expected given the importance of academic achievement in Chinese schools, the relation between popularity and academic achievement appears to be stronger in China than in the United States. Popular Chinese youth also appear to be prosocial, perhaps more so than popular American youth (Lu et al., 2018). Lu et al. (2018), for example, found that popularity was associated with prosocial behavior in a longitudinal study of seventh- through 12th-grade Chinese adolescents. The relation between popularity and prosocial behavior is particularly interesting given Confucian ideas that leaders are responsible for helping others.

Results from research in China and other countries (e.g., Indonesia, Europe) suggest that it is meaningful to think that peer groups in many parts of the world are organized by popularity. Popularity is particularly relevant to school peer groups in which large numbers of same-age youth come together, often with limited adult control. At the same time, however, it is likely that there are differences across cultures with regard to the characteristics of popular youth on such dimensions as aggression, academic success, athletic prowess, and physical attractiveness.

ORIGINS OF CULTURAL DIFFERENCES IN PEER RELATIONSHIPS

It is likely that the organization of peer groups is strongly associated with social organization of the culture. Some cultures that are organized based on the primacy of the family unit may also have very strong friendships. In these cultures, very close friends are often integrated into the family unit and are essentially treated as brothers or sisters. In other cultures, the primacy of the extended kinship group may leave little space for friends (Gaskins, 2006). In contrast, the social structure of some societies is more communal with the village, rather than the family, the essential unit of organization. For example, in Indonesia, wet rice agriculture relies on very strong interdependence of everyone in the village. Within this social structure, integration into the overall peer group is more strongly emphasized than developing specific dyadic friendships.

It does not appear that variation in individualism and collectivism fully accounts for the cultural differences in friendships. Consider the Triandis et al. (1988) argument that individuals from collectivist cultures are more likely to develop close relationships with a small group of peers whereas those from individualistic cultures develop relationships low in intimacy with a larger number of peers. In contrast to this opinion, students from different countries high in collectivism have been found to exhibit very different patterns of peer relationships from one another (French, Lee, et al., 2006). Thus, in asking the question of the origins of cultural differences in peer relationships, we return to the arguments presented in Chapter 1 that suggest factors associated with economic patterns, migration, and history may explain peer relationships as they do with other aspects of culture.

CONCLUSION

Peer relationships are embedded within cultural rule, value, and meaning systems that define the peers with whom children can and cannot form relationships and the parameters of these relationships. We have seen in this chapter how friendships, network affiliations, romantic relationships, and status systems are embedded in cultural systems.

We have also seen the applicability of the activity-setting analysis to understanding peer relationships. It is useful to understand the spaces that children typically occupy, the people who occupy these settings, the activities and interactions that occur within them, and the cultural meanings attached to these settings. Cultures differ in the extent to which parents and others value peer interaction and afford children access to peers and settings that facilitate various types of interaction.

Major gaps remain in our understanding of culture and peers given that most research is confined to North America, Europe, China, and a few other Asian countries. There is almost no information available on peer relationships in Africa, Mexico, and South America, creating a major impediment to understanding peer relationships across cultures.

For additional resources, see the Appendix.

DISCUSSION QUESTIONS

1. In addition to differences across cultures in qualities of friendship (e.g., intimacy, instrumental aid, exclusivity, conflict management), there are also individual differences within cultures. How large are within-culture differences in friendship in comparison with between-culture differences?

2. How are adolescents encouraged or discouraged to engage with peers within various ethnic or cultural groups?

3. What are the similarities and differences between the benefits of having a friend or being a member of a peer network?

4. How do selection and influence processes explain the impact of peers across multiple domains (e.g., academic success, religion, delinquency)?

5. What do children and adolescents derive from their relationships with peers that they do not obtain from other social relationships?

8

Culture and Conflict Management During Childhood and Adolescence

Although these low-income Indian children in India appear to be playing, they need to regulate their emotions and behavior so such episodes do not escalate into aggression.

Most guidebooks for conducting international business include a section on managing conflict. For example, the authors of the book *Working With Thais: A Guide to Managing in Thailand* (Holmes et al., 1997) warn people who are doing business in Thailand to avoid directly criticizing people or their ideas and instead urge them to compromise even if doing so is inefficient or requires a less-than-optimal solution. In contrast, another work suggests that people doing business in South Korea should socialize and build relationships with others throughout the office before bringing up problematic issues. How do these cultural variations in conflict management arise?

https://doi.org/10.1037/0000228-008
Child and Adolescent Development in Cultural Context, by J. E. Lansford, D. C. French, and M. Gauvain

In this chapter, we argue that cultural forms of conflict management are learned and practiced early in life. Thus, the conflict-management methods that are described in business guidebooks are often learned by 3- and 4-year-olds at home and on the playground. Some of these rules are actively taught, but most are learned by children in the cultural environments in which they practice managing conflict, learn from watching others, and polish their skills as their actions are gradually shaped by the reactions of others (e.g., parents, teachers, and peers) to their behavior.

CHILD AND ADOLESCENT CONFLICT MANAGEMENT

All cultures require their members to manage conflict and generally believe it is important to teach children these skills early in life (de Waal, 1996). In addition to teaching children valuable skills, it is also important to control conflict between children because unregulated conflict can be disruptive to the community and lead to conflicts between adults (W. W. Lambert, 1971).

At its most basic level, *conflict* is defined as opposition, which is often verbal (Shantz, 1987). The exchange below illustrates a typical conflict episode from a free-play session between two newly acquainted 4-year-old girls in the United States (Gottman & Parker, 1986). The dialogue of the girls as they experience conflict while attempting to agree on a common play activity (i.e., making a pretend dinner) illustrates a number of themes relevant to this chapter.

D: Oh. We've got to have our dinner.

D: I'm the mommy.

J: Who am I?

D: Um, the baby.

J: Daddy.

D: Sister.

J: I wanna be the daddy.

D: You're the sister.

J: Daddy.

D: You're the *big* sister.

J: Don't play house. I don't want to play house.

J: Just play eat-eat. We can play eat-eat. We have to play that way.

J: Look hungry!

D: Huh?

J: I said look hungry!

D: Look hungry? This is dumb.

J: Look hungry!

D: No!

The previous sequence was subsequently resolved when the two girls pretended to eat without assuming fantasy roles. The example above is typical of conflicts between children, which are usually mild, occur many times a day, and are usually settled without adult intervention.

Note that neither girl used aggression, which is also typical of most conflict episodes (Shantz, 1987). The distinction between conflict and aggression is particularly relevant for addressing the question of how children manage conflict in different cultures. Aggression is only one of many consequences of conflict, and most conflicts do not involve aggression. The probability that conflict will lead to aggression varies widely across cultures, with the likelihood that aggression will occur partly a function of cultural norms regarding the acceptability of using coercive control (Björkqvist, 1997; Bond, 2004; Fry, 1988). As noted in Chapter 13, some youth live in environments in which there is considerable conflict and aggression, and it is likely that youth reared in such environments will engage in more conflict with peers and more frequently employ aggression to settle conflicts. Support for this hypothesis comes from Huesmann et al.'s (2017) finding that Palestinian and Israeli children who were exposed to political conflict developed ideas about the acceptability of aggression and had aggressive fantasies that predicted increased aggression toward peers over a 3-year period.

Finally, the behavior of the two girls illustrates the important connection between conflict management and relationships. Gottman and his colleagues found conflict management to be essential for developing and maintaining close relationships such as friendships and marriages across the life span (Gottman & Parker, 1986). It is unlikely that these two girls will become friends unless they manage their conflicts sufficiently to enable them to enjoy playing together.

CULTURE AND CONFLICT

Conflict occurs within the context of cultural systems that include meanings, values, and beliefs (Fry, 2000; H. S. Ross & Conant, 1992). The broad cultural dimension of individualism/collectivism and hierarchical structure of the society are pertinent to understanding conflict. Cultural systems can influence how individuals interpret the behavior of others, the extent to which conflicts are permissible, the type of behavior exhibited during conflict, and the methods of resolution.

Conflict-Management Scripts

It is useful to employ Kitayama and Markus's (1994) conception of socially shared scripts for dealing with provocations to understand conflict and culture. *Scripts* are cognitive knowledge structures that organize sequences of everyday events. We can apply this model to conflict with the assumption that when children experience a provocation, they activate a well-practiced set of cognitions, emotions, and behaviors that are typically organized in the form of scripts. Children have multiple scripts available to them that use a variety of strategies (e.g., aggression, submission, compromise, or withdrawal) and select a response using criteria such as their goals for the interaction, the probability of success, relationship status, and situational factors. Children may employ multiple scripts within a single conflict episode so that if one script fails, they can shift to an alternative. The content of the scripts, the conditions under which they are employed, and the probability of use varies across cultures.

Earlier in this chapter, we mentioned the research from Huesmann et al. (2017) regarding the behavior of Palestinian and Israeli children who were exposed to political conflict. The authors suggested that in this high-conflict and sometimes violent environment, youth developed scripts that included aggressive responses to ambiguous provocations. The associations between script learning and aggression will be further developed in Chapter 13 on aggression, deviancy, and substance use. For now, it is important to appreciate the extent to which conflict management is associated with aggression and that similar processes (i.e., reaction to provocation, practice and use of cultural scripts) underlie both.

An important aspect of script selection is individuals' goals. A variety of goals might be relevant to any conflict. For example, children may seek to maintain positive relationships, achieve dominance, or resolve the problem by achieving a mutually acceptable solution. The relative attractiveness of these goals likely varies by culture. As will be discussed later in this chapter, Chinese and Indonesian children may approach conflict episodes with the goal of maintaining the relationships between participants and preserving harmony. In contrast, U.S. children may be more likely to approach conflicts with the goal of asserting their rights or achieving an optimal solution to the problem.

Cultural variation in conflict goals is illustrated by Medina et al.'s (2001) study of conflict of preschool children in the Netherlands and Andalusia (a region in southern Spain). The authors suggested that Dutch children entered into conflicts with the primary goal of controlling objects or space. In contrast, the Andalusian children focused on maintaining a positive relationship between the participants, as illustrated by the following two examples of conflict between Dutch and Andalusian children, respectively (Medina et al., 2001, p. 157).

In the Dutch example, a boy, Thijs, is playing with other children. They are playing with some blocks. Wietse approaches the group and takes one of the blocks:

1. THIJS: No, you must not take that. (*tries to take away the block that Wietse just took*)

2. WIETSE: Why not? (*holds the block out of Thijs's reach*)

3. THIJS: That's for (me) . . .

4. THIJS: (*now takes the block, grabbing it from Wietse's hands*)

5. THIJS: (*continues playing and Wietse turns his back on the group and walks away*)

Contrast the previous script with the following script, in which Andalusian children attempt to minimize conflict and find a common group activity. In this example, Maria and Ana Cecilia are deciding whether to play a game of Sleeping Beauty or Snow White.

1. ANA CECILIA: I want to play Snow White.

2. MARIA: Well you play, not me.

3. MARIA: (*lets go of Ana Cecilia and leaves upset*)

4. ANA CECILIA: (*goes after her*)

5. ANA CECILIA: Well, alright Maria. (*again takes her by the hand*)

6. MARIA: Do you want to play a game of Clowns?

7. ANA CECILIA: No, I don't feel like it.

8. MARIA: (*begins to act silly, imitating a clown, and they both end up laughing*)

Conflict Sequences

Conflicts unfold in a four-stage sequence that includes preconflict, mutual opposition, conflict termination, and postconflict periods (Shantz, 1987). In the following sections, we illustrate how cultural scripts differ across each of these stages.

Preconflict

During the initial preconflict stage, participants are confronted with provocation. If they react to this provocation with opposition, then a conflict ensues. Individuals, however, may elect not to react to this provocation and may ignore it, withdraw from the interaction, or engage in other actions, such as submission, that prevent the conflict from occurring.

There has been limited research exploring how individuals in different cultures behave during this preconflict period. Perhaps this is because it is difficult to study conflicts that do not occur. Nevertheless, there are major differences across cultures in the acceptability of conflict and in the actions that participants take to either initiate or mitigate the conflict (Fry, 2000). Rothbaum et al. (2000) suggested that North American culture tends to view conflict as desirable, and consequently, they are less likely than people in some other cultures to avoid conflicts. In contrast, Japanese cultural norms suggest that it is often preferable to avoid conflict even if the underlying issue is unresolved. A major component of conflict management in both Indonesia and China includes efforts to prevent overt conflict from occurring by avoiding people and issues that might precipitate a conflict, and withdrawing or submitting when presented with provocations.

Mutual Opposition

With the initiation of opposition, a conflict ensues. Sociolinguists have provided rich descriptions of how children in different cultures react to an initial opposition (A. R. Eisenberg & Garvey, 1981). Goodwin (1982), for example, described a process whereby inner-city African American youth engaged in confrontation and assertions of relative power.

Corsaro and Rizzo (1990) conducted an ethnographic study of the disputes between American and Italian children ages 2 to 4. They video- or audio-recorded the children's play and identified the disputes that arose. Across both countries, most disputes arose from controversies pertaining to the play activities. Similar to the play episode of the two 4-year-old girls that we presented at the beginning of this chapter, many of these disputes arose over possession of objects, occupancy of space, and the fantasy roles and activities of the persons involved.

Although there were many common features in the conflicts between the American and Italian children, Corsaro and Rizzo (1990) noted that the Italian children were more sophisticated in their language use during disputes than the American children. Italian preschool children engaged in "discussione," in which the act of participating in an elaborated argument, rather than the issue of contention, was the primary purpose. The authors suggested that this emphasis on style of discourse shown by the preschool children parallels the elaborated "discussione" of Italian adult discourse. It is also common for Italian children to introduce a repetitive sing-song chant into their dispute, a practice referred to as "cantilena." This is illustrated in the following segments from an elaborate dialogue by a group of 4-year-old Italian children (Corsaro & Rizzo, 1990, pp. 58–59).

1. **S:**   Wolves do not exist.

2. **GA:** Yes, wolves exist.

3. **S:**   They don't exist—only their bones.

6. **F:**   But, they do not exist . . . only in the mountains.

18. F: Yes. Yes, they exist. Ghosts however exist—

19. N: They are in the woods.

20. F: Eh, it's not true. Ghosts exist under the sea in houses—

23. GI: In—in abandoned houses.

24. S: It's true, underwater houses.

(*Sing-song cadence begins*)

25. S: In the—the dark houses. They stay in the dark—

26. GI: Yes, it's true.

27. F: And under the sea—it's dark.

28. N: Yes, it's true.

29. S: And under—they go there.

30. L: No, also crabs go there.

31. F: Submarines go there.

32. N: And also sharks.

These and other examples illustrate that conflict is an integral component of young children's play, and children are capable of using sophisticated strategies to manage conflict. These examples also illustrate that young children often deal with conflict in a similar manner as do adults in their culture (Garvey & Shantz, 1992).

Conflict Resolution

There is considerable diversity in the ways that conflicts are resolved across cultures. Fry (2000) proposed that there are five methods typically used to solve disputes; these include negotiation, coercion, avoidance, toleration, and third-party intervention (including mediation, or decision by a third party).

The likelihood that different methods will be employed varies across cultures. In individualistic cultures, for example, negotiation appears to be the preferred method, whereas in collectivist cultures, mediation, toleration, and third-party intervention are more prominent (Markus & Lin, 1999).

The form of these resolution methods also varies considerably across cultures. For example, third-party mediation in Indonesian villages has traditionally occurred through group discussion (Magnis-Suseno, 1997), whereas in traditional Chinese communities, this is more likely to be accomplished by an authority figure (Wall & Blum, 1991). It is also common for children to involve themselves as third parties in the conflicts of their peers. Such involvement, however, is often not effective. Chaux (2005) interviewed Colombian children between the ages of 8 and 14½ about their conflicts and found that third-party peers were involved in almost two thirds of the conflict episodes. Rather than mediate the dispute, the peers typically sided with one of the participants, and facilitated a peaceful outcome only 25% of the time.

Postconflict

The final stage, which has received little attention, is the postconflict period. This aspect of conflict has been most studied by de Waal and his colleagues (Aureli & de Waal, 2000; Butovskaya et al., 2000) under the label of "peacemaking." de Waal's interest in this phase of conflict emerged from observations of nonhuman primates who typically engaged in acts of reconciliation following acts of aggression. He suggested that it is evolutionarily adaptive for individuals to reconcile following conflict, and that peacemaking may be particularly common between people who have relationships with each other, such as friends and family members.

Butovskaya et al. (2000) observed the peacemaking of children between the ages of three and seven in Russia, Sweden, Italy, and the United States and witnessed both explicit and implicit peacemaking across the four cultures. In the United States, peacemaking activities included continued play, apologies, or hugs. The Russian children sometimes held hands and recited a peacemaking rhyme: "Make peace, make peace, don't fight, if you fight, I'll bite, and we cannot bite since we're friends" or "If you bite, I'll hit you with a brick, but the brick breaks, and the friendship begins again" (p. 249).

INDIVIDUAL DIFFERENCES IN CONFLICT MANAGEMENT

Although the major emphasis of this chapter is the cultural patterns of conflict management, it is important to recognize that within-culture differences exist in the extent to which children use various conflict-management scripts. Children also differ in their effectiveness of using these scripts. These variations have been most extensively studied in North America (Crick & Dodge, 1994; Spivack & Shure, 1974).

Common to the models of Crick and Dodge (1994) and Spivack and Shure (1974) is the view that individuals approach conflict situations with numerous alternative actions (i.e., scripts) available to them (see Chapter 13). Socially competent children are more likely than other children to use effective, prosocial, and nonaggressive scripts (Murphy & Eisenberg, 2002; Perry et al., 1992; Putallaz & Sheppard, 1992). Rose and Asher (1999), for example, found that children who had friends were less likely to select alternatives that involved hostility or sought revenge than those without friends. Research Highlight 8.1 describes another study linking conflict management with social competence.

Because the desirability and effectiveness of alternative scripts varies by culture, socially competent children are more likely to use problem-solving strategies that are consistent with cultural norms (Ogbu, 1981). If children select scripts that are well practiced and accepted within the community, groups of

RESEARCH HIGHLIGHT 8.1

Do Conflict Management Skills Enable Children to Handle Stress?

Z. Wang et al. (2020) explored the possibility that using effective conflict-management skills helps children deal with the stress brought on by being victimized by their peers. Fifth-grade Chinese children self-reported the extent to which they were victimized by peers, and their level of loneliness and depression. Children also rated their use of various conflict-management skills. Solution-focused conflict-management behavior included efforts to constructively solve conflicts by learning about the views of others and suggesting possible solutions that benefit both parties (e.g., "I suggest we work together to solve conflicts"; "I listen to my classmate's point of view when we disagree"). In contrast, other conflict-resolution behavior includes attempts to control others (e.g., "When my classmates and I disagree, I keep arguing until I get my way") and nonconfrontation ("I keep quiet about my views to avoid disagreements with my classmate").

Z. Wang et al. (2020) found that conflict resolution moderated the associations between victimization and depression and loneliness. Specifically, children who endorsed solution-focused conflict management experienced less depression and loneliness associated with victimization than those who used either control or nonconfrontation strategies. This provides further evidence that the successful management of conflict is an important aspect of social competence, and that children who effectively employ constructive methods are better adjusted than those who use less effective methods such as power assertion and submission and avoidance.

children are likely to agree quickly on a way to address the conflict. In the United States, examples of widely shared scripts include coin flipping, playing "rock-paper-scissors," or taking turns. By looking at the behavior of socially competent children, it is possible to obtain an insider's perspective of the meaning of conflict behavior in different cultures (French et al., 2008).

SOCIALIZATION OF CONFLICT MANAGEMENT

As we noted at the beginning of this chapter, it is essential that children learn conflict-management skills at an early age. Parents, teachers, and others spend considerable time teaching children these skills in an effort to maintain social harmony in the community as well as to teach young children the competencies that they will need to be successful throughout their lives.

Tobin et al.'s (2009) analyses of preschools in three cultures provide insight into how teachers in Japan and the United States react differently to children's conflict. The authors described an instance in which several 3-year-old Japanese girls tug on a teddy bear, attempting to gain possession. In this instance, the teacher watched but did not intervene, allowing the children to resolve the conflict by themselves. This strategy is described as "observing and standing guard" that is sometimes used by Japanese teachers with the understanding that children are often capable of resolving conflicts on their own and that it is often valuable for them to do so. American teachers, on the other hand, tend to respond quickly to physical altercations between children, encouraging them to explore the feelings of others and to consider alternative behaviors. Consider the following example in which an American teacher addresses Aaron, who has just thrown a plastic bowling pin in the direction of another child.

TEACHER: Do you think it was a good idea to throw two of these? What if when you threw it, it went over there and hit one of your friends? What would have happened to them?

AARON: They'd be hurt.

TEACHER: Would you be happy? Would they be happy? No, so a good idea . . . next time would be, if you want to throw something, what would you throw?

AARON: A ball.

TEACHER: Yes, there's a ball right there.

The work of Tobin et al. suggests that there may be cultural variation in how adults intervene in children's conflict and that the approach advocated in one country might not be universally endorsed.

RESEARCH HIGHLIGHT 8.2

Cultural Variation in Children's Reactions to Parental Conflict

Children's reactions to witnessing conflict may be related to cultural norms pertaining to conflict. Cummings et al. (2003) explored how 7- to 9- and 11- to 13-year-old children from the United States and Chile reacted to parental conflict. There were two components to this study.

First, parents reported on their marital conflict (specifically hostility, verbal aggression, and physical aggression). They then reported on their child's adjustment using a standardized rating scale. Children's adjustment was negatively associated with marital physical aggression in both counties. In contrast, however, hostility and verbal aggression were associated with adjustment problems in Chile but not in the United States. Cummings et al. (2003) suggested that these results reflected Chilean children's greater sensitivity to conflict.

In the second part of this study, children listened to several audio recordings of a man and a woman speaking in the children's native language; some recordings featured pleasant conversations, and others featured arguments. Children were asked to pretend that the people in the recordings were their parents and were then asked to report on the extent to which listening to each of these made them mad, sad, or scared. Although children in both countries reported feeling sad after listening to marital conflict, the Chilean children reported feeling sadder than the U.S. children.

As a result of these findings, Cummings et al. (2003) proposed that in the collectivist culture of Chile, conflict is less acceptable than in the individualistic culture of the United States. Because of this, parental deviations from the norm are associated with greater behavior problems and negative emotional reactions of Chilean than U.S. children. Thus, cultural conflict scripts are important not only for self-conflict behavior, but also are activated when children understand and react to the conflicts of others.

Cultural conflict scripts are not only invoked when children experience conflict, but also when children judge the conflict of others. This is illustrated in Research Highlight 8.2.

CONFLICT MANAGEMENT IN NORTH AMERICA, INDONESIA, AND CHINA

In this section, we apply the frameworks discussed previously to understand conflict management in North America, Indonesia, and China. As we shall see, conflict management in these countries appears to be roughly consistent with expectations derived from the individualism and collectivism framework of cultural conflict management (Markus & Lin, 1999). The differences between Indonesian and Chinese methods of conflict management illustrate, however, that there is considerable diversity within collectivist cultures.

North America

The conflict-management models endorsed by North Americans (particularly those of European ancestry) are based on the idea that there is an optimal solution to conflicts. People are assumed to have individual rights, and it is considered optimal for individuals to assert their views and then work toward finding a solution that addresses the needs of each party. Negotiation and compromise are presumed to be the preferred methods of resolving conflicts. Sternberg and Dobson (1987), for example, found that college students chose discussion and bargaining as appropriate methods of handling conflicts with roommates. This approach to conflict resolution is advocated in many books that teach conflict management (e.g., *Getting to Yes: Negotiating Agreement Without Giving in*; *Say What's Wrong and Make It Right: Proven Strategies of Teaching Children to Resolve Conflicts on Their Own*; and *People Skills: How to Assert Yourself, Listen to Others, and Resolve Conflicts*).

American children learn these cultural scripts for conflict management at an early age. Children as young as age 2½ learn principles of ownership and possession and use them to defend their use of objects or their occupation of space (Dunn & Munn, 1987; H. S. Ross & Conant, 1992). The success of entitlement claims likely emerges from the salience of the "ownership principle" in North America, and the fact that most children know and practice these scripts. In addition to rules of possession, young children employ sharing and turn-taking scripts, which are reinforced by parents and teachers (H. S. Ross, 1996). It is important to assess children's use of entitlement justifications and sharing routines to resolve conflicts in other countries where rules of possession and individual prerogatives are not as well established.

Preschool children in the United States also identify negotiation as a preferred method of dealing with hypothetical disputes (Iskandar et al., 1995), which is consistent with the theme that children learn cultural scripts for managing conflict at a young age and practice these throughout the life span.

Laursen et al. (2001) conducted a meta-analysis in which they aggregated the results from many studies of mostly European–North American youth and found that at all ages, negotiation is the preferred method for solving hypothetical conflicts. It is important to note, however, that although children say that negotiation is the ideal way to solve conflicts, they do not consistently use this approach. In fact, Laursen et al. found that children most often settled conflicts by using coercion.

Methods of conflict management that are typically used by European American youth may not be used to the same extent by people in other ethnic groups in the United States. Markus and Lin (1999) provided an overview of distinctive styles of conflict management existing among European American, Asian American, Hispanic, and African American adults. Although ethnic variation in conflict management of American children has received little study, it is reasonable to expect that the degree of variation that has emerged in adults would also be present in children.

Indonesia

Anthropologists have been fascinated by the processes that Javanese and those in other Indonesian ethnic groups use to minimize conflict (C. Geertz, 1976; Mulder, 1996). It is important in this culture to maintain the outward appearance of interpersonal harmony described by the Javanese word "Rukun" (Magnis-Suseno, 1997). Indonesians attain this state by using multiple methods including (a) avoiding topics of disagreement, (b) refraining from interacting with those with whom one has conflicts, (c) using polite and ritualized forms of interaction, (d) avoiding external displays of emotions, and (e) not expressing strong opinions.

H. Geertz (1961) described an important feature of Indonesian social interaction: the understanding that the social order is hierarchical, and one is required to show respect to those higher in this hierarchy and kindness to those below. It is particularly important to refrain from disagreeing with superiors. Leaders are responsible for maintaining order, and overt conflict is presumed to reflect poorly upon their power (Mulder, 1996). It is, however, acceptable to disagree privately and to covertly disobey the commands.

The findings from empirical studies of Indonesian youth are consistent with the idea that it is important to minimize conflict in this culture. Haar and Krahe (1999), for example, compared German and Indonesian adolescents' preferred methods for resolving hypothetical conflicts with parents, peers, and teachers. Indonesian youth elected to use confrontation less often than did German adolescents, and instead more often chose a solution that entailed submission. In other studies, Indonesian children and adolescents rated their friendships as being lower in conflict than did American youth (French, Pidada, & Victor, 2005; French et al., 2001).

French, Pidada, Denoma, et al. (2005) conducted an interview study of conflict management of 9- to 11-year-old Indonesian and American children in which researchers asked children to describe recent conflicts that they had with peers. The conflicts of children in both countries were short, nonaggressive, and settled amicably. Indonesian children reported using disengagement to deal with conflict more often than did American children. This disengagement sometimes took the form of a shared cultural script labeled by children as "acting enemies." Children who are "acting enemies" avoid the child with whom they have a quarrel for days and sometimes weeks, until the negative emotions dissipate. At the end of this period, there is typically no apology or resolution of the incident; the children resume interacting, sometimes saying that they stopped "acting enemies." These findings are consistent with the anthropological reports described earlier of the widespread practice of maintaining interpersonal harmony by avoiding the issue of contention as well as the party involved in the conflict. This style of conflict management is exhibited not only in daily life, but also in business and politics (Friend, 2003).

Additional analyses from this study provided evidence that disengagement is positively regarded as a culturally acceptable way to deal with conflict. Teacher ratings of children's social competence were positively associated with disengagement for Indonesian but not American children, suggesting that the meaning of the behavior differs in these two cultures. In the United States, disengagement appears to reflect low assertiveness and passivity. In contrast, Indonesians consider social withdrawal from conflict to be a socially competent way of maintaining interpersonal harmony.

China

Approaches to managing conflict in China are derived from Confucianism, which stipulates that it is important to maintain interpersonal harmony by compromising, forgiving others, and being tolerant (Wall & Blum, 1991). Chinese people tend to minimize overt conflict, relying instead on withdrawal or indirect methods of resolution (Bond, 1991). In this respect, there are similarities between Chinese and Indonesian approaches to conflict management. Hierarchies are central to Chinese models of conflict management; individuals are expected to acquiesce to the demands of higher status individuals.

Chinese children exhibit less conflict than do North American children. Navon and Ramsey (1989) observed that Chinese preschool children shared materials and reacted less defensively and aggressively to attempts by peers to take materials than did American children. Orlick et al. (1990) similarly found that Chinese kindergarten children exhibited less conflict and more cooperation than did American children.

Unlike Western models, Confucian models of conflict resolution are not based on conceptions of individual rights. Instead, morality and justness are thought to exist in the natural order of the universe, and it is assumed that the sage (i.e., a philosophically wise person) comprehends this order and applies it to specific situations. These assumptions underlie traditional community mediation systems that operate quite differently from the mediation systems that work to help individuals negotiate mutually beneficial solutions (Wall & Blum, 1991). These Chinese systems are not necessarily voluntary; mediators have authority to intervene in conflicts that come to their attention. Second, mediators may know the parties involved, and there is no presumption that they are neutral. Third, the goal of mediation is to settle the dispute, not necessarily to ensure that the participants are satisfied with the outcome. Fourth, the mediator often tells participants how they should think and behave and attempts to persuade the protagonists to adopt these views. The use of an authority to manage conflicts is widely used in Chinese society. It is typical for group leaders to assume responsibility for regulating conflict among persons in a group, mediating disputes, and keeping order (Bond & Hwang, 1986).

French and colleagues (2011) gained insight into the processes that Chinese children use to manage conflict by observing how quartets of unacquainted 9-year-old Chinese and Canadian children dealt with provocations that occurred after being presented with a highly attractive toy that only one child could play with at a time (French et al., 2011). Chinese children displayed behavior likely to reduce conflict by relinquishing control of the toy to others, whereas Canadian children assertively sought control. French et al. assessed perspectives on the meaning of these behaviors by comparing each individual's behavior in the group sessions with group members' ratings of each individual's likeability. Within the Chinese groups, group members liked children who displayed a somewhat reticent and cooperative style by making relatively few attempts to play with the toy and allowing others to do so. The opposite pattern emerged for Canadian children; group members liked children who were assertive and disliked those who were more passive. Thus, it appears that exhibiting cooperative behavior and avoiding conflict by acquiescence is associated with competence in China, whereas assertiveness and control of resources appear to be valued in Canada.

Also emerging from the French et al. (2011) study was evidence that children as well as adults use the "leadership conflict-management script." In 78% of the Chinese groups, a single child or pair of children attempted to structure the group actions; this behavior occurred in only 46% of Canadian groups. The exhibition of leadership behavior by these children is noteworthy given that they were age-mates and were previously unfamiliar with each other. This likely reflects that this script is prominent among children, perhaps because it is common for children to assume formal and informal leadership roles in Chinese schools and youth organizations.

CONCLUSION

We conclude this section by reviewing a few important themes. First, children learn conflict management at an early age. Parents and teachers actively teach some of these approaches, but for the most part, children learn them by watching others and practicing them in their daily interactions with peers and adults.

Many of the conflict-management techniques used by adults began in childhood.

Second, it is useful to think of the central role of well-practiced cultural scripts for managing conflict. The utility of these scripts stems partly from the fact that they are widely shared. For example, "rock-paper-scissors" is a common technique used in the United States for resolving conflicts because many people know this script and agree that it is a good way to solve disagreements. Thus, the child who says, "Let's do rock-paper-scissors" in the middle of a conflict may be greeted with widespread agreement.

Third, although the primary focus of this chapter is on conflict between children, the general principles of conflict management apply across the age span and generalize among a variety of situations. This is illustrated by the work of Markus and Lin (1999) who found that the cultural patterns of conflict management discussed in this chapter also pertain to adults. One of the remarkable aspects of research on child conflict is that children learn and practice the cultural conflict-management behavior at an early age. After defeating Napoleon, The Duke of Wellington famously said, "The battle of Waterloo was won on the playing fields of Eaton," meaning that the English officers learned and polished their skills during sport activities at this elite boarding school. We can adapt this to say that the conflict-management skills practiced daily in government offices and corporate boardrooms were learned and practiced by children on playgrounds throughout the world.

Fourth, it is valuable to explore how cultural approaches to conflict management are useful in explaining variations in the conflict that children have with their parents in different cultures (see Chapter 6 on family relationships). Although a full discussion of this issue is beyond the scope of this chapter, a few illustrations make these connections clear. The emphasis on negotiation and compromise that is the hallmark of conflict-management skills for European American adults is also pertinent to parent–child conflict in this culture. Ideally, parents support the developing child's increased needs for autonomy, and adolescents appreciate parents' responsibility to ensure their safety and optimal development. Within these parameters, it is assumed that parents and children can arrive at optimal solutions through negotiation and compromise (Branje, 2018). Thus, conflict occurs because of competing individual interests, and the solution lies in communication, negotiation, and compromise. This is somewhat different in China and Indonesia in which hierarchies are fundamental to conflict-management scripts. For example, the status difference between parents and children in traditional Javanese culture means that children must accept their parents' instructions without argument; disagreement brings shame to both parties. Fathers are often careful to avoid disagreements with their sons because of the risk of the child disobeying and shaming the father (Keeler, 1987). Discussions of parent–child relationships and conflict in China invariably invoke principles of filial piety that stem from Confucianism and serve as a template for parent–child relationships. This system requires children (even as adults) to obey their parents (Zhang et al., 2020).

Fifth, it is important to understand that some, but not all, of the cultural characteristics of conflict management align roughly with the individualism/collectivism model. Negotiation and assertiveness tend to be more common in individualistic cultures, whereas submission and third-party intervention are more common in collectivist cultures. The differences in the approaches used to deal with conflict in Indonesia and China, two cultures considered collectivist, however, reveal the limitations of relying upon this simplistic dichotomy.

Last, most conflict studies have been conducted in North America, so there is a need to conduct research on conflict management in other parts of the world. Little is known about conflict management of children in Africa, South America, and some parts of Europe. In addition, research is needed on conflict and culture across the life span. Most of our knowledge about conflict management outside of North America comes from the study of preschool children and adults, and we know little about how older children and adolescents manage conflict in diverse cultures.

For additional resources, see the Appendix.

DISCUSSION QUESTIONS

1. What are the implications of separating the study of culture and conflict from the study of culture and aggression?

2. How useful is the concept of scripts for understanding conflict? To what extent do people rely on well-practiced and culturally nested scripts for addressing conflicts?

3. Are there cultural scripts for addressing conflict used by ethnic groups and cultures not discussed in the chapter?

4. To what extent are the conflict-management methods used by children also used by adult members of the culture?

5. What are the implications of the viewpoint that children who have difficulty managing conflict have other adjustment difficulties? Are there implications for understanding psychopathology and developing interventions?

9

Development in Cultural Communities and Physical Spaces

Physical spaces affect child development within different cultural communities, as with this Navajo sister and brother who live in Monument Valley, Arizona, USA.

In many ways, communities, neighborhoods, physical environments and the social contexts they provide are the very crux of culture, so we devote considerable attention to social contexts in each chapter of this book. In contrast to the other chapters that position family relationships, peer relationships, behavioral development, and so forth within social contexts, this chapter focuses primarily on communities, neighborhoods, and physical environments as macrolevel contexts that have wide-ranging effects on child development both within and between cultural groups. First, we consider water, sanitation, and hygiene, which are strongly related to children's mortality,

https://doi.org/10.1037/0000228-009
Child and Adolescent Development in Cultural Context, by J. E. Lansford, D. C. French, and M. Gauvain

morbidity, physical growth, and cognitive development. Then we consider pollution, access to green space, and places that provide opportunities to retreat and to interact as features of physical environments with important implications for children's development. Next we turn to neighborhood danger, which affects children's development directly (e.g., increasing the likelihood that they will become a victim of crime) as well as indirectly (e.g., increasing parents' distress and harsh parenting, which increase children's emotional and behavioral problems). We then describe within-culture differences in children's experiences of communities that are tied to socioeconomic status, gender, and rural versus urban residence. We next discuss migration as one of the most drastic changes that can be made in children's communities as they move from one country to another. Finally, we summarize how climate change is affecting child development.

WATER, SANITATION, AND HYGIENE IN NEIGHBORHOODS AND COMMUNITIES

Communities and neighborhoods encompass both the physical and social environments to which children are exposed. The physical environment often has social implications, and the social environment often has physical implications. Consider two communities. In one community, families have purified water piped into their homes. In the other community, families must collect water from a river that is a mile from their homes. These differences in the physical environments have physical consequences for health (e.g., higher rates of diarrheal disease for families drinking water from the river), behavior (e.g., collecting water consumes a portion of time for families who must go to the river), and education (e.g., children who collect water have limited time for school). These differences in the physical environment also have social consequences (e.g., a young child in the community with piped water may not be allowed to cross the street alone, whereas a young child in the community with river water may be expected to walk long distances alone to collect water).

Even in the poorest neighborhoods in high-income countries, most residents have electricity, piped water, and flush toilets. These physical provisions are much less common in low-income countries. Globally, 11% of the population does not have access to electricity (World Bank, 2019b), 9% of the global population lacks access to water from improved sources (and 42% does not have water piped into their homes or yards), and 35% of the global population lacks improved sanitation to deal with waste (Centers for Disease Control and Prevention, 2019a). Access to electricity, clean water, and improved sanitation varies widely at the country level, between urban and rural areas, and as a function of socioeconomic status. The quality of resources available at the neighborhood level predicts child outcomes above and beyond the quality of resources available at the level of individual homes. For example, in an analysis of data from 73 health and demographic surveys, neighborhood factors predicted children's height-for-age in 22 samples, even after accounting for quality of the child's own housing (Montgomery & Hewett, 2004).

Sanitation Facilities

Each year, approximately 361,000 children under the age of 5 die from diarrhea that can be attributed to unclean water, lack of sanitation, and inadequate hygiene (World Health Organization, 2017b). Children who use toilets that are not connected to a sewer system or who share toilets with many members of the community (e.g., in the form of pit latrines where waste is collected in a hole in the ground) are at higher risk for diarrheal diseases, intestinal parasites, and other bacterial infections spread by contact with feces. Growth problems, including stunting (short height for age) and wasting (low weight for height), are more common in children not only with inadequate nutrition but also those who lack high quality hygiene and sanitation in their environments (Bradley & Putnick, 2016). In war-torn Baghdad City, Iraq, lacking access to services, including sewage drains, clean water, electricity, and a grocery store, predicted children's lower IQ scores, even controlling statistically for parents' education and household income (Ghazi et al., 2012).

Access to Clean Water

When water is not piped into homes, contamination is an important concern. For example, if children scoop water in their unwashed hands or drop water scoops onto unclean floors, drinking water can be contaminated. Improved access to clean water improves children's survival rates and decreases wasting and stunting (Mitra & Rodriguez-Fernandez, 2010). Contaminated water puts children at risk for physical health problems and cognitive decrements. For example, in Bangladesh, Mexico, Taiwan, and other countries, well water contaminated with arsenic has been related to decrements in children's IQ, with larger decrements associated with higher dose exposure to arsenic (Wasserman et al., 2004). Likewise, well water high in manganese is related to children's lower IQ scores, even after controlling for potential sociodemographic confounds (Wasserman et al., 2006). Improved access to clean water also affects children's cognitive development indirectly, as wasting and stunting impair cognitive development, and children who are ill miss more days of school. Particularly for girls, who are often the ones expected to walk long distances to collect water, lacking ready access to clean water can impact school attendance (Agesa & Agesa, 2019).

Because of the physical, social, and cognitive threats to children's development posed by unclean water, poor sanitation, and lack of hygiene, WASH (water, sanitation, and hygiene) initiatives have become among the most widely used interventions to try to decrease child mortality and morbidity and improve child development around the world (World Health Organization/ UNICEF, 2017). For example, the BabyWASH initiative in Nepal aims to improve nutrition and sanitation to prevent child stunting, which affects 38% of children from birth to age 5 in South Asia (Aguayo & Menon, 2016). The holistic 5-year program has targeted the most vulnerable children and has been successful in reducing children's stunting prior to age 2.

In any intervention, it is important to be sensitive to the cultural beliefs, prohibitions, and preferences of the community in which the intervention is attempted. For example, a WASH initiative in Bangladesh tested the efficacy of handwashing with soap compared with using waterless hand sanitizer and found that the waterless sanitizer was as effective at reducing hand contamination as traditional washing with water and soap (Luby et al., 2010). To be responsive to the reluctance of the local Muslim community to use any alcohol-based products, alcohol-free hand sanitizer was used in the intervention. Research Highlight 9.1 describes a study designed to evaluate whether interventions to improve access to clean water, sanitation, and hygiene in rural Bangladesh also improve children's development.

Sometimes interventions can be simple. For example, improving the design of buckets used for carrying water significantly reduced diarrheal diseases of children in Malawi (L. Roberts et al., 2001).

Other environmental threats to children's health and development come from diseases that are endemic in some parts of the world, such as malaria, which is a risk in 87 countries that encompass approximately 40% of the world's population (World Health Organization, 2018d). Children who contract malaria are at risk not only for physical health problems but also for

---

RESEARCH HIGHLIGHT 9.1

WASH Benefits in Bangladesh

Over 5,000 pregnant women in rural Bangladesh were enrolled in a study to evaluate the effectiveness of different water, sanitation, and hygiene (WASH) interventions on child outcomes (Tofail et al., 2018). During the first or second trimester of pregnancy, the women were randomly assigned to one of six intervention groups or a control group. Each group received a different intervention: chlorinated drinking water; improved sanitation; handwashing with soap; combined water, sanitation, and handwashing; improved nutrition through counseling and nutrient supplements; or combined water, sanitation, handwashing, and nutrition. Each intervention group also received a weekly visit from a community health promoter for 6 months and a visit every other week for the next 18 months. The control group received no intervention or community health promoter visits.

Researchers directly assessed the children's gross motor skills at the age of 1 year. Children whose mothers had participated in the combined water, sanitation, handwashing, and nutrition intervention group were more likely to be able to stand unassisted than children in the control group, and children whose mothers had received nutrition information and supplements were more able to walk without assistance. At age 2, children from all six intervention groups scored better on parent-report measures of communication, gross motor skills, and social development than children from the control group, with the largest effects for children whose mothers participated in the combined water, sanitation, handwashing, and nutrition intervention. These findings suggest that children's physical, cognitive, and social development benefit from improvements in sanitation, nutrition, and water quality.

---

impaired cognitive functioning (Boivin et al., 2019). A wide range of environmental threats can affect children's physical, cognitive, and socioemotional development, with many risks disproportionately affecting children in the poorest countries (Walker et al., 2007). Not only is understanding these environmental threats important for improving child development outcomes, understanding child development is also important for reducing environmental threats. For example, sleeping under bed nets treated with insecticide is a well-established intervention for reducing mosquito bites that can lead to malaria, but even when such bed nets are provided to families at no charge, estimates indicate that half of families do not use them (Kassam et al., 2015). Young children often do not understand the purpose of the nets and find them hot and uncomfortable, so getting families to use the nets is a challenge that can benefit from understanding child development and family relationships (Gauvain, 2018).

POLLUTION, ACCESS TO GREEN SPACE, AND FEATURES OF THE PHYSICAL ENVIRONMENT

Beyond water, sanitation, and hygiene, the physical environment is also characterized by a number of other features that are important to children's development, including pollution, access to green space, and other features of the physical environment that affect children's opportunities to retreat and interact with others. Let us consider each of these in turn.

Pollution

According to the World Health Organization (2017b), more than a quarter of child deaths worldwide are attributable to pollution (indoor and outdoor), secondhand smoke, unsafe water, lack of sanitation, and inadequate hygiene. For example, each year approximately 570,000 children under the age of 5 die of pneumonia and other respiratory infections resulting from indoor and outdoor air pollution and exposure to second-hand smoke. Because children's immune systems are still developing and their bodies are small, they are more susceptible to toxins than are adults. Interventions that provide clean fuels and eliminate the use of dung and coal for cooking and heating can reduce indoor air pollution and its associated risks to children's health (E. Thomas et al., 2015).

Exposure to pollution can also impact cognitive functioning. Exposure to nitrogen dioxide and polycyclic aromatic hydrocarbons in air pollution near industrial plants and from air and road traffic is related to cognitive delays and decrements, including memory problems, language delays, and lowered IQ (Ferguson et al., 2013). Air pollution has been thought to affect children's cognitive development by changing brain structure. For example, in highly polluted Mexico City, 57% of children had prefrontal white matter hyperintense lesions, compared with only 8% of children in less polluted Polotitlán (Calderón-Garcidueñas et al., 2011).

Like air pollution, noise pollution presents risks for children's physical and cognitive development. In studies in both laboratory and naturalistic settings, exposure to loud noise leads to children's elevated blood pressure and stress hormones (e.g., cortisol), which also interferes with learning to read and other cognitive skills (G. W. Evans & Hygge, 2007). For example, in a nationally representative sample of 8- to 14-year-old German children, those whose bedrooms faced a high-traffic street had higher blood pressure than children whose bedrooms faced a low-traffic street, even after statistically controlling for a number of other sociodemographic factors (Babisch et al., 2009). Noise exposure and physical and cognitive risks show a dose-response function, in that children who are exposed to noxious noises over longer periods of time (e.g., if they live by an airport or on a busy road), show worse physical and cognitive outcomes than children exposed to noxious noises over shorter periods of time. Children also show worse outcomes if they are exposed to noise in multiple settings, such as at home and at school.

Lead exposure has been estimated to account for 540,000 annual deaths and 13.9 million years of healthy life lost, primarily in low- and middle-income countries (World Health Organization, 2018c). Exposure can come from paint, toys, gasoline, and other products, as well as from living in proximity to industries such as mining and manufacturing that produce lead-contaminated byproducts. Because young children are more likely to put their hands and other objects in their mouths, they are more likely to ingest lead after touching peeling paint or mouthing toys than are older children and adults. Lead exposure can lead to lower IQ and elevated risk of cognitive and behavioral problems. For example, the World Health Organization (2018c) estimates that lead exposure accounts for 64% of the global incidence of developmental and intellectual nongenetic–origin disabilities.

Access to Green Space

The United Nations Educational, Scientific, and Cultural Organization (UNESCO) has led a project called "Growing Up in Cities" that is designed to give children and adolescents an opportunity to voice their opinions and participate in decisions about their neighborhood environments (Chawla & Driskell, 2006). When 10- to 15-year-olds in Argentina, India, and South Africa were asked about the physical quality of their neighborhoods, they were highly aware of the specific physical qualities of their neighborhoods, such as traffic, litter, poor sanitation, and lack of green spaces, all of which limited their opportunities to play (Ferguson et al., 2013). Children and adolescents in several other countries, including Australia, Norway, Poland, the United Kingdom, and the United States, also reported the importance of having access to green spaces to play (Ferguson et al., 2013).

Limited access to both green space and grocery stores with healthy food options has become a concern in the face of the growing worldwide obesity epidemic (G. W. Evans et al., 2010). Parents living close to street traffic in Zurich,

Switzerland, restricted their preschoolers' outdoor play, which was associated with children's reduced social and motor skills (Hüttenmoser, 1995). Other research suggests that exercising in nature has more benefits than exercising in urban settings. For example, researchers in Japan randomly assigned groups of young adults to walk in the city or in the forest, and then the next day, the groups were switched (B. J. Park et al., 2010). After walking in the forest, the participants reported that they experienced significant reductions in blood pressure, pulse rate, and stress hormones (e.g., cortisol) compared with when they walked in the city.

More access to green space also improves children's executive functioning, school performance, and psychological well-being (Bell & Dyment, 2008). Adults and children react less adversely to stressful life events when they are in proximity to nature. Adults perceive greater social cohesion and social control when they live in neighborhoods with more parks, suggesting that children who live close to green spaces may benefit from their parents' positive well-being (Ferguson et al., 2013). Likewise, playing on playgrounds with more vegetation improves children's mood and is more restorative, compared with playing in areas with less vegetation or in urban environments (Brunelle et al., 2018).

Access to green space is also important in the development of children's attitudes and behaviors related to the environment (Collado et al., 2015). Spending time enjoying nature or participating in activities that involve nature, such as fishing, as well as witnessing events that harm the environment, such as seeing a special part of nature commercially developed, are all related to the development of children's ecological beliefs and behaviors (Ewert et al., 2005). Youth movements have arisen in response to global climate change (UNICEF, 2013c). Adolescents' mental health and identity formation are fostered by the perceived ability to contribute to the environment, which can give adolescents a sense of personal control and belonging (G. W. Evans et al., 2005).

Opportunities to Retreat and Interact

Along with access to green spaces, children and adolescents also benefit from living in communities and neighborhoods that offer them opportunities to retreat from adults and spend time with peers, as well as opportunities to interact with adults in public spaces such as parks, beaches, markets, streets, squares, or other locations that are open to anyone. Although children are more likely to be in public spaces accompanied by their parents, adolescents in particular have needs for space that supports "hanging out" with peers (Brunelle et al., 2018). Participatory research with youth in low- and mixed-income neighborhoods in both high- and low-income countries found that the two main desired characteristics of urban environments were to have places to hang out and to be accepted by adults in their communities (Chawla & Malone, 2003). Being able to walk or ride bicycles in their communities is also important to teenagers, as it gives them some autonomy and improves access to public spaces.

Several design features of public spaces can either foster or hinder social interactions. For example, in public parks it is common to have benches spaced along a path that meanders through the park, which works well for individuals or couples, but not as well for groups of teenagers seeking a place to hang out and have large group conversations (Owens, 2002). Adolescents desire design features that make the public space easy to enter and exit and have anchoring objects that they can lean on while sitting or standing (Childress, 2000). Teenagers also value spaces that have definite boundaries on two or three sides and that offer a vantage point for watching other people.

As classic work in sociology (Jacobs, 1961) and contemporary research in a variety of fields (e.g., Brunelle et al., 2018) demonstrate, when designing public spaces, it is also important to be able to view the spaces from a variety of vantage points, for both safety and to reduce opportunities for crime and violence. Allowing adolescents to have unsupervised time to wander and "hang out" with peers can create opportunities for problem behaviors, such as substance use and risky sexual behavior (Dodge et al., 2006). Cultural groups vary in how much unsupervised free time children and adolescents are granted. For example, on average, East Asian adolescents are afforded less unsupervised time with peers than American and European adolescents (French & Cheung, 2018). In planning public spaces, taking into account needs of children and adolescents for both freedom and safety can help optimize their development.

NEIGHBORHOOD DANGER

Many studies have found that living in a dangerous neighborhood is related to a number of problems for youth development, including poor academic performance, more mental health issues, and risky behavior, such as violence and delinquency (Minh et al., 2017). Neighborhood danger is characterized by high-crime rates as well as deteriorating housing, abandoned buildings, vandalism, substance abuse, crowding, noise, lack of routines, and a variety of physical and psychological threats (C. E. Ross & Mirowsky, 2001). Living in a dangerous neighborhood makes it more difficult to parent effectively, in part because parents cannot rely on neighborhood resources to support their parenting instrumentally or emotionally (Deater-Deckard, 2008). Parents living in such neighborhoods may also experience more stress. Controlling for income, race, and neighborhood poverty, parents who lived in physically deteriorating New York neighborhoods were 30% more likely to have experienced depression in the previous 6 months than were parents who lived in neighborhoods of better physical quality (Galea et al., 2005).

Parents who live in more dangerous neighborhoods are less inclined to let their children play outside because of fears related to violence and drugs (Kimbro & Schachter, 2011). Dangerous neighborhoods pose risks for child development not only because of potential victimization but also because they provide more opportunities for children to perpetrate crimes and engage in delinquent behaviors (Chung & Steinberg, 2006). Children in these contexts may also be exposed to role models for risky behaviors, such as drug dealers or gang members who have access to money and other valued resources and draw children into their activities.

Despite the risks of living in a dangerous neighborhood, interpersonal and intrapersonal protective factors may help offset the risks. For example, religion and spirituality offer benefits both psychologically (reducing stress) and socially (offering a supportive community) that can help buffer both parents and children from the detrimental effects of living in a dangerous neighborhood (Lamis et al., 2014). African American fathers living in dangerous neighborhoods who were more spiritual monitored their children more closely and were more likely to teach them strategies to increase safety and protection than fathers who were less spiritual (Letiecq, 2007). For children, benefits to offset neighborhood danger may also be conferred by relationships with prosocial peers and high-quality relationships with parents (Criss et al., 2017).

Just as protective factors from other sources can offset risks of dangerous neighborhoods, positive neighborhood factors can offset risks from other sources. For example, children are less likely to affiliate with peers who engage in antisocial behavior if they live in neighborhoods that are high in social cohesion and trust among neighbors than those with low social cohesion and trust (Brody et al., 2001), suggesting that neighbors may collectively monitor children's behavior to reduce their opportunities for acting out. As another example of how neighborhoods can serve a protective function, living in an ethnically diverse neighborhood provided benefits of school readiness for children in Canada who spoke English as a second language. Upon kindergarten entry for children learning English as a second language who lived in ethnically diverse neighborhoods, there were smaller gaps between communication and general knowledge scores than for children in ethnically homogeneous neighborhoods (Puchala et al., 2010).

Characteristics of individual children can also affect how neighborhoods are related to various aspects of children's development (Minh et al., 2017). For example, the relation between neighborhood deprivation (indexed as a composite of deprivation related to income, employment, health, education, housing, other aspects of living environments, and high crime) and children's behavioral and emotional problems is attenuated for children with high cognitive abilities (Flouri et al., 2012). African American boys who grow up in disadvantaged environments (indexed as a composite of economic conditions, parenting quality, family structure and stability, and maternal depression) have been found to have shorter telomeres (a biomarker of stress exposure) than African American boys who grow up in advantaged environments; however, the relation between environment and telomere length is moderated by genetic factors related to serotonin and dopamine pathways (Mitchell et al., 2014). Boys who had the highest genetic sensitivity to context had the shortest telomeres when exposed to disadvantaged environments and the longest telomeres when exposed to advantaged environments. Thus, not all children are equally susceptible to risks associated with living in dangerous neighborhoods.

One difficulty in interpreting research findings linking neighborhood danger to child outcomes is that the studies generally rely on correlational data. Therefore, it is not possible to determine whether neighborhood danger causes these developmental problems or whether living in a dangerous neighborhood is merely correlated with other factors that play a role in the development of these problems. For example, parents in dangerous neighborhoods experience higher stress levels due to factors associated with low socioeconomic status such as not having enough money to make ends meet or being victims of crime. Parents who are experiencing high levels of stress are more likely to treat their children in harsh, punitive, and inconsistent ways than are parents in low-stress environments. Perhaps experiencing harsh parenting may be the proximal cause of children's developmental problems rather than neighborhood danger. Indeed, studies that have examined these kinds of developmental cascades find evidence for links from neighborhood danger to parents' distress to harsh parenting to child development problems (Jocson & McLoyd, 2015). For example, in more dangerous neighborhoods, caregivers provide less cognitive and linguistic stimulation, which predicts children's poorer academic achievement (Nieuwenhuis & Hooimeijer, 2016). In China, Colombia, Jordan, Kenya, the Philippines, and Thailand, both household chaos and neighborhood danger longitudinally predicted more maternal hostility, which predicted subsequent child externalizing and internalizing behaviors and worse school performance (Deater-Deckard et al., 2019).

Although most studies linking neighborhood danger to outcomes are correlational, there is evidence from experimental studies revealing causal links between neighborhood factors and child development outcomes. Research Highlight 9.2 describes findings from a housing mobility experiment aimed to improve child outcomes by moving families to neighborhoods with less poverty.

WITHIN-CULTURE DIFFERENCES IN COMMUNITY EXPERIENCES

Within a particular cultural group, community experiences often vary by socioeconomic status, gender, and urban versus rural residence. Let's consider each of these three types of within-culture factors in turn.

Socioeconomic Disparities

Most cultural groups have socioeconomic disparities among members of the group that can lead to within-culture differences in children's experiences. Colombia is a good example of how within-culture socioeconomic disparities at the neighborhood level can function. In the 1980s, the Colombian government implemented an administrative system that organized the population into six well-defined socioeconomic strata, defined based on the neighborhood characteristics rather than household income, education, or any other personal or family level characteristics. The assumption was that residents would choose to

RESEARCH HIGHLIGHT 9.2

Moving to Opportunity

In the United States, the U.S. Department of Housing and Urban Development funded a housing mobility experiment called "Moving to Opportunity," in which 4,604 families living in high-poverty housing projects in five cities were randomly assigned to one of the following three conditions: (a) a voucher for subsidized housing that could be used only in a census tract with a poverty rate less than 10%, (b) a voucher for subsidized housing that did not have a geographic restriction on where it could be used, or (c) a control group that did not receive a housing voucher. From the time of assignment to the age of 18, children in the control group lived in census tracts with poverty rates that averaged 41%, whereas children in the experimental groups lived in census tracts with lower poverty rates.

Data from tax records and other administrative records collected more than 10 years after the moves revealed that children in the experimental group who moved to a lower-poverty neighborhood before the age of 13 were 16% more likely to attend college, made 31% higher earnings, lived in lower-poverty neighborhoods as adults, and were less likely to become single parents than were children in the control group (Chetty et al., 2016). Moving to a lower poverty neighborhood improved adults' mental and physical health, sense of well-being, and safety, but did not affect adults' earnings or employment rates (Ludwig et al., 2013). Moving into a lower-poverty neighborhood as an adolescent had somewhat negative effects, perhaps because the move disrupted important social networks. Nevertheless, findings revealed that each year a child lives in a lower-poverty neighborhood increases college attendance rates and earnings in adulthood, suggesting that the duration of exposure to lower poverty neighborhoods during childhood is an important determinant of children's long-term developmental outcomes (Chetty et al., 2016).

live in the highest stratum they can afford. Residents who lived in strata 5 or 6 communities paid more for utilities (such as electricity and water) as a way to subsidize the expenses of the residents of the lower strata. An unintended consequence of this policy, however, has been stigmatization of individuals in the lower strata and more difficulty with social mobility because individuals become defined in terms of being from a certain stratum. Residents also sometimes lobby to keep their community labeled as being in a lower strata rather than being promoted to a higher strata to avoid paying higher costs (International Federation for Housing and Planning, 2019). Outcomes have been found to differ among children in Colombia's socioeconomic strata. For example, children in high strata are more likely than children in middle and low strata to have access to soap and water for regular handwashing, which can reduce illness and accompanying sequelae such as being absent from school (Lopez-Quintero et al., 2009).

Education is one way that socioeconomic status can affect the community experiences to which children are exposed. In some countries, neighborhoods are strongly tied to the quality of education children receive. In the United States, for example, 83% of funding for primary and secondary school comes from state and local taxes, with only 8% from the federal government, and 9% from private sources (United States Department of Commerce, 2010). Because families in neighborhoods with higher priced homes pay more in local property taxes, schools in these areas are better funded than schools in high-poverty neighborhoods where residents pay less in property taxes. In two adjacent school districts in the state of Illinois, for instance, the per-student spending differs by $18,000 per year, primarily because approximately half of the school funding is from local property taxes. Higher funded schools are able to hire better teachers, provide more instructional opportunities, and have more resources, all of which affect students' learning (A.T. Skinner et al., 2019). In contrast, China has a nationally standardized curriculum, textbooks, and pedagogy, which leads to a great deal of uniformity in education throughout the country, making students' educational experiences less dependent on the neighborhoods in which they live (Zhu & Chang, 2019).

Gender and Public Spaces

In many cultural contexts, concerns regarding safety prevent girls and women from venturing more into public spaces. For example, 92% of females in New Delhi report having been sexually harassed in public spaces (UN Women, 2013). Likely in part because of these harassment experiences, Indian women preferred being in groups and felt uncomfortable being alone in public spaces; in fact, only 5% of women in New Delhi reported feeling safe in public spaces (UN Women, 2013). Safety concerns for girls and women are not unique to India. International recommendations call on city planners, designers, and architects to attend to lighting, landscaping, visibility, traffic, security personnel, and other features of physical spaces with goals of keeping girls and women safe.

Gender is also relevant to the experience of the physical environment. In certain cultural groups, particularly after entering puberty, girls' access to public spaces is restricted because of norms about the need for teenage girls and women to remain sheltered in private domestic spaces (Dettori & Gupta, 2018). Menstrual taboos also keep girls out of public spaces, such as not being able to attend school while they are menstruating (Smiles et al., 2017). In countries where there are gender differences regarding access to public spaces, boys tend to be given more freedom following puberty whereas girls' freedom is restricted. In particularly conservative societies with restrictive gender norms, such as Afghanistan, historically, and even now in some rural areas, girls and women were forbidden from leaving the home unless accompanied by a male relative, which severely restricts girls' and women's mobility in public spaces. In a survey of more than 1,000 women in Afghanistan, 7% reported that they or a girl in their family had been raised as a boy at some point, largely for the greater access to education and mobility that was conferred by male gender in public spaces (Corboz et al., 2020).

Transgender and gender-nonconforming children and adolescents also face risks in public spaces, particularly when harassment is normalized and policies are not in place (or enforced) to prevent discrimination (Lubitow et al., 2017). Children's rights advocates have argued that the gender-binary structure of many public spaces, such as restrooms and changing rooms, creates inequalities and excludes transgender children (Sørlie, 2020). Cultures vary, however, in the extent to which gender is treated as a binary category (Vincent & Manzano, 2017). For example, the Buginese ethnic group in Indonesia recognizes five genders (S. G. Davies, 2010). Thus, children and adolescents' gendered experiences in public spaces vary depending on gender norms at the societal level.

Rural Versus Urban Residence

Whether children live in rural or urban areas is one of the major determinants of the availability of community and environmental resources that can affect their development. In most countries, children who live in urban areas have better access to clean water, sanitation, electricity, health care, and education than do children who live in rural areas (UNICEF, 2018). For example, children in urban areas are approximately 22% more likely to have access to clean water, 17% more likely to have improved sanitation, 2% more likely to be immunized, and 12% more likely to have access to education than those in rural areas. These urban advantages are primarily a result of the better infrastructure in urban than rural areas (e.g., 4/5 of people in urban areas have access to piped water compared with only 2/5 of people in rural areas; World Health Organization/UNICEF, 2017).

There are, however, wide disparities within urban areas between and across countries. In one in four countries, such as Congo and Haiti, the poorest urban children are more likely to die before the age of 5 than are the poorest children living in rural areas. In one in six countries, such as Mexico, the poorest urban children are less likely to complete primary school than are the poorest children living in rural areas (UNICEF, 2018). The distribution of rural and urban populations also differs across world regions. Only 43% of the population of Africa lives in urban areas, compared with 50% in Asia, 68% in Oceania, 74% in Europe, 81% in Latin America and the Caribbean, and 82% in North America (United Nations, 2018a).

MIGRATION TO A NEW COUNTRY

The most dramatic changes in neighborhoods and communities often occur when families migrate to a different country, either as voluntary immigrants or as refugees fleeing persecution, conflict, human rights violations, or other hardships. International estimates suggest that approximately 258 million people worldwide (3.4% of the world's population) currently live in a different country from the one in which they were born (International Organization for Migration, 2018). One third of immigrants move from a developing country to a developed one, one third move between developing countries, and one third originate in a developed country. Many nations are currently facing an overwhelming influx of immigrants and refugees, and the International Organization for Migration has described the situation as an emergency. Countries are struggling with both ethical and practical dilemmas regarding the humanitarian need to take in refugees fleeing from war and persecution while at the same time balancing the need to find jobs and social supports necessary to integrate refugees and immigrants into local communities. Fourteen percent of immigrants are younger than age 20 (International Organization for Migration, 2018). Given the large numbers of children and adolescents involved in international migration, countries face several pressing immigration policy questions, and developmental science research provides evidence regarding how to optimize adjustment of immigrant and refugee children.

A mission statement on positive adjustment of immigrant youth that was adopted by three leading professional organizations devoted to the study of child development (European Association for Developmental Psychology, European Association for Research on Adolescence, and Society for Research in Child Development) includes several recommendations for promoting the well-being of immigrant youth (García Coll et al., 2015). First, promoting non-segregated environments and opportunities to communicate with members of different ethnic and national backgrounds is important for helping children and adolescents integrate with others in their new communities. Second, providing economic opportunities helps immigrant families do well and contribute to the country. Third, children and adolescents should have access to childcare, education, health services, and other benefits to help them develop to their full potential. Fourth, public awareness campaigns can help show how immigrant families contribute to the host country and provide reminders of the importance of respecting diversity and the needs of different ethnic groups. Fifth, when countries make decisions about where to house refugees that have been taken in, the availability of economic, educational, and other opportunities in potential areas of settlement should be considered.

CLIMATE CHANGE

The United Nations Sustainable Development Goal 13, to take urgent action to combat climate change and its impacts, is one of 17 goals guiding the international agenda through 2030. Many of the other goals, including Goal 7, to "ensure access to affordable, reliable, sustainable and modern energy for all," and Goal 15, to "protect, restore and promote sustainable use of terrestrial ecosystems, sustainably manage forests, combat desertification, and halt and reverse land degradation and halt biodiversity loss," are closely connected to climate change. Doctors, scientists, and policy experts from 27 organizations around the world have called climate change the "biggest global health threat of the 21st century," because "a rapidly changing climate has dire implications for every aspect of human life, exposing vulnerable populations to extremes of weather, altering patterns of infectious disease, and compromising food security, safe drinking water, and clean air" (Watts et al., 2018, p. 2482).

Climate change involves both gradual changes, such as rising sea levels, droughts, and changes in growing seasons, as well as an increase in frequency and severity of extreme weather events, such as hurricanes and floods. Figure 9.1 illustrates how droughts can cause direct and indirect effects on children. Climate change is directly or indirectly responsible for increased mortality in extreme weather events, food shortages, economic hardship, forced migration, and other threats to children's well-being (U.S. Global Change Research Program, 2016). Figure 9.2 shows how and why children in low-income families are more vulnerable to and have worse outcomes from droughts than do children in higher-income families. Similar processes also occur in the face of other extreme weather events and climate-related changes. Children who live in low- and middle-income countries, which is about 85% of the world's children, are more vulnerable to the effects of climate change because these countries generally have weaker infrastructures, rely more on agriculture, and have fewer supports and services to be able to withstand extreme weather events and other effects of climate change (Sanson et al., 2018).

Children are more vulnerable to the effects of climate change than adults because of their immature immune systems, rapid growth, and greater direct contact with their physical environment (Garcia & Sheehan, 2016). Climate-related changes and extreme weather events present children with a number of risk factors, including food and water shortages, increased stress, violence stemming from competition for scarce resources, and forced migration. All of these factors pose physical as well as psychological risks for development. For example, extreme weather events linked to climate change have been related to posttraumatic stress disorder, depression, anxiety, sleep problems, and cognitive deficits in childhood (Garcia & Sheehan, 2016). Both quantitative and qualitative studies have demonstrated that children and adolescents are worried about the impact of climate change on their lives. For example, more than 60% of Australian 16- and 17-year-olds think that global warming is a serious threat to Australia (Tranter & Skrbis, 2014), and 74% of 11- to 16-year-olds in the United Kingdom worried about the effects of climate change on their future (UNICEF, 2013a). In South Africa, focus group discussions with 14- to 17-year-olds revealed concerns about the severe climate impacts their generation will suffer (UNICEF, 2011).

CONCLUSION

Communities, neighborhoods, and physical environments have important influences on child development that take various forms. Water, sanitation, and hygiene are critical aspects of communities that affect not only child growth and physical health but also cognitive and social development. Likewise, pollution, access to green space, neighborhood danger, and other aspects of the physical environment vary from community to community and affect many aspects of child development. Within a particular cultural group, not all individuals

FIGURE 9.1. Potential Impacts of Droughts and Water Stress on Children

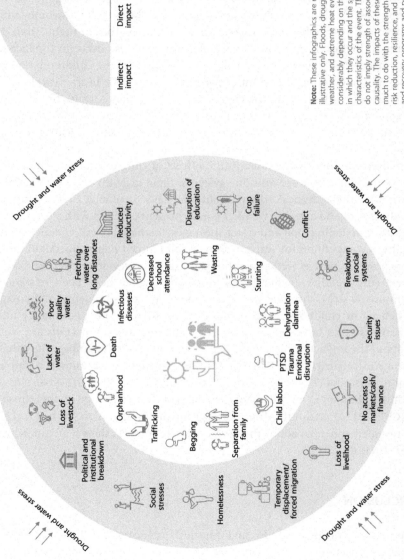

Note. PTSD = posttraumatic stress disorder. From *Unless We Act Now: The Impact of Climate Change on Children* (p. 25), by UNICEF, 2015. Copyright 2015 by UNICEF. Reprinted with permission.

FIGURE 9.2. Illustration of How Climate Change Can Exacerbate Inequities, Using the Example of Droughts and Water Stress Related to Climate Change

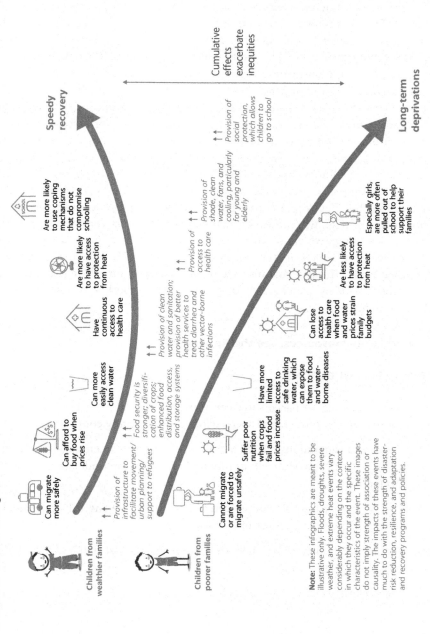

Note. From *Unless We Act Now: The Impact of Climate Change on Children* (p. 27), by UNICEF, 2015. Copyright 2015 by UNICEF. Adapted with permission.

experience communities in the same way or have the same access to neighborhood resources. Rather, socioeconomic status, gender, and rural versus urban residence play important roles in social contexts to which children are exposed. Migration to a different country is perhaps the most dramatic way in which a variety of community, neighborhood, and physical environments of child development change. Climate change is an aspect of the environment with global implications, yet children in low-income countries and from low-income families, even in high-income countries, are disproportionately affected by climate change because they have fewer resources with which to offset the negative effects of extreme weather events and other hardships brought about by climate change. Understanding how communities, neighborhoods, and physical environments affect child development is part of an ecological approach to child development that examines both direct effects of these environmental factors (e.g., pollution and environmental hazards directly harm children's health and impair cognitive development) and indirect effects of community factors on child development through the ways they affect parents' well-being and behavior (e.g., when neighborhood danger increases parents' distress and harsh parenting, which in turn increase children's adjustment problems). Countries vary widely in the physical environments to which children are exposed, and cultural norms and values play an important role in how children and their families experience communities, neighborhoods, and physical environments.

For additional resources, see the Appendix.

DISCUSSION QUESTIONS

1. Describe how lack of access to clean water affects children's physical health, cognitive development, and social experiences in many countries.

2. Why are considerations related to pollution, access to green space, and other features of the physical environment important for understanding child development?

3. How do socioeconomic status, gender, and rural versus urban residence affect children's experiences of physical spaces?

4. Why are all children not equally susceptible to risks associated with living in dangerous neighborhoods?

5. How is climate change affecting child and adolescent development?

10

Culture and Time Use

Play, Work, School, and Leisure

These Kuna children pick ripe coffee cherries during the coffee harvest season in the mountains of Panama. Cultural communities shape children's time spent in work, play, school, and leisure.

In this chapter, we expand on the concept of activity settings introduced in Chapter 1. Following the reasoning of B. B. Whiting and Whiting (1975), we argue that culture is reflected in the types of settings that individuals occupy, the time they spend in these settings, the tasks in which they engage, and the people with whom they interact. Activity settings are defined by cultural meanings and within these, children engage in routines that can be conceptualized as "scripts" (e.g., going to the movie scripts, arguing with a friend over activities scripts, and date scripts). Time spent in various activity settings affords individuals opportunities that have different implications for their development.

https://doi.org/10.1037/0000228-010
Child and Adolescent Development in Cultural Context, by J. E. Lansford, D. C. French, and M. Gauvain

Consider how Ji-yoo, a hypothetical 17-year-old South Korean high school girl, typically spends her Fridays and Saturdays. On Friday, she gets up at 6:00 a.m., eats breakfast, and arrives at school by 7:00 a.m. She remains in her classroom until 5:00 p.m., eating her lunch in the classroom. After class, she stays at school until 10:00 p.m. and during this time, studies under a teacher's supervision and eats dinner in the classroom. At 10:00 p.m., she returns home and studies until midnight. On Saturday, she sleeps a bit later and then goes to a private tutor or attends group study sessions beginning at 9:00 a.m. and continuing until she returns home for dinner. She then has a 3-hour break during which time she stays at home and watches television or socializes with her parents. After this break, she studies until about midnight.

Contrast the example above with the typical Friday and Saturday schedules of middle-class 17-year-old high school girls in the United States. They typically attend school and study much less than their Korean counterparts. On Friday school begins around 8:00 a.m. and goes until 3:00 p.m., with no school on Saturday. When not in school, they do homework and may work at part-time jobs, attend parties, go on dates, spend time at friends' homes, participate in organized sports, or perhaps hang out with friends at a restaurant or shopping mall. During their unscheduled times, they may or may not spend time eating or socializing with their parents, and on occasion may spend the night at a friend's home.

Consider the activity settings just described and the implications of these settings for the adjustment of teenagers in South Korea and the United States. As we will discuss later in this chapter, the intense studying and academic pressure reflected in the example of the South Korean girl's daily schedule can be associated with stress and depression for some students (M. Lee & Larson, 2000). The absence of time spent with peers in settings away from adult supervision provides them with limited opportunities to engage in deviant behavior or use tobacco or alcohol. In contrast, the girls in the United States have considerable time away from adults, affording them with opportunities to focus on their relationships with peers and romantic partners. They also spend time away from adult supervision and thus have the opportunity to engage in problem behavior. While their ability to engage in paid work can be enriching, it may also detract from schoolwork.

Larson and Verma (1999) suggested that it is important to understand how children and adolescents in different cultures spend their time and to consider the people with whom they interact and the settings in which this occurs. The previous examples illustrate the implications of time use for the socialization of children across cultures. As we discuss how children and adolescents in different cultures spend their time, it is helpful to think about this in the context of trade-offs. Time spent doing paid work means that there is less opportunity to pursue academic success and leisure, and time spent with parents and in adult-supervised settings means that less time is available to hang out with peers. These choices have implications for child development and adjustment. Children's time use is intertwined with other aspects of the culture, including economic structures, customs, and values. For example, the daily schedule of the South Korean girl reflects the cultural values of the importance of education and the Confucian perspective that educational achievement is the means of achieving status in this hierarchically structured society.

In the following sections, we discuss the large differences between how children in different cultures spend their time. We group our discussion into categories of play, work, school, and leisure.

PLAY

Major developmental theorists have argued that play is extremely important for the cognitive and social development of children. According to Swiss developmental psychologist Jean Piaget, "play is the work of childhood" and he postulated play to be a major element in his seminal theory of cognitive development. Piaget also argued that children learn morality at least partially through play with other children. Vygotsky, whose theories we discussed in Chapter 1, viewed play as a mechanism by which children develop new cognitive capacities. Beliefs about the importance of children's play, however, are not universal. Lancy (2015) reviewed the extensive anthropological literature exploring play in multiple countries and concluded that in some, people value play primarily because it occupies children and keeps them from interfering in adult productivity. Regardless of estimates of its importance, Lancy (2015) proposed that play occurs in all cultures and that children enact adult activities (e.g., farming, hunting, cooking, warfare, sexual reproduction, home building, etc.) in advance of the time they actually perform these activities for "real." Play occurs during childhood until other activities (i.e., work and school) crowd out the time available for play. In some cultures, this occurs earlier for girls than it does for boys because girls are often required at an early age to help with household and child care duties.

A focus on play in the context of cultural activity settings leads us to explore how ecological conditions affect children's play. For example, potential environmental dangers have an effect on the frequency and location of children's play. Parents' economic activities impact their availability as potential playmates, and economic parameters may require children to work rather than play.

Time for Play

There are considerable differences across cultures in the time that children engage in play. Edwards (2000) reanalyzed data from the Six Cultures Study discussed in Chapter 2 and in various places throughout this book to specifically explore children's play. Note that this study was conducted between the mid-1950s and mid-1970s, and with the exception of the United States, included communities that relied on subsistence agriculture. Children in Kenya and India engaged in the fewest observation sessions that included play (17% for girls and

20% for boys in Kenya; 18% for girls and 34% for boys in India). The highest play rates were observed in the United States (43% for girls and 55% for boys) and in Japan (79% for girls and 92% for boys). These differences in play are partially explained by variation in children's work demands. For example, the Kenyan children had little time to play because they cared for younger children, helped in the home, took care of animals, and worked in the field with their parents. Other variations in the amount of children's playtime can be explained by differences in their opportunities to interact with others (e.g., the Japanese children were in preschool programs with extensive opportunities to interact with other children). The availability of space, the presence of play materials, and parents' attitudes regarding the importance of play are other cultural factors that affect children's playtime. In all of the cultures studied, boys engaged in more play than did girls. This gender difference was partly a function of work demands as girls spent more of their time caring for younger children and doing household work. In addition, boys spent more time away from the home than did girls, providing them with enhanced opportunities to play.

Fantasy Play and Imagination

Among the most enchanting aspects of childhood are the construction of elaborate fantasy episodes. For example, consider Gottman's (1986, p. 159) observations of an American boy (Eric) and girl (Naomi) discussing their fears:

ERIC: Hold on there everyone. I am the skeleton, I'm the skeleton.

            ....

ERIC: [*Screams*] A skeleton, everyone, a skeleton!

NAOMI: I'm your friend. The dinosaur.

ERIC: Oh, hi, dinosaur. You know, no one likes me.

NAOMI: But I like you. I'm your friend.

ERIC: But none of my other friends like me. They don't like my new suit. They don't like my skeleton suit. It's really just me. They think I'm a dumb-dumb.

NAOMI: I know what. He's a good skeleton.

ERIC: [*Yelling*] I am not a dumb-dumb.

NAOMI: I'm not calling you a dumb-dumb. I'm calling you a friendly skeleton.

            ....

NAOMI: Huh, this is nice. Wow, where are you going we are going back to our house.

ERIC: This is my house, remember?

NAOMI: Where are your parents, remember?

ERIC: My parents? I don't have any parents. My mommy and daddy went; they don't like me anymore.

NAOMI: So they went somewhere else?

ERIC: I live here all alone. Hey, you can live with me.

NAOMI: Yes and keep you company. I'll cook the food.

Although it is reasonable to assume that episodes such as the one just presented are common across cultures, a surprising finding from the Six Cultures Study is the considerable variability in the extent that children engage in fantasy, defined as play in which children assume the role of an imaginary character or interact with an imaginary character. In the United States and Japan, fantasy play among 3- to 9-year-old children occurred in 37% to 50% of the episodes. In contrast, this type of play in Kenya, Mexico, and India ranged between 0% and 21%.

Cultural differences in fantasy play may exist for several reasons. The presence of objects such as dolls, costumes, and playhouses can facilitate fantasy play, so imaginative play likely occurs more frequently when such materials are present. Nevertheless, as every parent can attest, children readily use various objects in their environment (e.g., sticks used for guns, corncobs substituted for toy animals) or construct toys (e.g., mud forts or wire cars) to use in their play. Under some circumstances, the presence of companions (e.g., peers or adults) can facilitate fantasy play. Finally, adults can either facilitate or interfere with children's fantasy play to the extent that they allow children to be in settings conducive to fantasy play, or play without adult intervention and other distractions.

The importance of adult influence on fantasy play is illustrated by Farver and Shin's (1997) observations of children in European American and Korean American preschool classrooms. European American children engaged in more social pretend play than did the Korean American children. These results may be attributable to greater presence of materials amenable to fantasy play and the freedom allotted to children to move throughout the European American classrooms. In contrast, the Korean American students had few objects available to use in fantasy play, and children spent most of their time engaged in teacher-directed academic activities.

Play-Work or Role-Play

In their play, children in all the Six Cultures Study samples enacted behavior typically engaged in by adults, including activities such as pretend cooking, playing war, or "gardening." This type of play was more common for girls than boys, perhaps because girls frequently played cooking and infant care. It is common in many cultures for parents to provide young children with scaled-down objects (e.g., a miniature hoe, small cooking utensils) that they use until they are capable of using full-size objects. Sometimes children act out domestic scenes including marriage and even adultery, as in an example provided by Lancy (2015). These activities can facilitate the transition from play to work as young children sometimes make little distinction between playing at work and actually working. As children become older and more experienced, play morphs into work. This is illustrated by Lancy's (1977) observations of children in Sierra Leone learning blacksmithing:

> A child of three spends hours observing a blacksmith at work. A child of four brings his stick down on a rock repeatedly and says he is a blacksmith. A child of ten weaves with his friends an elaborate reconstruction of the blacksmith's craft, all in make believe. The child of ten is a blacksmith's helper in reality; he fetches wood for the forge and no more. At twelve, he begins to learn the skills of blacksmithing, adding a new one every few months or so. At age 18, he is a full-fledged blacksmith with his own forge. Parallel patterns can be observed for every class of work. (p. 75)

An additional illustration of play-work comes from Bloch and Adler's (1994) ethnographic study of girls in Senegal:

> At two years of age, little girls imitated older girls and women by carrying tiny cans of water on their heads from the village to their house. Progressively as they got older and more capable, they carried larger pots of water until by age seven, they could carry real buckets of water. (p. 171)

Games With Rules

Piaget theorized that children's participation in games with rules (specifically marbles) were important for the development of children's morality and social understanding. Edwards (2000) reported that children in the Six Cultures Study engaged in a variety of games including hide-and-seek, tag, and checkers. There was, however, considerable variation across cultures in the extent that children played such games. This variability was partly explained by the availability of free time, the presence or absence of partners, and the knowledge of such games.

Adults as Play Companions

There is wide variation across cultures in the extent to which parents participate in play with their children. Lancy (2015) reviewed the anthropological evidence regarding this topic and reported that in many cultures, parent–toddler play is almost nonexistent. For example, !Kung (South African food foragers) parents typically do not play with their children after infancy and believe that it is more beneficial for children's development for them to play with peers. Lancy (2007) concluded that children's play with parents was common only among educated, urban elite parents, a theme on which we will elaborate in the following sections. Another factor that contributes to the amount mothers play with their children is the availability of peer playmates.

Urban middle-class parents across multiple cultures play with their children as part of their efforts to support child development and educational attainment, a finding replicated in diverse countries including India, Turkey, the United States, and South Korea (Göncü et al., 2000). This is less the case in some non-Western countries and in particular, low-income populations. Farver and Howes (1993) conducted home observations of working-class American and Mexican mothers and their toddlers and found that American mothers encouraged their children to play by providing objects, suggesting activities, and participating in play with their child. In contrast, Mexican mothers seldom played with their children and expressed the belief that play was primarily important for the child's amusement but not for learning or development. Based on their observations of American, Mexican, and Indonesian parents, Farver and Wimbarti (1995) concluded the following:

> Mothers who valued play for its educational and cognitive benefits were more likely to join children's play activities and provide props and suggestions which encouraged the expression of pretend play. In contrast, mothers who viewed play as children's amusement or imitation of adult models were less likely to participate in their child's pretend play. (p. 19)

There are also cultural differences in the ways that parents play with their children and the goals for this activity, which is illustrated by Haight's (1999) comparisons of mothers' play with toddlers in Taiwan and the United States. Parents from Taiwan focused on teaching their children social rules and compliance through play as illustrated in the following example of a caregiver interacting with Angu, age 2½ (Haight, 1999, p. 128):

CAREGIVER: (*Smiling*) Stand up, bow, sit down, teacher is going to deliver a lesson. (*Angu, smiling, moves closer to her caregiver*)

CAREGIVER: Teacher is coming to the classroom, what should the class monitor say?

ANGU: Stand up!

CAREGIVER: OK. Stand up. (*Angu stands up and bows*)

CAREGIVER: Sit down. (*They read the story*)

CAREGIVER: We have finished the story. (*She claps her hands*) . . . Before we dismiss the class, the class monitor should say: "Stand up! Bow! Sit down! Stand up!" (*Angu stands up*)

CAREGIVER: Bow. (*Angu bows*)

CAREGIVER: Class dismissed. Go play on the slide. (*Indicates imaginary sliding board in the living room*)

In contrast to the example above, the U.S. parents were more likely to use imaginative play to support their children's individuality and self-expression.

Thus, parents from both Taiwan and the United States engaged in imaginative play with toddlers, but did so with the goal of teaching their children the competencies that are valued in their respective cultures.

At the beginning of this section, we noted that parents are likely to play with their children when they live in low-density environments in which few peer play companions are available. Edwards (2000), for example, cited this as one reason that American parents in the Six Cultures Study, who lived isolated from other families with children, played extensively with their children. An extreme example of this is evident in the play of Inuit mothers and their children (Lancy, 2015), which occurs partly because they live in low-density settlements in which children have few, if any, peers and are isolated with their mothers during periods of extreme weather.

Play as an Opportunity to Develop Culturally Valued Social Competencies

In several chapters of this book, we suggest that play and other forms of social interaction with peers provide important means by which children learn and practice cultural rules of social interaction. For example, in Chapter 8 we discussed research conducted by French et al. (2011) in which quartets of 7-year-old Canadian and Chinese children were given one attractive toy among them, and their behavior was observed. The Chinese children displayed cultural-typical patterns of behavior including peer leadership of group activities and willingness to give other group members opportunities to play with the toy. In contrast, Canadian children displayed an assertive interaction style, which is valued by their culture.

Play is a particularly important means by which children learn to display and regulate their aggression and learn culture-specific rules pertaining to this behavior. Across cultures, children engage in rough-and-tumble play (Lancy, 2015). This type of play was initially studied in nonhuman primates who display aggressive-type behavior accompanied by a playful expression and restraints on hurting the other. Such play is important for practicing fighting, establishing dominance hierarchies, training children for adult roles as warriors, and preparing them to engage in organized sports. Rough-and-tumble play is also a way for children to learn emotional and behavioral control as well as cooperation, which affords them the opportunity to practice multiple social skills (Pellegrini, 2009; Pellis & Pellis, 2011). As is the case for other types of social behavior, rough-and-tumble play exists within cultural rule and meaning systems.

The socialization of rough-and-tumble play within a cultural context is illustrated by Fry's (1988) comparison of two Mexican communities in which adults differed in their levels of aggression. Children from both communities engaged in rough-and-tumble play but rarely engaged in overt aggression. Nevertheless, children in the more peaceful community displayed less rough-and-tumble play and engaged in less threatening behavior during this play than did children living in the aggressive community. Thus, children's play reflected adult perspectives on aggression. At the same time, children were socialized through this play to display cultural patterns of aggression as adults and to transmit this into the next generation.

WORK

This discussion of play transitions us into the discussion of work in several ways. First, we discussed earlier how children's play could gradually morph into work. In addition, time spent working reduces the amount of time that children have available to play.

Lancy (2015) documented that in many cultures, children perform chores at a very young age. Running errands and fetching objects is one of the first childhood chores. He cited, for example, the observations of Nerlove et al. (1974) of children in Guatemala:

> The simplest and earliest task for which children are given actual responsibility is the running of errands, transporting objects to and from people's homes, and going to a local shop for a few cents' worth of goods. Considerably more difficult are the errands to the maize fields or other errands that require the child to go outside of the community. Selling items in the community may range in complexity from approximately the status of an errand to the cognitively complex task of soliciting buyers from anywhere in the community and making change. (Nerlove et al., 1974, p. 276)

In some cultures, children gradually progress from play to assuming adult work roles. In the previous section, we documented how children progress from blacksmith play to adult blacksmith expertise. Lancy (2015) described the processes used in a number of cultures to gradually introduce children to hunting. Children as young as age 3 are provided with scaled-down weapons such as bows and arrows or blowpipes, and children use these weapons to hunt small animals such as insects, birds, or lizards. As their skills improve, children may seek out bigger prey such as rabbits and squirrels and organize themselves into child hunting parties. With age and their development of enhanced skills, they may participate as peripheral members on adult hunts.

American children whose family lives on farms or owns a business may also gradually assume work responsibilities. For example, farm chores prepare some children for adult work as they engage in activities such as raising a calf as part of a youth organization (e.g., 4-H or Future Farmers of America, Boy or Girl Scouts), driving tractors, and operating machinery.

In some cultures, work outside of the home can begin with an apprenticeship in which the child is placed under the authority and tutelage of another adult (Lancy, 2015). Often these tasks are graded in ability such that the child initially takes on simple tasks (e.g., cleaning or working on small parts of large projects) that are within the child's capacity and will not be too costly if the child makes a mistake.

In many large cities, including in affluent countries, one may encounter children either living with their parents but spending significant time earning money on the street economy (children on the street) or living on the street. Approximately 100 million to 150 million children throughout the world work on the street. They earn money by selling small objects such as chewing gum or tissues, collecting recyclable objects, or performing tasks (e.g., shining shoes). Some children may engage in petty theft, begging, or prostitution. Research Highlight 10.1 describes one study of children working on the streets in Izmir, Turkey.

The World of Work

Based on data compiled by the United States Department of Labor, approximately 10% of the youth worldwide (64 million girls and 88 million boys) are engaged in labor. UNICEF defines labor for children ages 5 to 11 as doing more than 1 hour of economic work or 21 hours of unpaid household work per week. At ages 12 to 14, labor is defined as more than 14 hours of economic work or 21 hours of unpaid household work per week, and at ages 15 to 17, labor is defined as exceeding 43 hours per week. More boys than girls are child laborers, but because girls are more likely to work inside the home (either for their families or as domestic helpers), their efforts are underestimated. Note that many working children are uncounted because they work fewer hours than the threshold or their work is not public. Of these children, about 73 million are engaged in hazardous work, and a subset of these are engaged in the worst forms of labor, including prostitution, the illegal drug industry, child

---

RESEARCH HIGHLIGHT 10.1

Children Who Work in the Streets

Yilmaz and Dülgerler (2011) studied children working in the streets in Izmir, which is Turkey's third largest city, with a population of 3 million. They sought participants from areas where working children tended to congregate and distributed questionnaires to 226 children.

Most of these children were boys, ages 7 to 11. It is typical in many countries to have a higher proportion of boys than girls working in the streets. Most of the children lived with their families (94%). Thus, most of the children belonged in the UNICEF category of "working on the street" whereas 6% were in the category of "living on the street." Most children said their reason for working on the street was to give money to their families (66%). Almost all of the children attended school (48.4% regular school and 51.6% alternative school).

Children perceived their work to be dangerous, including exposure to physical assault (56%). This came largely from the police (42%) and/or older children (38%). The majority of the children had become sick or injured as a consequence of their street work. Among the factors associated with street work included family poverty, violence in their home, and paternal alcoholism. Most of the families were immigrants. These results suggest that efforts to assist these children will need to address family poverty issues.

---

soldiers, trafficking, or other forms of forced servitude (Koller et al., 2015). Children may also engage in labor activities that are dangerous such as mining or working with hazardous substances.

Children across all regions of the world are engaged in labor with prevalence rates that range from 2.9% in the Arab states to a high of 19.6% in Africa (International Labour Organization, 2020). Nine out of 10 child laborers live in either Africa or Asia. Nevertheless, child labor is not confined to low-income countries as 7% and 1%, respectively, of children in upper-middle and upper-income countries are in this category. Of the children involved in child labor, 48% were 5 to 11 years old, 28% were 12 to 14 years old, and 24% were 15 to 17 years old. Most children worked on family farms or in family businesses, and more than 70% of the child laborers worked in agriculture.

The United Nations Convention on the Rights of the Child treaty has been ratified by all countries except the United States. Article 32 pertains to child labor and states the following:

> Parties recognize the right of the child to be protected from economic exploitation and from performing any work that is likely to be hazardous or to interfere with the child's education, or to be harmful to the child's health or physical, mental, spiritual, moral or social development. (United Nations, 1990, Article 32, Section 1)

Despite the existence of this and other international agreements and country and local laws designed to protect children from engaging in excessive or harmful work, this practice nevertheless continues to exist for multiple reasons. In some countries, there is limited enforcement of these rules and the rules that do exist are often ignored. In addition, because most children work on family farms or in family businesses, there is not a clear distinction between "work" and "chores" (International Labour Office, 2017). Underlying the existence of child labor are problems of poverty. Some families do not see that the immediate advantages associated with the child's labor are offset by the long-term advantages associated with sending the child to school.

Child labor can be associated with various health problems. For example, a study of 10- to 15-year-old Indonesian children who attended school revealed that working to earn income was associated with health issues including fever and cough, among others (F.-C. Wolff & Maliki, 2008). There are a number of methodological problems, however, that make the study of work and health extremely complex (Levison & Murray-Close, 2005). For example, healthier children may be selected over unhealthy children to work. Conversely, children who work may be more economically disadvantaged than those who do not work, and poverty may also be associated with poor nutrition, low access to health services, and living in unsanitary environments. Because of the difficulty conducting research on the relation between health and working, some important questions have not been adequately explored, such as the relation between hours of work and health, type of work and health, and gender differences. Nevertheless, it appears that working long hours and in dangerous occupations is associated with health problems.

Work and School

In many regions of the world, children work and attend school. Depending on the type of work and number of hours worked, this can have negative consequences for both the children's health and education. Although most of the focus has been on the negative effects associated with work, there are also some potential positive effects (F.-C. Wolff & Maliki, 2008). For example, the extra money that children contribute to their family may provide the funding needed for siblings to attend school and receive adequate nutrition. In addition, work can provide students with valuable skills that enable them to secure employment as adults.

There are vast differences across countries in the extent to which children who attend school also work. Post and Pong (2000) reported statistics on the employment of eighth-grade children from the administration of the Third International Mathematics and Science Study in 40 countries. The percentage of boys and girls who engaged in paid work ranged from a low of 4% to 10% in some countries (e.g., South Korea, Hong Kong, and Portugal) to almost 50% in others (e.g., New Zealand, Philippines, Canada). The United States was in the middle of the range with 38% of boys and 31% of girls who worked. Information pertaining to the type of work is not available in these statistics and is important because some of this work may include babysitting and yard work for neighbors rather than regular employment. Although it is understandable that children in low- to lower-middle income countries (e.g., Thailand, Colombia, the Philippines) work, there is substantial variation in high-income countries. For example, there is low employment in countries including South Korea and Portugal and high employment in other countries (e.g., New Zealand, Canada). These differences between high-income countries likely reflect cultural values pertaining to how children should spend time, the importance of education, and the meaning and value of child work. For example, American parents may view work as a means of promoting individualistic values of self-sufficiency (White & Brinkerhoff, 1981). Some countries (e.g., Germany, Denmark) have strong vocational education programs that include paid work integrated with academic instruction.

Much of the international research pertaining to the effects of work on children has focused on educational achievement. Most researchers have found that work is negatively associated with school achievement, with the explanation that the time spent working reduces the time that children can devote to education. Post (2011) found that working more than four hours per day had a negative impact on the reading and mathematics achievement of 6th year primary school students in Chile, Colombia, Ecuador, and Peru.

Work also appears to interfere with the education of middle-school children. Analyses by Post and Pong (2000) provided evidence of the negative effects of work on the standardized assessments of mathematics and science achievement of middle-school children in the United States. Eighth-grade boys and girls who worked experienced lower concurrent math and science achievement. In other analyses, working in eighth grade predicted lower mathematics and science scores for boys and girls in 10th grade.

Post and Pong (2000) extended their analyses by looking at the associations between eighth graders who worked and mathematics and science achievement scores in 23 countries. Working part-time was negatively associated with mathematics learning of boys in 16 of the 23 countries and negatively associated with science learning in 14 countries. In these analyses, working 5 hours or more per day was associated with lower achievement than was working 1 to 4 hours per day. There was also a negative association between work and achievement for girls in mathematics (11 countries) and science (nine countries). Thus, there is consistency between these finding and those reported previously for American students. Across countries, employment of eighth-grade boys is negatively associated with both mathematics and science achievement. Similar effects emerged for girls, but the results were less consistent.

It is common for high school students in the United States to work part-time jobs. This, however, is not typical in some other regions of the world. Fuligni and Stevenson (1995) compared the time that high school students in the United States, China, and Japan worked. A substantial proportion of American students worked part-time (80%), compared with only 26% and 27% of Chinese and Japanese students, respectively. It is important to note, however, that all of the Chinese students and half of the Japanese students who worked were enrolled in vocational schools, and their work was associated with their studies.

There is evidence from the study of American adolescents that extensive work is associated with lower achievement. Steinberg and Dornbusch (1991) assessed American students in Grades 10, 11, and 12 and found that extensive working was associated with lower grades, less time spent on homework, and less effort directed toward education. These effects increased if students worked more than 10 hours per week. Similar results emerged from a large national longitudinal study of American students in Grades 8 through 12 (Quirk et al., 2001). The researchers controlled for both family background and past achievement and found that more than 11 to 13 hours of work per week was associated with lower grades for both boys and girls. Interestingly, students who worked fewer than 11 to 13 hours per week did not show decreased academic performance and in some cases outperformed those who did not work. In contrast, based on an extensive review of the empirical literature, Staff et al. (2015) concluded that the evidence regarding the advantages and disadvantages of working of American high school youth is more complex than presented by Steinberg and Dornbusch's (1991) analysis. There are potential advantages and disadvantages of working that vary depending on the type of work, the motivations of the worker, and the extent to which work interferes with education and participation in beneficial extracurricular activities.

In conclusion, the research reviewed in this section provides evidence supporting the tradeoff between time spent working and time devoted to education. A primary reason to limit how much children work is to provide them with time to study. For those children who work and attend school, long hours devoted to work are associated with lower levels of achievement in some cases. It is important, however, to determine the extent to which working leads to low academic performance or whether children with academic difficulties are more likely to work.

SCHOOL

One of the first things that comes to mind when one thinks of children's activities is school attendance. Although this is a common experience across the world for most children, the amount of time they spend in school and the characteristics of their school experience differ considerably across countries and social strata.

Almost all countries have laws mandating school attendance, with the required duration of schooling varying across countries. It is important to note, however, that government requirements for children to attend school do not mean that children necessarily attend. First, enforcement mechanisms in many countries are weak and as such, there are few if any consequences for parents who keep their children out of school to enable them to work. Second, despite school being compulsory, there may be financial barriers that prevent children from attending. For example, in Indonesia, children are required to buy uniforms, pay school fees, buy books and materials, and transport themselves to school; children who cannot afford these expenses may not attend school or instead may attend some type of alternative school. Third, there is wide variation across countries in the extent to which children with medical, physical, or intellectual disabilities attend school. The United Nations Education, Scientific, and Cultural Organization (UNESCO; 2017) reports that children with disabilities are less likely to be in school than children without disabilities (77% vs. 87%). The discrepancy is more pronounced in some countries such as Egypt (43% vs. 97%) and Indonesia (53% vs. 98%). These rates may overestimate the education of children with disabilities, as these children may not consistently attend school or graduate.

There are large differences across countries in the duration of compulsory school attendance. In the United States and many countries in Europe, compulsory education ranges between 11 and 13 years. In many other countries (e.g., Malaysia, China, the Czech Republic), compulsory education ranges between 6 and 9 years (UNESCO Institute for Statistics, 2019).

Particularly troubling is that many children in the world do not achieve minimum educational proficiency despite attending school (UNESCO Institute for Statistics, 2019). Across the world, by sixth grade, only 56% of girls and 55% of boys achieve minimal competency in mathematics, defined as the ability to translate verbal information into a mathematical operation, convert information into fractions, and interpret common units of measurement. Comparable figures for sixth-grade reading competency, defined as the ability to interpret the meaning of a short and simple text, are 55% of girls and 57% of boys. The distribution of educational competencies varies considerably across countries. For example, one out of three children in sub-Saharan Africa do not attain proficiency in reading, with similar percentages in central and southern Asia. Although about two thirds of these children attend school, their education does not lead to minimum knowledge proficiencies. Across almost all countries, children more often than adolescents meet minimal levels of academic competence. Girls are as likely as boys to attain minimal proficiency.

The diversity of time spent in educational activities is illustrated by the results of a series of time-use studies across India, Italy, Japan, and South Korea (Verma & Larson, 2003). The percentage of waking time devoted by high school students to academic pursuits (school attendance plus homework) varied from a high of 43% (South Korea) to a low of 29.5% (Japan), with both India (34%) and Italy (37.9%) falling in between. U.S. adolescents spent an average of 3 to 4.5 hours per day on academic pursuits, averaged across 7 days during periods when school was in session (Larson & Verma, 1999), which is less than students in Europe (4.5–6 hours) and East Asia (6–8 hours).

The time that students devote to academic pursuits (i.e., time in school plus time studying) varies dramatically. Lloyd et al. (2008) summarized a series of studies in which 15- to 19-year-old school-attending urban adolescents in multiple countries reported on their activities during 1 school day. Indian boys reported 8.9 hours of academic engagement compared with 8 hours for girls. We can compare this with the academic engagement of South African students of 5.7 hours for boys and 5.9 hours for girls. Respective reports for boys and girls in Nicaragua (7.7; 7.4) and Pakistan (6.8; 7.3) fell between these extremes.

Larson and Verma (1999) reviewed the benefits associated with the time that children and adolescents spend in academic activities. They concluded that time spent in education has clear benefits for both the individual and society. Time spent studying is associated with educational achievement and lifetime earnings. For some youth, however, there are negative effects associated with increased time devoted to studying, including boredom and lack of intrinsic motivation. Educational pressure may also be associated with high stress and depression. Research Highlight 10.2 illustrates the link between time spent studying and mental health in American and South Korean high school students.

Variations in time use have important implications for understanding the leisure activities of adolescents across countries. For those adolescents who do not work, time not engaged in academic activities leaves more time for leisure.

LEISURE

Given the previous discussion of differences across countries regarding time devoted to academics, it is not surprising that there are variations across countries in the time devoted to leisure. Larson and Verma (1999) aggregated findings from multiple studies and concluded that American adolescents had 6.5 to

RESEARCH HIGHLIGHT 10.2

The Korean "Examination Hell"

We began this chapter with a description of how Ji-yoo, a South Korean 17-year-old girl, spends her time. Although this example is hypothetical, it is a reflection of the activities of South Korean students who are preparing for the national exam. This exam, completed at the end of high school, determines whether or not students will be able to attend college, and if so, the status of the university. This is a critical point in the lives of South Korean youth because graduating from a high status college is critical for getting a good job, earning a good income, and for many, determining their marriage prospects. As such, both students and their parents are very stressed during this period. The common saying "pass with four and fail with five" reflects the view of many adolescents that they must curtail their sleep to spend more time studying.

M. Lee and Larson (2000) compared relations between time use and mood and depression of American and South Korean high school students using experience-sampling methods to evaluate time use and affect states. Students carried a "beeper" that signaled them 7–8 times a day, at which point they completed a self-report form recording what they were doing and how they were feeling at the time.

The first question pertains to the activities of students in the two countries. South Korean students spent much more time either in school or studying than did their American counterparts (44% vs. 19%). In contrast, the American students spent more than twice as much time engaged in socializing and leisure (49% vs. 23%).

The second question concerned affective states—how adolescents felt at the time they were beeped. South Korean students felt less positive when engaged in school-work than did American students, a finding that was attributed to stress. Interestingly, South Korean students were less happy during leisure as well, suggesting that there was a spillover effect from schoolwork to their discretionary time.

Finally, the authors compared the ratings of affect during each activity with students' depression scores. For South Korean students, depression was associated with their mood during studying. In other words, if students experienced negative emotions while studying, this was associated with depression. In contrast, for American students, depression was predicted by negative emotion during leisure. Although characteristics of leisure that were associated with depression are unknown, perhaps this arises from difficulties in relationships with parents, friends, or romantic partners.

8 hours of discretionary time daily. Leisure time for European youth ranged between 5.5 and 7.5 hours, and East Asian youth had between 4 and 5.5 hours. There are also differences in the amount of leisure within East Asian and European countries. For example, French adolescents have less than 3 hours per day leisure, whereas adolescents in Finland and Norway have 5 hours per day. There is also substantial variation within countries in the amount of adolescent leisure time, with some of this attributable to factors such as gender, social class, school enrollment, or employment. Nevertheless, European and American middle-class male and female adolescents appear to have more discretionary time than do their East Asian peers.

In addition to looking at the amount of leisure time that adolescents have available, it is important to look at how adolescents in different countries engage in leisure and the implications of participating in different activities for their development and adjustment. We separate our discussion of leisure activities into the following sections: organized activities, unsupervised socializing with peers, and computer use.

Time use during leisure is both a consequence of and a contributor to adolescent adjustment (Lam & McHale, 2015). What adolescents do with their discretionary time is partly determined by cultural scripts that define action settings including the location, companions, tasks, and the meanings and emotional experiences associated with them (Lam & McHale, 2015). Engagement in specific leisure activities is also determined by parameters such as availability of options and youth competencies and adjustment. For example, athletically skilled youth will likely choose to engage in sports to the extent that opportunities are available. Adolescents who engage in problem behavior and delinquency will likely gravitate toward other deviant youth in settings without adult supervision. Time use, however, is also a contributor to adjustment. To continue with the previous examples, adolescents who participate in sports are likely to become more skilled athletes, and adolescents who interact with deviant youth are likely to escalate their level of problem behavior.

Organized Activities

There are large cultural differences in the extent to which adolescents participate in organized activities such as sports, clubs, art and drama organizations, and religious groups. To illustrate the cultural differences in the time spent on these activities and their cultural meanings, researchers compared the leisure time of South Korean and Japanese adolescents.

M. Lee (2003) found that South Korean youth typically used their leisure time in passive activities including watching television, socializing, and idleness, and that the rates of these activities exceeded that of adolescents in other Asian countries. She suggested that South Korean youth are so exhausted by the effort and stress associated with studying that they have little energy to engage in active leisure. In addition, parents tend to view recreational activities as a distraction from studying, which is reflected in the lack of community organizations (e.g., sports, art) for adolescents to join.

Japan, in contrast to South Korea, provides extensive opportunities for adolescents to participate in organized activities through the Bundu-ryodo (pen and sword) organizations. Stemming from the samurai tradition in the 12th century, as suggested by Nishino and Larson (2003), it is important for adolescents, particularly boys, to enhance their academic and physical (particularly martial arts) skills. To achieve this goal, adolescent boys and girls participate in organized clubs and activities (busatsu) to enhance their athletic and cultural skills.

There is evidence that youth benefit from participating in organized activities, although in some cases, there are less positive effects as well. Fredricks and Eccles (2006) found that duration of participation (continued participation over multiple years) in high quality extracurricular activities was associated with American youths' academic and psychological adjustment. Lam et al. (2014) followed students from middle childhood into late adolescence using a methodology in which participants completed periodic telephone assessments. Participating in organized activities under adult supervision was associated with subsequent academic success. There appeared to be fewer benefits, however, associated with participating in organized sports. Although playing organized sports was associated with high social status and sense of belonging, it was also associated with increased alcohol use.

Active leisure is also associated with positive adjustment of South Korean adolescents. Although active leisure was uncommon for South Korean adolescents, it was associated with positive mood and low depression. In contrast, active leisure by Japanese students in connection with busatsu experiences was less positive. Adolescents described these activities as stressful and at times, leaving them fatigued (Nishino & Larson, 2003). Perhaps some of the negative mood associated with busatsu is that although they are "voluntary," there appears to be some pressure to participate.

Unsupervised Time With Peers

American adolescents experience considerable freedom to interact with their peers away from the scrutiny of adults. For example, Fuligni and Stevenson (1995) found that American high school students reported spending 23.1 hours per week with friends or going on dates compared with 9.7 hours and 13.5 hours per week, respectively, for students in Taiwan and Japan. There are also substantial differences across countries in the time that adolescents spend with members of the opposite sex. Fuligni and Stevenson found that American adolescents spent 4.7 hours per week dating, in contrast to 0.9 hours and 2.7 hours per week for adolescents in Taiwan and Japan, respectively. From their review of studies of adolescent time use, Larson and Verma (1999) concluded that American and European adolescents spend more time with peers of the opposite gender (e.g., 7% for American high school seniors and 4%–5% for older Italian adolescents) than do Asian adolescents (1%–2.4% for South Korean adolescents and less than 0.6% for Indian adolescents).

Underlying these cultural differences in the extent to which adolescents are allowed to interact with peers without adult supervision are cultural values regarding the importance of fostering autonomy in children. As discussed in Chapter 1 and throughout this book, values of independence and autonomy are present in the United States and many European countries, whereas values of interdependence are more prominent in other countries, including countries in Asia, Africa, and South America. These values of independence and interdependence are reflected in scripts and values pertaining to age and the domains over which adolescents are free to make independent decisions (Fuligni, 1998; Smetana, 2002). Consistent with these values, it is common for American adolescents to have unsupervised time and to be allowed to make decisions about their activities.

Larson and Verma (1999) concluded that unsupervised time with peers affords adolescents both developmental opportunities and risks. Peer interaction provides adolescents with opportunities to polish their social skills, including developing friendships, managing conflict, and behaving prosocially. On the negative side, however, extensive time with peers may be unproductive and may increase the likelihood of engaging in problem behavior.

The previous discussion pertains to the general argument that unsupervised time with peers presents youth with opportunities to engage in problem behavior that can include delinquent behavior, substance use, and risky sexual behavior. In a longitudinal study of American fourth- to eighth-grade boys, Stoolmiller (1994) showed that increases in wandering, defined as unsupervised time outside of the home, were associated with developmental changes in antisocial behavior and delinquent peer associations.

Computer Use and Online Socializing

Youth across the world are increasingly spending a portion of their leisure time in cyberspace. There are clear benefits associated with computer use. For example, in a study of American high school students, Willoughby (2008) found that moderate internet use was positively associated with academic orientation and higher grades, effects that were associated with either high or low use. Similarly, Chinese students' use of the internet to seek information was a protective factor against tobacco use (G. C. Huang et al., 2012).

As online activities have begun to occupy an increasing proportion of youth's leisure activities, questions regarding this activity have been raised. Multiple aspects of problematic online activity have been studied (e.g., bullying, online gambling, sexual-related online activities).

Computer use of 11- to 15-year-old adolescents in 30 countries was assessed as part of the World Health Organization's Health Behavior in School-Aged Children study (Bucksch et al., 2016). Comparisons of assessments conducted in 2002, 2006, and 2010 revealed an increase in weekday computer usage across all countries. Boys' use increased from a mean (averaged across countries) of 1.5 hours per day in 2002 to a mean of 3.67 hours per day in 2010. Girls' computer use also increased from a mean of 0.79 hours per day to 2.86 hours per day. Computer use was significantly higher during weekends; the mean across countries in 2010 was 4.93 hours per day for boys and 3.80 hours per day for girls. Note that computer use has increased since the time of this study. For example, in 2016, 17- to 18-year-old American youth spent about 6 hours per day of leisure time on their computers (Twenge, 2019).

Much of the concern about young people's extensive internet use pertains to "internet addiction," which is commonly defined in reference to its interference with other aspects of life (e.g., family and peer relationships, school, work, sleep) rather than the absolute time spent engaged in this activity. Concerns regarding internet addiction and efforts to treat it have become a major focus in China. L. Wang et al. (2013) used the Young Internet Addiction test to assess middle school, high school, and college students in seven Chinese cites. Sample questions from this instrument included "feeling preoccupied with the internet or online services and think about it when offline" and "lies to family members or friends to conceal excessive internet use." L. Wang et al. (2013) found that approximately 7.5% of adolescents exhibited this behavior. Internet-addicted adolescents were predominantly male (sex ratio of 1.9:1), had low academic achievement, and most were in high school.

Programs designed to treat internet addiction in China have been the subject of international media and a rather shocking documentary film (Rao, 2019). They report the existence of "boot camp" residential programs that resemble prisons in some aspects and include military training, drug treatment, family therapy, and in one notorious instance, electric shock for internet-addicted youth. Rao (2019) argued that concern over internet addiction in China is a manifestation of the salience of social control and child obedience in that culture.

Excessive internet use has also become a concern in countries outside of Asia. Blinka et al. (2015) assessed internet use by a representative sample of adolescents between the ages of 11 and 16 living in 25 European countries. Adolescents responded to a 5-item Excessive Internet Use Scale (e.g., "I have gone without eating or sleeping because of the internet," "I have tried unsuccessfully to spend less time on the internet"). They concluded that 4.4% and 1.4% of the population reported either moderate or excessive use and that adolescents in both of these groups exhibited both emotional and behavioral problems.

In addition to concerns regarding internet addiction, which most often involves gaming, there have also been concerns about extensive use of social media. A number of studies have reported that extensive time engaged in social media (e.g., Facebook, Instagram, Snapchat) is associated with depression (Twenge, 2019). One explanation of this finding is that people post selective information about themselves on social media (e.g., pictures showing them visiting interesting places with interesting looking people), and adolescents unfavorably compare themselves with these distorted profiles. The question remains, however, whether depressed adolescents simply spend more time on social media than do nondepressed adolescents, or instead, whether there is a causal relation such that hours engaged in social media predict subsequent increases in depression.

The question of the causal effects of social media use on depression was explored in two studies that yielded conflicting results. In a longitudinal study of adolescents and college students in the United States, girls' social media use was correlated with depression (Heffer et al., 2019). There was no evidence, however, that social media use predicted later increased depression. In contrast to these findings, in a 6-month longitudinal study of Norwegian adolescents, time engaged in social media predicted increased depression as well as conduct problems and heavy drinking (Brunborg & Burdzovic Andreas, 2019). In conclusion, although it appears that social media use is concurrently associated with depression, it is unclear whether social media use leads to increases in depression over time.

A number of additional questions require exploration, including the characteristics of youth that are negatively influenced by social media use and what types of social media activities (e.g., negative social comparison, bullying and victimization) are particularly problematic. There are also questions regarding sex differences in the associations between social media use and depression. Finally, it is important to understand how social media use might occupy time that could be spent doing other activities, some of which, such as physical activity, might have positive effects on well-being.

CONCLUSION

We have reviewed in this chapter how children and adolescents across the world differ in how they spend their time. Time is a limited resource, and time spent doing one activity limits opportunities to engage in another (Larson & Verma, 1999). Some activities provide opportunities for growth and enhancement of well-being, and others are either irrelevant or detrimental to well-being.

There are cultural differences in how youth spend their time. Some of these differences are explained by ecological parameters such as the wealth of the country and means of subsistence. Thus, children in poorer countries have limited access to school and likely attend for shorter amounts of time than children in more affluent countries. Children in societies in which the economy is based on family farming and businesses are more likely to work than are children in other countries.

The time that children engage in various activities is also a function of cultural norms and the value placed on different activities. For example, as we discussed previously, the considerable time that Chinese and South Korean students spend either attending school or studying can be traced to Confucian emphasis on learning and the view that official status in society is determined through educational achievement. To return to a theme that we first described in Chapter 1 and at the beginning of this chapter, activity settings are often infused with cultural meanings that have deep historical roots and are connected with the value systems of the culture.

Although the primary focus of this chapter has been on culture and time use, it is important to keep in mind that social class explains some of the within-culture variation in how children allocate their time. This is illustrated by Tudge et al.'s (2006) study of three-year-old children in the United Sates, Brazil, and Kenya. They found that activities were explained by a combination of culture and social class. For example, across cultural groups, children from middle class families were more likely than those from working class families to engage in academic lessons and to play with academic objects. There were also differences across cultures. For example, middle class children from Kenya engaged in more academic activities than did middle class children from Brazil.

Time use, however, is only one lens through which we can understand socialization experiences in relation to individual development and cultural patterns (Larson, 2001). For example, time attending school does not necessarily mean that children learn during this time. Time spent on the internet may be associated with different outcomes as a function of what children do during this time (e.g., conduct research for a school paper, watch pornography, bully others, communicate with friends). Despite this limitation, evaluating time use provides an important window into children's development both within (e.g., economic strata, ethnic group membership) and across cultures.

For additional resources, see the Appendix.

DISCUSSION QUESTIONS

1. What information does understanding children's time use provide for understanding culture and development? What are the limitations associated with this perspective?

2. Why do children differ across cultures in their amount and type of play?

3. What are the advantages and disadvantages associated with child work?

4. How is it possible to enhance the educational experiences of children across the world?

5. How much discretionary time do children and adolescents have? What are the advantages and disadvantages of having time away from adult supervision?

11

Culture and Academic Achievement

School is an important cultural institution that promotes child development, including for these children in Swaziland.

In Chapter 3, we reviewed learning in informal settings at home and in the community. In this chapter we describe learning and achievement in more formal settings, particularly in school. Formal learning has great importance in the lives of children and youth around the world. The primary goal is to prepare young people to take on responsible roles in society by the time they reach adulthood. Despite this common purpose, each culture has its own set of educational activities for youth. Cultures differ in the types of institutions provided for this purpose, the instructional methods used, and the number of years of training.

Research about education consists of a wide range of topics, including the role of schooling in society and the cognitive, social, and emotional consequences

https://doi.org/10.1037/0000228-011
Child and Adolescent Development in Cultural Context, by J. E. Lansford, D. C. French, and M. Gauvain

of attending school. We begin with some background on the establishment of required, or compulsory, schooling in the United States at the end of the 19th century. This historical context illustrates the close connections among schooling, larger societal goals, and child and youth development.

Then we discuss academic achievement, which is how well students meet the educational goals set forth for them by society. Here we concentrate on learning in the type of schools common in Western industrialized societies. Such schools exist around the world, and we describe research that compares academic achievement across several cultural contexts. Next, we discuss individual and social factors that are directly related to academic achievement. Although it is often assumed that academic achievement solely reflects an individual's cognitive capacity, this is not the case. Academic achievement is affected by many factors, including a person's desire to succeed in school or achievement motivation. Social experiences, including parental support, and societal factors, such as neighborhood and school characteristics, also contribute.

Toward the end of the chapter, we discuss formal learning arrangements in industrialized and nonindustrialized societies in the majority world. These various arrangements can differ greatly regarding what students learn and the consequences of the learning. We then look at what happens when cultures with different histories adopt educational practices based on the values and goals of Western industrialized societies. Lastly, we touch on recent efforts in the majority world to incorporate Indigenous cultural values and practices into formal schooling.

A BRIEF HISTORY OF COMPULSORY SCHOOLING IN THE UNITED STATES AND BEYOND

In the late 19th and early 20th centuries, the United States started requiring all young people to attend school. Compulsory education was going to play a major role in building the nation—a nation that was at a crossroads (Meyer et al., 1979). Huge changes in the lifestyle and economic base were underway (Hernandez, 1997; Stearns, 2015). The country was shifting from being primarily rural and agricultural to more urban and industrial. This change was not unique to the United States, it was also occurring in Western Europe and parts of Asia.

This shift had huge consequences for children and youth (Fass, 2007). Young people were no longer expected to take on farming and domestic responsibilities or join the labor force to help support their family. Rather, they were to attend school and learn knowledge and skills deemed valuable to society (Mayer et al., 1979). Lessons concentrated on literacy (reading and writing) and arithmetic—the proverbial three Rs. Students also learned civics, the rights and duties of citizenship. Academic lessons were aimed at preparing young people for emerging roles in the industrial and business sectors (mostly for boys) and social support occupations (e.g., teaching, nursing) and domestic sphere (mostly for girls). Civics served another purpose—to unify young people living in a nation that, for many, was divided and quite fragile.

Just a few decades earlier was the U.S. Civil War, which was followed by a massive migration of people from rural areas, many of whom had been enslaved on plantations, to urban centers. Toward the turn of the century, the country was experiencing a huge inflow of immigrants from around the globe. Thus, compulsory schooling was an effort to inculcate young society members into a common set of values while also equipping them with useful competencies for reaching societal goals. It also removed young people from the labor force, which protected them from hazardous workplace conditions and opened up jobs for unemployed adults. In short, compulsory education was a way to unify a large and changing nation, produce a skilled workforce, develop an informed and civically engaged populace, and safeguard children and youth (Crosnoe & Benner, 2015; Fass, 2007).

Compulsory education offered many benefits, but it also came with a cost for individuals, families, and society. Young people ended up spending a large part of their waking hours in school. As a result, their role changed from being a family member involved in the everyday activities of the home and community to one that entailed extensive training for the workforce, which would more than likely distance them from where they grew up and the life their parents had lived. Time at school was mainly spent with people other than kin and neighbors. Hence, new types of social relationships were introduced, based on a young person's societal role rather than personal connections, as was customary. The family was affected because its young members were no longer contributing to the household, while the cost of caring for them increased (Hernandez, 1997). Investment at the societal level was massive, including the cost of building many schools and then educating the students in them.

Other societal changes that impacted the lives of young people were occurring at the same time (Fass, 2007). The birth rate declined, and children now served a different function in the family. Also, more children were living past the critical early years—a change that coincided with the new field of pediatric medicine. School attendance also led to decreased play activities that young people created for themselves and increased play activities determined and monitored by adults (Stearns, 2015). Schools were age-graded; with so many students, it was an efficient way to teach them. Yet, because young people were living in smaller families with fewer siblings available for interaction, and associating mainly with same-age peers at school, children began spending more time with age-mates rather than in mixed-age groups as was previously the case (K. H. Rubin et al., 2015). This reduced the opportunity for them to learn from older children through instruction and modeling.

This history illustrates how the onset of compulsory schooling affected the experiences of children and youth, with consequences for social and psychological development. Again, these types of changes were occurring around the world in places that were shifting to a more urban and industrialized economic base and lifestyle (Stearns, 2015). Across societies, this change took a unique cultural cast. By the late 1800s, there was universal schooling in Japan, with an emphasis on traditional values of family and community. In 1917, the Communist Revolution in Russia ushered in compulsory schooling, which was considered vital for building the new socialist society. In 1923, Turkey became a republic and compulsory schooling based on a secular approach was introduced in an effort to integrate societal members from Islamic and non-Islamic backgrounds. In the 1940s, China adopted a Marxist political structure, which rejected traditional Confucian values that had been guiding family practices for centuries, and compulsory schooling was used to convey the values of the new communist society to its young members. Thus, as the 20th century advanced, more and more countries around the world introduced formal schooling to meet their societal goals of the time.

In 1989, the United Nations Convention on the Rights of the Child was signed by 189 world nations (Committee on the Rights of the Child, n.d.). Article 28 of this document identified education as a child's right and advocated that every nation provides free compulsory primary education to all its children. It also encouraged the development of different forms of secondary education, both general and vocational. Today, more children worldwide are attending school, and at earlier ages and for longer periods of time than ever before. That said, there are huge numbers of young people who do not attend school, and among those who attend school, there are substantial problems of underachievement in learning (UNESCO, 2017).

The Sustainable Development Goals adopted by the United Nations member states in 2015 are driving the international development agenda through 2030. Goal 4 is to ensure inclusive and equitable quality education and provide lifelong learning opportunities for all. To meet this goal, countries around the world have been striving to improve boys' and girls' access to free primary and secondary education. Nevertheless, children's participation in primary school has reached only 70% worldwide (United Nations, 2018b).

ACADEMIC ACHIEVEMENT

An outgrowth of the societal changes just described is concern with academic achievement—how well young people are meeting the educational goals of the school and society. Academic achievement is evaluated at the individual, school, and national levels (Crosnoe & Benner, 2015). At the individual level, the main question is how well a student is performing relative to same-age students. School assessments concentrate on the effectiveness of the school environment in delivering educational content and supporting student learning. National assessments look at student performance across countries.

Individual Achievement

Children's mastery of educational material is assessed in various ways. Teachers give incremental tests throughout the school year. The scores, reported in school grades, are useful for identifying how a student is performing relative to other students in the classroom and to determine if any students are exceling in certain areas or have special needs. Because the teachers (with whom the students have direct contact) complete these evaluations, there is a subjective element that may be affected by nonacademic information, such as a student's class behavior (M. K. Johnson et al., 2005). This type of grading may also reflect implicit biases regarding race and ethnicity. Teachers are more likely to give low grades to students from underrepresented minority groups (Girvan et al., 2017).

National assessments of individual achievement, typically conducted annually, evaluate students' scores on standardized tests relative to other students in the nation at their grade level. These assessments usually focus on two subject areas, mathematics and reading (or literacy). Recently, science has been added to track achievement in knowledge and skills relevant to science, technology, engineering, and mathematics, known as the STEM fields. These disciplines are foundational for many occupations in industrial and postindustrial (or information) societies.

A well-known assessment in the United States is the National Assessment of Educational Progress, which reports on nationwide trends in student achievement in mathematics, reading, and science (McFarland et al., 2019). The most recent assessments occurred in 2017 for fourth and eighth graders and in 2015 for 12th graders. Results show improvement over the past two decades at the primary and middle-school levels, but less improvement at the secondary level. The percentage of students who meet the level of proficiency, or competency, for their grade level is lower than desired, especially in mathematics and science.

Over the past decades, high-stakes standardized tests have been used in many countries to make important decisions about a student's future, such as promotion to the next educational level or the award of a diploma that recognizes student achievement and affects subsequent life chances (Stobart & Eggen, 2012). These tests are also used to determine if teachers are meeting certain educational goals, and, as a result, they can influence classroom experience as teachers "teach to the test" rather than cover a range of learning objectives. According to a survey of more than 8,000 educators in Australia, the majority of teachers felt that high-stakes test preparation interferes with the delivery of other curriculum areas (Polesel et al., 2014). Because scores on high-stakes tests affect students' future opportunities, these tests cause intense academic pressure on students and, in many cases, their families. Rather than increasing student success as claimed, high-stakes testing is related to a number of negative academic outcomes, including higher dropout rates and harmful psychological consequences like high levels of test anxiety and lower academic self-confidence when students do not do as well as hoped (Segool et al., 2013). Negative effects are especially pronounced for ethnic and language minority students and those from Indigenous and rural backgrounds for whom education is critical for advancing their future occupational and earning possibilities (Acosta et al., 2019; Altshuler & Schmautz, 2006; Wyman et al., 2010).

In many countries there is rising popularity in academic coaching and lessons outside of school to help students prepare for these tests. Although attendance in these so-called cram schools has, in some cases, improved test performance, enrollment is expensive and not widely available, which can exacerbate social inequities. Attendance in cram schools can also undermine student motivation to learn. A study conducted in Taiwan found that participation in this type of test preparation decreased students' intrinsic learning motivation and promoted the idea that learning is about test preparation and memorization rather than understanding, problem solving, and critical thinking (Tsai & Kuo, 2008).

School Effects

School quality is directly related to academic achievement. Students who attend higher-quality schools and spend more years in school perform better academically and earn higher wages in adulthood. More education in a population is also related to reduction in the national poverty rate (World Bank, 2018b). The contrary is also true. Deficits in education, including lack of formal education, dropping out, and too much time off from school, are related to lower academic achievement and lower wages in adulthood.

Educational attainment is compared internationally by the percentage of the adult population (ages 25–64) that has completed high school. In 2017, the Organisation for Economic Cooperation and Development (OECD, 2018b) reported secondary-school completion rates that ranged from under 40% in Mexico and Turkey to 90% or more in several nations including Canada, the Czech Republic, Finland, Poland, the Slovak Republic, and the United States. The proportion of adults who completed high school rose, on average, from 60% in 2000 to 79% in 2017. The OECD data do not include many countries from the majority world where the secondary-school achievement gap is considerable. According to the World Bank (2018a), secondary-school completion rates vary widely by regions in the majority world with 84% completion in eastern Europe and central Asia, 47% in east Asia and the Pacific, 42% in the Middle East and North Africa, 42% in Latin America and the Caribbean, 32% in South Asia, and 23% in sub-Saharan Africa.

Other than national differences, poor and minority students in rural and inner-city neighborhoods around the world often face substantial disadvantage in school quality compared with students in wealthier areas. In many countries, wealthier families can afford better schools for their children. For example, in Colombia 73% of public school students attend school for only half days, and the remaining 27% attend only 1 full day per week because of insufficient space and inadequate numbers of teachers (OECD, 2016a). In contrast, 60% of private school students in Colombia attend school for full days; however, the costs of private school are prohibitive for lower-income families.

Even when the cost of attending school is negligible or free, the cost of uniforms, books, and other supplies is sometimes prohibitively high for low-income families, leading to lower school enrollment rates for these students in many countries (e.g., Mutegi et al., 2017). Worldwide, financial barriers also pose a bigger problem for girls than for boys, as families with limited resources tend to prioritize their sons' education over their daughters' (United Nations, 2018b). Resulting from various environmental factors, poor students are also likely to start school with no preschool experience and lower skill levels compared with their middle-class peers. Disadvantaged students also tend to fall further behind as they advance in school (Molfese & Martin, 2001). Cultural differences and negative teacher attitudes may also hinder adjustment and learning for these children (Wigfield et al., 2015).

Peers influence children's attitudes toward and success in school. This influence is especially high at the secondary-school level because of the strong need for adolescents to belong to a peer group. For adolescents, feedback from peers often outweighs parental encouragement of academic achievement, with both positive and negative outcomes. Early research on this topic found that peer groups of Asian American students tend to support each other's academic pursuits and that these students often participate in education-related activities like studying together (Steinberg et al., 1992). In contrast, Ogbu (1988) reported anti-academic attitudes in other peer groups, including among African American students. However, more recent research involving African American students has found that the academic attitudes of elementary school students are achievement-oriented (Tyson, 2002) and that adolescents' perception of support from teachers can decrease negative school attitudes (Corprew & Cunningham, 2012).

The community can also have significant effects on a child's academic achievement. Poor children living in isolated rural areas or crowded inner cities tend to begin school with lower academic skills (P. Miller & Votruba-Drzal, 2013). Economically disadvantaged areas, both rural and urban, have fewer community resources, both cultural (e.g., museums) and natural (e.g., neighborhood parks), and more stressors, such as crime and pollution, that are associated with poorer academic achievement (P. Miller et al., 2019). In poor urban areas, inadequate nutrition, unsafe housing, and unemployment also contribute to lower academic achievement for children living in these environments (G. W. Evans, 2004).

National Comparisons

Since 2000 the OECD has assessed cross-national academic achievement in the Programme for Individual Student Assessment (PISA). Every 3 years, in more than 70 countries (including 27 low-income and 44 middle-income countries), the academic performance of 15-year-olds is compared in reading, mathematics, and science.

The 2015 PISA results (OECD, 2016b) indicated high levels of proficiency in the three subject areas in some countries. But overall student performance was quite low. Eighty percent of students in seven nations (Canada, Estonia, Finland, Hong Kong [China], Japan, Macao [China], Singapore) met or exceeded the baseline levels of proficiency in science, reading, and mathematics. There was a wide range of performance across the other nations. Of significant note, however, academic achievement on this test did not distinguish rich and well-educated nations from poor and less-educated nations. For example, achievement scores of 10% of the most disadvantaged students in Vietnam compared favorably with the average student in the OECD set of middle-income nations. As for the United States, in 2015 it ranked 25th in science, 24th in reading, and 40th in mathematics achievement.

PISA also assesses student interests and aspirations. The 2015 report emphasized science learning, which is expected to play an increasingly important role in economic success for individuals and nations. In most of the countries, students from advantaged backgrounds were more likely to expect to have a career in science than were less-advantaged students. This difference held regardless of students' scores on the science test or their self-reported enjoyment in learning science. Girls and boys performed similarly on the science test, but boys were more likely than girls to aim for science-related careers. This was true even for girls who reported that they enjoyed learning science.

Another cross-national project that compares academic achievement is the Trends in International Mathematics and Science Study (TIMSS; Provasnik et al., 2016). Every 4 years, in a large number of nations (ranging from 38 to more than 50 across assessments), the mathematics and science achievement of fourth and eighth graders is assessed. This project, which began in 1995, is funded by the U.S. Department of Education. Its primary impetus is to evaluate the academic achievement of U.S. students relative to students around the world.

In 2015, fourth-grade students in seven nations—Singapore, Hong Kong (China), Republic of Korea, Taipai (China), Japan, Northern Ireland, and the Russian Federation—performed better than U.S. fourth graders in mathematics. Eighth graders in eight nations (Singapore, Taipei [China], Hong Kong [China], Republic of Korea, Japan, Kazakhstan, the Russian Federation, and Israel) performed better than U.S. eighth-grade students in mathematics. As for science, fourth-grade students in four nations—Singapore, Republic of Korea, the Russian Federation, and Japan—scored better than their U.S. counterparts. Eighth graders in six nations (Singapore, Taipei [China], Japan, Republic of Korea, Slovenia, and Kazakhstan) performed better than U.S. eighth graders.

Going Beyond Test Scores in National Comparisons

The PISA and TIMSS projects provide insight about cross-national achievement in basic subject areas. However, they do not tell us about the psychological and social factors that underlie these patterns. Other studies do, however. A classic research project conducted by Harold Stevenson and his colleagues (Stevenson & Stigler, 1992), which was influential in launching the TIMMS project, investigated national differences in academic achievement in the United States and several other nations (Stigler & Hiebert, 1997).

This study was motivated by cross-national comparisons in which U.S. students scored lower than students in some Asian and Western European countries. Before this research was conducted, poor school achievement of American students was often attributed to failures of the school system. However, this research provided evidence that even in the earliest months of first grade, U.S. children already lag behind children in some Western and industrialized societies in academic achievement. This finding suggests that there is more involved in national comparisons of academic achievement than educational practices per se. Research Highlight 11.1 describes this study in detail. As you will read, two main themes emerged from these findings. First, children in various nations seem to be motivated in different ways to do well in school. Second, cultural values and practices, especially parental involvement, appear to relate to these differences.

PSYCHOLOGICAL AND SOCIAL FACTORS RELATED TO ACADEMIC ACHIEVEMENT

Academic achievement can reflect a number of factors, individual and social, related to the school experience. Much of the research on psychological factors has focused on how a student's motivation to learn and perform well in school contributes to academic achievement. Other research has looked closely at social factors, in particular how parental involvement contributes to students' academic achievement. In describing these areas of research, we look at findings from different ethnic communities in the United States and in different regions of the world.

Achievement Motivation

Achievement motivation is a set of goal-directed emotions and behaviors that energize an individual to act in certain ways in school-related learning activities. It includes the emotions that students associate with learning tasks, the way they view themselves and their abilities, and the responses they have to success and failure (Wigfield et al., 2015). In other words, achievement motivation reflects a student's views of him or herself as a person and a learner. For example, some children have negative feelings about certain learning tasks and believe they are unable to learn in these areas. Sometimes these feelings and beliefs are so strong that they distract the student from the task itself and impede further learning.

Early research on achievement motivation focused on internal needs and drives as a source (Graham & Weiner, 2012). This approach, derived from personality theory, considered motivation to be a dispositional trait of which individuals have certain amounts (e.g., low, high). It assumed universality, that motivation is a common human characteristic. Consequently, most of the research based on this view was not concerned with culture. More

RESEARCH HIGHLIGHT 11.1

Classroom Learning in China, Japan, and the United States

In the middle childhood years, classroom lessons concentrate on the further development and refinement of basic skills in mathematics and reading. If children do not develop strong skills in these areas at this time, they often face academic difficulties later (Hernandez, 2011; Siegler et al., 2012). In the latter part of the 20th century, educators and psychologists became concerned because children in the United States were not performing as well in these subject areas as their counterparts in China and Japan. These observations were the stimulus for a large project led by developmental psychologist Harold Stevenson that sought to understand the reasons for these achievement differences or gaps (Stevenson & Stigler, 1992; Stigler & Hiebert, 1997).

The researchers gave reading and mathematics tests to several thousand first, fifth, and 11th graders in two U.S. urban areas (Minneapolis, Minnesota; Fairfax County, Virginia), two East Asian cities (Beijing; Taipei, Taiwan), and Japan (Sendai). The U.S. sample included European, Chinese, African, and Latin American students. Teachers and students and their mothers were interviewed about the value of education, beliefs about learning, attitudes toward school, and family involvement in children's schoolwork.

There were differences in academic performance across the nations studied. Japanese first graders scored highest in reading, followed closely by Chinese American, Taiwanese, and European American students. By fifth grade, Taiwanese and European American students had jumped ahead of Japanese and Chinese Americans. On the mathematics test, American students scored considerably below the other students, and this difference became larger as children advanced from first to fifth grade. At both grade levels, Chinese (Beijing, Taiwan) and Japanese students had the highest mathematics scores, with Chinese Americans following close behind.

To understand what might explain these cultural differences, the researchers assessed the cognitive or intelligence scores of the children and found no evidence that the American children had lower intellectual levels. In addition, parental education levels were highest among European American students. There were, however, marked differences in parents' beliefs about learning, their school-related activities with their children, and how they interpreted their children's academic performance. Chinese and Japanese mothers generally viewed academic achievement as the child's most important pursuit and stressed the value of effort in academic learning. Once children entered school, the parents saw it as their duty to provide an environment conducive to achievement and to be available to assist, direct, and supervise their children's learning. American mothers were less likely to be actively involved in these ways and tended to put more emphasis on the importance of innate ability than effort in school learning. Children's behaviors also differed. American children spent much less time on homework and reading for pleasure and more time playing and doing chores than did Japanese or Taiwanese children.

This research is important for several reasons. It was one of the first studies to look closely at classroom practices across cultures and to try to connect these practices to children's academic achievement in specific subject areas. It also demonstrated how the classroom experience relates to the broader cultural context through the values that underlie school learning as well as family engagement in this process. Finally, it provided insight into the different ways that teachers teach the core academic curriculum, information that is useful for educators in designing ways to help children learn in school. The contribution of this work lives on in the Trends in International Mathematics and Science Study (Provasnik et al., 2016), a project committed to discovering and distributing information about best practices for classroom instruction from around the globe.

contemporary approaches assume that motivation varies across activities and learning environments. Many researchers adopt an Expectancy × Value approach in which motivation is conceptualized as the combination of expectancy—likelihood of goal attainment—and value—how much the goal is desired (Wigfield et al., 2015). This approach has been useful in educational research and has been found to predict students' academic interests and engagement.

Other contemporary research concentrates on learners' beliefs and evaluations of their achievement-related activities. Researchers have identified two response patterns among children when they work on a challenging task at which they could fail (Elliot et al., 2017). In a classic study on this topic, fifth- and sixth-grade children were given a series of difficult problems to solve, similar to a game of Twenty Questions (Diener & Dweck, 1978). At first the children were able to solve the problems, but then the experimenter presented several very hard problems that the children were not able to solve. Some children maintained or even improved their level of performance despite failure on some of the hard problems; these children were labeled as "mastery-oriented" because they were focused on gaining skill or mastery at the problems. In contrast, other children tended to give up easily or to show marked performance deterioration when working on challenging problems; these children were labeled as "helpless." When mastery-oriented children performed poorly, they expressed neutral or even positive emotions, attributed their failure to insufficient effort rather than to lack of ability, and maintained high expectations for future success. Helpless children, on the other hand, expressed negative emotions such as frustration, blamed their own lack of ability for their performance, and expressed low expectations for future performance.

The important point is that helpless and mastery-oriented children do not differ in their actual ability levels; rather, they *think* differently, or have different mindsets, about their ability and achievement (Dweck, 2006; Yeager & Dweck, 2012). And these beliefs affect children's motivation on later academic tasks. Mastery-oriented children tend to have *learning goals* and are concerned with improving their skills and learning new things rather than evaluating their ability. Children who show the helpless pattern, on the other hand, tend to have *performance goals*—that is, they are concerned with "looking smart," obtaining positive judgments, and avoiding negative judgments of their ability.

Sociocultural Context and Achievement Motivation

Research on achievement motivation was developed in Western societies, and the empirical support is mostly based on Western, middle-class samples (King et al., 2017). Recently, there has been increased attention on other populations, including young people living in certain environmental and cultural settings and students in ethnic minority and immigrant communities.

Achievement motivation is fostered in environments that encourage children and youth to develop interest and competence in academic learning along with a sense of internal control (e.g., effort, persistence) about their learning outcomes (Zusho et al., 2016). Children whose parents encourage more mastery-oriented behavior from them as toddlers, such as promoting independence and persistence in solving problems, show more mastery-oriented behaviors later on when they enter school (Pomerantz et al., 2005). Some environmental conditions may promote helplessness in children. In research on children in rural upstate New York, G. W. Evans (2004) found that those living in poverty who experienced a number of physical stresses, such as crowding and poor-quality housing, and psychosocial stresses, such as family turmoil or violence, were more likely to behave in a helpless manner when presented with a challenging puzzle task than were poor children who had fewer stresses in their lives.

Other differences between learning at home versus at school can emerge when parents are unfamiliar with what their children are learning or experiencing at school. Although some cross-generational differences in the content and process of learning are always expected, these differences may be exacerbated in families undergoing dramatic cultural change, such as immigrant families (Kagitçibasi, 2007).

In the United States, achievement gaps among children and youth from different racial and ethnic backgrounds have led researchers to investigate whether achievement motivation differs in these groups, and if so, why. Researchers have studied between-group and within-group differences (Wigfield et al., 2015). They are also interested in whether there are discontinuities, or dissonance, between informal learning practices at home and school learning, and if they impact the academic motivation and achievement of children from ethnic and racial groups (Kumar, 2006). Discontinuities can lead to tensions between home-based and school learning, especially when children first enter school. In earlier chapters we described a classic study by linguist Shirley Brice Heath (1983) that investigated this issue by looking at the early communicative experiences of African American and European American children living in working-class communities in the southeastern United States. The conversations between African American adults and children resembled storytelling, reflecting the oral tradition of the community. In contrast, adult–child talk in the European American group was more similar to the types of exchanges that occur in school, such as asking children questions to which the adult knows the answer. This type of talk may function as training for the types of exchanges children will experience later in school, which in this case was more similar for the European American children.

Because schools reflect society, children and youth from ethnic and racial minority communities may experience societal discrimination toward their group at school. As a result, they may feel like outsiders there and be more likely to experience home-school dissonance. These experiences, in turn, may affect their engagement with academic material and motivation to learn (Sue, 2004). Sometimes, in response to these experiences, young people develop coping strategies by creating different self-identities for home and school that help them navigate the school system. For example, Asian American students may respect cultural values of filial piety at home, including deference to elders, yet be more open in interactions with adults at school. There can also be negative outcomes from home-school dissonance. An early study of psychosocial pressures associated with academic achievement found that students who do not develop such strategies might show maladaptive behaviors, including low levels of achievement motivation (Phelan et al., 1991).

Ethnic and racial minority students may also show low levels of achievement motivation because they are vulnerable to stereotype threat, the awareness that some people have negative stereotypes about their group (Steele & Aronson, 1995). Students experiencing stereotype threat may perform poorly on academic tasks because of concern that they will be judged in relation to the stereotype of their group. For some students, this experience may lead them to devalue school and academics more generally, which can result in lower academic achievement. Students of color who are the most invested in schooling are especially vulnerable to the effects of negative stereotypes about achievement in their ethnic group (Osborne & Walker, 2006).

More research on academic motivation and achievement among ethnic and racial minority groups is needed to investigate individual differences in academic motivation and how motivation is affected in different classroom and school contexts (Graham & Weiner, 2012). Research is also needed on achievement motivation among immigrant youth, who comprise a sizable portion of societies in the world today. These youth are not only grappling with normative developmental challenges, they often have to navigate their home culture values and goals as well as those of the host country while living in a discriminatory context (Hernandez, & Napierala, 2013; Motti-Stefanidi, 2018). A recent meta-analysis on the experiences of immigrant youth in Europe found that they often have poor academic adjustment (Dimitrova et al., 2016). However, youth who have a higher sense of self-efficacy (Bandura, 1997), the belief that one has the capability to manage and accomplish a task, have higher academic achievement. This finding indicates that immigrant youth, who have learning and mastery goals they feel they are capable of achieving, adapt better to the new society.

Achievement Motivation Across Cultures

Research conducted across cultural settings has yielded valuable information about achievement motivation. By and large, results show positive relations between a mastery approach to learning and academic engagement. For example, research in Australia with third- to sixth-grade students from Aboriginal and non-Aboriginal backgrounds found that a mastery-oriented motivational approach to school learning was a positive predictor of academic engagement in both cultural groups (Mooney et al., 2016).

Researchers have studied how a culture's emphasis on individualism versus collectivism relates to achievement motivation. Results show that individual effort is more salient in students' motives to achieve academically in individualistic cultures, while fear of failure is more important in collectivist cultures because it is assumed that it helps maintain group harmony (Eaton & Dembo, 1997). Along these lines, a study involving Korean middle-school students found positive relations between academic motivation and conformity, but only when youth felt supported by parents, peers, and teachers (Jiang et al., 2015). These results are interesting because in Western samples conformity is usually negatively related to academic achievement.

Other research suggests that the relations between individualism and collectivism and academic motivation may not be so clear-cut. One study found that the academic motivation of Turkish adolescents, who live in a more collectivist culture, was affected by their social relationships with peers and teachers, whereas the academic motivation of German students, who live in an individualistic society, was based largely on their own efforts to learn (Raufelder et al., 2017). In another study with secondary-school students in two collectivist cultures, China and the Philippines, social goals, such as affiliation, concern for others, and approval, were more important than mastery-related achievement goals in predicting students' academic outcomes in both cultures (King et al., 2014). In yet another study, adolescents' perceptions of support from parents and peers were positively related to academic motivation in a sample that included Canadian (European and Chinese Canadian students), Cuban, and Spanish adolescents—societies that differ in individualism and collectivism (Vitoroulis et al., 2012).

Overall, the results indicate that, regardless of cultural orientation, a socially supportive learning environment is important for academic motivation (Kumar et al., 2018). To accomplish this goal, a supportive classroom environment that emphasizes individual achievement, rather than peer competition, is needed. This type of learning environment may be especially important for students from ethnic minority and immigrant communities who often feel marginalized at school (Suárez-Orozco et al., 2018).

Parental Involvement

In societies with formal schooling, parents contribute to their children's academic achievement in various ways (Hoover-Dempsey et al., 2005). Parents may provide financial and material support (e.g., school fees, workbooks, a desk or quiet place to study at home), although this type of support is contingent on the family's finances. Parents may also foster their children's engagement in school by encouraging them academically and by making their expectations for academic achievement known. Other forms of parental involvement pertain directly to learning class material, such as helping children with homework and providing enrichment experiences (e.g., after-school lessons). Parents with little formal education may have difficulty assisting their children with schoolwork, however, and single parents and parents who work long hours are limited in the support they can provide. Parents may also be involved with the school, including communicating with teachers about their child's learning and school performance. Parent involvement with the school is higher in schools that communicate clear expectations to parents about these behaviors. Research shows that not all types of parental involvement are linked positively to academic achievement, and also that positive relations are associated with the cultural background of the family (Holloway & Jonas, 2016).

Parental involvement in children's schooling varies across ethnic groups in the United States as well as across national groups. Earlier in this chapter we described research that found higher academic achievement among Chinese and Japanese students as compared with students in the United States (Stevenson & Stigler, 1992). The researchers identified some striking differences in parental involvement among the three cultures. Chinese and Japanese parents adopt what is called "learning-related parenting." These parents reported that they were expected to be involved in their children's education, create a home environment that supports learning, spend time working on homework with their children, and provide children with learning opportunities outside of school. Chinese and Japanese parents were also more involved with their children's teachers, with regular back-and-forth communication about children's school performance. All these behaviors occurred less often among American parents in this study.

Later research reported somewhat different patterns in China and the United States and also raised new issues, perhaps reflecting increased urbanization in China and higher educational expectations in the two countries over the past decades. In one study, middle-school children from both nations perceived that their parents valued educational achievement, which was positively related to children's academic achievement (Cheung & Pomerantz, 2014). Another study examined parental involvement in school learning of seventh and eighth graders, a time when schooling becomes more academically challenging (Cheung & Pomerantz, 2011). Again, in both cultural groups, parental involvement predicted children's academic engagement and achievement. However, only in the American sample did it predict higher levels of competence and positive emotional functioning in children.

To explain these results, the researchers looked closely at the types of control or support parents provided for their children. They found that Chinese parents used more psychological control in school-related interactions with their children. This type of control involves behaviors that try to manipulate the child's emotions such as making them feel worried or ashamed. In contrast, working- and middle-class parents in the United States tended to promote their children's autonomy, such as allowing choice and encouraging initiative, in school-related activities at home. When reacting to children's school performance, Chinese parents were more likely than American parents to emphasize their children's mistakes rather than their successes.

Thus, despite academic advantages among Chinese families, the method of control that parents use seems to have an emotional toll on children (Pomerantz et al., 2014). Parental use of control versus support may have been especially important because of the age of the children in this study, which averaged close to 13. They were right on the cusp of adolescence when striving for individual identity and autonomy occur. Building on these findings, Pomerantz and colleagues recommend that children's academic achievement and emotional well-being in China could be aided through parents' greater involvement in their children's education (as in traditional Chinese parenting), while at the same time using strategies that are more autonomy-promoting than controlling (as in traditional American parenting).

This recommendation is consistent with the idea, initially put forward by Erik Erikson (1968), that satisfying the need for autonomy is essential for individual psychological growth. However, researchers hold differing views about the importance of autonomy for academic achievement in Western and non-Western societies. For some, autonomy needs are consistent with the Western value of individualism, but contrary to values of interdependence and social conformity in collectivistic Eastern societies (Oishi, 2000). Researchers who subscribe to self-determination theory, which is relevant to achievement motivation, endorse a more universal view (Ryan & Deci, 2000). They see autonomy as an innate human need for self-determination (i.e., regulating behaviors in terms of one's internal volition) that is vital for individual growth and social integration, regardless of cultural context. Thus, in this view, social connections are not ignored; they are considered important contributors to individual autonomy.

Research with Chinese and South Korean children and youth found that autonomy support by parents and teachers positively predicted students' academic functioning and psychological well-being (d'Ailly, 2003; Jang et al., 2009). In other research, individual autonomy was found to be beneficial to academic motivation in Chinese children regardless of the quality of teacher–student relationships (Bao & Lam, 2008). In yet another study, Chinese parents' collectivistic tendency positively contributed to young adolescents' autonomous motivation, though this relation was mediated through parental autonomy-granting (Pan et al., 2013). Also, parents with higher levels of education granted more autonomy and exercised less psychological control with their children. These results suggest that autonomy is not unique to individualistic Western cultures; there is diversity among parents in collectivist societies in their emphasis on adolescents' autonomy, and autonomy support in non-Western societies has positive relations to academic motivation and achievement.

We now turn to parental involvement across ethnic groups in the United States. Among American students, Asian American children outperform children in other ethnic groups in mathematics and science. Although African American, European American, and Latin American parents also value education highly, their children do not experience the same level of academic success that is seen in Asian American families (Holloway & Jonas, 2016). One question that researchers have considered is whether Asian Americans' parental involvement in their children's schooling explains the children's high levels of performance. Much of this research has focused on Chinese American families, although the findings raise questions that are relevant for many ethnic groups.

Asian American parents hold high expectations for their children's education. Many of these parents tell their children that academic achievement is part of their duty to the family and parents also profess a learning-related view that emphasizes effort (Chao, 2001). Although these findings are consistent with earlier research conducted in China (Stevenson & Stigler, 1992), many of the behaviors related to children's academic success in China do not transfer to Chinese American families. For instance, parental school involvement, especially with teachers, is related to academic achievement in the United States, particularly among European Americans. Although Chinese parents are involved in their children's school, Chinese American parents attend fewer school events than parents from other ethnic groups in the U.S. (Holloway & Jonas, 2016). However, Chinese parents support their children's learning outside of school in other ways, such as arranging tutoring for their children.

It may be that parental involvement among Chinese Americans reflects cultural views about what the parents' role in children's schooling should be. Research on immigrant Mexican mothers in the United States found that these mothers consider the school, and not the parent, to be responsible for children's formal learning (Goldenberg et al., 2001). Given that parental involvement in children's schooling is associated with academic achievement in the United States, researchers suggest that schools should provide clear communication to parents to increase participation by immigrant parents (Hoover-Dempsey et al., 2005). Of course, there may be other reasons for low rates of school involvement among Chinese American parents. Chinese families that immigrate to the United States may differ from nonimmigrant Chinese families in their adherence to traditional cultural values of Confucianism or in their ideas about the purpose of schooling for their children's future.

To conclude this section, a few comments are in order. The psychological and social factors that contribute to achievement motivation and parental involvement across ethnic and cultural contexts are not well understood. This is partly because research participants are typically categorized by the social group with which they identify or the nation where they live. As we have stated in other parts of this book, treating ethnicity or culture as a single, overarching, and uniform feature of human psychological experience may not reveal the complex ways that these background experiences contribute to psychological development, which includes the academic motivation of an individual student or parental involvement in a family. In addition, according to cross-cultural research, cultures labeled "individualistic" and "collectivistic" are viewed as wholly distinct from each other, and the differences among societies grouped along these dimensions are ignored—differences that are known to exist. The type of collectivism practiced in China today, for example, differs from that found in Cuba and Turkey; individualism experienced in the United States differs from that found in Sweden and the Netherlands.

Finally, more research is needed regarding how parental involvement changes as children get older and confront new developmental challenges (Holloway & Jonas, 2016). It is likely that young children benefit most from parents' help in developing cognitive and social skills that are important during this growth period. Adolescents, on the other hand, may benefit more when parents support their autonomy and identity and, also, when they provide guidance and support regarding future educational and occupational goals.

A BROADER CULTURAL PERSPECTIVE ON FORMAL LEARNING

Around the world, there are various types of formal learning opportunities for young people in addition to the Western model we just discussed. There are highly specialized, one-on-one training situations, such as apprenticeships, that are devoted to passing on valued skills in the community. For example, Tanon (1994) observed how boys in the Dioula community in Cote d'Ivoire learn to weave traditional cloth patterns in one-on-one interactions with expert weavers. Other formal learning settings involve groups of children or youth who learn an important aspect of the culture, such as civic or religious instruction. Although this arrangement may seem similar to formal schooling based on the Western model, these schools differ in the scope of the lessons and the outcomes of the learning for the individuals and society. We must also be mindful that some children learn school-like skills outside the classroom. For instance, children who take on adult-like roles in society because of family hardship are often involved in commerce, which can teach them about mathematical reasoning. To illustrate, Research Highlight 11.2 describes the mathematics skills of Brazilian children who sell products on the street.

Variation in Settings of Formal Learning

To illustrate variation in formal group learning, we use Serpell and Hatano's (1997) description of the central themes and societal aspects of three formal schooling approaches found in cultures around the world. In the Western cultural tradition, previously discussed, the main themes are individual self-expression, technical expertise, and cognition as a personal and transforming accomplishment. Subject matter largely concentrates on the traditional topics of reading, writing, mathematics, and social studies. Over the last century, science has been added and has gradually assumed an increasingly larger role. Related societal impacts stressed by Serpell and Hatano include the social stigmatization of unschooled individuals as well as those who have fewer years of schooling than the societal norm. Also, the legitimization of exporting this educational approach beyond national borders has occurred. This practice has been forcefully critiqued as a form of intellectual colonialism and cultural imperialism (Carnoy, 1974; Freire, 1968).

The Sino-Japanese educational tradition emphasizes moral perfection, filial piety, and emulation of models and cultural norms. It is based on Confucian philosophy and its emphasis on the orderly nature of the universe, the

RESEARCH HIGHLIGHT 11.2

Learning and Using Mathematics Outside of School

Human beings use mathematical reasoning every day to carry out activities, such as calculating the costs of items in the supermarket, dividing a snack equally among friends, and estimating the distance to school and other destinations. In most cases, people learn the skills used to accomplish these mental acts in grade school, but not all children or adults have the opportunity to acquire a formal education. Yet even children who lack formal training or performed poorly in school can develop and use mathematical reasoning in everyday life. For instance, research has found that children who sell items on the street demonstrate the ability to use mathematics to support their livelihoods (Saxe, 1988).

Research with Brazilian children, between ages 9 and 15, who sell items on the streets illustrates these mathematical skills (Nunes et al., 1985, 1993). These young street vendors, who have limited experience with formal mathematics instruction, are nonetheless able to solve mathematics problems successfully when they are presented in a familiar form such as selling fruit or other products. In a way, this is not surprising because the children's success at their trade relies on mathematical reasoning. The researchers were interested in the types of mathematics problems the children tackled and the methods they used to solve them. One thing the researchers observed was that the children often sold items in bulk, such as three oranges for 10 cruzados (the monetary unit in Brazil). If a customer only wanted two oranges, the seller would need to figure out a fair price or risk losing the sale. The seller also needed to account for inflation, which is rampant in Brazil and prices 1 day may differ from the prices the day before. The children solved the problems mentally, rather than writing them down to calculate the answer. This approach allowed them to work quickly, which is important for making a sale, especially when a pedestrian is in a hurry or a driver is stopped in traffic.

To study the children's skill at mathematical calculation, the experimenters presented five young vendors with problems to solve either in the form of familiar commercial transactions or in a manner similar to how they would be presented in school. The children differed in their performance on these two types of problems. On the commercial transactions, the children were correct 98% of the time, and when the same problems were presented in a school-like format, the children were correct only 37% of the time. The children's methods for solving the problems also differed. As expected, they solved the commercial problems mentally, and used pencil and paper to solve the school-like problems. They also used different problem-solving strategies in the two situations. In the commercial calculations, the children used an "add-on" strategy to arrive at the correct answer (e.g., if the customer buys two coconuts at 40 cruzados each and pays with a 500-cruzado bill, the seller would count out the change beginning with 80 and ending at 500). For the school-like problems, the children used strategies similar to those taught in school, but they often did so incorrectly (e.g., writing down the subtraction problem on paper and doing an operation, such as borrowing [which is difficult for many children], in the wrong way).

This research shows that when young people with little or no schooling are confronted with problems involving mathematical reasoning, they use different skills from those taught in school, but are nonetheless effective for solving the problems (Nunes & Bryant, 1996, 2015). It also demonstrates children's resilience and their ability to survive and learn complex cognitive skills despite having limited access to formal schooling.

connection of human beings to the natural world, the importance of staying in harmony with the world, and the role of adults as role models for young people (Serpell & Hatano, 1997). Cultures with schools based on these ideas, such as China and Japan, stress the responsibility of teachers in conveying valued knowledge and modeling important cultural skills to young people. This approach has been identified as one of the reasons for the high levels of academic achievement in these cultures. However, the strong emphasis on transmitting established ways of thinking and acting has also generated societal concern about how to enhance creativity, intellectual exploration, and innovation in younger generations.

As a third example, Serpell and Hatano (1997) described the Islamic tradition practiced in Qur'anic schools. This form of education, which can differ considerably across the many cultures where it exists, concentrates on the teachings of the Prophet Muhammad in the Qur'an. Common features of these schools are the authority of the sacred text and memorization and recitation of this text. Individual and societal consequences of this education are complex. Wagner (1993) considered close examination of text as helping children develop skills for learning how to read in the more Western-style schools that many of them also attend. However, Serpell and Hatano contended that the large focus on prayer recitation may limit the types of cognitive skills developed by children and youth who attend these schools.

As these examples show, formal schooling of one sort or another exists around the world. Thus, although formal schooling is often conceptualized according to the Western cultural form, there are in actuality many types of educational traditions and practices. And different forms of schooling have different consequences for individual learning, child development, and society. To explore this issue further, next we will look at changes that occur when formal schooling based on the Western model of education is introduced in communities with very different histories.

What Happens When Communities Adopt Western-Style Schools?

As we described earlier, schooling of children and youth has changed dramatically over the last century. One such change was the introduction of the Western model of education to societies with very different histories and traditions, which greatly affected people's lives and the society at large.

Rogoff and colleagues (2005) studied the introduction of formal schooling in European-heritage families in the United States (using historical records) and in a traditional Guatemalan Maya community (using interview data collected over three generations, a 23-year period). In these two very different communities, the changes were remarkably similar and affected many aspects of children's lives. Children's involvement in certain activities declined, including work that contributed to the family both practically (e.g., household chores) and economically (e.g., child care responsibilities that allowed mothers to work for compensation). When schooling began, children of various ages were in the same classroom, but over time, classrooms were increasingly age-graded (Rogoff, 2003). As a result, children spent more time, both in and outside of school, with close-in-age peers rather than in mixed-age groups, with consequences for peer social relationships and peer learning. What and where children learned, and who taught them, also changed. School, rather than home, became the center for learning, and other changes followed, including behaviors central to socialization, such as modes of parent–child interaction that resemble school practices (e.g., sustained conversation on a single topic).

In such circumstances, young people's aspirations about their future schooling and occupations may change—often distancing them from their community and traditions, both literally and psychologically. This pattern has been reported in many places around the world. For instance, after the adoption of Western-style education in rural areas in many African nations, adolescents needed to move away from home to attend residential boarding schools for most of the year to advance in secondary education (Oburu & Mbagaya, 2019). Young people discovered that the village did not have sufficient work opportunities and they ended up leaving the community, often for urban centers, to find work (Nsamenang, 2005). In research conducted in Russia in the late 20th century shortly after the breakup of the Soviet Union, there were good and bad outcomes from schools adopting Western education values (Elliott & Tudge, 2007). Changes were evident in many behaviors of teachers and parents, as well as in their educational aspirations for children and youth.

The introduction of formal schooling is usually one part of a constellation of changes in a community (Rogoff et al., 2005). A related, societal-level change is the shift from subsistence to a market-based economy, which was studied by Greenfield (2004) and Saxe (2012). After a long absence from their respective field sites (around 25 years), these investigators returned and studied the cognitive processes they had studied earlier. Greenfield's research in a Maya community in southern Mexico focused on pattern representation and social learning of a traditional activity, weaving. She found that these skills changed substantially as community members became involved in a market economy and formal schooling. Saxe studied children's mathematics skills in the Oksapmin community in Papua New Guinea. He found significant change in mathematics practices (e.g., counting, arithmetic calculations) that were consistent with changes in economics and schooling at the societal level.

A related community-level change is urbanization, which is affecting child development and culture around the world. As is too often the case, the rapid pace of this change can alter a community significantly in the span of a single generation. Jukes et al. (2018) studied this process with a sample of 562 adolescents (average age of 17) in Gambia. Over the past decades, this African nation has seen dramatic growth in urban residence, and this trend is expected to continue for the foreseeable future. The participants were from the Mandinka and Wolof ethnic groups and lived in villages at the time of the study. About 42% of them had lived in an urban center for a short time (average of 4 months), close to one third had attended secular government schools, and the remainder had attended madrassas (religious Koranic schools). The researchers investigated relations between schooling and urban residence and performance on several cognitive tests (e.g., digit span, visual search, categorical frequency). They also asked adult villagers to rate the adolescents on various dimensions of social responsibility (e.g., cooperative, kind, patient) that are considered important to village life. The results showed that both urban residence and type of schooling affected the behaviors of the young people, and there were positive relations between these experiences and performance on the cognitive measures. Living in the city, however, was negatively associated with ratings of social responsibility. The researchers suggested that city life, where there are many people and few long-standing social connections, might have promoted more individualistic concerns among these youth. However, the researchers note that parents may be more willing to let offspring who are less socially connected to the village move to urban centers. Either or both explanations may hold, and the consequences for the village are the same. Schooling and urban experience, despite their benefits, can affect the cognitive skills and social connections that young people develop, and these changes have consequences for the social fabric and future of village culture.

Together, these studies indicate that the introduction of Western-style schooling and urban residence can have an enormous impact on young people's lives, with consequences for psychological development and the community at large. As Serpell (2018) wrote,

> During the 19th and 20th centuries, two social institutions were exported from the USA and Western Europe to the rest of the world: The factory and the school. The history of that export is heavy with political domination, economic exploitation, as well as religious proselytization. (p. 384)

In recent years, there have been efforts in the majority world to move beyond strict adoption of the Western educational model by incorporating a community's Indigenous culture and language into classroom practices and lessons (Serpell, 2018). For example, in the Philippines, recent reforms have provided for education in the local language in the first 4 years of primary school, which means that children are able to learn in one of 12 major languages in the country rather than only in English or Filipino, which remain the languages of instruction in later grades (Alampay & Garcia, 2019). In addition to incorporating more of the local language, local concepts, stories, and activities have been introduced to increase children's engagement in school and motivation to learn. Not only has this practice helped children during the transition to school by increasing their comprehension of material in the classroom, it has helped parents be more involved in their children's education when they understand the language of instruction and can identify with the concepts being taught (Abadzi, 2013).

Integrating Indigenous culture into formal learning has many benefits. First, it conveys respect for the heritage culture in a setting, the school, which is valued in the community. Second, it reinforces what young people have learned about traditional ideas and customs and provides them with the opportunity to discuss and practice these ideas in a social setting outside the home. Third, incorporating Indigenous culture in school can enhance learning because it draws from knowledge and experiences that are relevant to young people's everyday lives and the community. The emphasis on social responsibility in many cultures in Africa and elsewhere around the world is a case in point (Mpofu et al., 2012). Curriculum that builds on this Indigenous concept, for example, by promoting nurturant caring for others, especially younger children, affirms this important community value. This inclusion increases the social capital of the society by helping its young members maintain a valued cultural practice while at the same time acquiring abilities in school that will allow them to participate in modern economies (Super et al., 2011).

CONCLUSION

In this chapter, we have described formal schooling and its role in human development and society. We concentrated on the type of schooling seen in Western industrialized societies, and our description of academic achievement pertains to this setting. However, this emphasis is not intended to diminish the value of intellectual achievement, both in and outside of school, in cultural settings around the world. Indeed, in every society young people develop knowledge and skills that are valued and used in that culture. The important point is that academic achievement is only meaningful when it complements the values and goals of the cultural community in which individuals live and grow.

In the contemporary world, there are many different ways of educating young people. The type of schooling practiced in Western industrial societies is a particular approach—and a relatively recent one at that—of preparing young people for the societal roles they will be expected to occupy when they reach adulthood. This approach to schooling is assuming more and more significance worldwide in the context of globalization. The knowledge and skills taught there are considered valuable for preparing young people to participate in the world today. Efforts by societies to infuse Indigenous values into this form of educational practice are underway and represent a positive step forward for child and youth development. These efforts strive to equip young people with the knowledge and skills they will need in today's world while at the same time validating and building upon the heritage culture.

For additional resources, see the Appendix.

DISCUSSION QUESTIONS

1. How did changes in learning over the 20th century affect cultures?

2. Why do you think investment in formal schooling is decided at the national level and not at the local community or family level?

3. How do cultural values affect what is taught in school and how children learn there?

4. In what ways do cultural orientations of individualism and collectivism affect a student's achievement motivation?

5. How do children's lives in the majority world change when a culture adopts Western-style schooling?

12

Culture and Internalizing Symptomology

Shyness, Social Withdrawal, and Depression

This Swedish adolescent may or may not be alone by choice. Shyness, social withdrawal, and depression are manifested differently across cultures.

Enter the words "culture and introversion" into a search engine and you will encounter many articles and blogs by people sharing their impressions of the extent to which people in different cultures fit this characteristic. For example, a blogger on the site Some Call Me Adventurous (https://somecallmeadventurous.com/blog/2015/02/extroverted-introverted) describes him- or herself as an introvert and catalogs the extent to which his/her personality blends with styles of behavior in that country. The author suggests that there is a good fit with the United Kingdom, New Zealand, and Scandinavia,

https://doi.org/10.1037/0000228-012
Child and Adolescent Development in Cultural Context, by J. E. Lansford, D. C. French, and M. Gauvain

and a poorer fit with Spain, Brazil, and Australia. Why do country differences in introversion exist?

Introversion fits into a large category that includes normal personality characteristics and adjustment disorders that that are grouped under the category of "internalizing." This category incorporates a variety of subtypes (e.g., shyness, social withdrawal, depression), some of which reflect normal behavior and some that are problematic. These share the common feature of pertaining to processes that occur primarily within the self. This is in contrast to *externalizing*, a large category that includes aggression, delinquency, and other behaviors associated with actions directed toward others. Most of the research on culture and internalizing behavior has focused on shyness, social withdrawal, and depression, and from a review of this research, we can begin to understand how children's internalizing behavior develops within a cultural context.

GOODNESS-OF-FIT MODEL

As we discuss the associations between internalizing behavior and adjustment, it is helpful to think about A. Thomas and Chess's (1977) model detailing the importance of the fit between child characteristics and expectations and the demands of the environment. Originally developed to explore the relation between child temperament and environmental demands, this model is easily extended to explain the association between internalizing behavior and culture. In general, internalizing behavior will be associated with adjustment difficulties to the extent that there is a mismatch between the child's behavior and personality and the requirements of the environment and expectations of others. Difficulties arise when there is a mismatch between the child and the environment.

An illustration of the goodness-of-fit model comes from J. Liu et al.'s (2014) study of differences in the predictors of loneliness for Indonesian and Chinese adolescents. As noted in Chapter 7, dyadic friendships are more salient for Chinese adolescents than for Indonesian adolescents, and peer network membership is particularly important for Indonesian youth. Loneliness can be thought of as a sense of dissatisfaction with one's social relationships, which can arise either because of a lack of a close intimate relationship with another or a lack of involvement in a social network. Consistent with these features of cultural norms and expectations, loneliness was more strongly associated with the lack of friends for Chinese adolescents and with the lack of peer group acceptance for Indonesian adolescents. Thus, the fit between the child's social relationships and the cultural values pertaining to peer relationships (i.e., maintaining dyadic friendships or fitting into a social network) was associated with loneliness to differing extents in the two countries.

The goodness-of-fit model is useful for understanding which types of child behavior are problematic. Weisz et al. (1987) compared the characteristics of children and adolescents referred to mental health centers in Thailand and the

United States and found that American youth were more often referred to treatment agencies for externalizing behavior (e.g., disobedience, lying, fighting) than were Thai youth. In contrast, Thai youth were more likely to be referred for overcontrolled behavior (fearful or anxious, worrying, somatic problems including headaches). The authors suggested that the parenting practices of Thai parents incorporate the traditional Thai and Buddhist focus on quietness, inhibition, and deference. Parenting practices and the cultural focus on these qualities may discourage children from exhibiting undercontrolled behavior, such as aggression. In contrast, the cultural emphasis on behavioral restraint and emotional control may lead to problems of overcontrol in some Thai youth. This study illustrates that the features of cultures (i.e., values, meaning systems, child-rearing practices) may either facilitate or suppress different types of child problems and may influence adults' judgments about whether or not the child's behavior deviates from societal norms of acceptable behavior.

Chen and French (2008) proposed a model whereby cumulative social interactions mediate the associations between cultural values and child behavior. In this model, parents, teachers, and others respond to children's behavior based on cultural meaning systems, values, and characteristic cultural behavior patterns. Thus, adults and peers react to the child's daily behavior in culturally patterned ways that convey either approval or disapproval of the behavior. As a consequence of these cumulative interactions as well as their observations of others, children increasingly develop behavior patterns that are consistent with the norms of their culture. Note, however, that the processes are bidirectional as children engage in activities and social interactions, and through their participation, construct cultural norms. For example, as a consequence of their participation in the activity of dating, adolescents construct norms of behavior that are incorporated into the culture and are passed on to subsequent generations.

DISTINGUISHING INTERNALIZING PROBLEMS FROM PERSONALITY CHARACTERISTICS

In the next sections, we focus specifically on shyness, social withdrawal, and depression. In this discussion, it is important to note the large variability across studies in the ways that researchers have conceptualized and operationally defined internalizing behavior and personality characteristics. At one extreme are diagnosable psychiatric disorders, such as depression. At the other extreme are behavior and characteristics that are variations of normal personality. For example, it is common to categorize individuals as being either introverted or extroverted, and we use terms such as "socially sensitive," "slow to warm up," or "reticent" to describe such persons; these are viewed as variations of normal behavior and personality variations. Between these extremes are behaviors and characteristics that may or may not be concurrently and longitudinally associated with adjustment difficulties (e.g., shyness or social withdrawal). For example, it is common to study the presence of depression symptoms (e.g., problems with appetite or difficulty sleeping) within populations. In isolation, these symptoms are not necessarily signs of adjustment problems, but if they are sufficiently severe, impair successful functioning, and coexist with other symptoms, they may reflect serious difficulties.

The definition of constructs matters because different types of internalizing behavior are associated with adjustment, and some types of internalizing behavior and characteristics are more likely than other types to vary across cultures. Furthermore, as Research Highlight 12.1 shows, there may be culturally specific reasons, other than shyness or internalizing behavior, that explain why children spend little time playing with other children.

SHYNESS ACROSS CULTURES

Shy children desire to engage in social interaction, but are inhibited from doing so by anxiety and low self-confidence. Whereas most researchers use the term "shy" to describe this characteristic, others have preferred the labels "anxious avoidant" or "shyness-sensitivity."

Shyness has its roots in childhood temperament as some infants and toddlers approach or back away from unfamiliar people and objects (J. Kagan et al., 1988). This trait appears to have biological roots as evidenced by findings

---

RESEARCH HIGHLIGHT 12.1

Culturally Specific Reasons Children Withdraw From Social Interaction

Eggum-Wilkens et al. (2018) explored the social interaction of 11- to 17-year-old youth in eastern Uganda by presenting them with questionnaires. Students in both public and private schools were asked to provide written or oral answers to the following three questions:

1. Do you know any children your age who are alone more often than they are with other people? Write a word or phrase that describes this type of person.
2. Do you think some children want to play with and talk to other people, but do not because they are too afraid, nervous, or anxious? Write a word or phrase that describes this type of person.
3. Do you think some children do NOT want to play with and talk to other people?

Many of the comments were consistent with those of participants from other cultures, but the authors found some elements that appear to be specific to the cultural context of these adolescents. For example, some adolescents explained social withdrawal by describing the family and household circumstances of the individual, including being an orphan (e.g., lacks clothes, abused at home). Other descriptions included health problems (e.g., HIV), stigmatization, and shame.

These results suggest that social upheaval, such as existed in eastern Uganda at that time, can impact youth peer relationships. These results also illustrate that factors external to the peer group and school environment may impact children's social interactions.

---

that characteristics of the central nervous system (particularly the amygdala) differ in inhibited and uninhibited infants and toddlers. Although very young children can exhibit a tendency to either avoid or approach novelty, this behavior is highly malleable as children are exposed to different environments and challenges, and parents, peers, teachers, and others promote certain behaviors and attempt to change others. These efforts to either support or alter shy behavior are contextualized within a cultural framework that influences how others interpret, evaluate, and react to shy behavior.

Shy children often present a challenge for U.S. parents. Shy behavior can be viewed as inconsistent with cultural values of independence and assertiveness, and this behavior may be judged to be maladaptive and immature. This negative judgment applies to both boys and girls, but shy behavior exhibited by boys tends to be judged more negatively than comparable behavior by girls (K. H. Rubin & Coplan, 2004). A mismatch between parental expectations and child behavior may occur. For instance, parents who want their children to be outgoing and friendly may instead have children who are socially reticent and withdrawn. Such mismatches can lead to difficulties in relationships between the parent and child, and if this is extreme and persistent can interfere with the development of attachment relationships. Some U.S. parents react to their children's shy behavior by being controlling, overprotective, and micromanaging (Hastings et al., 2010). This pattern of behavior can begin in infancy and extend into childhood and adolescence. In contrast to North American parents, Chinese and South Korean parents tend to be more accepting of their children's shy behavior.

Chen et al. (1998) found that Canadian and Chinese parents reacted differently to their children's shy behavior. In this study, 2-year-old children participated in a laboratory session during which they were introduced to a stranger and provided with novel toys. In the Chinese sample, behavioral inhibition, which was indexed by shyness exhibited in the laboratory session, was positively associated with maternal acceptance, and negatively associated with maternal rejection. In contrast, however, there were no significant relations between children's inhibition and parent ratings in the Canadian sample, suggesting that parents viewed their children's shy behavior neutrally. The authors suggested that the reactions of Chinese parents to shy behavior were consistent with a Confucian view regarding the value of self-restraint.

Weisz et al.'s (1988) study of the reactions of American and Thai teachers and parents to descriptions of child behavior is another example of cultural differences in the extent to which parents tolerate various behaviors and want to change them. Adults from the two countries read vignette descriptions of both overcontrolled (e.g., shy, anxious) and undercontrolled (e.g., aggressive, disobedient) behavior exhibited by a 9-year-old child. They then rated the severity of the behavior, the extent that they would be concerned if a child behaved in this manner, and the likelihood that the behavior would improve without intervention as the child grew up. Thai parents and teachers rated both types of behavior as being of less concern than did their American counterparts.

In addition, Thai raters judged the problems to be less serious and more likely to improve over time than did the American raters. The authors interpreted these findings as suggesting that Thai parents adopt Buddhist perspectives of tolerance and the belief that things will improve on their own.

Shyness in Chinese Children

For almost 30 years, Chen and his colleagues have studied shyness in Chinese children and explored how it differs from shyness exhibited by North American children. They suggest that in traditional Chinese culture, modesty and behavioral control reflect maturity and competence, whereas such behavior in Western children reflects passivity and low assertiveness.

In an initial study, Chen et al. (1992) compared the associations between shyness and the social adjustment of 8- and 10-year-old Chinese and Canadian children. Classroom peers reported on their classmates' shyness and social adjustment using a peer nomination measure called the Revised Class Play (Masten et al., 1985). Class members identified peers who embodied various characteristics such as "feelings get hurt easily," "very shy," and "usually sad." In addition to measuring shyness, the researchers assessed adjustment by asking children to identify those classmates with whom they most like to play (positive playmate) and those they most wanted as friends (positive friendship).

Consistent with the view that shy behavior is not well accepted in North America, shyness of Canadian children was negatively associated with both positive playmate and positive friendship nominations. In contrast, the opposite patterns emerged for Chinese children, and shyness was associated with both peer acceptance and friendship. Thus, the meaning of shyness appeared to differ in these two countries. The researchers interpreted these results by suggesting that in the group-oriented (i.e., collectivist) culture of China, children are not encouraged to behave assertively or to freely express themselves; instead they are encouraged to stand back and fit into the group. In contrast, within individualistic cultures such as Canada, independence and assertiveness are valued, and consequently shyness is viewed negatively (Chen & French, 2008).

Cultural Change and Shyness in China

As noted in Chapter 1, cultures change, although they often do so slowly. Cultural change and the consequences of these changes for child behavior are reflected in the study of shyness in China. Beginning in the 1980s, Chinese society has been rapidly changing because of the introduction of a market structure into various economic sectors. This major societal and economic change has been accompanied by the increased emphasis and valuation of independence and individual assertiveness. These societal changes have been accompanied by educational practices whereby children are increasingly encouraged to express personal opinions and to acquire self-confidence. As shown in several studies, these changes have been associated with a decrease in the social acceptance of shyness.

Chen et al. (2005) compared cohorts of Shanghai children who were assessed in different years (1990, 1998, 2002) and found that the associations between shyness and adjustment changed over this time span. Whereas shyness was positively associated with positive nominations by classmates (i.e., "Who do you like most?") in both the 1990 and 1998 cohorts, this association was negative in the 2002 cohort. Similar patterns emerged for academic success. Whereas shyness was positively associated with school grades in the 1990 cohort, there was a negative association between shyness and grades in the 2002 cohort. These results suggest that the meaning of shyness changed during this 12-year time span.

Similar findings pertaining to historical changes in the relation between shyness and adjustment emerged for adolescents. J. Liu et al. (2012) compared the associations between shyness and adjustment in two cohorts (1994 and 2008) of sixth- and eighth-grade Chinese adolescents living in similar Shanghai neighborhoods at different times. Consistent with the previous findings, shyness was positively associated with teacher ratings of competence, academic achievement, and adjustment in the 1994 cohort. In contrast, shyness was negatively associated with peer ratings of acceptance and positively associated with self-ratings of loneliness in the 2008 cohort. This study provides further evidence that the rapid cultural changes that have occurred in China have been associated with changes in the meaning and acceptance of shyness.

Life Course of Shy Individuals in the United States and Sweden

What happens to shy children as they develop into adulthood? The answer to this question appears to be a function of culture, gender, and historical time.

Every third child born in Berkeley, California, in 1928 was recruited to participate in the Berkeley Growth Study in which they were assessed periodically from birth into adulthood. Caspi et al. (1988) analyzed these data to explore how children who were rated as "shy" by their parents at ages 10–12 fared when they were 30 and 40 years of age. Although there was no evidence that shy children experienced pathological outcomes, they differed from their peers in employment and relationships. The authors suggested that children who are shy during childhood sometimes continue to have difficulties managing new and unfamiliar situations and roles. These consequences of childhood shyness, however, differed for boys and girls.

Shy boys were more likely than nonshy boys to delay marriage, become parents, and achieve a stable career. They were also more likely than their peers to experience marital difficulties, perhaps because of their career difficulties. The authors suggested that shy men might have low assertiveness and trouble with courtship, which could interfere with their job advancement and delayed marriage.

Shy girls were more likely than nonshy girls to adopt a conventional lifestyle during their adulthood that included marriage and parenthood. Women who were shy as children were more likely to leave their employment (and not return to the workforce) after they married or had children. They also tended to marry men who were more successful.

The results from this U.S. study suggest that shyness had a greater impact on the later adjustment of shy boys than it did for shy girls. Note, however, that this study occurred at a historical time when it was less common for American women to have careers outside the home. As such, it is possible that some of the outcomes of this study would be different, particularly those that pertained to gender differences, had the study been conducted at a different time.

It is possible to compare the results from the U.S. sample with the results from a comparable Swedish study. Kerr et al. (1996) analyzed data from a longitudinal study of shy Swedish 8- to 10-year-old children who were initially assessed in the 1950s and followed as they transitioned into adulthood.

The authors suggested that several features of Swedish culture differed from the United States during these historical periods that could be pertinent to the associations between childhood shyness and adult outcomes. First, the authors suggested that Swedish people tend to view reticent behavior more positively than do Americans. In this egalitarian culture, Swedish people are encouraged to display moderation and to avoid strong assertive behavior. Because of this aspect of the culture, the authors hypothesized that shy Swedish men would be more successful in employment than would shy American men. Second, they suggested that the populations had different views regarding the role of women at the time the Swedish and American samples were assessed. In the 1960s, the Swedish government initiated a comprehensive program to establish economic equality between men and women by encouraging women to enter the workforce. Because both men and women were under pressure to succeed in the workplace, researchers hypothesized that childhood shyness would also interfere with women's academic and career progression.

Similarities and differences emerged regarding the outcomes of shyness in the two countries. In both countries, boys who were shy in childhood married and had children at a later age than their nonshy peers. In contrast to American men, Swedish men who were shy in childhood did not experience difficulties advancing in their careers. Both Swedish and American women who were shy in childhood married and had children at similar ages as their nonshy peers. Swedish women who were shy in childhood had a low level of academic attainment; whereas 44% of Swedish nonshy girls earned college degrees, none of the shy girls did.

The authors interpreted the results from Sweden and the United States as suggesting that the effects of shyness are dependent upon the expectations and demands of the culture in which the person lives. For men in both countries, assertive behavior was beneficial for successful courtship and dating, which put shy individuals at a disadvantage. Shyness similarly appeared to interfere with career advancement for American men and education advances for Swedish women. When assertiveness is not essential (e.g., marriage and parenthood for women in both cultures), shyness was not a barrier.

When interpreting these results, it is important to remember that the studies occurred at different historical times and in different countries. In particular, the educational and career opportunities for women were different at the time of the Swedish study than they were at the time of the Berkeley Growth Study. Current norms and practices in both the United States and Sweden as they pertain to marriage, parenting, employment, and education differ considerably from those that existed for participants in either country at the time of the study. Consequently, if the studies were conducted currently or at other historical times, we might find a different pattern of results.

Regulated Shyness

The complexity of understanding the meaning of "internalizing behavior" across cultures is illustrated by the research of Xu et al. (2007), who described a pattern of behavior they labeled "regulated shyness" that is associated with high self-control and low assertiveness. Children who fit this description tend to refrain from conflict and exhibit other behaviors that maximize their ability to get along with others. The authors suggested that this behavior pattern, although not reflected in Western conceptions of shyness, is present in China and other cultures that emphasize social harmony and interdependence. In contrast to shy children who desire to interact with others but are inhibited from doing so, regulated-shy children may seek to fit into the peer group by being unobtrusive, modest, attentive to others, and minimizing conflict.

Xu et al. (2009) found that teachers differentiated between these two types of shy Chinese children. Teachers rated regulated-shy children with items such as "behaves modestly," "does not show off," and "avoids conflict with peers." In contrast, anxious-shy children were described by items such as "is timid and fearful" and "is afraid to join or approach peer play groups."

These divergent patterns of shyness were also found in South Korean fourth and sixth graders. Children who were rated as "anxious-shy" by teachers and peers were lonely and poorly accepted by peers. In contrast, regulated-shy children were well accepted by peers and reported low levels of loneliness.

In sum, these results provide further evidence that the meaning of shyness varies across cultures. In particular, it appears that a type of shyness (i.e., regulated shyness) that is not typically seen in Western cultures is prominent in China and South Korea, and likely many other countries as well. Furthermore, in contrast to other forms of shyness, this type of shyness is associated with positive social adjustment.

SOCIAL WITHDRAWAL AND PREFERENCE FOR SOLITUDE

It is important to note that the previous findings pertained to shyness and not to social withdrawal (Asendorpf, 1991). J. M. Wang (2016) suggested that a preference for solitude is distinct from shyness. Whereas shy children do not necessarily choose to play alone but instead are inhibited from doing so, socially withdrawn children prefer to isolate themselves.

Chen (2019) suggested that in Western cultures, low sociability may be judged to be a consequence of personal choice. In other words, children may simply prefer to play alone rather than with others. These children are often capable of successfully interacting with peers when they desire to do so. As such, this type of internalizing behavior by children in Western cultures may be viewed as less problematic and less often associated with adjustment problems than shyness. Ladd et al. (2011), for example, found that unsociable American fifth graders were more likely to have friends than were their shy peers. Finally, although research has suggested that preference for solitude might not be particularly problematic for children in Western cultures, there is some evidence that it might be different for adolescents. J. M. Wang, Rubin, et al. (2013) found that preference for solitude was associated with anxiety/depression, low emotional regulation, and low self-esteem in American eighth and 10th graders.

Chen (2019) argued that in contrast to Western countries, in collectivist countries such as China, social isolation is incompatible with cultural values pertaining to the importance of integration into a group. As such, this behavior may be judged as being pathological and associated with adjustment problems.

J. Liu, Coplan, et al. (2014) provided evidence in support of this position in a study of fourth- through eighth-grade children living in Shanghai. Consistent with the findings presented earlier regarding shyness becoming negatively perceived in contemporary China, shyness was positively associated with victimization, loneliness, and depressive symptoms and negatively associated with peer acceptance and academic achievement. The authors then assessed the relation between unsociability and adjustment after controlling for the effects of shyness. Unsociability accounted for adjustment problems over and above the effects of shyness; unsociability positively predicted low peer acceptance, loneliness, and depressive symptoms and negatively predicted academic achievement.

Bowker and Raja (2011) studied how shyness and unsociability in 13-year-old Indian adolescents were associated with a variety of indices of adjustment, and they found distinctive profiles associated with these internalizing behaviors. Shyness was only slightly negatively associated with peer acceptance, providing some consistency with the earlier findings from China regarding the acceptability of this behavior in a collectivist culture. In contrast to the findings from China where unsociability was associated with a variety of adjustment difficulties, including low peer acceptance, this was not found in India. Consistent with the argument that shy children seek social interaction but are prevented from doing so because of anxiety or low confidence, shyness was associated with loneliness in this sample. Unsociability, however, was less strongly associated with loneliness. This finding is consistent with the argument that unsociable children choose to isolate themselves from others, and consequently, do not see the discrepancy between actual and desired social interaction that is associated with loneliness.

The similarities and differences between the results from India and China illustrate the dangers associated with assuming that findings obtained in one collectivist culture will be seen in others. Unfortunately, there are few studies of shyness and social withdrawal in India, and more research is needed.

DEPRESSION

Extensive research has been conducted to explore cultural variation in depression. The World Health Organization (2017a) estimated that approximately 4.4% of the world's population experiences diagnosable depression. The number of people who report depressive symptoms (e.g., feeling sad, trouble sleeping, or thinking of committing suicide) far exceeds these rates. Adolescents and children also experience depression. The rates of depression for children range between .03% and 2.1%. After puberty, however, depression rates approximate the 4.4% of adults (Fristad & Black, 2018). Boys and girls experience depression at relatively similar rates during childhood, but following puberty, there are consistent findings that girls experience depression more often than do boys. The finding that women experience higher rates of depression than men has emerged across all regions of the world (World Health Organization, 2017a).

The interest in culture and depression stems partly from consistent evidence of country differences in rates of depression. The World Health Organization estimates that rates of clinically diagnosed depression range from 5.4% in the African region to a low of 3.6% in the western Pacific region. It is also possible to look at depression rates obtained from community samples, which are higher than those of clinical depression because they do not require psychiatric diagnoses, and consequently less stringent criteria are used. Rates of reported depression from community samples also reflect large variation across countries. These range from a low of 1% in Taiwan to 16.4% in Paris. These numbers illustrate that depression appears to be universally present across regions but that there is variation in the rates of occurrence. This pattern has led to research to understand the reasons for these disparities.

The prevalence of poverty and life stress in a region is among the factors that account for disparities in depression rates across countries. Geopolitical stress, such as economic recession and war, is associated with increased rates of depression. In general, depression rates are lower in more wealthy countries than in poorer countries (Chentsova-Dutton & Tsai, 2009). These factors, however, explain only some of the worldwide variation in depression rates, and there is a search for other factors, such as culture, that explain the disparities.

It is particularly intriguing to consider the possibility that culture shapes the way that individuals experience and give meaning to the distress that is associated with depression. Because there are multiple criteria that define depression, some of which pertain to mental states (e.g., lack of pleasure, hopelessness) and others that refer to physical symptoms (e.g., loss of appetite, problems sleeping, low libido), it is possible for individuals who are depressed to show different symptomatology. It is also possible that people give meaning to their sense of distress using different explanations. In countries such as the United States that emphasize individualism, there is an emphasis on lack of pleasure and initiative in the diagnosis of depression. In other cultures, such as Japan, in which self tends to be conceptualized in relation to others, depression is more often viewed in terms of social withdrawal and the failure to maintain social obligations (Chentsova-Dutton et al., 2014).

Cultural variation in the interpretation and meaning of depression symptoms is reflected in local descriptions of the disorder. Kirmayer and Jarvis (2006) reported that people in Nigeria describe experiencing a "heat and a peppery feeling in the head" whereas in Iran, depression is described as "having a heavy heart" and "tightness in the chest." Thus, individuals in these different cultures interpret the distress associated with depression in various ways. In some cases, the tendency to identify physical symptoms may come about because it is considered more appropriate in a given culture to interpret depression in these terms.

This discussion reveals that cultural meanings define the extent to which individuals experience various depression symptoms and their severity. Although depression exists across cultures, individuals differ in how they interpret what is normal and abnormal. Cultural meaning systems define how discomfort is labeled and explained. Cultural norms also likely affect the extent to which individuals seek help. Factors that may influence seeking help include the stigma associated with mental illness, and ideas about when symptoms are sufficiently severe that help is needed.

Psychological Versus Somatic Symptoms of Depression

Much of the research pertaining to culture and depression has been conducted in China, with the primary focus on understanding the distinction between psychological and somatic (i.e., physical) symptoms of depression. The psychological aspects of depression include lack of pleasure, negative mood, hopelessness, guilt, and thoughts of suicide. The somatic aspects of depression include weight loss, sleep difficulties, fatigue, and diminished sexual interest, in addition to other bodily sensations like those described previously among people in Nigeria and Iran (Chentsova-Dutton & Tsai, 2009).

In a number of studies, it has been found that depressed Chinese participants more often referred to somatic complaints, whereas depressed Canadian participants focused more on psychological symptoms. With the accumulation of additional research findings from multiple countries, it now appears that a focus on somatic issues in depression is very common across the world, and the extensive focus on psychological symptoms in Western countries may be atypical. Chentsova-Dutton et al. (2014) suggest that the North American view of expecting positive emotions and distress being pathological is not widely shared in much of the world. Perhaps the focus on the individual in these cultures leads to a sense of the importance of self and individual happiness.

Correlates of Adolescent Depression

Depression rates increase substantially beginning at adolescence, and it is important to investigate whether the cultural patterns described previously for adults are associated with depressive symptoms among adolescents. Greenberger and Chen (1996) evaluated the extent to which various factors accounted for similarities and differences between symptoms of depression in school populations of 17-year-old U.S. and Chinese adolescents. A number of variables were similarly associated with depression across these two cultures, including being female, having experienced one or more negative life stresses (e.g., illness, death of a family member, family economic problems, school difficulties), perceived parental warmth or conflict, or reported peer warmth and conflict. Academic difficulties were more strongly associated with depression for Chinese adolescents than for American adolescents. Chinese students are under enormous pressure from their parents as well as themselves to succeed academically, and it is understandable that students who perceive themselves to be unsuccessful in this arena would experience symptoms of depression. Further research across different cultures is needed to determine the extent to which similar factors predict depressive symptoms.

One factor that may be associated with depression and culture is religion. There is a well-established small but consistent negative association between depression and religion in adults (Smith et al., 2003). The negative association between religion and depression has also been found in some studies of adolescents, as illustrated by Research Highlight 12.2.

CONCLUSION

We return to the question that we posed at the beginning of this chapter: Why do cultures differ in their exhibition of internalizing behavior and characteristics? From research on shyness, social withdrawal, and depression, we can begin to understand some answers.

As we discuss throughout this book, an important aspect of culture is a framework that provides people with ways to interpret behavior along with standards to enable them to judge whether a particular behavior is valued or not valued, appropriate or not appropriate, and within normal limits or reflects pathology. People respond to each other based on these judgments and either reinforce, ignore, or punish the behavior. Through these cumulative interactions that occur regularly in daily life, in addition to observational learning from the behavior of others, young people learn to regulate themselves and display behaviors that are characteristic of their culture. Individuals whose

RESEARCH HIGHLIGHT 12.2

Depression and Religiosity in Indonesian Muslim Adolescents

Purwono and French (2016) explored the association between depressive symptoms and religiosity in a sample of 13- and 16-year-old Muslim adolescents living in Indonesia. Although all of the participants in the study were practicing Muslims who were moderately to highly religious, there were individual differences in the consistency of their engagement in religious behavior.

The researchers assessed religiosity by asking youth multiple questions regarding the extent to which they engaged in religiously required behavior (e.g., fasting during Ramadan and consistently making the five daily prayers) as well as optional but recommended behavior (e.g., reading the Quran). They found that individual differences in religiosity were negatively associated with depressive symptoms such that more religious adolescents reported less depression than less religious adolescents. Most importantly, religiosity was not associated with loneliness, suggesting that the effects of religiosity were specific to depression.

The most intriguing question, one not answered in their study, is why religion appears to protect against experiencing symptoms of depression. Some of these explanations, such as the extent to which religion provides individuals with explanations for why negative events occur, and the hope that they will be reduced in the future, cut across multiple religions. Common to many religions is an emphasis on religion as a means of coping with negative events. There may also be positive effects of participating in a religious community.

Other effects, however, may be unique to Islam. Abdel-Khalek (2007) suggested that the regular pattern of religious behavior (e.g., performance of the five daily prayers; fasting during Ramadan; and for boys, attending the Friday mosque service) provides a structure that combats the lethargy that is associated with depression.

This study illustrates the important association between cultural and religious meaning systems (C. Geertz, 1973). Cultures vary in the importance of religion and the extent to which cultural and religious meaning systems and values are intertwined. In the homogenously religious communities that exist in countries such as Indonesia, there is often a very strong connection between religion and culture, such that it is often impossible and meaningless to differentiate between them.

behavior departs significantly from cultural standards may be identified as problematic or pathological (e.g., depressed), and interventions may be implemented.

As we noted previously, however, young people are not passive recipients of culture, which is pertinent to understanding internalizing behavior. Children create their social world as they engage in behavior patterns and decide which behaviors are appropriate and which are inappropriate. They then serve as models for others, actively shaping their behavior and opinions.

For additional resources, see the Appendix.

DISCUSSION QUESTIONS

1. What is an explanation for cultural differences in shyness?

2. How does the goodness-of-fit model explain cultural differences in shyness? Does it explain cultural differences in other behaviors?

3. What are the differences between shyness and social withdrawal? Based on your experience, is this distinction meaningful?

4. What would the life course of shy children in a particular culture be like if the studies had been conducted today?

5. Why are there differences across cultures in somatic and psychological symptoms of depression?

13

Culture and the Development of Aggression, Delinquency, and Substance Use

Two boys confront each other in Serbia.

Aggression is consistently defined across cultures as an act perpetrated by one individual that is intended to cause physical, psychological, or social harm to another (Ostrov et al., 2019). *Delinquency* is defined as antisocial behavior that breaks laws. Across cultures, substance use encompasses alcohol, tobacco, and other drug use, but the extent to which the use of these substances is deemed problematic varies. Collectively, antisocial behavior and externalizing problems encompass behaviors that involve acting out in ways that are not socially condoned, such as exhibiting aggression, delinquency, or other problem behavior. Behaving in oppositional or defiant ways, fighting

https://doi.org/10.1037/0000228-013
Child and Adolescent Development in Cultural Context, by J. E. Lansford, D. C. French, and M. Gauvain

with peers or adults, and breaking the law by stealing or vandalizing property are all examples of externalizing problems. Externalizing behaviors are common. For example, across 20 countries, 47% of 13- to 15-year-old boys and 26% of 13- to 15-year-old girls report having been in a physical fight in the past 12 months, motivating international campaigns to reduce externalizing behaviors and prevent youth violence (e.g., World Health Organization, 2015).

In this chapter, we first cover the forms and functions of aggression, and the motivation for engaging in such behavior. We next turn to understanding developmental trajectories of aggression and other antisocial behavior, including the extent to which these trajectories are similar across various cultural groups. Then we consider cultural risk factors for the development of aggression, including cultural norms related to violence and children's exposure to violence in real life and in the media. We then turn to understanding proximal cognitive mechanisms involved in processing social information that predict whether or not children will behave aggressively in particular situations. Finally, we consider substance use and other risky behaviors within diverse cultural contexts.

FORMS AND FUNCTIONS OF AGGRESSION

Imagine you are watching children playing outside. One girl wants another girl's toy, so she shoves the girl aside to take the toy. Across the yard, one boy tells another that he's terrible at the game they're playing. Another group of children excludes someone from playing with them. These are all examples of aggressive behavior.

Aggression can take physical, verbal, or relational forms (Little et al., 2003). Physical aggression involves hitting, pushing, kicking, or other actions that inflict bodily pain. Verbal aggression involves name-calling, taunting, or other actions that inflict hurt through words communicated directly to the victim. Relational aggression involves spreading rumors behind someone's back, excluding someone from a peer group, or other behaviors that inflict harm to someone's social relationships.

Aggression can also serve different functions (Little et al., 2003). The function of proactive aggression is to obtain a desired outcome. Prototypical examples would be hitting someone to take something in their possession or spreading a rumor about someone to elevate one's own position in the peer group. In contrast, the function of reactive aggression is to respond to a perceived wrong. Prototypical examples include hitting back after being hit first or retaliating after being insulted or left out of a peer group. Although these forms and functions of aggression appear to be generalizable across cultures, there are differences in the extent to which and situations in which aggression is considered to be acceptable. Children are socialized in their cultural group by their parents, peers, and other members in ways that increase or decrease their propensity for aggression.

DEVELOPMENTAL TRAJECTORIES OF AGGRESSION AND ANTISOCIAL BEHAVIOR

Because aggression is generally defined as the intention to cause harm, aggression cannot develop before the cognitive capacities associated with intentionality (DeWall et al., 2012). Therefore, although infants exhibit actions that might hurt, such as biting while nursing or pulling a parent's hair, such behavior is typically not defined as aggression because of the absence of intentionality. Indeed, parents who believe that their infants engage in such behaviors to cause harm are at heightened risk for abusing their infants compared with parents who understand that infants do not yet have the cognitive capabilities to cause harm intentionally (Rodriguez, 2010).

Intentionality emerges during the toddler years, and combined with toddlers' limited verbal abilities to express themselves and reason with others in complex ways, contributes to rates of aggression that are higher than at any other point in development (C. A. Anderson & Huesmann, 2003). For example, if a toddler wants a toy, she may take it by physical force, but after age 3, physical aggression generally declines (Tremblay, 2000). Between the ages of 3 and 4, developments in children's perspective-taking and theory of mind help them understand that others' thoughts and feelings are not the same as their own and lead to an increase in empathy and a decrease in physical aggression (see Chapter 3; Wellman, 2014). During middle childhood and adolescence, physical aggression continues to decline. Verbal aggression, however, increases after age 3 (Tremblay, 2000) and tends to peak during middle school (Poling et al., 2019). In addition, social-cognitive capacities that prompt decreases in physical aggression may actually prompt increases in relational aggression. Specifically, children's ability to manipulate social relationships to cause harm by excluding peers from a group, spreading rumors, or inflicting other social harm is improved when children's cognitive development helps them better understand others' perspectives and the nature of social relationships (Coyne & Ostrov, 2018).

Two prominent developmental models of antisocial behavior, including aggression but also delinquency and other forms of problem behaviors, share several features with one another. Both Moffitt's (1993) and Patterson's (1982) models describe two types of antisocial behavior. The first type begins early in childhood, increases in adolescence, and persists into adulthood. The second type begins in adolescence rather than childhood, and then desists with the transition to adulthood. The two models are similar in their times of onset and offset of antisocial behavior, but differ in the main causes offered for the developmental trajectories.

According to Moffitt (1993), life-course persistent antisocial behavior begins with neuropsychological problems that are present early in life paired with adverse environmental experiences. Adolescence-limited antisocial behavior, by contrast, begins when adolescents encounter a gap between their desires for independence and the reality that they are still dependent on and under the control of their parents and other adults. As adolescents begin spending more time with peers away from the direct supervision of parents, they may have more opportunities to engage in delinquency, substance use, and other problem behaviors, and peers may model these behaviors (Glaser et al., 2010). Adolescents may experiment with alcohol use, sexual relationships, and other behaviors that they perceive as being markers of adult status, and may engage in such behaviors in attempts to fit in with peers (M. L. Cooper et al., 2016). As adolescents move into early adulthood and have more independence and adult privileges, their antisocial behavior desists.

According to Patterson (1982), early starters begin exhibiting antisocial behavior because of coercive cycles of parenting that are initiated early in life. In a prototypical example, a child makes a request of the parent, the parent denies the request, and the child responds by whining or throwing a tantrum. The parent further escalates the interaction by yelling or spanking, and the cycle continues until the parent gives in to the child's original request (reinforcing the child's aversive behavior and increasing the likelihood that the child will behave in that manner in future situations) or the child stops the behavior but learns that aversive behavior can solve problems. Early starters generalize these coercive exchanges to other social situations and may behave similarly with teachers or peers. Late starters, however, exhibit relatively normal behavior during childhood, but affiliate with deviant peers in adolescence and begin to engage in aggressive and antisocial behaviors. When a shift in environmental contingencies makes other behaviors more attractive, the social and academic foundational skills of late starters typically enable them to adjust their behavior accordingly.

The cultural generalizability of the adolescence-limited or late-starter patterns of antisocial behavior is supported by international consistency in the age-crime curve, which shows an increase in crime through late adolescence and a decrease in crime thereafter (Britt, 2019). Cross-cultural consistency in the dual-systems model also provides an explanation for the adolescence-limited trajectory (Duell et al., 2016). The dual-systems model describes two distinct patterns of brain development during adolescence (Steinberg, 2008). The first system is characterized by growth in cognitive and impulse control and self-regulation, which improve steadily throughout adolescence before plateauing in adulthood. The second system is characterized by curvilinear growth in reward sensitivity and sensation seeking, which increase in early adolescence, peak in mid-to-late adolescence, and decrease in adulthood. Because these two systems show distinct developmental patterns and are not entirely aligned, the result is similar to a car with a fully functioning accelerator without a braking system. That is, adolescents are motivated to seek rewards (often through novel experiences and risky behaviors with peers) before they have the cognitive capacity to check their impulses and evaluate the risks relative to the rewards. In a study testing the generalizability of the dual-systems model in 11 countries, reward sensitivity predicted more risky behavior in all countries, but the associations between self-regulation and risky behavior were more variable (Duell et al., 2016). Although self-regulation follows similar developmental patterns tied to the maturation of the prefrontal cortex regardless of culture, there are cultural differences in norms regarding the acceptability of risky behavior, and there is variability in the opportunities adolescents have to engage in such behaviors. Therefore, some adolescents with immature self-regulation live in cultural environments that are less conducive to risky behavior than others.

Although there is general consistency in the developmental trajectories of aggressive and antisocial behavior across cultures, there are also cultural variations in the onset, peak, and offset of externalizing problems that are linked to specific cultural, parenting, and peer factors. Cultural differences in developmental trajectories of antisocial behavior are reflected primarily in mean-level differences and differences in stability across contexts.

For an example of cultural differences in aggression, we compare the development of aggression in Finland and the United States. The pathways of aggression from childhood to adulthood are less stable in Finland than they are in the United States (Kokko et al., 2014). Finland has a far-reaching social safety net and more social equality than the United States. Children from different socioeconomic backgrounds in Finland show few differences in school achievement, health, and social problems, whereas children from different social strata in the United States show large differences in these characteristics (Wilkinson & Pickett, 2010). Compared with the United States, schools in Finland are more socioeconomically mixed (Sahlberg, 2011), there is a higher graduation rate (respectively almost 100% vs. 84%; OECD, 2019), and the provision of free higher education facilitates upward social mobility. All of these factors may serve as protective factors for children in Finland, accounting for the lower stability in aggression from childhood to adulthood and homicide rates that are less than half of those in the United States (United Nations Office on Drugs and Crime, 2013). Factors other than culture can also affect the stability of trajectories of aggression. For example, compared with girls, boys showed more stability in externalizing behavior from childhood to adolescence in Canada, New Zealand, and the United States (Broidy et al., 2003).

CULTURAL RISK FACTORS FOR THE DEVELOPMENT OF AGGRESSION

Individual risk factors, such as male gender, and family risk factors, such as coercive parenting, can promote the development of aggression, but many cultural risk factors have also been found to affect the development of aggression. Authoritarianism and cultural norms that emphasize compliance can foster the development of aggression, as demonstrated in naturalistic settings as well as in classic psychology studies. For example, in Milgram's (1963) classic studies of obedience, subjects were willing to administer putatively painful shocks to others when told to do so by authority figures. In the Stanford Prison Experiment (Zimbardo, 2007), students who were randomly assigned to play the role of guards began verbally and physically abusing students who were randomly assigned to play the role of prisoners, to such an extent that the experiment, which was originally slated to last 2 weeks, had to be suspended after 6 days. Individuals generally adhere to cultural norms because they fear social disapproval for violating norms, and they feel guilt or shame after violating internalized cultural norms.

According to the World Health Organization (2009), certain cultural norms support different types of violence. For example, when children have low status in a society and corporal punishment is accepted as part of childrearing, children are more likely to be physically abused. When men have the right to exert power over women and physical violence is accepted as a legitimate way to resolve conflicts, women are more likely to be abused by intimate partners. When a particular ethnic group is shunned or ostracized, community violence against that group is more likely. Acceptance of one form of violence is related to acceptance of other forms of violence. For example, in an analysis of the acceptance of various forms of violence in 25 low- and middle-income countries, the acceptability for husbands to hit their wives was associated with beliefs in the appropriateness of using corporal punishment to rear children, and children were more likely to experience both physical and verbal aggression from their caregivers (Lansford, Deater-Deckard, et al., 2014). Children, in turn, learn to behave aggressively when they have experienced corporal punishment and witnessed violence between parents because children come to regard aggression as an appropriate, functional way to behave.

To reduce societal levels of violence, cultural norms must be changed so that violence in any form is regarded as unacceptable and irresponsible (Krug et al., 2002). Schools are an important context in which cultural norms and new patterns of behavior are learned. In a comparison of children's aggression in 62 countries, school principals rated children's behavior as more aggressive in countries with more individualistic than collectivist norms (Bergmüller, 2013).

Families can also socialize children in ways that alter norms about the acceptability of violence. Anger is the emotion most frequently linked to aggressive behavior, and there are cultural differences in how children are taught to manage this emotion. In a classic ethnographic study, Inuit parents displayed a socialization strategy that involves deliberately trying to elicit anger in young children, and if the child acts on the anger, calmly explaining why the angry or aggressive response is harmful (Briggs, 1971). For example, a parent may taunt a toddler and urge her to throw a rock at the parent. If the child throws the rock, the parent will explain that getting hit by a rock hurts and that the child should not do that in the future. Through repeated experiences with the deliberate elicitation of anger and then training children to deal with anger in non-aggressive ways, Inuit children become adept at anger management. Displays of anger, including toward children, are almost unheard of among Inuit adults; even the display of irritation is considered to be weak and childlike.

Overall, aggression tends to increase over time when youth are raised in risky environments, such as during middle school for adolescents who live in dangerous neighborhoods (Romero et al., 2015). For example, Israeli and Palestinian youth who are exposed to chronic ethnic and political conflict and violence exhibit an increase in aggression that is predicted by beliefs that aggression is normative, rehearsal of aggressive scripts, and emotional distress (Huesmann et al., 2017). Externalizing behaviors similarly increased among Kenyan youth who were exposed to time-limited but intense violence following a disputed political election (A. T. Skinner, Oburu, et al., 2014).

As was just discussed, among the primary ways in which culture affects the development of aggression is the presence of risk factors, such as dangerous neighborhoods and political conflict, as well as through protective factors, such as social safety nets, to which children and adolescents are exposed. Although these risk and protective factors may be related to aggressive behavior in similar ways in various cultural contexts, they likely contribute to mean differences across countries and cultural groups in levels of aggressive behavior.

Exposure to violence and aggressive models is one of the most important risk factors for the development of children's aggression because children learn, in part, through observing others in real life and in the media. For example, the strength of the association between children's exposure to violent media, including watching violent movies and television programs and playing violent video games, and the development of aggressive behavior is nearly as strong as the association between smoking and the development of lung cancer, and stronger than many other health-related links such as the association between using condoms and reduced risk of sexually transmitted infections (Bushman & Anderson, 2001). Research Highlight 13.1 provides examples of study designs that have investigated relations between playing violent video games and subsequent aggressive behavior. Some specificity of observed input and behavioral output was found; viewing television programs depicting relational aggression is associated with subsequent relationally aggressive behavior in adolescence (Coyne, 2016). More relationally aggressive adolescents, however, have not been found to seek out media depicting relational aggression.

Peer associations can have a large impact on the development of aggression and antisocial behavior. In particular, children who engage in antisocial behavior are likely to seek friends who also engage in antisocial behavior (Dijkstra et al., 2011), and these affiliations increase antisocial behavior through processes of reinforcement and deviancy training (Dishion & Patterson, 2006). Deviancy training refers to a process in which peers reinforce one another's antisocial beliefs and behaviors, leading to the spread and escalation of antisocial behavior. Deviancy is, by necessity, culturally defined because it involves deviating from some culturally prescribed standard. If one adolescent tells a story about skipping school and vandalizing a building, for example, and a peer laughs and chimes in with a story about another antisocial act, the interaction reinforces both adolescents' antisocial behavior. Through repeated similar interactions, group norms about the desirability of antisocial behavior develop, and over time the group might define itself in terms of deviancy. These processes can be accentuated when societal structures facilitate the interaction of antisocial

---

RESEARCH HIGHLIGHT 13.1

Violent Video Games and Aggressive Behavior

A meta-analysis of 24 studies including more than 17,000 participants from a variety of countries and ethnic groups concluded that playing violent video games is related to aggressive behavior in the future (Prescott et al., 2018). How have researchers designed studies to rule out the possibility of children and adolescents who are more aggressive merely choosing to play violent video games more often than do children and adolescents who are not prone to aggression? In one laboratory experiment, eight- to 12-year-old children in the United States were randomly assigned to play a violent video game or an equally exciting nonviolent video game. Physiologic measures were obtained before and after children played the game, and children engaged in other tasks, such as completing words when they were provided with only some of the letters. Cortisol (a stress hormone related to fight-or-flight responses) increased for children who played the violent game, but not the nonviolent game, and children who played the violent game showed evidence of activating more aggressive thoughts, such as generating violent words like "KILL" rather than nonviolent words like "KISS" when prompted to finish a four-letter word beginning with "KI" (Gentile et al., 2017).

Experimental studies such as the one just described have the strength of random assignment to different conditions, but they generally test only short-term effects. In longitudinal studies, researchers can test correlations over longer periods of time and statistically control for prior levels of aggression when testing associations between video game play and subsequent aggression during a specific time period. For example, in a study of 1,340 12- to 19-year-olds in China who were assessed three times at 6-month intervals, adolescents who played more violent video games at Time 1 reported more moral disengagement (a cognitive strategy used to justify why "good" people engage in "bad" behavior) at Time 2, which in turn predicted more aggressive behavior at Time 3, taking into account Time 1 aggressive behavior (Teng et al., 2019). When research findings using different methods and participants from a variety of cultural backgrounds converge, the findings are more robust and trustworthy.

---

youth. For example, it is common to group antisocial youth together through the juvenile justice system where youth learn to be delinquent and tough from other deviant youth (L. M. Johnson et al. 2004). Schools sometimes group antisocial children together in alternative schools or classrooms. Some youth grow up in very high-crime neighborhoods in which they learn from older antisocial youth and adults and have few options to escape the cycle of delinquency and crime because of poor schools and limited job prospects. In contrast, social structures that establish prosocial group norms and are carefully supervised by adults who can disrupt the deviancy training that begins to occur will be more successful in preventing the dispersion and escalation of antisocial behavior (Dishion et al., 2006).

SOCIAL INFORMATION PROCESSING AND AGGRESSION

Although risk factors such as exposure to coercive parent–child interactions, deviant peer affiliations, witnessing real-life or media violence, and cultural norms that endorse aggression all predict the development of aggression in the long term, what accounts for whether an individual aggresses in the moment? Several social-cognitive models explain how individuals cognitively process social information, which in turn predicts their likelihood of behaving aggressively. Social information–processing theory proposes a set of six steps through which individuals proceed subconsciously when they encounter an ambiguous social situation (Crick & Dodge, 1994). Emotion can affect the social-cognitive processes at each step (Lemerise & Arsenio, 2000).

The first step is *encoding*, in which individuals take in information about the situation. Individuals are more likely to behave aggressively if they take in only some of the relevant information rather than all of it, particularly if they are overly aware of hostile cues, unaware of nonhostile cues, or both (Lansford, Malone, Dodge, Pettit, & Bates, 2010). For example, if a boy trips and spills milk on a girl, the girl is more likely to behave aggressively if she encodes only the spill and not the trip. In addition, individuals are more likely to encode information that is compatible with their current mood, so they will be more likely to encode hostile cues if they enter a situation feeling angry or emotionally aroused, but will be more likely to encode nonhostile cues if they enter a situation feeling happy or content.

The second step is *making attributions*, in which individuals decide whether others were acting with hostile or benign intent. Individuals are more likely to behave aggressively if they believe that others behaved with hostile intent rather than with benign intent (Orobio de Castro et al., 2002). Accurately interpreting others' emotions helps in making accurate attributions. For example, if a peer is angry, hostile intent is more likely than if a peer is happy. Individuals who are less skilled at reading their own and others' emotions are more likely to behave aggressively (Lemerise & Arsenio, 2000). In the tripping/milk-spilling example, the girl is more likely to respond aggressively if she thinks the boy spilled milk on her purposely to be mean than if she thinks it was an accident.

The third step is *clarifying and selecting goals*, in which individuals decide what outcome they desire. Individuals who have goals involving retaliation, obtaining an instrumental end, showing dominance, or demonstrating status are more likely to behave aggressively than are individuals who have goals of affection and intimacy (Sijtsema et al., 2020). If individuals feel angry or frustrated, they are more likely to select instrumental goals that involve using force, if necessary, to get what they want (Lemerise & Arsenio, 2000).

The fourth step is *response generation*, in which individuals generate possible behavioral responses to the situation. Individuals are more likely to behave aggressively if they generate few possible responses, if they generate a preponderance of aggressive responses, or both (Dodge et al., 2013). For instance, if the girl from the previous example can think of only two ways to respond— yelling at the boy or spilling her milk on him to retaliate—she is more likely to respond aggressively than if she can think of multiple possible responses, several of which are not aggressive, such as getting something to clean up the milk, ignoring the boy, or making a joke to diffuse the situation. Individuals are better able to generate various possible responses if they are better at regulating their emotions and are not overwhelmed by negative emotions (Lemerise & Arsenio, 2000).

The fifth step is *response evaluation*, in which individuals evaluate different possible responses in terms of how others will react, how they will feel about themselves, and how likely it is for a given response to work. Individuals are more likely to behave aggressively if they think others will respect them for that response; if they will feel good about themselves if they react that way; and if they believe that behaving aggressively will lead to desired instrumental, interpersonal, or intrapersonal outcomes (Fontaine et al., 2009). If the girl from the previous example, for instance, thinks that others will respect her for not being a pushover if she yells at the boy, if she will feel good about herself for not letting him get away with spilling milk on her, and if she believes that yelling at the boy will prevent him from spilling milk on her in the future, she will be more likely to yell.

The sixth step is *enactment* in which individuals behave aggressively or not. If individuals are skilled at behaving aggressively but lack the communication, interpersonal, or self-regulatory skills to behave nonaggressively, they are more likely to aggress. In addition, if children are calm rather than emotionally aroused, they may be better able to control their behavior so as not to behave aggressively (Lemerise & Arsenio, 2000). Social information–processing theory has been used primarily to account for the enactment of physical aggression, but related steps may ultimately lead to enactment of relational aggression. For example, in situations involving relational rather than physical provocations, children who ultimately use relational aggression make more hostile attributions and feel more distressed than nonaggressive children (Leff et al., 2010).

These social information–processing steps are interrelated. For example, the failure to encode all of the relevant information about the situation in the first step can increase the likelihood of making a hostile attribution in the second step. If one does not generate numerous possible responses in the fourth step, there will not be many options to evaluate in the fifth step. The basic steps of the model and relations with aggressive behavior appear to be consistent across cultures. In one study, children in nine countries (China, Colombia, Italy, Jordan, Kenya, the Philippines, Sweden, Thailand, and the United States) were presented with 10 hypothetical vignettes that depicted an ambiguous situation (Dodge et al., 2015). Children were asked why the provocateur behaved as he or she did, and the responses were coded as hostile or benign. Children were also asked to predict how they would react if they were in that situation, and responses were coded as aggressive or nonaggressive. Children's hostile attributions were related to more aggressive behaviors at three levels. Among cultures, cultural groups that were higher than average in making hostile attributions were also higher than average in mothers' and children's reports of children's aggressive behavior. Within cultures, children who were higher than average in making hostile attributions were also higher than average in aggressive behavior. At the individual level, during situations in which the child made a hostile attribution, he or she was more likely to respond aggressively than in situations in which the child made a benign attribution.

Despite the cross-cultural consistency in links between social-cognitive processes and aggressive behavior, cultural differences exist in the likelihood of having social information–processing patterns that increase the likelihood of aggressive behavior. Cultural differences are also found in evaluations of aggressive responses, with some cultural groups showing more support of aggression than others (Ramírez et al., 2001). Children who live in societies that endorse aggression are more likely to behave aggressively (A. T. Skinner, Bacchini, et al., 2014).

Some cultural groups are more attuned to threats to honor than are other cultural groups, which increases the likelihood of making hostile attributions and, thereby, aggressive behavior. As noted in Chapter 1, Nisbett and Cohen (1996) suggested that many individuals in the southern United States brought with them the herder culture developed in Scotland and Ireland, a culture in which aggression and retaliation were rewarded. In a classic laboratory-based study in the United States, a researcher the participant did not realize was affiliated with the experiment provoked white male college students (Nisbett & Cohen, 1996). Compared with men from the north, men from the southern United States were more likely to attribute hostile intent to the provocateur, were more than twice as likely to become angry, and were almost twice as likely to respond aggressively to a hypothetical provocative vignette (Nisbett & Cohen, 1996). Following provocation, men from the south had an increase in testosterone and the stress hormone cortisol, and were more likely to feel that their honor had been threatened, thereby becoming physiologically primed for aggression.

CULTURAL NORMS PERTAINING TO THE ACCEPTABILITY OF AGGRESSION AND VIOLENCE

There are large differences between cultures regarding the acceptability of using aggression. As we noted in Chapter 1, some of these norms likely stem from ecological conditions and associated community structures in which aggression is more or less adaptive, as well as factors such as cohesiveness of family relationships and religion. Compared with Western European and other high-income countries such as Australia, Canada, and New Zealand, people in the United States are considerably more violent. In several countries in Africa, Asia, Eastern Europe, and South America, however, people are more violent than in the United States. At a national level, these differences in violent crime, homicide, and other less extreme forms of violence demonstrate that cultural groups differ regarding the level of aggression members express toward each another.

Cultures can be conceptualized as conveying from generation to generation sets of opportunities and constraints that affect if and how members of the culture can control other members through coercive means (Bond, 2004). When norms guiding the distribution of limited material or social resources are violated, such violations are often defined as "aggression" and attempts to restore harmony and social order follow, or the aggression is used as a justification for reacting with further aggression, which escalates the conflict.

Cultural groups differ regarding the acceptability of coercive behavior and aggression, and adults convey these beliefs to children. For example, two neighboring Zapotec communities in Mexico that had varied levels of adult violence differed regarding play fighting and actual fighting among 3- to 8-year-old children, in ways that mirrored the behavior of adults in their respective communities (Fry, 1988). From an early age, children learn ways of expressing aggression (or not) that are appropriate in their communities.

Cultures of honor exist in communities around the world. There is an extreme manifestation of these values in honor killings that involve homicide committed by a family member who thinks that the victim has dishonored or shamed the family. Endorsement of violence in certain situations that violate social expectations can lead people to be more accepting of aggression (Chesler, 2010). Cultural spillover theories of violence have been supported by empirical findings indicating that cultural groups in which aggression is tolerated or endorsed in one domain are more accepting of violence in other domains (Lysova & Straus, 2019). For example, combative sports, severe punishment of criminals, homicide, and war tend to co-occur at a societal level, and corporal punishment of children is more likely in societies in which these other forms of aggression are prevalent (Ember & Ember, 2005). Anthropological data from 186 cultural groups demonstrated that corporal punishment of children was harsher and more frequent in cultural groups that had more societal-level endorsement of violence and more prevalent violence, as indicated by warfare, interpersonal aggression between adults, and socialization of aggression in children (Lansford & Dodge, 2008). Adults are more likely to use physical and psychological aggression toward children in countries that have a higher tolerance of violence between spouses (Lansford, Deater-Deckard, et al., 2014). In addition, data from college students in 19 countries suggested that countries in which large proportions of students experienced corporal punishment as children also had large proportions of students report assaulting or injuring a romantic partner (Douglas & Straus, 2006).

Social-learning mechanisms can account for the ways that children model the aggressive behaviors of adults around them. Individuals who witness aggressive behaviors in various situations also hold cognitions that normalize aggression, increasing the likelihood that they will behave aggressively (Ng-Mak et al., 2002). In social groups with strict demarcations of ingroups and outgroups, norms justifying aggression toward the outgroup increase the likelihood of violence between gangs, ethnic groups, and tribes that fuel actions as extreme as genocide in some cases (Staub, 2019).

Some beliefs in the acceptability of aggression are transmitted to children through parenting. For example, parents who positively evaluate aggressive responses in social situations are more likely to use aggression, such as corporal punishment, in response to their children's misbehaviors (Lansford, Deater-Deckard, et al., 2014), and are more likely to have children who behave aggressively (Huesmann & Kirwil, 2007). If children observe their parents behaving aggressively, they are likely to internalize beliefs about the acceptability of using aggression. In addition, parents who evaluate aggression positively may intentionally or unintentionally reinforce aggression in their children, such as by encouraging them to fight back when provoked. Culture-level norms can either reinforce or mitigate effects of family-level socialization. For example, parents' use of corporal punishment socializes children to use aggression to deal with interpersonal conflicts. If cultural norms also support the use of aggression, intergenerational transmission of aggression is further socialized (Wright & Fagan, 2013).

Thus, at least two mechanisms can account for how children internalize cultural norms in ways that increase their aggressive behavior. First, according to social-learning theories, children learn by observing others and modeling their own behavior on the behaviors of others. Therefore, if children grow up in violent neighborhoods, homes, or cultures where they observe others behaving aggressively, they will model that aggression. Second, according to the General Aggression Model (C. A. Anderson & Bushman, 2002), being exposed to aggression leads individuals to internalize knowledge structures and aggressive scripts that increase the likelihood of aggression when these scripts are activated in new situations. Exposure to violence can be either direct (being bullied by peers, abused by parents, or witnessing neighborhood crime) or indirect (watching violent television shows or playing violent video games). Repeated exposure to aggression shapes the ways that children perceive, interpret, make decisions about, and behave in social situations. If children hold knowledge structures primed for aggression through prior experiences, then new situations are more likely to elicit affective and behavioral scripts, such as anger and retaliation, which prompt aggressive behavior. For instance, if children are rejected by peers or abused by their parents, they expect that others will behave with hostile intent, and they accept the use of aggression in social interactions (Dodge et al., 2003). Children are then more likely to behave aggressively in the future because aggression becomes a readily accessible response in their cognitive repertoire.

In addition to social information–processing, emotional and cognitive mediators can serve as mechanisms through which exposure to risk factors for aggression ultimately leads to aggressive behavior in certain situations. For example, moral disengagement involves a separation between oneself and ethical standards in a certain context or at a particular time (Bandura, 2016). Adolescents are especially more likely to behave aggressively if they are morally disengaged (Gini et al., 2014). In addition, other risk factors, such as exposure to violent video games, are more likely to lead to aggressive behavior in individuals who are high in moral disengagement (Gabbiadini et al., 2014). Children's self-regulation and emotion dysregulation also mediate links between exposure to risk factors and ultimately behaving aggressively (Cui et al., 2014).

Latent mental structures and online processing are both important aspects of social cognition (Happé et al., 2017). Latent mental structures encompass general knowledge and cognitive schemas that provide mental shortcuts in new situations by reducing the complexity of new information individuals need to process in the moment as they draw from their existing knowledge database. Cognitive schemas are mental representations that develop through previous experiences in certain social situations. For example, individuals may develop cognitive schemas that involve normative beliefs about aggression, which can be either specific to certain situations (If someone hits me, it's okay for me to hit back) or general (It's okay to hit other people; Huesmann et al., 2017). People are more likely to behave aggressively if they hold normative beliefs about the acceptability of aggression.

Individuals in social situations may engage in either controlled or automatic processing (Schneider & Chein, 2003). Controlled processing occurs when an individual carefully considers different options and evaluates the situation before responding. In contrast, automatic processing occurs when an individual responds quickly without stopping to think consciously through options and evaluate the situation. Unless they make a deliberate decision to act otherwise, children's processing generally becomes more automatic with age because they develop a knowledge base of how they have reacted to similar situations in the past, which they then apply to respond more quickly in new social situations. If children have developed aggressive schemas in the context of previous social interactions, they will become increasingly reliant on those schemes and use them automatically in future situations.

Like social information–processing theory, the general aggression model describes cognitive mechanisms in the development of aggression (C. A. Anderson & Bushman, 2002). According to the model, knowledge structures develop through social experiences and affect perceptions, interpretations, decisions, and behaviors in future situations. If a new situation activates scripts regarding anger and revenge based on prior experience, then aggression is more likely to result in the new situation. In the case of violent media, for example, individuals who have been exposed repeatedly to violent television programs or played violent video games will develop attitudes endorsing aggression, will begin to expect aggression, will become desensitized to aggression, and will learn ways to aggress (C. A. Anderson & Bushman, 2001). Aggressive children are already more likely to choose to watch violent television programs and play violent video games than are nonaggressive children, but exposure to violent media escalates aggression above and beyond these initial proclivities (Bushman & Anderson, 2001).

SUBSTANCE USE AND OTHER RISKY BEHAVIORS

Rates of substance use vary widely across countries (World Health Organization, 2018b). Research Highlight 13.2 describes the International Self-Report

RESEARCH HIGHLIGHT 13.2

International Self-Report Delinquency Study
The International Self-Report Delinquency Study is an international collaboration that aims to understand substance use, delinquency, and victimization during early-to-mid adolescence (Enzmann et al., 2018). Three rounds of surveys have been conducted to date, first in 1991–1992, second in 2006–2008, and third in 2012–2019. A fourth round of surveys is being planned. In the most recent round of the survey, representative samples of seventh, eighth, and ninth graders were recruited from at least two cities in each of 35 countries, primarily in Europe but also in North and South America, the Caribbean, Africa, Australia, and Asia. At least 900 children (300 per grade) were recruited in each city, for a sample of at least 1,800 per country. Adolescents completed either paper-and-pencil or online versions of questionnaires that ask whether, when, and how often they have engaged in a number of behaviors, such as stealing, fighting, drinking alcohol, and using illegal drugs, as well as ways they may have been victimized (e.g., robbed, bullied). Findings from the study are used to understand trends in substance use, delinquent behaviors, and victimization over time and to make international comparisons. The findings are also used to shape policies and prevention strategies related to substance use and delinquency.

Delinquency Study to illustrate one way that countries collect data about substance use and other risky behaviors. Countries differ in cultural norms about the acceptability of substance use and potentially risky behaviors, access to risk-taking opportunities, and resources to prevent risky behaviors. For example, consistent with Islamic principles forbidding the use of intoxicants, alcohol use in predominantly Muslim countries is low in comparison with other countries (AlMarri & Oei, 2009). In Jordan, for instance, 73% of adolescents reported believing that even occasional use of alcohol is extremely harmful, and 87% of adolescents reported believing that occasional use of other drugs is extremely harmful (Haddad et al., 2010). In contrast, 33% of 17- to 18-year-olds in the United States reported having been drunk in the past year (Johnston et al., 2020), even though the legal drinking age is 21, suggesting that cultural norms play an important role in substance use. Substance use also changes over time. For example, vaping more than doubled between 2017 and 2019 among eighth-, 10th-, and 12th-grade students in the United States (approximately ages 14, 16, and 18), whereas the use of marijuana and most illicit drugs changed little over this time period (Johnston et al., 2020).

Similarly, nonmarital sex is common in Italy, Sweden, and the United States (Capuano et al., 2009; Holmberg & Hellberg, 2004; Guttmacher Institute, 2016, respectively), but is illegal in some countries, such as Saudi Arabia and the United Arab Emirates, with penalties as severe as jail or lashings for citizens or deportation for noncitizens (e.g., Santos, 2017). Even in countries with norms that are similarly accepting of nonmarital sex, different societal-level resources make nonmarital sex less risky in some countries than others. For example, condoms and comprehensive sex education are widely available to adolescents in Sweden but not in the United States. The consequences are evident in teen birth rates of 5.9 per 1,000 in Sweden compared with 41.9 per 1,000 in the

United States (United Nations Statistics Division, 2006) as well as the prevalence of sexually transmitted infections (e.g., among adolescents the rates are 10 times higher for syphilis and more than 300 times higher for gonorrhea in the United States than in Sweden; Panchaud et al., 2000). Recognizing that adolescents are developmentally more likely to engage in risky behaviors than are younger children or adults, societies that are able to change environments to reduce detrimental outcomes are likely to be more successful. For example, providing adolescents with access to long-acting reversible contraceptives, such as intrauterine devices and subdermal contraceptive implants, in nonthreatening, confidential settings has been found to be one of the most effective ways to reduce unplanned pregnancies and abortions (Ricketts et al., 2014). Because cultural groups have various norms about the acceptability of certain behaviors, a child or an adolescent who engages in behavior not condoned by the cultural group is likely to be on a more problematic developmental trajectory than a child or an adolescent who engages in more culturally normative behavior.

Life-history theory provides an evolutionary explanation for why some environments are more conducive to aggression and other externalizing behaviors than others (Kaplan et al., 2000). According to the theory, survival and reproductive advantages are optimized differently depending on environmental constraints involving food and safety. When food is plentiful and safety is relatively assured, individuals adopt slow life-history strategies that include maturing late, delaying reproduction, prolonging development, and being highly involved in the development of offspring, as well as related behaviors, such as exploring and learning (Chang et al., 2019). However, when survival is at risk because of inadequate food, safety risks, or both, individuals adopt fast life-history strategies that include maturing early, developing rapidly, mating early and frequently, being less involved with offspring, and engaging in aggression and other behaviors that are conducive to a present-oriented lifestyle (Belsky et al., 2012).

In a study comparing fast versus slow life-history strategies in nine countries, living in unsafe neighborhoods, family chaos, fluctuating income, and experiencing stressful life events during childhood were related to adopting fast life-history strategies, including more aggressive behavior and poorer school performance, later in childhood and adolescence (Chang et al., 2019). Consistent with life-history theory, growing up in unpredictable and unreliable environments was related to children focusing on immediate instrumental goals rather than on longer term academic goals. For children raised in stable environments, however, long-term goals involving academic achievement and socially affiliative behaviors were more prominent.

CONCLUSION

Overall, children who grow up in different cultures show similarities in the physical, verbal, and relational forms of aggression they exhibit and the reactive or proactive functions that aggression serves. Likewise, tied to their cognitive capacities, children in different cultural groups show similar developmental trajectories of aggressive and antisocial behavior. In particular, adolescence (vs. earlier or later in development) is a time of increased antisocial and risky behavior. Across cultures, risk factors for the development of aggression include exposure to violence in the family, the community, and the media, as well as social information–processing patterns that include making hostile attributions and positively evaluating aggressive responses. Culture affects the development of aggression, delinquency, substance use, and other forms of risky behavior in several ways. In particular, children develop beliefs about the acceptability of aggression; an understanding of norms about substance use and other potentially risky behaviors; and cognitive schemas that increase or decrease the likelihood of aggressive behavior by observing others in their cultural group, being reinforced by parents and peers for behaving in particular ways, and by learning the cultural constraints on particular behaviors in their cultural group.

For additional resources, see the Appendix.

DISCUSSION QUESTIONS

1. How do cultural norms related to violence and children's exposure to violence in real life and in the media contribute to the development of aggression?

2. Why do changes in brain development and cognition make adolescents in a variety of cultural contexts vulnerable to peer influence?

3. Describe how cultural context could affect each step of the social information–processing model to increase or decrease the likelihood that children would behave aggressively.

4. What factors contribute to differences between countries in rates of substance use, risky sexual behaviors, and other forms of risky behavior during adolescence?

5. How could interventions designed to prevent or reduce adolescents' aggression, delinquency, and substance use be developed to take advantage of knowledge about culture and adolescent development?

14

Prosocial Behavior, Morality, and Positive Youth Development in Cultural Context

These teenagers in the United Kingdom are volunteering their time creating a mural for a community art project.

As children and adolescents develop, clearly the goal is for them to avoid aggression, deviancy, and substance use (as described in Chapter 13), but also for them to behave prosocially and morally, with a host of characteristics that constitute positive youth development. In this chapter we will consider which aspects of prosocial behavior, morality, and positive youth development are consistent across cultures and which aspects differ, as well as how their predictors are shaped by the cultural contexts in which children develop. Prosocial

https://doi.org/10.1037/0000228-014
Child and Adolescent Development in Cultural Context, by J. E. Lansford, D. C. French, and M. Gauvain

behavior, morality, and positive youth development are all desirable aspects of child development, yet they differ in their characteristics and the extent to which they develop within the context of culture. We will consider each in turn.

DEVELOPMENT OF PROSOCIAL BEHAVIOR

Prosocial behavior is generally defined as voluntary, desirable actions aimed to help others and can include sharing, offering assistance, and other acts of kindness (N. Eisenberg et al., 2015). Prosocial behavior is positive in its own right and also promotes positive future developmental outcomes.

As we discussed in Chapter 1, Fiske (1992) argued that there are cultural rules about how resources are distributed within relationships. Thus, communal sharing relationships entail providing resources to others regardless of their contribution. Authority-ranking relationships entail distribution of resources based on status-related criteria. In equality-matching relationships there is an emphasis on equal distribution, whereas in market-pricing relationships, the emphasis is on providing resources in proportion to some criterion (e.g., need, merit, contribution). All of these forms of relationships exist within cultures, and children's socialization requires them to differentiate between people and the circumstances under which different types of relationships and distribution arrangements pertain. Underlying judgments about the appropriateness of different forms of sociability are judgments about ingroup and outgroup membership.

As early as the first year of life, infants are aware of differences between prosocial and antisocial behavior (Kuhlmeier et al., 2003). By 15 months of age, children prefer peers who are fair and share toys with others (Schmidt & Sommerville, 2011). By 19 months, children expect others to be fair in sharing, as indicated by their look of surprise when an experimenter distributes resources such as toys or cookies unequally to puppets in an experimental paradigm (Sloane et al., 2012). By age 2 or 3, children generally protest when others violate the norms they have come to expect in their cultural group (e.g., for rules or prosocial behavior), which generally have not been taught explicitly but rather learned through observation (Schmidt et al., 2011). Even preschoolers try to comfort peers who are sad or hurt and are able to share their toys with others. Prosocial behavior becomes more sophisticated, and motivations for prosocial behavior change developmentally. For example, prosocial behavior increases as children become better at considering other people's perspectives and understanding that others have beliefs and feelings apart from their own (theory of mind, as described in Chapter 3). By the time they are 5 years old, children generally believe that they should share with others as much as others share with them (Paulus, 2014).

All of these demonstrations of preferences for prosocial behavior in early childhood suggest some cross-cultural commonalities in the bases of prosocial behavior. But, children's ideas about what is fair and just, as well as various aspects of prosocial behavior (e.g., sharing, sympathy) also depend on their cultural context (Robbins & Rochat, 2011). For example, sharing depends on both affective and cognitive processes that are guided by culturally based representations of group norms regarding expectations in particular situations (Jensen et al., 2014), as illustrated by findings that children in Eastern cultures are more likely to share with peers than are children in Western cultures (Stewart & McBride-Chang, 2000). There is also variation within cultures. For example, British children from higher socioeconomic backgrounds are more likely to share than children from lower socioeconomic backgrounds (Benenson et al., 2007), perhaps because these children have more resources to share. Research Highlight 14.1 describes a study comparing children's sharing behavior in three cultural groups

Several studies have shown that the development of ideas of distributive justice (how resources should be divided) is more culturally similar when the resources being distributed are abstract rather than culturally meaningful. For example, in a comparison of 3- and 5-year-old American children and Palestinian refugees in Lebanon, researchers used puppets and a three-dimensional scene with houses and an empty plot of land between them to see how the children thought land should be distributed between neighbors who varied on

---

RESEARCH HIGHLIGHT 14.1

Children's Sharing in Different Cultural Groups

The ways in which children share and the amount of sharing vary across cultures. One study compared the sharing habits of 4- to 11-year-old children from Germany, a rural foraging tribe in Namibia, and a rural area in Kenya that depends on livestock and gardening for food (Schäfer et al., 2015). Children were asked to use a magnetic rod to fish for metal objects in a fish tank. The children completed the task in pairs, fishing next to each other in adjacent tanks. The researchers rigged the experiment so that sometimes the children caught the same number of fish, but sometimes one child caught 3 times as many fish as the other child. In a third experimental condition, the children were given an unequal number of objects from the tanks without fishing for them.

The researcher then gave each pair of children the same number of sweets as the total number of fish they had and asked the children to divide the sweets between them. The German children followed principles of merit and distributive justice (e.g., within Fiske's system, "market pricing") when dividing the sweets, so the children who caught 3 times as many fish received three times as many sweets.

In contrast, children from the rural foraging tribe in Namibia and the rural area in Kenya divided the sweets equally between themselves, regardless of who caught more fish (i.e., communal sharing or equity matching). One explanation is that children in the rural groups that depend on foraging and farming for food were socialized to share equally to maintain social harmony and to balance inequalities for the good of the group. Similar findings have been reported comparing how 3- and 5-year-olds from seven cultural groups share candies. Across cultures, the 5-year-olds generally shared more equally than the 3-year-olds (who are more likely to maximize their own gain), but the children in rural areas of Peru and Fiji, characterized by more collectivist values, were more likely to distribute candies equally than were children in urban areas of Brazil, China, and the United States (Rochat et al., 2009).

several dimensions. Both American and Palestinian children advocated distributing more land to poor neighbors than to rich neighbors, but Palestinian children were more likely than American children to advocate distributing more land to an ingroup member of their own nationality than to an outgroup member, perhaps because of the political salience of land distribution for Palestinian children (Zebian & Rochat, 2012). Research Highlight 14.2 describes a study in five countries illustrating the development of generosity, which is related to the idea of distributive justice.

Research on the development of empathy and compassion can highlight when children are more likely to behave prosocially and toward whom. Empathy involves adopting the feelings of other people. For example, if a child becomes sad after seeing a peer cry, he or she is showing empathy with the other child. Compassion, by contrast, involves considering another person's feelings but not taking on the other's emotions. Empathy and compassion activate different parts of the brain (Singer & Klimecki, 2014). People are more empathetic with people with whom they share a common cultural background, race, ethnicity, or language, and this differentiation predicts later proclivities to help ingroup members more than outgroup members (Singer & Klimecki, 2014). In addition, empathy and compassion often lead to different behavioral responses. People are more likely to help others when they feel compassion

---

RESEARCH HIGHLIGHT 14.2

The Development of Generosity

Urban samples in Canada, China, South Africa, Turkey, and the United States were recruited to compare the development of generosity in children ages 5 to 12 (Cowell et al., 2017). In a laboratory-based task, children were given 30 stickers and told that they could choose their favorite 10 to keep. After one child selected 10 stickers, the experimenter said that there was not time for all children to complete the game but that the child could choose to give some of the stickers to another child who would be unable to play. The child was instructed to put stickers to keep in one envelope and the ones to give to other children in a different envelope; experimenters turned their backs to do other tasks while the child completed the sorting. Generosity was operationalized as the number of stickers the child chose to share, out of a possible of 10. Subsequent analyses categorized children as "hoarders" if they shared three or fewer stickers, "egalitarians" if they shared four to six stickers, and "ultra-sharers" if they shared seven or more stickers. Children in all five countries became more generous with age, consistent with the idea that developmentally, as children become better able to consider other people's perspectives, they become more generous and better at sharing (Cowell et al., 2017). However, differences were also found between countries. The variation at the country-level could contribute to these differences in generosity, but it is notable that a broad individualistic versus collectivistic orientation cannot account for the findings. That is, children in China (a country traditionally labeled as collectivistic) had more similar sharing behavior to children in Canada and the United States (countries traditionally labeled as individualistic) than to children in Turkey (another traditionally collectivistic country). The market economies of South Africa and Turkey are less developed than those in Canada, China, and the United States, which is an alternate explanation for differences in children's sharing behavior.

---

rather than empathic distress (N. Eisenberg, 2000). According to Bloom (2016), empathy can lead people to care more about one person with whom they identify than for thousands of more distant people who are culturally dissimilar. Bloom argues for using reasoning rather than empathy as the basis for morality, especially when the goal is to do the most good for the most people.

Some prosocial behavior comes at a cost to oneself, whereas other prosocial behavior does not. To understand this distinction, one study examined prosocial behavior of 3- to 14-year-old children in six cultural groups: Aka (nomadic hunter–gatherers living in the Congo Basin), Himba (seminomadic agro-pastoralists in Namibia), Shuar (slash and burn horticulturalists from Amazonia), Martu (sedentized foragers from Australia), marine forager–horticulturalists from Yasawa Island, Fiji, and urban Americans in Los Angeles (House et al., 2013). In one experimental condition, children received a food reward for engaging in a task and could decide whether or not a peer should also receive a food reward, without giving up their own reward. There were no differences in prosocial behavior for children of any age in this condition when prosocial behavior (rewarding the peer) did not involve personal sacrifice. In a different experimental condition, children could decide whether to retain two food rewards for themselves, or to give one of their food rewards to a peer. There were no cultural differences for the youngest children, and children in all six cultural groups became more prosocial with age. In addition, cultural differences emerged by middle childhood, and children began to more closely resemble adults from their respective cultural groups in their prosocial behavior regarding whether or not they distributed food rewards equally between themselves and a peer, even if it meant less food for them.

Volunteering is a specific aspect of prosocial behavior that becomes developmentally more salient in adolescence. A number of studies have investigated youth volunteering and their motivation to volunteer (e.g., Grönlund et al., 2011). Volunteering benefits other people but has costs for the volunteer (e.g., time). Underlying motivations for volunteering have generally been grouped into three types: altruistic or values-based, utilitarian, and social (Handy et al., 2010). Altruistic or values-based volunteering is driven by religious beliefs, the desire to help others, or embracing a particular cause. Utilitarian volunteering is driven by more self-serving factors such as building a resume to get into college, gaining job skills, or making contacts that could be useful for paid work in the future. Social volunteering is motivated by social norms or expectations about volunteering or the desire to be with friends who are volunteering. Country-level factors affect youth motivation to volunteer. For example, in countries in which the government has a larger role in providing a social safety net, individuals are less likely to be motivated to volunteer for altruistic reasons, such as helping the poor, because that is perceived as being the role of the government (Ziemek, 2006).

Differences in prosocial behavior may develop as children passively observe the behaviors of others in their cultural group, as adults explicitly socialize prosocial behavior, or as a result of variations in other culture-specific experiences.

For example, children's typical experiences in various cultural contexts elicit different types of prosocial behavior. In cultures that expect young children to care for even younger siblings or expect children to engage in labor that benefits the entire family, and on which the family's survival sometimes depends, prosocial behavior that is characterized by helping others and attending to others' needs occurs in meaningful everyday contexts (de Guzman et al., 2005). Among the Ngecha people in Gikuyu, Kenya, for instance, children demonstrated less prosocial behavior in situations that did not involve family obligations than in situations in which they were engaged in labor for their family's benefit, such as caring for younger siblings or performing household chores (de Guzman et al., 2005). However, in cultures in which children have more limited opportunities to contribute to the family's livelihood, parents try to socialize their children to behave prosocially in more abstract situations, such as discussing how their actions (after misbehaving) made others feel (Hastings et al., 2007).

Differences in prosocial behavior between countries depend on a number of factors, such as the beneficiary of the prosocial behavior (ingroup or outgroup, family, friends), the situation (spontaneity, costs), and the type of prosocial behavior (helping, sharing, being cooperative; N. Eisenberg et al., 2015). An experimental paradigm was used in 21 countries to investigate adults' behavior when offering help to a stranger, a form of prosocial behavior (Knafo et al., 2009). In both high- and low-income countries, individuals who lived in cultures characterized by social embeddedness—which value social order, obedience, security, tradition, and emphasize the welfare of one's ingroup—made fewer offers to help the stranger. Thus, to understand the development of prosocial behavior, it is important to understand the cultural rules regarding expected prosocial behavior with other people. Consistent with the early analysis by Fiske (1992), these rules differ as a function of culture and relationship type.

DEVELOPMENT OF MORALITY

Prosocial behavior is the outward manifestation of actions that benefit other people, whereas *morality* is the underlying mental framework that involves reasoning about right and wrong. Morality guides behavior, but one could behave prosocially without having an underlying moral reason for doing so. Likewise, moral reasoning does not guarantee that one will behave prosocially.

A major theory of moral development was proposed by Kohlberg (1981), who posited that moral development proceeds in six stages among three levels, with two stages in each level:

1. preconventional level characterized by an obedience and punishment orientation at Stage 1 (e.g., thinking something is morally wrong because of a resulting punishment) and a self-interest orientation at Stage 2 (e.g., not

being concerned with the interests of others but only in what's in it for oneself);

2. conventional level characterized by an orientation toward interpersonal accord and conformity at Stage 3 (e.g., behaving in a way that will be perceived by society as being a good girl or boy) and an authority and social-order maintaining orientation at Stage 4 (e.g., recognizing the importance of following laws to maintain a well-functioning society); and

3. postconventional level characterized by a social contract orientation at Stage 5 (e.g., considering different individuals' rights and perspectives and believing that laws should be changed when they are not in the majority's best interests) and universal ethical principles at Stage 6 (e.g., holding a commitment to justice that can involve disobeying laws if they are unjust).

Kohlberg's theory generated a large body of empirical research that addressed the extent to which the theorized stages of moral development characterized development in different cultural groups. Very few individuals consistently operate at the highest stage of moral development proposed by Kohlberg, and in many cultures (and for European American women, the ethnic group for which the theory was primarily developed), the majority of adults do not reach the highest two stages of moral development proposed by Kohlberg (Gibbs et al., 2007). In a review of 45 studies from 27 primarily non-European cultural groups, researchers found support for Kohlberg's first four stages of moral development (Snarey, 1985). However, higher stages of moral reasoning may be more culturally nuanced. For example, lying to benefit oneself or one's social group and lying to avoid taking credit for a good deed are examples of moral decisions that vary across cultural groups, in part depending on whether behavior to benefit oneself is socially encouraged or discouraged (Helwig, 2017).

Beyond Kohlberg's (1981) theory, according to the domain theory of moral development, children use different reasoning for behaviors in moral, social-conventional, and personal domains (Turiel & Gingo, 2017). The moral domain includes ethical issues that could hurt someone, such as stealing, cheating, or lying. The social-conventional domain includes social norm issues involving behaviors such as manners and expectations about how to act in certain situations, which help to maintain harmony in social systems, but the norms are somewhat arbitrary (e.g., shaking someone's right hand and looking in their eyes when meeting). The personal domain involves issues that are largely individual preferences, such as music choice or what clothes to wear. Children and adolescents (as well as adults) generally consider violations of expectations in the moral domain to be more serious than violations in the social-conventional or personal domains. Moral rules are less arbitrary than social-conventional rules and are more widely accepted across cultures and individuals within cultures (Dahl & Killen, 2018). Children in all cultures learn similar moral codes that involve not hurting other people, whereas social conventions and personal domains vary widely across cultures.

In Kohlberg's (1981) theory, social-conventional reasoning was simply at an earlier stage of moral development than more sophisticated moral reasoning, but according to the domain theory of moral reasoning, moral and social-conventional domains are two separate entities rather than points on the same developmental continuum (Turiel & Gingo, 2017). Thus, children and adolescents reason differently on moral and social-conventional issues (Dahl & Killen, 2018). Reasons for engaging in both moral and socially accepted behaviors vary developmentally and culturally. For example, in Hong Kong, both 4- and 6-year-olds considered social convention violations to be less wrongful and less serious than moral transgressions, regardless of how authorities reacted. Compared with 6-year-olds, however, 4-year-olds were more likely to report that they would adhere to social conventions to avoid punishment and because authorities prohibited certain behaviors (Yau & Smetana, 2003). Compared with 4-year-olds, 6-year-olds were more likely to report justifications involving the accepted nature of the acts for adhering to social conventions (Yau & Smetana, 2003). Furthermore, children and adolescents generally regard moral and social-conventional domains to be under the legitimate control of adults, whereas they regard personal domain issues as those that adults should leave to children's discretion rather than try to control (Turiel & Gingo, 2017). Some developmental differences in reasoning about different domains have been found across cultures. For example, in both China and the United States, older children are more likely than younger children to say that they should have control over personal-domain decisions (Smetana et al., 2014). Despite these developmental similarities across cultures, there are also differences across cultures regarding which domains are considered to be under the control of parents versus children, and in how parents respond when children violate expectations. For example, when children's disobedience results from expressions of individuality, middle-class Israeli mothers are more tolerant than are middle-class Japanese mothers (Osterweil & Nagano, 1991).

Conversations between parents and children about morally laden topics are an important way that children are socialized into the moral thinking of their respective cultural groups (Wainryb & Recchia, 2014). Such conversations are an important context for moral development because they provide opportunities to share ideas about how one's behavior makes oneself and others feel, and parents may be more likely than peers to challenge children's immoral behaviors. Morality thus provides the mental framework underlying the development of children's behaviors.

There is some evidence that underlying the cultural differences in moral development, as just described, are cultural differences in the philosophical underpinnings of morality (J. G. Miller, 2015). Underlying Kohlberg's (1981) stage theory of moral development is a philosophical view of the autonomy of the individual and a reliance on abstract principles of justice. There is evidence that this view is not shared across cultures. For example, in China there is little sense that moral decisions are based on abstract rules that pertain to individual rights. Instead, individuals learn systems of obligations and responsibilities derived from Confucianism that describe the obligations of people to each other and rely on the advice of superiors to resolve moral issues and conflicts.

It is useful to consider how children and adolescents in India and the United States conceptualize moral issues differently. Shweder and Haidt (2000) suggested that the Indian concept of morality is based on community ethics and responsibilities rather than on the more abstract codes of individual rights. As such, actions that might be considered disgusting or disrespectful but not necessarily immoral in the United States (e.g., cleaning a toilet with the national flag) were viewed as immoral in India. Morality is also conceptualized in relational terms, which stems from the aspect of self that is embedded in a network of social roles and relationships. Thus, morality is expressed as performance of responsibilities consistent with relationships and roles, and a focus exclusively on self-needs is viewed as immoral (Kapadia & Bhangaokar, 2015). In addition, J. G. Miller et al. (1990) found that children and adults from the United States and India use different criteria to determine prosocial and moral behavior. They argue that Americans tend to categorize helping others as "moral" only under circumstances in which others experience extreme need, such as a life-threatening emergency. In contrast, Indian people tend to view helping others as a broader moral imperative and an obligation that is present regardless of the relationship and the extremity of the need. Thus, views of morality in India typically differ considerably from those of the United States.

POSITIVE YOUTH DEVELOPMENT

Both prosocial behavior and morality can be indicators of positive youth development, but positive youth development is broader than prosocial behavior and morality. *Positive youth development* has been defined in various ways in different cultural contexts, but one useful way to understand it is in the 5-Cs framework (competence, confidence, connection, character, and caring or compassion; e.g., Lerner et al., 2005). According to the 5-Cs theory, each of the Cs represents the contributions that children and adolescents can make to their families, schools, and communities (Lerner et al., 2015). Another framework of positive youth development incudes 24 moral competences, or character strengths, clustered in six groups: (a) wisdom (e.g., creativity, curiosity); (b) courage (e.g., persistence, zest); (c) humanity (e.g., kindness, social intelligence); (d) justice (e.g., fairness); (e) temperance (e.g., self-regulation); and (f) transcendence (e.g., hope, spirituality; N. Park & Peterson, 2006).

When attempting to understand positive youth development, it is important to delve into Indigenous concepts to avoid being "underinclusive" (van de Vijver, 2017). For example, the following 10 constructs might characterize positive youth development in China better than the five constructs in the 5-Cs model (Gai & Lan, 2013):

1. active and optimistic view,

2. striving and insistence,

3. leadership,

4. caring,

5. confidence,

6. autonomy,

7. prudence,

8. love of learning,

9. flexibility and innovation, and

10. interests and curiosity.

Some of those constructs overlap across models (caring, confidence), but others are not explicitly singled out in the 5-Cs model (e.g., flexibility and innovation). Open-ended interviews in which Swedish fathers were asked how they could tell if their teenager was developing well and whether or not things were going well in all areas of life revealed responses related to four aspects of well-being: cognitive, emotional and psychological, physical, and social (Mansoory et al., 2019). Some of the themes that fathers described related to the four aspects of well-being were congruent with themes identified in other research, whereas other themes were more novel. For example, with respect to cognitive well-being, the descriptions of academic achievement and intelligence were similar to aspects of cognitive well-being that are often included in other models, but curiosity and openness to the surrounding world were more novel aspects of cognitive well-being. Similarly, Swedish fathers' descriptions of emotional and psychological well-being included characteristics frequently noted in other contexts, such as happiness and confidence, as well as less frequently noted characteristics, such as calmness, optimism, and contentment. These findings suggest that specific features of positive youth development may be more or less salient in different cultural contexts. Beyond these specific characteristics of positive youth development, cultural expectations for the development of youth may also differ. For example, in the United States, adolescents are often regarded as being rebellious, impulsive, and likely to engage in problem behavior, whereas in China, adolescents are regarded as being filled with hope, vitality, vigor, and optimism (Chen et al., 2017).

Although the 5-Cs characterize positive youth development in many different cultural groups, the specific ways that these Cs are defined sometimes differs. For example, competence is often defined in terms of success in school, athletics, music, or other hobbies that are valued by a cultural group. Cultural groups sometimes develop particular tests or rituals that serve as markers of competence in particular domains. High-stakes academic testing is common in many countries to enable children to advance from one level of education to the next or to enter different tracks of the education system. A student's score on the Tawjihi, for example, is the sole criterion for admission to higher-education institutions in Jordan (Al-Hassan, 2019), and a student's score on the examination organized by the Kenya National Examination Council determines whether the student will be admitted to a high-performing boarding school or a lower-performing local day school in Kenya (Oburu & Mbagaya, 2019). As discussed in Chapter 11, academic achievement is important in all countries for future occupational, financial, and health outcomes (Robert Wood Johnson Foundation, 2013). Nevertheless, cultural groups place different emphasis on academic achievement as an indicator of positive youth development. For example, in the Ivory Coast, only 13% of survey respondents rated education as the most important factor for life success, compared with 73% of survey respondents in Botswana (Crabtree, 2014). Other markers of competence are demonstrated through rituals rather than standardized tests or academic achievement. The Maasai people in Kenya, for example, value high jumping as a marker of adolescent and young adult males' competence, and males who can jump higher are given higher status (Sobania, 2003). Among Indonesian Muslim youth, religiosity is an important component of social competence (French et al., 2012).

Just as competence can be demonstrated in different ways in different cultural contexts, so too can other Cs in the 5-Cs model. For example, although positive interpersonal relationships are important indicators of positive youth development in all countries, the specific features of these relationships may differ. For example, as described in Chapter 7, adolescents in South Korea expect their friendships to be intimate and exclusive in a way that is not expected in Indonesia (French, 2015). It is notable in all of these examples that the Cs themselves are consistent across cultural groups but the manifestations of the Cs may differ (Akinsola, 2013). This is similar to the distinction between forms and functions of parenting presented in Chapter 6. That is, the form taken by competence, confidence, connection, character, and caring or compassion may differ, but the underlying function of each of those aspects of positive youth development may be similar in signaling and promoting not just the absence of problems, but the presence of thriving. Positive youth development across cultures is demonstrated by the contributions one makes to society and positive relationships with other people. Experiences (such as being part of a team) and attributes (such as kindness) build interpersonal connections and contribute to a sense of purpose beyond the self (Gillham et al., 2011). Thus, understanding positive youth development is dependent on core features that generalize across cultures as well as culture-specific features that depend on values and norms within a particular context (Kagitcibasi, 2013).

Differences have been found among countries regarding numerous indicators of positive youth development. For example, countries are increasingly interested in reports of happiness or subjective well-being as indicators of how their citizens are faring, along with more traditional indices, such as infant mortality and life expectancy. The annual World Happiness Report rank-orders happiness in 156 countries based on survey data from youth and adults ages 15 and older (Helliwell et al., 2019). In the most recent ranking, Finland is the happiest country, followed by Denmark, Norway, Iceland, Netherlands, Switzerland, Sweden, New Zealand, Canada, and Austria in the top 10, with the United States in 19th place. According to data from Yemen, India, Syria,

Botswana, and Venezuela (countries at the bottom of the happiness ranking), violence, political turmoil, and social stress are often associated with decreases in happiness. A country's overall level of wealth and affluence of families are correlated with adolescents' happiness, but once a threshold of basic needs has been met, additional increases in income are not necessarily associated with increases in happiness (Levin et al., 2011). Instead, the countries that rank highest on happiness are characterized not only by high gross domestic product, but also by low corruption, high life expectancy, freedom, generosity, and high levels of social support. Thus, positive youth development may not only show similarities and differences across cultures, but also may be predicted by factors that show consistencies as well as differences across cultures.

PREDICTORS OF PROSOCIAL BEHAVIOR, MORALITY, AND POSITIVE YOUTH DEVELOPMENT

Thus far, we have focused on cultural similarities and differences in how prosocial behavior, morality, and positive youth development are manifested. Next, we turn to how predictors of prosocial behavior, morality, and positive youth development may be similar or different across cultures. Families, schools, religion, and other community contexts are among the potential predictors.

Positive youth development is predicted by many of the same factors across cultures. For example experiencing interpersonal violence, material deprivation, and living in dangerous neighborhoods impede positive youth development, whereas supportive family relationships and friendships enhance positive youth development consistently across cultures (e.g., Currie et al., 2012). Each of these predictors encompasses a host of others. For example, living in safer neighborhoods affords children more opportunities to play outside (Carver et al., 2008), positive adult role models (Galster, 2014), and freedom from chronic stressors of crime and violence (Finkelhor et al., 2015). Supportive, responsive relationships with caregivers in infancy and early childhood predict long-term positive youth development (Schoenmaker et al., 2015), and positive social relationships are more important predictors of well-being in adulthood than academic performance (Olsson et al., 2013). The importance of interpersonal acceptance as a predictor of positive development has been demonstrated in meta-analyses that include samples from many countries (Khaleque & Rohner, 2012).

Despite many consistencies in predictors of positive youth development across cultures, certain predictors are more important in some cultures than in others. For example, Asian American adolescents' academic aspirations are predicted by values related to family obligations (Kiang et al., 2013), and Mexican American adolescents' prosocial behaviors are predicted by familism values (Calderón-Tena et al., 2011). In contrast, individual agency is a more salient predictor of positive youth development in Sweden (Sorbring & Gurdal, 2011), where parental warmth has indirect effects on children's adjustment through the development of children's agency, which involves self-esteem, self-efficacy, an internal locus of control, and a sense of purpose in life (Gurdal et al., 2016).

Both cognitive and affective aspects of interacting with parents foster children's moral development (Jambon & Smetana, 2019). Children are more motivated to attend to their parents and respond favorably to socialization attempts when they have warm, loving relationships with their parents. The manner in which parents and children react following a child misbehaving can also affect how children process the misbehavior. Cognitively, children's moral behavior is promoted when parents explain to them why they should behave in particular ways, and when parents help reason with their children about how to behave in various social situations (Jambon & Smetana, 2019). Inductive reasoning, particularly when parents explain how children's behaviors affect other people, promotes children and adolescents' prosocial behavior (Mounts & Allen, 2019). By contrast, power-assertive forms of discipline, such as corporal punishment and yelling, are unlikely to promote children's prosocial behavior (Mounts & Allen, 2019). In addition, adults who experienced more power-assertive discipline as children show less empathy even into adulthood (Lopez et al., 2001). One of the most important ways that cultural representations of morality and behavioral expectations are passed from one generation to the next is through parent–child interactions.

Parents' discipline might also affect children's future moral behavior by promoting the development of conscience (Kochanska et al., 2003). For example, through parental socialization, children often develop feelings of guilt and anxiety when they misbehave, which can lead them to control their future behaviors to avoid misbehavior and behave prosocially instead. When parents are socializing children in conflict episodes, referring to emotions rather than to rules or consequences is more likely to promote conscience development (Laible & Thompson, 2002). The development of conscience begins very early. For example, preschoolers who are securely attached to their mothers (as described in Chapter 6) are more likely than insecurely attached children to have conversations regarding feelings and moral evaluations after misbehaving, which contributes to conscience development (Laible & Thompson, 2000). The reactions of parents and other authority figures depend on the nature of children's transgressions. For example, when children fail to behave prosocially, parents are likely to respond with other-oriented induction, but when children behave antisocially, parents are likely to respond with punishment (Grusec, 2019). In turn, the manner in which children respond to their parents' discipline depends on both the discipline type and the nature of the child's transgressions (Padilla-Walker, 2008), as well as the cultural normativeness of their parents' discipline (Lansford et al., 2005).

In addition to the important role of families, schools can also foster beliefs and behaviors deemed to be desirable by a society. For example, 90,000 14-year-olds in 28 countries were assessed on surveys of their attitudes toward government, knowledge of civic content, concepts of citizenship, and political actions (Torney-Purta, 2002). Adolescents' civic engagement was higher in countries with schools that teach civic content, have open discussions of political issues, and foster participation in the school culture. Sweden, a country that has long emphasized children's rights and equality with adults, is an example of how this can work in practice. The curriculum in Swedish schools explicitly covers children's rights and tenets of major rights legislation and conventions, such as the United Nations Convention on the Rights of the Child (Harcourt & Hägglund, 2013). Democracy in Swedish schools is promoted through collaboration, discussion, and meetings (Zackari & Modigh, 2000). The messages conveyed to students in school teach them values in particular cultural contexts.

In many cultures, religion and spirituality are also important influences promoting morality and prosocial behavior (Saroglou, 2013). Religion can give children and adolescents more social capital, including social relationships with caring adults, which in turn promotes positive youth development (Ebstyne King & Furrow, 2004). In addition, most religions explicitly advocate prosocial behavior, such as helping people who need food, shelter, or clothing, and many provide concrete opportunities for doing so. For example, giving is one of the five pillars of Islam, charity is a central teaching in Christianity, and *tzedakah* (literally, justice) prioritizes helping the poor in Judaism. In a study of nine countries that varied in predominant religious affiliations, including Buddhist, Catholic, Muslim, and Protestant, parents' religiousness predicted subsequently higher parental efficacy and better school performance and social competence of their children (Bornstein, Putnick, Lansford, et al., 2017). Religious institutions can promote the development of morality and engagement in prosocial behaviors, and spirituality can be one facet of positive youth development.

Research has focused on what children and adolescents need to be able to thrive in different cultural contexts. For example, adolescents in the United States were more likely to thrive if they had relationships and resources that could nurture their "sparks" (deep passions or interests), and if they were empowered to make civic contributions (Scales et al., 2011). The Developmental Assets Profile measures both external (supports, relationships, and opportunities that families and communities afford) and internal (skills and characteristics that young people bring to their own development) assets to predict positive youth adjustment (Scales et al., 2017). Data using the Developmental Assets Profile have been collected in more than 30 countries and show that the more external and internal developmental assets young people have, the more positive their development is over time.

Furthermore, in emergency situations, such as humanitarian crises and natural disasters, children and adolescents fare better when they have developmental assets that can serve as buffers. The following 13 developmental assets are particularly important in emergency settings (Scales et al., 2015):

1. I feel good about my future (positive identity).

2. I think it is important to help other people (positive values).

3. I feel safe and secure where I currently live (empowerment).

4. I resolve conflicts without anyone getting hurt (social competencies).

5. I am actively engaged in learning new things (commitment to learning).

6. I am involved in a religious group or activity (constructive use of time).

7. I participate in music, dance, art, sports, or other play (constructive use of time).

8. I am involved in meaningful tasks (empowerment).

9. I am eager to do well in school (commitment to learning).

10. I have friends who set good examples for me (boundaries and expectations).

11. I have adults who are good role models for me (boundaries and expectations).

12. I have support from teachers and adults, other than my parents (support).

13. I have a family that gives me love and support (support).

For 10- to 18-year-old Syrian refugees in Iraq, Jordan, and Lebanon and youth in areas of the Philippines that had been destroyed by Typhoon Haiyan in 2013, responses to these questions were a good indication of how young people were faring in humanitarian crises (Scales et al., 2015).

CONCLUSION

Across cultural groups, prosocial behavior, morality, and positive youth development are desired elements of child development. Prosocial behavior, such as sharing, is demonstrated from an early age in all cultural groups, but as children develop, their prosocial behavior takes on culture-specific features, such as sharing resources in proportion to merit or dividing resources evenly. Likewise, most cultural groups socialize children with moral codes that involve not hurting other people, and morality progresses through similar stages of development in many cultural groups. Domain theories of morality differentiate reasoning about moral issues versus issues that are social conventions or personal preferences; moral reasoning is more similar cross-culturally than is reasoning about social conventions or personal preferences. Positive youth development is often characterized by competence, confidence, connection, character, and caring/compassion across cultures, but the specific features of each characteristic may differ. Prosocial behavior, morality, and positive youth development are affected by children's experiences in families, schools, religion, and other community contexts.

For additional resources, see the Appendix.

DISCUSSION QUESTIONS

1. Which aspects of prosocial behavior, morality, and positive youth development are consistent across cultures? Which aspects differ?

2. How are predictors of prosocial behavior, morality, and positive youth development shaped by the cultural contexts in which children develop?

3. How do researchers know that infants and young children already have conceptions of prosocial behavior and fairness that are aligned with norms in their cultural group?

4. Why might behaviors in the moral domain show more cross-cultural similarities than behaviors in the social-conventional or personal domains?

5. What can parents, teachers, and other adults do to promote the development of children and adolescents' prosocial behavior? How are adults guided in their efforts to promote children and adolescents' prosocial behavior by the cultural context in which they live?

15

Culture and the Transition to Adulthood

This Hindu couple on their wedding day is marking a major milestone in the transition to adulthood.

What milestones must you reach before you become an adult? Being financially independent from your parents? Finishing your education? Getting a job? Marrying? Respond to the questions in Table 15.1, which were generated from theoretical and empirical work in sociology, psychology, and anthropology, to indicate whether you think the item must be achieved before a person can be considered an adult, and whether you believe you have reached each of the milestones (Arnett, 1998).

The answers to these questions have changed historically and vary in different cultural contexts. Adolescence is often defined as beginning in biology and

https://doi.org/10.1037/0000228-015
Child and Adolescent Development in Cultural Context, by J. E. Lansford, D. C. French, and M. Gauvain

TABLE 15.1. Becoming an Adult

Milestone	Is this a milestone that defines adulthood?		Do you believe you have achieved this milestone?	
1. Accept responsibility for the consequences of your actions	Yes	No	Yes	No
2. Decide on personal beliefs and values independently of parents or other influences	Yes	No	Yes	No
3. Financially independent from parents	Yes	No	Yes	No
4. Capable of running a household	Yes	No	Yes	No
5. Establish a relationship with parents as an equal adult	Yes	No	Yes	No
6. No longer living in parents' household	Yes	No	Yes	No
7. Capable of keeping family physically safe	Yes	No	Yes	No
8. Learn to always have good control of your emotions	Yes	No	Yes	No
9. Capable of supporting a family financially	Yes	No	Yes	No
10. Capable of caring for children	Yes	No	Yes	No
11. Reached age 18	Yes	No	Yes	No
12. Drive an automobile safely and close to the speed limit	Yes	No	Yes	No
13. Avoid becoming drunk	Yes	No	Yes	No
14. Capable of fathering/bearing children	Yes	No	Yes	No
15. Have no more than one sexual partner	Yes	No	Yes	No
16. Obtained driver's license	Yes	No	Yes	No
17. Settle into a long-term career	Yes	No	Yes	No
18. Not deeply tied to parents emotionally	Yes	No	Yes	No
19. Avoid using profanity/vulgar language	Yes	No	Yes	No
20. Married	Yes	No	Yes	No
21. Employed full time	Yes	No	Yes	No
22. Purchased a home	Yes	No	Yes	No
23. Committed to a long-term love relationship	Yes	No	Yes	No
24. Have at least one child	Yes	No	Yes	No
25. Grow to full height	Yes	No	Yes	No
26. Finished with education	Yes	No	Yes	No
27. Have had sexual intercourse	Yes	No	Yes	No

ending in culture. That is, the beginning of adolescence is generally marked by the onset of puberty, but the ending of adolescence and beginning of adulthood can be harder to define because cultures differ regarding the ages at and circumstances in which young people take on adult roles and responsibilities. In this chapter we define adulthood from the perspectives of international laws, historical and traditional milestones, and self-perceptions. We then consider mismatches between adult roles and adult status, particularly in terms of child marriage, child labor, child soldiers, and teen parenthood. We next describe the "Big 5" roles of early adulthood: education, work, residential independence, marriage or cohabitation, and parenthood. We conclude by focusing on well-being during the transition to adulthood.

DEFINING ADULTHOOD

International law sets the age of 18 as the line differentiating childhood and adulthood. The United Nations Convention on the Rights of the Child, ratified by all countries except the United States, defines a *child* as anyone under the age of 18, and advances the rights of children to protection from abuse and exploitation and to contribute to decisions affecting their lives. A number of other laws and policies, both internationally and in specific countries, recognize age 18 as the legal onset of adulthood, but some countries set other ages as the legal definition of adult status. For example, in Tehran, according to sharia law, Islamic law derived from the Quran, sayings of the Prophet Muhammad, and rulings of Islamic scholars, a girl under the age 18 can be tried as a legal adult (with potential penalties of stoning for behaviors such as using intoxicants) and can enter into marriage with her father's consent at the age of 8 years 9 months (9 lunar years), and a boy can be tried as a legal adult at the age of 14 years 7 months (Mendoza-Denton & Boum, 2015). Despite variation in legal definitions of adulthood, rarely do individuals consider themselves to be fully an adult just because they have turned 18, or another age at which one is determined to be a legal adult in their jurisdiction. Instead, the transition to adulthood is generally a more gradual process characterized by a number of milestones rather than a single defining moment.

Historically, and even today in many traditional societies, marriage has been considered the major milestone that defines the beginning of adulthood (Tillman et al., 2019). In Erikson's (1963) classic theory of developmental stages, achieving intimacy in a romantic relationship is the chief developmental task for individuals ages 18 to 35, with failure to achieve intimacy resulting in isolation. In an anthropological analysis of 186 traditional, preindustrial cultures, most women married between the ages of 16 and 18, and most men married between the ages of 18 and 20 (Schlegel & Barry, 1991). In these cultures, decisions about marriage were generally made by the family according to financial interests and cultural expectations, rather than by the couple. Young people in these cultures are socialized to believe that the group, rather than individuals, will be responsible for many decisions.

Even when marriage is the milestone defining the beginning of adulthood, most societies have expectations about other psychological, behavioral, or social characteristics that individuals must possess before they are deemed ready for marriage. For example, traditionally, in many cultures, men were expected to be able to achieve the "three Ps" before they could marry (Gilmore, 1990). That is, they had to be able to provide, protect, and procreate. This means that they needed to develop skills in hunting, fishing, farming, or other tasks that would enable them to provide financially for a wife and children; skills in warfare or defense to be able to physically protect a family; and physical ability to father children.

Women were traditionally expected to achieve a complementary set of skills enabling them to care for children and run a household (Schlegel & Barry, 1991). Researchers have hypothesized that young people in traditional cultures might feel like adults at a younger age than do young people in industrialized cultures because they have had work and family responsibilities from an early age (B. B. Whiting & Edwards, 1988). Taking on these responsibilities and learning specific skills that enable the transition to adulthood also require the development of particular character traits, such as consideration for others (Sharon, 2016). For example, being diligent and reliable is necessary for both men and women to be able to provide and care for their children.

Similar findings regarding the importance of both role transitions and the development of character traits were generated in ethnographic research with Inuit teenagers from the Canadian Arctic (Condon, 1987). Teenagers said that adulthood was defined by living in a separate household (from their parents) with a potential spouse (regardless of whether a legal marriage occurred), parenthood, employment, and age. Character traits, particularly self-restraint, reliability, and seriousness of purpose, were also considered defining features of adulthood, resulting in a change in behavior that involved spending more time at home with a partner and less time running around with peers and playing team sports.

In a rural, traditional Moroccan culture, the transition to adulthood was defined by marriage, according to adults (Davis & Davis, 1989). However, most 9- to 20-year-olds reported physical development and chronological age or behavioral, moral, or mental changes as the indicators that defined them as being "grown up." Even adults often referred to the development of character traits as being important in defining adulthood, particularly the quality of *aql*, an Arabic word that means being able to make rational, informed decisions and to control impulses and passions. Adolescents were regarded as lacking aql, whereas adults possessed it. Females generally developed aql at an earlier age than males.

Likewise, ethnographic research in the Marquesas Islands of Polynesia suggests that character traits are also important to defining adulthood (Kirkpatrick, 1987). In this culture, girls and boys are believed to be capable of adult work by the age of 14, and they often work with adults at this age. However, these young people are described as *taure'are'a*—unreliable, lazy, and lacking impulse control—considered by the people of the Marquesas Islands to be characteristics of adolescents rather than adults. Young people are considered to be adults when they have become reliable, hard working, and able to control their impulses, outgrowing taure'are'a.

In most industrialized societies today, marriage is no longer one of the milestones individuals use to define adulthood. For example, in Argentina, 43% of married couples ages 18 to 27 did not feel they had reached full adulthood (Facio et al., 2007). Instead, in a wide range of cultures, three of the top defining features of adulthood are (a) accepting responsibility for the consequences of one's actions, (b) deciding on personal beliefs and values independently of parents or other influences, and (c) being financially independent from parents (Arnett & Schwab, 2012). American males and females responded similarly when rating milestones for the transition to adulthood for both men and women (Arnett, 1998). For example, 50% of men and 42% of women considered the ability to provide financially for a family to be an important milestone, and both men and women equally perceived being able to care for children as an important milestone. Accepting responsibility for the consequences of one's actions and being financially independent from parents were also among the top three endorsed milestones in China, along with learning to always have good control of one's emotions (L. J. Nelson et al., 2004). Notably, these markers of adult status reflect internal milestones rather than role transitions related to education, career, marriage, or parenthood, which rank low as markers of adult status in the United States, China, and many other industrialized countries.

Cultural similarities may be undergirded by either similarities or differences in motivation. For example, the milestones may reflect a motivation to become independent and self-sufficient, or they may reflect a motivation to be in control of oneself so as not to be a burden on others or disrupt the social order. Some evidence indicates that different motivations may underlie the milestones in the United States and China. For example, in addition to the three similar milestones, 93% of college students in China said that becoming less self-oriented and developing greater concern for others was important to becoming an adult, compared with only 73% of European American students (L. J. Nelson et al., 2004). This pattern suggests that motivation to place family and community needs above one's own goals and needs is more salient in China than in the United States.

There are also a number of differences between countries in which milestones are considered important in defining adulthood. For example, in a sample from Beijing, China, 89% of college students deemed being able to support their parents financially as a defining milestone of adulthood (L. J. Nelson et al., 2004), compared with only 16% of students in the United States (Arnett, 2003). These differences can be understood in the context of Confucian doctrine, which stresses the importance of filial piety and placing the needs of the family above one's own. The majority of young people in China expect to take care of their parents in the future and know that their own or their spouse's parents will ultimately live with them, expectations that are codified in Chinese law stipulating that one role of the family is to take care of aging parents when they are no longer able to earn a living on their own (L. J. Nelson et al., 2004).

Romanian college students are more likely than college students in other cultural groups to rank norm-following behaviors, including using contraception and avoiding being drunk, as important criteria for adulthood, perhaps because in their society the consequences of not adhering to these norms are salient (L. J. Nelson, 2009). In particular, during the former president Nicolae Ceauşescu's time in power, birth control was illegal. Families did not have the resources to care for all of the children who were born, leading to the proliferation of orphanages in which children lacked stimulation and adult interaction to such a degree that they often developed long-term psychological, social, and cognitive problems (Humphreys et al., 2015). The deplorable conditions of the orphanages came to international attention, international adoptions ensued, and the crisis has had political implications even since Ceauşescu's death in 1989 by execution. Thus, because of the visible and dire social consequences of not using birth control, when considering criteria that are important for adulthood, using contraception when not trying to conceive a child is especially salient for Romanians.

Some cultural groups also have important rites of passage that serve as milestones defining adulthood. For example, 2 to 3 years of military service is mandatory for males and females in Israel, serving as an important milestone defining adulthood (Scharf & Mayseless, 2010). High school students often plan and prepare for military service to such an extent that they give less consideration to their goals following military service. In this way, the rigid requirements of military service can constrict the freedom to explore alternate identities related to education and work early in adulthood (Scharf & Mayseless, 2010). During the transition to adulthood, Israeli individuals regard following social norms and rules, such as safe driving and responsible drinking, and social roles of employment and marriage as important, perhaps because of the communal structure of Israeli society (Mayseless & Scharf, 2003).

In the Church of Jesus Christ of Latter-day Saints (LDS, Mormon) religious community, missionary work may be a defining milestone. Males between the ages of 18 and 27 are expected to do 2 years of missionary work, and females are encouraged to do 18 months of missionary work (Barry & Nelson, 2005). This missionary work, during which visits home to family are not permitted, along with other religious rites of passage, structures the transition to adulthood for LDS youth, and they report feeling more certain of their beliefs and that they have taken on adult roles at younger ages than non-LDS young people (Barry & Nelson, 2005).

As a result of cultural variations in milestones deemed to be important for reaching adulthood, rites of passage, and other factors, cultures may differ widely regarding whether individuals of a given age are considered to be adults. For example, 59% of 18- to 25-year-old Chinese college students believed they had reached adulthood compared with only 24% to 36% of 18- to 25-year-old

RESEARCH HIGHLIGHT 15.1

The Transition to Adulthood for Individuals With Disabilities
The transition to adulthood poses developmental challenges even when young people are well supported and progressing through life in ways expected by their culture.
Challenges can be exacerbated in circumstances in which young people have disabilities that make it more difficult for them to attain the social roles and psychological
and behavioral characteristics that often mark the transition to adulthood. Qualitative
case studies of young adults with intellectual disabilities in Spain highlighted three
main areas of concern for the young adults and their families (Pallisera et al., 2016).
First, the young adults had difficulties completing secondary education and continuing with higher education. Second, participants expressed concerns about the young
adults' ability to be integrated into the labor market and to live independently. Third,
young adults and their families had concerns about the lack of support services
needed to provide training opportunities and help plan for the future. UNICEF (2013c)
has published guidelines for engaging young people with disabilities in decisions
affecting their lives.

American students (Arnett, 2003; L. J. Nelson et al., 2004). Achieving psychosocial maturity depends on both autonomy, such as being able to control one's
behavior, and social responsibility, such as contributing to the well-being of the
social group (Benson et al., 2012). When individuals take on adult roles without psychosocial maturity, this creates a mismatch that is often harmful to individuals and possibly to entire societies. Research Highlight 15.1 describes
research on challenges faced by individuals with disabilities during the transition to adulthood.

MISMATCHES BETWEEN ADULT ROLES AND ADULT STATUS

Sometimes individuals take on adult roles before they have adult status or have
developed the character traits deemed important for adulthood, which can lead
to poorer developmental outcomes and a range of conflicts with others. In
some cases, the social group or society imposes these adult roles on young
people. Child marriage, child labor, child soldiers, and teen pregnancy involve
such mismatches, as do mismatches between expectations of young people and
others in their social circles. Let's take a closer look at each.

Child Marriage

A poignant example of a mismatch between an adult role and character traits
important for adulthood is in the case of child marriage. Worldwide, 20% of
girls are married before the age of 18, but the prevalence rates vary widely by
geographic region. As many as 76% of girls in Niger marry before the age of 18,
and over 50% of girls marry before the age of 18 in eight other countries around
the world (Girls Not Brides, 2019). Although marriage has historically been and
in many cultural groups is still considered a milestone for attaining adulthood,

in the case of child marriage, girls are generally married for financial reasons to benefit their families, rather than by personal choice. These young brides generally have not attained other milestones of adulthood that would psychologically prepare them to marry. For example, child brides generally have low educational attainment and poor work prospects, leaving them financially dependent on their husbands. Child brides are at higher risk of physical and sexual abuse, and are more likely to have complications and die during childbirth because their bodies are often not physically ready to bear children. The international community has rallied around the importance of ending child marriage. Yet even when countries outlaw child marriage, local norms and customs as well as dire economic circumstances in a girl's family, still lead to child marriages outside of the law or in exceptions to the law. For example, 93 countries allow girls under the age 18 to marry with their parents' consent. Other than cases of child marriage, girls generally are allowed to marry 1 to 3 years earlier than boys (Girls Not Brides, 2019).

Child Labor

The International Labor Organization, UNICEF, and the World Bank define child labor as employment below the minimum age of 15; work likely to harm children's health, safety, or morals; illicit activity; and hazardous unpaid household work, including chores performed for long hours, in dangerous locations or unhealthy environments, and using unsafe equipment or heavy loads (UNICEF, 2019). An estimated 168 million children worldwide are possibly engaged in child labor. Children are vulnerable not only to direct threats from this kind of labor, such as threats to their physical safety in mines or threats of sexual exploitation when working as domestic servants, but also indirect threats, primarily because child labor often curtails children's education and leaves them unable to escape a life of poverty.

Child Soldiers

Although international law stipulates that 18 should be the minimum age for military service, children have been recruited or kidnapped into armed conflict in a number of countries, including 18 countries since 2016 (Child Soldiers International, 2019). The militaries of 46 countries do not hold to the strict standard of 18 as the minimum recruitment age. Even adult soldiers are at risk for post-traumatic stress disorder following armed conflict, but both short- and long-term outcomes are even worse for children who participate in armed conflict. For example, in Sierra Leone, individuals who were age 28 on average, reported on their current adjustment as well as experiences when they were child soldiers between the ages of 10 and 17 (T. S. Betancourt et al., 2020). Former child soldiers experienced trauma not just related to killing and injuring others but also from being the victims of life-threatening violence; in addition, 45% of females and 5% of males had been raped. Even 15 years after their reintegration into society, 47% of former child soldiers experienced clinical levels of anxiety/depression, and 28% experienced clinical levels of posttraumatic stress disorder.

Teen Pregnancy

Teen pregnancy is common even in some countries in which child marriage is not. In qualitative interviews asking what experiences most made them feel like an adult, both males and females often spontaneously mentioned the birth of a child (Arnett, 1998). However, taking on the adult role of parenting as a teenager poses developmental risks for the teen as well as for the offspring. In particular, teen parents, especially teen mothers, are at high risk of dropping out of school, and with little education are likely to struggle to support themselves and their child financially. Teen parents also engage in harsher parenting than older parents and are less likely to provide cognitively stimulating environments for their children. Offspring of teen parents, in turn, generally perform more poorly in school and have more behavior problems than offspring of older parents. In this way, taking on an adult role without having achieved many of the other markers of adulthood makes teen parenthood developmentally premature and a risk to both the teen and the child.

Mismatched Expectations

Other mismatches do not necessarily involve major life events but can involve differences in expectations between young people and others in their social circles. Some of these mismatches become particularly salient during late adolescence or early adulthood when children are still living with their parents. Parents may have certain expectations for their (young adult) child who is still living at home, and the young adult child may have different expectations. For example, the young adult child may want to have control over his or her own decisions, whereas the parent may want to retain some control. Cultural groups differ regarding how legitimate parental authority is perceived to be at different ages, and in the extent to which adolescents and young adults believe they must obey their parents in cases of disagreement (Darling et al., 2005). Conflict may occur when young people have different expectations about their roles and adult status than others do.

BIG 5 ROLES OF ADULTHOOD

Life-span psychologists and sociologists have described the "Big 5" roles in adulthood, which include education, work, residential independence, marriage or cohabitation, and parenthood (Settersten & Ray, 2010). These roles have changed historically over time and differ across cultural groups. In particular, compared with previous generations, individuals today, on average, are older at the time they finish their education, attain residential independence, marry, and become parents. In addition, the sequence of these social roles is more variable than in the past. For example, marriage formerly preceded parenthood, and still does in many cultural groups, but in other cultural groups many individuals who are not married become parents. Each of these major roles will be considered in turn.

Education

Countries vary widely with respect to the percentage of students in secondary school and who go on to tertiary education, including colleges, universities, and technical training programs. For example, 9% of students in sub-Saharan Africa enroll in tertiary education, compared with 69% of students in Europe and central Asia (World Bank, 2019a). Tertiary education is important for both individuals and entire societies. The transition to adulthood takes a different shape for individuals who continue their education than for those who are no longer in formal education, with differences directly related to education extending far into adulthood. For example, in Latin America and the Caribbean, an individual with a tertiary degree can expect to earn twice as much as someone with a high school diploma (World Bank, 2018a). Countries benefit from additional tax revenues from citizens who are more educated and also incur fewer costs related to health care and criminal justice, as more educated individuals generally have healthier lifestyles and engage in less crime.

Financing higher education and how admittance to higher education is handled vary across countries. One of the major determinants of students being able to continue into tertiary school is cost and whether individuals and their families are responsible for paying the tuition or whether it is paid for by the state. Clearly, lack of finances can be a major barrier to higher education. Another barrier is acceptance into higher education institutions. For example, toward the end of secondary school in China (around age 17 or 18), students take a high-stakes exam that determines not only which university they can attend but also their major (L. J. Nelson et al., 2004). Because of this exam system, it is very difficult for a Chinese student to change majors or transfer to a different university, making the college years less about exploring career interests and options and more about taking the prerequisite steps to achieve a particular career (L. J. Nelson et al., 2004). In contrast, 33% of American students change majors during the course of their college years, and 10% change majors more than once (U.S. Department of Education, 2017). Thirty-seven percent of American students transfer to a different university (Shapiro et al., 2015), making the education experience of American college students less linear than that of Chinese college students.

Work

Work constitutes a major role in adulthood that can take many forms. In traditional societies, men and women take on different work roles, with men more often working for pay outside the home and women working in the home to take care of children and run the household. In hunter–gatherer societies, men generally hunt and women generally gather. In industrialized societies, jobs are less strictly stratified by gender, but countries typically enact policies, such as paid paternity and maternity leave, to enable gender equality in the workplace and at home (Bartel et al., 2018). During childhood and adolescence, young people in many cultures engage in labor in various forms, including farm work in agrarian societies, and part-time jobs while attending school in urban societies (Putnick & Bornstein, 2016). Even after entering full-time employment, changing jobs is common during the transition to adulthood in many countries (e.g., Fuller, 2008).

Mendoza-Denton and Boum (2015) have used the terms "delaying," "hopscotching," and "opting out" to characterize the ways that individuals alter their progression and sequencing of milestones in the transition to adulthood. Delaying involves putting off a role either voluntarily or involuntarily. For example, during college, students generally delay work voluntarily because they are finishing education that will enable them to eventually enter a chosen career. Work can also be delayed involuntarily, though, when unemployment rates are high and young people have a hard time finding work. Work or lack of it can also lead to delays in other roles. For example, many low-income young adults delay marriage until they have found stable work or achieved other financial goals, an effect that applies to marriage but not cohabitation (Gibson-Davis et al., 2018).

Hopscotching involves moving in and out of roles without following a traditional linear sequence (Mendoza-Denton & Boum, 2015). In the case of work, hopscotching may involve alternating between education and work, as when financial constraints make it impossible to continue school without breaks to earn money to support continued education. Hopscotching may also involve leaving a job to take a new job or to take a break to care for children and then reentering the workforce.

Opting out involves a more politicized choice that young people make to avoid the status quo if it limits their political, economic, and social freedom and participation (Mendoza-Denton & Boum, 2015). Young adults have led several social movements protesting political and economic conditions that limit their employment opportunities, among other factors. For example, the revolts that were part of the Arab Spring in several nations from 2010 to 2012 arose largely because of frustrations with governments that did not meet the needs of unemployed and educated young adults. The Occupy Wall Street movement during that same period in the United States focused on economic inequality, a pressing concern for young people (Dube & Kaplan, 2012). When young people opt out, they are civically engaged in an attempt to improve their future work (and other) prospects.

Residential Independence

The age at which young people begin living in a separate residence from their parents varies widely across cultures, even between Western, industrialized countries. For example, in Italy, most people live with their parents until after the age of 30, whereas in Sweden, most people move out of their parents' home before the age of 20 (Eurostat, 2015). Economic factors, such as the availability of jobs, and demographic trends, such as the increase in the average age at first marriage, have implications for residential independence. Cultural factors, such as whether it is acceptable for young people, especially females, to live alone before marriage, also affect residential independence.

Even when young people no longer live with their parents, most remain in close contact. For example, in the United States, half of 26- to 29-year-olds have daily contact with their parents (Arnett & Schwab, 2012). Sixty-six percent of American parents report that the amount of contact they have with their young adult children is generally "about right," but 24% would like to have more contact, and 10% would like to have less contact. Eighty percent of American parents report that their 18- to 29-year-old children rely on them at least occasionally for emotional support, and 44% report that they provide either frequent financial support or regular support for living expenses. Even at ages 26 to 29, 56% of Americans still receive at least occasional financial support from their parents. Compared with during the midteenage years, 66% of American parents and 75% of 18- to 29-year-olds believe that their current relationship is better. Some of the key improvements include having more adult conversations, enjoying time together more, and having fewer conflicts.

In the United States, 40% to 47% of African American, European American, and Latin young adults live with their parents, but 49% of Latino parents, 34% of African American parents, and 21% of European American parents agree that in their culture it is common for grown children to remain at home (Arnett & Schwab, 2012). Continued interdependence of parents and young adult children has been described as being more common in parts of Africa (Abebe, 2019), India (Jackson et al., 2016), and the Philippines (Alampay, 2014) than in the United States, Canada, and Western Europe. Likewise, perceptions of closeness between parents and their young adult children are shaped by broader cultural contexts (Alavi et al., 2020). Feelings of closeness to family members can affect other adult roles and milestones. For example, almost half of 18- to 21-year-old Argentinian young adults reported believing that family responsibilities should be more important than future career plans, and more than half reported believing that they should try to live near their parents in the future despite opportunities in other areas of the country (Facio et al., 2007).

Descriptions of residential independence generally focus on moving out of one's parents' home, but such a move affects not only relationships between parents and young adult children but also relationships between siblings and other family members. Sibling relationships during the transition to adulthood vary widely depending on how close or conflicted the sibling relationship was during childhood and adolescence, how often the siblings see one another after they no longer live together, and other demographic and interpersonal factors (Conger & Little, 2010). In some cultural groups, rituals established between siblings during childhood continue into adulthood. For example, in a Muslim community in Sri Lanka, as adults, brothers are expected to provide gifts and services to their sisters, and sisters often cook for and nurture their brothers (de Munck, 1993). Sibling relationships are generally the only relationships that individuals maintain from infancy through late adulthood, contributing to their importance even during the transition to adulthood.

Marriage and Cohabitation

Romantic relationships during the transition to adulthood often last longer than such relationships earlier in adolescence. They are also increasingly likely to include cohabitation or marriage. The path to marriage varies widely across countries in terms of average age at the time of marriage; appropriate marriage partners; how romantic relationships develop: and whether other forms of intimate partnerships, such as cohabitation without marriage, are acceptable. As described previously, child marriage continues to be common in many parts of the world, and such marriages are generally arranged between families for economic purposes rather than between two individuals who have fallen in love. Even into adulthood, marriages in many countries continue to be arranged by parents or other family members.

Regardless of whether adult marriages are arranged by family members, most adults end up marrying individuals who resemble themselves with respect to sociodemographic and cultural factors (Coontz, 2006). For example, husbands and wives tend to have similar levels of education; economic and religious backgrounds; and be from the same ethnic group, even in ethnically diverse countries such as the United States (e.g., Qian et al., 2018). Thus, even when family members do not arrange marriages, individuals tend to select mates who are similar to those their families may have selected for them, in part because social circles tend to be populated by individuals who are similar to each other.

Cultural groups may differ regarding marriage and cohabitation during the transition to adulthood in part because of differences in national laws. For example, in the Gulf countries (Bahrain, Kuwait, Oman, Qatar, Saudi Arabia, and the United Arab Emirates), it is illegal for a couple to live together unless they are married. Penalties for pregnancy outside of marriage are severe, including lashings, imprisonment, and deportation (Santos, 2017). In China, marriage regulations include a law enacted by the Chinese Department of Education prohibiting college entrance for anyone who is married and possibly dismissing students (at the discretion of individual colleges) who marry before finishing their degree (L. J. Nelson et al., 2004). Thus, although universities are where people in many cultures develop intimate relationships, laws discourage such relationships by penalizing them in other cultures. Seventeen percent of Chinese college students report that they are uncertain about whether they want to marry, and 28% report being uncertain about whether they want to have children (L. J. Nelson et al., 2004). In contrast, marriage is endorsed in other college settings. At Brigham Young University in the United States where nearly all of the students are LDS members, 60% of males and 45% of females are married by the time they graduate (Barry & Nelson, 2005). Average ages of marriage for LDS men and women are 23 and 21, respectively, considerably lower than the average for the United States population as a whole (Barry & Nelson, 2005).

Although historically, marriage was the major milestone in the transition to adulthood, and continues to be a major milestone in many cultural groups today, cohabitation without marriage has also become common. For example, in the United States, 9% of 18- to 24-year-olds are cohabiting, and 7% are married; 14% of 25- to 35-year-olds are cohabiting, and 41% are married (Stepler, 2017). In France and Norway, more than 90% of individuals ages 15 to 24 who are partnered are cohabiting rather than married, as are approximately 40% of individuals ages 25 to 44 (Sánchez Gassen & Perelli-Harris, 2015). Cultural groups differ regarding whether cohabitation is viewed primarily as a precursor to marriage or as an alternative to marriage (Dronkers, 2016).

To date, 30 countries have legalized same-sex marriage, beginning with the Netherlands in 2000 (Pew Research Center, 2019), marking an important shift in a milestone characterizing the transition to adulthood for gay men and lesbian women. Support from both family members and at the societal level is important for the well-being of sexual minority adolescents and young adults (Needham & Austin, 2010). Qualitative interviews with lesbian, gay, bisexual, transgender, and queer (LGBTQ) young adults identified four themes deemed important in relation to their transition to adulthood (Wagaman et al., 2016). These included (a) community-supported independence, (b) close relationships with family and friends, (c) personal preservation and self-fulfillment, and (d) strength to engage with heteronormative and cisnormative contexts. LGBTQ adolescents and young adults continue to face discrimination in many cultural contexts. Homosexual activity is illegal in 72 countries and carries penalties as severe as life imprisonment or execution in some countries (76 Crimes, 2019). The transition to adulthood for LGBTQ youth clearly varies widely depending on national laws. There are better mental health and social outcomes for LGBTQ individuals in countries that provide protection and support rather than persecution, which led the United Nations Human Rights Council to pass a resolution promoting the rights of LGBTQ individuals globally (United Nations, 2014).

Parenthood

In many countries, the average age at which individuals first become parents has increased over time. For example, the average age of women when they first give birth is 30 in the Organization for Economic Cooperation and Development (OECD) middle- and high-income countries, an increase of 2 to 5 years, on average, since 1970 (OECD, 2018a). Even in low-income countries, on average, women are well into their 20s at the time of first becoming a parent. Males, on average, are older than females at the time of first becoming a parent.

Many men and women also choose to remain childless. For example, in high-income countries, about 10% of women in their late-40s do not have children, and in some countries (e.g., Italy and Switzerland), as many as 25% of women in their late-40s do not have children (Chamie & Mirkin, 2012). Conversely, in countries such as India, Indonesia, Pakistan, South Africa, and Turkey, fewer than 5% of women in their late-40s are childless (Chamie & Mirkin, 2012). In many countries, becoming a parent is increasingly disentangled from the transition to adulthood as individuals wait until later to have children or decide not to have children at all.

Parenthood is related to other major roles during the transition to adulthood. For example, more educated men and women often delay parenthood as they complete their education, launch their careers, or both (Neels et al., 2017). Historically, and in many present cultures, parenthood follows marriage. In fact, one of the main functions of marriage was to create a family unit for the purposes of procreation (Carlson, 2007). In many cultural groups today, parenthood and marriage are uncoupled so that individuals become parents without being married, and married couples choose not to have children. Decisions about becoming a parent depend not only on personal choice but also on the availability of reliable birth control, national policies regarding abortion, and societal norms and values.

In cases of infertility, individuals are not childless by choice. Infertility is defined as not being able to conceive a child after 12 months of unprotected, regular sexual intercourse. One consequence of the increased average age at the time of first trying to conceive has been an increase in the infertility rate, as infertility increases with age for both women and men. For example, about one third of couples in which the woman is over age 35 have fertility problems, and infertility for men increases after about age 40 (Centers for Disease Control and Prevention, 2019b). In some cultural contexts, women are not considered to have reached full adulthood until becoming a mother, partly because few other adult roles are available to them if their education and employment are restricted (Batool & de Visser, 2016). In Pakistan and many other countries, infertility is generally deemed to be a woman's problem (even if the infertility stems from the man), women are taunted and shamed for not having children, and men may be encouraged to divorce their wife and remarry to be able to continue the family line (Mumtaz et al., 2013). In this context, becoming a mother is the only way for a woman to secure her marriage and status in adult society.

The importance of particular social roles depends on a variety of events and values at a societal level. For example, political and economic instability in Argentina have created a context in which individuals may be more likely to prioritize family goals, which are regarded as more attainable and stable, than goals related to education or work, which are regarded as less predictable in the uncertain political and economic climate (Facio et al., 2007). Socioeconomic status is one of the main factors affecting the opportunities available for many social roles during the transition to adulthood. Research Highlight 15.2 illustrates

RESEARCH HIGHLIGHT 15.2

Young Lives Study

Consider the following two examples from Young Lives, a longitudinal study that has followed 12,000 children through adolescence and into early adulthood in Ethiopia, India, Peru, and Vietnam (Rojas et al., 2016). The study includes both quantitative questionnaires and qualitative interviews conducted at ages 12 through 19. These scenarios illustrate the intersection of different roles and how they shape the transition to adulthood in Peru.

Diana is a 19-year-old girl from a rural area in Peru. She became pregnant at the age of 14 and decided to drop out of school to run away to a city to live with her baby's father, at which point she lost her family's support. She has been working in factories and fields since then and never returned to school. She has separated from her baby's father and feels many responsibilities related to motherhood, taking care of a home, and financially supporting her son.

Carmen is a 19-year-old girl from an urban area in Peru. Her parents both have university degrees and expect Carmen to earn a university degree, too. Carmen's parents pay for her tuition and living expenses so that Carmen does not have to work while at the university. Carmen is now studying law at one university and social work at another. Her parents want her to be able to earn a living at a good job so she does not have to be financially dependent on a future husband.

Both Diana and Carmen are 19 now, adults according to international law. Their transitions to adulthood have followed different paths with respect to education, work, residential independence, intimate partnerships, and parenthood. Differences in Diana's and Carmen's developmental trajectories are, in part, a function of differences in socioeconomic status, support from their parents, and rural versus urban residence. Their lives illustrate ways in which different turning points can help or hinder long-term development and well-being.

findings from the Young Lives study of how a variety of socioeconomic and other factors intersect during the transition to adulthood in ways that are important for long-term well-being.

WELL-BEING DURING THE TRANSITION TO ADULTHOOD

Using nationally representative samples of 18-year-olds from the United States who were followed until age 26, well-being in terms of self-efficacy, self-esteem, and social support was predicted by trajectories of major developmental tasks during this developmental period (Schulenberg et al., 2004). Well-being during the transition to adulthood was particularly related to functioning in the areas of work, romantic relationships, and citizenship. Success in one domain could compensate for not succeeding in other domains (e.g., pursuing higher education compensated for not advancing in a career), but well-being was particularly bolstered by success in different domains, such as in both education and romantic relationships.

According to Arnett's (2000) theory of emerging adulthood, the period of life from age 18 to the mid-to-late 20s is characterized by five features. First, emerging adults feel "in-between" in that they no longer regard themselves as adolescents but also do not yet feel that they have reached full adulthood. Second, emerging adults explore identities in the areas of work, love, and worldviews. Third, emerging adults are self-focused in that they often lack obligations to others. Fourth, emerging adulthood is an age of possibilities in which individuals can direct their lives in a number of different directions. Fifth, emerging adulthood is characterized by instability in education, work, residential status, and social relationships. Each of these features has the potential to influence well-being during the transition to adulthood.

Consider as an example how the feature of instability may be related to well-being. Instability in social roles from ages 18 to 25 can be indicative of exploration of social roles that can be beneficial for long-term well-being, even when the instability involves moving into and out of social roles rather than just from a child-like role (e.g., single) to an adult-like role (e.g., partnered). For example, instability in romantic relationships may make it easier to leave abusive or otherwise problematic relationships to enter healthier relationships or remain single, both of which are related to better well-being than remaining in an unhealthy relationship (A. B. Barr et al., 2013). Likewise, delaying some social roles to focus on others may optimize long-term well-being (Settersten & Ray, 2010). For example, delaying marriage and full-time employment to focus on completing more education might be adaptive in the long run, and delaying residential independence to save money to pay for education may be a wise decision. Thus, thinking about the entire constellation of social roles and developmental tasks in which young people are involved during the transition to adulthood may be the best way to understand current and future well-being.

The feature of emerging adulthood characterized as feeling "in-between" may be especially pronounced in college student samples that have been the focus of many research studies on emerging adulthood (L. J. Nelson, 2009). Because college is a time when students are working to complete their education and prepare for a future career, the feeling of not quite being an adult may be more pronounced than for individuals of the same age who are not attending college and instead have taken on other adult roles, such as work. Nevertheless, even after taking on other adult roles, young people who are not in college often still report feeling as though they have not yet fully reached adulthood.

A longitudinal study that examined how American 20-year-olds were functioning in the domains of friendship, academics, conduct, work, and romance and then reassessed their development at age 30 found that well-being at age 30 was better predicted by roles at age 20 that had been established during adolescence than roles that were newly emerging at age 20 (Roisman et al., 2004). Romantic relationships and work were salient roles at age 20 but had not yet become developmentally entrenched, whereas friendship quality, academic success, and behavioral adjustment had been well established during adolescence, perhaps giving them more predictive power later in adulthood compared with those roles that were being newly established.

In addition to being a time of changing roles, the transition to adulthood often also functions as a time to explore beliefs and values, as more independence from parents provides enough distance to question some of the world-views characterizing a particular upbringing (L. J. Nelson et al., 2004). However, some cultural contexts are more conducive to this kind of exploration than others. For example, when governments ban or persecute certain religious groups and promote others, freedom to explore individual beliefs related to religion is curtailed. In cultural groups where individuals have fewer opportunities to explore different beliefs, educational options, or career paths, there is evidence that the lack of exploration may be more a function of lack of opportunity than lack of desire to explore options (L. J. Nelson et al., 2004).

Socioemotional selectivity theory is a way to understand exploration of options and social relationships within a life-course perspective (Carstensen, 2006). According to the theory, during the transition to adulthood, young adults are motivated to socialize with a wide range of people, partly to advance their educational and work prospects and partly to seek a potential life partner. As individuals progress through adulthood and their social roles become more stable, they typically prune their social networks to maintain relationships with family members and friends with whom they are emotionally close rather than more distant acquaintances. Individuals' prioritization of goals during the transition to adulthood compared with later in adulthood reflects their desire to gather information and expand their horizons when the future is perceived as being long and full of possibilities versus focusing on meaning and emotional satisfaction in close relationships when future time is more limited. Thus, knowledge-oriented goals are more prevalent in early adulthood, whereas emotion-related goals are more prevalent later in adulthood. Empirical support has been found for socioemotional selectivity theory in several cultural groups, in that as individuals move from early to later adulthood, they selectively prioritize a smaller number of emotionally close social relationships, but cultures differ regarding which relationships are deemed as emotionally meaningful (Fung et al., 2008).

CONCLUSION

International law defines adulthood as beginning at the age of 18, but very few 18-year-olds perceive themselves to be full adults. Instead, the transition to adulthood is defined by a variety of internal and external milestones. Historically, marriage was the major marker of adult status in most societies, but today in most cultural groups, adulthood is defined more by internal factors such as accepting responsibility for the consequences of one's actions, deciding on personal beliefs and values independently from parents or other influences, and being financially independent from parents. Motivation for achieving these characteristics may differ across cultures, and certain factors, such as being capable of financially supporting one's parents, are more important in defining adulthood in some cultures than in others. Mismatches between adult roles and adult status, particularly in terms of child marriage, child labor, child soldiers, and teen parenthood, are problematic for long-term development and well-being. The "Big 5" roles of education, work, residential independence, marriage, and parenthood are important during the transition to adulthood and are characterized by many cultural differences in terms of the percent of the population that enters a particular role, the average age of achieving each milestone, and the constraints and opportunities that surround each role. Achievement and relationships in each social role affect individuals' well-being during the transition to adulthood.

For additional resources, see the Appendix.

DISCUSSION QUESTIONS

1. Describe how social roles and psychosocial maturity are both important during the transition to adulthood. How do those social roles and characteristics of psychosocial maturity differ across cultures? In what ways are they the same?

2. How do cultural norms regarding the timing of developmental milestones affect individuals who attain those milestones either before or after others in their cultural group?

3. Discuss the international arguments for eliminating child marriage and child labor in relation to arguments sometimes made by local cultural groups that child marriage and child labor are accepted and financially necessary in their local community.

4. Gender, sexual orientation, religion, and other social identities in addition to ethnicity and country of origin can be important markers of cultural experiences. Describe how the intersection of these identities can shape individuals' transition to adulthood.

5. In what ways has the transition to adulthood changed historically over time in a variety of cultural contexts?

APPENDIX

Resources for Further Research

BRAIN DEVELOPMENT

Blakemore, S. J. (2012, June). *The mysterious workings of the adolescent brain* [Video]. TED Conferences. https://www.ted.com/talks/sarah_jayne_blakemore_the_mysterious_workings_of_the_adolescent_brain

TED Talk on adolescent brain development.

CAREGIVERS

Chai, M. (n.d.). *Goats as nannies? Childhood in the Himalayan desert* [Blog post]. Masala Chai: Musings about our relationships with little people. https://masalachaimusings.com/2020/06/05/goats-as-nannies-childhood-in-the-himalayan-desert/

This blog post describes cultures in which multiple caregivers of young children are the norm.

CHILD LABOR

International Labour Organization. (n.d.). *Child labour*. https://www.ilo.org/global/topics/child-labour/lang--en/index.htm

Information about child labor across the world.

CHILD MARRIAGE

Girls Not Brides. (n.d.). *What is child marriage*. https://www.girlsnotbrides.org/

Information about child marriage.

CHILD SOLDIERS

Ferguson, S. (2020). *UNICEF is working to free child soldiers around the world*. UNICEF USA. https://www.unicefusa.org/stories/unicef-working-free-child-soldiers-around-world/35474

Information about child soldiers.

CHILD WELL-BEING

United Nations. (n.d.). *United Nations Children's Fund*. https://www.un.org/youthenvoy/2013/09/unicef-the-united-nations-childrens-fund/

Reports and data pertaining to education, health, refugees, and other aspects of child development across the world.

United Nations. (n.d.). *Universal Declaration of Human Rights*. https://www.un.org/en/universal-declaration-human-rights/

This document outlines fundamental human rights to be protected in all regions of the world.

COGNITION

Child and Family Blog. (n.d.). https://www.childandfamilyblog.com

Features short articles and photos on a range of topics, including an entire set of articles on cognitive development from ages 4 to 12.

Drew, A. (2019). *Pulling together: Michael Tomasello on how shared intentionality and social coordination set humans apart*. Association for Psychological Science. https://www.psychologicalscience.org/observer/tomasello-keynote

In this presentation Michael Tomasello, a leading scholar of evolution and the development of human cognition, talks about shared understanding and cooperation as distinctive human characteristics that are fostered in every human culture.

CONFLICT

Aureli, F., & de Waal, F. (Eds.). (2000). *Natural conflict resolution*. University of California Press.

Edited volume connecting primate and human conflict.

Marcus, H. R., & Lin, L. R. (1999). Conflictways: Cultural diversity in the meanings and practices of conflict. In D. A. Prentice & D. T. Miller (Eds.), *Cultural divides: Understanding and overcoming group conflict* (pp. 302–333). Russell Sage Foundation.

Discussion of conflict from the perspective of social psychology and independent and interdependent views of self.

CULTURE

American Psychological Association, Division of International Psychology. (n.d.). *Four corners conversations: Perspectives on psychology from around the world* [Webinar]. http://div52.net/4-corners-div7/

> Conversations with psychologists from many backgrounds of study working around the world. Each is interviewed about what psychologists do in their region and how they are trained.

Best Documentary. (December 23, 2018). *Animals like us - Animal culture* [Video]. YouTube. https://www.youtube.com/watch?v=DRktP16kajA

> A film about culture in nonhuman animals.

International Association for Cross-Cultural Psychology. (n.d.). *Online readings in psychology and culture.* https://scholarworks.gvsu.edu/orpc/

> This website is an archive of online readings on psychology and culture. The articles are written in an engaging fashion and cover a broad range of topics.

Roell, C. (2010). Intercultural training with films. *English Teaching Forum* (Number 2). https://americanenglish.state.gov/files/ae/resource_files/48_2-etf-intercultural-training-with-films.pdf

> Techniques to enhance cultural learning with films. List of films that are useful for provoking discussion about selected issues.

TEDx. (August 15, 2016). *Tom Weisner: What is the most important influence on child development?* [Video]. YouTube. https://www.youtube.com/watch?v=gIZ8PkLMMUo

> TEDx talk by UCLA anthropologist Thomas Weisner about the role of culture in development.

DISASTER RELIEF

International Rescue Committee. (n.d). *Who we are.* https://www.rescue.org/who-we-are

> Website of the International Rescue Committee, an organization that helps people whose lives have been disrupted by conflict and disasters.

EDUCATION

DataBank. (n.d.). *Education statistics.* World Bank. https://databank.worldbank.org/databases/education

> World Bank reports and data pertaining to education across the world.

National Academies of Sciences, Engineering, and Medicine. (2017). *Promoting the educational success of children and youth learning English: Promising futures.* The National Academies Press. https://doi.org/10.17226/24677

Book published by the National Academy of Sciences, Engineering and Medicine about promoting educational success among children and youth learning English. A free PDF copy of the book can be downloaded from the website.

Organisation for Economic Co-operation and Development. (n.d.). *Programme for International Student Assessment.* https://www.oecd.org/pisa/

Homepage for the Programme for International Student Assessment (PISA) with links to projects and data reports as well as videos about student learning and general information about the PISA program.

TIMSSVIDEO. (n.d.). *The TIMSS Video Study.* http://www.timssvideo.com

Website with public use videos collected as part of the TIMSS project.

University-Based Child and Family Policy Consortium and the Society for Research in Child Development. (2017). *Excellence for all children: Addressing issues of equity and culture in teaching* [Webinar]. Society for Research in Child Development. https://www.srcd.org/event/excellence-all-children-addressing-issues-equity-and-culture-teaching

This series of presentations focuses on culture and equity in the classroom.

EMOTIONS

Association of Psychological Science. (2015). *Inside the psychologist's studio: Paul Ekman* [Video]. https://www.psychologicalscience.org/video/inside-the-psychologists-studio-paul-ekman.html#.WI925mCV6Uk

Interview with Paul Ekman, who developed research on assessing emotions across cultures.

International Society for the Study of Behavioural Development. (2006, May). Culture and the development of emotions. *International Society for the Study of Behavioural Developemet Newsletter, 1*(Serial No. 49). https://issbd.org/resources/files/newsletter_0606.pdf

International Society for the Study of Behavioural Development special section on culture and the development of emotions. Interesting articles by internationally respected developmental scientists, with commentaries by renowned scholars in this area of research.

Tronick, E. (2009). *Still face experiment* [Video]. YouTube. https://www.youtube.com/watch?v=apzXGEbZht0

Video illustrating infant emotional responsiveness in the still-face paradigm.

ETHICS

UNESCO. (n.d.). *Culture speaks*. https://en.unesco.org/themes/protecting-our-heritage-and-fostering-creativity/talking-about-culture

Series of podcasts discussing safeguarding Indigenous rights, cultural heritage, and sustainable tourism.

United Nations. (n.d.). *Universal Declaration of Human Rights*. https://www.un.org/en/universal-declaration-human-rights/

This document outlines fundamental human rights to be protected in all regions of the world.

World Health Organization. (n.d.). *Ensuring ethical standards and procedures for research with human beings*. https://www.who.int/ethics/research/en/

Information on ethical standards to protect the rights and well-being of humans as research participants.

GENDER

Association of Psychological Science. (2014). *Inside the psychologist's studio: Eleanor Maccoby* [Video]. https://www.psychologicalscience.org/observer/eleanor-maccoby-itps

Interview with Eleanor Maccoby, who helped launch research on the development of gender in childhood.

INFANCY

Gottlieb, A., & DeLoache, J. (2017). *A world of babies: Imagined childcare guides for eight societies*. Cambridge University Press.

Book written by anthropologists with guides for child-rearing from the perspective of eight cultural groups.

INTERNALIZING PROBLEMS

Big Think. (2008). *John Cacioppo on American loneliness* [Video]. https://bigthink.com/videos/john-cacioppo-on-american-loneliness

Professor John Cacioppo from the University of Chicago talks about loneliness in America and its association with a culture of individualism.

World Health Organization. (2020). *Depression fact sheet*. https://www.who.int/news-room/fact-sheets/detail/depression

World Bank data on depression around the world.

INTERNATIONAL PSYCHOLOGY

American Psychological Association Division of International Psychology. https://div52.net/webinars/

> Division 52 of the American Psychological Association is devoted to international psychology. This webpage has a number of hour-long informational and skill-building webinars.

LANGUAGE

BBC Earth. *Dog understands 1022 words* [Video]. YouTube. https://www.youtube.com/watch?v=Ip_uVTWfXyI

> The mutual exclusivity bias is used as a method to discover intelligence in dogs.

BBC Four. (2010). *Julia's guide Willie Komani describes the Xhosa 'click' language – South Africa walks* [Video]. https://www.youtube.com/watch?v=lrK-XVCwGnI

> Video illustrating the Xhosa language that has syllables that use the click sound.

Child Language Data Exchange System. https://childes.talkbank.org

> Online archive and data storage website of child language, including data from many languages.

TED. (2016). *John McWhorter: 4 reasons to learn a new language* [Video]. YouTube. https://www.youtube.com/watch?v=VQRjouwKDlU

> A TEDx talk with John McWhorter, a professor of English and comparative literature at Columbia University, that describes the close connection between language and thought and human experience both within and across cultures.

Zero to Three. (n.d.). *Language and communication.* https://www.zerotothree.org/espanol/language-and-communication

> Zero to Three engages in policy discussions and distributes information for professionals and parents about children's early years. This webpage provides information on language and communication.

LEARNING

Columbia University. (2010). *Claude M. Steele, "Identity and stereotype threat"* [Video]. YouTube. https://www.youtube.com/watch?v=q1fzIuuXlkk

> This video is a presentation by Claude Steele about the concept of stereotype threat.

Rogoff, B. (2020.) *Strengths for learning among Indigenous- and Mexican-heritage children and families.* SRCD Commons. https://commons.srcd.org/viewdocument/strengths-for-learning-among-indige?CommunityKey=b098f303-d3eb-46cd-962d-1b05006fd6c5&tab=librarydocuments

> Information and videos about the strengths of learning among Indigenous- and Mexican-heritage Mexican families.

Saxe, G. B. (n.d.). *Culture and thought*. https://culturecognition.com

    Short video showing a child in the Oksapmin community of Papua New Guinea teaching another child the 27-body-part counting system.

LGBTQ YOUTH

Herdt, G. H. (Eds.). (2012). *Gay and lesbian youth*. Harrington Park Press.

    Edited book that provides an overview of issues pertaining to gay and lesbian youth worldwide, along with reports from various countries.

METHODS FOR STUDYING CULTURE

National Research Council. (2008). *International collaborations in behavioral and social sciences: Report of a workshop*. The National Academies Press. https://doi.org/10.17226/12053

    This website describes a book published by the National Academy of Sciences, Engineering and Medicine about international collaborations in the behavioral and social sciences. A free PDF copy of the book can be downloaded from the website.

SRCD Ethnic & Racial Issues Committee. (2019, March 20). *Conceptualizing and measuring culture, context, race and ethnicity: A focus on science, ethics, and collaboration in the spirit of 2044*. Society for Research in Child Development Preconference, Baltimore, MD, United States. https://www.srcd.org/event/conceptualizing-and-measuring-culture-context-race-and-ethnicity-focus-science-ethics-and

    Series of presentations by developmental scientists about how to measure culture, context, race, and ethnicity.

Wang, Q. (2016). *Five myths about the role of culture in psychological research*. Association for Psychological Science. https://www.psychologicalscience.org/observer/five-myths-about-the-role-of-culture-in-psychological-research

    A short paper by Qi Wang, professor of developmental psychology in the Department of Human Development at Cornell University, describing five myths about studying culture in psychological research.

PARENTING

Save the Children. (2019). *Raising children without violence is possible: How positive discipline leads to change and benefits society* [Webinar]. https://resourcecentre.savethechildren.net/library/raising-children-without-violence-possible-how-positive-discipline-leads-change-and-benefits

    Webinar and resources from Save the Children on positive parenting and nonviolent discipline.

PEER RELATIONSHIPS

Chen, X., French, D. C., & Schneider, B. (Eds.). (2006). *Child and adolescent peer relationships in cultural context*. Cambridge University Press.

    Edited book that combines research on peer relationships from multiple countries.

PHYSICAL ENVIRONMENT

UNICEF. (2007). *Climate change and children.* https://www.unicef.org/publications/files/Climate_Change_and_Children.pdf

UNICEF report on climate change and child development.

World Health Organization. (n.d.). *Children's environmental health.* https://www.who.int/health-topics/children-environmental-health#tab=tab_1

World Health Organization resources on children's health in relation to the physical environment.

PLAY

International Play Association. https://ipaworld.org

Website of the International Play Association, a nongovernmental organization dedicated to supporting and fostering the right for children around the world to have time for play and leisure.

POLICIES

Garcia, M., Pence, A., & Evans, J. L. (2008). *Africa's future, Africa's challenge: Early childhood care and development in sub-Saharan Africa.* World Bank. https://openknowledge.worldbank.org/handle/10986/6365

A book on early childhood care and development in sub-Saharan Africa.

Society for Research in Child Development. (2017). Goals for sustainable development: Focusing on children and youth. *Social Policy Report Brief, 30*(3). https://www.srcd.org/research/goals-sustainable-development-focusing-children-and-youth

Social policy report published by the Society for Research in Child Development on United Nations Sustainable Development Goals focusing on children and youth.

POSITIVE YOUTH DEVELOPMENT

John Templeton Foundation. https://www.templeton.org/discoveries

Learn more about research on forgiveness, gratitude, generosity, and other domains of positive development through the John Templeton Foundation.

Petersen, A. C. (2015). *Promoting positive youth development globally* [Video]. YouTube. https://www.youtube.com/watch?v=EJN_gp2iHUE

Vodcast on promoting positive youth development produced by the International Society for the Study of Behavioural Development.

UNICEF. https://www.unicefusa.org/unite/events-trainings

Learn more about training opportunities and volunteering through UNICEF.

RISK AND RESILIENCE

Briski, Z., & Kauffman, R. (Directors). (2004). *Born Into Brothels: Calcutta's red light kids* [Film]. ThinkFilm.

This Oscar-winning film portrays the lives of some of the children who live in Calcutta's red light district, where their mothers work as prostitutes. The film was originally part of director Zana Briski's photography project. She gave cameras to some of the children, and in recording much of the film's footage, they facilitated a closer look at life in the area than would have otherwise been possible. The film also illustrates the resilience of these children.

VIOLENCE PREVENTION

Ludwig, J. (2012). *Preventing crime and violence* [Video]. YouTube. https://www.youtube.com/watch?v=NFV_uVIGQG8

TED-style talk on how to use behavioral science to prevent youth violence and delinquency.

REFERENCES

Abadzi, H. (2013). Education for all in low-income countries: A crucial role for cognitive scientists. *British Journal of Education, Society & Behavioral Science, 3*, 1–23.

Abdel-Khalek, A. M. (2007). Religiosity, happiness, health, and psychopathology in a probability sample of Muslim adolescents. *Mental Health, Religion & Culture, 10*, 571–583. https://doi.org/10.1080/13674670601034547

Abebe, T. (2019). Reconceptualising children's agency as continuum and interdependence. *Social Sciences, 8*(3), 81. https://doi.org/10.3390/socsci8030081

Acosta, S., Garza, T., Hsu, H.-Y., Goodson, P., Padrón, Y., Goltz, H. H., & Johnston, A. (2020). The accountability culture: A systematic review of high-stakes testing and English learners in the United States during No Child Left Behind. *Educational Psychology Review, 32*, 327–352.

Adamson, L. B., Bakeman, R., & Deckner, D. F. (2005). Infusing symbols into joint engagement: Developmental themes and variations. In L. Namy (Ed.), *Symbol use and symbolic representation: Developmental and comparative perspectives* (pp. 171–195). Erlbaum.

Adamson, L. B., & McArthur, D. (2014). Joint attention, affect, and culture. In C. Moore & P. J. Dunham (Eds.), *Joint attention: Its origins and role in development* (pp. 205–222). Psychology Press.

Adler, P. A., & Adler, P. (2001). *Peer power: Preadolescent culture and identity.* Rutgers University Press.

Agesa, R. U., & Agesa, J. (2019). Time spent on household chores (fetching water) and the alternatives forgone for women in sub-Saharan Africa: Evidence from Kenya. *Journal of Developing Areas, 53*(2), 29–42. https://doi.org/10.1353/jda.2019.0019

Aguayo, V. M., & Menon, P. (2016). Stop stunting: Improving child feeding, women's nutrition and household sanitation in South Asia. *Maternal and Child Nutrition, 12*(Suppl 1), 3–11. https://doi.org/10.1111/mcn.12283

Ahmed, R. A. (2010). North Africa and the Middle East. In M. H. Bornstein (Ed.), *Handbook of cultural developmental science* (pp. 359–381). Taylor and Francis.

Ainsworth, M. D. (1963). The development of infant-mother interaction among the Ganda. In D. M. Foss (Ed.), *Determinants of infant behavior* (Vol. 2, pp. 67–104). Wiley.

Ainsworth, M. D. S., Blehar, M. C., Waters, E., & Wall, S. (1978). *Patterns of attachment: A psychological study of the strange situation*. Erlbaum.

Akhtar, N. (2005). The robustness of learning through overhearing. *Developmental Science, 8*, 199–209. https://doi.org/10.1111/j.1467-7687.2005.00406.x

Akinsola, E. F. (2011). "Omoluwabi's approach" to educating the African child. In A. B. Nsamenang & T. M. S. Tchombe (Eds.), *Handbook of African educational theories and practices: A generative teacher education curriculum* (pp. 221–232). Human Development Resource Centre.

Akinsola, E. F. (2013). Cultural variations in parenting styles in the majority world: Evidences from Nigeria and Cameroon. In M. L. Seidl-de-Moura (Ed.), *Parenting in South American and African contexts*. IntechOpen. https://doi.org/10.5772/57003

Alampay, L. P. (2014). Parenting in the Philippines. In H. Selin (Ed.), *Parenting across cultures: Childrearing, motherhood and fatherhood in non-Western cultures* (pp. 105–121). Springer. https://doi.org/10.1007/978-94-007-7503-9_9

Alampay, L. P., & Garcia, A. S. (2019). Education and parenting in the Philippines. In E. Sorbring & J. E. Lansford (Eds.), *School systems, parent behavior, and academic achievement* (Vol. 3, pp. 79–94). Springer. https://doi.org/10.1007/978-3-030-28277-6_7

Alavi, M., Latif, A. A., Ninggal, M. T., Mustaffa, M. S., & Amini, M. (2020). Family functioning and attachment among young adults in Western and non-Western societies. *The Journal of Psychology, 154*, 346–366. https://doi.org/10.1080/00223980.2020.1754153

Al-Hassan, S. (2019). Education and parenting in Jordan. In E. Sorbring & J. E. Lansford (Eds.), *School systems, parent behavior, and academic achievement* (Vol. 3, pp. 55–65). Springer. https://doi.org/10.1007/978-3-030-28277-6_5

Allen, J. P., & Antonishak, J. (2008). Adolescent peer influences: Beyond the dark side. In M. Prinstein & K. A. Dodge (Eds.), *Understanding peer influence in children and adolescents* (pp. 141–160). Guilford Press.

Allwood, C. M., & Berry, J. W. (2006). Origins and development of Indigenous psychologies: An international analysis. *International Journal of Psychology, 41*, 243–268. https://doi.org/10.1080/00207590544000013

AlMarri, T. S. K., & Oei, T. P. S. (2009). Alcohol and substance use in the Arabian Gulf region: A review. *International Journal of Psychology, 44*, 222–233. https://doi.org/10.1080/00207590801888752

Altshuler, S. J., & Schmautz, T. (2006). No Hispanic student left behind: The consequences of "high stakes" testing. *Children & Schools, 28*, 5–14. https://doi.org/10.1093/cs/28.1.5

American Psychological Association. (2017). *Ethical principles of psychologists and code of conduct* (2002, amended effective June 1, 2010, and January 1, 2017). http://www.apa.org/ethics/code/index.aspx

Andersen, E. S. (1990). *Speaking with style: The socio-linguistic skill of children*. Routledge.

Anderson, C. A., & Bushman, B. J. (2001). Effects of violent video games on aggressive behavior, aggressive cognition, aggressive affect, physiological arousal, and prosocial behavior: A meta-analytic review of the scientific literature. *Psychological Science, 12*, 353–359. https://doi.org/10.1111/1467-9280.00366

Anderson, C. A., & Bushman, B. J. (2002). Human aggression. *Annual Review of Psychology, 53*, 27–51. https://doi.org/10.1146/annurev.psych.53.100901.135231

Anderson, C. A., & Huesmann, L. R. (2003). Human aggression: A social-cognitive view. In M. A. Hogg & J. Cooper (Eds.), *Sage handbook of social psychology* (pp. 296–323). Sage.

Arnett, J. J. (1998). Learning to stand alone: The contemporary American transition to adulthood in cultural and historical context. *Human Development, 41*, 295–315. https://doi.org/10.1159/000022591

Arnett, J. J. (2000). Emerging adulthood. A theory of development from the late teens through the twenties. *American Psychologist, 55*, 469–480. https://doi.org/10.1037/0003-066X.55.5.469

Arnett, J. J. (2003). Conceptions of the transition to adulthood among emerging adults in American ethnic groups. *New Directions for Child and Adolescent Development, 2003*(100), 63–76. https://doi.org/10.1002/cd.75

Arnett, J. J. (2008). The neglected 95%: Why American psychology needs to become less American. *American Psychologist, 63*(7), 602–614. https://doi.org/10.1037/0003-066X.63.7.602

Arnett, J. J., & Schwab, J. (2012). *The Clark University Poll of Emerging Adults: Thriving, struggling, and hopeful.* Clark University.

Asendorpf, J. B. (1991). Development of inhibited children's coping with unfamiliarity. *Child Development, 62*, 1460–1474. https://doi.org/10.2307/1130819

Asher, S. R., & Coie, J. D. (Eds.). (1990). *Peer rejection in childhood.* Cambridge University Press.

Aslin, R. (1987). Visual and auditory development in infancy. In J. Osofsky (Ed.), *Handbook of infant development* (2nd ed., pp. 5–97). Wiley.

Aslin, R. N., & Newport, E. L. (2012). Statistical learning: From acquiring specific items to forming general rules. *Current Directions in Psychological Science, 21*, 170–176. https://doi.org/10.1177/0963721412436806

Aukrust, V. G., Edwards, C. P., Aslye, K., Knoche, L., & Msuk, K. (2003). Young children's close relationships outside the family: Parental ethnotheories in four communities in Norway, United States, Turkey, and Korea. *International Journal of Behavioral Development, 27*, 481–494. https://doi.org/10.1080/01650250344000109

Aureli, F., & de Waal, F. B. M. (Eds.). (2000). *Natural conflict resolution.* University of California Press.

Babatunde, E. D., & Setiloane, K. (2014). Changing patterns of Yoruba parenting in Nigeria. In H. Selin (Ed.), *Parenting across cultures: Childrearing, motherhood and fatherhood in non-Western cultures* (pp. 241–252). Springer. https://doi.org/10.1007/978-94-007-7503-9_18

Babisch, W., Neuhauser, H., Thamm, M., & Seiwert, M. (2009). Blood pressure of 8–14 year old children in relation to traffic noise at home—Results of the German Environmental Survey for Children (GerES IV). *The Science of the Total Environment, 407*, 5839–5843. https://doi.org/10.1016/j.scitotenv.2009.08.016

Baguma, P., & Aheisibwe, I. (2011). Issues in African education. In A. B. Nsamenang & T. M. S. Tchombe (Eds.), *Handbook of African educational theories and practices: A generative teacher education curriculum* (pp. 21–34). Human Development Resource Centre.

Bakeman, R., Adamson, L. B., Konner, M., & Barr, R. G. (1990). Kung infancy: The social context of object exploration. *Child Development, 61*, 794–809. https://doi.org/10.2307/1130964

Bandura, A. (1986). *Social foundations of thought and action: A social cognitive theory.* Prentice-Hall.

Bandura, A. (1997). *Self-efficacy.* Freeman.

Bandura, A. (2016). *Moral disengagement: How people do harm and live with themselves.* Worth.

Bao, X.-H., & Lam, S.-F. (2008). Who makes the choice? Rethinking the role of autonomy and relatedness in Chinese children's motivation. *Child Development, 79*(2), 269–283. https://doi.org/10.1111/j.1467-8624.2007.01125.x

Barr, A. B., Culatta, E., & Simons, R. L. (2013). Romantic relationships and health among African American young adults: Linking patterns of relationship quality over time to changes in physical and mental health. *Journal of Health and Social Behavior, 54*, 369–385. https://doi.org/10.1177/0022146513486652

Barr, R., & Hayne, H. (2003). It's not what you know, it's who you know: Older siblings facilitate imitation during infancy. *International Journal of Early Years Education, 11,* 7–21.

Barry, C. M., & Nelson, L. J. (2005). The role of religion in the transition to adulthood for young emerging adults. *Journal of Youth and Adolescence, 34,* 245–255. https://doi. org/10.1007/s10964-005-4308-1

Bartel, A. P., Rossin-Slater, M., Ruhm, C. J., Stearns, J., & Waldfogel, J. (2018). Paid family leave, fathers' leave-taking, and leave-sharing in dual-earner households. *Journal of Policy Analysis and Management, 37,* 10–37. https://doi.org/10.1002/pam. 22030

Bates, E. (1976). *Language and context: The acquisition of pragmatics.* Academic Press.

Batool, S. S., & de Visser, R. O. (2016). Experiences of infertility in British and Pakistani women: A cross-cultural qualitative analysis. *Health Care for Women International, 37,* 180–196. https://doi.org/10.1080/07399332.2014.980890

Bauer, P. J., & Fivush, R. (2010). Context and consequences of autobiographical memory development. *Cognitive Development, 25,* 303–308. https://doi.org/10.1016/j. cogdev.2010.08.001

Baumrind, D. (1967). Child care practices anteceding three patterns of preschool behavior. *Genetic Psychology Monographs, 75,* 43–88.

Bell, A. C., & Dyment, J. E. (2008). Grounds for health: The intersection of green school grounds and health-promoting schools. *Environmental Education Research, 14,* 77–90. https://doi.org/10.1080/13504620701843426

Bellmore, A., Nishina, A., & Graham, S. (2011). Peer popularity in the context of ethnicity. In A. H. N. Cillessen, D. Schwartz, & L. Mayeux (Eds.), *Popularity in the peer system* (pp. 193–215). Guilford Press.

Belsky, J., Schlomer, G. L., & Ellis, B. J. (2012). Beyond cumulative risk: Distinguishing harshness and unpredictability as determinants of parenting and early life history strategy. *Developmental Psychology, 48,* 662–673. https://doi.org/10.1037/a0024454

Benenson, J. F., Pascoe, J., & Radmore, N. (2007). Children's altruistic behavior in the dictator game. *Evolution and Human Behavior, 28,* 168–175. https://doi.org/10.1016/j. evolhumbehav.2006.10.003

Bennett, L. (2005). *Maidenhood, Islam and modernity: Single women, sexuality and reproductive health in contemporary Indonesia.* Routledge/Curzon. https://doi.org/10.4324/ 9780203391389

Benson, J. E., Johnson, M. K., & Elder, G. H., Jr. (2012). The implications of adult identity for educational and work attainment in young adulthood. *Developmental Psychology, 48*(6), 1752–1758. https://doi.org/10.1037/a0026364

Bergmüller, S. (2013). The relationship between cultural individualism-collectivism and student aggression across 62 countries. *Aggressive Behavior, 39,* 182–200. https:// doi.org/10.1002/ab.21472

Betancourt, H., & López, S. R. (1993). The study of culture, ethnicity, and race in American psychology. *American Psychologist, 48*(6), 629–637. https://doi.org/10.1037/ 0003-066X.48.6.629

Betancourt, T. S., Thomson, D. L., Brennan, R. T., Antonaccio, C. M., Gilman, S. E., & VanderWeele, T. J. (2020). Stigma and acceptance of Sierra Leone's child soldiers: A prospective longitudinal study of adult mental health and social functioning. *Journal of the American Academy of Child & Adolescent Psychiatry, 59,* 715–726. https://doi.org/ 10.1016/j.jaac.2019.05.026

Bialystok, E., & Craik, F. I. M. (2010). Cognitive and linguistic processing in the bilingual mind. *Current Directions in Psychological Science, 19,* 19–23. https://doi.org/ 10.1177/0963721409358571

Bianchi, S. M., & Milkie, M. A. (2010). Work and family research in the first decade of the 21st century. *Journal of Marriage and the Family, 72,* 705–725. https://doi.org/ 10.1111/j.1741-3737.2010.00726.x

Bickerton, D. (1983). Creole languages. *Scientific American, 249*, 116–122. https://doi.org/10.1038/scientificamerican0783-116

Bickerton, D. (1990). *Language and species*. University of Chicago Press. https://doi.org/10.7208/chicago/9780226220949.001.0001

Björkqvist, K. (1997). The inevitability of conflict, but not of violence: Theoretical considerations on conflict and aggression. In D. Fry & K. Björkqvist (Eds.), *Cultural variation in conflict resolution: Alternatives to violence* (pp. 25–37). Erlbaum.

Blicharska, M., Smithers, R. J., Kuchler, M., Agrawal, G. K., Gutiérrez, J. M., Hassanali, A., Huq, S., Koller, S. H., Marjit, S., Mshinda, H. M., Masjuki, H. H., Solomons, N. W., Staden, J. V., & Mikusiński, G. (2017). Steps to overcome the North–South divide in research relevant to climate change policy and practice. *Nature Climate Change, 7*, 21–27. https://doi.org/10.1038/nclimate3163

Blinka, L., Škařupová, K., Ševčíková, A., Wölfling, K., Müller, K. W., & Dreier, M. (2015). Excessive internet use in European adolescents: What determines differences in severity? *International Journal of Public Health, 60*, 249–256. https://doi.org/10.1007/s00038-014-0635-x

Bloch, M. N., & Adler, S. M. (1994). African children's play and the emergence of sexual division of labor. In J. L. Roopnarine, J. E. Johnson, & F. H. Hooper (Eds.), *Children's play in diverse cultures* (pp. 148–178). State University of New York Press.

Bloom, L. (1970). *Language development: Form and function in emerging grammars*. MIT Press.

Bloom, L. (1991). *Language development from two to three*. Cambridge University Press.

Bloom, P. (2016). *Against empathy: The case for rational compassion*. HarperCollins.

Bock, J., & Johnson, S. E. (2004). Subsistence ecology and play among the Okavango Delta Peoples of Botswana. *Human Nature, 15*, 63–81. https://doi.org/10.1007/s12110-004-1004-x

Boisvert, S., & Poulin, F. (2016). Romantic relationship patterns from adolescence to emerging adulthood: Associations with family and peer experiences in early adolescence. *Journal of Youth and Adolescence, 45*, 945–958. https://doi.org/10.1007/s10964-016-0435-0

Boivin, M. J., Mohanty, A., Sikorskii, A., Vokhiwa, M., Magen, J. G., & Gladstone, M. (2019). Early and middle childhood developmental, cognitive, and psychiatric outcomes of Malawian children affected by retinopathy positive cerebral malaria. *Journal of Child Neuropsychology, 25*, 81–102. https://doi.org/10.1080/09297049.2018.1451497

Bond, M. H. (1991). *Beyond the Chinese face: Insights from psychology*. Cambridge University Press.

Bond, M. H. (2004). Culture and aggression-from context to coercion. *Personality and Social Psychology Review, 8*, 62–78. https://doi.org/10.1207/s15327957pspr0801_3

Bond, M. H., & Hwang, K. (1986). The social psychology of the Chinese people. In M. H. Bond (Ed.), *The psychology of the Chinese people* (pp. 213–266). Oxford University Press.

Borke, H. (1971). Interpersonal perception of young children: Egocentrism or empathy. *Developmental Psychology, 5*, 263–269. https://doi.org/10.1037/h0031267

Bornstein, M. H. (1995). Form and function: Implications for studies of culture and human development. *Culture and Psychology, 1*(1), 123–137. https://doi.org/10.1177/1354067X9511009

Bornstein, M. H. (2002). Toward a multiculture, multiage, multimethod science. *Human Development, 45*, 257–263. https://doi.org/10.1159/000064986

Bornstein, M. H. (2012). Cultural approaches to parenting. *Parenting: Science and Practice, 12*, 212–221. https://doi.org/10.1080/15295192.2012.683359

Bornstein, M. H. (2015). Children's parents. In M. H. Bornstein & T. Leventhal (Eds.), *Handbook of child psychology and developmental science: Vol. 4. Ecological settings and processes in developmental systems* (7th ed., pp. 55–132). Wiley. https://doi.org/10. 1002/9781118963418.childpsy403

Bornstein, M. H., Cote, L. R., Haynes, O. M., Suwalsky, J. T., & Bakeman, R. (2012). Modalities of infant–mother interaction in Japanese, Japanese American immigrant, and European American dyads. *Child Development, 83*, 2073–2088. https://doi.org/ 10.1111/j.1467-8624.2012.01822.x

Bornstein, M. H., & Putnick, D. L. (2012). Cognitive and socioemotional caregiving in developing countries. *Child Development, 83*, 46–61. https://doi.org/10.1111/j.1467-8624.2011.01673.x

Bornstein, M. H., & Putnick, D. L. (2016). Mothers' and fathers' parenting practices with their daughters and sons in low- and middle-income countries. *Monographs of the Society for Research in Child Development, 81*(1), 60–77. https://doi.org/10.1111/ mono.12226

Bornstein, M. H., Putnick, D. L., Cote, L. R., Haynes, O. M., & Suwalsky, J. T. D. (2015). Mother-infant contingent vocalizations in 11 countries. *Psychological Science, 26*, 1272–1284. https://doi.org/10.1177/0956797615586796

Bornstein, M. H., Putnick, D. L., & Lansford, J. E. (2011). Parenting attributions and attitudes in cross-cultural perspective. *Parenting: Science and Practice, 11*, 214–237. https://doi.org/10.1080/15295192.2011.585568

Bornstein, M. H., Putnick, D. L., Lansford, J. E., Al-Hassan, S. M., Bacchini, D., Bombi, A. S., Chang, L., Deater-Deckard, K., Di Giunta, L., Dodge, K. A., Malone, P. S., Oburu, P., Pastorelli, C., Skinner, A. T., Sorbring, E., Steinberg, L., Tapanya, S., Tirado, L. M. U., Zelli, A., & Alampay, L. P. (2017). 'Mixed blessings': Parental religiousness, parenting, and child adjustment in global perspective. *Journal of Child Psychology and Psychiatry, and Allied Disciplines, 58*, 880–892. https://doi.org/10.1111/ jcpp.12705

Bornstein, M. H., Putnick, D. L., Lansford, J. E., Deater-Deckard, K., & Bradley, R. H. (2015). A developmental analysis of caregiving modalities across infancy in 38 low- and middle-income countries. *Child Development, 86*, 1571–1587. https://doi. org/10.1111/cdev.12402

Bornstein, M. H., Putnick, D. L., Lansford, J. E., Deater-Deckard, K., & Bradley, R. H. (2016). Gender in low- and middle-income countries: Introduction. *Monographs of the Society for Research in Child Development, 81*(1), 7–23. https://doi.org/10.1111/ mono.12223

Bornstein, M. H., Putnick, D. L., Park, Y., Suwalsky, J. T. D., & Haynes, O. M. (2017). Human infancy and parenting in global perspective: Specificity. *Proceedings of the Royal Society B: Biological Sciences, 284*, 2017–2168. https://doi.org/10.1098/rspb. 2017.2168

Bornstein, M. H., Tal, J., & Tamis-LeMonda, C. (1991). Parenting in cross-cultural perspective. In M. H. Bornstein (Ed.), *Cultural approaches to parenting* (pp. 69–90). Erlbaum.

Bowerman, M., & Choi, S. (2003). Space under construction: Language-specific spatial categorization in first language acquisition. In D. Gentner & S. Goldin-Meadow (Eds.), *Language in mind: Advances in the study of language and thought* (pp. 387–427). MIT Press.

Bowker, J. C., & Raja, R. (2011). Social withdrawal subtypes during early adolescence in India. *Journal of Abnormal Child Psychology, 39*, 201–212. https://doi.org/10.1007/ s10802-010-9461-7

Bowlby, J. (1969). *Attachment and loss: Vol. 1. Attachment*. Basic Books.

Bowlby, J. (1973). *Attachment and loss: Vol. 2. Separation*. Basic Books.

Bowlby, J. (1980). *Attachment and loss: Vol. 3. Loss, sadness and depression*. Basic Books.

Boyd, R., Richerson, P., & Henrich, J. (2011). The cultural niche: Why social learning is essential for human adaptation. *Proceedings of the National Academy of Sciences*, 1–8.

Bradley, R. H., & Putnick, D. L. (2016). The role of physical capital assets in young girls' and boys' mortality and growth in low- and middle-income countries. *Monographs of the Society for Research in Child Development, 81*(1), 33–59 . https://doi.org/10.1111/mono.12225

Brain, R. (1976). *Friends and lovers*. Basic Books.

Branje, S. (2018). Development of parent–adolescent relationships: Conflict interactions as a mechanism of change. *Child Development Perspectives, 12*, 171–176. https://doi.org/10.1111/cdep.12278

Branje, S. J. T., van Lieshout, C. F. M., van Aken, M. A. G., & Haselager, G. J. T. (2004). Perceived support in sibling relationships and adolescent adjustment. *Journal of Child Psychology and Psychiatry, 45*, 1385–1396. https://doi.org/10.1111/j.1469-7610.2004.00332.x

Bridges, L. J., & Grolnick, W. S. (1995). The development of emotional self-regulation in infancy and early childhood. In N. Eisenberg (Ed.), *Social development* (pp. 185–211). Sage.

Briggs, J. L. (1971). *Never in anger*. Harvard University Press.

Britt, C. L. (2019). Age and crime. In D. P. Farrington, L. Kazemian, & A. R. Piquero (Eds.), *The Oxford handbook of developmental and life-course criminology* (pp. 13–33). Oxford University Press.

Brody, G. H., Ge, X., Conger, R., Gibbons, F. X., Murry, V. M., Gerrard, M., & Simons, R. L. (2001). The influence of neighborhood disadvantage, collective socialization, and parenting on African American children's affiliation with deviant peers. *Child Development, 72*, 1231–1246. https://doi.org/10.1111/1467-8624.00344

Broidy, L. M., Nagin, D. S., Tremblay, R. E., Bates, J. E., Brame, B., Dodge, K. A., Fergusson, D., Horwood, J. L., Loeber, R., Laird, R., Lynam, D. R., Moffitt, T. E., Pettit, G. S., & Vitaro, F. (2003). Developmental trajectories of childhood disruptive behaviors and adolescent delinquency: A six-site, cross-national study. *Developmental Psychology, 39*, 222–245. https://doi.org/10.1037/0012-1649.39.2.222

Bronfenbrenner, U. (1979). *The ecology of human development*. Harvard University Press.

Brooker, R. J., Buss, K. A., Lemery-Chalfant, K., Aksan, N., Davidson, R. J., & Goldsmith, H. H. (2013). The development of stranger fear in infancy and toddlerhood: Normative development, individual differences, antecedents, and outcomes. *Developmental Science, 16*, 864–878. https://doi.org/10.1111/desc.12058

Brownell, C. A., Ramani, G. B., & Zerwas, S. (2006). Becoming a social partner with peers: Cooperation and social understanding in one- and two-year-olds. *Child Development, 77*, 803–821. https://doi.org/10.1111/j.1467-8624.2006.t01-1-.x-i1

Brunborg, G. S., & Burdzovic Andreas, J. (2019). Increase in time spent on social media is associated with modest increase in depression, conduct problems, and episodic heavy drinking. *Journal of Adolescence, 74*, 201–209. https://doi.org/10.1016/j.adolescence.2019.06.013A

Brunelle, S., Brussoni, M., Herrington, S., Matsuba, M. K., & Pratt, M. W. (2018). Teens in public spaces and natural landscapes: Issues of access and design. In J. E. Lansford & P. Banati (Eds.), *Handbook of adolescent development research and its impact on global policy* (pp. 361–379). Oxford University Press.

Bruner, J. S. (1964). The course of cognitive growth. *American Psychologist, 19*, 1–15. https://doi.org/10.1037/h0044160

Bruner, J. S. (1983). *Children's talk*. Norton.

Bruner, J. S., & Sherwood, V. (1976). Peek-a-boo and the learning of rule structures. In J. S. Bruner, A. Jolly, & K. Sylva (Eds.), *Play: Its role in development and evolution* (pp. 277–285). Basic Books.

Bucksch, J., Sigmundova, D., Hamrik, Z., Troped, P. J., Melkevik, O., Ahluwalia, N., Borraccino, A., Tynjälä, J., Kalman, M., & Inchley, J. (2016). International trends in adolescent screen-time behaviors from 2002 to 2010. *The Journal of Adolescent Health, 58*, 417–425. https://doi.org/10.1016/j.jadohealth.2015.11.014

Burdelski, M. (2010). Socializing politeness routines: Action, other-orientation, and embodiment in a Japanese preschool. *Journal of Pragmatics, 42*, 1606–1621. https://doi.org/10.1016/j.pragma.2009.11.007

Burr, R. (2014). The complexity of morality: Being a 'good child' in Vietnam? *Journal of Moral Education, 43*, 156–168. https://doi.org/10.1080/03057240.2014.893421

Bushman, B. J., & Anderson, C. A. (2001). Media violence and the American public. Scientific facts versus media misinformation. *American Psychologist, 56*, 477–489. https://doi.org/10.1037/0003-066X.56.6-7.477

Butler, L. P., Ronfard, S., & Corriveau, K. H. (Eds.). (2020). *The questioning child: Insights from psychology and education.* Cambridge University Press. https://doi.org/10.1017/9781108553803

Butovskaya, M., Verbeek, P., Ljungberg, T., & Lundarini, A. (2000). A multicultural view of peacemaking among young children. In A. Filippo & F. B. M. de Waal (Eds.), *Natural conflict resolution* (pp. 243–258). University of California Press.

Butterworth, B., Reeve, R., & Reynolds, F. (2011). Using mental representations of space when words are unavailable: Studies of enumeration and arithmetic in Indigenous Australia. *Journal of Cross-Cultural Psychology, 42*, 630–638. https://doi.org/10.1177/0022022111406020

Calderón-Garcidueñas, L., Engle, R., Mora-Tiscareño, A., Styner, M., Gómez-Garza, G., Zhu, H., Jewells, V., Torres-Jardón, R., Romero, L., Monroy-Acosta, M. E., Bryant, C., González-González, L. O., Medina-Cortina, H., & D'Angiulli, A. (2011). Exposure to severe urban air pollution influences cognitive outcomes, brain volume and systemic inflammation in clinically healthy children. *Brain and Cognition, 77*, 345–355.

Calderón-Tena, C. O., Knight, G. P., & Carlo, G. (2011). The socialization of prosocial behavioral tendencies among Mexican American adolescents: The role of familism values. *Cultural Diversity & Ethnic Minority Psychology, 17*, 98–106. https://doi.org/10.1037/a0021825

Callaghan, T. (2013). Symbols and symbolic thought. In P. D. Zelazo (Ed.), *The Oxford handbook of developmental psychology: Body and mind* (Vol. 1, pp. 974–1005). Oxford University Press.

Callaghan, T., Moll, H., Rackoczy, H., Warneken, F., Lizskowski, U., Behne, T., & Tomasello, M. (2011). *Monographs of the Society for Research in Child Development: Vol. 76. Early social cognition in three cultural contexts.* Wiley.

Camras, L. A., Malatesta, C., & Izard, C. (1991). The development of facial expressions in infancy. In R. Feldman & B. Rime (Eds.), *Fundamentals of nonverbal behavior* (pp. 73–105). Cambridge University Press.

Camras, L. A., Oster, H., Campos, J. J., Miyake, K., & Bradshaw, D. (1992). Japanese and American infants' responses to arm restraint. *Developmental Psychology, 28*, 578–583. https://doi.org/10.1037/0012-1649.28.4.578

Capuano, S., Simeone, S., Scaravilli, G., Raimondo, D., & Balbi, C. (2009). Sexual behaviour among Italian adolescents: Knowledge and use of contraceptives. *The European Journal of Contraception & Reproductive Health Care, 14*, 285–289. https://doi.org/10.1080/13625180902926920

Carey, S. (1978). The child as a word learner. In M. Halle, J. Bresnan, & G. Miller (Eds.), *Linguistic theory and psychological reality* (pp. 264–293). MIT Press.

Carlson, A. C. (2007). *Conjugal America: On the public purposes of marriage.* Routledge.

Carnoy, M. (1974). *Education as cultural imperialism.* David McCay.

Carpenter, M., Akhtar, N., & Tomasello, M. (1998). 14- through 18-month-old infants differentially imitate intentional and accidental actions. *Infant Behavior and Development, 21*, 315–330. https://doi.org/10.1016/S0163-6383(98)90009-1

Carruthers, P. (2020). Questions in development. In L. P. Butler, S. Ronfard, & K. H. Corriveau (Eds.), *The questioning child: Insights from psychology and education* (pp. 6–28). Cambridge University Press. https://doi.org/10.1017/9781108553803.002

Carstensen, L. L. (2006). The influence of a sense of time on human development. *Science, 312*, 1913–1915. https://doi.org/10.1126/science.1127488

Carver, A., Timperio, A., & Crawford, D. (2008). Playing it safe: The influence of neighbourhood safety on children's physical activity. A review. *Health & Place, 14*, 217–227. https://doi.org/10.1016/j.healthplace.2007.06.004

Caspi, A., Elder, G. H., Jr., & Bem, D. J. (1988). Moving away from the world: Life-course patterns of shy children. *Developmental Psychology, 24*, 824–831. https://doi.org/10.1037/0012-1649.24.6.824

Cassidy, J., & Shaver, P. R. (Eds.). (2008). *Handbook of attachment: Theory, research, and clinical applications* (2nd ed.). Guilford Press.

Centers for Disease Control and Prevention. (2019a). *Global WASH fast facts.* https://www.cdc.gov/healthywater/global/wash_statistics.html

Centers for Disease Control and Prevention. (2019b). *Infertility FAQs.* https://www.cdc.gov/reproductivehealth/infertility/index.htm

Central Intelligence Agency. (2019). *World factbook.* https://www.cia.gov/library/publications/the-world-factbook/rankorder/2091rank.html

Chamie, J., & Mirkin, B. (2012). *Childless by choice.* Yale Center for the Study of Globalization.

Chang, L., Lu, H. J., Lansford, J. E., Skinner, A. T., Bornstein, M. H., Steinberg, L., Dodge, K. A., Chen, B. B., Tian, Q., Bacchini, D., Deater-Deckard, K., Pastorelli, C., Alampay, L. P., Sorbring, E., Al-Hassan, S. M., Oburu, P., Malone, P. S., Di Giunta, L., Tirado, L. M. U., & Tapanya, S. (2019). Environmental harshness and unpredictability, life history, and social and academic behavior of adolescents in nine countries. *Developmental Psychology, 55*, 890–903. https://doi.org/10.1037/dev0000655

Chao, R. K. (2001). Extending research on the consequences of parenting style for Chinese Americans and European Americans. *Child Development, 72*, 1832–1843. https://doi.org/10.1111/1467-8624.00381

Chao, R. K., & Otsuki-Clutter, M. (2011). Racial and ethnic differences: Sociocultural and contextual explanations. *Journal of Research on Adolescence, 21*, 47–60. https://doi.org/10.1111/j.1532-7795.2010.00714.x

Chatwin, B. (1987). *The songlines.* Viking Penguin.

Chaux, E. (2005). Role of third parties in conflicts among Colombian children and early adolescents. *Aggressive Behavior, 31*, 40–55. https://doi.org/10.1002/ab.20031

Chavajay, P. (2006). How Maya mothers with different amounts of schooling organize a problem-solving discussion with children. *International Journal of Behavioral Development, 30*, 371–382. https://doi.org/10.1177/0165025406066744

Chavajay, P., & Rogoff, B. (1999). Cultural variation in management of attention by children and their caregivers. *Developmental Psychology, 35*, 1079–1090. https://doi.org/10.1037/0012-1649.35.4.1079

Chawla, L., & Driskell, D. (2006). The Growing Up in Cities Project: Global perspectives on children and youth as catalysts for community change. *Journal of Community Practice, 14*, 183–200. https://doi.org/10.1300/J125v14n01_11

Chawla, L., & Malone, K. (2003). Neighbourhood quality in children's eyes. In P. Christensen & M. O'Brien (Eds.), *Children in the city: Home, neighbourhood and community* (pp. 118–141). RoutledgeFalmer.

Cheah, C. S. L., & Li, J. (2010). Parenting of young immigrant Chinese children: Challenges facing their social emotional and intellectual development. In E. L. Grigorenko & R. Takanishi (Eds.), *Immigration, diversity, and education* (pp. 225–241). Routledge.

Cheah, C. S. L., Li, J., Zhou, N., Yamamoto, Y., & Leung, C. Y. Y. (2015). Understanding Chinese immigrant and European American mothers' expressions of warmth. *Developmental Psychology, 51*, 1802–1811. https://doi.org/10.1037/a0039855

Cheah, C. S. L., & Rubin, K. H. (2004). European American and Mainland Chinese mothers' responses to aggression and social withdrawal in preschoolers. *International Journal of Behavioral Development, 28*, 83–94. https://doi.org/10.1080/01650250344000299

Chen, B.-B., Li, X., & Chen, N. (2017). Positive youth development in China. In R. Dimitrova (Ed.), *Well-being of youth and emerging adults across cultures* (pp. 35–48). Springer. https://doi.org/10.1007/978-3-319-68363-8_3

Chen, C., Lee, S. Y., & Stevenson, H. W. (1995). Response style and cross-cultural comparisons of rating scales among East Asian and North American students. *Psychological Science, 6*, 170–175. https://doi.org/10.1111/j.1467-9280.1995.tb00327.x

Chen, S. H., Zhou, Q., Eisenberg, N., Valiente, C., & Wang, Y. (2011). Parental expressivity and parenting styles in Chinese families: Prospective and unique relations to children's psychological adjustment. *Parenting: Science and Practice, 11*, 288–307. https://doi.org/10.1080/15295192.2011.613725

Chen, X. (2011). Culture and children's socioemotional functioning: A contextual-developmental perspective. In X. Chen & K. H. Rubin (Eds.), *Socioemotional development in cultural context* (pp. 29–52). Guilford Press.

Chen, X. (2012). Culture, peer interaction, and socioemotional development. *Child Development Perspectives, 6*, 27–34. https://doi.org/10.1111/j.1750-8606.2011.00187.x

Chen, X. (2015). Exploring the implications of social change for human development: Perspectives, issues and future directions. *International Journal of Psychology, 50*, 56–59. https://doi.org/10.1002/ijop.12128

Chen, X. (2019). Culture and shyness in childhood and adolescence. *New Ideas in Psychology, 53*, 58–66. https://doi.org/10.1016/j.newideapsych.2018.04.007

Chen, X., Cen, G., Li, D., & He, Y. (2005). Social functioning and adjustment in Chinese children: The imprint of historical time. *Child Development, 76*, 182–195. https://doi.org/10.1111/j.1467-8624.2005.00838.x

Chen, X., French, D., & Schneider, B. H. (Eds.). (2006). *Peer relationships in cultural context.* Cambridge University Press. https://doi.org/10.1017/CBO9780511499739

Chen, X., & French, D. C. (2008). Children's social competence in cultural context. *Annual Review of Psychology, 59*, 591–616. https://doi.org/10.1146/annurev.psych.59.103006.093606

Chen, X., Hastings, P. D., Rubin, K. H., Chen, H., Cen, G., & Stewart, S. L. (1998). Child-rearing attitudes and behavioral inhibition in Chinese and Canadian toddlers: A cross-cultural study. *Developmental Psychology, 34*, 677–686. https://doi.org/10.1037/0012-1649.34.4.677

Chen, X., Kaspar, V., Zhang, Y., Wang, L., & Zheng, S. (2004). Peer relationships among Chinese and North American boys: A cross-cultural perspective. In N. Way & J. Chu (Eds.), *Adolescent boys: Exploring diverse cultures of boyhood* (pp. 197–218). New York University Press.

Chen, X., Rubin, K. H., & Li, Z. (1995). Social functioning and adjustment in Chinese children: A longitudinal study. *Developmental Psychology, 31*, 531–539. https://doi.org/10.1037/0012-1649.31.4.531

Chen, X., Rubin, K. H., & Sun, Y. (1992). Social reputation and peer relationships in Chinese and Canadian children: A cross-cultural study. *Child Development, 63*, 1336–1343. https://doi.org/10.2307/1131559

Chen, Z., Mo, L., & Honomichl, R. (2004). Having the memory of an elephant: Long-term retrieval and the use of analogues in problem solving. *Journal of Experimental Psychology: General, 133*, 415–433. https://doi.org/10.1037/0096-3445.133.3.415

Chentsova-Dutton, Y. E., & Tsai, J. L. (2009). Understanding depression across cultures. In I. H. Gotlib & C. L. Hammen (Eds.), *Handbook of depression* (2nd ed., pp. 363–385). Guilford Press.

Chentsova-Dutton, Y. E., Ryder, A. G., & Tsai, J. L. (2014). Understanding depression across cultural contexts. In I. H. Gotlib & C. L. Hammen (Eds.), *Handbook of depression* (3rd ed., pp. 337–354). Guilford Press.

Chesler, P. (2010). Worldwide trends in honor killings. *Middle East Quarterly, 17*, 3–11.

Chess, S., & Thomas, A. (1986). *Temperament in clinical practice*. Guilford Press.

Chetty, R., Hendren, N., & Katz, L. F. (2016). The effects of exposure to better neighborhoods on children: New evidence from the Moving to Opportunity experiment. *The American Economic Review, 106*, 855–902. https://doi.org/10.1257/aer.20150572

Cheung, C. S., & Pomerantz, E. M. (2011). Parents' involvement in children's learning in the United States and China: Implications for children's academic and emotional adjustment. *Child Development, 82*, 932–950. https://doi.org/10.1111/j.1467-8624.2011.01582.x

Cheung, C. S.-S., & Pomerantz, E. M. (2015). Value development underlies the benefits of parents' involvement in children's learning: A longitudinal investigation in the United States and China. *Journal of Educational Psychology, 107*(1), 309–320. https://doi.org/10.1037/a0037458

Child Soldiers International. (2019). *Where are child soldiers?* https://www.child-soldiers.org/where-are-there-child-soldiers

Childers, J. B., & Tomasello, M. (2002). Two-year-olds learn novel nouns, verbs, and conventional actions from massed or distributed exposures. *Developmental Psychology, 38*, 967–978. https://doi.org/10.1037/0012-1649.38.6.967

Childers, J. B., Vaughan, J., & Burquest, D. A. (2007). Joint attention and word learning in Ngas-speaking toddlers in Nigeria. *Journal of Child Language, 34*, 199–225. https://doi.org/10.1017/S0305000906007835

Childress, H. (2000). *Landscapes of betrayal, landscapes of joy: Curtisville in the lives of its teenagers*. State University of New York Press.

Childs, C. P., & Greenfield, P. M. (1980). Informal modes of learning and teaching: The case of Zinacanteco weaving. In N. Warren (Ed.), *Studies in cross-cultural psychology* (pp. 269–316). Academic Press.

Chiu, L. (1972). A cross-cultural comparison of cognitive styles in Chinese and American children. *International Journal of Psychology, 7*, 235–242. https://doi.org/10.1080/00207597208246604

Chomsky, N. (1968). *Language and mind*. Harcourt, Brace & World.

Chouinard, M. M. (2007). Children's questions: A mechanism for cognitive development. *Monographs of the Society for Research in Child Development, 72*(1), vii–ix.

Chung, H. L., & Steinberg, L. (2006). Relations between neighborhood factors, parenting behaviors, peer deviance, and delinquency among serious juvenile offenders. *Developmental Psychology, 42*, 319–331. https://doi.org/10.1037/0012-1649.42.2.319

Cillessen, A. H. N., Schwartz, D., & Mayeux, L. (Eds.). (2011). *Popularity in the peer system*. Guilford Press.

Clahsen, H., Aveledo, F., & Roca, I. (2002). The development of regular and irregular verb inflection in Spanish child language. *Journal of Child Language, 29*, 591–622. https://doi.org/10.1017/S0305000902005172

Clancy, P. (1985). Acquisition of Japanese. In D. I. Slobin (Ed.), *The cross-linguistic study of language acquisition: Vol. 1. The data* (pp. 323–524). Erlbaum.

Clancy, P. (1999). The socialization of affect in Japanese mother-child conversation. *Journal of Pragmatics, 31*, 1397–1421. https://doi.org/10.1016/S0378-2166(98)00112-X

Cleveland, E. S., & Reese, E. (2005). Maternal structure and autonomy support in conversations about the past: Contributions to children's autobiographical memory. *Developmental Psychology, 41*(2), 376–388. https://doi.org/10.1037/0012-1649.41.2.376

Cocq, C. (2015). Mobile technology in Indigenous landscapes. In L. E. Dyson, S. Grant, & M. Hendriks (Eds.), *Indigenous people and mobile technologies* (p. 9). Routledge.

Cogos, S., Roué, M., & Roturier, S. (2017). Sami place names and maps: Transmitting knowledge of a cultural landscape in contemporary contexts. *Arctic, Antarctic, and Alpine Research, 49*, 43–51. https://doi.org/10.1657/AAAR0016-042

Cohen, D. (2001). Cultural variation: Considerations and implications. *Psychological Bulletin, 127*, 451–471. https://doi.org/10.1037/0033-2909.127.4.451

Cole, M. (1966). *Cultural psychology: A once and future discipline*. Harvard University Press.

Cole, M. (2005). Putting culture in the middle. In M. Cole (Ed.), *An introduction to Vygotsky* (2nd ed., pp. 199–226). Routledge.

Cole, M. (2006). Culture and cognitive development in phylogenetic, historical, and ontogenetic perspective. In D. Kuhn, R. S. Siegler, W. Damon, & R. M. Lerner (Eds.), *Handbook of child psychology: Vol. 2. Cognition, perception, and language* (6th ed., pp. 636–683). Wiley.

Cole, M., Gay, J., Glick, J., & Sharp, D. W. (1971). *The cultural context of learning and thinking*. Basic Books.

Cole, M., & Scribner, S. (1974). *Culture and thought*. Wiley.

Cole, P. M., Bruschi, C. J., & Tamang, B. L. (2002). Cultural differences in children's emotional reactions to difficult situations. *Child Development, 73*, 983–996. https://doi.org/10.1111/1467-8624.00451

Cole, P. M., & Tamang, B. L. (1998). Nepali children's ideas about emotional displays in hypothetical challenges. *Developmental Psychology, 34*, 640–646. https://doi.org/10.1037/0012-1649.34.4.640

Cole, P. M., & Tan, P. Z. (2015). Emotion socialization from a cultural perspective. In J. E. Grusec & P. D. Hastings (Eds.), *Handbook of socialization: Theory and research* (2nd ed., pp. 499–519). Guilford Press.

Collado, S., Corraliza, J. A., Staats, H., & Ruiz, M. (2015). Effect of frequency and mode of contact with nature on children's self-reported ecological behaviors. *Journal of Environmental Psychology, 41*, 65–73. https://doi.org/10.1016/j.jenvp.2014.11.001

Collins, L. (2018). The impact of paper versus digital map technology on students' spatial skill acquisition. *The Journal of Geography, 117*, 137–152. https://doi.org/10.1080/00221341.2017.1374990

Committee on the Rights of the Child. (n.d.). *Convention on the Rights of the Child*. United Nations Human Rights Office of the High Commissioner. https://www.ohchr.org/EN/ProfessionalInterest/Pages/CRC.aspx

Conant, L. L., Fastenau, P. S., Giordani, B., Boivin, M. J., Chounramany, C., Xaisida, S., Choulamountry, L., & Pholsena, P. (2003). Environmental influences on primary memory development: A cross-cultural study of memory span in Lao and American children. *Journal of Clinical and Experimental Neuropsychology, 25*, 1102–1116. https://doi.org/10.1076/jcen.25.8.1102.16722

Condon, R. G. (1987). *Inuit youth: Growth and change in the Canadian Arctic*. Rutgers University Press.

Conger, K. J., & Little, W. M. (2010). Sibling relationships during the transition to adulthood. *Child Development Perspectives, 4*, 87–94. https://doi.org/10.1111/j.1750-8606.2010.00123.x

Connolly, J., Furman, W., & Konarski, R. (2000). The role of peers in the emergence of heterosexual romantic relationships in adolescence. *Child Development, 71*, 1395–1408. https://doi.org/10.1111/1467-8624.00235

Coontz, S. (2006). *Marriage, a history: How love conquered marriage*. Penguin Books.

Cooper, M. L., Kuntsche, E., Levitt, A., Barber, L. L., & Wolf, S. (2016). A motivational perspective on substance use: Review of theory and research. In K. J. Sher (Ed.), *Oxford handbook of substance use disorders* (pp. 375–421). Oxford University Press.

Cooper, R. P., & Aslin, R. N. (1990). Preference for infant-directed speech in the first month after birth. *Child Development, 61,* 1584–1595. https://doi.org/10.2307/1130766

Corboz, J., Gibbs, A., & Jewkes, R. (2020). *Bacha posh* in Afghanistan: Factors associated with raising a girl as a boy. *Culture, Health & Sexuality, 22,* 585–598. https://doi.org/10.1080/13691058.2019.1616113

Corprew, C. S., III, & Cunningham, M. (2012). Educating tomorrow's men: Perceived school support, negative youth experiences, and bravado attitudes in African American adolescent males. *Education and Urban Society, 44,* 571–589. https://doi.org/10.1177/0013124511406534

Correa-Chávez, M., Mangione, H., & Black, K. (2015). In and out of the classroom: The intersection of learning and schooling across cultural communities. In L. A. Jensen (Ed.), *The Oxford handbook of human development and culture: An interdisciplinary perspective* (pp. 292–306). Oxford University Press.

Corsaro, W., & Rizzo, T. A. (1990). Disputes in the peer culture of American and Italian nursery-school children. In A. Grimshaw (Ed.), *Conflict talk: Sociolinguistic investigations of arguments in conversations* (pp. 21–66). Cambridge University Press.

Cote, L. R., Kwak, K., Putnick, D. L., Chung, H. J., & Bornstein, M. H. (2015). The acculturation of parenting cognitions: A comparison of South Korean, Korean immigrant, and European American mothers. *Journal of Cross-Cultural Psychology, 46,* 1115–1130. https://doi.org/10.1177/0022022115600259

Cowell, J. M., Lee, K., Malcolm-Smith, S., Selcuk, B., Zhou, X., & Decety, J. (2017). The development of generosity and moral cognition across five cultures. *Developmental Science, 20,* e12403. https://doi.org/10.1111/desc.12403

Coyne, S. M. (2016). Effects of viewing relational aggression on television on aggressive behavior in adolescents: A three-year longitudinal study. *Developmental Psychology, 52,* 284–295. https://doi.org/10.1037/dev0000068

Coyne, S. M., & Ostrov, J. M. (Eds.). (2018). *The development of relational aggression.* Oxford University Press.

Crabtree, S. (2014). *Value Africans place on education varies widely by country.* Gallup. http://www.gallup.com/poll/174332/value-africans-place-education-varies-widely-country.aspx

Crain-Thoreson, C., & Dale, P. S. (1992). Do early talkers become early readers? Linguistic precocity, preschool language and emergent literacy. *Developmental Psychology, 28,* 421–429. https://doi.org/10.1037/0012-1649.28.3.421

Crampton, J. W., & Krygier, J. (2006). An introduction to critical cartography. *ACME: An International E-Journal for Critical Geographies, 4,* 11–33.

Crick, N. R., & Dodge, K. A. (1994). A review and reformulation of social information-processing mechanisms in children's social adjustment. *Psychological Bulletin, 115,* 74–101. https://doi.org/10.1037/0033-2909.115.1.74

Criss, M. M., Smith, A. M., Morris, A. S., Liu, C., & Hubbard, R. L. (2017). Parents and peers as protective factors among adolescents exposed to neighborhood risk. *Journal of Applied Developmental Psychology, 53,* 127–138. https://doi.org/10.1016/j.appdev.2017.10.004

Crosnoe, R., & Benner, A. D. (2015). Children at school. In M. H. Bornstein & T. Leventhal (Eds.), *Handbook of child psychology and developmental science: Vol. 4. Ecological settings and processes* (7th ed., pp. 268–204). Wiley. https://doi.org/10.1002/9781118963418.childpsy407

Cui, L., Morris, A. S., Criss, M. M., Houltberg, B. J., & Silk, J. S. (2014). Parental psychological control and adolescent adjustment: The role of adolescent emotion regulation. *Parenting: Science and Practice, 14,* 47–67. https://doi.org/10.1080/15295192.2014.880018

Cummings, E. M., Wilson, J., & Shamir, H. (2003). Reactions of Chilean and US children to marital discord. *International Journal of Behavioral Development, 27,* 437–444. https://doi.org/10.1080/01650250344000055

Currie, C., Zanotti, C., Morgan, A., Currie, D., de Looze, M., Roberts, C., Samdal, O., Smith, O. R. F., & Barnekow, V. (2012). *Social determinants of health and well-being among young people. Health Behaviour in School-aged Children (HBSC) study: International report from the 2009/2010 survey.* World Health Organization.

Dahl, A., & Killen, M. (2018). A developmental perspective on the origins of morality in infancy and early childhood. *Frontiers in Psychology, 9,* 1736. https://doi.org/10.3389/fpsyg.2018.01736

d'Ailly, H. (2003). Children's autonomy and perceived control in learning: A model of motivation and achievement in Taiwan. *Journal of Educational Psychology, 95*(1), 84–96. https://doi.org/10.1037/0022-0663.95.1.84

Daiute, C. (2014). *Narrative inquiry: A dynamic approach.* Sage. https://doi.org/10.4135/9781544365442

D'Andrade, R. G. (1984). Cultural meaning systems. In R. A. Shweder & R. A. LeVine (Eds.), *Culture theory: Essays on mind, self, and emotion* (pp. 88–119). Cambridge University Press.

Daniels, H. (Ed.). (2017). *Introduction to Vygotsky* (3rd ed.). Routledge/Taylor and Francis. https://doi.org/10.4324/9781315647654

Darling, N., Cumsille, P., & Peña-Alampay, L. (2005). Rules, legitimacy of parental authority, and obligation to obey in Chile, the Philippines, and the United States. In J. Smetana (Ed.), *New directions for child and adolescent development. Changing boundaries of parental authority during adolescence* (pp. 47–60). Jossey-Bass. https://doi.org/10.1002/cd.127

Darling, N., & Steinberg, L. (1993). Parenting style as context: An integrative model. *Psychological Bulletin, 113,* 487–496. https://doi.org/10.1037/0033-2909.113.3.487

Darwin, C. (1872). *The expression of emotion in man and animals.* John Murray. https://doi.org/10.1037/10001-000

Dasen, P. R. (1974). The influence of ecology, culture, and European contact on cognitive development in Australian Aborigines. In J. W. Berry & P. R. Dasen (Eds.), *Culture and cognition: Readings in cross-cultural psychology* (pp. 381–408). Methuen.

Dasen, P. R. (1977). *Piagetian psychology: Cross-cultural contributions.* Gardner Press.

Dasen, P. R., Inhelder, B., Lavallée, M., & Retschitzki, J. (1978). *Naissance de l'intelligence chez l'enfant Bauolé de Côte d'Ivoire* [Birth of intelligence with the child Bauolé from Ivory Coast]. Hans Huber.

Davies, P. T., & Cummings, E. M. (1994). Marital conflict and child adjustment: An emotional security hypothesis. *Psychological Bulletin, 116,* 387–411. https://doi.org/10.1037/0033-2909.116.3.387

Davies, S. G. (2010). *Gender diversity in Indonesia: Sexuality, Islam and queer selves.* Routledge. https://doi.org/10.4324/9780203860953

Davis, S. S., & Davis, D. A. (1989). *Adolescence in a Moroccan town.* Rutgers University Press.

Deater-Deckard, K. (2008). *Parenting stress.* Yale University Press.

Deater-Deckard, K., Godwin, J., Lansford, J. E., Bacchini, D., Bombi, A. S., Bornstein, M. H., Chang, L., Di Giunta, L., Dodge, K. A., Malone, P. S., Oburu, P., Pastorelli, C., Skinner, A. T., Sorbring, E., Steinberg, L., Tapanya, S., Alampay, L. P., Uribe Tirado, L. M., Zelli, A., & Al-Hassan, S. M. (2018). Within- and between-person and group variance in behavior and beliefs in cross-cultural longitudinal data. *Journal of Adolescence, 62,* 207–217. https://doi.org/10.1016/j.adolescence.2017.06.002

Deater-Deckard, K., Godwin, J., Lansford, J. E., Tirado, L. M. U., Yotanyamaneewong, S., Alampay, L. P., Al-Hassan, S. M., Bacchini, D., Bornstein, M. H., Chang, L., Di Giunta, L., Dodge, K. A., Oburu, P., Pastorelli, C., Skinner, A. T., Sorbring, E., Steinberg, L., & Tapanya, S. (2019). Chaos, danger, and maternal parenting in families: Links with adolescent adjustment in low- and middle-income countries. *Developmental Science, 22*(5), e12855. https://doi.org/10.1111/desc.12855

Deater-Deckard, K., Lansford, J. E., Malone, P. S., Alampay, L. P., Sorbring, E., Bacchini, D., Bombi, A. S., Bornstein, M. H., Chang, L., Di Giunta, L., Dodge, K. A., Oburu, P., Pastorelli, C., Skinner, A. T., Tapanya, S., Tirado, L. M., Zelli, A., & Al-Hassan, S. M. (2011). The association between parental warmth and control in thirteen cultural groups. *Journal of Family Psychology, 25*, 790–794. https://doi.org/10.1037/a0025120

De Boysson-Bardies, B., Vihman, M., Roug-Hellichius, L., Durand, C., Landberg, I., & Arao, F. (1992). Material evidence of infant selection from target language: A cross-linguistic study. In C. A. Ferguson, L. Menn, & C. Stoel-Gammon (Eds.), *Phonological development* (pp. 369–391). York Press.

de Castro, B., Veerman, J. W., Koops, W., Bosch, J. D., & Monshouwer, H. J. (2002). Hostile attribution of intent and aggressive behavior: A meta-analysis. *Child Development, 73*, 916–934. https://doi.org/10.1111/1467-8624.00447

de Guzman, M. R. T., Edwards, C. P., & Carlo, G. (2005). Prosocial behaviors in context: A study of the Gikuyu children of Ngecha, Kenya. *Journal of Applied Developmental Psychology, 26*, 542–558. https://doi.org/10.1016/j.appdev.2005.06.006

de Jong-Gierveld, J., & Merz, E. M. (2013). Parents' partnership decision making after divorce or widowhood: The role of the (step)children. *Journal of Marriage and the Family, 75*, 1098–1113. https://doi.org/10.1111/jomf.12061

DeLay, D., Shen, M., Cook, R. E., Zhao, S., Logis, H., & French, D. C. (2020). Peer relationship dynamics associated with the onset and progression of adolescents' tobacco and alcohol use in China.

de Léon, L. (1998). The emergent participant: Interactive patterns in the socialization of Tzotzil (Maya) infants. *Journal of Linguistic Anthropology, 8*, 131–161. https://doi.org/10.1525/jlin.1998.8.2.131

Delgado-Gaitan, C. (1994). Socializing young children in Mexican-American families: An intergenerational perspective. In P. M. Greenfield & R. R. Cocking (Eds.), *Cross-cultural roots of minority child development* (pp. 55–86). Erlbaum.

de Munck, V. C. (1993). The dialectics and norms of self interest: Reciprocity among cross-siblings in a Sri Lankan Muslim community. In C. W. Nuckolls (Ed.), *Siblings in South Asia: Brothers and sisters in cultural context* (pp. 143–162). Guilford Press.

Denham, S. A., Bassett, H. H., & Wyatt, T. (2015). The socialization of emotional competence. In J. E. Grusec & P. D. Hastings (Eds.), *Handbook of socialization: Theory and research* (2nd ed., pp. 590–613). Guilford Press.

Dennis, W. (1940). Does culture appreciably affect patterns of infant behavior? *The Journal of Social Psychology, 12*, 305–317. https://doi.org/10.1080/00224545.1940.9921475

DeRosier, M. E., & Kupersmidt, J. B. (1991). Costa Rican children's perceptions of their social networks. *Developmental Psychology, 27*, 656–662. https://doi.org/10.1037/0012-1649.27.4.656

de Tocqueville, A. (2000). *Democracy in America* (S. D. Grant, Trans.). Hackett Publishing. https://doi.org/10.7208/chicago/9780226924564.001.0001

Dettori, E., & Gupta, G. R. (2018). Gender equity and the SDGs: Collective impact for change. In J. E. Lansford & P. Banati (Eds.), *Handbook of adolescent development research and its impact on global policy* (pp. 412–431). Oxford University Press.

deVries, M. W. (1984). Temperament and infant mortality among the Masai of East Africa. *The American Journal of Psychiatry, 141*, 1189–1194. https://doi.org/10.1176/ajp.141.10.1189

deVries, M. W., & Sameroff, A. J. (1984). Culture and temperament: Influences on infant temperament in three East African societies. *American Journal of Orthopsychiatry, 54*, 83–96. https://doi.org/10.1111/j.1939-0025.1984.tb01477.x

de Waal, F. B. M. (1996). Conflict as negotiation. In W. C. McGrew, L. F. Marchant, & T. Nishida (Eds.), *Great ape societies* (pp. 159–172). Cambridge University Press. https://doi.org/10.1017/CBO9780511752414.014

DeWall, C. N., Anderson, C. A., & Bushman, B. J. (2012). Aggression. In H. Tennen, J. Suls, & I. B. Weiner (Eds.), *Handbook of psychology* (2nd ed., Vol. 5, pp. 449–466). Wiley.

Diamond, J. (2012). *The world until yesterday: What can we learn from traditional societies?* Penguin Books.

Diaz, R. M. (1983). Thought and two languages: The impact of bilingualism on cognitive development. *Review of Research in Education, 10,* 23–54. https://doi.org/10.2307/1167134

Diener, C. I., & Dweck, C. S. (1978). An analysis of learned helplessness: Continuous changes in performance, strategy and achievement cognitions following failure. *Journal of Personality and Social Psychology, 36,* 451–462. https://doi.org/10.1037/0022-3514.36.5.451

Dijkstra, J. K., Berger, C., & Lindenberg, S. (2011). Do physical and relational aggression explain adolescents' friendship selection? The competing roles of network characteristics, gender, and social status. *Aggressive Behavior, 37,* 417–429. https://doi.org/10.1002/ab.20402

Dimitrova, R., Chasiotis, A., & van de Vijver, F. (2016). Adjustment outcomes of immigrant children and youth in Europe: A meta-analysis. *European Psychologist, 21,* 150–162. https://doi.org/10.1027/1016-9040/a000246

Dishion, T. J., Dodge, K. A., & Lansford, J. E. (2006). Findings and recommendations: A blueprint to minimize deviant peer influence in youth interventions and programs. In K. A. Dodge, T. J. Dishion, & J. E. Lansford (Eds.), *Deviant peer influences in programs for youth* (pp. 366–394). Guilford Press.

Dishion, T. J., & Patterson, G. R. (2006). The development and ecology of antisocial behavior in children and adolescents. In D. Cicchetti & D. J. Cohen (Eds.), *Developmental psychopathology* (pp. 503–541). Wiley.

Dishion, T. J., Spacklen, K. M., Andrews, D. W., & Patterson, G. R. (1996). Deviancy training in male adolescent friendships. *Behavior Therapy, 27,* 373–390. https://doi.org/10.1016/S0005-7894(96)80023-2

Dittrichova, J. (1969). The development of sleep in infancy. In R. J. Robinson (Ed.), *Brain and early behaviour* (pp. 193–200). Academic Press.

Dodge, K. A., Dishion, T. J., & Lansford, J. E. (Eds.). (2006). *Deviant peer influences in programs for youth.* Guilford Press.

Dodge, K. A., Godwin, J., & Conduct Problems Prevention Research Group. (2013). Social-information-processing patterns mediate the impact of preventive intervention on adolescent antisocial behavior. *Psychological Science, 24,* 456–465. https://doi.org/10.1177/0956797612457394

Dodge, K. A., Lansford, J. E., Burks, V. S., Bates, J. E., Pettit, G. S., Fontaine, R., & Price, J. M. (2003). Peer rejection and social information-processing factors in the development of aggressive behavior problems in children. *Child Development, 74,* 374–393. https://doi.org/10.1111/1467-8624.7402004

Dodge, K. A., Malone, P. S., Lansford, J. E., Sorbring, E., Skinner, A. T., Tapanya, S., Tirado, L. M., Zelli, A., Alampay, L. P., Al-Hassan, S. M., Bacchini, D., Bombi, A. S., Bornstein, M. H., Chang, L., Deater-Deckard, K., Di Giunta, L., Oburu, P., & Pastorelli, C. (2015). Hostile attributional bias and aggressive behavior in global context. *Proceedings of the National Academy of Sciences of the United States of America, 112,* 9310–9315. https://doi.org/10.1073/pnas.1418572112

Douglas, E. M., & Straus, M. A. (2006). Assault and injury of dating partners by university students in 19 countries and its relation to corporal punishment experienced as a child. *European Journal of Criminology, 3,* 293–318. https://doi.org/10.1177/1477370806065584

Downs, R. M. (2014). Coming of age in the geospatial revolution: The geographic self re-defined. *Human Development, 57,* 35–57. https://doi.org/10.1159/000358319

Dronkers, J. (2016). *Cohabitation, marriage, and union instability in Europe.* Institute for Family Studies.

Dube, A., & Kaplan, E. (2012). Occupy Wall Street and the political economy of inequality. *The Economists' Voice, 9*(3). https://doi.org/10.1515/1553-3832.1899

Duell, N., Steinberg, L., Chein, J., Al-Hassan, S. M., Bacchini, D., Lei, C., Chaudhary, N., Di Giunta, L., Dodge, K. A., Fanti, K. A., Lansford, J. E., Malone, P. S., Oburu, P., Pastorelli, C., Skinner, A. T., Sorbring, E., Tapanya, S., Uribe Tirado, L. M., & Alampay, L. P. (2016). Interaction of reward seeking and self-regulation in the prediction of risk taking: A cross-national test of the dual systems model. *Developmental Psychology, 52,* 1593–1605. https://doi.org/10.1037/dev0000152

Duku, E., Janus, M., & Brinkman, S. (2015). Investigation of the cross-national equivalence of a measurement of early child development. *Child Indicators Research, 8,* 471–489. https://doi.org/10.1007/s12187-014-9249-3

Dunn, J. (1988). *The beginnings of social understanding.* Harvard University Press. https://doi.org/10.4159/harvard.9780674330610

Dunn, J. (2004). *Children's friendships.* Blackwell.

Dunn, J., & Kendrick, C. (1982). The speech of two- and three-year-olds to infant siblings: 'Baby talk' and the context of communication. *Journal of Child Language, 9,* 579–595. https://doi.org/10.1017/S030500090000492X

Dunn, J., & Munn, P. (1987). The development of justification in disputes. *Developmental Psychology, 23,* 791–798. https://doi.org/10.1037/0012-1649.23.6.791

Dunsmore, J. C., Her, P., Halberstadt, A. G., & Perez-Rivera, M. B. (2009). Parents' beliefs about emotions and children's recognition of parents' emotions. *Journal of Nonverbal Behavior, 33,* 121–140. https://doi.org/10.1007/s10919-008-0066-6

Duranti, A., Ochs, E., & Schieffelin, B. (Eds.). (2011). *The handbook of language socialization.* Wiley-Blackwell. https://doi.org/10.1002/9781444342901

Dweck, C. A. (2006). *Mindset: The new psychology of success.* Random House.

Dyson, J. (2010). Friendship in practice: Girls' work in the Indian Himalayas. *American Ethnologist, 37,* 482–498. https://doi.org/10.1111/j.1548-1425.2010.01267.x

Eaton, M. J., & Dembo, M. H. (1997). Differences in the motivational beliefs of Asian-American and non-Asian students. *Journal of Educational Psychology, 89,* 433–440. https://doi.org/10.1037/0022-0663.89.3.433

Ebstyne King, P., & Furrow, J. L. (2004). Religion as a resource for positive youth development: Religion, social capital, and moral outcomes. *Developmental Psychology, 40*(5), 703–713. https://doi.org/10.1037/0012-1649.40.5.703

Edwards, C. P. (2000). Children's play in cross-cultural perspective: A new look at the "Six Cultures" study. *Cross-Cultural Research: The Journal of Comparative Social Science, 34,* 318–338. https://doi.org/10.1177/106939710003400402

Eggum-Wilkens, N. D., Zhang, L., & An, D. (2018). An exploratory study of Eastern Ugandan adolescents' descriptions of social withdrawal. *Journal of Adolescence, 67,* 153–157. https://doi.org/10.1016/j.adolescence.2018.06.011

Eisenberg, A. R., & Garvey, C. (1981). Children's use of verbal strategies in resolving disputes. *Discourse Processes, 4,* 149–170. https://doi.org/10.1080/01638538109544512

Eisenberg, N. (2000). Emotion, regulation, and moral development. *Annual Review of Psychology, 51,* 665–697. https://doi.org/10.1146/annurev.psych.51.1.665

Eisenberg, N., Spinrad, T. L., & Knafo-Noam, A. (2015). Prosocial development. In M. E. Lamb & C. Garcia Coll (Eds.), *Handbook of child psychology and developmental science: Vol. 3. Social, emotional, and personality development* (7th ed., pp. 610–656). Wiley. https://doi.org/10.1002/9781118963418.childpsy315

Ekman, P. (1994). Strong evidence for universals in facial expressions: A reply to Russell's mistaken critique. *Psychological Bulletin, 115,* 268–287. https://doi.org/10.1037/0033-2909.115.2.268

Ekman, P., Friesen, W. V., O'Sullivan, M., Chan, A., Diacoyanni-Tarlatzis, I., Heider, K., Krause, R., LeCompte, W. A., Pitcairn, T., Ricci-Bitti, P. E., Scherer, K., Tomita, M., & Tzavaras, A. (1987). Universals and cultural differences in the judgments of facial expressions of emotion. *Journal of Personality and Social Psychology, 53*, 712–717. https://doi.org/10.1037/0022-3514.53.4.712

Eldering, L. (1995). Child-rearing in bi-cultural settings: A culture-ecological approach. *Psychology and Developing Societies, 7*, 133–153. https://doi.org/10.1177/097133369500700203

Elliot, A. J., Dweck, C. S., & Yeager, D. S. (Eds.). (2017). *Handbook of competence and motivation: Theory and application* (2nd ed.). Guilford Press.

Elliott, J., & Tudge, J. (2007). The impact of the west on post-Soviet Russian education: Change and resistance to change. *Comparative Education, 43*, 93–112. https://doi.org/10.1080/03050060601162420

Ellis, S., & Gauvain, M. (1992). Social and cultural influences on children's collaborative interactions. In L. T. Winegar & J. Valsiner (Eds.), *Children's development within social context* (pp. 155–180). Erlbaum.

Ellsworth, C. P., Muir, D. W., & Hains, S. M. J. (1993). Social competence and person-object differentiation: An analysis of the still-face effect. *Developmental Psychology, 29*, 63–73. https://doi.org/10.1037/0012-1649.29.1.63

Ember, C. R. (1973). Feminine task assignment and the social behavior of boys. *Ethos, 1*(4), 424–439. https://doi.org/10.1525/eth.1973.1.4.02a00050

Ember, C. R., & Ember, M. (2001a). *Cross-cultural research methods*. AltaMira.

Ember, C. R., & Ember, M. (2001b). Father absence and male aggression: A re-examination of the comparative evidence. *Ethos, 29*(3), 296–314. https://doi.org/10.1525/eth.2001.29.3.296

Ember, C. R., & Ember, M. (2005). Explaining corporal punishment of children: A cross-cultural study. *American Anthropologist, 107*, 609–619. https://doi.org/10.1525/aa.2005.107.4.609

Endendijk, J. J., Groeneveld, M. G., & Mesman, J. (2018). The gendered family process model: An integrative framework of gender in the family. *Archives of Sexual Behavior, 47*, 877–904. https://doi.org/10.1007/s10508-018-1185-8

Engle, P. L., Black, M. M., Behrman, J. R., Cabral de Mello, M., Gertler, P. J., Kapiriri, L., Martorell, R., Young, M. E., & the International Child Development Steering Group. (2007). Strategies to avoid the loss of developmental potential in more than 200 million children in the developing world. *The Lancet, 369*, 229–242. https://doi.org/10.1016/S0140-6736(07)60112-3

Ensor, R., Marks, A., Jacobs, L., & Hughes, C. (2010). Trajectories of antisocial behaviour towards siblings predict antisocial behaviour towards peers. *Journal of Child Psychiatry and Psychology, 51*, 1208–1216. https://doi.org/10.1111/j.1469-7610.2010.02276.x

Enzmann, D., Kivivuori, J., Haen Marshall, I., Steketee, M., Hough, M., & Killias, M. (2018). *A global perspective on young people as offenders and victims: First results from the ISRD3 Study*. Springer. https://doi.org/10.1007/978-3-319-63233-9

Erikson, E. H. (1963). *Childhood and society* (2nd ed.). W.W. Norton.

Erikson, E. H. (1968). *Identity, youth, and crisis*. Norton.

Ervin-Tripp, S. (1979). Children's verbal turn taking. In E. Ochs & B. Schieffelin (Eds.), *Developmental pragmatics* (pp. 391–414). Academic Press.

Ervin-Tripp, S. M. (1982). Ask and it shall be given you: Children's requests. In H. Byrnes (Ed.), *Contemporary perceptions of language: Interdisciplinary dimensions* (pp. 232–245). Georgetown University Press.

Eurostat. (2015). *Being young in Europe today: Family and society*. http://ec.europa.eu/eurostat/statistics-explained/index.php/Being_young_in_Europe_today_-_family_and_society

Evans, G. W. (2004). The environment of childhood poverty. *American Psychologist, 59*, 77–92. https://doi.org/10.1037/0003-066X.59.2.77

Evans, G. W., & Hygge, S. (2007). Noise and performance in children and adults. In L. M. Luzon & D. Prasher (Eds.), *Noise and its effects* (pp. 549–566). Wiley.

Evans, G. W., Wells, N. M., & Schamberg, M. A. (2010). The role of the environment in SES and obesity. In L. Dube, A. Bechara, A. Dagher, D. Drewnoski, J. LeBel, J. P. James, D. Richard, & R. Y. Yada (Eds.), *Obesity prevention: The role of society and brain on individual behavior* (pp. 713–725). Elsevier. https://doi.org/10.1016/B978-0-12-374387-9.00057-X

Evans, W. P., Owens, P. E., & Marsh, S. C. (2005). Environmental factors, locus of control, and adolescent suicide risk. *Child & Adolescent Social Work Journal, 22*, 301–319. https://doi.org/10.1007/s10560-005-0013-x

Ewert, A., Place, G., & Sibthorp, J. (2005). Early-life outdoor experiences and an individual's environmental attitudes. *Leisure Sciences, 27*, 225–239. https://doi.org/10.1080/01490400590930853

Facio, A., Resett, S., Micocci, F., & Mistrorigo, C. (2007). Emerging adulthood in Argentina: An age of diversity and possibilities. *Child Development Perspectives, 1*, 115–118. https://doi.org/10.1111/j.1750-8606.2007.00025.x

Farver, J. A. M. (1999). Activity setting analysis: A model for examining the role of culture in development. In A. Göncü (Ed.), *Children's engagement in the world: Sociocultural perspectives* (pp. 99–127). Cambridge University Press.

Farver, J. A. M., & Howes, C. (1993). Cultural differences in American and Mexican mother-child pretend play. *Merrill-Palmer Quarterly, 39*, 344–358.

Farver, J. A. M., & Shin, Y. L. (1997). Social pretend play in Korean- and Anglo-American preschoolers. *Child Development, 68*, 544–556. https://doi.org/10.2307/1131677

Farver, J. A. M., & Wimbarti, S. (1995). Paternal participation in toddlers' pretend play. *Social Development, 4*, 17–31. https://doi.org/10.1111/j.1467-9507.1995.tb00048.x

Fass, P. S. (2007). *Children of a new world: Essays in society, culture, and the world.* New York University Press.

Feinberg, M. E., Solmeyer, A. R., & McHale, S. M. (2012). The third rail of family systems: Sibling relationships, mental and behavioral health, and preventive intervention in childhood and adolescence. *Clinical Child and Family Psychology Review, 15*, 43–57. https://doi.org/10.1007/s10567-011-0104-5

Feinman, S. (1982). Social referencing in infancy. *Merrill-Palmer Quarterly, 28*, 445–470.

Feng, W., Gu, B., & Cai, Y. (2016). The end of China's one-child policy. *Studies in Family Planning, 47*, 83–86. https://doi.org/10.1111/j.1728-4465.2016.00052.x

Fenson, L., Dale, P. S., Reznick, S. J., Bates, E., Thal, D. J., & Pethick, S. J. (1994). Variability in early communicative development. *Monographs of the Society for Research in Child Development, 59* (Serial No. 242).

Ferguson, K. T., Cassells, R. C., MacAllister, J. W., & Evans, G. W. (2013). The physical environment and child development: An international review. *International Journal of Psychology, 48*, 437–468. https://doi.org/10.1080/00207594.2013.804190

Fernald, A. (1992). Meaningful melodies in mothers' speech to infants. In H. Papousek, U. Jurgens, & M. Papousek (Eds.), *Nonverbal vocal communication* (pp. 262–282). Cambridge University Press.

Fernald, A., & Morikawa, H. (1993). Common themes and cultural variations in Japanese and American mothers' speech to infants. *Child Development, 64*, 637–656. https://doi.org/10.2307/1131208

Finkelhor, D., Turner, H., Shattuck, A., Hamby, S., & Kracke, K. (2015). *Children's exposure to violence, crime, and abuse: An update.* U.S. Department of Justice, Office of Justice Programs, Office of Juvenile Justice and Delinquency Prevention.

Fiske, A. P. (1992). The four elementary forms of sociality: Framework for a unified theory of social relations. *Psychological Review, 99*, 689–723. https://doi.org/10.1037/0033-295X.99.4.689

Fitneva, S. A., & Matsui, T. (2015). The emergence and development of language across cultures. In L. A. Jensen (Ed.), *The Oxford handbook of human development and culture* (pp. 111–126). Oxford University Press.

Flege, J. E., Yeni-Komshian, G. H., & Liu, S. (1999). Age constraints on second-language acquisition. *Journal of Memory and Language, 41*, 78–104. https://doi.org/10.1006/jmla.1999.2638

Flouri, E., Mavroveli, S., & Tzavidis, N. (2012). Cognitive ability, neighborhood deprivation, and young children's emotional and behavioral problems. *Social Psychiatry and Psychiatric Epidemiology, 47*, 985–992. https://doi.org/10.1007/s00127-011-0406-4

Flynn, E. G., Laland, K. N., Kendal, R. L., & Kendal, J. R. (2013). Target article with commentaries: Developmental niche construction. *Developmental Science, 16*, 296–313. https://doi.org/10.1111/desc.12030

Fontaine, R. G., Yang, C., Dodge, K. A., Pettit, G. S., & Bates, J. E. (2009). Development of Response Evaluation and Decision (RED) and antisocial behavior in childhood and adolescence. *Developmental Psychology, 45*, 447–459. https://doi.org/10.1037/a0014142

Fredricks, J. A., & Eccles, J. S. (2006). Extracurricular involvement and adolescent adjustment: Impact of duration, number of activities, and breadth of participation. *Applied Developmental Science, 10*, 132–146. https://doi.org/10.1207/s1532480xads1003_3

Freedman, D. G. (1974). *Human infancy: An evolutionary perspective*. Erlbaum.

Freire, P. (1968). *Pedagogy of the oppressed*. Seabury Press.

French, D. C. (2015). Cultural templates for child and adolescent friendships. In L. A. Jensen (Ed.), *Oxford handbook of human development and culture: An interdisciplinary perspective* (pp. 425–437). Oxford University Press.

French, D. C., Bae, A., Pidada, S., & Lee, O. (2006). Friendships of Indonesian, South Korean, and U.S. college students. *Personal Relationships, 13*, 69–81. https://doi.org/10.1111/j.1475-6811.2006.00105.x

French, D. C., Chen, X., Chung, J., Li, M., Chen, H., & Li, D. (2011). Four children and one toy: Chinese and Canadian children faced with potential conflict over a limited resource. *Child Development, 82*, 830–841. https://doi.org/10.1111/j.1467-8624.2011.01581.x

French, D. C., & Cheung, H. S. (2018). Peer relationships. In J. E. Lansford & P. Banati (Eds.), *Handbook of adolescent development research and its impact on global policy* (pp. 130–149). Oxford University Press.

French, D. C., Eisenberg, N., Purwono, U., & Sallquist, J. A. (2012). Indonesian Muslim adolescents and the ecology of religion. In G. Trommsdorff & X. Chen (Eds.), *Values, religion, and culture in adolescent development* (pp. 146–163). Cambridge University Press. https://doi.org/10.1017/CBO9781139013659.009

French, D. C., Eisenberg, N., Vaughan, J., Purwono, U., & Suryanti, T. A. (2008). Religious involvement and the social competence and adjustment of Indonesian Muslim adolescents. *Developmental Psychology, 44*, 597–611. https://doi.org/10.1037/0012-1649.44.2.597

French, D. C., Lee, O., & Pidada, S. (2006). Friendships of Indonesian, South Korean, and U. S. youth: Exclusivity, intimacy, enhancement of worth, and conflict. In X. Chen, D. C. French, & B. H. Schneider (Eds.), *Peer relationships in cultural context* (pp. 379–402). Cambridge University Press. https://doi.org/10.1017/CBO9780511499739.017

French, D. C., Pidada, S., Denoma, J., McDonald, K., & Lawton, A. (2005). Reported peer conflicts of children in the United States and Indonesia. *Social Development, 14*, 458–472. https://doi.org/10.1111/j.1467-9507.2005.00311.x

French, D. C., Pidada, S., & Victor, A. (2005). Friendships of Indonesian and United States youth. *International Journal of Behavioral Development, 29*, 304–313. https://doi.org/10.1177/01650250544000080

French, D. C., Purwono, U., & Rodkin, P. (2014). Indonesian Muslim adolescents' use of tobacco and alcohol: Associations with use by friends and network affiliates. *Merrill-Palmer Quarterly, 60*, 385–402. https://doi.org/10.13110/merrpalmquar1982.60.4.0385

French, D. C., Riansari, M., Pidada, S., Nelwan, P., & Buhrmester, D. (2001). Social support of Indonesian and U.S. children and adolescents by family members and friends. *Merrill-Palmer Quarterly, 47*, 377–394. https://doi.org/10.1353/mpq.2001.0015

Friedlmeier, W., Corapci, F., & Benga, O. (2015). Early emotional development in cultural perspective. In L. A. Jensen (Ed.), *The Oxford handbook of human development and culture* (pp. 127–148). Oxford University Press.

Friedlmeier, W., & Trommsdorff, G. (1999). Toddler's emotion regulation in stressful situations: A cross-cultural comparison between Japanese and German children. *Journal of Cross-Cultural Psychology, 30*, 684–711. https://doi.org/10.1177/0022022199030006002

Friend, T. (2003). *Indonesian destinies*. Harvard University Press.

Fristad, M. A., & Black, S. R. (2018). Mood disorders in childhood and adolescence. In J. N. Butcher & P. C. Kendall (Eds.), *APA handbook of psychopathology: Vol. 2. Child and adolescent psychopathology* (pp. 253–277). American Psychological Association. https://doi.org/10.1037/0000065-013

Fry, D. P. (1988). Intercommunity differences in aggression among Zapotec children. *Child Development, 59*, 1008–1019. https://doi.org/10.2307/1130267

Fry, D. P. (2000). Conflict management in cross-cultural perspective. In F. Aureli & F. B. M. de Waal (Eds.), *Natural conflict resolution* (pp. 334–351). University of California Press.

Fukuyama, F. (2011). *The origins of political order: From prehumen times to the French revolution*. Farrar, Straus, and Giroux.

Fuligni, A. J. (1998). Authority, autonomy, and parent-adolescent conflict and cohesion: A study of adolescents from Mexican, Chinese, Filipino, and European backgrounds. *Developmental Psychology, 34*, 782–792. https://doi.org/10.1037/0012-1649.34.4.782

Fuligni, A. J., & Stevenson, H. W. (1995). Time use and mathematics achievement among American, Chinese, and Japanese high school students. *Child Development, 66*, 830–842. https://doi.org/10.2307/1131953

Fuller, S. (2008). Job mobility and wage trajectories for men and women in the United States. *American Sociological Review, 73*, 158–183. https://doi.org/10.1177/000312240807300108

Fung, H. H., Stoeber, F. S., Yeung, D. Y.-I., & Lang, F. R. (2008). Cultural specificity of socioemotional selectivity: Age differences in social network composition among Germans and Hong Kong Chinese. *The Journals of Gerontology, Series B, 63*, P156–P164. https://doi.org/10.1093/geronb/63.3.P156

Gabbiadini, A., Riva, P., Andrighetto, L., Volpato, C., & Bushman, B. J. (2014). Interactive effect of moral disengagement and violent video games on self-control, cheating, and aggression. *Social Psychological & Personality Science, 5*, 451–458. https://doi.org/10.1177/1948550613509286

Gai, X., & Lan, G. (2013). Development of the positive development questionnaire for college students. *Studies of Psychology and Behavior, 11*, 786–791.

Galea, S., Ahern, J., Rudenstine, S., Wallace, Z., & Vlahov, D. (2005). Urban built environment and depression: A multilevel analysis. *Journal of Epidemiology and Community Health, 59*, 822–827. https://doi.org/10.1136/jech.2005.033084

Galla, C. K. (2016). Indigenous language revitalization, promotion, and education: Functions of digital technology. *Computer Assisted Language Learning, 29*, 1137–1151. https://doi.org/10.1080/09588221.2016.1166137

Galster, G. C. (2014). *How neighborhoods affect health, well-being, and young people's futures.* MacArthur Foundation.

Ganong, L. H., Coleman, M., & Russell, L. T. (2015). Children in diverse families. In M. H. Bornstein & T. Leventhal (Eds.), *Handbook of child psychology and developmental science: Vol. 4. Ecological settings and processes* (7th ed., pp. 1–42). Wiley. https://doi.org/10.1002/9781118963418.childpsy404

Garcia, D. M., & Sheehan, M. C. (2016). Extreme weather-driven disasters and children's health. *International Journal of Health Services, 46*, 79–105. https://doi.org/10.1177/0020731415625254

García Coll, C., Motti-Stefanidi, F., Oppedal, B., Pavlopoulos, V., Strohmeier, D., & van de Vijver, F. (2015). *Positive development of immigrant youth: Why bother?* Mission statement formulated in Hydra, Greece, at the Experts' Meeting on Immigrant Youth Adaptation and Well-Being.

Gartstein, M. A., Gonzalez, C., Carranza, J. A., Ahadi, S. A., Ye, R., Rothbart, M. K., & Yang, S. W. (2006). Studying cross-cultural differences in the development of infant temperament: People's Republic of China, the United States of America, and Spain. *Child Psychiatry and Human Development, 37*, 145–161.

Garvey, C., & Shantz, C. U. (1992). Conflict talk. In C. U. Shantz & W. W. Hartup (Eds.), *Conflict in child and adolescent development* (pp. 93–121). Cambridge University Press.

Gaskins, S. (2000). Children's daily activities in a Maya village: A culturally grounded description. *Cross-Cultural Research: The Journal of Comparative Social Science, 34*, 375–389. https://doi.org/10.1177/106939710003400405

Gaskins, S. (2006). The cultural organization of Yucatec Maya children's social interaction. In X. Chen, D. C. French, & B. H. Schnieder (Eds.), *Peer relationships in cultural context* (pp. 283–309). Cambridge University Press. https://doi.org/10.1017/CBO9780511499739.013

Gaskins, S., & Paradise, R. (2010). Learning through observation in daily life. In D. F. Lancy, S. Gaskins, & J. Bock (Eds.), *The anthropology of learning in childhood* (pp. 85–117). Alta-Mira Press.

Gatta, M., Miscioscia, M., Svanellini, L., Peraro, C., & Simonelli, A. (2017). A psychological perspective on preterm children: The influence of contextual factors on quality of family interactions. *BioMed Research International, 2017*, 9152627. https://doi.org/10.1155/2017/9152627

Gauvain, M. (1993). Spatial thinking and its development in sociocultural context. In R. Vasta (Ed.), *Annals of child development* (pp. 67–102). Jessica Kingsley Publishers.

Gauvain, M. (2001). *The social context of cognitive development.* Guilford Press.

Gauvain, M. (2005). Scaffolding in socialization. *New Ideas in Psychology, 23*, 129–139. https://doi.org/10.1016/j.newideapsych.2006.05.004

Gauvain, M. (2009). Social and cultural transitions in cognitive development: A cross-generational view. In A. J. Sameroff (Ed.), *The transactional model of development: How children and contexts shape each other* (pp. 163–182). American Psychological Association. https://doi.org/10.1037/11877-009

Gauvain, M. (2016). Peer contributions to cognitive development. In K. R. Wentzel & G. B. Ramani (Eds.), *Handbook of social influences in school contexts: Social-emotional, motivation, and cognitive outcomes* (pp. 80–95). Routledge, Taylor & Francis.

Gauvain, M. (2018). From developmental psychologist to water scientist and back again: The role of interdisciplinary research in developmental science. *Child Development Perspectives, 12*, 45–50. https://doi.org/10.1111/cdep.12255

Gauvain, M., & Munroe, R. L. (2019). Children's experience during cultural change. *Child Development Perspectives, 13*, 65–70. https://doi.org/10.1111/cdep.12318

Gauvain, M., & Munroe, R. L. (2020). Children's questions in social and cultural perspective. In S. Ronfard, L. Butler, & K. Corriveau (Eds.), *The questioning child: Insights from psychology and education* (pp. 183–211). Cambridge University Press. https://doi.org/10.1017/9781108553803.010

Gauvain, M., Munroe, R. L., & Beebe, H. (2013). Children's questions in cross-cultural perspective: A four-culture study. *Journal of Cross-Cultural Psychology, 44*, 1148–1165. https://doi.org/10.1177/0022022113485430

Gauvain, M., & Nicolaides, C. (2015). Cognition in childhood across cultures. In L. A. Jensen (Ed.), *The Oxford handbook of human development and culture: An interdisciplinary perspective* (pp. 198–213). Oxford University Press.

Gauvain, M., & Perez, S. M. (2015). The socialization of cognition. In J. Grusec & P. Hastings (Eds.), *Handbook of socialization: Theory and research* (2nd ed., pp. 566–589). Guilford Press.

Gay, J., & Cole, M. (1967). *The new mathematics and an old culture.* Holt, Rinehart, & Winston.

Geertz, C. (1973). *The interpretation of cultures.* Basic Books.

Geertz, C. (1976). *The religion of Java.* University of Chicago Press.

Geertz, H. (1961). *The Javanese family: A study of kinship and socialization.* The Free Press.

Gentile, D. A., Bender, P. K., & Anderson, C. A. (2017). Violent video game effects on salivary cortisol, arousal, and aggressive thoughts in children. *Computers in Human Behavior, 70*, 39–43. https://doi.org/10.1016/j.chb.2016.12.045

Gerbault, P., Liebert, A., Itan, Y., Powell, A., Currat, M., Burger, J., Swallow, D. M., & Thomas, M. G. (2011). Evolution of lactase persistence: An example of human niche construction. *Philosophical Transactions of the Royal Society B: Biological Sciences, 366*, 863–877. https://doi.org/10.1098/rstb.2010.0268

Gewirtz, J. L. (1967). The course of infant smiling in four child-rearing environments in Israel. In B. M. Foss (Ed.), *Determinants of infant behavior* (Vol. 3, pp. 105–258). Methuen.

Ghazi, H. F., Isa, Z. M., Aljunid, S., Shah, S. A., Tamil, A. M., & Abdalqader, M. A. (2012). The negative impact of living environment on intelligence quotient of primary school children in Baghdad City, Iraq: A cross-sectional study. *BMC Public Health, 12*, 562. https://doi.org/10.1186/1471-2458-12-562

Gibbs, J. C., Basinger, K. S., Grime, R. L., & Snarey, J. (2007). Moral judgment development across cultures: Revisiting Kohlberg's universality claims. *Developmental Review, 27*, 443–500. https://doi.org/10.1016/j.dr.2007.04.001

Gibson-Davis, C., Gassman-Pines, A., & Lehrman, R. (2018). "His" and "hers": Meeting the economic bar to marriage. *Demography, 55*, 2321–2343. https://doi.org/10.1007/s13524-018-0726-z

Gillham, J., Adams-Deutsch, Z., Werner, J. K., Reivich, K., Coulter-Heindl, V., Linkins, M., Winder, B., Peterson, C., Park, N., Abenavoli, R., Contero, A., & Seligman, M. E. P. (2011). Character strengths predict subjective well-being during adolescence. *The Journal of Positive Psychology, 6*, 31–44. https://doi.org/10.1080/17439760.2010.536773

Gilmore, D. (1990). *Manhood in the making: Cultural concepts of masculinity.* Yale University Press.

Gini, G., Pozzoli, T., & Hymel, S. (2014). Moral disengagement among children and youth: A meta-analytic review of links to aggressive behavior. *Aggressive Behavior, 40*, 56–68. https://doi.org/10.1002/ab.21502

Girls Not Brides. (2019). *Child marriage around the world*. https://www.girlsnotbrides. org/where-does-it-happen/

Girvan, E. J., Gion, C., McIntosh, K., & Smolkowski, K. (2017). The relative contribution of subjective office referrals to racial disproportionality in school discipline. *School Psychology Quarterly, 32*, 392–404. https://doi.org/10.1037/spq0000178

Glaser, B., Shelton, K. H., & van den Bree, M. B. M. (2010). The moderating role of close friends in the relationship between conduct problems and adolescent substance use. *The Journal of Adolescent Health, 47*, 35–42. https://doi.org/10.1016/j. jadohealth.2009.12.022

Goldberg, S. (1977). Ethics, politics and multicultural research. In P. H. Leiderman, S. R. Tulkin, & A. Rosenfeld (Eds.), *Culture and infancy: Variations in the human experience* (pp. 587–598). Academic Press.

Goldenberg, C., Gallimore, R., Reese, L., & Garnier, H. (2001). Cause or effect? A longitudinal study of Latino parents' aspirations and expectations, and their children's school performance. *American Educational Research Journal, 38*, 547–582. https://doi.org/10.3102/00028312038003547

Goldin-Meadow, S. (2009). How gesture promotes learning throughout childhood. *Child Development Perspectives, 3*, 106–111. https://doi.org/10.1111/j.1750-8606. 2009.00088.x

Goldin-Meadow, S. (2015). Gesture and cognitive development. In L. Liben & U. Müller (Eds.), *Handbook of child psychology and developmental science: Vol. 2. Cognitive processes* (7th ed., pp. 339–380). Wiley. https://doi.org/10.1002/9781118963418. childpsy209

Goldschmidt, W. (1966). *Comparative functionalism: An essay in anthropological theory*. University of California Press.

Golinkoff, R. M. (1983). The preverbal negotiation of failed messages: Insights into the transition period. In R. M. Golinkoff (Ed.), *The transition from prelinguistic to linguistic communication* (pp. 57–78). Erlbaum.

Golinkoff, R. M., Hirsh-Pasek, K., Bailey, L. M., & Wenger, N. R. (1992). Young children and adults use lexical principles to learn new words. *Developmental Psychology, 28*, 99–108. https://doi.org/10.1037/0012-1649.28.1.99

Golombok, S., Mellish, L., Jennings, S., Casey, P., Tasker, F., & Lamb, M. E. (2014). Adoptive gay father families: Parent–child relationships and children's psychological adjustment. *Child Development, 85*, 456–468. https://doi.org/10.1111/cdev.12155

Göncü, A., & Gaskins, S. (2006). *Play and development: Evolutionary, sociocultural, and functional perspectives*. Erlbaum.

Göncü, A., Jain, J., & Tuermer, U. (2007). Children's play as cultural interpretation. In A. Göncü & S. Gaskins (Eds.), *Play and development: Evolutionary, sociocultural, and functional perspectives* (pp. 155–178). Erlbaum. https://doi.org/10.4324/ 9780203936511

Göncü, A., Mistry, J., & Mosier, C. (2000). Cultural variations in the play of toddlers. *International Journal of Behavioral Development, 24*, 321–329. https://doi.org/10. 1080/01650250050118303

GonzáLez, Y., Moreno, D. S., & Schneider, B. H. (2004). Friendship expectations of early adolescents in Cuba and Canada. *Journal of Cross-Cultural Psychology, 35*, 436–445. https://doi.org/10.1177/0022022104264127

Goodnow, J. J. (1976). The nature of intelligent behavior: Questions raised by cross-cultural studies. In L. B. Resnick (Ed.), *The nature of intelligence* (pp. 169–188). Erlbaum.

Goodnow, J. J. (1990). The socialization of cognition: What's involved? In J. W. Stigler, R. A. Shweder, & G. Herdt (Eds.), *Cultural psychology* (pp. 259–286). Cambridge University Press. https://doi.org/10.1017/CBO9781139173728.008

Goodwin, M. (1982). Process of dispute management among urban Black children. *American Ethnologist, 9*, 76–96. https://doi.org/10.1525/ae.1982.9.1.02a00050

Gottman, J. M. (1983). How children become friends. *Monographs of the Society for Research in Child Development, 48*(3), 1–86. https://doi.org/10.2307/1165860

Gottman, J. M. (1986). The world of coordinated play: Same and cross-sex friendships. In J. M. Gottman & J. G. Parker (Eds.), *Conversations of friends: Speculations on affective development* (pp. 139–191). Cambridge University Press.

Gottman, J. M., & Parker, J. G. (1986). *Conversations of friends: Speculations on affective development.* Cambridge University Press.

Graham, S., & Weiner, B. (2012). Motivation: Past, present, and future. In K. R. Harris, S. Graham, & T. Urdan (Eds.), *APA educational psychology handbook: Vol. 1. Theories, constructs, and critical issues* (pp. 366–396). American Psychological Association.

Greenberger, E., & Chen, C. (1996). Perceived family relationships and depressed mood in early and late adolescence: A comparison of European and Asian Americans. *Developmental Psychology, 32,* 707–716. https://doi.org/10.1037/0012-1649.32.4.707

Greenfield, P. M. (1974). Comparing dimensional categorization in natural and artificial contexts: A developmental study among the Zinacantecos of Mexico. *The Journal of Social Psychology, 93,* 157–171. https://doi.org/10.1080/00224545.1974.9923149

Greenfield, P. M. (1997). You can't take it with you: Why ability assessments don't cross cultures. *American Psychologist, 52,* 1115–1124. https://doi.org/10.1037/0003-066X.52.10.1115

Greenfield, P. M. (2004). *Weaving generations together: Evolving creativity in the Maya of Chiapas.* School of American Research Press.

Greenfield, P. M. (2009). Linking social change and developmental change: Shifting pathways of human development. *Developmental Psychology, 45,* 401–418. https://doi.org/10.1037/a0014726

Greenfield, P. M., & Childs, C. P. (1977). Understanding sibling concepts: A developmental study of kin terms in Zinacantecan. In P. R. Dasen (Ed.), *Piagetian psychology: Cross-cultural contributions* (pp. 335–338). Gardner.

Greenfield, P. M., Keller, H., Fuligni, A., & Maynard, A. (2003). Cultural pathways through universal development. *Annual Review of Psychology, 54,* 461–490. https://doi.org/10.1146/annurev.psych.54.101601.145221

Greif, E. B., & Gleason, J. B. (1980). Hi, thanks, and goodbye: More routine information. *Language in Society, 9,* 159–166. https://doi.org/10.1017/S0047404500008034

Groh, A. M., Fearon, R. P., Bakermans-Kranenburg, M. J., van IJzendoorn, M. H., Steele, R. D., & Roisman, G. I. (2014). The significance of attachment security for children's social competence with peers: A meta-analytic study. *Attachment & Human Development, 16,* 103–136. https://doi.org/10.1080/14616734.2014.883636

Grönlund, H., Holmes, K., Kang, C., Cnaan, R. A., Handy, F., Brudney, J. L., Haski-Leventhal, D., Hustinx, L., Kassam, M., Meijs, L. C. P. M., Pessi, A. B., Ranade, B., Smith, K. A., Yamauchi, N., & Zrinščak, S. (2011). Cultural values and volunteering: A cross-cultural comparison of students' motivation to volunteer in 13 countries. *Journal of Academic Ethics, 9,* 87–106. https://doi.org/10.1007/s10805-011-9131-6

Grusec, J. E. (2019). Domains of socialization: Implications for parenting and the development of children's moral behavior and cognitions. In D. Laible, G. Carlo, & L. M. Padilla-Walker (Eds.), *Oxford handbook of parenting and moral development* (pp. 73–90). Oxford University Press.

Grusec, J. E., & Davidov, M. (2007). Socialization in the family: The roles of parents. In J. E. Grusec & P. D. Hastings (Eds.), *Handbook of socialization: Theory and research* (pp. 284–308). Guilford Press.

Grusec, J. E., & Davidov, M. (2010). Integrating different perspectives on socialization theory and research: A domain-specific approach. *Child Development, 81*(3), 687–709. https://doi.org/10.1111/j.1467-8624.2010.01426.x

Grusec, J. E., & Hastings, P. (2015). *Handbook of socialization: Theory and research* (2nd ed.). Guilford Press.

Guidetti, M., Conner, M., Prestwich, A., & Cavazza, N. (2012). The transmission of attitudes towards food: Twofold specificity of similarities with parents and friends. *British Journal of Health Psychology, 17*, 346–361. https://doi.org/10.1111/j.2044-8287.2011.02041.x

Gummerum, M., & Keller, M. (2008). Affection, virtue, pleasure, and profit: Developing an understanding of friendship closeness and intimacy in Western and Asian societies. *International Journal of Behavioral Development, 32*, 218–231. https://doi.org/10.1177/0165025408089271

Gunnar, M. R. (2000). Early adversity and the development of stress reactivity and regulation. In C. A. Nelson (Ed.), *The Minnesota symposia on child psychology: Vol. 31. The effects of early adversity on neurobehavioral development* (pp.163–200). Erlbaum.

Gurdal, S., Lansford, J. E., & Sorbring, E. (2016). Parental perceptions of children's agency: Parental warmth, school achievement and adjustment. *Early Child Development and Care, 186*, 1203–1211. https://doi.org/10.1080/03004430.2015.1083559

Guttmacher Institute. (2016). *American teens' sexual and reproductive health.* https://www.guttmacher.org/fact-sheet/american-teens-sexual-and-reproductive-health

Haar, B. F., & Krahe, B. (1999). Strategies for resolving interpersonal conflicts in adolescence: A German–Indonesian comparison. *Journal of Cross-Cultural Psychology, 30*, 667–683. https://doi.org/10.1177/0022022199030006001

Haddad, L., Shotar, A., Umlauf, M., & Al-Zyoud, S. (2010). Knowledge of substance abuse among high school students in Jordan. *Journal of Transcultural Nursing, 21*, 143–150. https://doi.org/10.1177/1043659609357632

Hagerman, M. A. (2017). White racial socialization: Progressive fathers on raising "antiracist" children. *Journal of Marriage and the Family, 79*, 60–74. https://doi.org/10.1111/jomf.12325

Haight, W. L. (1999). The pragmatics of caregiver–child pretending at home: Understanding culturally specific socialization practices. In A. Göncü (Ed.), *Children's engagement in the world: Sociocultural perspectives* (pp. 128–147). Cambridge University Press.

Halberstadt, A. G., Denham, S. A., & Dunsmore, J. C. (2001). Affective social competence. *Social Development, 10*, 79–119. https://doi.org/10.1111/1467-9507.00150

Hamadani, J. D., & Tofail, F. (2014). Childrearing, motherhood and fatherhood in Bangladeshi culture. In H. Selin (Ed.), *Parenting across cultures: Childrearing, motherhood and fatherhood in non-Western cultures* (pp. 123–144). Springer. https://doi.org/10.1007/978-94-007-7503-9_10

Hammons, A. J., & Fiese, B. H. (2011). Is frequency of shared family meals related to the nutritional health of children and adolescents? *Pediatrics, 127*, e1565–e1574. https://doi.org/10.1542/peds.2010-1440

Handy, F., Hustinx, L., Kang, C., Brudney, J. L., Haski-Leventhal, D., Holmes, K., Meijs, L. C. P. M., Pessi, A. B., Ranade, B., Yamauchi, N., & Zrinscak, S. (2010). A cross-cultural examination of student volunteering: Is it all about résumé building? *Nonprofit and Voluntary Sector Quarterly, 39*, 498–523. https://doi.org/10.1177/0899764009344353

Happé, F., Cook, J. L., & Bird, G. (2017). The structure of social cognition: In(ter) dependence of sociocognitive processes. *Annual Review of Psychology, 68*, 243–267. https://doi.org/10.1146/annurev-psych-010416-044046

Harcourt, D., & Hägglund, S. (2013). Turning the UNCRC upside down: A bottom-up perspective on children's rights. *International Journal of Early Years Education, 21*, 286–299. https://doi.org/10.1080/09669760.2013.867167

Harkness, S., & Super, C. M. (1985). The cultural context of gender segregation in children's peer groups. *Child Development, 56*, 219–224. https://doi.org/10.2307/1130188

Harter, S. (2006). The self. In N. Eisenberg (Ed.), *Handbook of child psychology: Vol. 3. Social, emotional, and personality development* (pp. 505–570). Wiley.

Hastings, P. D., Nuselovici, J. N., & Cheah, C. S. L. (2010). Shyness, parenting, and parent-child relationships. In K. H. Rubin & R. J. Coplan (Eds.), *The development of shyness and social withdrawal* (pp. 107–130). Guilford Press.

Hastings, P. D., Utendale, W. T., & Sullivan, C. (2007). The socialization of prosocial development. In J. E. Grusec & P. D. Hastings (Eds.), *Handbook of socialization: Theory and research* (pp. 638–664). Guilford Press.

Hau, K. T., & Ho, I. T. (2010). Chinese students' motivation and achievement. In M. H. Bond (Ed.), *The Oxford handbook of Chinese psychology* (pp. 187–204). Oxford University Press.

Haun, D. B. M. (2015). Comparative and developmental anthropology: Studying the origins of cultural variability in cognitive function. In L. A. Jensen (Ed.), *The Oxford handbook of human development and culture: An interdisciplinary perspective* (pp. 94–110). Oxford University Press.

Haun, D. B. M., Rapold, C. J., Janzen, G., & Levinson, S. C. (2011). Plasticity of human spatial cognition: Spatial language and cognition covary across cultures. *Cognition, 119*, 70–80. https://doi.org/10.1016/j.cognition.2010.12.009

Hawley, P. H. (2003). Prosocial and coercive configurations of resource control in early adolescence: A case for the well-adapted Machiavellian. *Merrill-Palmer Quarterly, 49*, 279–309. https://doi.org/10.1353/mpq.2003.0013

Heath, S. B. (1983). *Ways with words: Language, life and work in communities and classrooms.* Cambridge University Press. https://doi.org/10.1017/CBO9780511841057

Heath, S. B. (1984). Oral and literate traditions. *International Social Science Journal UNESCO, 99*, 1–41.

Heffer, T., Good, M., Daly, O., MacDonell, E., & Willoughby, T. (2019). The longitudinal association between social-media use and depressive symptoms among adolescents and young adults: An empirical reply to Twenge et al. (2008). *Clinical Psychological Science, 7*, 462–470. https://doi.org/10.1177/2167702618812727

Helliwell, J., Layard, R., & Sachs, J. (2019). *World happiness report 2019.* Sustainable Development Solutions Network.

Helwig, C. C. (2017). Identifying universal developmental processes amid contextual variations in moral judgment and reasoning. *Human Development, 60*, 342–349. https://doi.org/10.1159/000485453

Henrich, J., Heine, S. J., & Norenzayan, A. (2010). The weirdest people in the world? *Behavioral and Brain Sciences, 33*(2-3), 61–83. https://doi.org/10.1017/S0140525X0999152X

Herdt, G. H. (1989). *Gay and lesbian youth.* Hayworth Press.

Hernandez, D. J. (1997). Child development and the social demography of childhood. *Child Development, 68*, 149–169. https://doi.org/10.2307/1131933

Hernandez, D. J. (2011). *Double jeopardy: How third-grade reading skills and poverty influence high school graduation.* The Annie E. Casey Foundation.

Hernandez, D. J., & Napierala, J. S. (2013). *Diverse children: Race, ethnicity, and immigration in America's non-majority generation.* Foundation for Child Development.

Hetherington, E. M. (2006). The influence of conflict, marital problem solving, and parenting on children's adjustment in nondivorced, divorced, and remarried families. In A. Clarke-Stewart & J. Dunn (Eds.), *Families count* (pp. 203–237). Cambridge University Press. https://doi.org/10.1017/CBO9780511616259.010

Hewlett, B. S. (1991). *Intimate fathers: The nature and context of Aka Pygmy paternal infant care.* University of Michigan Press. https://doi.org/10.3998/mpub.13211

Hewlett, B. S. (1992). Husband-wife reciprocity and the father-infant relationship among Aka Pygmies. In B. S. Hewlett (Ed.), *Father-child relations* (pp. 153–176). Aldine de Gruyter.

Hewlett, B. S., & Lamb, M. E. (2002). Integrating evolution, culture and developmental psychology: Explaining caregiver-infant proximity and responsiveness in central Africa and the USA. In H. Keller, Y. H. Poortinga, & A. Schölmerich (Eds.), *Between culture and biology: Perspectives on ontogenetic development* (pp. 241–269). Cambridge University Press. https://doi.org/10.1017/CBO9780511489853.012

Hewlett, B. S., Lamb, M. E., Shannon, D., Leyendecker, B., & Schölmerich, A. (1998). Culture and early infancy among central African foragers and farmers. *Developmental Psychology, 34,* 653–661. https://doi.org/10.1037/0012-1649.34.4.653

Hewlett, B. S., Lamb, M. E., Shannon, D., Leyendecker, B., & Schölmerich, A. (2000). Parental investment strategies among Aka foragers, Ngandu farmers, and Euro-American urban-industrialists. In L. Cronk, N. Chagnon, & W. Irons (Eds.), *Adaptation and human behavior: An anthropological perspective* (pp. 155–178). Aldine de Gruyter.

Hoff, E. (2014). *Language development* (5th ed.). Wadsworth.

Hofstede, G. (1980). *Culture's consequences.* Sage.

Hofstede, G. (1991). *Cultures and organizations: Software of the mind.* McGraw Hill.

Hollan, D. (1988). Staying "cool" in Toraja: Informal strategies for the management of anger and hostility in a nonviolent society. *Ethos, 16,* 52–72. https://doi.org/10.1525/eth.1988.16.1.02a00030

Hollich, G., Golinkoff, R. M., & Hirsh-Pasek, K. (2007). Young children associate novel words with complex objects rather than salient parts. *Developmental Psychology, 43,* 1051–1061. https://doi.org/10.1037/0012-1649.43.5.1051

Holloway, S. D., & Jonas, M. (2016). Families, culture, and schooling. In K. R. Wentzel & G. B. Ramani (Eds.), *Handbook of social influences in school contexts: Social-emotional, motivation, and cognitive outcomes* (pp. 258–272). Taylor and Francis.

Holmberg, L. I., & Hellberg, D. (2004). Teenagers' sexual behavior in Sweden, Europe. *Journal of Reproduction and Contraception, 16,* 157–166.

Holmes, H., Tangtongtavy, S., & Tomizawa, R. (1997). *Working with the Thais: A guide to managing Thailand.* White Lotus Press.

Holowka, S., Brosseau-Lapre, F., & Petitto, L. A. (2002). Semantic and conceptual knowledge underlying bilingual babies' first signs and words. *Language Learning, 52*(2), 205–262. https://doi.org/10.1111/0023-8333.00184

Hoover-Dempsey, K. V., Walker, J. M. T., Sandler, H. M., Whetsel, D., Green, C. L., Wilkins, A. S., & Closson, K. (2005). Why do parents become involved? Research findings and implications. *The Elementary School Journal, 106,* 105–130. https://doi.org/10.1086/499194

House, B. R., Silk, J. B., Henrich, J., Barrett, H. C., Scelza, B. A., & Boyette, A. H., Hewlett, B. S., McElreath, R., & Laurence, S. (2013). Ontogeny of prosocial behavior across diverse societies. *Proceedings of the National Academy of Sciences, 110,* 14586–14591. https://doi.org/10.1073/pnas.1221217110

Howe, M. L., Courage, M. L., & Edison, S. C. (2003). When autobiographical memory begins. *Developmental Review, 23,* 471–494. https://doi.org/10.1016/j.dr.2003.09.001

Huang, C. Y., Cheah, C. S. L., Lamb, M. E., & Zhou, N. (2017). Associations between parenting styles and perceived child effortful control within Chinese families in the United States, the United Kingdom and Taiwan. *Journal of Cross-Cultural Psychology, 48,* 795–812. https://doi.org/10.1177/0022022117706108

Huang, G. C., Okamoto, J., Valente, T. W., Sun, P., Wei, Y., Johnson, C. A., & Unger, J. B. (2012). Effects of media and social standing on smoking behaviors among adolescents in China. *Journal of Children and Media, 6,* 100–118. https://doi.org/10.1080/17482798.2011.633411

Huesmann, L. R., Dubow, E. F., Boxer, P., Landau, S. F., Gvirsman, S. D., & Shikaki, K. (2017). Children's exposure to violent political conflict stimulates aggression at peers by increasing emotional distress, aggressive script rehearsal, and normative beliefs favoring aggression. *Development and Psychopathology, 29,* 39–50. https://doi.org/10.1017/S0954579416001115

Huesmann, L. R., & Kirwil, L. (2007). Why observing violence increases the risk of violent behavior by the observer. In D. J. Flannery, A. T. Vazsony, & I. Waldman

(Eds.), *The Cambridge handbook of violent behavior and aggression* (pp. 545–570). Cambridge University Press. https://doi.org/10.1017/CBO9780511816840.029

Hughes, C. (2011). *Social understanding and social lives: From toddlerhood through to the transition to school.* Psychology Press. https://doi.org/10.4324/9780203813225

Hughes, D., Rodriguez, J., Smith, E. P., Johnson, D. J., Stevenson, H. C., & Spicer, P. (2006). Parents' ethnic-racial socialization practices: A review of research and directions for future study. *Developmental Psychology, 42,* 747–770. https://doi.org/10.1037/0012-1649.42.5.747

Hughes, D. L., Watford, J. A., & Del Toro, J. (2016). A transactional/ecological perspective on ethnic–racial identity, socialization, and discrimination. *Advances in Child Development and Behavior, 51,* 1–41. https://doi.org/10.1016/bs.acdb.2016.05.001

Humphreys, K. L., Gleason, M. M., Drury, S. S., Miron, D., Nelson, C. A., III, Fox, N. A., & Zeanah, C. H. (2015). Effects of institutional rearing and foster care on psychopathology at age 12 years in Romania: Follow-up of an open, randomised controlled trial. *The Lancet: Psychiatry, 2,* 625–634. https://doi.org/10.1016/S2215-0366(15)00095-4

Hund, A. M., Schmettow, M., & Noordzij, M. L. (2012). The impact of culture and recipient perspective on direction giving in the service of wayfinding. *Journal of Environmental Psychology, 32*(4), 327–336. https://doi.org/10.1016/j.jenvp.2012.05.007

Hurtado, N., Marchman, V. A., & Fernald, A. (2008). Does input influence uptake? Links between maternal talk, processing speed and vocabulary size in Spanish-learning children. *Developmental Science, 11,* F31–F39. https://doi.org/10.1111/j.1467-7687.2008.00768.x

Hutchins, E. (1983). Understanding Micronesian navigation. In D. Gentner & A. Stevens (Eds.), *Mental models* (pp. 191–226). Erlbaum.

Huttenlocher, J., Smiley, P., & Charney, R. (1983). Emergence of action categories in the child: Evidence from verb meanings. *Psychological Review, 90,* 72–93. https://doi.org/10.1037/0033-295X.90.1.72

Hüttenmoser, M. (1995). Children and their living surroundings: Empirical investigations into the significance of living surroundings for the everyday life and development of children. *Children's Environments, 12,* 403–413.

Hyde, J. S. (2014). Gender similarities and differences. *Annual Review of Psychology, 65,* 373–398. https://doi.org/10.1146/annurev-psych-010213-115057

Hymes, D. (1974). *Foundations in sociolinguistics: An ethnographic approach.* University of Pennsylvania Press.

Hyson, M. (2017, March). *Observing teachers' practices with MELE in Indonesia: Why, what, and what next?* Paper presented at the Comparative and International Education Society conference, Atlanta, GA.

Ingram, D. (1989). *First language acquisition: Methods, description, and explanation.* Psychology Press.

International Federation for Housing and Planning. (2019). *Colombia: Social stratification by law.* https://www.ifhp.org/ifhp-blog/colombia-social-stratification-law

International Labour Office. (2017). *Global estimates of child labor: Results and trends, 2012–2016.* https://www.ilo.org/wcmsp5/groups/public/---dgreports/---dcomm/documents/publication/wcms_575499.pdf

International Labour Organization. (2014). *Maternity and paternity at work: Law and practice across the world.* https://www.ilo.org/global/topics/equality-and-discrimination/maternity-protection/publications/maternity-paternity-at-work-2014/lang--en/index.htm

International Labour Organization. (2020). *Youth employment databases and platforms.* https://www.ilo.org/global/topics/youth-employment/databases-platforms/lang--en/index.htm

International Organization for Migration. (2018). *Global migration indicators*. International Organization for Migration.

Irwin, M. H., & McLaughlin, D. H. (1970). Ability and preference in category sorting by Mano schoolchildren and adults. *The Journal of Social Psychology, 82,* 15–24. https://doi.org/10.1080/00224545.1970.9919926

Iskandar, N., Laursen, B., Finkelstein, B., & Fredrickson, L. (1995). Conflict resolution among preschool children: The appeal of negotiation in hypothetical disputes. *Early Education and Development, 6,* 359–376. https://doi.org/10.1207/s15566935eed0604_5

Iverson, J. M., Capirci, O., Volterra, V., & Goldin-Meadow, S. (2008). Learning to talk in a gesture-rich world: Early communication in Italian vs. American children. *First Language, 28,* 164–181. https://doi.org/10.1177/0142723707087736

Izard, C. E., Hembree, E., & Huebner, R. (1987). Infants' emotional expressions to acute pain: Developmental changes and stability of individual differences. *Developmental Psychology, 23,* 105–113. https://doi.org/10.1037/0012-1649.23.1.105

Jack, F., MacDonald, S., Reese, E., & Hayne, H. (2009). Maternal reminiscing style during early childhood predicts the age of adolescents' earliest memories. *Child Development, 80*(2), 496–505. https://doi.org/10.1111/j.1467-8624.2009.01274.x

Jackson, E. F., Raval, V. V., Bendikas-King, E. A., Raval, P. H., & Trivedi, S. S. (2016). Cultural variation in reports of subjective experience of parent–child boundary dissolution among emerging adults. *Journal of Family Issues, 37,* 671–691. https://doi.org/10.1177/0192513X15576280

Jacobs, J. (1961). *The death and life of great American cities*. Random House.

Jambon, M., & Smetana, J. (2019). Socialization of moral judgments and reasoning. In D. Laible, G. Carlo, & L. M. Padilla-Walker (Eds.), *Oxford handbook of parenting and moral development* (pp. 375–390). Oxford University Press.

Jang, H., Reeve, J., Ryan, R. M., & Kim, A. (2009). Can self-determination theory explain what underlies the productive, satisfying learning experiences of collectivistically-oriented South Korean adolescents? *Journal of Educational Psychology, 101,* 644–661. https://doi.org/10.1037/a0014241

Jensen, K., Vaish, A., & Schmidt, M. F. H. (2014). The emergence of human prosociality: Aligning with others through feelings, concerns, and norms. *Frontiers in Psychology, 5,* 822. https://doi.org/10.3389/fpsyg.2014.00822

Jiang, Y., Bong, M., & Li, S. (2015). Conformity of Korean adolescents in their perceptions of social relationships and academic motivation. *Learning and Individual Differences, 40,* 41–54. https://doi.org/10.1016/j.lindif.2015.04.012

Jocson, R. M., & McLoyd, V. C. (2015). Neighborhood and housing disorder, parenting, and youth adjustment in low-income urban families. *American Journal of Community Psychology, 55,* 304–313. https://doi.org/10.1007/s10464-015-9710-6

Johnson, L. M., Simons, L., & Conger, R. D. (2004). Criminal justice system involvement and continuity of youth crime: A longitudinal analysis. *Youth & Society, 36,* 3–29. https://doi.org/10.1177/0044118X03260323

Johnson, M. H. (2010). Understanding the social world: A developmental neuroscience approach. In M. H. Johnson (Ed.), *Child development at the intersection of emotion and cognition* (pp. 153–174). American Psychological Association. https://doi.org/10.1037/12059-009

Johnson, M. K., McCue, M., & Iacono, W. G. (2005). Disruptive behavior and school grades: Genetic and environmental relations in 11-year-olds. *Journal of Educational Psychology, 97,* 391–405. https://doi.org/10.1037/0022-0663.97.3.391

Johnson, W. F., Emde, R. N., Pannabecker, B. J., Stenberg, C. R., & Davis, M. H. (1982). Maternal perception of infant emotion from birth to 18 months. *Infant Behavior and Development, 5,* 313–322. https://doi.org/10.1016/S0163-6383(82)80041-6

Johnston, L. D., Miech, R. A., O'Malley, P. M., Bachman, J. G., Schulenberg, J. E., & Patrick, M. E. (2020). *Monitoring the Future national survey results on drug use*

1975-2019: Overview, key findings on adolescent drug use. Institute for Social Research, University of Michigan.

Jones, S. S. (2007). Imitation in infancy: The development of mimicry. *Psychological Science, 18*, 593–599. https://doi.org/10.1111/j.1467-9280.2007.01945.x

Jourdan, C. (1991). Pidgins and creoles: The blurring of categories. *Annual Review of Anthropology, 20*, 187–209. https://doi.org/10.1146/annurev.an.20.100191.001155

Juang, L. P., & Nguyen, H. H. (2009). Misconduct among Chinese American adolescents. *Journal of Cross-Cultural Psychology, 40*, 649–666. https://doi.org/10.1177/0022022109335185

Juang, L. P., Qin, D., & Park, I. K. (2013). Deconstructing the myth of the "tiger mother": An introduction to the special issue on tiger parenting, Asian-heritage families, and child/adolescent well-being. *Asian American Journal of Psychology, 4*, 1–6. https://doi.org/10.1037/a0032136

Jukes, M. C. H., Zuilkowski, S. S., & Grigorenko, E. L. (2018). Do schooling and urban residence develop cognitive skills at the expense of social responsibility? A study of adolescents in Gambia, West Africa. *Journal of Cross-Cultural Psychology, 49*, 82–98. https://doi.org/10.1177/0022022117741989

Jusczyk, P. W., Friederici, A. D., Wessels, J., Svenkerud, V. Y., & Jusczyk, A. M. (1993). Infants' sensitivity to the sound patterns of native language words. *Journal of Memory and Language, 32*, 402–420. https://doi.org/10.1006/jmla.1993.1022

Kagan, J. (2010). Emotions and temperament. In M. H. Bornstein (Ed.), *Handbook of cultural developmental science* (pp. 175–194). Taylor and Francis.

Kagan, J., Reznick, J. S., & Snidman, N. (1988). Biological bases of childhood shyness. *Science, 240*, 167–171. https://doi.org/10.1126/science.3353713

Kagan, J., & Snidman, N. (2004). *The long shadow of temperament*. Harvard University Press.

Kagan, J. J., Kearsley, R. B., & Zelazo, P. R. (1978). *Infancy: Its place in human development*. Harvard University Press.

Kagitçibasi, Ç. (1994). A critical appraisal of individualism and collectivism: Toward a new formulation. In U. Kim, H. C. Triandis, Ç. Kagitçibasi, S. Choi, & G. Yoon (Eds.), *Individualism and collectivism: Theory, method, and application* (pp. 52–65). Sage.

Kagitçibasi, Ç. (2005). Autonomy and relatedness in cultural context: Implications for self and family. *Journal of Cross-Cultural Psychology, 36*, 403–422. https://doi.org/10.1177/0022022105275959

Kagitçibasi, Ç. (2007). *Family, self, and human development across cultures: Theory and applications* (2nd ed.). Erlbaum. https://doi.org/10.4324/9780203937068

Kagitcibasi, Ç. (2013). Adolescent autonomy-relatedness and the family in cultural context: What is optimal? *Journal of Research on Adolescence, 23*, 223–235. https://doi.org/10.1111/jora.12041

Kapadia, S., & Bhangaokar, R. (2015). An Indian moral worldview: Developmental patterns in adolescents and adults. In L. A. Jensen (Ed.), *Moral development in a global world: Research from a cultural-developmental perspective* (pp. 69–91). Cambridge University Press. https://doi.org/10.1017/CBO9781139583787.005

Kaplan, H., Hill, K., Lancaster, J., & Hurtado, A. M. (2000). A theory of human life history evolution: Diet, intelligence, and longevity. *Evolutionary Anthropology, 9*, 156–185. https://doi.org/10.1002/1520-6505(2000)9:4<156::AID-EVAN5>3.0.CO;2-7

Karasik, L. B., Tamis-LeMonda, C. S., Adolph, K. E., & Bornstein, M. H. (2015). Places and postures: A cross-cultural comparison of sitting in 5-month-olds. *Journal of Cross-Cultural Psychology, 46*, 1023–1038. https://doi.org/10.1177/0022022115593803

Kassam, R., Collins, J. B., Liow, E., & Rasool, N. (2015). Narrative review of current context of malaria and management strategies in Uganda (Part I). *Acta Tropica, 152*, 252–268. https://doi.org/10.1016/j.actatropica.2015.07.028

Kawabata, Y., Alink, L. R. A., Tseng, W.-L., van IJzendoorn, M. H., & Crick, N. R. (2011). Maternal and paternal parenting styles associated with relational aggression in children and adolescents: A conceptual analysis and meta-analytic review. *Developmental Review, 31,* 240–278. https://doi.org/10.1016/j.dr.2011.08.001

Kazi, S., Demetriou, A., Spanoudis, G., Zhang, X., & Wang, Y. (2012). Mind–culture interactions: How writing molds mental fluidity in early development. *Intelligence, 40,* 622–637. https://doi.org/10.1016/j.intell.2012.07.001

Kearins, J. (1986). Visual spatial memory in Aboriginal and White Australian children. *Australian Journal of Psychology, 38,* 203–214. https://doi.org/10.1080/00049538608259009

Keeler, W. (1987). *Javanese shadow plays, Javanese selves.* Princeton University Press.

Keller, H. (2002). Development as the interface between biology and culture: A conceptualization of early ontogenetic experience. In H. Keller, Y. H. Poortinga, & A. Schölmerich (Eds.), *Between culture and biology: Perspectives on ontogenetic development* (pp. 215–240). Cambridge University Press. https://doi.org/10.1017/CBO9780511489853.011

Keller, H., & Chaudhary, N. (2017). Is the mother essential for attachment? Models of care in different cultures. In H. Keller & K. A. Bard (Eds.), *The cultural nature of attachment: Contextualizing relationships and development* (pp. 109–138). MIT Press. https://doi.org/10.7551/mitpress/11425.003.0007

Keller, H., & Otto, H. (2009). The cultural socialization of emotion regulation in infancy. *Journal of Cross-Cultural Psychology, 40,* 996–1011. https://doi.org/10.1177/0022022109348576

Kent, R. (2005). Speech development. In B. Hopkins (Ed.), *The Cambridge encyclopedia of child development* (pp. 257–264). Cambridge University Press.

Kerr, M., Lambert, W. W., & Bem, D. J. (1996). Life course sequelae of childhood shyness in Sweden: Comparison with the United States. *Developmental Psychology, 32,* 1100–1105. https://doi.org/10.1037/0012-1649.32.6.1100

Khaleque, A., & Ali, S. (2017). A systematic review of meta-analyses of research on interpersonal acceptance-rejection theory: Constructs and measures. *Journal of Family Theory & Review, 9,* 441–458. https://doi.org/10.1111/jftr.12228

Khaleque, A., & Rohner, R. P. (2012). Transnational relations between perceived parental acceptance and personality dispositions of children and adults: A meta-analytic review. *Personality and Social Psychology Review, 16,* 103–115. https://doi.org/10.1177/1088868311418986

Kiang, L., Andrews, K., Stein, G. L., Supple, A. J., & Gonzalez, L. M. (2013). Socioeconomic stress and academic adjustment among Asian American adolescents: The protective role of family obligation. *Journal of Youth and Adolescence, 42,* 837–847. https://doi.org/10.1007/s10964-013-9916-6

Killion, C. M. (2017). Cultural healing practices that mimic child abuse. *Annals of Forensic Research and Analysis, 4*(2), 1042.

Kim, K. (1996). The reproduction of Confucian culture in contemporary Korea: An anthropological study. In T. Wei-Ming (Ed.), *Confucian traditions in East Asian modernity: Moral education and economic culture in Japan and the four mini-dragons* (pp. 202–227). Harvard University Press.

Kim, S., & Kochanska, G. (2012). Child temperament moderates effects of parent-child mutuality on self-regulation: A relationship-based path for emotionally negative infants. *Child Development, 83,* 1275–1289. https://doi.org/10.1111/j.1467-8624.2012.01778.x

Kimbro, R. T., & Schachter, A. (2011). Neighborhood poverty and maternal fears of children's outdoor play. *Family Relations, 60,* 461–475. https://doi.org/10.1111/j.1741-3729.2011.00660.x

King, R. B., Ganotice, F. A., Jr., & Watkins, D. A. (2014). A cross-cultural analysis of achievement and social goals among Chinese and Filipino students. *Social Psychology of Education, 17,* 439–455. https://doi.org/10.1007/s11218-014-9251-0

King, R. B., McInerney, D. M., & Nasser, R. (2017). Different goals for different folks: A cross-cultural study of achievement goals across nine cultures. *Social Psychology of Education, 20*, 619–642. https://doi.org/10.1007/s11218-017-9381-2

Kinzler, K. D., Corriveau, K. H., & Harris, P. L. (2011). Children's selective trust in native-accented speakers. *Developmental Science, 14*, 106–111. https://doi.org/10.1111/j.1467-7687.2010.00965.x

Kirkpatrick, J. (1987). Taure'are'a: A liminal category and passage to Marquesan adulthood. *Ethos, 15*, 382–405. https://doi.org/10.1525/eth.1987.15.4.02a00030

Kirmayer, L. J., & Jarvis, G. E. (2006). Depression across cultures. In D. J. Stein, D. J. Kupfer, & A. F. Schatzberg (Eds.), *The American Psychiatric Publishing textbook of mood disorders* (pp. 699–715). American Psychiatric Publishing.

Kisilevsky, B. S., Hains, S. M., Lee, K., Xie, X., Huang, H., Ye, H. H., Zhang, K., & Wang, Z. (2003). Effects of experience on fetal voice recognition. *Psychological Science, 14*, 220–224. https://doi.org/10.1111/1467-9280.02435

Kita, S. (2009). Cross-cultural variation of speech-accompanying gesture: A review. *Language and Cognitive Processes, 24*, 145–167. https://doi.org/10.1080/01690960802586188

Kitayama, S., & Markus, H. R. (1994). Introduction to cultural psychology and emotion research. In S. Kitayama & H. R. Markus (Eds.), *Emotion and culture: Empirical studies of mutual influence* (pp. 1–22). American Psychological Association. https://doi.org/10.1037/10152-010

Kjørholt, A.-T. (2019). Early childhood and children's rights: A critical perspective. In A.-T. Kjørholt & H. Penn (Eds.), *Early childhood and development work: Theories, policies, and practices* (pp. 17–37). Palgrave MacMillan. https://doi.org/10.1007/978-3-319-91319-3_2

Knafo, A., Schwartz, S. H., & Levine, R. V. (2009). Helping strangers is lower in embedded cultures. *Journal of Cross-Cultural Psychology, 40*, 875–879. https://doi.org/10.1177/0022022109339211

Knight, G. P., & Zerr, A. A. (2010). Introduction to the special section: Measurement equivalence in child development research. *Child Development Perspectives, 4*, 1–4. https://doi.org/10.1111/j.1750-8606.2009.00108.x

Kochanska, G., Aksan, N., & Nichols, K. E. (2003). Maternal power assertion in discipline and moral discourse contexts: Commonalities, differences, and implications for children's moral conduct and cognition. *Developmental Psychology, 39*, 949–963. https://doi.org/10.1037/0012-1649.39.6.949

Koentjaraningrat (1985). *Javanese culture*. Oxford University Press.

Kohlberg, L. (1981). *Essays on moral development: Vol. I. The philosophy of moral development*. Harper & Row.

Kokko, K., Simonton, S., Dubow, E., Lansford, J. E., Olson, S. L., Huesmann, L. R., Boxer, P., Pulkkinen, L., Bates, J. E., Dodge, K. A., & Pettit, G. S. (2014). Country, sex, and parent occupational status: Moderators of the continuity of aggression from childhood to adulthood. *Aggressive Behavior, 40*, 552–567. https://doi.org/10.1002/ab.21546

Koller, S. H., Dutra-Thomé, L., Morais, N. A., Silva, C. J. N., & Santana, J. P. (2015). Child labor: Homes, streets, factories, and stores. In L. A. Jensen (Ed.), *Child handbook of human development and culture: An interdisciplinary perspective* (pp. 456–470). Oxford University Press.

Koller, S. H., Motti-Stefanidi, F., Petersen, A. C., & Verma, S. (2017). Achieving positive development for youth globally: How far have we come and what is yet needed. In A. C. Petersen, S. H. Koller, F. Motti-Stefanidi, & S. Verma (Eds.), *Positive youth development in global contexts of social and economic change* (pp. 301–310). Taylor & Francis.

Konner, M. (1975). Relations among infants and juveniles in comparative perspective. In M. Lewis & L. A. Rosenblum (Eds.), *The origins of behavior* (pp. 99–129). Wiley.

Konner, M. (1977). Evolution of human behavior development. In P. H. Leiderman, S. Tulkin, & A. Rosenfeld (Eds.), *Culture and infancy: Variations in the human experience* (pp. 69–109). Academic Press.

Kramer, L., & Hamilton, T. (2019). Sibling caregiving. In M. H. Bornstein (Ed.), *Handbook of parenting: Vol. 3. Being and becoming a parent* (3rd ed., pp. 372–408). Taylor and Francis. https://doi.org/10.4324/9780429433214-11

Kroeber, A. L., & Kluckhohn, C. (1952). *Culture: A critical review of concepts and definitions* (Vol. 47, no. 1). Peabody Museum.

Kroll, J., & Tokowicz, N. (2005). Bilingual lexical processing. In J. F. Kroll & A. M. B. DeGroot (Eds.), *Handbook of bilingualism: Psycholinguistic approaches* (pp. 531–554). Oxford University Press.

Krug, E. G., Mercy, J. A., Dahlberg, L. L., & Zwi, A. B. (2002). The world report on violence and health. *The Lancet, 360,* 1083–1088. https://doi.org/10.1016/S0140-6736(02)11133-0

Kuhl, P. K. (2009). Linking infant speech perception to language acquisition: Phonetic learning predicts language growth. In J. Columbo, P. McCardle, & L. Freund (Eds.), *Infant pathways to language: Methods, models, and research directions* (pp. 213–244). Psychology Press.

Kuhl, P. K., Williams, K. A., Lacerda, F., Stevens, K. N., & Lindblom, B. (1992). Linguistic experience alters phonetic perception in infants by 6 months of age. *Science, 255,* 606–608. https://doi.org/10.1126/science.1736364

Kuhlmeier, V., Wynn, K., & Bloom, P. (2003). Attribution of dispositional states by 12-month-olds. *Psychological Science, 14,* 402–408. https://doi.org/10.1111/1467-9280.01454

Kuhns, C., & Cabrera, N. (2018). Fathering. In M. H. Bornstein (Ed.), *The SAGE encyclopedia of lifespan human development* (pp. 858–860). Sage.

Kumar, R. (2006). Students' experiences of home-school dissonance: The role of school academic culture and perceptions of classroom goal structures. *Contemporary Educational Psychology, 31,* 253–279. https://doi.org/10.1016/j.cedpsych.2005.08.002

Kumar, R., Zusho, A., & Bondie, R. (2018). Weaving cultural relevance and achievement motivation into inclusive classroom cultures. *Educational Psychologist, 53,* 78–96. https://doi.org/10.1080/00461520.2018.1432361

Kwan, V. S. Y., Hui, C., & McGee, J. A. (2010). What do we know about the Chinese self? Illustrations with self-esteem, self-efficacy, and self-enhancement. In M. H. Bond (Ed.), The *Oxford handbook of Chinese psychology* (pp. 279–294). Oxford University Press. https://doi.org/10.1093/oxfordhb/9780199541850.013.0018

Kwon, A. Y., Vallotton, C. D., Kiegelmann, M., & Wilhelm, K. H. (2018). Cultural diversification of communicative gestures through early childhood: A comparison of children in English-, German-, and Chinese- speaking families. *Infant Behavior and Development, 50,* 328–339. https://doi.org/10.1016/j.infbeh.2017.10.003

Kyratzis, A., & Cook-Gumperz, J. (2015). Child discourse. In D. Tannen, H. E. Hamilton, & D. Schriffin (Eds.), *The handbook of discourse analysis* (2nd ed., Vol. 1, pp. 681–704). Wiley Blackwell.

LaBarbera, J. D., Izard, C. E., Vietze, P., & Parisi, S. A. (1976). Four- and six-month-old infants' visual responses to joy, anger, and neutral expressions. *Child Development, 47,* 535–538. https://doi.org/10.2307/1128816

Ladd, G. W., Kochenderfer-Ladd, B., Eggum, N. D., Kochel, K. P., & McConnell, E. M. (2011). Characterizing and comparing the friendships of anxious-solitary and unsociable preadolescents. *Child Development, 82,* 1434–1453. https://doi.org/10.1111/j.1467-8624.2011.01632.x

LaFrance, M., Hecht, M. A., & Paluck, E. L. (2003). The contingent smile: A meta-analysis of sex differences in smiling. *Psychological Bulletin, 129,* 305–334. https://doi.org/10.1037/0033-2909.129.2.305

LaFreniere, P. J. (2000). *Emotional development: A biosocial perspective.* Wadsworth.

Lagattuta, K. H. (2007). Thinking about the future because of the past: Young children's knowledge about the causes of worry and preventative decisions. *Child Development, 78*, 1492–1509. https://doi.org/10.1111/j.1467-8624.2007.01079.x

Laible, D. J., & Thompson, R. A. (2000). Mother-child discourse, attachment security, shared positive affect, and early conscience development. *Child Development, 71*(5), 1424–1440. https://doi.org/10.1111/1467-8624.00237

Laible, D. J., & Thompson, R. A. (2002). Mother–child conflict in the toddler years: Lessons in emotion, morality, and relationships. *Child Development, 73*(4), 1187–1203. https://doi.org/10.1111/1467-8624.00466

Lam, C. B., & McHale, S. M. (2015). Time use as a cause and consequence of youth development. *Child Development Perspectives, 9*, 20–25. https://doi.org/10.1111/cdep.12100

Lam, C. B., McHale, S. M., & Crouter, A. C. (2014). Time with peers from middle childhood to late adolescence: Developmental course and adjustment correlates. *Child Development, 85*, 1677–1693. https://doi.org/10.1111/cdev.12235

Lamb, M. E. (2010). How do fathers influence child development? Let me count the ways. In M. E. Lamb (Ed.), *The role of the father in child development* (5th ed., pp. 1–26). Wiley.

Lambert, W. E. (1987). The effects of bilingual and bicultural experiences on children's attitudes and social perspectives. In P. Homel, M. Palij, & D. Aronson (Eds.), *Childhood bilingualism* (pp. 197–221). Erlbaum.

Lambert, W. W. (1971). Cross-cultural backgrounds to personality development and the socialization of aggression: Findings from the Six Cultures Study. In W. W. Lambert & R. Weisbrod (Eds.), *Comparative perspectives on social psychology* (pp. 49–61). Little, Brown.

Lamis, D. A., Wilson, C. K., Tarantino, N., Lansford, J. E., & Kaslow, N. J. (2014). Neighborhood disorder, spiritual well-being, and parenting stress in African American women. *Journal of Family Psychology, 28*, 769–778. https://doi.org/10.1037/a0036373

Lamm, B., Keller, H., Teiser, J., Gudi, H., Yovsi, R. D., Freitag, C., Poloczek, S., Fassbender, I., Suhrke, J., Teubert, M., Vöhringer, I., Knopf, M., Schwarzer, G., & Lohaus, A. (2018). Waiting for the second treat: Developing culture-specific modes of self-regulation. *Child Development, 89*, e261–e277. https://doi.org/10.1111/cdev.12847

Lancy, D. (1977). The play behavior of Kpelle children during rapid cultural change. In D. F. Lancy & B. A. Tindall (Eds.), *The anthropological study of play: Problems and prospects* (pp. 84–91). Leisure Press.

Lancy, D. F. (1980). Play in species adaptation. *Annual Review of Anthropology, 9*, 471–495. https://doi.org/10.1146/annurev.an.09.100180.002351

Lancy, D. F. (1983). *Studies in cognition and mathematics.* Academic Press.

Lancy, D. F. (1996). *Playing on the mother-ground: Cultural routines for children's development.* Guilford Press.

Lancy, D. F. (2007). Accounting for variability in mother-child play. *American Anthropologist, 109*, 273–284. https://doi.org/10.1525/aa.2007.109.2.273

Lancy, D. F. (2008). *The anthropology of childhood: Cherubs, chattel, changelings.* Cambridge University Press.

Lancy, D. F. (2015). *The anthropology of childhood: Cherubs, chattel, changelings* (2nd ed.). Cambridge University Press.

Lancy, D. F. (2018). *Anthropological perspectives on children as helpers, workers, artisans, and laborers.* Palgrave/MacMillan. https://doi.org/10.1057/978-1-137-53351-7

Lancy, D. F., Bock, J., & Gaskins, S. (2010). *The anthropology of learning in childhood.* Alta Mira Press.

Laniran, Y. O., & Clements, G. N. (2003). Downstep and high raising: Interacting factors in Yoruba tone production. *Journal of Phonetics, 31*, 203–250. https://doi.org/10.1016/S0095-4470(02)00098-0

Lansford, J. E. (2009). Parental divorce and children's adjustment. *Perspectives on Psychological Science, 4*, 140–152. https://doi.org/10.1111/j.1745-6924.2009.01114.x

Lansford, J. E., Bornstein, M. H., Deater-Deckard, K., Dodge, K. A., Al-Hassan, S. M., Bacchini, D., Bombi, A. S., Chang, L., Chen, B. B., Di Giunta, L., Malone, P. S., Oburu, P., Pastorelli, C., Skinner, A. T., Sorbring, E., Steinberg, L., Tapanya, S., Alampay, L. P., Tirado, L. M., & Zelli, A. (2016). How international research on parenting advances understanding of child development. *Child Development Perspectives, 10*, 202–207. https://doi.org/10.1111/cdep.12186

Lansford, J. E., Chang, L., Dodge, K. A., Malone, P. S., Oburu, P., Palmérus, K., Bacchini, D., Pastorelli, C., Bombi, A. S., Zelli, A., Tapanya, S., Chaudhary, N., Deater-Deckard, K., Manke, B., & Quinn, N. (2005). Physical discipline and children's adjustment: Cultural normativeness as a moderator. *Child Development, 76*, 1234–1246. https://doi.org/10.1111/j.1467-8624.2005.00847.x

Lansford, J. E., & Deater-Deckard, K. (2012). Childrearing discipline and violence in developing countries. *Child Development, 83*, 62–75. https://doi.org/10.1111/j.1467-8624.2011.01676.x

Lansford, J. E., Deater-Deckard, K., Bornstein, M. H., Putnick, D. L., & Bradley, R. H. (2014). Attitudes justifying domestic violence predict endorsement of corporal punishment and physical and psychological aggression towards children: A study in 25 low- and middle-income countries. *The Journal of Pediatrics, 164*, 1208–1213. https://doi.org/10.1016/j.jpeds.2013.11.060

Lansford, J. E., & Dodge, K. A. (2008). Cultural norms for adult corporal punishment of children and societal rates of endorsement and use of violence. *Parenting: Science and Practice, 8*, 257–270. https://doi.org/10.1080/15295190802204843

Lansford, J. E., Gauvain, M., Koller, S. H., Daiute, C., Hyson, M., Motti-Stefanidi, F., Smith, O., Verma, S., & Zhou, N. (2019). The importance of international collaborative research for advancing understanding of child and youth development. *International Perspectives in Psychology: Research, Practice, Consultation, 8*, 1–13. https://doi.org/10.1037/ipp0000102

Lansford, J. E., Godwin, J., Al-Hassan, S. M., Bacchini, D., Bornstein, M. H., Chang, L., Chen, B. B., Deater-Deckard, K., Di Giunta, L., Dodge, K. A., Malone, P. S., Oburu, P., Pastorelli, C., Skinner, A. T., Sorbring, E., Steinberg, L., Tapanya, S., Alampay, L. P., Uribe Tirado, L. M., & Zelli, A. (2018). Longitudinal associations between parenting and youth adjustment in twelve cultural groups: Cultural normativeness of parenting as a moderator. *Developmental Psychology, 54*, 362–377. https://doi.org/10.1037/dev0000416

Lansford, J. E., Godwin, J., Alampay, L. P., Uribe Tirado, L. M., Zelli, A., Al-Hassan, S. M., Bacchini, D., Bombi, A. S., Bornstein, M. H., Chang, L., Deater-Deckard, K., Di Giunta, L., Dodge, K. A., Malone, P. S., Oburu, P., Pastorelli, C., Skinner, A. T., Sorbring, E., & Tapanya, S. (2016). Mothers', fathers' and children's perceptions of parents' expectations about children's family obligations in nine countries. *International Journal of Psychology, 51*, 366–374. https://doi.org/10.1002/ijop.12185

Lansford, J. E., Malone, P. S., Dodge, K. A., Chang, L., Chaudhary, N., Tapanya, S., Oburu, P., & Deater-Deckard, K. (2010). Children's perceptions of maternal hostility as a mediator of the link between discipline and children's adjustment in four countries. *International Journal of Behavioral Development, 34*, 452–461. https://doi.org/10.1177/0165025409354933

Lansford, J. E., Malone, P. S., Dodge, K. A., Pettit, G. S., & Bates, J. E. (2010). Developmental cascades of peer rejection, social information processing biases, and aggression during middle childhood. *Development and Psychopathology, 22*, 593–602. https://doi.org/10.1017/S0954579410000301

Lansford, J. E., Woodlief, D., Malone, P. S., Oburu, P., Pastorelli, C., Skinner, A. T., Sorbring, E., Tapanya, S., Tirado, L. M., Zelli, A., Al-Hassan, S. M., Alampay, L. P., Bacchini, D., Bombi, A. S., Bornstein, M. H., Chang, L., Deater-Deckard, K., Di Giunta, L., & Dodge, K. A. (2014). A longitudinal examination of mothers' and fathers' social information processing biases and harsh discipline in nine countries. *Development and Psychopathology, 26,* 561–573. https://doi.org/10.1017/S0954579414000236

Larsen, J. T., To, Y. M., & Fireman, G. (2007). Children's understanding and experience of mixed emotions. *Psychological Science, 18,* 186–191. https://doi.org/10.1111/j.1467-9280.2007.01870.x

Larson, R. W. (2001). How U.S. adolescents spend their time: What it does (and doesn't) tell us about their development. *Current Directions in Psychological Science, 10*(5), 160–164. https://doi.org/10.1111/1467-8721.00139

Larson, R. W., & Verma, S. (1999). How children and adolescents spend time across the world: Work, play, and developmental opportunities. *Psychological Bulletin, 125,* 701–736. https://doi.org/10.1037/0033-2909.125.6.701

Laursen, B., Finkelstein, B. D., & Betts, N. T. (2001). A developmental meta-analysis of peer conflict resolution. *Developmental Review, 21,* 423–449. https://doi.org/10.1006/drev.2000.0531

Lee, M. (2003). Korean adolescents' "examination hell" and their use of free time. In S. Verma & R. Larson (Eds.), Examining adolescent leisure time across cultures: Developmental opportunities and risks. *New Directions for Child and Adolescent Development,* no 99 (pp. 9–22). Jossey Bass. https://doi.org/10.1002/cd.63

Lee, M., & Larson, R. (2000). The Korean "examination hell": Long hours of studying, distress, and depression. *Journal of Youth and Adolescence, 29,* 249–271. https://doi.org/10.1023/A:1005160717081

Lee, S. (1994). The *cheong* space: A zone of non-exchange in Korean human relationships. In G. Yoon & S. Choi (Eds.), *Psychology of the Korean people: Collectivism and individualism* (pp. 85–99). Dong-A Publishing.

Lee, S., Davis, B. L., & MacNeilage, P. F. (2008). Segmental properties of input to infants: A study of Korean. *Journal of Child Language, 35,* 591–617. https://doi.org/10.1017/S0305000908008684

Leff, S. S., Waasdorp, T. E., Paskewich, B., Gullan, R. L., Jawad, A. F., Macevoy, J. P., Feinberg, B. E., & Power, T. J. (2010). The preventing relational aggression in schools everyday program: A preliminary evaluation of acceptability and impact. *School Psychology Review, 39,* 569–587.

Lemerise, E. A., & Arsenio, W. F. (2000). An integrated model of emotion processes and cognition in social information processing. *Child Development, 71,* 107–118. https://doi.org/10.1111/1467-8624.00124

Lerner, R. M., Almerigi, J. B., Theokas, C., & Lerner, J. V. (2005). Positive youth development: A view of the issues. *The Journal of Early Adolescence, 25,* 10–16. https://doi.org/10.1177/0272431604273211

Lerner, R. M., Lerner, J. V., Bowers, E., & Geldhof, G. J. (2015). Positive youth development: A relational developmental systems model. In W. F. Overton & P. C. Molenaar (Eds.), *Handbook of child psychology and developmental science: Vol. 1. Theory and method* (7th ed., pp. 607–651). Wiley. https://doi.org/10.1002/9781118963418.childpsy116

Letiecq, B. L. (2007). African American fathering in violent neighborhoods: What role does spirituality play? *Fathering, 5,* 111–128. https://doi.org/10.3149/fth.0502.111

Levin, K. A., Torsheim, T., Vollebergh, W., Richter, M., Davies, C. A., Schnohr, C. W., Due, P., & Currie, C. (2011). National income and income inequality, family affluence and life satisfaction among 13-year-old boys and girls: A multilevel study in 35 countries. *Social Indicators Research, 104,* 179–194. https://doi.org/10.1007/s11205-010-9747-8

LeVine, R. A. (2007). Ethnographic studies of childhood: A historical overview. *American Anthropologist, 109*, 247–260. https://doi.org/10.1525/aa.2007.109.2.247

LeVine, R. A., Dixon, S., LeVine, S., Richman, A., Leiderman, P. H., Keefer, C. H., & Brazelton, T. B. (1994). *Child care and culture: Lessons from Africa.* Cambridge University Press. https://doi.org/10.1017/CBO9780511720321

Levinson, S. C. (1996). Frames of reference and Molyneux's question: Crosslinguistic evidence. In P. Bloom, M. A. Peterson, L. Nadel, & M. F. Garrett (Eds.), *Language and space* (pp. 109–169). MIT Press.

Levison, D., & Murray-Close, M. (2005). Challenges in determining how child work affects child health. *Public Health Reports, 120*, 614–620. https://doi.org/10.1177/003335490512000609

Lewis, M. (2000). Self-conscious emotions: Embarrassment, pride, shame, and guilt. In M. Lewis & J. Haviland (Eds.), *Handbook of emotions* (2nd ed., pp. 623–636). Guilford Press.

Lewis, M. (2014). *The rise of consciousness and the development of emotional life.* Guilford Press.

Lewis, M. (2015). Emotional development and consciousness. In W. F. Overton & P. C. M. Molenaar (Eds.), *Handbook of child psychology and developmental science: Vol. 1. Theory and method* (7th ed., pp. 407–451). Wiley. https://doi.org/10.1002/9781118963418.childpsy111

Lewis, M., Alessandri, S. M., & Sullivan, M. W. (1992). Differences in shame and pride as a function of children's gender and task difficulty. *Child Development, 63*, 630–638. https://doi.org/10.2307/1131351

Lewis, M., & Ramsay, D. (2002). Cortisol response to embarrassment and shame. *Child Development, 73*, 1034–1045. https://doi.org/10.1111/1467-8624.00455

Lewis, M., Takai-Kawakami, K., Kawakami, K., & Sullivan, M. W. (2010). Cultural differences in emotional responses to success and failure. *International Journal of Behavioral Development, 34*, 53–61. https://doi.org/10.1177/0165025409348559

Li, J. (2012). *Cultural foundations of learning: East and West.* Cambridge University Press. https://doi.org/10.1017/CBO9781139028400

Li, W., Woudstra, M. J., Branger, M. C. E., Wang, L., Alink, L. R. A., Mesman, J., & Emmen, R. A. G. (2019). The effect of the still-face paradigm on infant behavior: A cross-cultural comparison between mothers and fathers. *Infancy, 24*, 893–910. https://doi.org/10.1111/infa.12313

Li, Z. H., Connolly, J., Jiang, D., Pepler, D., & Craig, W. (2010). Adolescent romantic relationships in China and Canada: A cross-national comparison. *International Journal of Behavioral Development, 34*, 113–120. https://doi.org/10.1177/0165025409360292

Liben, L. S. (2001). Thinking through maps. In M. Gattis (Ed.), *Spatial schemas and abstract thought* (pp. 45–77). MIT Press.

Liben, L. S. (2009). The road to understanding maps. *Current Directions in Psychological Science, 18*, 310–315. https://doi.org/10.1111/j.1467-8721.2009.01658.x

Liben, L. S., & Christensen, A. E. (2010). Spatial development: Evolving approaches to enduring questions. In U. Goswami (Ed.), *Blackwell handbook of childhood cognitive development* (2nd ed., pp. 446–472). Wiley-Blackwell. https://doi.org/10.1002/9781444325485.ch17

Liben, L. S., & Downs, R. M. (2015). Map use skills. In M. Monmonier (Ed.), *Cartography in the twentieth century* (pp. 1074–1080). University of Chicago Press.

Lieven, E., & Stoll, S. (2010). Language. In M. H. Bornstein (Ed.), *Handbook of cultural developmental science* (pp. 143–173). Psychology Press.

Liszkowski, U., Brown, P., Callaghan, T., Takada, A., & de Vos, C. (2012). A prelinguistic gestural universal of human communication. *Cognitive Science, 36*, 698–713. https://doi.org/10.1111/j.1551-6709.2011.01228.x

Liszkowski, U., Carpenter, M., Henning, A., Striano, T., & Tomasello, M. (2004). Twelve-month-olds point to share attention and interest. *Developmental Science, 7*, 297–307. https://doi.org/10.1111/j.1467-7687.2004.00349.x

Little, T. D., Henrich, C. C., Jones, S. M., & Hawley, P. H. (2003). Disentangling the 'whys' from the 'whats' of aggressive behavior. *International Journal of Behavioral Development, 27*, 122–133. https://doi.org/10.1080/01650250244000128

Liu, C., Cox, R. B., Jr., Washburn, I. J., Croff, J. M., & Crethar, H. C. (2017). The effects of requiring parental consent for research on adolescents' risk behaviors: A meta-analysis. *The Journal of Adolescent Health, 61*, 45–52. https://doi.org/10.1016/j.jadohealth.2017.01.015

Liu, J., Chen, X., Li, D., & French, D. (2012). Shyness-sensitivity, aggression, and adjustment in urban Chinese adolescents at different historical times. *Journal of Research on Adolescence, 22*, 393–399. https://doi.org/10.1111/j.1532-7795.2012.00790.x

Liu, J., Coplan, R. J., Chen, X., Li, D., Ding, X., & Zhou, Y. (2014). Unsociability and shyness in Chinese children: Concurrent and predictive relations with indices of adjustment. *Social Development, 23*(1), 119–136. https://doi.org/10.1111/sode.12034

Liu, J., Li, D., Purwono, U., Chen, X., & French, D. C. (2015). Loneliness of Indonesian and Chinese adolescents as predicted by relationships with friends and parents. *Merrill-Palmer Quarterly, 61*, 362–382. https://doi.org/10.13110/merrpalmquar1982.61.3.0362

Livingston, G. (2011). *In a down economy, fewer births*. Pew Research Center.

Lloyd, C. B., Grant, M., & Ritchie, A. (2008). Gender differences in time use among adolescents in developing countries: Implications of rising school enrollment rates. *Journal of Research on Adolescence, 18*, 99–120. https://doi.org/10.1111/j.1532-7795.2008.00552.x

Lopez, N. L., Bonenberger, J. L., & Schneider, H. G. (2001). Parental disciplinary history, current levels of empathy, and moral reasoning in young adults. *North American Journal of Psychology, 3*, 193–204.

Lopez-Quintero, C., Freeman, P., & Neumark, Y. (2009). Hand washing among school children in Bogotá, Colombia. *American Journal of Public Health, 99*, 94–101. https://doi.org/10.2105/AJPH.2007.129759

Lu, T., Jin, S., Li, L., Niu, L., Chen, X., & French, D. C. (2018). Longitudinal associations between popularity and aggression in Chinese middle and high school adolescents. *Developmental Psychology, 54*, 2291–2301. https://doi.org/10.1037/dev0000591

Lu, T., Li, L., Niu, L., Jin, S., & French, D. C. (2018). Relations between popularity and prosocial behavior in middle and high school Chinese adolescents. *International Journal of Behavioral Development, 42*, 175–181. https://doi.org/10.1177/0165025416687411

Lubitow, A., Carathers, J., Kelly, M., & Abelson, M. (2017). Transmobilities: Mobility, harassment, and violence experienced by transgender and gender nonconforming public transit riders in Portland, Oregon. *Gender, Place and Culture, 24*, 1398–1418. https://doi.org/10.1080/0966369X.2017.1382451

Luby, S. P., Kadir, M. A., Yushuf Sharker, M. A., Yeasmin, F., Unicomb, L., & Sirajul Islam, M. (2010). A community-randomised controlled trial promoting waterless hand sanitizer and handwashing with soap, Dhaka, Bangladesh. *Tropical Medicine & International Health, 15*, 1508–1516. https://doi.org/10.1111/j.1365-3156.2010.02648.x

Ludwig, J., Duncan, G. J., Gennetian, L. A., Katz, L. F., Kessler, R. C., Kling, J. R., & Sanbonmatsu, L. (2013). Long-term neighborhood effects on low-income families: Evidence from Moving to Opportunity. *The American Economic Review, 103*, 226–231. https://doi.org/10.1257/aer.103.3.226

Luria, A. R. (1976). *Cognitive development: Its cultural and social foundations*. Harvard University Press.

Lysova, A., & Straus, M. A. (2019). Intimate partner violence: A multinational test of cultural spillover theory. *Journal of Interpersonal Violence.* https://doi.org/10.1177/0886260519839421

Maccoby, E. E. (1990). Gender and relationships. A developmental account. *American Psychologist, 45,* 513–520. https://doi.org/10.1037/0003-066X.45.4.513

Maccoby, E. E., & Martin, J. A. (1983). Socialization in the context of the family: Parent-child interaction. In E. M. Hetherington (Ed.), *Handbook of child psychology: Vol. 4. Socialization, personality, and social development* (4th ed., pp. 1–101). Wiley.

Mackie, D. (1980). A cross-cultural study of intra-individual and interindividual conflicts of centrations. *European Journal of Social Psychology, 10,* 313–318. https://doi.org/10.1002/ejsp.2420100310

MacWhinney, B. (2015). Language development. In L. Liben & U. Müller (Eds.), *Handbook of child psychology and developmental science: Vol. 2. Cognitive processes* (7th ed. pp. 296–338). Wiley. https://doi.org/10.1002/9781118963418.childpsy208

Maddieson, I. (2005). Consonant inventories. In M. Haspelmath, M. S. Dryer, D. Gil, & B. Comrie (Eds.), *The world atlas of language structures* (pp. 10–14). Oxford University Press.

Magnis-Suseno, F. (1997). *Javanese ethics and world-view: The Javanese idea of the good life.* Gramedia Pustaka Utama.

Majid, A., Bowerman, M., Kita, S., Haun, D. B., & Levinson, S. C. (2004). Can language restructure cognition? The case for space. *Trends in Cognitive Sciences, 8*(3), 108–114. https://doi.org/10.1016/j.tics.2004.01.003

Mangelsdorf, S. C., Shapiro, J. R., & Marzolf, D. (1995). Developmental and temperamental differences in emotion regulation in infancy. *Child Development, 66,* 1817–1828. https://doi.org/10.2307/1131912

Mansoory, S., Ferrer-Wreder, L., & Trost, K. (2019). Youth well-being contextualized: Perceptions of Swedish fathers. *Child and Youth Care Forum, 48,* 773–795. https://doi.org/10.1007/s10566-019-09508-6

Maphalala, Z., Pascoe, M., & Smouse, M. R. (2014). Phonological development of first language isiXhosa-speaking children aged 3;0-6;0 years: A descriptive cross-sectional study. *Clinical Linguistics & Phonetics, 28,* 176–194. https://doi.org/10.3109/02699206.2013.840860

Marey-Sarwan, I., Keller, H., & Otto, H. (2016). Stay close to me: Stranger anxiety and maternal beliefs about children's socio-emotional development among Bedouins in the unrecognized villages in the Naqab. *Journal of Cross-Cultural Psychology, 47*(3), 319–332. https://doi.org/10.1177/0022022115619231

Marfo, K. (2011). Envisioning an African child development field. *Child Development Perspectives, 5,* 140–147. https://doi.org/10.1111/j.1750-8606.2011.00169.x

Markman, E. M. (1991). The whole-object, taxonomic, and mutual exclusivity assumptions as initial constraints on word meaning. In S. A. Gelman & J. P. Byrnes (Eds.), *Perspectives on language and thought: Interrelations in development* (pp. 72–106). Cambridge University Press. https://doi.org/10.1017/CBO9780511983689.004

Markowitsch, H. J., & Röttger-Rössler, B. (Eds.). (2009). *Emotions as bio-cultural processes.* Springer-Verlag. https://doi.org/10.1007/978-0-387-09546-2

Marks, A. K, & Garcia Coll, C., (2018). Education and developmental competencies of ethnic minority children: Recent theoretical and methodological advances. *Developmental Review, 50,* 90–98. https://doi.org/10.1016/j.dr.2018.05.004

Markus, H. R., & Kitayama, S. (1991). Culture and the self: Implications for cognition, emotion, and motivation. *Psychological Review, 98,* 224–253. https://doi.org/10.1037/0033-295X.98.2.224

Markus, H. R., & Lin, L. R. (1999). Conflictways: Cultural diversity in the meanings and practices of conflict. In D. A. Prentice & D. T. Miller (Eds.), *Cultural divides: Understanding and overcoming group conflict* (pp. 302–333). Russell Sage Foundation.

Marsh, V., Mwangome, N., Jao, I., Wright, K., Molyneux, S., & Davies, A. (2019). Who should decide about children's and adolescents' participation in health research? The views of children and adults in rural Kenya. *BMC Medical Ethics, 20*, 41. https://doi.org/10.1186/s12910-019-0375-9

Martin, J. A., Hamilton, B. E., Osterman, M. J. K., Driscoll, A. K., & Mathews, T. J. (2017). Births: Final data for 2015. *National Vital Statistics Reports, 66*(1). National Center for Health Statistics.

Martini, M., & Kirkpatrick, J. (1992). Parenting in Polynesia: A view from the Marquesas. In J. L. Roopnarine & D. B. Carter (Eds.), *Parent-child socialization in diverse cultures: Annual advances in applied developmental psychology* (Vol. 5, pp. 199–222). Ablex.

Masten, A. S., Morison, P., & Pellegrini, D. S. (1985). A revised class play method of peer assessment. *Developmental Psychology, 21*(3), 523–533. https://doi.org/10.1037/0012-1649.21.3.523

Matsumoto, D. (1999). Culture and self: An empirical assessment of Markus and Kitayama's theory of independent and interdependent self-construal. *Asian Journal of Social Psychology, 2*, 289–310. https://doi.org/10.1111/1467-839X.00042

Mayer, J. D., Roberts, R. D., & Barsade, S. G. (2008). Human abilities: Emotional intelligence. *Annual Review of Psychology, 59*, 507–536. https://doi.org/10.1146/annurev.psych.59.103006.093646

Maynard, A. E. (2002). Cultural teaching: The development of teaching skills in Maya sibling interactions. *Child Development, 73*, 969–982. https://doi.org/10.1111/1467-8624.00450

Mayseless, O., & Scharf, M. (2003). What does it mean to be an adult? The Israeli experience. *New Directions for Child and Adolescent Development, 2003*, 5–20. https://doi.org/10.1002/cd.71

McCall, G. J. (1988). The organizational life cycle of relationships. In S. Duck (Ed.), *Handbook of personal relationships: Theory, research, and interventions* (pp. 467–486). Wiley.

McCormack, T., O'Connor, E., Beck, S., & Feeney, A. (2016). The development of regret and relief about the outcomes of risky decisions. *Journal of Experimental Child Psychology, 148*, 1–19. https://doi.org/10.1016/j.jecp.2016.02.008

McFarland, J., Hussar, B., Zhang, J., Wang, X., Wang, K., & Hein, S., Diliberti, M., Forrest Cataldi, E., Bullock Mann, F., & Barmer, A. (2019). *The condition of education 2019*. U.S. Department of Education, National Center for Education Statistics. https://nces.ed.gov/pubsearch/pubsinfo.asp?pubid=2019144

McHale, J. P., & Sirotkin, Y. (2019). Coparenting in diverse family systems. In M. H. Bornstein (Ed.), *Handbook of parenting: Vol. 3. Being and becoming a parent* (3rd ed., pp. 137–166). Taylor and Francis. https://doi.org/10.4324/9780429433214-4

McLoyd, V. C. (1990). The impact of economic hardship on black families and children: Psychological distress, parenting, and socioemotional development. *Child Development, 61*, 311–346. https://doi.org/10.2307/1131096

McNeill, D. (1992). *Hand and mind*. University of Chicago Press.

Medin, D., Bennis, W., & Chandler, M. (2010). Culture and the home-field disadvantage. *Perspectives on Psychological Science, 5*, 708–713. https://doi.org/10.1177/1745691610388772

Medina, J. A. M., Lozano, V. M., & Goudena, P. P. (2001). Conflict management in preschoolers: A cross cultural perspective. *International Journal of Early Years Education, 9*, 153–160.

Meltzoff, A. N., Kuhl, P. K., Movellan, J., & Sejnowski, T. J. (2009). Foundations for a new science of learning. *Science, 325*, 284–288. https://doi.org/10.1126/science.1175626

Mendoza-Denton, N., & Boum, A. (2015). Breached initiations: Sociopolitical resources and conflicts in emergent adulthood. *Annual Review of Anthropology, 44*, 295–310. https://doi.org/10.1146/annurev-anthro-102214-014012

Mercken, L., Snijders, T. A. B., Steglich, C., & de Vries, H. (2009). Dynamics of adolescent friendship networks and smoking behavior: Social network analyses in six European countries. *Social Science & Medicine, 69*, 1506–1514. https://doi.org/10.1016/j.socscimed.2009.08.003

Mesman, J., Minter, T., Angnged, A., Cissé, I. A. H., Salali, G. D., & Migliano, A. B. (2018). Universality without uniformity: A culturally inclusive approach to sensitive responsiveness in infant caregiving. *Child Development, 89*, 837–850. https://doi.org/10.1111/cdev.12795

Messinger, D. S., Fogel, A., & Dickson, K. L. (2001). All smiles are positive, but some smiles are more positive than others. *Developmental Psychology, 37*, 642–653. https://doi.org/10.1037/0012-1649.37.5.642

Meyer, J. W., Tyack, D., Nagel, J., & Gordon, A. (1979). Public education as nation-building in America: Enrollments and bureaucratization in the American States, 1870-1930. *American Journal of Sociology, 85*, 591–613. https://doi.org/10.1086/227051

Milevsky, A., & Levitt, M. J. (2005). Sibling support in early adolescence: Buffering and compensation across relationships. *European Journal of Developmental Psychology, 2*, 299–320. https://doi.org/10.1080/17405620544000048

Milgram, S. (1963). Behavioral study of obedience. *Journal of Abnormal Psychology, 67*, 371–378. https://doi.org/10.1037/h0040525

Miller, J. G. (2015). Taking culture and context into account in understanding moral development. In L. A. Jensen (Ed.), *Moral development in a global world: Research from a cultural-developmental perspective* (pp. 195–203). Cambridge University Press. https://doi.org/10.1017/CBO9781139583787.010

Miller, J. G., Bersoff, D. M., & Harwood, R. L. (1990). Perceptions of social responsibilities in India and in the United States: Moral imperatives or personal decisions? *Journal of Personality and Social Psychology, 58*, 33–47. https://doi.org/10.1037/0022-3514.58.1.33

Miller, J. G., Goyal, N., & Wice, M. (2015). Ethical considerations in research on human development and culture. In L. A. Jensen (Ed.), *The Oxford handbook of human development and culture* (pp. 14–27). Oxford University Press.

Miller, J. L., & Eimas, P. D. (1994). Observations on speech perception, its development, and the search for a mechanism. In J. C. Goodman & H. C. Nusbaum (Eds.), *The development of speech perception: The transition from speech sounds to spoken words* (pp. 37–56). MIT Press.

Miller, P., & Sperry, L. L. (1987). The socialization of anger and aggression. *Merrill-Palmer Quarterly, 33*, 1–31.

Miller, P., & Votruba-Drzal, E. (2013). Early academic skills and childhood experiences across the urban-rural continuum. *Early Childhood Research Quarterly, 28*, 234–248. https://doi.org/10.1016/j.ecresq.2012.12.005

Miller, P., Votruba-Drzal, E., & Coley, R. L. (2019). Poverty and academic achievement across the urban to rural landscape: Associations with community resources and stressors. *Russel Sage Foundation Journal of the Social Sciences, 5*, 106–122. https://doi.org/10.7758/rsf.2019.5.2.06

Miller, P. J., Fung, H., Lin, S., Chen, E. C.-H., & Boldt, B. R. (2012). How socialization happens on the ground: Narrative practices as alternate socializing pathways in Taiwanese and European-American families. *Monographs of the Society for Research in Child Development, 77*(1), 1–140. https://doi.org/10.1111/j.1540-5834.2011.00642.x

Miller, P. J., Wiley, A. R., Fung, H., & Liang, C. H. (1997). Personal storytelling as a medium of socialization in Chinese and American families. *Child Development, 68*, 557–568. https://doi.org/10.2307/1131678

Miller, S., Lansford, J. E., Costanzo, P., Malone, P. S., Golonka, M., & Killeya-Jones, L. A. (2009). Early adolescent romantic partner status, peer standing, and problem behaviors. *The Journal of Early Adolescence, 29*, 839–861. https://doi.org/10.1177/0272431609332665

Mills-Koonce, W. R., Willoughby, M. T., Zvara, B., Barnett, M., Gustafsson, H., Cox, M. J., & the Family Life Project Key Investigators. (2015). Mothers' and fathers' sensitivity and children's cognitive development in low-income, rural families. *Journal of Applied Developmental Psychology, 38*, 1–10. https://doi.org/10.1016/j.appdev.2015.01.001

Minh, A., Muhajarine, N., Janus, M., Brownell, M., & Guhn, M. (2017). A review of neighborhood effects and early child development: How, where, and for whom, do neighborhoods matter? *Health & Place, 46*, 155–174. https://doi.org/10.1016/j.healthplace.2017.04.012

Mistry, J. (1997). The development of remembering in cultural context. In N. Cowan & C. Hulme (Eds.), *The development of memory in childhood* (pp. 343–368). Psychology Press.

Mitchell, C., Hobcraft, J., McLanahan, S. S., Siegel, S. R., Berg, A., Brooks-Gunn, J. Garfinkel, I., & Notterman, D. (2014). Social disadvantage, genetic sensitivity, and children's telomere length. *Proceedings of the National Academy of Sciences, 111*, 5944–5949. https://doi.org/10.1073/pnas.1404293111

Mitra, A. K., & Rodriguez-Fernandez, G. (2010). Latin America and the Caribbean: Assessment of the advances in public health for the achievement of the Millennium Development Goals. *Journal of Environmental Research and Public Health, 7*, 2238–2255. https://doi.org/10.3390/ijerph7052238

Moffitt, T. E. (1993). Adolescence-limited and life-course-persistent antisocial behavior: A developmental taxonomy. *Psychological Review, 100*, 674–701. https://doi.org/10.1037/0033-295X.100.4.674

Molfese, V. J., & Martin, T. B. (2001). Intelligence and achievement: Measurement and prediction of developmental variations. In D. L. Molfese & V. J. Molfese (Eds.), *Developmental variations in learning* (pp. 1–22). Erlbaum. https://doi.org/10.4324/9781410604644

Montague, D. R., & Walker-Andrews, A. S. (2002). Mothers, fathers, and infants: The role of person familiarity and parental involvement in infants' perception of emotion expressions. *Child Development, 73*, 1339–1352. https://doi.org/10.1111/1467-8624.00475

Montgomery, M. R., & Hewett, P. C. (2004). *Urban poverty and health in developing countries: Household and neighborhood effects.* Policy Research Division Working Paper No. 184. Population Council. https://knowledgecommons.popcouncil.org/departments_sbsr-pgy/54/

Mooney, J., Seaton, M., Kaur, G., Marsh, H. W., & Yeung, A. S. (2016). Cultural perspectives on Indigenous and non-Indigenous Australian students' school motivation and engagement. *Contemporary Educational Psychology, 47*, 11–23. https://doi.org/10.1016/j.cedpsych.2016.04.006

Moore, C., & Dunham, P. J. (2014). *Joint attention: Its origins and role in development.* Psychology Press. https://doi.org/10.4324/9781315806617

Motti-Stefanidi, F. (2018). Resilience among immigrant youth: The role of culture, development and acculturation. *Developmental Review, 50*, 99–109. https://doi.org/10.1016/j.dr.2018.04.002

Motti-Stefanidi, F., & Asendorpf, J. B. (2017). Adaptation during a great economic recession: A cohort study of Greek and immigrant youth. *Child Development, 88*, 1139–1155. https://doi.org/10.1111/cdev.12878

Mounts, N. S., & Allen, C. (2019). Parenting styles and practices: Traditional approaches and their application to multiple types of moral behavior. In D. Laible, G. Carlo, & L.

M. Padilla-Walker (Eds.), *Oxford handbook of parenting and moral development* (pp. 41–56). Oxford University Press.

Mpofu, E., Ntinda, K., & Oakland, T. (2012). Understanding human abilities in sub-Saharan African settings. *Online Readings in Psychology and Culture, 4*(3). https://doi.org/10.9707/2307-0919.1036

Mpogole, H., Usanga, H., & Tedre, M. (2008). Mobile phones and poverty alleviation: A survey study in rural Tanzania. *Proceedings of 1st International Conference on M4D Mobile Communication Technology for Development*, 2008.

Mulder, N. (1996). *Inside Indonesian society: Cultural change in Indonesia.* Pepin Press.

Mullen, M. K., & Yi, S. (1995). The cultural context of talk about the past: Implications for the development of autobiographical memory. *Cognitive Development, 10*, 407–419. https://doi.org/10.1016/0885-2014(95)90004-7

Müller-Wille, L. (Ed.). (1998). *Franz Boas among the Inuit of Baffin Island 1883-84: Journals and letters.* University of Toronto Press. https://doi.org/10.3138/9781442675049

Mumtaz, Z., Shahid, U., & Levay, A. (2013). Understanding the impact of gendered roles on the experiences of infertility amongst men and women in Punjab. *Reproductive Health, 10*, 3. https://doi.org/10.1186/1742-4755-10-3

Munroe, R. H., & Munroe, R. L. (1971). Household density and infant care in an East African society. *The Journal of Social Psychology, 83*, 3–13. https://doi.org/10.1080/00224545.1971.9919967

Munroe, R. H., Munroe, R. L., & Brasher, A. (1985). Precursors of spatial ability: A longitudinal study among the Logoli of Kenya. *The Journal of Social Psychology, 125*, 23–33. https://doi.org/10.1080/00224545.1985.9713505

Munroe, R. H., Shimmin, H. S., & Munroe, R. L. (1984). Gender understanding and sex role preference in four cultures. *Developmental Psychology, 20*, 673–682. https://doi.org/10.1037/0012-1649.20.4.673

Munroe, R. L., & Gauvain, M. (2010). Cross-cultural study of children's learning and socialization: A short history. In D. F. Lancy, J. Bock, & S. Gaskins (Eds.), *Anthropological perspectives on learning in childhood* (pp. 35–63). Alta Mira Press.

Munroe, R. L., & Munroe, R. H. (1971). Effect of environmental experience on spatial ability in an East African society. *The Journal of Social Psychology, 83*, 15–22. https://doi.org/10.1080/00224545.1971.9919968

Murdock, G. P., Ford, C. S., Hudson, A. E., Kennedy, R., Simmons, L. W., & Whiting, J. W. M. (2000). *Outline of cultural materials* (5th ed. revised). Human Relations Area Files.

Murphy, B. C., & Eisenberg, N. (2002). An integrative examination of peer conflict: Children's reported goals, emotions, and behaviors. *Social Development, 11*, 534–557. https://doi.org/10.1111/1467-9507.00214

Murry, V. M., & Lippold, M. A. (2018). Parenting practices in diverse family structures: Examination of adolescents' development and adjustment. *Journal of Research on Adolescence, 28*, 650–664. https://doi.org/10.1111/jora.12390

Mutegi, R. G., Muriithi, M. K., & Wanjala, G. (2017). Education policies in Kenya: Does free secondary education promote equity in public secondary schools? *International Journal of Developmental Research, 7*, 16696–16699.

Nakamura, K. (1996). The use of polite language by Japanese preschool children. In Slobin, D. I., Gerhardt, J., Kyratzis, A., & Guo, J. (Eds.), *Social interaction, social context, and language: Essays in honor of Susan Ervin-Tripp* (pp. 235–250). Erlbaum.

Navon, R., & Ramsey, P. G. (1989). Possession and exchange of materials in Chinese and American preschools. *Journal of Research in Childhood Education, 4*, 18–29. https://doi.org/10.1080/02568548909594942

Needham, B. L., & Austin, E. L. (2010). Sexual orientation, parental support, and health during the transition to young adulthood. *Journal of Youth and Adolescence, 39*, 1189–1198. https://doi.org/10.1007/s10964-010-9533-6

Neels, K., Murphy, M., Ní Bhrolcháin, M., & Beaujouan, É. (2017). Rising educational participation and the trend to later childbearing. *Population and Development Review, 43,* 667–693. https://doi.org/10.1111/padr.12112

Nelson, K. (1996). *Language in cognitive development: The emergence of the mediated mind.* Cambridge University Press. https://doi.org/10.1017/CBO9781139174619

Nelson, K. (2007). Becoming a language user: Entering a symbolic world. In C. A. Brownell & C. B. Kopp (Eds.), *Socioemotional development in the toddler years: Transitions and transformations* (pp. 221–240). Guilford Press.

Nelson, L. J. (2009). An examination of emerging adulthood in Romanian college students. *International Journal of Behavioral Development, 33,* 402–411. https://doi.org/10.1177/0165025409340093

Nelson, L. J., Badger, S., & Wu, B. (2004). The influence of culture in emerging adulthood: Perspectives of Chinese college students. *International Journal of Behavioral Development, 28,* 26–36. https://doi.org/10.1080/01650250344000244

Nerlove, S. B., Roberts, J. M., Klein, R. E., Yarbrough, C., & Habicht, J.-P. (1974). Natural indicators of cognitive development: An observational study of rural Guatemalan children. *Ethos, 2,* 265–295. https://doi.org/10.1525/eth.1974.2.3.02a00040

Newport, E. L. (1990). Maturational constraints on language learning. *Cognitive Science, 14,* 11–28. https://doi.org/10.1207/s15516709cog1401_2

Ng-Mak, D. S., Salzinger, S., Feldman, R., & Stueve, A. (2002). Normalization of violence among inner-city youth: A formulation for research. *American Journal of Orthopsychiatry, 72,* 92–101. https://doi.org/10.1037/0002-9432.72.1.92

Niedźwiecka, A. (2020). Look me in the eyes: Mechanisms underlying the eye contact effect. *Child Development Perspectives, 14,* 78–82. https://doi.org/10.1111/cdep.12361

Nielsen, M., Haun, D., Kärtner, J., & Legare, C. H. (2017). The persistent sampling bias in developmental psychology: A call to action. *Journal of Experimental Child Psychology, 162,* 31–38. https://doi.org/10.1016/j.jecp.2017.04.017

Nielsen, M., & Tomaselli, K. (2010). Overimitation in Kalahari Bushman children and the origins of human cultural cognition. *Psychological Science, 21,* 729–736. https://doi.org/10.1177/0956797610368808

Nieuwenhuis, J., & Hooimeijer, P. (2016). The association between neighbourhoods and educational achievement, a systematic review and meta-analysis. *Journal of Housing and the Built Environment, 31,* 321–347. https://doi.org/10.1007/s10901-015-9460-7

Nisbett, R. E., & Cohen, D. (1996). *Culture of honor: The psychology of violence in the South.* Westview Press.

Nishino, H., & Larson, R. (2003). Japanese adolescents' free time: Juku, bukatsu, and government efforts to create more meaningful leisure. *New Directions for Child and Adolescent Development, 99,* 23–36. https://doi.org/10.1002/cd.64

Noesjirwan, J. (1978). A rule-based analysis of cultural differences in social behavior: Indonesia and Australia. *International Journal of Psychology, 13,* 305–316. https://doi.org/10.1080/00207597808246634

Norton, I. M., & Manson, S. M. (1996). Research in American Indian and Alaska Native communities: Navigating the cultural universe of values and process. *Journal of Consulting and Clinical Psychology, 64,* 856–860. https://doi.org/10.1037/0022-006X.64.5.856

Nsamenang, A. B. (1992). *Human development in cultural context: A third world perspective.* Sage. https://doi.org/10.4135/9781483326030

Nsamenang, A. B. (2005). Educational development and knowledge flow: Local and global forces in human development in Africa. *Higher Education Policy, 18,* 275–288. https://doi.org/10.1057/palgrave.hep.8300090

Nsamenang, A. B. (2015). Indigenous social science at the intersection with human development: Implications for lessons from African ecocultures. In L. A. Arnett

(Ed.), *The Oxford handbook of human development and culture* (pp. 61–76). Oxford University Press.

Nunes, T., & Bryant, P. (1996). *Children doing mathematics*. Blackwell.

Nunes, T., & Bryant, P. (2015). The development of mathematical reasoning. In L. Liben & U. Müller (Eds.), *Handbook of child psychology and developmental science: Vol. 2. Cognitive processes* (7th ed., pp. 715–762). Wiley. https://doi.org/10.1002/9781118963418.childpsy217

Nunes, T., Carraher, D. W., & Schliemann, A. D. (1985). Mathematics in the streets and in schools. *British Journal of Developmental Psychology, 3*, 21–29. https://doi.org/10.1111/j.2044-835X.1985.tb00951.x

Nunes, T., Schliemann, A. D., & Carraher, D. W. (1993). *Street mathematics and school mathematics*. Cambridge University Press.

Nydegger, W. F., & Nydegger, C. (1963). Tarong: An Ilocos barrio in the Philippines. In B. B. Whiting (Ed.), *Six cultures: Studies of child rearing* (pp. 693–868). Wiley.

Oburu, P., & Mbagaya, C. (2019). Education and parenting in Kenya. In E. Sorbring & J. E. Lansford (Eds.), *School systems, parent behavior, and academic achievement* (pp. 67–78). Springer. https://doi.org/10.1007/978-3-030-28277-6_6

Oburu, P. O. (2011). Attributions and attitudes of mothers and fathers in Kenya. *Parenting: Science and Practice, 11*, 152–162. https://doi.org/10.1080/15295192.2011.585561

Ochs, E. (1986). From feelings to grammar: A Samoan case study. In B. B. Schieffelin & E. Ochs (Eds.), *Language socialization across cultures* (pp. 251–272). Cambridge University Press.

Ochs, E. (1990). Indexicality and socialization. In J. W. Stigler, R. A. Shweder, & G. Herdt (Eds.), *Cultural psychology: Essays on comparative human development* (pp. 287–308). Cambridge University Press. https://doi.org/10.1017/CBO9781139173728.009

Ochs, E. (2002). Becoming a speaker of culture. In C. Kramsch (Ed.), *Language acquisition and language socialization: Ecological perspectives* (pp. 99–120). Continuum.

Ochs, E., & Schieffelin, B. B. (2016). *Acquiring conversational competence*. Routledge. https://doi.org/10.4324/9781315401621

Odling-Smee, F. J., Laland, K. N., & Feldman, M. W. (2003). Niche construction: The neglected process in evolution. *Monographs in Population Biology, 37*. Princeton University Press.

OECD. (2016a). *Education in Colombia: Reviews of national policies for education*. OECD Publishing. https://doi.org/10.1787/9789264250604-en

OECD. (2016b). *PISA 2015 results (Volume I): Excellence and equity in education*. OECD Publishing. https://doi.org/10.1787/9789264266490-en

OECD. (2018a). *Age of mothers at childbirth and age-specific fertility*. http://www.oecd.org/els/soc/SF_2_3_Age_mothers_childbirth.pdf

OECD. (2018b). *Online education database*. https://www.oecd.org/education/database.htm

OECD. (2019). *Secondary graduation rate*. https://doi.org/10.1787/b858e05b-en

Ogbu, J. (1981). Origins of human competence: A cultural–ecological perspective. *Child Development, 52*, 413–429. https://doi.org/10.2307/1129158

Ogbu, J. (1988). Black education: A cultural-ecological perspective. In H. P. McAdoo (Ed.), *Black families* (pp. 169–186). Sage.

Oishi, S. (2000). Goals as cornerstones of subjective well-being: Linking individuals and cultures. In E. Diener & E. M. Suh (Eds.), *Culture and subjective well-being* (pp. 87–112). Bradford.

Olson, K. R., & Gülgöz, S. (2018). Early findings from the TransYouth Project: Gender development in transgender children. *Child Development Perspectives, 12*, 93–97. https://doi.org/10.1111/cdep.12268

Olson, K. R., Key, A. C., & Eaton, N. R. (2015). Gender cognition in transgender children. *Psychological Science, 26*, 467–474. https://doi.org/10.1177/0956797614568156

Olsson, C. A., McGee, R., Nada-Raja, S., & Williams, S. M. (2013). A 32-year longitudinal study of child and adolescent pathways to well-being in adulthood. *Journal of Happiness Studies, 14,* 1069–1083. https://doi.org/10.1007/s10902-012-9369-8

Orlick, T., Zhou, Q. Y., & Partington, J. (1990). Co-operation and conflict within Chinese and Canadian kindergarten settings. *Canadian Journal of Behavioural Science, 22,* 20–25. https://doi.org/10.1037/h0078933

Osborne, J. W., & Walker, C. (2006). Stereotype threat, identification with academics, and withdrawal from school: Why the most successful students of colour might be the most likely to withdraw. *Educational Psychology, 26,* 563–577. https://doi.org/10.1080/01443410500342518

Osgood, C. E., May, W. H., & Miron, M. S. (1975). *Cross-cultural universals of affective meaning.* University of Illinois Press.

Osterweil, Z., & Nagano, K. N. (1991). Maternal views on autonomy: Japan and Israel. *Journal of Cross-Cultural Psychology, 22,* 362–375. https://doi.org/10.1177/0022022191223003

Ostrov, J. M., Kamper-DeMarco, K. E., Blakely-McClure, S. M., Perry, K. J., & Mutignani, L. (2019). Prospective associations between aggression/bullying and adjustment in preschool: Is general aggression different from bullying behavior? *Journal of Child and Family Studies, 28,* 2572–2585. https://doi.org/10.1007/s10826-018-1055-y

Otto, H., & Keller, H. (2015). A good child is a calm child: Mothers' social status, maternal conceptions of proper demeanor, and stranger anxiety in one-year-old Cameroonian Nso children. *Psihologijske Teme, 1,* 1–25.

Owens, P. E. (2002). No teens allowed: The exclusion of adolescents from public spaces. *Landscape Journal, 21,* 156–163. https://doi.org/10.3368/lj.21.1.156

Oyserman, D., Coon, H. M., & Kemmelmeier, M. (2002). Rethinking individualism and collectivism: Evaluation of theoretical assumptions and meta-analyses. *Psychological Bulletin, 128,* 3–72. https://doi.org/10.1037/0033-2909.128.1.3

Padilla, J., Jager, J., Updegraff, K. A., McHale, S. M., & Umaña-Taylor, A. J. (2020). Mexican-origin family members' unique and shared family perspectives of familism values and their links with parent-youth relationship quality. *Developmental Psychology, 56,* 993–1008. https://doi.org/10.1037/dev0000913

Padilla-Walker, L. M. (2008). Domain-appropriateness of maternal discipline as a predictor of adolescents' positive and negative outcomes. *Journal of Family Psychology, 22,* 456–464. https://doi.org/10.1037/0893-3200.22.3.456

Pallisera, M., Fullana, J., Puyaltó, C., & Vilà, M. (2016). Changes and challenges in the transition to adulthood: Views and experiences of young people with learning disabilities and their families. *European Journal of Special Needs Education, 31,* 391–406. https://doi.org/10.1080/08856257.2016.1163014

Palmer, S. B., Fais, L., Golinkoff, R. M., & Werker, J. F. (2012). Perceptual narrowing of linguistic sign occurs in the 1st year of life. *Child Development, 83,* 543–553. https://doi.org/10.1111/j.1467-8624.2011.01715.x

Pan, Y., Gauvain, M., & Schwartz, S. J. (2013). Do parents' collectivistic tendency and attitudes toward filial piety facilitate autonomous motivation among young Chinese adolescents? *Motivation and Emotion, 37,* 701–711. https://doi.org/10.1007/s11031-012-9337-y

Panchaud, C., Singh, S., Feivelson, D., & Darroch, J. E. (2000). Sexually transmitted diseases among adolescents in developed countries. *Family Planning Perspectives, 32,* 24–32, 45.

Park, B. J., Tsunetsugu, Y., Kasetani, T., Kagawa, T., & Miyazaki, Y. (2010). The physiological effects of Shinrin-yoku (taking in the forest atmosphere or forest bathing): Evidence from field experiments in 24 forests across Japan. *Environmental Health and Preventive Medicine, 15,* 18–26. https://doi.org/10.1007/s12199-009-0086-9

Park, N., & Peterson, C. (2006). Character strengths and happiness among young children: Content analysis of parental descriptions. *Journal of Happiness Studies, 7,* 323–341. https://doi.org/10.1007/s10902-005-3648-6

Parke, R. D., McDowell, D. J., Cladis, M., & Leidy, M. (2006). *Family and peer relationships: The role of emotion regulatory processes.* American Psychological Association.

Parker, A. E., Halberstadt, A. G., Dunsmore, J. C., Townley, G., Bryant, Jr. A., Thompson, J. A, & Beale, K. S. (2012). "Emotions are a window into one's heart": A qualitative analysis of parental beliefs about children's emotions across three ethnic groups. *Monographs of the Society for Research in Child Development, 77*(3), 1–136. https://doi.org/10.1111/j.1540-5834.2012.00676.x

Parrish-Morris, J., Golinkoff, R. M., & Hirsh-Pasek, K. (2013). From coo to code: A brief story of language development. In P. D. Zelazo (Ed.), *The Oxford handbook of developmental psychology, Vol. 1: Body and mind* (pp. 867–908). Oxford University Press.

Patterson, G. R. (1982). *Coercive family process.* Castalia.

Paugh, A. L. (2005). Multilingual play: Children's code-switching, role play, and agency in Dominica, West Indies. *Language in Society, 34,* 63–86. https://doi.org/10.1017/S0047404505050037

Paulus, M. (2014). The emergence of prosocial behavior: Why do infants and toddlers help, comfort, and share? *Child Development Perspectives, 8,* 77–81. https://doi.org/10.1111/cdep.12066

Pearson, B. Z., Fernandez, S. C., Lewedeg, V., & Oller, D. K. (1997). The relation of input factors of lexical learning by bilingual infants (ages 8 to 30 months). *Applied Psycholinguistics, 18,* 41–58. https://doi.org/10.1017/S0142716400009863

Pellegrini, A. D. (2009). *The role of play in human development.* Oxford University Press. https://doi.org/10.1093/acprof:oso/9780195367324.001.0001

Pellis, S. M., & Pellis, V. C. (2011). Rough and tumble play: Training and using the social brain. In A. D. Pellegrini (Ed.), *The Oxford handbook of play* (pp. 245–259). Oxford University Press.

Peng, Y., & Wong, O. M. H. (2016). Who takes care of my left-behind children? Migrant mothers and caregivers in transnational child care. *Journal of Family Issues, 37,* 2021–2044. https://doi.org/10.1177/0192513X15578006

Penn, H. (2019). Patronage, welfare, tenders, private consultancies and expert measurement: What is happening in early childhood education and care. In A.-T. Kjørholt & H. Penn (Eds.), *Early childhood and development work: Theories, policies, and practices* (pp. 1–15). Palgrave MacMillan. https://doi.org/10.1007/978-3-319-91319-3_1

Perry, D. G., Perry, L. C., & Kennedy, E. (1992). Conflict and the development of antisocial behavior. In C. U. Shantz & W. W. Hartup (Eds.), *Conflict in child and adolescent development* (pp. 301–329). Cambridge University Press.

Petersen, S. (2017). Human subjects review standards and procedures in international research: Critical ethical and cultural issues and recommendations. *International Perspectives in Psychology: Research, Practice, Consultation, 6,* 165–178. https://doi.org/10.1037/ipp0000072

Pew Research Center. (2019). *Same-sex marriage around the world.* Pew Research Center.

Phelan, D., Davidson, A. L., & Cao, H. T. (1991). Students' multiple worlds: Negotiating the boundaries of family, peer, and school cultures. *Anthropology & Education Quarterly, 22,* 224–250. https://doi.org/10.1525/aeq.1991.22.3.05x1051k

Pinquart, M., & Kauser, R. (2018). Do the associations of parenting styles with behavior problems and academic achievement vary by culture? Results from a meta-analysis. *Cultural Diversity & Ethnic Minority Psychology, 24,* 75–100. https://doi.org/10.1037/cdp0000149

Plomin, R., DeVries, J. C., Knopik, V. S., & Neiderhiser, J. M. (2016). *Behavioral genetics* (7th ed.). Worth.

Polesel, J., Rice, S., & Dulfer, N. (2014). The impact of high-stakes testing on curriculum and pedagogy: A teacher perspective from Australia. *Journal of Education Policy*, *29*, 640–657. https://doi.org/10.1080/02680939.2013.865082

Pomerantz, E. M., Grolnick, W. S., & Price, C. E. (2005). The role of parents in how children approach achievement: A dynamic process perspective. In A. J. Elliot & C. S. Dweck (Eds.), *Handbook of competence and motivation* (pp. 229–278). Guilford Press.

Pomerantz, E. M., Ng, F., Cheung, C. S.-S., & Qu, Y. (2014). Raising happy children who succeed in school: Lessons from China and the United States. *Child Development Perspectives*, *8*, 71–76. https://doi.org/10.1111/cdep.12063

Post, D. (2011). Primary school student employment and academic achievement in Chile, Colombia, Ecuador, and Peru. *International Labour Review*, *150*, 255–278. https://doi.org/10.1111/j.1564-913X.2011.00116.x

Post, D., & Pong, S. (2000). Employment during middle school: Effects on academic achievement in the U. S. and abroad. *Educational Evaluation and Policy Analysis*, *22*, 273–298.

Prescott, A. T., Sargent, J. D., & Hull, J. G. (2018). Metaanalysis of the relationship between violent video game play and physical aggression over time. *Proceedings of the National Academy of Sciences of the United States of America*, *115*, 9882–9888. https://doi.org/10.1073/pnas.1611617114

Price-Williams, D. R. (1962). Abstract and concrete modes of classification in a primitive society. *The British Journal of Educational Psychology*, *32*, 50–61. https://doi.org/10.1111/j.2044-8279.1962.tb01732.x

Provasnik, S., Malley, L., Stephens, M., Landeros, K., Perkins, R., & Tang, J. H. (2016). *Highlights from TIMSS and TIMSS Advanced 2015: Mathematics and science achievement of U.S. students in Grades 4 and 8 and in advanced courses at the end of high school in an international context*. U.S. Department of Education. http://nces.ed.gov/pubsearch

Pruden, S. M., Levine, S. C., & Huttenlocher, J. (2011). Children's spatial thinking: Does talk about the spatial world matter? *Developmental Science*, *14*, 1417–1430. https://doi.org/10.1111/j.1467-7687.2011.01088.x

Puchala, C., Vu, L. T., & Muhajarine, N. (2010). Neighbourhood ethnic diversity buffers school readiness impact in ESL children. *Canadian Journal of Public Health*, *101* (Suppl. 3), S13–S18.

Purwono, U., & French, D. C. (2016). Depression and its relation to loneliness and religiosity in Indonesian Muslim adolescents. *Mental Health, Religion & Culture*, *19*(3), 218–228. https://doi.org/10.1080/13674676.2016.1165190

Putallaz, M., & Sheppard, B. H. (1992). Conflict management and social competence. In C. U. Shantz & W. W. Hartup (Eds.), *Conflict in child and adolescent development* (pp. 330–355). Cambridge University Press.

Putnam, S. P., Sanson, A. V., & Rothbart, M. (2002). Child temperament and parenting. In M. Bornstein (Ed.), *Handbook of parenting* (2nd ed., pp. 255–278). Erlbaum.

Putnick, D. L., & Bornstein, M. H. (2016). Girls' and boys' labor and household chores in low- and middle-income countries. In M. H. Bornstein, D. L. Putnick, J. E. Lansford, K. Deater-Deckard, & R. H. Bradley, Gender in low- and middle-income countries. *Monographs of the Society for Research in Child Development*, *81*(1), 104–122. https://doi.org/10.1111/mono.12228

Qian, Z., Lichter, D. T., & Tumin, D. (2018). Divergent pathways to assimilation? Local marriage markets and intermarriage among U.S. Hispanics. *Journal of Marriage and the Family*, *80*, 271–288. https://doi.org/10.1111/jomf.12423

Qin, L., Pomerantz, E. M., & Wang, Q. (2009). Are gains in decision-making autonomy during early adolescence beneficial for emotional functioning? The case of the United States and china. *Child Development*, *80*, 1705–1721. https://doi.org/10.1111/j.1467-8624.2009.01363.x

Quirk, K. J., Keith, T. Z., & Quirk, J. T. (2001). Employment during high school and student achievement: Longitudinal analysis of national data. *The Journal of Educational Research, 95*, 4–10. https://doi.org/10.1080/00220670109598778

Raikes, A. (2017). Measuring child development and learning. *European Journal of Education Research, 52*, 511–522. https://doi.org/10.1111/ejed.12249

Ramírez, J. M., Fujihara, T., & van Goozen, S. (2001). Cultural and gender differences in anger and aggression: A comparison between Japanese, Dutch, and Spanish students. *The Journal of Social Psychology, 141*, 119–121. https://doi.org/10.1080/00224540109600528

Rao, Y. (2019). From Confucianism to psychology: Rebooting Internet addicts in China. *History of Psychology, 22*, 328–350. https://doi.org/10.1037/hop0000111

Raufelder, D., Bakadorova, O., Yalcin, S., Dibek, M. I., & Yavuz, H. C. (2017). Motivational relations with peers and teachers among German and Turkish adolescents: A cross-cultural perspective. *Learning and Individual Differences, 55*, 13–20. https://doi.org/10.1016/j.lindif.2017.02.004

Raval, V. V., & Martini, T. S. (2009). Maternal socialization of children's anger, sadness, and physical pain in two communities in Gujarat, India. *International Journal of Behavioral Development, 33*, 215–229. https://doi.org/10.1177/0165025408098022

Ravindran, N., Berry, D., & McElwain, N. L. (2019). Dynamic bidirectional associations in negative behavior: Mother-toddler interaction during a snack delay. *Developmental Psychology, 55*, 1191–1198. https://doi.org/10.1037/dev0000703

Reed, J., Hirsh-Pasek, K., & Golinkoff, R. M. (2017). Learning on hold: Cell phones sidetrack parent-child interactions. *Developmental Psychology, 53*, 1428–1436. https://doi.org/10.1037/dev0000292

Ricketts, S., Klingler, G., & Schwalberg, R. (2014). Game change in Colorado: Widespread use of long-acting reversible contraceptives and rapid decline in births among young, low-income women. *Perspectives on Sexual and Reproductive Health, 46*, 125–132. https://doi.org/10.1363/46e1714

Rivers, S. E., Brackett, M. A., Reyes, M. R., Mayer, J. D., Caruso, D. R., & Salovey, P. (2012). Measuring emotional intelligence in early adolescence with the MSCEIT-YV: Psychometric properties and relationship with academic performance and psychosocial functioning. *Journal of Psychoeducational Assessment, 30*, 344–366. https://doi.org/10.1177/0734282912449443

Robbins, E., & Rochat, P. (2011). Emerging signs of strong reciprocity in human ontogeny. *Frontiers in Psychology, 2*(2), 353. https://doi.org/10.3389/fpsyg.2011.00353

Robert Wood Johnson Foundation. (2013). *Why does education matter so much to health?* http://www.rwjf.org/content/dam/farm/reports/issue_briefs/2012/rwjf403347

Roberts, L., Chartier, Y., Chartier, O., Malenga, G., Toole, M., & Rodka, H. (2001). Keeping clean water clean in a Malawi refugee camp: A randomized intervention trial. *Bulletin of the World Health Organization, 79*, 280–287.

Roberts, M. E., Nargiso, J. E., Gaitonde, L. B., Stanton, C. A., & Colby, S. M. (2015). Adolescent social networks: General and smoking-specific characteristics associated with smoking. *Journal of Studies on Alcohol and Drugs, 76*, 247–255. https://doi.org/10.15288/jsad.2015.76.247

Rochat, P., Dias, M. D. G., Guo, L., Broesch, T., Passos-Ferreira, C., Winning, A., & Berg, B. (2009). Fairness in distributive justice by 3- and 5-year-olds across seven cultures. *Journal of Cross-Cultural Psychology, 40*, 416–442. https://doi.org/10.1177/0022022109332844

Rodriguez, C. M. (2010). Parent-child aggression: Association with child abuse potential and parenting styles. *Violence and Victims, 25*, 728–741. https://doi.org/10.1891/0886-6708.25.6.728

Rogoff, B. (1981). Schooling and the development of cognitive skills. In H. C. Triandis & A. Heron (Eds.), *Handbook of cross-cultural psychology* (Vol. IV, pp. 233–294). Allyn & Bacon.

Rogoff, B. (1990). *Apprenticeship in thinking: Cognitive development in social context.* Oxford University Press.

Rogoff, B. (2003). *The cultural nature of human development.* Oxford University Press.

Rogoff, B., Coppens, A. D., Alcalá, L., Aceves-Azurara, I., Ruvalcaba, O., López, A., & Dayton, A. (2017). Noticing learners' strengths through cultural research. *Perspectives on Psychological Science, 12,* 876–888. https://doi.org/10.1177/1745691617718355

Rogoff, B., Correa-Chávez, M., & Cotuc, M. N. (2005). A cultural/historical view of schooling in human development. In D. B. Pillemer & S. H. White (Eds.), *Developmental psychology and social change* (pp. 225–263). Cambridge University Press. https://doi.org/10.1017/CBO9780511610400.011

Rogoff, B., Dahl, A., & Callanan, M. (2018). The importance of understanding children's lived experiences. *Developmental Review, 50,* 5–15. https://doi.org/10.1016/j.dr.2018.05.006

Rogoff, B., Paradise, R., Arauz, R. M., Correa-Chávez, M., & Angelillo, C. (2003). Firsthand learning through intent participation. *Annual Review of Psychology, 54,* 175–203. https://doi.org/10.1146/annurev.psych.54.101601.145118

Rohner, R. P. (2004). The parental "acceptance-rejection syndrome": Universal correlates of perceived rejection. *American Psychologist, 59,* 830–840. https://doi.org/10.1037/0003-066X.59.8.830

Rohner, R. P., & Lansford, J. E. (2017). Deep structure of the human affectional system: Introduction to interpersonal acceptance-rejection theory. *Journal of Family Theory & Review, 9,* 426–440. https://doi.org/10.1111/jftr.12219

Roisman, G. I., & Groh, A. M. (2011). Attachment theory and research in developmental psychology: An overview and appreciative critique. In M. K. Underwood & L. H. Rosen (Eds.), *Social development: Relationships in infancy, childhood, and adolescence* (pp. 101–126). Guilford Press.

Roisman, G. I., Masten, A. S., Coatsworth, J. D., & Tellegen, A. (2004). Salient and emerging developmental tasks in the transition to adulthood. *Child Development, 75,* 123–133. https://doi.org/10.1111/j.1467-8624.2004.00658.x

Rojas, V., Guerrero, G., & Vargas, J. (2016). *Gendered trajectories through education, work and parenthood in Peru.* Young Lives.

Romero, E., Richards, M. H., Harrison, P. R., Garbarino, J., & Mozley, M. (2015). The role of neighborhood in the development of aggression in urban African American youth: A multilevel analysis. *American Journal of Community Psychology, 56,* 156–169. https://doi.org/10.1007/s10464-015-9739-6

Roopnarine, J. L. (2011). Cultural variations in beliefs about play, parent–child play, and children's play: Meaning for childhood development. In A. D. Pellegrini (Ed.), *The Oxford handbook of the development of play* (pp. 19–27). Oxford University Press.

Rose, A. J., & Asher, S. R. (1999). Children's goals and strategies in response to conflicts within a friendship. *Developmental Psychology, 35,* 69–79. https://doi.org/10.1037/0012-1649.35.1.69

Ross, C. E., & Mirowsky, J. (2001). Neighborhood disadvantage, disorder, and health. *Journal of Health and Social Behavior, 42,* 258–276. https://doi.org/10.2307/3090214

Ross, H. S. (1996). Negotiating principles of entitlement in sibling property disputes. *Developmental Psychology, 32,* 90–101. https://doi.org/10.1037/0012-1649.32.1.90

Ross, H. S., & Conant, C. L. (1992). The social structure of early conflict: Interaction, relationships, and alliances. In C. U. Shantz & W. H. Hartup (Eds.), *Conflict in child and adolescent development* (pp. 153–185). Cambridge University Press.

Rothbart, M. K., & Bates, J. (2006). Temperament. In N. Eisenberg (Ed.), *Handbook of child psychology: Vol. 3. Social, emotional, and personality development* (6th ed., pp. 99–166). Wiley.

Rothbaum, F., Pott, M., Azuma, H., Miyake, K., & Weisz, J. (2000). The development of close relationships in Japan and the United States: Paths of symbiotic harmony and generative tension. *Child Development, 71*, 1121–1142. https://doi.org/10.1111/1467-8624.00214

Rothbaum, F., Weisz, J., Pott, M., Miyake, K., & Morelli, G. (2000). Attachment and culture. Security in the United States and Japan. *American Psychologist, 55*, 1093–1104. https://doi.org/10.1037/0003-066X.55.10.1093

Rubin, D. C. (1995). *Memory in oral traditions: The cognitive psychology of epic, ballads, and counting-out rhymes.* Oxford University Press.

Rubin, K. H., Bukowski, W. M., & Bowker, J. C. (2015). Children in peer groups. In M. H. Bornstein & T. Leventhal (Eds.), *Handbook of child psychology and developmental science: Vol. 4. Ecological settings and processes* (7th ed., pp. 175–222). Wiley. https://doi.org/10.1002/9781118963418.childpsy405

Rubin, K. H., & Coplan, R. J. (2004). Paying attention to and not neglecting social withdrawal and social isolation. *Merrill-Palmer Quarterly, 50*, 506–534. https://doi.org/10.1353/mpq.2004.0036

Rudolph, K. D., Lansford, J. E., & Rodkin, P. (2017). Interpersonal theories of developmental psychopathology. In D. Cicchetti (Ed.), *Developmental psychopathology* (pp. 243–311). Wiley.

Russell, D. W. (1996). UCLA Loneliness Scale (Version 3): Reliability, validity, and factor structure. *Journal of Personality Assessment, 66*, 20–40. https://doi.org/10.1207/s15327752jpa6601_2

Rutter, M. (2006). *Genes and behavior.* Blackwell.

Ruvolo, P., Messinger, D., & Movellan, J. (2015). Infants time their smiles to make their moms smile. *PLOS ONE, 10*(9), e0136492. https://doi.org/10.1371/journal.pone.0136492

Ryan, R. M., & Deci, E. L. (2000). Self-determination theory and the facilitation of intrinsic motivation, social development, and well-being. *American Psychologist, 55*, 68–78. https://doi.org/10.1037/0003-066X.55.1.68

Saarni, C., Campos, J. J., & Camras, L. (2006). Emotional development: Action, communication, and understanding. In N. Eisenberg (Ed.), *Handbook of child psychology: Vol. 3. Social, emotional, and personality development* (6th ed., pp. 226–299). Wiley.

Saffran, J. R., Aslin, R. N., & Newport, E. L. (1996). Statistical learning by 8-month-old infants. *Science, 274*, 1926–1928. https://doi.org/10.1126/science.274.5294.1926

Sahlberg, P. (2011). *Finnish lessons: What can the world learn from educational change in Finland?* Teachers College, Columbia University.

Salmivalli, C., Kaukiainen, A., & Lagerspetz, K. (2000). Aggression and sociometric status among peers: Do gender and type of aggression matter? *Scandinavian Journal of Psychology, 41*, 17–24. https://doi.org/10.1111/1467-9450.00166

Salomo, D., & Liszkowski, U. (2013). Sociocultural settings influence the emergence of prelinguistic deictic gestures. *Child Development, 84*, 1296–1307. https://doi.org/10.1111/cdev.12026

Sameroff, A. (Ed.). (2009). *The transactional model of development: How children and contexts shape each other.* American Psychological Association. https://doi.org/10.1037/11877-001

Sameroff, A. J., & Haith, M. M. (1996). *The five to seven year shift: The age of reason and responsibility.* University of Chicago Press.

Sánchez Gassen, N., & Perelli-Harris, B. (2015). The increase in cohabitation and the role of union status in family policies: A comparison of 12 European countries. *Journal of European Social Policy, 25*, 431–449. https://doi.org/10.1177/0958928715594561

Sanson, A. V., Burke, S. E. L., & Van Hoorn, J. (2018). Climate change: Implications for parents and parenting. *Parenting: Science and Practice, 18*, 200–217. https://doi.org/10.1080/15295192.2018.1465307

Santos, A. P. (2017). *Low income expat women pay the price for unmarried sex in Qatar*. Pulitzer Center. https://pulitzercenter.org/reporting/low-income-expat-women-pay-price-unmarried-sex-qatar

Saroglou, V. (2013). Religion, spirituality, and altruism. In K. I. Pargament, J. J. Exline, & J. W. Jones (Eds.), *APA handbook of psychology, religion, and spirituality: Vol. 1. Context, theory, and research* (pp. 439–457). American Psychological Association.

Saxe, G. B. (1981). Body parts as numerals: A developmental analysis of enumeration among a village population in Papua New Guinea. *Child Development, 52,* 306–316. https://doi.org/10.2307/1129244

Saxe, G. B. (1988). The mathematics of child street vendors. *Child Development, 59,* 1415–1425. https://doi.org/10.2307/1130503

Saxe, G. B. (2014). *Cultural development of mathematical ideas: Papua New Guinea studies.* Cambridge University Press.

Scales, P. C., Benson, P. L., & Roehlkepartain, E. C. (2011). Adolescent thriving: The role of sparks, relationships, and empowerment. *Journal of Youth and Adolescence, 40,* 263–277. https://doi.org/10.1007/s10964-010-9578-6

Scales, P. C., Roehlkepartain, E. C., & Shramko, M. (2017). Aligning youth development theory, measurement, and practice across cultures and contexts: Lessons from use of the Developmental Assets Profile. *Child Indicators Research, 10,* 1145–1178. https://doi.org/10.1007/s12187-016-9395-x

Scales, P. C., Roehlkepartain, E. C., Wallace, T., Inselman, A., Stephenson, P., & Rodriguez, M. (2015). Brief report: Assessing youth well-being in global emergency settings: Early results from the Emergency Developmental Assets Profile. *Journal of Adolescence, 45,* 98–102. https://doi.org/10.1016/j.adolescence.2015.09.002

Schäfer, M., Haun, D. B. M., & Tomasello, M. (2015). Fair is not fair everywhere. *Psychological Science, 26,* 1252–1260. https://doi.org/10.1177/0956797615586188

Scharf, M., & Mayseless, O. (2010). Finding the authentic self in a communal culture: Developmental goals in emerging adulthood. *New Directions for Child and Adolescent Development, 130,* 83–95.

Schieffelin, B. B., & Ochs, E. (1986). *Language socialization across cultures.* Cambridge University Press.

Schlegel, A., & Barry, H., III. (1991). *Adolescence: An anthropological inquiry.* Free Press.

Schmidt, M. F. H., Rakoczy, H., & Tomasello, M. (2011). Young children attribute normativity to novel actions without pedagogy or normative language. *Developmental Science, 14,* 530–539. https://doi.org/10.1111/j.1467-7687.2010.01000.x

Schmidt, M. F. H., & Sommerville, J. A. (2011). Fairness expectations and altruistic sharing in 15-month-old human infants. *PLOS ONE, 6*(10), e23223. https://doi.org/10.1371/journal.pone.0023223

Schneider, W. (2010). Memory development in childhood. In U. Goswami (Ed.), *The Wiley-Blackwell handbook of childhood cognitive development* (2nd ed., pp. 347–376). Blackwell. https://doi.org/10.1002/9781444325485.ch13

Schneider, W., & Chein, J. M. (2003). Controlled and automatic processing: Behavior, theory, and biological mechanisms. *Cognitive Science, 27,* 525–559. https://doi.org/10.1207/s15516709cog2703_8

Schoenmaker, C., Juffer, F., van IJzendoorn, M. H., Linting, M., van der Voort, A., & Bakermans-Kranenburg, M. J. (2015). From maternal sensitivity in infancy to adult attachment representations: A longitudinal adoption study with secure base scripts. *Attachment & Human Development, 17,* 241–256. https://doi.org/10.1080/14616734.2015.1037315

Schröder, L., Kärtner, J., Keller, H., & Chaudhary, N. (2012). Sticking out and fitting in: Culture-specific predictors of 3-year-olds' autobiographical memories during joint reminiscing. *Infant Behavior and Development, 35,* 627–634. https://doi.org/10.1016/j.infbeh.2012.06.002

Schulenberg, J. E., Bryant, A. L., & O'Malley, P. M. (2004). Taking hold of some kind of life: How developmental tasks relate to trajectories of well-being during the transition to adulthood. *Development and Psychopathology, 16*, 1119–1140. https://doi.org/10.1017/S0954579404040167

Schwartz, R. G., & Leonard, L. B. (1984). Words, objects, and actions in early lexical acquisition. *Journal of Speech and Hearing Research, 27*, 119–127. https://doi.org/10.1044/jshr.2701.119

Sear, R. (2016). Beyond the nuclear family: An evolutionary perspective on parenting. *Current Opinion in Psychology, 7*, 98–103. https://doi.org/10.1016/j.copsyc.2015.08.013

Segool, N. K., Carlson, J. S., Goforth, A. N., von der Embse, N., & Barterian, J. A. (2013). Heightened test anxiety among young children: Elementary school students' anxious responses to high-stakes testing. *Psychology in the Schools, 50*, 489–499. https://doi.org/10.1002/pits.21689

Selin, H., & Stone, P. K. (Eds.). (2009). *Childbirth across cultures: Ideas and practices of pregnancy, childbirth and the postpartum.* Springer. https://doi.org/10.1007/978-90-481-2599-9

Senghas, A., & Coppola, M. (2001). Children creating language: How Nicaraguan sign language acquired a spatial grammar. *Psychological Science, 12*, 323–328. https://doi.org/10.1111/1467-9280.00359

Serpell, R. (1979a). *Culture's influence on behavior.* Methuen.

Serpell, R. (1979b). How specific are perceptual skills? A cross-cultural study of pattern reproduction. *British Journal of Psychology, 70*, 365–380. https://doi.org/10.1111/j.2044-8295.1979.tb01706.x

Serpell, R. (2011). Social responsibility as a dimension of intelligence, and as an educational goal: Insights from programmatic research in an African society. *Child Development Perspectives, 5*, 126–133. https://doi.org/10.1111/j.1750-8606.2011.00167.x

Serpell, R. (2018). Situated understanding of human development in Africa: Systematic inquiries at the nexus of psychology, social science and history. *Culture and Psychology, 24*, 382–397. https://doi.org/10.1177/1354067X18779034

Serpell, R., & Hatano, G. (1997). Education, schooling, and literacy. In J. W. Berry, P. R. Dasen, & T. S. Saraswathi (Eds.), *Handbook of cross-cultural psychology: Vol. 2. Basic processes and human development* (pp. 339–376). Allyn and Bacon.

Settersten, R. A., & Ray, B. E. (2010). *Not quite adults: Why 20-somethings are choosing a slower path to adulthood, and why it's good for everyone.* Bantam Books.

76 Crimes. (2019). *72 countries where homosexuality is illegal.* https://76crimes.com/76-countries-where-homosexuality-is-illegal/

Shantz, C. U. (1987). Conflicts between children. *Child Development, 58*, 283–285. https://doi.org/10.2307/1130507

Shapiro, D., Dundar, A., Wakhungu, P. K., Yuan, X., & Harrell, A. (2015, July). *Transfer and mobility: A national view of student movement in postsecondary institutions, fall 2008 cohort* (Signature Report No. 9). National Student Clearinghouse Research Center.

Sharabany, R. (2006). The cultural context of children and adolescents: Peer relationships and intimate friendships among Arab and Jewish children in Israel. In X. Chen, D. C. French, & B. H. Schneider (Eds.), *Peer relationships in cultural context* (pp. 452–478). Cambridge University Press. https://doi.org/10.1017/CBO9780511499739.020

Sharma, D., & Verma, S. (2013). Street girls and their fight for survival across four developing countries. *Psychological Studies, 58*, 365–373. https://doi.org/10.1007/s12646-013-0226-6

Sharon, T. (2016). Constructing adulthood: Markers of adulthood and well-being among emerging adults. *Emerging Adulthood, 4*(3), 161–167. https://doi.org/10.1177/2167696815579826

Shatz, M. (1983). Communication. In P. Mussen (Ed.), *Handbook of child psychology* (pp. 841–889). Wiley.

Shatz, M. (1994). Theory of mind and the development of sociolinguistic intelligence in early childhood. In C. Lewis & P. Mitchell (Eds.), *Children's early understanding of mind: Origins and development* (pp. 311–329). Erlbaum.

Shen, M., Purwono, U., & French, D. C. (2020). Romance, religion, and problem behavior in Indonesian Muslim adolescents. *Journal of Adolescence, 81,* 87–95. https://doi.org/10.1016/j.adolescence.2020.04.001

Shen, M., Purwono, U., Liu, J., Li, D., Zhao, S., Chen, X., Gest, S., & French, D. C. (March, 2019). Children's friendships and networks in China, USA, and Indonesia. In D. Delay (Chair), *Considering the impact of social context and group norms across cultures.* Symposium conducted at the biennial meeting of the Society for Research in Child Development, Baltimore, MD.

Sherman, N. (1993). Aristotle on the shared life. In N. K. Badhwar (Ed.), *Friendship: A philosophical reader* (pp. 91–107). Cornell University Press. https://doi.org/10.7591/9781501741104-007

Shultz, S., & Vouloumanos, A. (2010). Three-month olds prefer speech to other naturally occurring signals. *Language Learning and Development, 6,* 241–257. https://doi.org/10.1080/15475440903507830

Shwalb, D. W., Shwalb, B. J., Nakazawa, J., Hyun, J.-H., Le, H. V., & Satiadarma, M. P. (2010). East and Southeast Asia: Japan, South Korea, Vietnam, and Indonesia. In M. H. Bornstein (Ed.), *Handbook of cultural developmental science* (pp. 445–464). Taylor and Francis.

Shweder, R. A. (2003). *Why do men barbecue: Recipes for cultural psychology.* Harvard University Press.

Shweder, R. A., & Haidt, J. (2000). The cultural psychology of the emotions: Ancient and new. In M. Lewis & J. M. Haviland-Jones (Eds.), *Handbook of emotions* (2nd ed., pp. 397–414). Guilford Press.

Siegler, R. S., Duncan, G. J., Davis-Kean, P. E., Duckworth, K., Claessens, A., Engel, M., Susperreguy, M. I., & Chen, M. (2012). Early predictors of high school mathematics achievement. *Psychological Science, 23,* 691–697. https://doi.org/10.1177/0956797612440101

Sijtsema, J. J., Lindenberg, S. M., Ojanen, T. J., & Salmivalli, C. (2020). Direct aggression and the balance between status and affection goals in adolescence. *Journal of Youth and Adolescence, 49,* 1481–1491. https://doi.org/10.1007/s10964-019-01166-0

Singelis, T. M., Triandis, H. C., Bhawuk, D. P. S., & Gelfand, M. J. (1995). Horizontal and vertical dimensions of individualism and collectivism: A theoretical and measurement refinement. *Cross-Cultural Research: The Journal of Comparative Social Science, 29,* 240–275. https://doi.org/10.1177/106939719502900302

Singer, T., & Klimecki, O. M. (2014). Empathy and compassion. *Current Biology, 24,* R875–R878. https://doi.org/10.1016/j.cub.2014.06.054

Skinner, A. T., Bacchini, D., Lansford, J. E., Godwin, J., Sorbring, E., Tapanya, S., Tirado, L. M., Zelli, A., Alampay, L. P., Al-Hassan, S. M., Bombi, A. S., Bornstein, M. H., Chang, L., Deater-Deckard, K., Giunta, L. D., Dodge, K. A., Malone, P. S., Miranda, M. C., Oburu, P., & Pastorelli, C. (2014). Neighborhood danger, parental monitoring, harsh parenting, and child aggression in nine countries. *Societies, 4,* 45–67. https://doi.org/10.3390/soc4010045

Skinner, A. T., Lansford, J. E., Bornstein, M. H., Deater-Deckard, K., Dodge, K. A., Malone, P. S., & Steinberg, L. (2019). Education and parenting in the United States. In E. Sorbring & J. E. Lansford (Eds.), *School systems, parent behavior, and academic achievement* (Vol. 3, pp. 123–138). Springer. https://doi.org/10.1007/978-3-030-28277-6_10

Skinner, A. T., Oburu, P., Lansford, J. E., & Bacchini, D. (2014). Childrearing violence and child adjustment following exposure to Kenyan post-election violence. *Psychology of Violence, 4,* 37–50. https://doi.org/10.1037/a0033237

Skinner, B. F. (1957). *Verbal behavior.* Appleton-Century-Crofts. https://doi.org/10.1037/11256-000

Sloane, S., Baillargeon, R., & Premack, D. (2012). Do infants have a sense of fairness? *Psychological Science, 23,* 196–204. https://doi.org/10.1177/0956797611422072

Slobin, D. I. (1985). *The cross-linguistic study of language acquisition* (Vols. 1 & 2). Erlbaum.

Slobin, D. I. (1992). *The cross-linguistic study of language acquisition* (Vol. 3). Erlbaum.

Slobodskaya, H. R., Gartstein, M. A., Nakagawa, A., & Putnam, S. P. (2013). Early temperament in Japan, the United States, and Russia: Do cross-cultural differences decrease with age? *Journal of Cross-Cultural Psychology, 44,* 438–460. https://doi.org/10.1177/0022022112453316

Smetana, J. G. (2002). Culture, autonomy, and personal jurisdiction in adolescent-parent relationships. *Advances in Child Development and Behavior, 29,* 51–87. https://doi.org/10.1016/S0065-2407(02)80051-9

Smetana, J. G., Wong, M., Ball, C., & Yau, J. (2014). American and Chinese children's evaluations of personal domain events and resistance to parental authority. *Child Development, 85,* 626–642. https://doi.org/10.1111/cdev.12140

Smiles, D., Short, S., & Sommer, M. (2017). "I didn't tell anyone because I was very afraid": Girls' experiences of menstruation in contemporary Ethiopia. *Women's Reproductive Health, 4,* 185–197. https://doi.org/10.1080/23293691.2017.1388721

Smith, T. B., McCullough, M. E., & Poll, J. (2003). Religiousness and depression: Evidence for a main effect and the moderating influence of stressful life events. *Psychological Bulletin, 129,* 614–636. https://doi.org/10.1037/0033-2909.129.4.614

Snarey, J. R. (1985). Cross-cultural universality of social-moral development: A critical review of Kohlbergian research. *Psychological Bulletin, 97,* 202–232. https://doi.org/10.1037/0033-2909.97.2.202

Snow, C. E. (1977). The development of conversation between mothers and babies. *Journal of Child Language, 4,* 1–22. https://doi.org/10.1017/S0305000900000453

Sobania, N. (2003). *Culture and customs of Kenya.* Greenwood Press.

Sokolov, J. L. (1993). A local contingency analysis of the fine-tuning hypothesis. *Developmental Psychology, 29,* 1008–1023. https://doi.org/10.1037/0012-1649.29.6.1008

Sorbring, E., & Gurdal, S. (2011). Attributions and attitudes of mothers and fathers in Sweden. *Parenting: Science and Practice, 11,* 177–189. https://doi.org/10.1080/15295192.2011.585565

Sørlie, A. (2020). Transgender children's right to non-discrimination in schools: The case of changing-room facilities. *International Journal of Children's Rights, 28,* 221–242. https://doi.org/10.1163/15718182-02802001

Speidel, G. E., Farran, D. C., & Jordan, C. (1989). On the learning and thinking styles of Hawaiian children. In G. E. Speidel, D. C. Farran, & C. Jordan (Eds.), *Thinking across cultures: The third international conference on thinking* (pp. 55–77). Erlbaum.

Spivack, G., & Shure, M. B. (1974). *Social adjustment of young children: A cognitive approach to solving real life problems.* Jossey Bass.

Sroufe, L. A. (1996). *Emotional development: The organization of emotional life in the early years.* Cambridge University Press. https://doi.org/10.1017/CBO9780511527661

Staff, J., Mont'alvao, A., & Mortimer, J. T. (2015). Children at work. In M. H. Bornstein & T. Leventhal (Eds.), *Handbook of child psychology and developmental science: Vol. 4. Ecological settings and processes* (7th ed., pp. 1–30). Wiley. https://doi.org/10.1002/9781118963418.childpsy409

Staub, E. (2019). Promoting healing and reconciliation in Rwanda, and generating active bystandership by police to stop unnecessary harm by fellow officers. *Perspectives on Psychological Science, 14,* 60–64. https://doi.org/10.1177/1745691618809384

Stearns, P. N. (2015). Children in history. In M. H. Bornstein & T. Leventhal (Eds.), *Handbook of child psychology and developmental science: Vol. 4. Ecological settings and processes* (7th ed., pp. 787–810). Wiley. https://doi.org/10.1002/9781118963418. childpsy420

Steele, C. M., & Aronson, J. (1995). Stereotype threat and the intellectual test performance of African Americans. *Journal of Personality and Social Psychology, 69*, 797–811. https://doi.org/10.1037/0022-3514.69.5.797

Stein, G. L., Coard, S. I., Kiang, L., Smith, R. K., & Mejia, Y. C. (2018). The intersection of racial–ethnic socialization and adolescence: A closer examination at stage-salient issues. *Journal of Research on Adolescence, 28*, 609–621. https://doi.org/10.1111/jora.12380

Steinberg, L. (2008). A social neuroscience perspective on adolescent risk-taking. *Developmental Review, 28*, 78–106. https://doi.org/10.1016/j.dr.2007.08.002

Steinberg, L., & Dornbusch, S. M. (1991). Negative correlates of part-time employment during adolescence: Replication and extension. *Developmental Psychology, 27*, 304–313. https://doi.org/10.1037/0012-1649.27.2.304

Steinberg, L., Dornbusch, S. M., & Brown, B. B. (1992). Ethnic differences in adolescent achievement: An ecological perspective. *American Psychologist, 47*, 723–729. https://doi.org/10.1037/0003-066X.47.6.723

Stenberg, C. R., Campos, J. J., & Emde, R. N. (1983). The facial expression of anger in seven-month-old infants. *Child Development, 54*, 178–184. https://doi.org/10.2307/1129875

Stepler, R. (2017). *Number of U.S. adults cohabiting with a partner continues to rise, especially among those 50 and older*. Pew Research Center.

Sternberg, R. J., & Dobson, D. M. (1987). Resolving interpersonal conflicts: An analysis of stylistic consistency. *Journal of Personality and Social Psychology, 52*, 794–812. https://doi.org/10.1037/0022-3514.52.4.794

Sterponi, L. (2010). Learning communicative competence. In D. F. Lancy, J. Bock, & S. Gaskins (Eds.), *The anthropology of learning in childhood* (pp. 235–259). Alta Mira Press.

Stevenson, H. W., & Stigler, J. W. (1992). *The learning gap: Why our schools are failing and what we can learn from Japanese and Chinese education*. Summit Books.

Stewart, S. M., & McBride-Chang, C. (2000). Influences on children's sharing in a multicultural setting. *Journal of Cross-Cultural Psychology, 31*, 333–348. https://doi.org/10.1177/0022022100031003003

Stigler, J. W., & Hiebert, J. (1997). Understanding and improving classroom mathematics instruction: An overview of the TIMSS video study. *Phi Delta Kappan, 79*, 14–21.

Stobart, G., & Eggen, T. (2012). High-stakes testing – value, fairness and consequences. *Assessment in Education: Principles, Policy & Practice, 19*, 1–6. https://doi.org/10.1080/0969594X.2012.639191

Stoolmiller, M. (1994). Antisocial behavior, delinquent peer association, and unsupervised wandering for boys: Growth and change from childhood to early adolescence. *Multivariate Behavioral Research, 29*, 263–288. https://doi.org/10.1207/s15327906mbr2903_4

Suárez-Orozco, C., Motti-Stefanidi, F., Marks, A., & Katsiaficas, D. (2018). An integrative risk and resilience model for understanding the adaptation of immigrant-origin children and youth. *American Psychologist, 73*, 781–796. https://doi.org/10.1037/amp0000265

Sue, D. W. (2004). Whiteness and ethnocentric monoculturalism: Making the "invisible" visible. *American Psychologist, 59*, 761–769. https://doi.org/10.1037/0003-066X.59.8.761

Sullivan, H. S. (1953). *The interpersonal theory of psychiatry*. Norton.

Super, C. M., Axia, G., Harkness, S., Welles-Nystrom, B., Zylicz, P. O., Parmar, P., Bonichini, S., Bermúdez, M. R., Moscardino, U., Kolar, V., Palacios, J., Eliasz, A., &

McGurk, H. (2008). Culture, development, and the "difficult child": A study of seven Western cultures. *European Journal of Developmental Science, 2,* 136–157. https://doi.org/10.3233/DEV-2008-21209

Super, C. M., & Harkness, S. (1986). The developmental niche: A conceptualization at the interface of child and culture. *International Journal of Behavioral Development, 9,* 545–569. https://doi.org/10.1177/016502548600900409

Super, C. M., & Harkness, S. (1994). Temperament and the developmental niche. In W. B. Carey & S. C. McDevitt (Eds.), *Prevention and early intervention: Individual differences as risk factors for the mental health of children* (pp. 115–125). Brunner/Mazel.

Super, C. M., & Harkness, S. (2009). The developmental niche of the newborn in rural Kenya. In K. J. Nugent, B. J. Petrauskas, & T. B. Brazelton (Eds.), *The newborn as a person: Enabling healthy infant development worldwide* (pp. 85–97). Wiley.

Super, C. M., Harkness, S., Barry, O., & Zeitlin, M. (2011). Think locally, act globally: Contributions of African research in child development. *Child Development Perspectives, 5,* 119–125. https://doi.org/10.1111/j.1750-8606.2011.00166.x

Szechter, L. E., & Liben, L. S. (2004). Parental guidance in preschoolers' understanding of spatial-graphic representations. *Child Development, 75,* 869–885. https://doi.org/10.1111/j.1467-8624.2004.00711.x

Tager-Flusberg, H. (1985). The conceptual basis for referential word meaning in children with autism. *Child Development, 56,* 1167–1178. https://doi.org/10.2307/1130231

Talhelm, T., & Oishi, S. (2018). How rice farming shaped culture in Southern China. In A. K. Üskül & S. Oishi (Eds.), *Socio-economic environment and human psychology: Social, ecological, and cultural perspectives* (pp. 53–76). Oxford University Press.

Talhelm, T., Zhang, X., Oishi, S., Shimin, C., Duan, D., Lan, X., & Kitayama, S. (2014). Large-scale psychological differences within China explained by rice versus wheat agriculture. *Science, 344,* 603–608. https://doi.org/10.1126/science.1246850

Tanon, F. (1994). *A cultural view on planning: The case of weaving in Ivory Coast.* Tilburg University Press.

Tardif, T. (1996). Nouns are not always learned before verbs: Evidence from Mandarin speakers' early vocabularies. *Developmental Psychology, 32,* 492–504. https://doi.org/10.1037/0012-1649.32.3.492

Taylor, M. (2013). Imagination. In P. D. Zelazo (Ed.), *The Oxford handbook of developmental psychology: Vol. 1. Body and mind* (pp. 791–831). Oxford University Press.

Teng, Z., Nie, Q., Guo, C., Zhang, Q., Liu, Y., & Bushman, B. J. (2019). A longitudinal study of link between exposure to violent video games and aggression in Chinese adolescents: The mediating role of moral disengagement. *Developmental Psychology, 55,* 184–195. https://doi.org/10.1037/dev0000624

Tetahiotupa, E. (2000). *Bilinguisme et scolarisation en Polynésie Française* [Bilingualism and schooling in French Polynesia; Doctoral dissertation]. Université de Paris.

Tharp, R. G., & Gallimore, R. (1988). *Rousing minds to life: Teaching, learning, and schooling in social context.* Cambridge University Press.

Tharp, R. G., Jordan, C., Speidel, G. E., Au, K. H.-P., Klein, T. W., Calkins, R. R., Sloat, K. C. M., & Gallimore, R. (2007). Education and Native Hawaiian children: Revisiting KEEP. *Hulili: Multidisciplinary Research on Hawaiian Well-Being, 4,* 269–317.

Thevenin, D. M., Eilers, R. E., Oller, D. K., & LaVoie, L. (1985). Where's the drift in babbling drift? A cross-linguistic study. *Applied Psycholinguistics, 6,* 3–15. https://doi.org/10.1017/S0142716400005981

Thomas, A., & Chess, S. (1977). *Temperament and development.* Brunner/Mazel.

Thomas, E., Wickramasinghe, K., Mendis, S., Roberts, N., & Foster, C. (2015). Improved stove interventions to reduce household air pollution in low and middle income countries: A descriptive systematic review. *BMC Public Health, 15,* 650. https://doi.org/10.1186/s12889-015-2024-7

Thompson, R. A. (1989). Causal attributions and children's emotional understanding. In C. Saarni & P. L. Harris (Eds.), *Children's understanding of emotions* (pp. 117–150). Cambridge University Press.

Thompson, R. A. (2015). The development of the person: Social understanding, relationships, conscience, self. In M. E. Lamb (Ed.), *Handbook of child psychology and developmental science: Vol. 3. Socioemotional processes* (7th ed., pp. 201–246). Wiley.

Tietjen, A. M. (1989). The ecology of children's social support networks. In D. Belle (Ed.), *Children's social networks and social support* (pp. 37–69). Wiley.

Tillman, K. H., Brewster, K. L., & Holway, G. V. (2019). Sexual and romantic relationships in young adulthood. *Annual Review of Sociology, 45*, 133–153. https://doi.org/10.1146/annurev-soc-073018-022625

Tobin, J., Hsueh, Y., & Karasawa, M. (2009). *Preschool in three cultures revisited: China, Japan, and the United States.* University of Chicago Press. https://doi.org/10.7208/chicago/9780226805054.001.0001

Tofail, F., Fernald, L. C. H., Das, K. K., Rahman, M., Ahmed, T., Jannat, K. K., Unicomb, L., Arnold, B. F., Ashraf, S., Winch, P. J., Kariger, P., Stewart, C. P., Colford, J. M., Jr., & Luby, S. P. (2018). Effect of water quality, sanitation, hand washing, and nutritional interventions on child development in rural Bangladesh (WASH Benefits Bangladesh): A cluster-randomised controlled trial. *The Lancet: Child & Adolescent Health, 2*(4), 255–268. https://doi.org/10.1016/S2352-4642(18)30031-2

Tomasello, M. (1995). Language is not an instinct. *Cognitive Development, 10*, 131–156. https://doi.org/10.1016/0885-2014(95)90021-7

Tomasello, M. (2003). *Constructing a language: A usage-based theory of language acquisition.* Harvard University Press.

Tomasello, M. (2016). Cultural learning redux. *Child Development, 87*, 643–653. https://doi.org/10.1111/cdev.12499

Tomasello, M., Carpenter, M., Call, J., Behne, T., & Moll, H. (2005). Understanding and sharing intentions: The origins of cultural cognition. *Behavioral and Brain Sciences, 28*, 675–691. https://doi.org/10.1017/S0140525X05000129

Tomasello, M., Carpenter, M., & Liszkowski, U. (2007). A new look at infant pointing. *Child Development, 78*, 705–722. https://doi.org/10.1111/j.1467-8624.2007.01025.x

Tönnies, F. (1957). *Community and society: Gemeinschaft und Gesellschaft* (C. P. Loonmis, Trans.). Michigan State University Press.

Topping, K., Dekhinet, R., & Zeedyk, S. (2013). Parent–infant interaction and children's language development. *Educational Psychology, 33*, 391–426. https://doi.org/10.1080/01443410.2012.744159

Torney-Purta, J. (2002). The school's role in developing civic engagement: A study of adolescents in twenty-eight countries. *Applied Developmental Science, 6*, 203–212. https://doi.org/10.1207/S1532480XADS0604_7

Tõugu, P., Tulviste, T., Schröder, L., Keller, H., & De Geer, B. (2012). Content of maternal open-ended questions and statements in reminiscing with their 4-year-olds: Links with independence and interdependence orientation in European contexts. *Memory, 20*, 499–510. https://doi.org/10.1080/09658211.2012.683009

Tranter, B., & Skrbis, Z. (2014). Political and social divisions over climate change among young Queenslanders. *Environment and Planning A: Economy and Space, 46*(7), 1638–1651. https://doi.org/10.1068/a46285

Tremblay, R. E. (2000). The development of aggressive behavior during childhood: What have we learned in the past century? *International Journal of Behavioral Development, 24*, 129–141. https://doi.org/10.1080/016502500383232

Triandis, H. C. (1994). *Culture and social behavior.* McGraw Hill.

Triandis, H. C. (1995). *Individualism & collectivism.* Westview Press.

Triandis, H. C., Bontempo, R., Villareal, J. J., Asai, M., & Lucca, N. (1988). Individualism and collectivism: Cross-cultural perspectives on self-ingroup relationships.

Journal of Personality and Social Psychology, 54, 323–338. https://doi.org/10.1037/0022-3514.54.2.323

Triandis, H. C., & Gelfand, M. J. (2012). A theory of individualism and collectivism. In P. Van Lange (Ed.), *Handbook of theories of social psychology* (pp. 498–520). Sage. https://doi.org/10.4135/9781446249222.n51

Tronick, E. (2007). *The neurobiological and social-emotional development of infants and children.* Norton.

Tronick, E. Z., Morelli, G. A., & Ivey, P. K. (1992). The Efe forager infant and toddler's pattern of social relationships: Multiple and simultaneous. *Developmental Psychology, 28,* 568–577. https://doi.org/10.1037/0012-1649.28.4.568

Tsai, C.-C., & Kuo, P.-C. (2008). Cram school students' conceptions of learning and learning science in Taiwan. *International Journal of Science Education, 30,* 353–375. https://doi.org/10.1080/09500690701191425

Tudge, J. R. H., Odero, D. A., Hogan, D. M., & Etz, K. E. (2003). Relations between the everyday activities of preschoolers and their teachers' perceptions of their competence in the first years of school. *Early Childhood Research Quarterly, 18,* 42–64. https://doi.org/10.1016/S0885-2006(03)00005-X

Tudge, J. R. H., Odera, D., Piccinini, C. A., Doucet, F., Sperb, T. M., & Lopes, R. S. (2006). A window into different cultural worlds: Young children's everyday activities in the United States, Brazil, and Kenya. *Child Development, 77,* 1446-1469. https://doi.org/10.1111/j.1467-8624.2006.00947.x

Turiel, E., & Gingo, M. (2017). Development in the moral domain: Coordination and the need to consider other domains of social reasoning. In N. Budwig, E. Turiel, & P. D. Zelazo (Eds.), *New perspectives on human development* (pp. 209–228). Cambridge University Press. https://doi.org/10.1017/CBO9781316282755.013

Twenge, J. M. (2019). More time on technology, less happiness? Associations between digital-media use and psychological well-being. *Current Directions in Psychological Science, 28,* 372–379. https://doi.org/10.1177/0963721419838244

Tyson, K. (2002). Weighing in: Elementary-age students and the debate on attitudes toward school among Black students. *Social Forces, 80,* 1157–1189. https://doi.org/10.1353/sof.2002.0035

UN Women. (2013). *Annual report 2012–2013.* https://www.unwomen.org/en/digital-library/publications/2013/6/annual-report-2012-2013

UNESCO. (2017). *Global Education Monitoring Report. Accountability in education: Meeting our commitments.* https://unesdoc.unesco.org/ark:/48223/pf0000259338.pdf

UNESCO Institute for Statistics. (2019). *Compulsory education, duration (years).* https://data.worldbank.org/indicator/SE.COM.DURS

UNICEF. (2011). *Exploring the impact of climate change on children in South Africa.* https://www.unicef.org/southafrica/reports/exploring-impact-climate-change-children-south-africa

UNICEF. (2012). *School readiness: A conceptual framework.* UNICEF.

UNICEF. (2013a). *Climate change: Children's challenge.* https://www.unicef.org.uk/publications/climate-change-report-jon-snow-2013/

UNICEF. (2013b). *Take us seriously! Engaging children with disabilities in decisions affecting their lives.* https://www.unicef.org/disabilities/files/Take_Us_Seriously.pdf

UNICEF. (2013c). *Youth in action on climate change: Inspirations from around the world.* United Nations Joint Framework Initiative on Children, Youth and Climate Change. https://sgp.undp.org/images/Publication%20Youth%20in%20Action%20on%20Climate%20Change%20Inspirations%20from%20Around%20the%20World%20English-%20SGP%20examples.pdf

UNICEF. (2015). *Unless we act now: The impact of climate change on children.* https://www.unicef.org/reports/unless-we-act-now-impact-climate-change-children

UNICEF. (2016). *The state of the world's children 2016: A fair chance for every child.* https://www.unicef.org/publications/files/UNICEF_SOWC_2016.pdf

UNICEF. (2018). *Advantage or paradox: The challenge for children and young people of growing up urban.* https://www.unicef.org/media/60451/file/Advantage-or-paradox-2018.pdf

UNICEF. (2019). *Child labor.* https://www.unicef.org/protection/57929_child_labour.html

United Nations. (1990). *Convention on the Rights of the Child.* UNICEF. https://www.unicef.org/child-rights-convention/convention-text

United Nations. (2014). *Resolution on human rights, sexual orientation, and gender identity.* United Nations.

United Nations. (2018a). *68% of the world population projected to live in urban areas by 2050, says UN.* https://www.un.org/development/desa/en/news/population/2018-revision-of-world-urbanization-prospects.html

United Nations. (2018b). *Sustainable development goals report.* https://www.un.org/development/desa/publications/the-sustainable-development-goals-report-2018.html

United Nations Office on Drugs and Crime. (2013). *Homicide statistics, 2013.* http://www.unodc.org/unodc/en/data-and-analysis/homicide.html

United Nations Statistics Division. (2006). *Demographic yearbook 2006.* https://unstats.un.org/unsd/demographic/products/dyb/dyb2006.htm

United States Department of Commerce. (2010). *School districts.* https://www.census.gov/did/www/schooldistricts/data/

U.S. Department of Education. (2017). *Beginning college students who change their majors within 3 years of enrollment.* National Center for Education Statistics. https://nces.ed.gov/pubs2018/2018434.pdf

U.S. Global Change Research Program. (2016). *The impacts of climate change on human health in the United States: A scientific assessment.* https://health2016.globalchange.gov

Uttal, D. (2005). Spatial symbols and spatial thought: Cross-cultural, developmental, and historical perspectives on the relation between map use and spatial cognition. In L. Namy (Ed.), *Symbol use and symbolic representation: Developmental and comparative perspectives* (pp. 3–23). Erlbaum.

van de Vijver, F. J. R. (2017). Contextualized positive youth development: A SWOT analysis. In R. Dimitrova (Ed.), *Well-being of youth and emerging adults across cultures* (pp. 299–308). Springer. https://doi.org/10.1007/978-3-319-68363-8_19

van de Vijver, F. J. R., Hofer, J., & Chasiotis, A. (2010). Methodology. In M. H. Bornstein (Ed.), *Handbook of cultural developmental science* (pp. 21–37). Taylor & Francis.

van de Vijver, F. J. R., & Leung, K. (1997). *Methods and data analysis for cross-cultural research.* Sage.

van de Vijver, F. J. R., & Leung, K. (2000). Methodological issues in psychological research on culture. *Journal of Cross-Cultural Psychology, 31,* 33–51. https://doi.org/10.1177/0022022100031001004

van de Waal, E., Borgeaud, C., & Whiten, A. (2013). Potent social learning and conformity shape a wild primate's foraging decisions. *Science, 340,* 483–485. https://doi.org/10.1126/science.1232769

Verma, S., & Cooper, C. R. (2017). Optimizing development following disasters and traumatic experiences among children, adolescents, and adults: Useful frameworks and promising research directions. *ISSBD Bulletin, 1*(71), 3–6.

Verma, S., & Larson, R. (Eds.). (2003). *Examining adolescent leisure time across cultures: Developmental opportunities and risks.* Jossey-Bass.

Vihman, M. (2004). Review of input-based phonological acquisition. *First Language, 24,* 373–376. https://doi.org/10.1177/014272370402400307

Vincent, B., & Manzano, A. (2017). History and cultural diversity. In C. Richards, W. Bouman, & M. J. Barker (Eds.), *Genderqueer and non-binary genders: Critical and applied approaches in sexuality, gender and identity* (pp. 11–30). Palgrave Macmillan. https://doi.org/10.1057/978-1-137-51053-2_2

Vitoroulis, I., Schneider, B. H., Vasquez, C. C., del Pilar Soteras de Toro, M., & Gonzales, Y. (2012). Perceived parental and peer support in relation to Canadian, Cuban, and Spanish adolescents' valuing of academics and intrinsic academic motivation. *Journal of Cross-Cultural Psychology, 43*, 704–722. https://doi.org/10.1177/0022022111405657

Vuolo, M., & Staff, J. (2013). Parent and child cigarette use: A longitudinal, multigenerational study. *Pediatrics, 132*, e568–e577. https://doi.org/10.1542/peds.2013-0067

Vygotsky, L. S. (1978). *Mind in society: The development of higher psychological processes.* Harvard University Press.

Vygotsky, L. S. (1987). *The collected works of L. S. Vygotsky. Vol. 1: Problems of general psychology.* Plenum Press.

Wagaman, M. A., Keller, M. F., & Cavaliere, S. J. (2016). What does it mean to be a successful adult? Exploring perceptions of the transition into adulthood among LGBTQ emerging adults in a community-based service context. *Journal of Gay & Lesbian Social Services, 28*, 140–158. https://doi.org/10.1080/10538720.2016.1155519

Wagner, D. A. (1978). Memories of Morocco: The influence of age, schooling, and environment on memory. *Cognitive Psychology, 10*, 1–28. https://doi.org/10.1016/0010-0285(78)90017-8

Wagner, D. A. (1981). Culture and memory development. In H. C. Triandis & A. Heron (Eds.), *Handbook of cross-cultural psychology* (Vol. 4, pp. 178–232). Allyn & Bacon.

Wagner, D. A. (1993). *Literacy, culture, and development: Becoming literate in Morocco.* Cambridge University Press.

Wahler, R. G. (1967). Infant social attachments: A reinforcement theory interpretation and investigation. *Child Development, 38*, 1079–1088. https://doi.org/10.2307/1127105

Wainryb, C., & Recchia, H. (2014). Parent-child conversations as contexts for moral development: Why conversations, and why conversations with parents? In C. Wainryb & H. Recchia (Eds.), *Talking about right and wrong: Parent-child conversations as contexts for moral development* (pp. 3–18). Cambridge University Press. https://doi.org/10.1017/CBO9781139207072.002

Walker, S. P., Wachs, T. D., Gardner, J. M., Lozoff, B., Wasserman, G. A., Pollitt, E., Carter, J. A., & the International Child Development Steering Group. (2007). Child development: Risk factors for adverse outcomes in developing countries. *The Lancet, 369*, 145–157. https://doi.org/10.1016/S0140-6736(07)60076-2

Wall, J. A., Jr., & Blum, M. (1991). Community mediation in the People's Republic of China. *The Journal of Conflict Resolution, 35*, 3–20. https://doi.org/10.1177/0022002791035001001

Wang, J. M. (2016). Preference-for-solitude and depressive symptoms in Chinese adolescents. *Personality and Individual Differences, 100*, 151–156. https://doi.org/10.1016/j.paid.2015.09.033

Wang, J. M., Rubin, K. H., Laursen, B., Booth-LaForce, C., & Rose-Krasnor, L. (2013). Preference-for-solitude and adjustment difficulties in early and late adolescence. *Journal of Clinical Child and Adolescent Psychology, 42*, 834–842. https://doi.org/10.1080/15374416.2013.794700

Wang, L., Luo, J., Yu, B., Kong, J., Luo, J., Gao, W., & Sun, X. (2013). Internet addiction of adolescents in China: Prevalence, predictors, and association with well-being. *Addiction Research and Theory, 21*, 62–69. https://doi.org/10.3109/16066359.2012.690053

Wang, Q. (2001). Culture effects on adults' earliest childhood recollection and self-description: Implications for the relation between memory and the self. *Journal of Personality and Social Psychology, 81*, 220–233. https://doi.org/10.1037/0022-3514.81.2.220

Wang, Q. (2013). Chinese socialization and emotion talk between mothers and children in native and immigrant Chinese families. *Asian American Journal of Psychology, 4*, 185–192. https://doi.org/10.1037/a0030868

Wang, Q., Doan, S. N., & Song, Q. (2010). Talking about internal states in mother-child reminiscing influences children's self-representations: A cross-cultural study. *Cognitive Development, 25*, 380–393. https://doi.org/10.1016/j.cogdev.2010.08.007

Wang, Q., Hutt, R., Kulkofsky, S., McDermott, M., & Wei, R. (2006). Emotion situation knowledge and autobiographical memory in Chinese, immigrant Chinese, and European American 3-year-olds. *Journal of Cognition and Development, 7*(1), 95–118. https://doi.org/10.1207/s15327647jcd0701_5

Wang, Q., Leichtman, M. D., & Davies, K. I. (2000). Sharing memories and telling stories: American and Chinese mothers and their 3-year-olds. *Memory, 8*, 159–177. https://doi.org/10.1080/096582100387588

Wang, Z., Chen, X., Liu, J., Bullock, A., Li, D., Chen, X., & French, D. (2020). Moderating role of conflict resolution strategies in the links between peer victimization and psychological adjustment among youth. *Journal of Adolescence, 79*, 184–192. https://doi.org/10.1016/j.adolescence.2020.01.002

Wasserman, G. A., Liu, X., Parvez, F., Ahsan, H., Factor-Litvak, P., van Geen, A., Slavkovich, V., LoIacono, N. J., Cheng, Z., Hussain, I., Momotaj, H., & Graziano, J. H. (2004). Water arsenic exposure and children's intellectual function in Araihazar, Bangladesh. *Environmental Health Perspectives, 112*, 1329–1333. https://doi.org/10.1289/ehp.6964

Wasserman, G. A., Liu, X., Parvez, F., Ahsan, H., Levy, D., Factor-Litvak, P., Kline, J., van Geen, A., Slavkovich, V., LoIacono, N. J., Cheng, Z., Zheng, Y., & Graziano, J. H. (2006). Water manganese exposure and children's intellectual function in Araihazar, Bangladesh. *Environmental Health Perspectives, 114*, 124–129. https://doi.org/10.1289/ehp.8030

Watts, N., Amann, M., Arnell, N., Ayeb-Karlsson, S., Belesova, K., Berry, H., Bouley, T., Boykoff, M., Byass, P., Cai, W., Campbell-Lendrum, D., Chambers, J., Daly, M., Dasandi, N., Davies, M., Depoux, A., Dominguez-Salas, P., Drummond, P., Ebi, K. L., . . . Costello, A. (2018). The 2018 report of the *Lancet* Countdown on health and climate change: Shaping the health of nations for centuries to come. *The Lancet, 392*, 2479–2514. https://doi.org/10.1016/S0140-6736(18)32594-7

Way, N. (2006). The cultural practice of close friendships among urban adolescents in the United States. In X. Chen, D. C. French, & B. H. Schneider (Eds.), *Peer relationships in cultural context* (pp. 403–425). Cambridge University Press. https://doi.org/10.1017/CBO9780511499739.018

Weisner, T. S. (1979). Urban-rural differences in sociable, aggressive, and dominant behaviors of Kenya children. *Ethnology, 18*, 153–172. https://doi.org/10.2307/3773288

Weisner, T. S. (1997). The ecocultural project of human development: Why ethnography and its findings matter. *Ethos, 25*, 177–190. https://doi.org/10.1525/eth.1997.25.2.177

Weisner, T. S. (2001). Children investing in their families: The importance of child obligation in successful development. In A. J. Fuligni (Ed.), *Family obligation and assistance during adolescence: Contextual variations and developmental implications* (pp. 77–84). Wiley. https://doi.org/10.1002/cd.32

Weisner, T. S., Gallimore, R., Bacon, M. K., Barry, H., III, Bell, C., Novaes, S. C., Edwards, C. P., Goswami, B. B., Minturn, L., Nerlove, S. B., Koel, A., Ritchie, J. E., Rosenblatt, P. C., Singh, T. R., Sutton-Smith, B., Whiting, B. B., Wilder, W. D., & Williams, T. R. (1977). My brother's keeper: Child and sibling caretaking. *Current Anthropology, 18*, 169–190. https://doi.org/10.1086/201883

Weisz, J. R., Chaiyasit, W., Weiss, B., Eastman, K. L., & Jackson, E. W. (1995). A multimethod study of problem behavior among Thai and American children in school: Teacher reports versus direct observations. *Child Development, 66,* 402–415. https://doi.org/10.2307/1131586

Weisz, J. R., Suwanlert, S., Chaiyasit, W., & Walter, B. R. (1987). Over- and undercontrolled referral problems among children and adolescents from Thailand and the United States: The *wat* and *wai* of cultural differences. *Journal of Consulting and Clinical Psychology, 55,* 719–726. https://doi.org/10.1037/0022-006X.55.5.719

Weisz, J. R., Suwanlert, S., Chaiyasit, W., Weiss, B., Walter, B. R., & Anderson, W. W. (1988). Thai and American perspectives on over- and undercontrolled child behavior problems: Exploring the threshold model among parents, teachers, and psychologists. *Journal of Consulting and Clinical Psychology, 56,* 601–609. https://doi.org/10.1037/0022-006X.56.4.601

Wellman, H. M. (2014). *Making minds: How theory of mind develops.* Oxford University Press. https://doi.org/10.1093/acprof:oso/9780199334919.001.0001

Wellman, H. M., & Lempers, J. D. (1977). The naturalistic communicative abilities of two-year-olds. *Child Development, 48,* 1052–1057. https://doi.org/10.2307/1128359

Wenger, M. (1989). Work, play, and social relationships among children in a Giriama community. In D. Belle (Ed.), *Children's social networks and social supports* (pp. 91–115). Wiley.

Werker, J. F., Pegg, J. E., & McLeod, P. J. (1994). A cross-language investigation of infant preference for infant-directed communication. *Infant Behavior and Development, 17,* 323–333. https://doi.org/10.1016/0163-6383(94)90012-4

Werker, J. F., Pons, F., Dietrich, C., Kajikawa, S., Fais, L., & Amano, S. (2007). Infant-directed speech supports phonetic category learning in English and Japanese. *Cognition, 103,* 147–162. https://doi.org/10.1016/j.cognition.2006.03.006

White, L. K., & Brinkerhoff, D. R. (1981). Children's work in the family: Its significance and meaning. *Journal of Marriage and the Family, 43,* 789–798. https://doi.org/10.2307/351336

Whiting, B. B. (1975). The problem of the packaged variable. In K. F. Riegel & J. A. Meacham (Eds.), *The developing individual in a changing world: Vol. 1. Historical and cultural issues* (pp. 303–309). Mouton.

Whiting, B. B. (1963). *Six cultures: Studies of child rearing.* Wiley.

Whiting, B. B., & Edwards, C. P. (1988). *Children of different worlds: The formation of social behavior.* Harvard University Press.

Whiting, B. B., & Whiting, J. W. M. (1975). *Children of six cultures: A psycho-cultural analysis.* Harvard University Press.

Whiting, J. W. M., & Child, I. L. (1953). *Child training and personality.* Yale University Press. https://doi.org/10.2307/3537788

Whiting, J. W. M., Child, I. L., & Lambert, W. W. (1966). *Field guide for a study of socialization.* Wiley

Whitten, A., Goodall, J., McGrew, W. C., Nishida, T., Reynolds, V., Sugiyama, Y., Tutin, C. E., Wrangham, R. W., & Boesch, C. (1999). Cultures in chimpanzees. *Nature, 399,* 682–685.

Wigfield, A., Eccles, J. S., Fredricks, J. A., Simpkins, S., Roeser, R. W., & Schiefele, U. (2015). Development of achievement motivation and engagement. In M. E. Lamb (Ed.), *Handbook of child psychology and developmental science: Vol. 3. Socioemotional processes* (pp. 657–700). Wiley. https://doi.org/10.1002/9781118963418.childpsy316

Wikan, U. (1989). Managing the heart to brighten face and soul: Emotions in Balinese morality and health care. *American Ethnologist, 16*(2), 294–312.

Wilbert, J. (1979). To become a maker of canoes: An essay on Warao enculturation. In J. Wilbert (Ed.), *Enculturation in Latin America* (pp. 303–358). Latin American Press.

Wilkinson, R., & Pickett, K. (2010). *The spirit level: Why equality is better for everyone.* Penguin Books.

Willoughby, T. (2008). A short-term longitudinal study of Internet and computer game use by adolescent boys and girls: Prevalence, frequency of use, and psychosocial predictors. *Developmental Psychology, 44*, 195–204. https://doi.org/10.1037/0012-1649.44.1.195

Witkow, M. R., Huynh, V., & Fuligni, A. J. (2015). Understanding differences in college persistence: A longitudinal examination of financial circumstances, family obligations, and discrimination in an ethnically diverse sample. *Journal of Applied Developmental Science, 19*, 4–18. https://doi.org/10.1080/10888691.2014.946030

Wolff, F.-C., & Maliki. (2008). Evidence on the impact of child labor on child health in Indonesia, 1993–2000. *Economics and Human Biology, 6*, 143–169. https://doi.org/10.1016/j.ehb.2007.09.003

Wolff, P. H. (1987). *The development of behavioral states and the expression of emotions in early infancy: New proposals for investigation*. University of Chicago Press.

Wood, D. (1993). The fine line between mapping and mapmaking. *Cartographica, 30*, 50–60. https://doi.org/10.3138/N70Q-0R5X-694T-7868

Wood, D., & Middleton, D. (1975). A study of assisted problem-solving. *British Journal of Psychology, 66*(2), 181–191. https://doi.org/10.1111/j.2044-8295.1975.tb01454.x

World Bank. (2018a). *World Bank education overview: Higher education*. http://documents.worldbank.org/curated/en/610121541079963484/World-Bank-Education-Overview-Higher-Education

World Bank. (2018b). *World development report 2018: Learning to realize education's promise*. https://www.worldbank.org/en/publication/wdr2018

World Bank. (2019a). Education statistics. https://databank.worldbank.org/indicator/SE.TER.ENRR?id=c755d342&report_name=EdStats_Indicators_Report&populartype=series

World Bank. (2019b). *The Energy progress report 2019*. https://www.worldbank.org/en/topic/energy/publication/tracking-sdg7-the-energy-progress-report-2019

World Economic Forum. (2014). *The global gender gap report 2014*. https://www.weforum.org/reports/global-gender-gap-report-2014

World Health Organization. (2009). *Changing cultural and social norms that support violence*. https://apps.who.int/iris/handle/10665/44147

World Health Organization. (2015). *Preventing youth violence: An overview of the evidence*. https://apps.who.int/iris/handle/10665/181008

World Health Organization. (2017a). *Depression and other common mental disorders: Global health estimates*. https://apps.who.int/iris/handle/10665/254610

World Health Organization. (2017b). *Inheriting a sustainable world: Atlas on children's health and the environment*. https://www.who.int/publications/i/item/inheriting-a-sustainable-world

World Health Organization. (2018a). *Breastfeeding*. http://www.who.int/topics/breastfeeding/en/

World Health Organization. (2018b). *Global status report on alcohol and health 2018*. https://www.who.int/publications/i/item/9789241565639

World Health Organization. (2018c). *Lead poisoning and health*. https://www.who.int/news-room/fact-sheets/detail/lead-poisoning-and-health

World Health Organization. (2018d). *World malaria report 2018*. https://www.who.int/publications/i/item/9789241565653

World Health Organization/UNICEF. (2017). *Progress on drinking water, sanitation and hygiene: 2017 update and SDG baselines*. https://www.who.int/water_sanitation_health/publications/jmp-2017/en/

World Population Review. (2019). Fertility rate by country. http://worldpopulationreview.com/countries/total-fertility-rate/

Wörmann, V., Holodynski, M., Kärtner, J., & Keller, H. (2012). A cross-cultural comparison of the development of the social smile: A longitudinal study of maternal and infant imitation in 6- and 12-week-old infants. *Infant Behavior and Development, 35*, 335–347. https://doi.org/10.1016/j.infbeh.2012.03.002

Worthman, C. M. (2010). The ecology of human development: Evolving models for cultural psychology. *Journal of Cross-Cultural Psychology, 41*, 546–562. https://doi.org/10.1177/0022022110362627

Wright, E. M., & Fagan, A. A. (2013). The cycle of violence in context: Exploring the moderating roles of neighborhood disadvantage and cultural context. *Criminology, 51*, 217–249. https://doi.org/10.1111/1745-9125.12003

Wu, C., & Chao, R. K. (2011). Intergenerational cultural dissonance in parent-adolescent relationships among Chinese and European Americans. *Developmental Psychology, 47*, 493–508. https://doi.org/10.1037/a0021063

Wyman, L., Marlow, P., Andrew, C. F., Miller, G., Nicholai, C. R., & Readen, Y. N. (2010). High stakes testing, bilingual education and language endangerment: A Yup'ik example. *International Journal of Bilingual Education and Bilingualism, 13*, 701–721. https://doi.org/10.1080/13670050903410931

Xu, Y. (1997). Contextual tonal variations in Mandarin. *Journal of Phonetics, 25*, 61–83. https://doi.org/10.1006/jpho.1996.0034

Xu, Y., Farver, J. A. M., Chang, L., Zhang, Z., & Yu, L. (2007). Moving away or fitting in? Understanding shyness in Chinese children. *Merrill-Palmer Quarterly, 53*, 527–556. https://doi.org/10.1353/mpq.2008.0005

Xu, Y., Farver, J. A. M., Yu, L., & Zhang, Z. (2009). Three types of shyness in Chinese children and the relation to effortful control. *Journal of Personality and Social Psychology, 97*, 1061–1073. https://doi.org/10.1037/a0016576

Yap, M. B., Pilkington, P. D., Ryan, S. M., & Jorm, A. F. (2014). Parental factors associated with depression and anxiety in young people: A systematic review and meta-analysis. *Journal of Affective Disorders, 156*, 8–23. https://doi.org/10.1016/j.jad.2013.11.007

Yau, J., & Smetana, J. G. (2003). Conceptions of moral, social-conventional, and personal events among Chinese preschoolers in Hong Kong. *Child Development, 74*, 647–658. https://doi.org/10.1111/1467-8624.00560

Yeager, D. S., & Dweck, C. S. (2012). Mindsets that promote resilience: When students believe their personal characteristics can be developed. *Educational Psychologist, 47*, 302–314. https://doi.org/10.1080/00461520.2012.722805

Yilmaz, H. B., & Dülgerler, Ş. (2011). Children who work in the street in Izmur, Turkey. *Social Behavior and Personality, 39*, 129–144. https://doi.org/10.2224/sbp.2011.39.1.129

Yoon, S., Lam, W. W. T., Sham, J. T., & Lam, T. H. (2015). Learning to drink: How Chinese adolescents make decisions about the consumption (or not) of alcohol. *The International Journal on Drug Policy, 26*, 1231–1237. https://doi.org/10.1016/j.drugpo.2015.09.001

Zackari, G., & Modigh, F. (2000). *Värdegrundsboken, om samtal för demokrati i skolan* [Values, about conversations for democracy in school]. Regeringskansliet.

Zajac, L., Bookhout, M. K., Hubbard, J. A., Carlson, E. A., & Dozier, M. (2020). Attachment disorganization in infancy: A developmental precursor to maladaptive social information processing at age 8. *Child Development, 91*, 145–162. https://doi.org/10.1111/cdev.13140

Zebian, S., & Rochat, P. (2012). Judgment of land ownership by young refugee Palestinian and U.S. children. *International Journal of Behavioral Development, 36*, 449–456. https://doi.org/10.1177/0165025412450526

Zhang, M., Lin, T., & Jao, W. (2020). Filial piety dilemma solutions in Chinese adult children: The role of contextual theme, filial piety beliefs, and generation. *Asian Journal of Social Psychology, 23*, 227–237. https://doi.org/10.1111/ajsp.12395

Zhu, N., & Chang, L. (2019). Education and parenting in China. In E. Sorbring & J. E. Lansford (Eds.), *School systems, parent behavior, and academic achievement* (Vol. 3, pp. 15–28). Springer.

Ziemek, S. (2006). Economic analysis of volunteers' motivations: A cross-country study. *Journal of Socio-Economics, 35*, 532–555. https://doi.org/10.1016/j.socec.2005.11.064

Zimba, R. F. (2002). Indigenous conceptions of childhood development and social realities in southern Africa. In H. Keller, Y. P. Poortinga, & A. Scholmerish (Eds.), *Between cultures and biology: Perspectives on ontogenetic development* (pp. 89–115). Cambridge University Press. https://doi.org/10.1017/CBO9780511489853.006

Zimbardo, P. (2007). *The Lucifer effect: Understanding how good people turn evil*. Random House.

Zusho, A., Daddino, J., & Barcia, C.-B. (2016). Culture, race, ethnicity, and motivation. In K. R. Wentzel & G. B. Ramani (Eds.), *Handbook of social influences in school contexts: Social-emotional, motivation, and cognitive outcomes* (pp. 273–292). Routledge, Taylor and Francis.

INDEX

ABOUT THE AUTHORS

Jennifer E. Lansford, PhD, is a research professor at the Sanford School of Public Policy and faculty fellow of the Center for Child and Family Policy at Duke University. She earned her PhD in developmental psychology from the University of Michigan, and she has authored more than 200 publications that focus on the development of aggression and other behavioral problems during childhood and adolescence. She leads the Parenting Across Cultures Project, a longitudinal study of mothers, fathers, and children from nine countries (China, Colombia, Italy, Jordan, Kenya, Philippines, Sweden, Thailand, and the United States).

In addition, Dr. Lansford has consulted for UNICEF on the evaluation of parenting programs in several low- and middle-income countries and on the development of a set of international standards for parenting programs. She serves in editorial roles for several academic journals and has served in a number of national and international leadership roles, including chair of the U.S. National Institutes of Health Psychosocial Development, Risk and Prevention Study Section; U.S. National Committee for Psychological Science of the National Academies of Sciences, Engineering, and Medicine; and Society for Research in Child Development International Affairs Committee.

Doran C. French, PhD, is a professor in the Department of Child Development and Family Studies at Purdue University. He earned his PhD in child psychology from the Institute of Child Development at the University of Minnesota. His research focuses on child and adolescent social competence with an emphasis on peer relationships, conflict, developmental psychology, and religion. Since his 1994 Fulbright Fellowship to Indonesia, his research has addressed the cultural context of social competence.

Dr. French has ongoing longitudinal studies of child and adolescent development in Indonesia and China and has previously studied youth in Thailand and South Korea. His work on culture has focused on friendship, conflict, peer status, social networks, tobacco and alcohol use, and loneliness. He has published several studies assessing the relation between Islam and social competence in Indonesian youth, including associations between religious practices and friendship, loneliness, effortful control, depression, substance use, and prosocial behavior.

Mary Gauvain, PhD, is a distinguished professor of Psychology at the University of California, Riverside (UCR). She received her MA in sociology of education from Stanford University and her PhD in developmental psychology from the University of Utah. Dr. Gauvain is a developmental psychologist whose research investigates social and cultural contributions to cognitive development. She has studied children's planning, spatial thinking, and learning in and outside of school, and her recent research focuses on children's knowledge of water and food contamination in the United States and Africa and child development during cultural change.

Dr. Gauvain is the author of *The Social Context of Cognitive Development* (2001), and was an associate editor of *Child Development* and the principal investigator on an interdisciplinary NSF-IGERT award, *Water SENSE: Social, Engineering, and Natural Sciences Engagement*. She is a fellow of the American Association for the Advancement of Science, the American Educational Research Association, the American Psychological Association, and the Association for Psychological Science. She has been on the UCR faculty for over 2 decades, where she has also served as chair of the Academic Senate, associate vice provost for Faculty Success and Development, and codirector of the UC Global Health Center of Expertise on One Health.